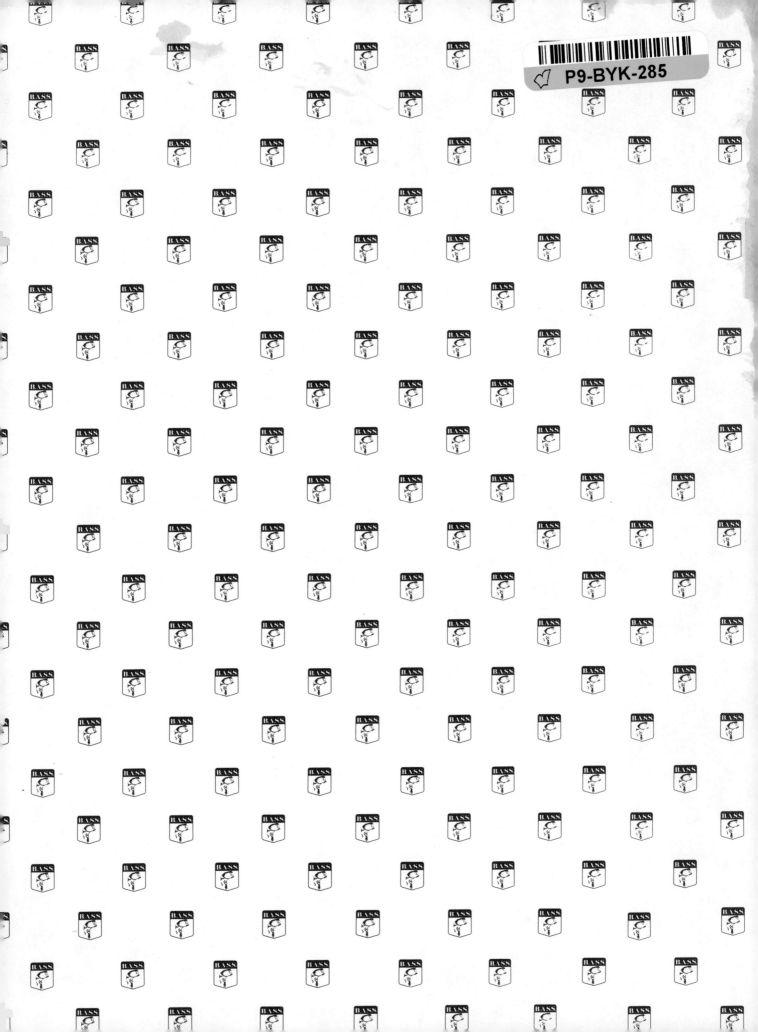

BASSMASTER'S

BEST TACTICS & TECHNIQUES

A "How-To" Treasury

CONTENTS

BASSMASTER'S BEST TACTICS & TECHNIQUES
A "How-To" Treasury

EDITOR: Colin Moore

PUBLISHER: Helen Sevier
PRESIDENT, BASS ANGLERS SPORTSMAN SOCIETY:
Ray Scott
EDITOR, BASSMASTER MAGAZINE:
Dave Precht

ASSOCIATE EDITOR:
Susan Shehane

ART DIRECTOR:
Scott Hughes

DESIGNER:
Glo Fomby

ARTISTS:
Carol Boatright, Leah Cochrane

ILLUSTRATORS:
Rebecca Hockman-Carlisle
Emily Craig, Scott Hughes, Bernie Schultz

COMPOSITION:
Marge Stanfield
COPY DIRECTOR:
Laura Harris
COPY ASSISTANT:
Lorene Hamner

PRODUCTION MANAGER:
Jane Rea
MARKETING AND SALES DIRECTOR:
Anita Capouano
ASSISTANT CREATIVE DIRECTOR:
Karen Gaston
SENIOR MARKETING WRITER:
Stacy Bromberg
MARKETING ASSISTANT:
Emily Bentley
BOOK FULFILLMENT:
Martha Thornburgh

COVER PHOTOGRAPH:
Glenn Lau Productions

PREFACE

A Storehouse of Bassing Lore

The Texas angler, a loyal member of Bass Anglers Sportsman Society and a student of bass-fishing techniques, should have been pleased to receive a deluxe edition of the *BASSMASTER's Best Of Lures* book for Christmas. Yet he complained. "For years I've been clipping articles out of my BASSMASTER® magazines and filing them for later reference," he said. "If I had known you were going to publish the stories in book form, I wouldn't have gone to all the trouble of clipping and filing and organizing them.

He is not alone in his penchant for saving articles from the magazine *Time* once called "the Bible of bass fishing." Frequently, long-time B.A.S.S. members write to tell about their filing systems for BASSMASTER stories. Others complain that an advertiser's coupon is printed on the back of an article they wanted to keep. Still others plead for copies of old stories that were thrown away mistakenly.

With *BASSMASTER's Best Tactics And Techniques*, there need be no worry about filing, cross-referencing or coupon-clipping. And certainly no one would throw away a handsome, 352-page volume like the one you're now reading.

Not only will bassin' bibliophiles treasure this latest volume in the Best of BASSMASTER series, but newcomers to the sport also will find this book to be an invaluable aid to a higher education in bass fishing.

Editor Colin Moore scoured the pages of 23 years' worth of BASSMASTER Magazines to select representative stories on the best bass-fishing techniques ever devised. Included here are illustrated mini-manuals on everything from flipping and pitching to stream-fishing strategies. The reader will learn how to "shake" a worm for suspended bass, how to work spinnerbaits in deep water, how to set a hook more effectively, how to use tackle to best advantage, and more. There's even a topical index at the end to help you find each reference to a technique you may want to study in greater detail.

I think you'll agree with me that Colin Moore has done a commendable job of planning and organizing *BASSMASTER's Best Tactics And Techniques*. The result of his labor — and of the contributions of some of America's best fishing writers — is a helpful, enjoyable and treasurable addition to bass-fishing literature.

Dave Precht, *Editor*
BASSMASTER Magazine

Photo: Gerald Crawford

Photo: Ronnie Arthur

CHAPTER ONE

OVERVIEW:
How Bassing Techniques Have Developed

A review of fishing techniques of the past 20 years, and what's ahead.

Photo: Tom Evans

How Bassin' Techniques Have Developed

By WADE BOURNE

Over the past two decades, new techniques have been devised as solutions to age-old bass-fishing riddles ...

It was early 1975 when Californian Dee Thomas decided to head east and try his luck on the Bass Anglers Sportsman Society®'s Tournament Trail.

He had a technique the circuit regulars hadn't seen before, an offshoot of a West Coast bassin' method called "tule dipping." The good ol' boys just snickered.

Thomas first competed at Toledo Bend in March, and he failed to finish in the money. His new technique was designed to catch bass from individual, scattered pieces of cover, and The Bend's flooded jungles were too large a maze.

But in his second tournament, in April on Arkansas' Bull Shoals, the snickering stopped, and the bass fishing world took note. Dee Thomas found the conditions he liked, and he won by a heavy margin, this when many "name pros" scratched.

Thomas dubbed his new long-rod technique "flipping," and as Paul Harvey says, "Now you know the rest of the story."

Flipping was quickly adopted by anglers around the country, and it has subsequently revolutionized the sport of catching bass. In the last 10 years, flipping has produced enough fish to win more tournaments than any comparable method.

In 1967, the year BASSMASTER® Magazine was born, flipping, skipping, kneeling-and-reeling, "doing nothing" and a host of other modern techniques had not even been conceived.

The past two decades have seen an enormous evolution in bassing knowledge, strategies, and baits and tackle with which to employ them. New techniques have been conjured up as solutions to formerly unsolved fishing riddles.

What's a better way to catch bass holding tight in thick cover? Flipping.

What's a more efficient, faster means of catching bass on sunken creek channels? Deep-cranking.

What's the best way to reach bass hiding deep beneath boat docks? Skipping.

A few of these techniques were discovered by accident, but most of them were devised and refined by anglers who possessed the vision and daring to try something different.

And undoubtedly, as this trying has been so rampant since '67, so will it be in the next 20 years. Anglers will continue to explore new frontiers. Present-day techniques will be altered to match emerging challenges. And when these alterations won't turn the trick, entirely new methods will be developed.

Deep water, clear water, heavy cover and suspended bass are examples of fishing perplexities which may give rise to new techniques in the future.

Following is BASSMASTER's 20th Anniversary look at how popular bassin' techniques have developed since 1967, plus a forecast of what's ahead in the next 20 years. Looking back can be fun but, more importantly, it can also be instructional. For by noting how techniques have changed, farsighted anglers might anticipate what lies ahead and thus get a jump on the future.

What Constitutes a "Technique"

In bass angling, a "technique" is a combination of three elements: the tools (tackle and bait), a spot, and the method by which the first are employed in the second to take fish. Flipping is a good example. This technique involves a long, stiff rod, heavy line and a jig or plastic worm; shallow cover (weeds, brush, stumps, etc.); and the close-quarters, pendulum-type lob

Photo: Charles Beck

Photo: Steve Price

Among the side effects of the bass-fishing boom in the past couple of decades is more sophisticated tackle that accommodates a variety of new techniques. Likewise, the evolution of lures and how they're presented has helped anglers derive more enjoyment and reward from the sport.

Photo: Bob McNally

that drops the bait in front of fish holding around this cover. Eliminate any of these elements, and you're not flipping.

Therefore, the evolution of bassin' techniques over the last 20 years has involved a lot more than simple bait presentations. In many cases new techniques, or refinements in techniques, have resulted from changes in tackle, lures or the bass' environment, which alters its behavior.

Using this definition as a foundation, here is how various bass fishing techniques have developed since Ray Scott's first All American bass tournament on Beaver Lake, Ark.

Flipping

"Back in the 1950s, I met a guy named O.C. McGhee who had moved to California from Arkansas. We became friends and started fishing together, and he taught me his long-pole technique for bass. Basically, it was just jig-poling," says Dee Thomas. "We used it to dip jigs down into the tules where the fish lay in pockets."

When tournament fishing came to the West Coast, Thomas began competing, and he was consistently successful with his "tule-dipping" method. Soon other anglers started complaining that his 12-foot pole gave him an unfair advantage over those who used "standard" tackle.

"I was scheduled to fish a U.S. Bass tournament in 1973, and the man who owned this circuit called me and said he was getting a lot of protests. He asked what was the minimum length pole I would consent to and still fish the tournament. I said 7 1/2 feet, and he agreed. That's how that rule got into effect."

Thomas mounted a casting reel on a 7 1/2-foot saltwater rod, and he began stripping out line and experimenting with an underhand lob presentation. He soon found that he could fish from farther away, more accurately and deeper than he had been able to with the 12-foot pole. He named this new method "flipping," and in 1975 he headed east to test it on the BASS-MASTER® Tournament Trail. In a couple of years, his technique had become the rage among bass fishermen nationwide.

From that time until now, the flipping technique has undergone several alterations. One pro responsible for several of them is Basil Bacon of Springfield, Mo. Bacon immediately recognized the potential in Thomas' style of fishing, and he adapted and refined it to several new situations, particularly to

grasslines in Florida and milfoil in the Tennessee River system. Eventually flipping was applied to almost every dingy-water, shallow-cover situation.

When flipping's popularity was on the rise, tackle manufacturers began supplying this new market with graphite rods and special thumb-bar flipping reels (another innovation attributed to Bacon).

Flipping baits also went through an evolution. Dee Thomas first used a hair leadhead jig and plastic-worm trailer. But through the years, living-rubber skirts replaced the hair skirt, and pork frogs replaced worms as the No. 1 add-on. (Pork provides greater buoyancy than plastic, thus slowing the fall of the bait and giving a bass longer to decide to strike it.)

In warm-water situations, plastic worms with pegged slip sinkers are now favored by knowledgeable flippers, and a few anglers are also flipping spinnerbaits, spoons and other "non-traditional" lures (for this technique) into tight cover.

One early 1980s offshoot of flipping was a technique called "pitching." Basil Bacon describes this as "long-range flipping." Basically, this is a specialized casting method utilizing flipping tackle and baits. It requires disengaging the reel and letting the spool turn as the bait is pitched underhand toward a target. It is designed to take bass holding along outside edges of grass or timber lines, where moving the boat into standard flipping range might spook the fish.

Nowadays, specialized tackle is available to serve a fisherman's every need. Photo: Gerald Crawford

Plastic-Worm Techniques

Every pro who's ever been interviewed has probably been asked the question, "If you had to choose one bait . . .?" It's safe to bet that nine out of 10 pros answered "plastic worms." These lures are standards for bass fishermen, both because of their great adaptability and their productivity. Few would argue that plastic worms will catch more bass in a broader range of conditions than any other lure type.

These baits were the offspring of World War II plastics technology. The first models were pre-rigged worms sporting exposed hooks, propellers and beads. They were fished by trolling or by casting out and reeling back in with a steady, straight pull. If they brushed up against cover, they'd hang.

Then, around 1960, the Texas-rigged worm made its debut, and suddenly bass anglers were able to cast into the thickest cover. This was the standard, widely practiced technique for wormin' in 1967.

"The slip-sinker weighted, lift-and-drop method is still extremely popular today," says Jim Ising (formerly of the ZetaBait Worm Co. in Jacksonville, Fla.). "Drop-offs, humps, heavy vegetation, brush, treetops and other types of structure are still largely fished by anglers using this traditional rig. The main difference in how they use them is that today they set the hook as soon as they feel a bite, whereas back in the '60s, most fishermen let a bass run with the worm before they'd strike."

Ising is confident that anglers are an inventive group, and despite their continued dependence on the Texas rig, over the years they've devised numerous other ways to fish plastic worms. Most of these new techniques were designed to be more efficient than the Texas rig in specific cover situations.

"Doodlesocking" was an early example of this inventiveness. This technique entailed vertically lowering plastic worms through the branches of Sam Rayburn's and Toledo Bend's submerged timber. By tightlining and jiggling worms straight under the boat, anglers could skin bass off the tree trunks that couldn't be reached any other way.

"Skipping" is another good example. This is a technique for shooting a worm back under overhanging objects like tree branches or piers. Pro angler Ron Shearer of Kentucky is credited with popularizing this method in the late 1970s. He used a long spinning rod, a worm with a pegged bullet sinker and a powerful sidearm cast. "It's just like skipping a rock across the water," Shearer describes. "If you do it right, you can skip a worm 15 to 20 feet back up under cover."

A third example of how plastic-worm techniques have been altered to fit different fishing conditions is the Carolina rig. This setup consists of a heavy sinker run up the line, a barrel swivel tied on behind, a 2- to 4-foot leader tied below the barrel swivel, and a worm on the end of the leader. The technique is to cast this rig out, allow it to sink to the bottom and then drag or hop it back in. The heavy sinker digs into the bottom, while the worm skitters along behind on the leader. The Carolina-rig technique emanated from the region for which it's named, and it was designed to catch bass off deep, relatively snag-free bars and drop-offs. It became famous when pro angler Jack Chancellor of Alabama used it to win the 1985 BASS Masters Classic® on the Arkansas River.

In many cases, the evolution of certain techniques is actually an evolution of the acceptance of those techniques. The floating worm is a case in point. Since plastic worms have been available, a handful of anglers have always fished them as slithering topwater tempters. Yet only recently has this technique become widely accepted. Today, weightless worms frequently are snaked across thick vegetation or through heavy brush.

Still other techniques have been developed in recent years by inventive anglers. Running grasslines (moving steadily along edges of vegetation and fan-casting worms into borderline pockets) is an effective way of covering lots of territory and catching scattered fish. Each cast is pumped only two or three times before the worm is water-skiied back to the rod tip in preparation for the next cast.

"Deadsticking" (casting a worm, allowing it to settle to the bottom and not moving it for 30 to 40 seconds) is a recent technique which is gaining a large following as a producer of spawning and/or reluctant bass. And skidding a Texas-rigged worm along a clean bottom (no hopping or swimming) is another non-standard method which is earning a reputation as a catcher of inactive fish.

Jigging

"Jigging" is a term which describes a lure's action produced by a lift-and-drop retrieve. While being jigged, a lure may also be pulled horizontally along the lake bottom, or it may be jigged up and down in the same spot ("vertical jigging.") Two bait types are traditionally used for jigging: leadhead jigs and jigging spoons. For standard jigging, the leadhead jig with a pork rind or plastic grub trailer is the preferred bait, while the jigging spoon is routinely used for vertical jigging. However, either lure can be adapted to either retrieve method.

Bass pro and lure consultant Bobby Murray grew up in Arkansas, where jigging for bass with leadheads first started. He says, "The original leadhead jigs were bucktails that came out of old Army surplus survival kits. After World War II the sale of these jigs coincided with the boom years of bass fishing on Ouachita and Bull Shoals and other Arkansas lakes. Those first jigs were flatheaded, like a butter bean, and they'd lay over and catch on anything. They were designed to hang up."

Despite this flaw, the basic jigging technique was devised. Its intent was to allow anglers to maintain bottom contact and to massage likely structure for deep-water bass. The original pick-up-the-bait, swim-it, let-it-fall method is intact today, but innovations in lure and tackle design have opened new jig-fishing panoramas.

Bobby Murray continues, "By the early to mid-60s, we'd progressed to using the round- and banana-head jigs, but none of them had weedguards. When fishing timber, we'd have to make short casts. A long one would hang up every time. But then weedguards came along, and this allowed us to start casting right into the brush. Not having to worry about hanging so often made jig-fishing a lot more effective, because we could probe the cover better."

One subsequent change in the bait has been the switch from bucktail and polar-bear-hair dressings to living rubber, which offers a more lifelike appearance in the water and longer life in the tacklebox.

Murray says that improvement in rods has been the largest significant change in jig fishing in the past 20 years. Graphite models offer the sensitivity needed to detect subtle strikes, and rods can now be built with the proper combination of butt strength and fast-tapered tip that this technique requires.

Besides the switch to fishing in heavier cover, Murray says there is one other trend in the use of jigs.

"Jigs have always been thought of as cold-weather baits, but now more anglers are learning that they're just as effective in hot weather, and day in and day out, they'll catch bigger bass than will plastic worms."

Jigging spoons were originally used in salt water, but some unknown angler adapted them to largemouths in South Carolina's Santee-Cooper lakes about the time of BASSMASTER's first issue. Vertical jigging with spoons was localized to this area for a few years, and then Blake Honeycutt of Hickory, N.C., exported the technique via tournaments into other parts of the South. It soon earned a small but devoted group of followers. It has never gained great popularity among the bassing masses, but those who know how to use the jigging spoon say that, when bass are bunched up on deep structure, it's one of the deadliest of all lures.

"We started out jigging along deep structure in cold weather," Honeycutt remembers. "We'd find a school of bass with our depthfinder, and then we'd drop a spoon down into them, let it sink to the bottom, rip it back up 3 to 4 feet and then ride it back down with a semi-slack line. Strikes would almost always come when the spoon was falling.

"From this technique we progressed to casting and jig-hopping it back along sand bars, gravel bars and other smooth structure types. And eventually we started fishing it in warm weather along drop-offs, places where other anglers would fish a worm. With a jigging spoon, we could get right over the drop and jig vertically along it. This way we could work a drop-off a lot faster and cover it better than a worm-fisherman could. And we could fish deeper. We could fish 40 to 50 feet down with 17-pound-test line and still be effective."

Spinnerbait Techniques

Since the mid-1960s, spinnerbait techniques have been altered according to fundamental changes which have occurred in bass fishing. Modern-day spinnerbait experts utilize these new methods to take fish their predecessors never even knew were around.

Pro angler Guy Eaker of Cherryville, N.C., is a longtime spinnerbait devotee who has seen these changes take place. "Twenty years ago, everybody fished a spinnerbait along the outside edges of cover. You'd cast close to a bush or brushpile or grassline, and if there was a feeding bass hanging just inside it, you'd have a chance at it.

"But today, the fish are subjected to a lot more pressure. The ones holding on the outside edges get caught or spooked pretty fast. That means the spinnerbait fisherman has to cast back into the middle of the cover to get the ones that were thought to be inaccessible before. This is the biggest difference between now and 1967. Today more people are casting right into the thick stuff."

Eaker says new techniques for fishing grass or weedlines are a good example of this change. Rather than staying out away from these vegetation lines and casting to their edges, modern anglers are positioning their boats closer to the cover and tossing spinnerbaits several yards back into it to holes or pockets where "inside" bass lie. Eaker adds that a major switch to willowleaf spinnerbaits in a tandem-blade configuration facilitates fishing in the heavier cover, since the long, slender willowleaf spins easier in the salad.

Another change in spinnerbait techniques is how today's anglers fish stumps, logs and other solid objects. "We've finally realized how important it is to actually *hit* the cover, to bump it, and then to allow the bait to 'die off' toward the bottom. I'm not sure why, but this bumping, falling action seems to trigger more strikes."

Eaker says a similar technique applies to downed treetops or standing timber. "We used to swim the bait through the limbs and then let it drop at the end of the tree. Now we're easing it up over every limb, and then letting it sink back down. You might pull it up, crawl it over a stick and let it fall 10 times before clearing the tree."

And one recent spinnerbait technique that's gaining in popularity is what Eaker calls "slow-rolling" on deep structure. Formerly considered shallow-water lures, spinnerbaits are increasingly being recognized as good lures on submerged points, creek channels and other spots once reserved for diving crankbaits and plastic worms.

One other change in spinnerbait techniques is how these baits are actually cast out to target zones. The old, standard overhand cast is now giving way to an underhand roll cast. "You can be a lot more accurate with an underhand cast. You can keep the bait low to the water, which means you can shoot it back up under bushes, docks and other overhanging cover. And since you don't cast the bait as high, it lands softer, which is less likely to scare nervous fish. All these things help you catch the tighter-holding bass that we're seeing more and more these days," Eaker concludes.

Crankbait Techniques

In 1967, crankbaits weren't exactly ignored, but neither did they figure prominently in many BASSers' fishing plans. The old, metal-lipped Bombers and Hellbenders were overshadowed by plastic worms and spinnerbaits. A handful of anglers cranked, but there were few spots or situations that couldn't be fished better with some other type lure.

Tennessean Fred Young changed all this when his hand-carved Big O arrived on the scene in the early 1970s. A whole new style of fishing evolved around this fat, wobbling, shallow-running plug. Suddenly tournament anglers were putting their trolling motors on high and fast-cranking these baits past as many spots as they could. They were after the "instinct-biters" or active bass, and they caught enough fish to cause a whole new legion to convert to being "crankbait fishermen," as opposed to "worm fishermen" or "spinnerbait fishermen."

As crankbaiting caught on in the bassin' ranks, lure companies generated a whole new family of balsa and plastic "alphabet" plugs. By the mid-1970s, many bait designers were experimenting with different bodies, diving lips, weights, rattles, paint and other features to learn which combinations would produce more fish.

Paul Elias of Laurel, Miss., is recognized as one of the country's best crankbait fishermen, and he remembers when these changes were taking place. "This experimentation with crankbaits coincided with the big boom in knowledge about bass habits, especially the discovery that a lot of fish lived out away from the banks in deeper water. Pretty soon crankbait companies were turning out lures that would dive deeper, and this trend hasn't let up since," Elias notes.

The BASSMASTER® Tournament Trail became the proving grounds for new deep-water crankbait techniques. The pros learned that they could cover deep-water structure faster with crankbaits than with plastic worms and other, slower types of lures. They began experimenting with lighter lines, longer rods and what later came to be known as the "kneel and reel" technique of poking the rod tip down into the water to gain additional retrieve depth. Combining the best of these modifications, they could now crank structure as deep as 14 feet. (This is the method Paul Elias used to win the 1982 BASS Masters Classic® on the Alabama River.) The race for depth has continued, and today lure makers are turning out baits purported to reach 20 feet and deeper.

Besides the deep technique, several other specialty methods have evolved for crankbaits over the years, and anglers routinely experiment to see which is most effective on any given day. One such retrieve is the stop-and-go method, momentarily stopping the retrieve whenever the lure bumps into a stump, rock or other underwater object. Another involves intentionally "mistuning" the bait so it will veer offline and scrape around bridge or dock pilings, riprap and other types of vertical structure. A third is random search-casting on flats with vibrating crankbaits.

Topwater Techniques

One angler with a great perspective on the subject of fishing topwater baits over the last 20 years is Dick Kotis of the Fred Arbogast Co. A longtime proponent of topwaters, he's seen trends come and go, and he's watched the techniques change.

When plastic worms and crankbaits became the vogue, the use of topwater lures diminished.

"Actually, the way you use these baits is probably less conducive to change than the other lure categories. I mean, there are only a certain number of ways you can work topwaters, and they don't vary much from one year to the next," Kotis says.

"But what does change is the degree of intelligence with which fishermen select and use topwater baits. In 1987, the average angler is much smarter in this area than his predecessor of 20 years ago. Modern fishermen know how to choose the right colors and actions to suit water conditions and moods of the fish," Kotis continues.

He says when plastic worms and then crankbaits became the vogue in the '60s and '70s, topwater use slacked off to a great degree. The established method of casting a bait out and waiting until the ripples disappeared was too slow for run-and-gun anglers who kept a stopwatch to see how many casts they could cram into a minute.

"Today, though, we're seeing a move back to topwaters. Some tournament fishermen are using subsurface baits to catch a limit of fish, and then they're going to a topwater plug to upgrade their weight. It's a fact that you'll catch bigger bass on topwaters than you will on underwater lures."

One current topwater technique which does lend itself to run-and-gun fishermen is fast-casting small poppers or chugger baits. This method is an effective means of searching for (or attracting) bass on feeding flats, points, in stumpfields or other large, relatively shallow areas where the fish may be holding. Another topwater technique which accomplishes this purpose is buzzbaiting. And Tennessee tackle maker Billy Phillips was responsible to a large extent for making this lure and method a standard in the bassing world. In the mid-1970s, Phillips used his own Buzz Jewel to win several regional tournaments. But what got everybody's attention was when he relied on the buzzbait to qualify as a B.A.S.S. Federation angler for two separate BASS Masters Classics.

"Buzzbaits have been around for a long time, but they'd mostly been worked on a long pole and a short line," Phillips says. "I just designed a bait that you could cast and keep up on top of the water. I adapted it to my style of fishing (short, fast casts around submerged, shallow cover)."

Phillips continues that the basic buzzbait technique hasn't changed since the mid-70s. "There are a lot of three-bladed baits out now, and modern reels with faster retrieve speeds make it easier to hold the bait on the surface. But there's not a lot to change about casting it out and cranking it back in. You just keep moving and covering a lot of water with it."

"Finessing" bass with lighter lines and lures is popular among modern fishermen.

Photo: Gerald Crawford

Light-Tackle Techniques

Twenty years ago, light spinning tackle in bass boats was fodder for hard-core jokesters. Theirs was a "real men don't eat quiche; real BASSers don't use wimp tackle" mentality. In '67, most anglers pursued bucketmouths with broomstick rods and well-rope lines.

Today, though, the lightweight rigs are included in most every bassin' man's arsenal, and they're being used more and more. This switch to light line and small, subtle baits is one of the major trends in the sport.

Charlie Brewer is the guru of light-tackle users. It was back in the early 1960s that this Tennessean figured out that, day in and day out, thin lines and little lures attract more bites. He started designing baits in the mid-60s, and in 1970 he founded the Crazy Head Lure Co. (later renamed Charlie Brewer Slider Co.). Since that time he has crusaded for light tackle, and his message is finally getting through.

"It was back in the '60s that I came up with the Slider worm and the 'do-nothing' way of fishing it. The actual technique hasn't changed much since then. You still use light spinning tackle, and you make a slow, no-action retrieve. You just crank with the reel. You don't put any action into the Slider with the rod tip.

"But there is one big difference in where it's fished today and where it was back then. Now, more fishermen are casting Sliders and other small baits right into thick cover. They've learned how to play big fish on light tackle, and they understand now that they can effectively use the light stuff anywhere they can throw heavier baits. Sure, they'll break a fish off once in a while, but if they get twice as many strikes on the light baits, they can more than make up the difference in what they catch."

Charlie Brewer adds that the quality of light tackle has undergone vast improvements in the past 20 years. Graphite rods are much more sensitive and lighter in weight. New spinning reels are also lighter, and they have better gear and drag systems. And finally, lines have greater strength and abrasion resistance, less twist and better sensitivity to soft strikes.

Extensions of Charlie Brewer's light-tackle philosophy are the "finesse techniques" spawned in the western United States and now working their way east. California pro Rich Tauber is a practitioner of the finesse methods, and he says they're meant for such situations as clear water, heavy-pressure lakes and post-cold-front bass. Basically, finesse techniques are designed for when the fish are deep, spooky and reluctant to hit larger baits with more pronounced actions.

Tauber says there are three main finesse techniques in current popular use. The first is a jig/squid-type grub combo (such as Bass'n Man's Fat Gitzit) free-falling on slack line beside cover spots. The angler rarely feels the pickup. Instead, he simply detects a heavy sensation when he starts to move the bait, and that's when he sets the hook.

The second finesse technique is bumping a dart-head jig and 4-inch worm down steep, vertical structure, such as bluffs or rock walls. And the third finesse method is called "doodling" or "shaking." This involves lowering a 4-inch worm (often a paddletail design) down to deep structure (rockpiles, treetops, etc.), and then just shaking it right in the cover with subtle, 1-inch flips of the rod tip. All three finesse techniques require medium length/action spinning tackle, no heavier than 6-pound-test line, a reel with a smooth drag, and the patience of Job.

Techniques of the Future

So much for recent history of bassin' techniques. What about the future? How will techniques evolve, and what will the most successful BASSers be doing to take fish two decades from now? Following are predictions of the experts cited in this article as to how techniques will develop by the year 2007.

Flipping: "This technique may decrease some in popularity in the next few years. The cover in a lot of lakes is starting to rot away, and as these lakes grow older, many of them are also clearing up. Both these conditions decrease the opportunity for flipping. The result is that all the flippers may get crowded into smaller areas where the conditions are still right. The fish in these areas will get hammered, and this technique will become less productive. When this happens, I think we'll see some fishermen turn to other methods," predicts Basil Bacon.

"I'm not saying flipping will go away, though," he continues. "We'll still have a lot of vegetation and some timber and other types of shallow cover, and when you've got this situation, you'll have some bass that can be caught by flipping. I just think the use of this technique may be at its peak right now, and it might slide back a little in the next 20 years."

Plastic-Worm Techniques: Jim Ising notes, "It's a fact that more good fishermen are fishing for fewer bass. Some biologists are starting to wonder if we're catching most of the 'active biters,' if we're taking the aggressive bass out of the gene pool and leaving only the reticent, reluctant fish.

The effect of this would be the breeding of a strain of super-hesitant bass. If this is so, and it may very well be, then anglers of the future are going to have to be even more conscious of their lures' speed, action, color, hook size and a lot of other factors to imitate *exactly* the different forage the bass want. Translate this into plastic worms, and I think you'll see a lot more of the slow, subtle techniques like dragging and deadsticking."

Jigging: Bobby Murray doesn't expect jig-fishing techniques to change much in the next 20 years, though he does foresee more anglers turning to them. "People can learn so much faster now from magazines, seminars and videos. They understand that a lot of fish live down deep, and that the lead-head jig is a good way to catch them. Also, I think improvements in tackle may make jig fishing more effective. In 20 years we might see 20-pound line that feels like it's 10-pound-test."

"I think that, as people learn more about spoons, they'll be turning to them," predicts Blake Honeycutt. "In my opinion, fishing pressure is outgrowing the fishery. The last great untapped opportunity in bass fishing might be suspended bass, and sooner or later somebody's going to figure out how to get these spooky, inactive fish to strike spoons. When they do, it'll open a big, new frontier."

Spinnerbaits: "I don't think shallow-water fishing with spinnerbaits will change all that much. But I do think we'll see a lot more fishermen using spinnerbaits deep. This bait is very effective on deep ledges and drops. I don't think many fishermen are aware of how much feeding goes on down there. I'm guessing that 20 years from now more people will understand that, and they'll be crawling spinnerbaits along spots where they're fishing plastic worms or deep crankbaits right now," forecasts Guy Eaker.

Crankbaits: "I'd guess we'll see a continuation of the present trends — deeper and maybe smaller baits," states Paul Elias. "I don't know how much deeper than 20 feet we can go, but we can learn to refine our techniques in those depths, to learn even more about when and where bass can be caught in deep water and how to keep the bait in the strike zone longer."

Topwater: "One real possibility for change in topwater fishing is the use of these baits over deeper water," says Dick Kotis. "We know that bass will come up from great depths to strike topwaters, but not many people have tried this technique. This might be a good method to take suspended fish or fish holding along deep river ledges. The problem that fishermen are going to have to overcome is that foolish feeling that comes with working a surface bait over 20-foot structure."

Light Tackle: "I think light-tackle techniques will definitely become more and more prevalent as the years go on. The future of bass fishing lies with light tackle," says Rich Tauber. "We are going to see lighter varieties of the 'finesse' baits and probably miniatures of traditional large plugs. Light tackle will continue to improve in quality, and more and more fishermen will learn to handle it as well as they do heavy tackle."

Now let's review these answers collectively. The major trend is evident. In 20 years, more anglers will be fishing deeper, and they will be intent on catching many of these bass via subtle, light-tackle techniques.

Rick Clunn agrees with this. Often described as the "thinking man's bass pro," Clunn acknowledges having spent hours pondering the future of the sport, trying to decide what skills he needs to work on to stay competitive as tournament bassin' heads toward the 21st century.

Clunn says, "On a scale of 1 to 10, right now I'd rate our knowledge about bass and our skills for catching them at around 3 1/2. We've learned a lot in the past 20 years, but we've still got a long way to go.

"I think by the year 2007, we might be up to about a level 6. We'll understand a bass' senses better, and we'll know more about what makes it strike. And we'll probably be a lot better at adapting our techniques to the different moods of the fish. When they're shallow and active, we'll still be using heavy tackle and 'power techniques' like we do today. But when they're deep and not so active, we won't be trying to force them to do something they don't want to do. We'll be better at adapting to what the fish want, and we'll be making those changes quicker."

So in sum, the successful fisherman of 2007 will be the one who is adept at both the heavy/shallow/fast and light/deep/slower techniques, and who knows when to use each. He will be a lot more versatile than we are today, and he won't be afraid to change techniques when his instincts tell him it's time to do so. And even then, according to Clunn, he still won't know all there is to know about catching bass.

— JUNE/JULY 1987

Photo: Mercury Marine

Photo: Grady Allen

CHAPTER TWO

TACKLE TIPS

The evolution of tackle and how it can be used to the best advantage of fishermen.

CANE-POLE TALES

By BYRON W. DALRYMPLE

Old-timers well remember how, with cane pole and bait, they sacked up the bass. The method is by no means out of business . . .

The average, impeccably equipped bass fisherman of today would about as soon be caught wearing button shoes as fishing with a cane pole. Many might tell you that very few bass could be — or ever were —caught that way, anyway. How could anyone possibly find and get close enough to take fish under such handicaps?

Indeed, to the Bassmaster using all the accoutrements of modern bassin', the thought of cane-poling does seem a bit ridiculous.

However, there are many older heads and less-than-elite bass enthusiasts of all ages who would just smile. The old-timers know what happened years ago, before the deluge of innovations, and they know how they sacked up bass, how crafty one had to be to accomplish it with a cane pole, and all about the unique joys and thrills of this homely fishing. Other younger but bumpkin types from down the country, who still swear by and use the cane pole for their bassin', would do their smiling because they'd consider the modern zoom-around, equipment-mesmerized bassmen as dudes who never "learnt much about ordinary fishin'."

The fact is that the cane pole is a truly deadly bass-catching instrument. It is also surprisingly sporty, and requires of its manipulator true craft.

Naturally, most of us are bound to move along with progress. The cane pole did to a large extent "go out with button shoes." But there was a time when it was the mainstay of bassmen's tackle, and we might learn from it. Highly skilled technicians adeptly hauled out scads of bass using it. In addition, though few of today's anglers are aware of it, the groundwork for many of the techniques of modern bass fishing were laid by cane-pole fishermen.

When I was a youngster, the angler who used tackle other than the cane pole was the exception. There wasn't much else available. When you went fishing it was assumed you fished with standard equipment: a cane pole, 10 or 12 feet long, and a length of stout, braided, salt-'n-pepper cotton line about as long as the pole. Bobbers often were employed, and I can assure you they were not brightly colored plastic. They were whittled from dry stick, sometimes, on the spot, or else a bottle cork was employed, split halfway through with a sharp pocketknife and the line pulled into the slot.

Nobody bought sinkers. In small towns they weren't available. The nut of a stove bolt served perfectly.

What purchase early-day cane-polers did dote on were their hooks. Oddly, in today's fishing world, hook names seldom mean much to the average bass angler, but in the heyday of the cane pole there were heated discussions over which was best, an Aberdeen or a Sproat, a Limerick, Carlisle or Kirby. The long-shanked, thin-wire, straight-bend Aberdeen was sworn by among those who dabbled baits onto the brush because, hung up, it would bend and pull free. The Kirby, with its offset bend, was the favorite of many, but some minnow fishermen swore its point gouged back into the bait, killing it.

"Good Ol' Ways" — Certain methods taken for granted during cane-pole days would be considered by today's standards impossible to use successfully. As I write this, I envision a pair of bass fishermen I watched often. Both were bib-overall farmers who lived in the vicinity of a small bass lake near my home and fished as a team. They kept an old flat-bottomed wooden rowboat on the lake, with a coffee can in it to bail out water coming in from leaks.

One man handled the oars. The other stood up front holding a long cane pole. Their expertly expedited system put them practically within reach of every bass they caught. It was like bowhunting compared to hunting with a rifle. They invariably carried a bucket of crawdads in wet moss. The lake shore was studded with submerged and partially submerged stumps and blowdowns. With no bobber on the line, just the sinker and the terminal-kicking crawdad on a hook, the pole man stood poised and quiet in the prow. The skill with which the oarsman worked was phenomenal. Not a splash, barely a ripple.

Jockeying to utilize breeze and keep the sun right so the fisherman's shadow didn't touch the water, the boatman would glide the boat within reach of a stump or log. In slow-motion, like a gunner stalking a buck, the cane-poler eased his implement forward and slipped the crawdad quietly into the water right against the stump. Today's long-distance lure casters couldn't sit in the same league. He moved it up and down a couple of times. If no strike occurred, he dropped it in on the other side of the stump.

The stealthy system was utterly lethal. When a bass lolling in its lair seized the kicking crawdad, the fisherman abruptly rammed the hook home.

Such splashing and cavorting! The pole man didn't fool around with the quarry. The wildly floundering bass was held at surface until its strength ebbed somewhat, then was swung into the boat. After the pole man had caught a couple, he and the boatman changed places.

Points to Ponder — The points to note that made this system so deadly are several. The silent movement of the boat gliding within reach and avoiding shadows was a classic technique. Further, by no other method and with no other tackle could the bait be presented so precisely and the bass so adroitly, and without hangups, removed from its lair. The challenge was in the stalk and the close approach, the excitement in outwitting the fish. Although most of the present-day bass-boat and electronic-gadget crowd are unaware of it, thousands of big bass still succumb annually to similar cane-pole approaches — in the "backwoods and down-home" bailiwicks of bass fishing where modernism has failed to take hold.

It amused me recently to read a story in a highly touted national magazine telling in detail how a certain astute Southern bass fisherman had — get this — within the past few seasons pioneered and perfected a new, surefire method for trophy bass. This is the technique of using large baitfish — usually shiners — up to a foot long and letting them run under weedbeds and in other places likely to harbor mounting-size bass.

I could hardly believe what I was reading when I noted the young fellow's picture and came to that "pioneered and perfected" part. Go on now! A half-century or more ago both blacks and whites in the South were butchering shoat-sized bass via the outsize-baitfish technique, and they used no souped-up modern bass tackle, just the trusty old cane pole.

Cane-Poling Memories — The first experience I ever had with this fishing was on Florida's Lake Panasofkee over 30 years ago. A young black man named George Mobley worked occasionally as a guide out of a rather broken-down fishing camp near the mouth of Pana Creek. He took me out in an old wooden boat whose paint was peeling. Mobley practically lived off the swamp and the lake. He carried a cane pole, and I insisted that he fish as much as he wanted to right along with me.

I remember how, when we walked through a section of swamp to get to the boat, Mobley slid his cane pole ahead of him and tapped the vines and roots. "Lookin' for cottonmouths," he explained. At first we caught so-so bass, or I did. But as we became better acquainted Mobley asked if I'd like

Cane-pole fishing can teach an angler a lot about bass, and hone his tackle-handling skills in the process.
Photo: Byron Dalrymple

him to show me how to catch big bass.

He could scull a boat masterfully. He sat in the bow, the haft of a short paddle thrust into his armpit, the blade working silently in a half circle around the prow. He could guide the craft anywhere he wanted it, stop it, back it, and with never so much as the sound of a droplet of water falling. In a shallow place he stopped and threw out some oatmeal from a tin can. Then he sat immobile for 10 minutes, after which he produced a small thrownet, flared it expertly and dropped it over the spot he'd baited with oatmeal. He hauled it in, flopping with golden shiners.

I recall with a chuckle that I sat there waiting for him to throw back the 10- or 12-inchers and keep the small ones. He did just the opposite, plopping those broiling-size baitfish into a big bucket. It was now late afternoon, and he sculled silently up near a mass of hyacinths, put a baseball-size cork bobber in his line 10 inches or so up from the hook, and skewered a monster bait beneath the back fin.

Reaching out his cane pole, he dropped the lively giant shiner at the edge of the weeds. The big bobber swirled and jiggled along the edge. There was suddenly an awesome but muffled *kerchug* under the weeds and they, too, jiggled over a yard-square expanse. In high excitement now, Mobley raised to a crouch and reached the long pole ahead as far as he could. A bass had seized the bait and had run back under the floating mat. The bobber had disappeared.

Mobley deftly picked up his sculling paddle and gave the boat a thrust toward the hyacinths to gain a few feet for the bass to run. Then, with pole tip at the water and weeds, he reared back. The pole arched over in an anguished bend but Mobley kept right on putting pressure to it. There was an awesome commotion under the hyacinths and Mobley brought the bass out into the open, keeping its head up, forcing it to run on tether round and round, throwing spray by the bucketful. Its tail looked, to me in my excitement, a foot broad at least.

Back at camp, that bass weighed a few ounces over 10 pounds. After that I was a convert. Mobley and I brought in bass and put them in a big cement bait tank to keep them alive. In three days we had more than a dozen above 6 pounds, several of them 8- and 9-pounders. I used my regular bass tackle, and was quickly convinced that by using the cane pole, Mobley landed big bass 2-to-1 over me. For this big-bait method, it is one of the most effective rods ever invented — able to precisely place and control both bait and bass. And that method definitely was not pioneered in modern times.

The great-grandfathers of many of today's Bassmasters were catching big bass with their big canes and big baitfish when this century was young.

Flippin' A Frog — Some early-days cane-pole experts specialized in using frogs. When I was in grade school in the Thumb area of Michigan, a lad several years older, one of the Richardson boys, used to take me fishing. His family were all outdoorsmen of the old-time school who made it up from experience rather than reading about it.

His father had taught him how to walk a riverbank and drop a frog hooked through the lips into likely holes and runs. He used no sinker. He could swing that frog out and plop it pinpoint, maneuvering often on hands and knees. The bass in that oxbowed river were smallmouths, and I marveled at how he could flip 'em out by the dozens.

Lake fishermen also used frogs in like manner, quietly drifting a boat along a lily-pad patch and "dapping" the frog — reached and swung out from the tip of the pole — out among the pads. It was a deadly technique, partly because placement and movement of the bait could be so exactly manipulated by the angler. However, not all cane-poling bass fishermen of those times used bait.

When surface bass plugs first became popular, numerous fishermen who owned no casting tackle used them with a cane and a length of line. They'd flip or swing the plug into small pockets, give it a chug or two, and repeat.

Cane-Pole Innovators — The first so-called "figure-eighting" ever done with bass lures was accomplished with a long cane pole and a short length of line. The line often was only 2 or 3 feet long. Various plugs and spinners were used. Some anglers swore by the Dowagiac plug with fore-and-aft spinners. They called the method "Dijacking." The boat was eased close to where a bass might lie — a log, pile of brush, a stump, a patch of lily pads. The short line and 12-foot pole allowed reaching and easing the lure into the water gingerly. When bass were very shallow, that was important. Then it was skittered in a figure-eight pattern back and forth, or sometimes simply drawn along near the possible lie of a bass.

As a young fellow I once fished with an old gent in Michigan whose only approach to bass fishing was to ease along in an old wooden boat around dense weedbeds and pads, looking for small holes among them. He loved summer fishing and was in his glory because, at that time, weeds were so heavy the other fishermen shied from them. He simply dunked his lure, usually a spinner and bucktail, down into small openings, using 3 feet of line at pole's end, jigging the lure a few times in each hole.

An immense advantage of this approach is that the instant a bass strikes, it isn't allowed to get into the weeds. Instead, the bass is heaved up out of them as soon as the hook is set. By no other method I know of can bass be taken so efficiently from such places.

It is the very handicap and restrictions of the cane pole that add to the sport and challenge of using it. I think, too, it is doubtful that modern BASSers quite realize the specialized excitement and joys of, for example, bait fishing for bass with cane pole and bobber. One is, first of all, very close to his quarry — a pole length or slightly more distant. One watches the bobber and suddenly it begins to jiggle a bit, sending out warning circles upon the surface.

When casting a lure with modern tackle, remember that the strike is a split-second thrill. But when bobber fishing, one watches with exquisite anguish the first jiggle of the bobber, then it moves a bit, begins to travel over the surface, goes down, comes back up, goes down and moves away as a bass runs with the bait. The strike excitement is drawn out into all but unbearable seconds of tension.

To be sure, the battle, once entered, is not likely to be long. No runs or deep soundings can occur. But the jumps do materialize, and the drama and delightful suffering of the "take," as if in ultraslow-motion on a movie screen, imparts an inner agitation and bright excitement within the angler unknown elsewhere in bass fishing.

This is not to say, of course, that we all should revert to cane-poling. I am convinced, nonetheless, that a step back to the old-time tackle on an experimental basis can teach modern BASSers much they don't know about bass fishing, and perhaps make them better fishermen. They learn, among other things, how to be quiet, how to stalk bass, and how to handle really difficult tackle and succeed under severe restrictions.

Fishing with a cane pole involves hours of quiet vigilance mixed with a few moments of frantic excitement.   Photo: Dave Precht

Years ago, for instance, I watched two fellows on a small Michigan lake casting deerhair bugs of the type then most often used, and when I saw the action of a surface strike and a fish fought and landed on a fly rod, I was so excited I had to somehow try this.

Alas, I had no fly-fishing tackle. I was still at the cane-pole stage. I bought a single deerhair bass bug, tied it to the end of my salt-'n-pepper cane-pole line, and swished and whooshed my long pole in an attempt to cast. Of course, a real fly line, which is heavy and carries the light lure, would have placed it where I wanted it. All I had was muscle to overcome wind resistance. Even that did not suffice very well. Still, I caught bass! Not large, but that was my launching into fly fishing for largemouths.

Unique Technique — That may have been a high point of innovation in the world of cane-poling for bass. But a method I observed in detail years ago, popular at that time in central Ohio and as far as I know never known elsewhere, was one of the cleverest uses of the cane pole I've ever seen. It also employed a lure, and the technique of using it required such expertise — and resulted in such devastation among big bass

— that it should at least be recorded in bassin' history.

Baby-bottle nipples were at that time available in almost any small-town general store. They were made of white rubber. Some obscure and ingenious bass angler of the region had conceived the idea of turning a nipple into a killer bass lure. Various models evolved, but the basic one was formed as follows:

A bit of weight was fixed to the shaft of a treble hook. The nipple was set down over the shank, the hooks curving out around the collar that fitted onto the bottle, and the shank brought out through the top by enlarging the sucking holes slightly. The line was, of course, tied to the eye of the treble.

The manipulation of the lure was as ingenious as its conception. It was an art. One man handled the boat, another the pole. The line was roughly as long as the pole. The shallow hangouts of bass were stealthily approached. Obviously the method was practiced only during seasons and hours of the day when bass were in shallow places around cover. The fisherman reached out just the same as the crawdad-dropper did, as his partner maneuvered the boat into position. He then dapped the nipple lure onto — but never under — the surface.

A skilled and practiced nipple fisherman could dance the lure over a small area of surface so that it dimpled the water in a little circle and meanwhile produced a continuous sucking sound, the bottom opening creating a surface suction. The light touch upon the surface had to be exact, and the tip of the cane pole had to move with practiced precision in order to produce the proper action, sound, and result.

The result was often phenomenal. Big bass would slam upward to seize this dancing, escaping white morsel. Strikes were spectacular, hookups virtually certain. Nipple fishermen of that day and place took great pride in the artistry of their performances.

Bass fishing has certainly moved a long way since the decades when the cane pole reigned as standard tackle. I doubt, however, that the ingenuity and expertise of the men who handled this simple tool so successfully years ago, and of those who continue to do so today, has been — considered its handicaps — vastly improved. A study of its history and methods might prove valuable to all of us.

— MARCH 1983

BASSers And The Long Rod

By BOB GWIZDZ

Longer bass fishing rods aren't being used just for flipping anymore. There's a trend to general bassin' use . . .

Paul Elias was on fish. Big fish. Competing in a B.A.S.S. tournament on Lake Eufaula on the Alabama-Georgia border in midspring, Elias had located a concentration of huge largemouths in shallow water. His only problem was he couldn't reach them. And not because they weren't cooperating; the bass were taking his offerings eagerly. He just couldn't get his hook sunk firmly in *Ol' Micropterus'* jaw. Elias takes it from there:

"The wind was blowing like 25 miles an hour. The only way you could fish was to get upwind and drift in the direction you wanted to fish and try to guide the boat with the trolling motor. The fish were hitting my spinnerbait and running toward me with it. There just wasn't any way I could stick the fish," says Elias.

That's when the proverbial light bulb came on and burnt brightly in Elias' head.

"I switched to a 7-foot flipping stick," the 31-year-old reigning BASS Masters Classic® champion from Laurel, Miss., recalls. "And I caught two 7-pounders just like that," he concluded with a snap of his fingers.

Though he didn't know it at the time, Elias was taking part in one of the most sweeping trends to hit bass fishing since short, stiff poles became standard tackle. Flipping sticks, those lengthy, long-handled weapons which became the rage for several years because they gave anglers the ability to present baits to fish at close range and in tight cover, aren't just for flipping anymore. Long rods are becoming more accepted all the time as substitutes for basic casting rods.

"I just felt like it was the shortness of the rod that was

doing it," says Elias, reflecting on his tackle adjustment that propelled him from far back in the pack into a third-place finish at the Eufaula tournament. "I figured a longer rod would give those fish a bigger jolt. It worked."

Why Use A Longer Rod — Now anytime he's fishing in a heavy wind — and a lot of times when there isn't any wind at all — Elias switches to a flipping rod. "It stands to reason," he says, "that if you've got a foot- to a foot-and-a-half longer rod, you're going to pull more slack out of the line when you set the hook."

Elias is only one of a number of Tournament Trail anglers who have gone to using the longer rod in any number of fishing situations. Ronnie Young of Wichita Falls, Texas, is another. Young, who qualified for and finished fourth in the BASS Masters Classic on Montgomery Lake, Ala., in his rookie season on the B.A.S.S. tour, says using a flipping stick under most conditions is part of the reason he did so well.

It took Young just a couple of hours of fishing with Elias to become a convert to the long rod. "Paul wore me out when I fished with him in Missouri (Lake of the Ozarks)," says Young, a 35-year-old welder. "It was really windy and we were fishing a jig. I got the hits to catch Paul, but I just couldn't hook the fish. There was too much slack in that line."

So Young took up casting with his flipping stick. Now he rarely puts it down. And he thinks it has made all the difference in his fishing.

"It's helped me a lot," the quiet, confident BASSer says. "I don't think I've lost a fish since I started using it. I

The advantages of using a long rod are a matter of basic geometry — the longer the rod, the farther the cast. Presenting baits from a distance lessens the chance of spooking a school of fish.
Photo: Gerald Crawford

might have missed a few bites, but as far as hooking a fish and losing it, no, I don't think I've lost one."

It's the same principle at work as fishing in a wind — taking more slack out of the line on the strike — that's played a big role in his success, says Young. He estimates that he takes up twice as much line when setting the hook with a flipping stick than with an ordinary casting rod.

"And you can really whack 'em," he adds. "You can use your forearm and really put your weight behind it. I'd say the biggest advantage of a flipping stick is the hookset you get. You can really hurt them with it. A lot of times I have to dig that dadgum hook right out of their heads."

Bully Bass Around — Hooking the fish isn't the only secret, either, thinks Young. He believes that an angler can hit the fish so hard that it becomes too disoriented to fight and is in the boat before it knows what hit it. Kenneth Walker, an Austin, Texas, machinist and three-time

Classic® contender, agrees wholeheartedly.

"A fish is not excited when it bites," notes Walker. "The bass is not ready to fight until you hit it. If you can get it moving toward you, all its strength is helping you get it.

"What you do in the first five seconds after you stick a fish determines whether or not you're going to catch it," concludes Walker, who uses the long rod when he fishes vertically in deep water and anytime he's working heavy cover. "It helps you get a big fish out of tight cover. You can move a fish farther after you stick it. And you have more control over the fish once you stick it, too."

With all the talk about setting the hook, you'd think that's the only advantage the long rod might have. You'd be sadly mistaken. A flipping stick also offers opportunities for presenting the bait that the shorter rod doesn't.

Longer Rod Advantages — It's basic geometry. The longer length of the rod causes the tip to travel farther on the cast, resulting in greater distance. The advantage is most obvious with schooling fish — and not just black bass, but with whites and stripers, too. By presenting the bait from afar, there's less chance of drifting into the school and spooking the fish. But that's by no means the only advantage. Catching deep or suspended fish is another plus.

Elias proved that at the 1982 Classic. His winning fish were caught about 14 feet deep and he was catching them on a crankbait. In order to maximize the amount of time Elias had his bait in the strike zone, he tossed the bait well past the target, cranked it quickly to attain the proper depth, then moseyed it back to the boat. He kept it at maximum depth for as long as possible. It resulted in enough strikes to win the Classic.

Another advantage is depth. By fishing from a kneeling position and keeping the rod tip in the water, anglers can work a crankbait in areas that have never been searched with such a lure. "I've been using a flipping stick with a crankbait longer than I have with a worm, mainly to get the crankbait deeper," says Young. "I can get that crankbait 4 or 5 feet deeper with it. I guarantee you I've bumped bottom 15 feet deep with a (Bagley) DB3."

Zell Rowland "kneels and reels" with a long rod to get the lure deeper.
Photo: Gerald Crawford

The longer rod has an advantage in that it allows an angler to reel down and punch off a lure that's hung up on the bottom in deeper water than if he used a shorter rod. That's why, Bo Dowden said after his 1980 Classic victory on the Thousand Islands area of the St. Lawrence River in New York, he used a flipping stick to work a jig and pork frog over the rocks and through the weedbeds. But Dowden admits it wasn't his only reason.

"A flipping stick, to me, is a better piece of equipment to work a jig with," Dowden says. "I can swim it a long distance with that long length. It works real good with a worm, too. When I'm worm fishing, about 95 percent of the time I'm using a long rod."

The same applies if you fish buzzbaits or plastic frogs in heavy vegetation, and even to tailspinners in open water.

"Ninety percent of your fish will hit on the drop," believes Elias, who never fishes a Whing Ding, his favorite tailspinner, with anything but a long rod. "If you've got a longer rod you can pick the bait up higher and get a longer drop."

Awkward At First — Anglers attempting to use a flipping stick as a casting rod for the first time will, for the most part, find it a bit awkward. Most begin by using a two-handed power cast, similar to that used by a surf fisherman. It takes a little practice before using a flipping stick as a casting rod becomes as natural as, well, using a casting rod.

"Now I feel funny without it," says Elias. "From the time I started using it, from that first brainstorm, I've felt more and more comfortable. One day of throwing it and I had it down."

Certainly there has to be a disadvantage to using a flipping stick. It's heavier, right? Less sensitive? But ask proponents of the long rod and about all you hear are more accolades.

"It's definitely more strenuous, but it's no big deal," states Elias. "And if you're going along a bank casting, you don't have to switch rods if you come to a treetop and want to flip into it. You're ready."

Adds Young: "I don't think I lose any sensitivity. Basically I'm a line watcher anyway — I'd rather see them than feel them. The only disadvantage I can think of is it's kind of hard on your stomach (where the rod butt rests) when you hit a good fish."

"You're going to see a definite trend toward a bigger bass rod," Elias opines. "No doubt about it." He should know. His title as the reigning BASS Masters Classic champion should be enough to make him a trendsetter.

— FEBRUARY 1983

FLY-ROD CASTS THAT TAKE MORE BASS

By C. BOYD PFEIFFER

Learn these three fly casts — Double Haul, Lazy "S," Curve — to catch more bass . . .

Problem — You are waist-deep in water in a famed smallmouth river, fly rod in hand, with a rising fish a good cast away. And you suspect that the small-mouth would take your offering, if only you could get the fly to drift naturally for a few feet over the fish, rather than the fly being immediately dragged downstream by the belly of the line caught in the fast current between you and the fish.

Solution — The Lazy "S" cast to get a drag-free drift of the fly on moving water.

Problem — You have worked your bass boat into the weeds as far as it will go, but you still can't quite reach the spot you just *know* harbors a good-size largemouth bass. Short of lengthening your cast, there is no way to reach the bass.

Solution — The double haul, which will allow you to build up more line speed and, thus, more casting distance.

Problem — You can see a largemouth bass scurrying around on the far side of a stump, but by the time you move the boat to get into the proper casting position the bass will proba-bly have stopped chasing minnows. And, you can't cast over the stump or reach the fish by normal casting means. You're stumped, if you'll pardon the pun.

Solution — The left-hand-curve cast, to get the fly around the stump and to the bass.

The point is that fly fishing has a lot of advantages when it comes to swinging around a fly or popper to get to the fish quickly and easily. As pointed out in previous articles in BASSMASTER® Magazine, it has the advantage of allowing you to pick up an offering in the middle of a retrieve and drop it immediately down in another, more productive spot, should the fishing conditions require.

However, fly rods are not unlike all those modern 35mm cameras. The cameras have lots of fancy controls, but if you don't know how to use them, they are no better than an inex-pensive model. Fly rods allow you to have a lot of control of the fly to get the bass, but if you don't know these capabilities, a fly rod is nothing more than a long, expensive, funny-looking stick with which you try to catch bass.

The Basic Fly Cast — It pays to take a look at what fly casting is and how to properly make a straightforward regular cast, before looking at a few of the many variations. First, fly casting is really a misnomer, since the weight necessary to all casting methods is really in the line, not in the lightweight fly or bug. Second, the fly is not cast off the reel, as with spinning, spincast or casting, but the line is gradually lengthened while casting until the casting distance is reached.

There are two basic mistakes common to most beginning flyfishermen, or to those who use fly tackle only occasionally. First, there is a tendency to swing the rod through too wide an arc when making each cast, and second (and closely associated with the above) is the tendency to bring the backcast to or beyond horizontal, causing the fly line or bug to hit the water on the backcast and ruining any casting efforts.

While books could be written about fly casting (and some have — *Fly Casting With Lefty Kreh,* by Lefty Kreh, Lippen-cott, paperback and hardback, is excellent), some basics can be briefly discussed to get both the embryonic fly caster and the fly off the ground, so to speak. While it is best to practice and perfect your technique over water, you can practice ade-quately in the backyard, with the exception of some casts and casting methods.

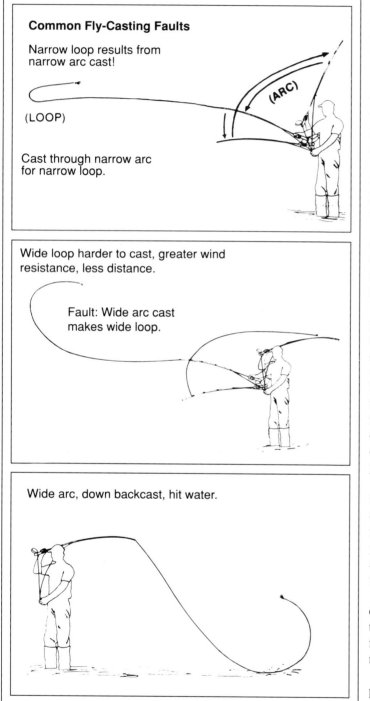

Common Fly-Casting Faults

Narrow loop results from narrow arc cast!

(ARC)

(LOOP)

Cast through narrow arc for narrow loop.

Wide loop harder to cast, greater wind resistance, less distance.

Fault: Wide arc cast makes wide loop.

Wide arc, down backcast, hit water.

you think of yourself standing at the center of a giant clock, with the rod pointing to the left (at 9 o'clock), you can think of raising and flexing the rod between the 9 o'clock and 1 o'clock positions.

Done properly, the line should straighten out over your shoulder in a smooth arc as the line flows out behind you to straighten out in the air. (You can turn around to watch the line while this takes place, both in practice and while fishing — there is nothing illegal, immoral or fattening about this practice.)

If the line does not flow back horizontally in the air, but instead angles down to the ground or water, it means that you have extended the force of the rod through a wider arc and used the rod to "push" the line toward the ground.

One easy way to think of the correct technique, described once by a beginner just getting into the sport, is to think of the cast at this point as a "back lift," in which the line is lifted up in the air, rather than the traditional term "backcast."

Once the backcast rolls out straight (pause during this period), reverse the casting force on the rod to push the rod forward and cause the line to roll out in front of the caster. Here, too, a short arc of force on the rod is best, since it will create a narrow loop cast. A tight loop particularly is important in bass fly casting, since much of the fishing is on open water, under slight or high wind situations, and with big bugs that require the most force and energy transmission to get the fly, leader and line to "turn over" completely and straighten out at the end of each cast you make.

The Double Haul — One easy way to make straightforward casting even easier, however, is to develop the double haul. While initially this technique seems to be the fly caster's equivalent of the kid's trick of trying to pat your head and rub your stomach (or is it the other way around?) at the same time, it is easy to learn, once you understand the principle.

The technique of the double haul is one that will accelerate line speed, which is the only way to get more distance, often necessary in bass-fishing situations, whether fishing a large nymph on a smallmouth river or plopping a rubber-legged bug next to a stump in a largemouth slough.

There are two ways to develop line speed. One is to push the rod through the arcs described above, to cause line to follow, almost like slowly cracking a whip. The second is to pull on the line. You can prove this to yourself by holding the rod stationary, parallel to the ground, and give the line a good, sharp tug. The results will be line that travels rapidly back toward you.

Now, place these two techniques together and pull on the line as you raise the line up off the water to make the backcast. Then, as the line flows back, allow your line hand to move up the rod with the pull of the line. Once at the end of the backcast,

Begin by working with a short length of line (about 30 feet), which you can control. Too many anglers try to extend their distance capability during practice when the time should be spent on technique. With the proper technique, the distance will come.

Begin by flipping the line in a straight line in front of you. Then, to pick up the line, raise the rod sharply and with increasing force until the rod is slightly over your shoulder. If

push the rod forward while simultaneously pulling down with your hand to pull the line forward. The result is an acceleration of the line through both the movement of the rod and the sharp, short pull of the line at the same time.

As a result, you will be able to propel your bass bug or fly farther than you might if not using this trick. Also, when making false casts (several casts in the air to lengthen line or to get the fly over the target area), you must use the double haul on both the forward and backcasts for maximum efficiency.

The Lazy "S" Cast — Once this method of increased line acceleration is basic to your casting, other casts make additional presentation and tricks while bass fishing easy. Take, for example, our first problem outlined, where you wish to make a cast to a rising smallmouth, but the river current keeps washing out the line and preventing a lifelike float of the fly. The solution here is the Lazy "S" cast, in which you make a cast using the double haul, but at the end of the forward cast and as the line is rolling out to the target, shake the rod horizontally back and forth to create horizontal waves in the line as it falls.

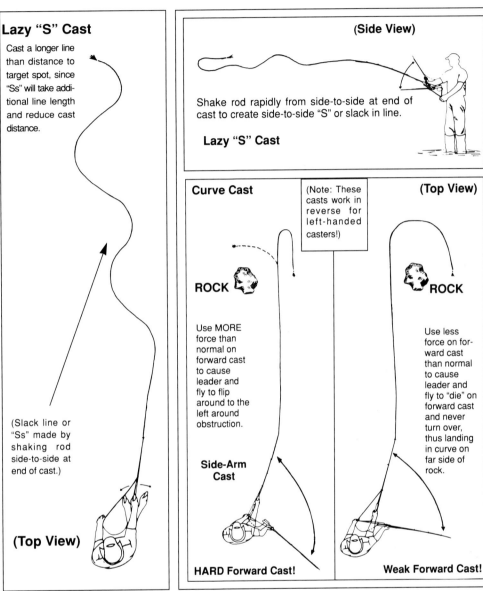

Lazy "S" Cast

Cast a longer line than distance to target spot, since "Ss" will take additional line length and reduce cast distance.

(Slack line or "Ss" made by shaking rod side-to-side at end of cast.)

(Top View)

(Side View)

Shake rod rapidly from side-to-side at end of cast to create side-to-side "S" or slack in line.

Lazy "S" Cast

Curve Cast

(Note: These casts work in reverse for left-handed casters!)

(Top View)

ROCK

Use MORE force than normal on forward cast to cause leader and fly to flip around to the left around obstruction.

Side-Arm Cast

HARD Forward Cast!

ROCK

Use less force on forward cast than normal to cause leader and fly to "die" on forward cast and never turn over, thus landing in curve on far side of rock.

Weak Forward Cast!

The result will be a line on the water with a series of "Ss" throughout its length. The current will wash out the slack "Ss" in the line while not disturbing the leader or fly floating down to that waiting smallmouth. Presto, by the time the line slack is completely washed out by the current, the fly will have reached the fish, the smallmouth taken the fly (hopefully), and you'll be fighting a fish.

Admittedly, the cast is a specialized one, but one that is easy to do any time current requires a natural float to reach a bass.

The "Curve Cast" — That same forceful double-haul cast can also be used to cast a fly around the far side of a stump, rock, log or other obstruction to present a lure to a bass that otherwise couldn't be reached. By making a cast in which you use more force to propel the line, you can cause the bug to turn and make a loop in the end of the leader and line. Now, by casting

with the rod held at your side or at a slight angle, you can make the cast so that the bug will pull the leader around the corner.

While the above cast is best for casting to the left by right-handed casters, (or casting to the right with left-handed casters), reverse loops can also be made by making a cast horizontal to the water, but putting less power into the cast than necessary. The result will be a cast that never straightens out and casts a loop to the right for right-handed casters and to the left for left-handed casters.

These three casts enable you to reach bass farther away, reach them around the corner, and to get a proper float for smallmouth on fast-river situations. They are just a few fly-casting solutions for bass-fishing problems; other casts can solve other problems equally well, but then that's another story, for another issue.

— JULY/AUGUST 1983

ULTRALIGHT IS RIGHT FOR BIGMOUTH BASSIN'

By DAVE BOWRING

Why should you add another outfit to your bass tackle? Because lighter wands, minisize lures, and scaled-down tactics are often the only solution to a tough bass problem . . .

The best reason for using ultralight tackle is that the gossamer gear catches fish when other tackle won't. All other reasons are secondary, to my way of thinking.

But get into the reasons why ultralight tackle works, when and where it works, and things get very complex very quickly. To my mind, the light gear is what I go to when the more common heavier bass tackle has been tried without success. This generally means the fish are in water requiring special tactics, and perhaps in a mood requiring the same thing. Then is when the light stuff shows its worth.

The best example I know of was the set of conditions encountered at the BASS Masters Classic® several years ago. It was held on Lake Mead, under high skies with bright, direct sunlight and water as clear as dry martinis. The bass were super-wary, to say the least, and the usual 15- to 20-pound-test monofilament hit the water like steel cable. So the tourney anglers went to ultralight gear, lighter lines, long casts and smaller lures — and they caught bass.

Rods, reels, lines, lures, accessories, and tactics . . . all these parts of the problem of catching bass change with the seasons, water conditions, weather fronts, and fish moods. Decide one is more important than any of the others, and you've broken the string between you and continued success on the water. It is as simple as that.

Fishing rods of all types have come an awfully long way. Today's newest interest is in lighter, but stronger, graphite rods. However, fiberglass makes up most of today's rods, and is malleable enough in manufacturing to

appear in ultralight sizes and weights without giving up the guts needed to handle heavy fish. B.A.S.S. President Ray Scott's fiberglass Mini-Stix is a fine example of good power in a 5 1/2-foot small package. A newer line of 100 percent graphite rods just being introduced will interest Bassmasters.

Even light tackle meant for bass fishing must have two main ingredients — guts in the lower section to rough-house big fish in cover, and a handle section large enough to give the angler something to hang onto. Some custom-rod builders reduce the weight even further by taping the reel to the handle rather than using conventional reel seats; this practice is preferred by many BASS pros on the cast-for-cash Tournament Trail.

Line guides should be of the improved type for even line flow, low friction, and reduced wear. The new Speed Guides, available on many modern rods or separately from good dealers, fill this requirement nicely.

Reels — and here we're talking strictly about the open-face spinning types — are more critical than you might think, mainly because their ruggedness is of great importance. The smaller the reel (and all ultralight spinning reels are small), the more critical their quality under stress.

There are several things to look for in the ultralight reel intended for bass fishing. These include ball-bearing construction to assure smooth operation; a good, smooth drag system that won't freeze up at the wrong time; quality springing in the bail system; and an outer cowling or outer surface that is tough enough to withstand minor shocks and abrasions without becoming chipped. And make sure the reel handle is large enough for easy handling when a heavy fish is on the line. Small handles slip out of fingers.

One good reel filling those requirements is the Cardinal 3 ultralight reel by Zebco. The Cardinal 3 features a double spring system (in case one spring should malfunction on the water, there's a backup), excellent smoothness, and spools offering varied line sizes and capacities, which are interchangeable. The smaller open-face reels by Quick also are worth attention.

Now then, what about line for the ultralight outfit you're building? Are some lines better than others, is there a place in bass worming for 4-pound-test mono, and how critical is knot strength and knots in general?

The move toward 4- and 6-inch plastic worms has brought this most popular type of fishing to the ultralight-tackle users. This in turn has made the quality of monofilament lines, particularly in the 4- to 12-pound-test class, all the more critical. Today, if a mono line allows much stretch at all, it's no good for worming. Moreover, today's lighter mono must be relatively limp (for good worm detection), and possess excellent knot strength.

And, it's a good idea to choose a mono line with a memory loss. Memory is the term used to describe the line's retention of coils it developed on the manufacturer's plastic shipping spool. Take a new mono line from its spool and drop it on the floor. Only

Ultralight tackle can often bring bites from bass with lockjaw, particularly in clearwater lakes.

Photo: Dave Precht

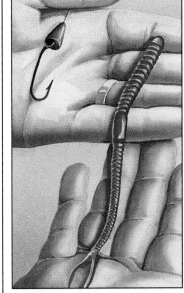

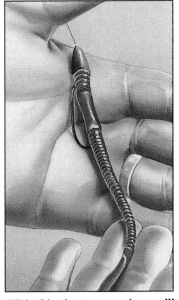

Here's veteran B.A.S.S. tournament pro Tom Mann's favorite worm rig for taking hard-to-get tournament limits. It's a standard 6-inch Jelly Worm he scales down to a short-worm rig.

Illustrations: Emily Craig

Pinch the worm off about 1/2 inch above the egg sac. Use a No. 2 Eagle Claw 295JB hook with a 1/8-ounce slip sinker. Rig the worm with a conventional self-weedless Texas-rig method.

With this short-worm rig, you'll seldom miss a strike. Hit the fish as soon as you feel the "tap." With light line, you must "sweep" the hook into the fish. Hard hooksets will usually pop the smaller 4- to 6- pound lines.

the limpest, most "forgetful" lines will drop in anything except a huge bird's nest of a tangle. Choose lighter line carefully, then be sure to install it on a reel with the coils going in the same direction they came off the commercial spool. This helps prevent those "wild" strands of line ballooning off a reel spool.

Tip: Fill the reel spool to within 1/8 inch of the outer lip. Doing so should lengthen the casts you make by (1) increasing the diameter of the line's coils as they come off the reel, and (2) decreasing the total number of coils off the reel per cast.

Another tip for tying the best possible knots in fine monofilament is to moisten the untightened knot just before you draw it tight. This makes the mono slippery and permits the hardest possible knot. Also, draw the knot tight with one gradual pull, rather than a series of short, hard jerks.

Lures and lure manufacturers just now are catching up with the idea of catching largemouth black bass on ultralight tackle. Not too long ago it was either use the featherweight spinners and jigs on your light rig, or nothing at all.

Among the scaled-down versions are the ultralight sizes of the Big-O, Big-B, Big Jim, Mann's Razor Back, and Rebel's Wee-R series of plugs. These are baits that either float or suspend themselves at rest, then dig for the depths when retrieved. Tom Mann has introduced his new Razor Back Pig size, a 1/4-ounce version of the crankbait-type craze, designed for ultralight largemouthing. The highly engineered bait contains two separate sound chambers (rattler), a scaled finish, double trebles and a new, longer diving bill. The manufacturer claims it will drop down to depths approaching 14 feet when used on 6-pound-test line. Now *that's* gettin' down there.

Also making a big splash among pro BASS anglers are the small, 4- to 6-inch plastic worms. Baits this size are easily cast with microgear and can be very effective when waters are super-clear or the bass are finicky.

Some of the small worms already come rigged with two or three hooks attached to mono threaded through the worm body, while others come unrigged to suit the angler's personal fancy. I prefer the latter because it gives me a greater latitude in which to match the prevailing conditions.

One accessory I've found invaluable for ultralight bassin', particulary when throwing a variety of plugs, is the snap, which is too light to affect the action of most plugs, while facilitating changing lures. It's still a good idea, however, to break off the snap every hour or so, then tie it back on again to assure a good knot.

Okay, the rod box of your bass boat, van or family station wagon is filled to bristling with baitcasting rods and reels, medium-weight spinning outfits, and maybe a fly rod and a spincast outfit. Why should you add still another outfit, the ultralight?

Because it catches fish, that's why, and often when no

other method will produce. I think you'll agree that's the best of reasons to make the change.

The secret is presentation, and visibility. These are the factors facing every bass angler, eventually, which makes ultralight gear the only logical choice.

Let's run through them.

Presentation means the way a lure is cast over the water, and how it lands on the water. Simply put, today's 1/2-ounce bass plugs make a considerable shadow over the water, and a heckuva splash on the surface, under the best of conditions. Some waters are so clear and shallow, and therefore contain bass so wary, that standard bass gear just won't do the job.

Take an afternoon near my Dayton, Ohio, home early last spring. I was fishing a one-acre farm pond, and the water was so clear I could plainly see bass as they swam by some 30 feet offshore. Standard bass plugs and worms merely spooked them into flight. I was stumped after two fruitless hours.

Then, I spotted three good bass lying in shallow, ginclear water under an overhanging bush. Just lying there, finning in place. The sight made my mouth water.

I put away my casting outfit and rigged a little 5-foot wand with a 1/8-ounce Burke curly-tail on a leadhead jig. I made a long, arching cast well past the bass' holding spot, but one saw it fly past and actually chased it, tracking the lure through the air and striking as it hit the water. I was able to catch three other bass in this manner the same day.

Had I been using standard gear, I think my 20-pound mono and heavier lure would have put these bass, too, off their feed. As it was, the will'-o-the-wisp line and bait *caused*, or rather *permitted*, the bass to strike. It looked good enough to eat, even though the water was super-clear.

This "trick" has produced for me several times since that afternoon, on waters often too clear and airy for the regular tackle. But I keep my ultralight handy for those days when it's ultralight or nothing for largemouth.

Light tackle, microline, and tiny lures may not appeal to some hairy-chested bass anglers, but it does appeal to fish. This method of fishing a small worm and jig will pay off in winter, and is often the answer for clearwater lakes and finicky feeders.

A twist to the light-tackle game spawned in the older clearwater lakes of Tennessee is a method called "Do-Nothing" fishing. This special style of light-tackle bassin' was developed by Charlie Brewer of Lawrenceburg, Tenn. On days when bass have lockjaw, Brewer's crazy-lookin' flathead "Slider" and miniworms can turn the trick.

Brewer calls this style of fishin' "Do-Nothing," because his idea is to play nature. Instead of hopping, jumpin', wigglin', and bouncin' this little worm bait, you slide it through the water. This is the action that best describes the movement of small minnows.

— MARCH/APRIL 1976

A FLIPPER NAMED FLOYD

By STAN FAGERSTROM

This new "Fly Rod Flipper" technique offers some advantages over the standard system . . .

I ran into a Bassmaster friend, Pete, the day after he'd participated in our area's largest bass tournament.

I slid into the coffee shop booth next to him. "Pete," I asked, "how'd it go for you over the weekend? Did you win that contest?"

My friend grunted. Then he held up his left hand. His first two fingers were freshly bandaged. "Look at that," he said as he wiggled the two digits. "Not only did I get skunked both days, those dang bass almost cut off my fingers!"

It didn't take long to get the full story. My bassin' buddy is into flipping for bass. He'd bought a couple of new graphite rods designed for that purpose and equipped them with levelwind reels loaded with 25-pound-test line.

Pete is a good fisherman. And it didn't take him long to get the hang of flipping. Within a couple of months, he was getting as many bass using that procedure as anything else. It was flipping that almost cost him a couple of fingers.

"I was in the south end of the lake where those pilings are," he said, "and I was flipping a jig-and-pork-chunk around the old duck blind that's in behind the wood. My line looped around the reel handle just as I flipped the lure out. As I tried to take it off the handle, I got the line wrapped around these two fingers. I guess I must have lifted the rod tip a little and made the jig-and-rind bounce. Anyhow, the first thing I know, I feel this tug. Instinctively, I jerked with the rod in my right hand while the line was still wrapped around my fingers." Pete paused and shook his head.

"You can guess what happened. That was probably the largest fish I've hooked in three years. The monofilament cut into both fingers and I thought I was going to lose one of them before the fish came off."

The "Flipper's Lament" — I'm not the only bass fisherman who has heard that kind of story. And one of the guys who had heard similar tales decided to do something about it. He's a man I've known for some time. You might have heard about him: Pat Floyd, inventor of the famous Floyd's Buzzer and a lure maker who has attracted the attention of plug pitchers all

The Floyd Flipping System utilizes a No. 10 floating fly line. The graphite rod is built with the reel seat constructed like that of a fly rod.   Photo: Stan Fagerstrom

over the country.

Floyd and I have never eyeballed one another face to face. He headquarters in Royal Center, Ind., and I'm across the country to the west at Silver Lake in Washington. Despite the distance, I feel as if I know Floyd better than some of the bass fishermen in my hometown. We've been swapping letters and ideas for years, and I think sometimes you learn more about another human being from the way he expresses himself on paper than you do in a one-on-one conversation.

Floyd is an unusual individual. If my sink stops up, I can't get to a telephone quickly enough to call a plumber. A guy like Pat Floyd would fix it himself, then he'd spend the next couple of weeks figuring how to design one that wouldn't stop up in the first place.

The same thing applies to fishing. When an inventive genius like Floyd sees a piece of equipment, or tries an angling technique that doesn't grab him just right, the wheels in his head start turning and eventually he'll come up with something that's more to his liking.

Like I said, Floyd has heard those stories about fishermen getting their fingers cut while handling monofilament in the process of flipping for bass. Once he observed a couple of tournament fishermen taping their fingers prior to a contest to avoid just such a problem should they hook really good fish.

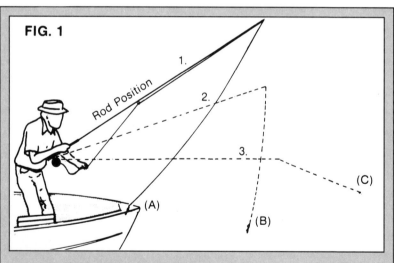

With the "Floyd Flipping System" the lure presentation is similar to flippin'; (A) let the lure swing toward you, (B) flip the lure toward the target , (C) as the lure hits, drop the rod to position 3. Let the line run through the fingers of the right hand (FIG. 2), then manipulate the lure by tugs of the fly line with the left hand.

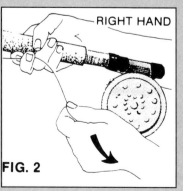

"Everyone builds flipping sticks in one of two ways," Floyd says. "They set them up either for spinning reels or for casting reels. Both have reel seats positioned in the usual fashion."

The Indiana lure maker also asks a couple of questions about the standard type of flipping rod. "Have you," he asks, "ever picked up a flipping rod with a casting reel on it that ever felt really comfortable or that the line didn't loop around the reel handle when you started fishing?"

Floyd's Flipping System — Pat Floyd didn't just sweat and swear when his flipping rigs wouldn't work to suit him. He set out to do something about it. The result is the *Floyd Flipping System* and it's a technique bass fishermen anywhere might want to try, especially if they've not been comfortable with the usual approach to this type of bass angling.

"The more I thought about flipping, the more it brought back memories of when I was a kid and had only one outfit," Floyd says. "It was an old bamboo fly rod and a J.C. Higgins fly reel. I could lay a fishworm under a hanging tree limb better with that old rig than any I've had since."

Those memories set the stage for the new method. Floyd got a tubular glass blank and mounted a reel seat on the extreme butt end in the same fashion you'd place the reel seat on a fly rod. Then he built up a cork handle like a fly rod has. On the business end, he used ceramic guides instead of standard fly-rod guides.

That was the beginning. To complete the outfit, he loaded an automatic fly reel with No. 9 fly line and hung a 30-pound-test leader at the end. The result was a flipping rod built like a fly rod and equipped with a fly reel. That setup, while it won't appeal to everyone, does have certain advantages.

Anybody who has done enough flipping to know what it's all about soon discovers that he's dead in the water unless he learns to watch the line like a fox eyeballing the henhouse on Saturday night. A good share of the time, a slight movement of the line is the only indication that a fish is there.

That's not always easy when a standard flipping outfit and a reel loaded with monofilament is used. I dislike a fluorescent monofilament, and the clear variety — which is least visible to the fish — can also be difficult for a fisherman to spot.

That's no problem with the Floyd flipping system. Remember, this procedure uses a No. 9 or 10 floating fly line with a leader on the end. The jig-and-pork or whatever lure used takes the line and leader down, but the part above the water floats up there where it's easy to see.

New Fly Rod Flipper — Floyd sent me one of his new rods, after he'd played around with it for a while, and asked me to try it. I found the blank he was using too heavy for my own tastes. Anytime I run into a rod problem I can't solve, I head for the nearby community of Woodland, Wash., to visit my friend Dick Posey, president of Lamiglas Inc., one of the leading rod builders.

I outlined Floyd's flipping system for Posey and he perked up like a rose in the rain. Together we picked out a graphite blank that has a lighter action than the usual flipping rod, yet one that has sufficient backbone to turn a 5-pounder if it's headed for cover.

I've thoroughly tested this new rod and it's a dandy. Like I said, it's a bit lighter than most flipping sticks and it's also lighter in weight because the rod is constructed without the collapsible butt section. That makes it a little less convenient to carry, but I'll accept that because I like the lightness.

Dick Posey is calling the new rod the Lamiglas Fly Rod Flipper. It's 7 1/2 feet long. For the do-it-yourself bassin' man, the blank number is a Lamiglas GLB901M. Bass Anglers Sportsman Society® members can get details and prices on either the complete rod or blank by writing to Dick Posey, president, Lamiglas Inc., Dept. B.A.S.S., P.O. Box 148, Woodland, WA 98674.

What Floyd's System Offers — I mentioned the advantage of having a floating line so those little "tics" can be spotted more easily. That's a great help. There's also darn little problem with line wrapping around reel handles or otherwise getting screwed up as at times when flipping with monofilament.

About the only thing I didn't do the way Floyd had suggested was select the same type of reel he likes. I've been using a single-action instead of an automatic. That wasn't through choice. I didn't have an automatic available. While the single-action fly reel hasn't been any problem, it isn't as convenient to use as an automatic would be. But in this kind of flipping all the reel is doing is storing line, anyway.

I've been using a weight-forward No. 10 floating fly line. Certainly the tapered line isn't a necessity. A No. 10 level floater ought to work every bit as well and would cost a whole lot less. With any kind of fly line, it pays to keep the line cleaned and dressed. It will flow through the guides more readily and float better.

Floyd told me he thinks it is the balance of the Fly Rod Flipper that makes it more pleasant to use. "I think it will catch more fish because your feel is better," is the way he put it.

Another advantage is the angler can be ready to strike constantly because the rod tip is always in position. With a conventional flipping setup, the cast is made and the lure worked back by lifting the rod tip. As the lure nears the boat, the fisherman's rod tip gets higher. I've watched some of the top B.A.S.S. pros wind up with a flipping rod tip so high when a hit came that they really didn't have anyplace to go with it. The result was a poor hookset.

That's not a problem with the Lamiglas Fly Rod Flipper. As soon as the flip is made, the rod tip is lowered so it points out along the line. Let the heavy fly line run through the fingers of the right hand, which is holding the rod handle. Retrieve the lure by little twitches of the line held in the left hand. Note carefully the illustrations that accompany this article because they are extremely important in getting the proper technique for the use of this system.

The line isn't gripped with the fingers of the right hand. Just hold it there loosely. The manipulation of the lure is done with the tugs of the left hand. As I mentioned, the rod tip is pointing out along the line. The advantage of this becomes apparent when a bass picks up the lure. The rod tip is down so it can be snapped. At the same time, the line is jerked backward with the left hand. It's sort of a double whammy and I'll guarantee it's possible to nail Ol' Bucketmouth to the wall when done properly.

Consider The Negatives — Those are the big advantages of the Floyd flipping system as I see them. There are a couple of negatives. One is that it's cumbersome to flip anything lighter than 1/4 ounce. The fly line, while it's easy to control and easy to see in the water, doesn't flow through the guides anywhere near as smoothly as monofilament. While it works beautifully in heavy cover where so much flipping is done, I haven't found it as good as the standard approach where the waters are clear and greater distance on the flip is a necessity.

One thing sure, that heavy fly line isn't going to slice fingers the way monofilament can, and will, if they get tangled at the wrong time. My early experiments with the Floyd system indicate that a fairly short leader, something less than 5 feet, is most satisfactory.

I've always regarded a fisherman's rod selection as something where personal preference is most important. The kind of rod I use might not appeal to somebody else and what he selects might not be my choice at all.

I haven't retired my conventional flipping outfits since Floyd introduced me to his flipping system nor do I have any intention of doing so. As I've pointed out, there are jobs the conventional rig will do better than the new method. I find any kind of flipping tiring after a time and it has been fun to switch from one technique to the other since Floyd introduced me to his own special approach.

He told me once that he really didn't enjoy yanking a bass from cover to the livewell in "two seconds flat" and that's about what flipping amounts to some of the time. But his mind is far too active, and his curiosity too great, not to try to figure out how it might be done even more efficiently.

The Floyd flipping system is his answer. And it will work. I've proved that to my own satisfaction. For more details, Floyd can be contacted at (219) 643-6215 or write him at Floyd's Baits & Services, Dept B.A.S.S., P.O. Box 326, Royal Center, IN 46978.

In a way, I always get a little ticked off at fellows like Pat Floyd. They're forever coming up with something I wish I'd thought of myself. But then I've had a little more fun with my flipping since Floyd shared his procedures with me.

— JANUARY 1983

Photo: Kitty Pearson-Vincent

CHAPTER THREE

PRESENTATIONS

Finding a bass is one thing, putting a lure in front of it is quite a different matter.

Photo: Glenn Lau Productions

THE INNOVATORS: ZANY TACTICS FOR BASS

By JOHN WEISS

"Gardening," "Wire-Lining," and casting "Judas Plugs" are off-beat methods some creative BASSers use to catch more bass . . .

For every bass angler who takes a new lure out of a box and merely begins chunking, there are 10 other BASSers who are not so content with traditional style. Almost nothing satisfies their incessant urge to experiment, improve upon an existing lure or technique, or even devise an altogether new method of lure presentation that will dupe more bass than ever before.

These anglers are "The Innovators," the ones who make bassin' the great, exciting, diversified, unpredictable madness it is today. It's a good thing we have so many non-conformists in our rank and file too, because how else would we ever have acquired such lethal strategies as flippin', yo-yoing, doodle-socking, deadsticking or walking the dog?

Indeed, if one thumbs back the pages of bass fishing annals to only 20 years ago, even the use of plastic worms rigged Texas-style was an unprecedented idea many said would never catch on. Yet today, what Bassmaster does not have and rely upon at least a modest assortment of the fake wigglers in his or her tacklebox?

All of this makes it worthwhile to look at a few surprises the 1980s may hold. They are revolutionary — even wacky — bassin' methods several tournament pros, guides and just average weekend anglers are refining, using with success, and hoping will eventually receive national acceptance.

There are two reasons why these tactics work. First, they are different. This is important because almost every popular body of water these days is filled with wall-to-wall bass hunters. Consequently, fish that have grown to lunker size undoubtedly know the catalog numbers and retail prices of virtually everything whizzing past their noses. Therefore,

catching them very often requires something out of the ordinary to attract their interest.

Also, the largest bass typically like to take up residence in special places where they are the least accessible to run-of-the-mill plug pitchers. They go into, behind, or underneath places that cannot effectively be fished by standard methods: places where lure presentation tests a Bassmaster's ingenuity to the limit.

So here is the pick of the litter, an array of positively outlandish angling methods presently being used by only a handful of enterprising fishermen, that may well prove to be commonplace tactics in the new decade. Go ahead and have a good laugh, just like you hee-hawed the prospect of using rubber (plastic) worms long ago. But when you're through, rig up and give these new ideas a try. You may be very glad you did.

• **Gardening** — An incredibly unorthodox idea that has nothing to do with planting tomatoes or sweet corn, but there is indeed an impressive harvest to be savored: big bass!

Also sometimes referred to as "raking" or "potholing," a Bassmaster uses a garden rake with an extension handle to uncover thick surface weeds to effectively fish the places gargantuan bass like to hide during midsummer.

You've seen, and despaired over, these waters many times before. They are usually quite shallow, and typically located south of the Mason-Dixon line, although the situation occasionally reveals itself on many small lakes and farm ponds throughout the North and Midwest.

These are the waters you travel to with high expectations, only to find entirely matted, dense vegetation. In some cases there may be a small winding channel here and there, but

mostly there are wide expanses of thoroughly carpeted, impenetrable hyacinth, hydrilla or coontail moss. The water temperature is warm. The sun is high and bright. And you just absolutely know the biggest bass are tucked way back under that cool, shaded canopy.

To catch those bass, you have to somehow get a lure to them. You could do that if only there were potholes in the weeds. There are none. So you make your own.

There are certain places where bass like to congregate under such matted expanses of weeds, and those are the recommended locations to undertake your "gardening" efforts. A few examples include wherever you know there to be a ditch, flooded stream channel, drop-off, natural spring or perhaps several stumps.

Then merely reach out over the bow of your boat and begin pulling clumps of weeds away to form a 3- or 4-foot diameter pothole. If a long reach is necessary, you can bolt a length of lightweight aluminum tubing (available at any junkyard) to the handle of the garden rake. In a relatively small patch of matted weeds, just one opening may suffice. But if an entire embayment is covered with the green stuff, you may wish to create a series of openings spaced every 10 to 15 yards apart.

The effectiveness of this far-out fishing tactic has to do with the nature of bass themselves. During the very early and late hours of dawn and dusk, big fish may prowl the outside edges of matted weedbeds. But during the remainder of the day, they do not like to have themselves so well exposed. They like to retreat far back underneath the cover to keep tabs on just tiny openings, and slurp in hapless food items that chance by.

Since "gardening" tends to temporarily disturb the area, it is best to wait about one-half hour before actually fishing the potholes you've created. When things quiet down, any bass spooked from the area by your activity will eventually return to the ditch, spring or whatever attracted them in the first place.

Use a plastic worm first. Cast it slightly beyond the potholes, crawl it to the edge, and then let it slither down into the dark opening. If that doesn't work, try a weedless spoon with pork rind or a spinnerbait.

This is no place for "toy tackle." Go armed with a heavy-duty rod and monofilament line strong enough to winch the prize out of the salad when the "go-rilla" wallops the offering.

• **Wire-Lining** — "Wire-Lining" is catching on fast in California's San Diego reservoirs and the deep canyon lakes of Nevada, Utah and Arizona as well as a smattering of other

The development of techniques such as crashing and kissing opened the door to anglers who wanted to fish cover like this.

Photo: Grady Allen

spots in the South and upper Midwest. Yet it is a method that should work equally well on any body of water that has extreme depths, a marked lack of cover, and, in addition to the bass, the presence of several cold-water fish species. (We're referring to other game fish like trout, panfish such as perch, or baitfish species such as smelt, ciscoes, alewives or perhaps herring.)

In cases like this, the largest bass, even though they are a warm-water fish, are nevertheless encouraged to live deep-water lives throughout much of the year. Many anglers, in fact, are catching bass from 12 to 18 pounds as deep as 80 feet!

The bass retreat to these levels for two reasons:

• Such waters generally are gin clear, and the fish feel a greater sense of security where underwater light intensities are minimum.

• Also, due to the nature of the inhabiting fish populations, much of the bass' forage base remains in deeper water due to their preferences for much cooler temperatures.

This is a situation in which conventional cast-and-retrieve tactics using monofilament lines are not as successful for reaching the largest fish. But wire line can indeed be used to present lures as deep as 120 feet.

Wire cannot be cast, however, so trolling is the *modus operandi*. The wire is spooled on a standard levelwind reel and a short, stiff trolling rod comes into play that is equipped with special guides to withstand the cutting torture the wire otherwise would inflict.

Tied to the terminal end of the wire is a 10-foot length of monofilament. The most effective lures are those which closely represent forage upon which the bass in that particular water are accustomed to dining. In the case of southern California waters, BASSers are painting minnow-shaped plugs such as Rapalas and Rebels in rainbow trout colors.

And in some cases they even are creating unique lures by first cutting off the front half of a slim-minnow plug and then cementing a soft plastic tail in place that gives a realistic swimming motion in the water. (See, *"Where The Lunkers Lurk,"* BASSMASTER® Magazine, Jan. 1980 issue.)

The most productive places to carry out these trolling maneuvers include deep shoreline points, underwater stair-step ledges and rocky outcroppings, submerged islands, and deep bars.

One variation of this strategy is to use a graph recorder to locate schools of trout or baitfish, and then lower plugs to that level by means of downriggers. A downrigger is a spool filled with wire line, a crank handle and a "cannonball" weight that

Judas plugs are used to find bass in a hurry. They're cast into thick cover where lunkers are likely to be holding.

Photo: John Weiss

is lowered into the water. The angler's monofilament line is attached to the cannonball with a quick-release mechanism that separates the fisherman from the wire at the same time as the strike. This allows the fisherman to enjoy a more spirited fight from his quarry with a lighter line, instead of the fish being encumbered by the heavy wire.

• **Crashing** — This off-beat technique is a shallow-water, heavy-cover type of bassin' that has to be seen to be believed. It comes into play when bass are on the flats but hiding smack-dab in the middle of button bushes, willows, stick-ups, brushpiles and hedgerows.

Less adventuresome anglers throw lures around the edges of the cover, fearful of hanging up and losing expensive baits. Now and then they'll entice a small bass that is prowling the perimeter of the cover. But if there is a buster bigmouth hanging around, you can count on that bass not venturing far from its lair. You have to go to the heart of the matter; almost hit it on the head, hoping for an involuntary, reflexive strike. The way to do this is with "crashing."

The tactic definitely requires a stout rod, a reel with guts

and line testing at least 30 pounds. A heavy 5/8-ounce spinnerbait in the color of your choice is the recommended lure.

Fish the edges of the bush first, in the traditional manner. Then ease the bow of the boat to within several yards of the cover. Hold your rod tip high, and let the lure hang down on about 6 feet of slack line.

Then, sweep the rod in an around-the-clock motion, and slam the bait right down in the middle of the cover. The idea is to use the weight and force of the downcoming lure and literally crash through, breaking the small, dead, brittle twigs and branches so the spinnerbait eventually penetrates the bass' hiding place.

If you don't succeed on the first attempt, crash the bait down again and again. Then, after the spinner has found its way through the overhead cover, pump it up and down on a tight line so it flutters seductively right in the middle of the bush or brushpile.

"Crashing" works, yet, strangely, doesn't seem to alarm bass, because it is apparently a simulation of spawning shad. In the late spring and early summer, swarms of the baitfish venture onto shallow flats, snug up close to woody cover, and then violently thrash around to loosen and expel their eggs.

Eventually the commotion is too much for a big bass to take and it goes berserk in an attempt to maul the prey. (See "Pro-Style Techniques For The New Breed Of Bass," March-April 1977 BASSMASTER Magazine.)

Be sure to check the terminal end of your line after every two or three "crashing" attempts. This tactic inflicts a tremendous amount of abrasion on monofilament lines.

• *Slip-Corking* — This change-of-pace bassin' idea was originally devised as a means of fishing rivers where logs, driftwood and other debris have a way of piling up like pickup-stix along various stretches of shoreline.

Bass like to hide deep in the logjams, but conventional lure presentation is almost impossible due to the presence of the current. It simply sweeps the lure out of position before it has had time to sink to the level where the bass are holding.

First thread onto the line a cylindrical cork bobber of the type that has a hole running lengthwise through its center. Then thread onto the line a heavy sliding sinker, 3/4 to 1 ounce in weight, depending upon how swift the current is. Finally, tie on a 4/0 Sproat hook, and rig a plastic worm Texas-style.

By next positioning the boat slightly upstream from the tangled logs you wish to fish (you may have to anchor), and then slowly paying out line, it is easy to work the bobber into the midst of the logs, hover it in place, and then vertically dance the worm around deep in the logs below.

This takes a bit of manual dexterity and rod-tip manipulation. And one key is the weight of the sliding sinker in accordance with how fast the current is running. But with a little practice it is possible to work the worm several feet within the jumbled logs.

Fishing in thick grass or moss is no problem when you can rake away your obstacles. Photo: John Weiss

Watch both the line and bobber for signs of a pickup. Strike the instant you think a bass has taken the worm.

Slip-corking also works on lakes and reservoirs where there is no current, but where there exists deep logjams or other cover in which usual cast-and-retrieve methods would snag on every cast.

• **"Judas Plugs"** — These special plugs are rapidly gaining in popularity. And they're free — you make them yourself from 6-inch lengths from a broom handle or wooden dowel. And they are just the ticket for locating bass as quickly as possible, because these lures have no hooks!

So-called because they "betray" bass, Judas plugs are used by those BASSers who are looking for one big, special fish but have only a limited amount of time and therefore must work fast.

Likely, that trophy bass will be in the thickest cover it can find. Yet working such cover with conventional lures is bound to result in many snags, and that spells plenty of wasted time. A "Judas plug" eliminates the need to retrieve the tangled lure, cut back the terminal end of the line, retie knots, and all the rest.

Most "Judas plus" are painted light blue, silver or other baitfish color. The only hardware is an eyelet at the front for tying the line. With the bait, the angler first spends time trying to find a bass he wants to catch. He tosses it into the thickest cover he can find, and seductively retrieves it through brush, drowned treetops and thick matted weeds.

When a bass gives itself away, it invariably bulges the water with its broad shoulders in an attempt to capture the minnow-look-alike. The "Judas plug" is quickly returned to the boat, and replaced in the water with a worm or buzzbait. A hookup is almost guaranteed. The advantage of a "Judas plug" for so-so casters is that they can cover far more territory in a day's fishing because of the zero number of snags and hangups that otherwise would result in casting stock lures with hooks. And in the case of professional anglers looking for fish during pretournament practice days, such deception won't "sting" the fish, which means those bass likely will strike again a day or two later.

• **Kissing** — Here is another off-beat ruse that allows aggressive Bassmasters to get cozy with increasing numbers of big bass every year. The type of cover best suited for courting is standing trees in about 5 feet of water, such as willows or cypress, but especially those with branches flaring out from the trunk, then drooping, almost touching the surface.

Bass like to hug the base of the tree, right next to the trunk, where it is shady. And seldom is a lunker largemouth inclined to swim 6 or 8 feet away from its hideout to inspect lures cast around the outside perimeter of the drooping branch tips. Big bass want the menu items served right in the dining room.

Another spot to "kiss" bass is where there are tangled logjams in shallow water, and getting plastic worms under the overhead latticework of woody cover is difficult.

An ideal rod for "kissing" can be a spinning or baitcasting model, but it should be short and stiff. A limber rod that flexes easily won't work because "kissing" requires a fast, snapping wrist motion that will quickly transmit as much energy as possible from the butt to the rod tip. I use 30-pound-test line and rig a 7-inch worm "Texas-style," but the real secret to this method is a light, sliding sinker, no more than 3/16 ounce.

The essence of "kissing" is causing the bogus wiggler, at the very moment it slaps the water after the cast, to "kiss off" the surface and skip along the water for an additional 6 or 8 feet. I recommend a floating worm because, when rigged with a 4/0 hook, there is just enough weight to cause it to slowly flutter and sink at the end of the "kiss."

A short cast is desirable. The worm is traveling at a high rate of speed and will therefore slide a farther distance when it kisses off the surface, as compared to a worm cast a long distance with a higher arc and has lost momentum when it touches down.

Ease the bow of the boat to within 15 or 20 feet of the cover, hold the rod low and parallel to the water, and, with a brisk side-arm motion, cast right to the edge of the branch tips that are hanging low to the water. When the worm sinker assembly strikes the water, the weight quickly meets resistance, stops and begins to descend. But the plastic worm continues, sliding across the water and pulling line through the hole in the sinker.

How far a worm will "kiss and run" depends upon the amount of muscle put into the cast, but it is also important to give line the instant the lure hits the water, or it will stop dead in its tracks. With spinning tackle, this maneuver comes automatically. With baitcasting gear, it takes an educated thumb to release pressure on the reel spool at the precise moment without backlashing.

With a little practice it's possible to slide a worm under the overhanging branches right to the base of the trunk or under jack-strawed logs to the center of the cover. This idea also is a super way to fish underneath docks and piers.

On the strike, the rod tip should not be raised in a vertical motion. The line and worm are under the cover, and raising the rod would only serve to pull the line up and into the overhead obstructions. Instead, the rod should be kept low to the water and swept sideways to set the hook and pull the fish out from beneath the cover.

"Kissing" is also the perfect method to try when fishing cover in shallow, vodka-clear water where the fish are shy. In this case, a lure splashing down on the noggin' of a bass is sure to spook it. Yet, by casting short of the intended target, and gently "kissing" the lure an additional 6 or 8 feet to a likely bass hangout, the presentation is less alarming. And the largemouth wastes no time grabbing it.

• **Calling** — Also sometimes known as "slamming," this tactic is similar to "crashing" in that an angler slaps an oversize spinnerbait upon the surface with all the strength the BASSer can muster. However, this is the technique to use when bushes, felled trees or stick-ups are not dry and brittle as encountered in crashing, but instead are alive, green, springy, and too resilient to successfully smash a bait down through.

"Calling" also can be used along the edges of dense weeds, fields of lily pads, or anywhere else the cover is so junglelike it's impossible to present a lure to bass hiding underneath. In a situation like this, the angler "calls" the bass out by repeatedly making that same spawning-baitfish sound described earlier.

The spinner is slammed down right beside the boat. It's best to use a heavy, tandem spinnerbait with the biggest Colorado blades available. After loudly TH-WACKing the water three or four times, cast the spinner as close as possible to the edge of the cover, let it sink, and then bring the lure back with an intermittent stop-and-go retrieve.

The unique technique works especially well in muddy water. And, honestly, I have seen some anglers "call" out as many as three good bass from the same tangle of cover

—JANUARY 1981

SPINNERFLIPPING FOR BASS

By GERRY KINGDOM

*In some situations, flipping with spinning gear
is the best remedy
for uncooperative bass . . .*

Tons of articles have been written about flipping," said George Locke, as he reached his 7-foot Loomis muskie rod out over the weed-rich waters of New York's Saratoga Lake, "but this is different . . . really different. And if more bass anglers knew about it, they'd be haulin' in more bass. It's as simple as that."

A blazing sun beat down overhead, sending the lake's sizeable population of largemouths deep into clusters of long, shade-giving cabbage weed.

Saratoga has high, dense weed growth, sometimes filling the water in 10- to 15-foot depths. The weeds make it impossible to offer a lure properly to bass lying close to the bottom. But Locke has a good solution.

"We've got lakes like this one all over the North, and there are a good many down South, too," he began to explain. "You'll have one devil of a time presenting a bait so that it plops right in front of a bass' nose and triggers a strike."

Locke watched the line spiral off the rod tip and then lowered his eyes to the waterline, looking intently for any unnatu-

New York BASSer George Locke uses his shaking method, in which he allows his lure to settle to the bottom, and gently shakes the rod tip, to take big bass like this one.   Photo: Gerry Kingdom

ral movement, however slight, to signal a hit.

Suddenly, his right forearm shot upward. "See what I mean?" he said as his jaw muscles grew taut and his teeth clenched for battle.

Minutes before, a pair of well-equipped but fishless anglers had complained to us that action was slow.

Locke smiled and played out his adversary in that casual manner that suggests there's a lot more action yet to be had.

"Now you see the difference?" he asked, dropping to one knee and grabbing the lip of a 4-pounder. "Those guys are flipping, but they're not *spinnerflipping,* and on a lake like this, that's all the difference in the world."

George Locke, a Schenectady, N.Y., BASSer and member of the Albany Area Bassmasters, knows the difference well. He's done extremely well in local and regional bass tournaments, and he's won at least one club tournament in each of the past 11 years, a feat that requires not only bassin' savvy, but also a great deal of consistency.

And Locke is high on spinnerflipping.

Locke, who has done extremely well in bass tournaments, is high on spinnerflipping — a technique that appeals to even an inactive bass' reflex action.

Photo: Gerry Kingdom

Another Way To Flip

According to Locke, spinnerflipping is a new application of an old technique: flipping.

In flipping, which was spawned more than a decade ago on the West Coast, the angler strips extra line off his baitcasting reel and swings his lure toward a shallow target.

But in spinnerflipping, the fisherman uses a spinning reel instead of the traditional baitcasting reel. Why? Because the open-face, fixed-spool reel enables a lure to drop vertically, right in front of a bass, even at depths that are as great as a traditional flip-cast is long. The silent lure entry and vertical drop of the bait appeals to a bass' reflex action, even in times when the fish is holed up in deep cover and is least likely to strike the lure.

Too often in the standard flipping technique, the bait begins to swing back through the water toward the angler before it reaches the deep-holding bass. If a bass is in a negative feeding stage, it isn't inclined to waste energy surging after a grub or worm that's swinging past its weed-framed window like a watch on a hypnotist's chain.

But put the meal instantly in front of its nose, and more often than not the fish will accept the offering — out of instinct, if not out of hunger.

Spinnerflipping is also advantageous for fishing vertical structures such as seawalls and bulkheads, where deep pilings offer good bass habitat but make for difficult lure presenta-

tions. Other upright structures like bridge abutments, docks and boathouses are best fished by this method, too.

Pennsylvania bass fisherman Ted Nielson once told me that he used a similar, albeit less sophisticated, approach to take hundreds of smallmouths from the many abutments on the Susquehanna River.

"You'll rarely see guys fishing right down next to the concrete," he said. "They either cast to it, which is foolish, since they are only covering a few feet near the surface, or they drop a bait down near the abutment. You've got to get the bait down right alongside that slab, and that's not easy."

Locke's system does makes it easy, though, in part because of the gear he uses.

Spinnerflipping Gear

Locke's 7 1/2-foot muskie blank has been cut down to 7 feet, a length he feels more comfortable working all day, and seven oversized guides have been added to facilitate an easy pay-out of line. Because the rod is graphite and light in weight, it can be used over extended periods without causing undue arm fatigue. A 1 1/2-inch-thick cork handle adds strength and provides a comfortable grip.

In reels, Locke chooses a Cardinal 4 for its lightness and smoothness. He strongly recommends backreeling, with the anti-reverse feature turned off, instead of using a drag. With practice in the backreeling technique, you can learn to give line quickly during power surges.

A reel-related tip that's also worth noting is to make certain the reel handle is rotated toward you when making your initial flip. This prevents the line from catching on the handle. Of course, once you've done this a few dozen times, it will become instinctive.

Besides enabling a vertical drop with a lure, a spinning reel has another major advantage: It lets you detect a strike more easily than you can with a baitcasting reel, Locke says. That's because the lure falls on a slack line rather than a semi-tight line. Any lateral movement of the line will indicate a fish has taken the bait.

Naturally, the system isn't foolproof. One of the sacrifices that has to be made is in accuracy. You can only control line momentum with your left hand, not with the thumb as in baitcasting or pitching.

Tips On Line

When spinnerflipping, the strength of the line you choose should be based primarily on cover thickness. Lines can vary in color and visibility because the strike will be a reflex strike, not one in which the fish has a great deal of time to study a lure or be frightened by highly visible line.

In spooling line onto a reel used in spinnerflipping, Locke suggests that you underfill the spool slightly. The manuals say to spool line to within 1/8 inch of the lip, but that isn't necessary with this technique because long casts aren't required. Less line on the spool helps eliminate those troublesome tangles and loops.

Also, soaking your line the night before you fish makes it supple enough not to spring off the spool just when you don't want it to.

Spinnerflipping Lures

Although a wide range of lures can be used when spinnerflipping, a few work best.

First is the plastic worm with a 1/4- to 5/8-ounce bullet-shaped slip sinker. A heavier weight will help the worm burrow deeper in thicker weed cover.

If you're after heftier bass, the "jig-and-pig" is your surest bet.

And if you happen to be fishing man-made, vertical structures such as docks or abutments, go with worms or soft-plastic grubs on exposed hooks.

As in line selection, lure-color selection is less important in spinnerflipping than in other techniques because of the instantaneous reflex action that causes bass to strike.

Ways To Work Baits

If your lure is not being taken on the initial drop, several other tricks can be used to entice a bass into striking. Of course, if a bass doesn't bite on the first drop, odds are reduced that one will hit because of anything else you might try.

Locke recommends three alternate maneuvers that will work under these circumstances.

First, hop your lure off the bottom two or three times and allow it to fall back completely to the bottom each time. As the lure descends, be certain to watch the line right where it meets the water; look for a tick, a jump or a tightening in the line. If you see it, set the hook.

The second approach may seem a bit unorthodox to some, but it definitely works: Allow your lure to settle to the bottom and *gently* shake the rod tip. Note the emphasis on the word, "gently." It should move only a couple of inches, and will take some practice to accomplish proficiently.

On the afternoon of my latest fishing outing with George Locke, he used this shaking method to take the biggest largemouth of the day.

A final approach to take, and this should be done when all else fails, is to spinnerflip into the desired weed hole and allow your lure to lie on the bottom for about 30 seconds. (Locke actually counts out precisely 30 seconds each time.) This "dead-sticking" technique can be frustrating, and it's guaranteed to test both your patience and your fishing faith. But it does work, so it's worth a shot.

If all else fails, experiment with various second-effort movements of your own, but keep in mind that all of these secondary approaches still come after the vertical drop. That is the starting point.

Try It Yourself

After hearing of Locke's system from some upstate New York anglers, I decided to test it on a lake that always had posed problems for me because of its thick weed content — northeastern Pennsylvania's White Oak Pond.

The waterway is more noted for its pickerel than for its bass, although I've taken enough good bass to know that the fish are present.

Locke's system proved hearsay true. In a three-hour fishing safari there, I netted more bass than I had in a half-dozen or so previous trips combined. The spinnerflipping and the vertical drop did the trick.

The lesson learned was to carry at least one spinning outfit among my baitcasting rigs, just in case I come across the type of vertical structure that merits its use. Other bass anglers would be well-advised to do likewise.

It's a trick that pays off in enough fishing situations — in dense weed cover, where there is heavy fishing pressure and in vertical, deep structure — to warrant its use.

Obviously, spinnerflipping is not the be-all or end-all of bassing, but it is a fairly new application of an old technique that should be a part of every Bassmaster's repertoire.

— MARCH 1989

Dabblin' For Big Bass, Texas-Style

By GUY W. McCARTY

Long before flipping came along, Texans were dabbling for bass with broomstick-stiff rods and dyed monofilament line …

A number of things are of utmost importance to be successful at this art of "dabbling" for bass. Yes, it truly is an art. Many who have been trying it for years have yet to become successful at it. Catch a few bass — yes, but lunkers — no. Of course, you first must know and convince yourself that what you are looking for are *big* bass, and you also must know where to look.

I may seem to bore you from time to time repeating myself on some of the more important points in order to become effective at this method but be assured that slow, methodical pinpoint fishing is a must as big bass did not get that way being dumb. Once you have convinced yourself of this, then one's equipment and the location of these lunkers come into focus, but that's later in the battle and let's first learn how to be an excellent dabbler.

The bait must be presented to the hunted black beauty in the proper manner, or you might as well be home playing gin rummy with the baby's mother. This is not accomplished overnight and a good place to start is in front of the TV.

Start with a bucket or, to be quieter so as not to disturb the little woman (in all probability she ain't much for this fishing), a foot-square piece of paper on the floor in front of the TV. Of course, the depth of water will depend on how much line you need. But a good place to start is to let your practice plug out about the length of the rod, then grab the line in front of the reel and pull off line until your arm is about fully extended to the side of your body. You should have about 3 feet of line between your hand and levelwind in a V-type position from reel to hand then back to the rod at the first guide.

This, with the line you have already let out, would put your bait on the bottom with your rod tip just above the water in about 9 feet of water. Seldom do we dabble in water that deep, but you must remember you have got to get the bait there. Most successful dabblers usually fish in water from 2 to 8 feet deep. Start with a little less if you wish and add a little along as you begin to get the feel.

I would strongly recommend that you learn how to dabble with the left hand. If you are beginning, it will be about as easy left as right, and because of where you are going to take most of your fish, the quick ability to grab the reel handle and get it out of its natural habitat will be a tremendous advantage. The straight-up-and-down dabble will come fairly simple (remember, we choose murky water so a bush or likely spot immediately under the boat can produce fish), but the swinging or pendulum-type dabble is where the practice comes in.

Start the bait slowly swinging forward and backward and keep your eye on the bucket or piece of paper. As it swings away from you, lower the rod tip, let the line you have in the other hand glide over your fingers, but don't turn it loose. The objective is to see how close and how quietly you can get the bait to the target.

In all probability, it bounced and made some noise. A lighter, quieter landing can be accomplished by very gently raising the rod tip with your wrist just before the bait hits the target. Never, unless of course the depth of the water demands it, let the line go completely from your hand. If you happen not to be watching the line, the twitch or strike can be felt by hand.

The bait has entered the water very quietly. It is slowly sinking. The bass doesn't think the bait has seen it and so is in no big hurry to get the bait before it gets away. Because of this, your strike may be very soft, similar to a bream pecking at the end of a worm. When you do get the twitch or strike, jerk, and I mean now and not one second later. Cross its eyes, so to speak, and get the bass out of its hiding place as quickly as possible.

Whoever said practice makes perfect was a dabbler, I assure you, and when you can consistently hit your target (quietly) at 7 to 10 feet, it's time to discard the bucket or piece of paper, take off a little more line, and replace the target with your fishing cap. Nope, you ain't ready yet, but you will be when you can hit a coffee cup six to nine times out of 10 at about 12 to 15 feet.

This is not necessarily a one-man-to-the-boat method, although I will admit the man in front has a definite advantage. So much so that I fish alone in all tournaments that allow it. I have a foot-controlled trolling motor, with my seat high and very near the front of the boat. This enables me to fish over the bow as well as to either side.

Equipment is of utmost importance. Use a 6-foot Heddon No. 6319 rod. Athough

Because dabblin' cover usually is so thick, a weedless jig is the lure of choice.

any good stiff worm rod will do, the 6-foot rod gives me a little more advantage on the longer dabbles. My choice of reels is the Abu Garcia 2650 with a power handle. Yeah, you can make one fit.

I choose this reel for its weight, which gives the rig more balance as your arms are extended nearly 100 percent of the time, and you can thumb down on ol' iron jaw and move it on out of its "hideyhole" with more authority.

Twenty-five-pound-test mono is my line preference from December through mid-April. Then I graduate down to 20-pound-test. I use a black line altogether. It is much easier to see, and my eyes never leave the line where it enters the water. The reason for this is the lightness of most strikes using the dabblin' method.

The way I teach others to recognize the strike is tell 'em to take their thumb and forefinger of one hand and reach over and hold their other sleeve between them. Then, with a downward motion, see how lightly they can tug on the sleeve. Ninety percent of your strikes will come like that.

Where do you get black monofilament? To my knowledge there is none on the market today, but don't let that stop you. Dye your own as I do. The Lowrance depthfinder instruction book tells how, only do the entire spool instead of the 5-foot intervals. If you don't want to go to the trouble, use a dark green or the new Stren Mod II with the purple glow. But be assured that the black dye job will be worth the effort and result in more strikes. The Shakespeare 6100 is a fine line to dye.

The perfect dabble is to let the bait straight down into the likely hiding place. The tube boys are much more capable of this than the boat boys. Sometimes the bush or target is large

When weeds are so thick you can hardly move, you're in a good dabblin' spot.

Photo: Gerald Crawford

and the most likely place for Mr. Bass is far back in the hole and you certainly don't want to hit the brush or target with the boat or rod tip. The element of surprise to the fish is one of the secrets. Here again is the main reason you want to place the bait in the target area slowly, quietly and with pinpoint accuracy.

The more the target is obstructed or the harder it is to reach makes it a more likely spot for lunkers. This makes it necessary to use the swing or pendulum dabble you practiced in front of the TV.

When the bait reaches the bottom and line goes slack, lift your rod tip 6 to 12 inches. Then lower it quickly to make the bait move up and down with a yo-yo action. When you drop the rod tip, don't forget to watch the line. Of course, on longer dabbles you must work the bait back to you, more like fishing a worm.

LURES — This is nearly 100 percent jig-and-lizard fishing with an exception now and then, such as a spinner of some sort in front of your jig and lizard. This particularly is true in the dead of winter.

I use a 4/0 hook on a banana jig I make myself (not for sale as they are too darned hard to make) with two stainless-steel wire guards on it for size .022, a rubber skirt put on backward, and a variety of articles on the hook.

Tie your line directly to the jig and use no swivel. Of course, you can buy jigs with weedguards but most of them are of a one-piece loop design that hooks under the barb, and this restricts your hook-setting should the fish strike from the side. The wire tends to lodge under the barb in such cases.

My favorite trailer is the bottom two-thirds of an Action Worm or a No. 3 Pedigo Liz. The Action Worm is locally made with a string about midway and has two tails from the string to the end, and comes in a multiple of colors, which at times makes it my choice over the Pedigo Liz. The new Liz No. 2 and Liz No. 5 show a great deal of merit. Some days the fish seem to want a smaller bait while on others they prefer a larger-something one. Why this is, I would certainly like to know, but I'd be quick to admit that I don't.

My favorite jig-and-lizard color is black, and in my part of the country, probably the bait running second is all white. Hair jigs are very successful, and weedguards are optional. The jig with no weedguard has much more chance of hanging. With the locally made Action Worm I can fish a black jig, black skirt, and black worm with yellow or white tips, or the white with black or yellow tips, among many other varied color combinations.

By the time of season that the fluorescent worm comes in handy, the spawn usually is over and dabblin' involves fishing the worm in deeper water. The worm itself (no jig or skirt, just slip weight, hook and worm) has produced many fine catches with the dabblin' method in deeper water.

The dabblin' method is most productive during the spawning season and in the early fall. The fish seem to be much deeper during the summer and dead-of-winter months.

Once more I emphasize the importance of the slow and precise method of the delivery of the bait as well as where you put it.

AREAS — Trees, bushes, cattails, at the edge of lily pads or weedbeds, brushpiles, pilings, old piers, old boat houses (preferably sunken), stick-ups or any other obstacles are good dabblin' spots. Although I seldom fish water over 8 feet deep, I like my fishing water to be near much deeper water. In all probability, if I had to pick out a favorite spot, it would be a single heavy bush, or when fishing a line of brush, the one at each end or the ones with the most pockets deep back into them.

A long brushy point starting at the shoreline and protruding far out into the lake with deep water at its end or on one or both sides of it is great. An old roadbed, long covered with water, but having once had fences and trees or brush on each side is possibly just as great. Both banks of a small tributary stream, where the stream might be up to 20 feet deep, but the water around the trees and brush at each side ranges from 2 to 8 feet, also can be good. Be certain not to overlook any promising areas.

I am one who doesn't believe the Almighty intended for fish to go hungry when the water was murky, and if I can look down and see their nests in 4 to 6 feet of water, then most certainly they can look up and see me in pursuit of them. If you want a stringerful of tournament-sized fish (we call them racers out here in Texas) then rush to clear water, but if you want some braggin'-size lunkers, start dabblin' in off-color or murky water.

— MARCH/APRIL 1972

A Pitch
For Invisible Bass

By LOUIE STOUT

This technique catches bass where they aren't
supposed to be — in clear,
shallow water . . .

Three things in life drive Bassmasters up the wall: 1) water-skiers, 2) a list of weekend chores and 3) clearwater lakes.

Some fishermen will take either or both of the first two headaches over the third. There's something about clear water that drives confidence levels deeper than the bass.

We all suffer from clearwater phobia. It's hard to accept watching a spinnerbait throb its way to the boat on a 30-yard cast. When a Bassmaster pulls onto a shallow flat and sees nothing but a clean bottom, he breaks out in a cold sweat.

Well, stop shaking and read on. There's hope for shallow-water bassers on clear lakes if they're willing to be a little more open-minded.

First, you have to believe in "ghosts" — invisible bass, to be specific. If you don't, then nothing here will make sense.

Where I live, clearwater lakes are the norm, not the exception. In the North, if you refuse to fish clear water then you'd best take up golf.

It's true that lighter line, smaller baits and a more meticulous approach catch cautious, clearwater bass. But if you're willing to believe in ghosts, then add another tactic to your repertoire. You might find a cure for the clearwater phobia, especially on days when deep-water techniques are not doing the job.

My first encounter with an invisible bass came a few years ago on a transparent Michigan lake. Fishing was slow and I was itching to try out a new flipping rod — and to smooth out my awkward lobs.

I eased near an old boat dock sitting high over 2 feet of water — a good practice pier for a beginner. I could see bottom all the way to shore, which made it easier for me to practice getting the lure in close.

My first try was simply awful, falling a foot short of the dock and crashing to the bottom directly in front of me. I glanced around to see if anyone saw the clumsy attempt, then looked back at the jig resting on bottom. In the blink of an eye, there was a bass. And then another one. As I studied one, the other vanished as quickly as it appeared. And then I realized my jig was gone, too.

Sure, I told my buddies I caught the 4-pounder flipping. And I kept the embarrassing details to myself. I wrote it off as a fluke until I talked with Max Glenn, an Indiana angler who also believes in ghostly bass.

"After I caught a few invisible bass, it changed my attitude about clearwater tactics," he says. "We tend to think that just because we can't see the bass in clear water, they aren't there. These fish have good camouflage. You think you can see them, but in fact, they can blend in well with the environment."

So what about fishermen's belief that bass can't be caught in thin, clear water? Larry Stanley, another northern shallow-water advocate, says it's mostly in the minds of the anglers.

"Let's not forget the fact that bass are primarily shallow-water predators," Stanley says. "They prefer dark water and cover, but in some lakes, those conditions can't be found. I think a large percentage of bass feed shallow, so they make do with whatever cover is available."

Stanley believes that any fish found shallow in clear lakes usually can be provoked to strike; rarely are inactive fish found in shallow water.

Just because you can't see bass in clear water doesn't mean they aren't there. By backing off from your target and using an underhand pitch-cast, you can cover a lot of clear water effectively. Photo: Louie Stout

He says there are two kinds of fish in the shallows: feeding fish and active fish. A feeding fish will move away from its cover to feed. An active fish may not be feeding, but it will take a bait if it's presented close by.

"You can't just start flailing away in shallow water and expect to catch fish," he adds. "Casts must be precise and you must work whatever cover is available."

Stanley and Glenn have discovered a modified jig-flipping technique to be the most effective way to catch bass in clear water. Neither believes long casts are crucial.

"When the flipping technique was first publicized I really didn't think it was suitable for our clear lakes," Glenn recalls. "But then I got to fooling around with a spinning outfit and discovered I could back off from a target and with an underhand pitch cover as much water with the same effectiveness as the guys using traditional baitcasting outfits in darker water."

He prefers the old Mitchell 300 spinning reel on 7- and 8-foot spinning rods with medium-heavy actions. The 7-foot rod provides better bait control than the long one when he skips jigs under docks. He tightens the spool drag and "back-reels" if a fish is too heavy or powerful for his line.

"I have never seen a more productive way than this of catching quality bass from areas most people avoid," Glenn says.

His tactic is most effective once the water temperature rises to 60 degrees, and he uses it well into the fall. During one period in October last year, 50 of the 78 keeper bass he caught were 3 pounds or better, and all came from clear water on pitched jigs.

Piers aren't his only targets. Boats, pumps, pipes and tiny weed clumps are all viable targets. Surprisingly, he has more success around pontoons or piers that are as far as 100 yards from deep water, especially if that boat or dock is the only cover on the shoreline.

"I've discovered the best pontoon boats are those sitting on shorelines where there is no cover," he says. "If there are weeds around the boat, the bass are more likely to be in them. Even though you can see bottom all around a pontoon, the bass are there. They tend to rest high and off bottom under those boats; that's why you can't see them.

"Many times I've pitched a jig along a pontoon and watched it swim all the way back to my boat — then it disappeared. The bass took the bait while I was watching, and I never saw the fish hit."

Glenn says he sees about half of his strikes. And he takes pains to keep the bass from seeing him. He conceals himself by pitching around boats and piers, often from about 10 feet away and at an angle, when possible. The quality fish, he adds, usually are on the shallow end of boats and piers.

While large pontoon boats are his favorite target, he fishes other boats, too. He prefers rowboats over runabouts and bass boats tied to docks and shorelines. The pontoon boat offers a bigger surface, but he believes rowboats are productive because they are kept close to shore.

When piers or boats aren't available, he looks for other cover.

"I've caught 4-pound bass on a 2-foot sandy flat where there was just one weed sticking up," Glenn says. "I've caught them from under water hoses and pipes along a residential shoreline, too. It doesn't take much to hold a bass."

Stanley agrees. Some of his better bass have come from small patches of weeds, such as a couple of lily pads that sit alone offshore.

"Those spots are especially good if weeds have been chopped up by excessive boat traffic and are blown against the shore," he explains. "We've caught a lot of bass by dropping a jig right down in the middle of the weeds."

Interestingly, both Glenn and Stanley prefer the shoreline shallows during the middle of the day in bright sunlight.

"On cloudy days, the fish seem to scatter on the flats," Stanley says. "But on a bright day, they seek whatever cover is available. We have some of our best fishing between 1 p.m. and 4 p.m. on bright summer days."

Glenn says a jig fisherman doesn't have to be on the water at daylight. "If you're fishing a crankbait or other fast-moving lures, then yes, I think it's important to be out early. But this style is targeted toward the less aggressive fish. I'm fishing for bass in a holding situation — they're not feeding, nor are they inactive. That's why I think jigs catch more quality fish than do faster-moving baits."

Neither Stanley nor Glenn thinks line size is critical in the clear shallows.

"I've not noticed a difference," says Stanley. "I've caught just as many fish on 20-pound-test line as I have on light line. I think the shallow water brings out the predatory instincts in a bass. It doesn't think before it strikes a jig or a worm in the shallows — it's purely a reflex strike, especially when you drop it in on its nose."

Glenn uses 12-pound-test Stren Class line because he says it gives him the strength he needs and is easier to handle on a spinning outfit.

"Really, the bass concentrate on the jig, not the line," he explains. "I've watched them follow it 5 feet into the open. They can't help but see me, but they're concentrating on the

jig, particularly when they aren't overly aggressive. I've watched them actually 'stand' on their noses, looking down at the jig. You see some strange things and learn a lot about bass when you fish clear, shallow water."

If a lake has a rim of weeds offshore, as many northern lakes do, Glenn pitches to shallow weed pockets when the shoreline structure isn't producing. The best weeds are usually adjacent to a drop-off.

"It's a technique I like for lakes that get a lot of pressure," he says. "I can go behind other boats that are running buzzbaits, spinnerbaits and crankbaits over the top of weeds and catch the more wary fish. I also cover a lot of productive water that way."

Glenn keeps a 1/4-ounce and a 3/8-ounce jig tied on his rods at all times.

"If I'm fishing really shallow and the bass are a little spooky, I may even fish a 1/8-ounce jig," he explains. "But most of the time 1/4 ounce works fine. It falls a little slower and gives them a little longer look. If the fish are aggressive and I can fish faster, I'll go to the 3/8-ounce jig."

Not everyone uses jigs in clear, shallow water. Some, like Al Gearheart, believe plastic worms are even more effective.

"In early-morning hours and after dark, I find large worms catch bigger bass and are easier for the bass to find," he says. "When the sun gets up, I scale down the size of the worm, and when it's high overhead, I prefer smaller, pre-rigged worms for shallows. You catch a lot of small bass, but that's better than nothing."

When he fishes with a partner, Stanley says, one works a jig and the other uses a worm.

"We've had days when the worm produced and the jig didn't," he explains. "The worm is better in early spring when bass move tight to cover under the piers. You can get right next to the pier and shoot the worm all the way back under it."

All three fishermen admit that you mustn't get too close to shallow structure, because the bass there are more easily spooked than those in dingy water. However, pier bass can get used to people and noise.

For example, Glenn once caught and released a dozen bass from a lake rimmed with homes and piers. As he pitched under one pier, the property owner, fishing off the other side, told him he was wasting his time.

"Been fishing here for two days," the man said. "They just aren't biting."

Glenn didn't have time to respond. A 3-pounder grabbed his jig, zipped to open water and bounded across the surface. The man was flabbergasted.

"Happens to me all the time," Glenn says. "You just have to have confidence and not let the clear shallows or the opinions of others bother you."

And, he says with a wink, it helps to believe in "ghosts."

— MAY 1988

SKIP YOUR WAY TO HIDDEN BASS

By STEVE VANTREESE

You've heard of "flipping." Now BASSers are "skipping" plastic worms to catch more hard-to-reach bass . . .

Every kid knows that if you throw a flat rock just right you can make it skip a long way on the surface of water. One kid figured out how to do the same with a plastic worm.

Ron Shearer was that kid. He's not anymore. Now he's a bassin' pro, a regular on the Bass Anglers Sportsman Society's professional circuit. But what he learned as a kid about flat rocks and plastic worms helps him make a living catching fish today.

The 27-year-old Shearer lives in the western Kentucky community of Hardin, near the timbered shores of Kentucky Lake where he guides for black bass. As a youngster, Shearer lived near Winchester in the eastern end of the Bluegrass State.

The son of a bass fisherman, Shearer, at an early age, learned to pursue fish of the *Micropterus* genus on the Kentucky River near his home. It was there he learned that bass prefer the thickest of cover when in a neutral or non-aggressive mood. He watched bass taking refuge along the quiet edges of the river, lurking below overhanging limbs, root tangles and undercut banks.

Knowing the fish were there, the young Shearer pondered the riddle of how to get at them. Much of the cover in which the bass held positions was too low to the water, often nearly touching the surface, to make a conventional cast. By the same token, the limbs, roots and other obstructions that gave the fish security from above prevented the presentation of lures vertically.

He finally fell upon the solution in the form of a straight, beeline cast made on/or just clearing the sur-

face. The way a flat rock can be skipped along the surface, low and with a flat trajectory, seemed the closest thing to the answer.

• **In The Beginning** — Shearer's equipment of that earlier day consisted of a Zebco 33 spincast reel secured to a long self-harvested native Kentucky cane to which an inexpensive set of guides were taped. Rigged to the business end was, most of the time, an early version of the plastic worm.

So armed, Shearer found that by using a hard, sidearm cast, he could slap the worm across the surface, just clearing obstacles inches above the waterline. And "skipping" was born.

As the years passed, the boy Shearer became a full-grown BASSer. His angling skills increased and his techniques took on more sophistication. But he never abandoned skipping.

Shearer came to a personal decision to "go pro" in 1974. He launched into his chosen career by spending "250 days on the water" the first year learning all the specialized techniques utilized by renowned tournament circuit fishermen. These assorted techniques, like his own skipping, were filed away as tools of the trade.

"I thought everybody skipped," Shearer now recalls. But the more he saw, the more he realized he was on to something unique — a trick that gives him an advantage over non-skippers when conditions are right.

Now a well-rounded, tournament-fired professional, Shearer made the elite field for the 1980 BASS Masters Classic®. En route to securing his Classic® berth, Shearer finished as runner-up in total poundage in the B.A.S.S. Western Division for the 1980 season.

His first major laurel, however, came in 1978 when he won a major tournament on his home waters of Kentucky Lake, against a field of top "name" anglers. The conditions were ripe for skipping, and skip Shearer did . . . to the tune of just under 58 pounds of bass in three days. And that's not to mention the 20 or so bass in the 6-pound class Ron Shearer swears he hooked and lost to heavy brush cover.

• **Skipping How-To** — Skipping is a deceiving technique in the visual sense. "It looks complicated," Shearer says. "That's the trouble."

However, with the right tackle, and the proper approach, skipping is little more difficult than standard casting. That's for achieving the basic skip, mind you. Precision placement of the lure is something that takes some practice.

Shearer, leaving the cane-pole stage behind, graduated to long spinning rods — stiff ones that he wrapped himself from blanks. Then, when he began making inroads in tournament bassin' with skipping, things got easier.

Shearer designed his idea of the ideal "skippin' rod" and Skyline Industries made it. The rod has since been placed on the open market. It is a 7-foot, two-handed stick of 100 percent graphite construction. The tip end is of a fast-taper action. The big wand, dubbed appropriately the "Skippin' Rod" (Model No. SKS7002), is relatively light despite a stiff butt section for jaw-wrench, hook-setting power.

Shearer mates the stick with a medium heavy-duty spinning reel. He has experimented with several and recently settled on the Daiwa BG15, a fast-retrieve model in the "Black Gold" series.

So equipped, Shearer casts with a "two-handed, gold-type swing." The rod travels sidearm — parallel to the surface of the water and roughly belt-buckle high. Instead of facing his target, Shearer, a right-hander, comes closer to aiming his left shoulder at the chosen casting target.

The delivery is sharp and with gusto.

"You get your snap from the right hand and your power from the left hand," Shearer explains.

He advises student skippers to concentrate on keeping the rod level and rolling the arms and wrist over when the swing is made. He cautions that early efforts should be directed toward merely getting the worm to skip .

Noting that accuracy in cast placement comes with

As Hank Parker knows, a skipped plastic worm can crawl under overhanging obstacles and reach bass in out-of-the-way places.   Photo: Ted Ancher

time, Shearer says many badly aimed skips will produce fish in the right type of cover at the appropriate time.

"The hardest thing to learn is how to feather the line with a finger against the spool of the reel to stop the worm just where you want it," he says.

A plastic worm, hook and slip sinker fired over the water in this manner will, like a rifle bullet, skip when it hits the surface. The lure may travel 10 to 15 feet or more after it first contacts the water, depending upon how much power is put into the cast, the angle of trajectory and how smooth the surface is.

The length of Shearer's "Skippin' Rod" enhances accuracy in the sidearm casting and permits long, sweeping hook-sets which help bring fish out of heavy cover quickly before they have the opportunity to decide otherwise.

The fixed-spool spinning reel is essential with the skipping technique practiced by Shearer. A form of this maneuver has been used for some time with casting reels on certain southern impoundments, such as Santee-Cooper Reservoir in South Carolina. But skipping with casting gear is strictly a short-range trick. A bait can only be skipped a time or two on a cast before the line feeding off a revolving spool can generate a backlash of monumental proportions.

There is skipping as practiced with casting gear, and then there is Shearer's skipping. To see both is to know that Shearer's approach is a whole different ball game, and a superior one at that.

• **Why Skip?** — Shearer is the first to admit that skipping is a specialty that should be utilized only when conditions warrant.

How far a skipped bait travels under an overhanging obstruction depends largely on the force of the cast and the angle of the trajectory.

Illustration: Bernie Schultz

"It doesn't do you any good to go out and skip when you can catch bass faster some other way," he explains.

As a tournament angler, he knows the virtues of fishing in the most efficient manner. When bass are active and "chasing," he jumps on them with a spinnerbait or crankbait which produces fish quickly.

But when the fish become sluggish and reluctant to sock a fleeing piece of hardware, they are apt to seek out places to take up refuge in comfort and security. Non-aggressive fish often move from the outside edges of cover, such as flooded bushes, brush tops, boathouses, and undercut banks, to the sheltered inside positions — places most methods of lure presentation cannot reach.

Flipping — the technique of swinging a lure into pockets of cover via a long rod — is a good method to pick up these fish. A good method, that is, if the bass remain on or near the edge. However, bass often move up under struc-

ture far enough to even put flippers out of range.

Then comes skipping. When other approaches draw nil results, and when there is even an inch or two of clearance above the water surface over which to skitter a worm, the skipper can get to these seemingly immune bass.

"I can catch a whole lot of fish that others can't reach," Shearer says. Referring to scattered, inactive bass, he adds, "It's probably the best 'junk fish' method there is."

Too, flipping requires that the fisherman get rather close to his quarry. This can be a disarming factor if the water is relatively clear. Skipping, meanwhile, can and should be done from a more remote position.

Shearer says spooky fish — those that tend to vacate for parts unknown when a lure plops down from a conventional cast — can be bamboozled better by a skipped worm. The wiggler loses its momentum while skipping and just seems to "settle" when it reaches the end of its travel. Extra-wary bass appear to be less apprehensive of the presentation, Shearer says.

Another advantage that skipping provides over other methods of fishing heavy cover is that, when the fish does hit, the line is flat on the water. The skipping BASSer won't have his line strewn over the tops of bushes, limbs and other abrasive awfuls. Hit the fish hard, and fast, and chances are good that the bass can be relocated in a straight path without sawing the monofilament into or on the structure.

• **The Fine Points** — Shearer's favorite bait for "skipping" is a paddle-tailed, 6-inch Ding-A-Ling worm made by J.W. Lures. He rigs it self-weedless on a 5/0 stainless-steel hook.

A 3/16- or 1/4-ounce slip sinker is pegged with the tip of a wooden toothpick to the head of the worm. Shearer, when rigging, first pegs the sinker on the 17-pound-test Du Pont Stren line and slides it with firm pressure up and down a few times to form a "seat" inside the pegged sinker. His next step is to glide it up to a fresh section of line and cut off the discards that used to seat the sinker. The result is a grooved sinker that stays tight against the worm, but not so tight as to damage the line and lower its breaking strength.

Shearer says he favors Stren line because he finds that it has minimal stretch. This, combined with the stout character of the "Skippin' Rod" and having the drag on the Daiwa reel tightened down all the way gives him plenty of thunder when it comes to setting the hook into the jaw of a surly largemouth and dragging it from the boonies.

Obviously, when a guy bounces a bait 15 feet into the midst of a tangle of bushes and hooks a big fish, there are bound to be odds on the fish making an escape.

Shearer admits that he does lose a fair number of bass, especially when he is encountering thick-shouldered sows in very heavy cover. However, he plays the odds himself.

Shearer catches a good percentage of what he sticks with a worm hook and, by fishing this method, he figures to encounter many more fish than the conventional caster. If he hooks 20 fish and loses half of them, Shearer still beats the guy fishing the outside edge of the cover who lands all the bass he hooks, but only happens upon five fish.

• **Skipping The Skids** — Conditions that make for the best skipping are some of those that usually put the skids to most fishing. Bluebird skies and burning sunshine are two factors which can send bass to hideouts in thick cover, places where the skipper can zero in on them. Cold fronts can be ideal.

Very clear water is a drawback to skipping, but probably not as much as it is to other methods.

Shearer surmises, "You can find skippin' water on just about any lake."

Ron Shearer, who perfected the skipping technique, delivers a plastic worm to bass holding under the branches of a fallen tree at Kentucky lake.   Photo: Steve Vantreese

But some lakes offer types of cover which are better than others. Some cover, meanwhile, is a dead end for his specialty — like grassbeds, solid walls of vegetation that grow from below the surface.

"You can't skip grass at all," Shearer says.

Structure, such as grass, can often be flipped with success instead. So Shearer, using his same outfit, flips. He points out that the "Skippin' Rod" is a specialty tool, but lends itself to other purposes. Versatility is not to be shrugged off when a BASSer invests hard-earned dollars in a precision, high-ticket item.

And just as versatility is desirable in fishing tackle, it can mean the difference in success and failure in a fisherman. Ron Shearer thinks of skipping as a tool, and uses it when the bassin' job calls for it. And because skipping opens doors to fish seemingly otherwise untouchable, time could show an increasing number of anglers adding this tool to their own bag of tricks.

— JANUARY 1981

HOT-WEATHER FLIPPING TACTICS

By CHRIS ALTMAN

Basil Bacon demonstrates that flipping is more than a cold-weather technique . . .

The sun was angry. By noon on that August day on Kentucky's Lake Barkley, the fireball in the cloudless sky had already shoved the mercury over the 100-degree mark, and Basil Bacon's digital surface temperature gauge read 95 degrees.

Barkley was low and muddy, a result of consumer demand for hydroelectric power to run air conditioners. Noting the current and the falling water, I suggested tossing crankbaits over a few river ledges.

"Nah," Bacon said. "Let's go flipping."

To be honest, flipping was one of the last tactics I would have considered on that brutally hot day. Hot water, hot weather, a falling lake level and a bluebird sky spelled deepwater fishing to me. Little did I know that I was in for a lesson of a lifetime.

Our coolerful of iced tea lasted just four hours, but in that time some three dozen bucketmouths, including a few 4- and 5-pound line stretchers, fell to the flip of a Craw Worm over fallen logs. A repeat performance the next day, this time flipping milfoil beds on Kentucky Lake, proved just how valuable Bacon's hot-weather flipping techniques can be to every Bassmaster who tries them.

"One of the greatest misconceptions is that bass cannot tolerate hot water," Bacon says. "As a result, most fishermen look to deep water during the hottest months of summer, but they're fishing under many of the feeding fish. Bass will move to deep water when they cannot find cover to escape the sun, and they'll follow baitfish into deeper water. But in muddy water with an abundance of shallow cover, you will find plenty of feeding fish in water less than waist-deep. In muddy water, without exception, most of the feeding fish will be shallow all of the time."

Basil Bacon is a fixture on the BASSMASTER® Tournament Trail, having competed in well over 100 contests and qualified for eight BASS Masters Classic® championships in his 20-year stint of professional angling. Though the 53-year-old angler from Springfield, Mo., is highly regarded as a topwater specialist and a jig wizard, Bacon's first love is flipping. For that, anglers across the country should be thankful, for it was Bacon who developed the first flipping switch for Abu Garcia, a device that is now a "must-have" option on any flipping reel.

What is more, Bacon added the first flipping deck to his Ranger bass boat, and that, too, has since been duplicated by most boat companies.

When he is not fishing or speaking at fishing shows for Ranger boats, Bacon builds performance propellers. His company, Hi-Performance Industries, maker of Protester props, pioneered the four-bladed prop — yet another reason to appreciate the creative mind of this ingenious angler.

He is as knowledgeable about bass behavior as he is about performance boating. "There will always be more forage available to the bass in shallow water than in deeper water," Bacon says. "Crawfish, baitfish and everything else that the bass most often eat are, like the largemouth, predominantly shallow-water creatures.

"And as long as there is suitable cover and shade in the shallows, you can find largemouths there — no matter how warm the water gets. Some people say that the bass become stressed in warm water, but I haven't found that to be true. In fact, the fish I catch from hot, shallow water are the hardest-fighting bass I have ever encountered."

For the most part, Bacon's tackle is standard flipping gear. A 7 1/2- or 8-foot graphite flipping rod is the backbone

of the system. He chooses graphite, not because of its lighter weight and increased sensitivity, but because of its more rapid reflex as compared to fiberglass.

"When I hook a big fish in heavy cover, I need to move it out of there as quickly as possible, and I just cannot rely on fiberglass to do that job as well as graphite," he says. "The weight of the rod is inconsequential, because if you flip correctly, the technique is one of the easiest and least-tiring modes of fishing I know of. And the sensitivity of the rod is meaningless, since 99 times out of 100, you won't feel the fish hit your lure."

A baitcasting reel with a flipping switch and spooled with 30-pound-test line completes the rig.

Bacon follows a general rule in regard to lure selection when flipping: When the surface temperature is less than 70 degrees, he uses a jig. When it's above 70 degrees, he uses a soft-plastic bait. During the summer months, he most often flips a plastic bait of some sort, and two of his favorites are crawfish-type lures like Hale's 4 1/2-inch Craw Worm and worms with a large, curled tail like Ditto's Gator Tail. A 1/2-ounce bullet weight is pegged above the bait, although Bacon sometimes switches to a 1-ounce weight when needed to penetrate thick or matted vegetation.

He reports landing better than nine out of every 10 fish that strike his soft-plastic baits — a remarkable feat for which he credits the unique design of his hook. The Alron flipping hook, which Bacon helped to design, is a modified version of the hook incorporated in Alron's Basil Bacon Super Jig. It differs from other hooks on the market in that the eye is perpendicular to the hook's point. In most hooks, the eye is parallel to the point. Bacon says the design offers more leverage, resulting in deep, sure penetration. A series of well-placed reverse barbs on the shank hold the soft-plastic bait in place, and Bacon

Despite hot water and hot weather, Basil Bacon's flipping technique works on largemouth bass in log-jams, as this catch from Kentucky's Lake Barkley shows.

Photo: Chris Altman

Bacon suggests thick cover is essential for productive flipping and points out that the clearer the water, the thicker the cover needs to be.

Photo: Chris Altman

reports that most fish are hooked deep in the upper jaw with this hook. For all of his flipping utilities, Bacon opts for 5/0 and 6/0 hooks. (Write Alron Lures, Dept. B.A.S.S., 705 Cardinal, Clinton, MO 64735.)

Bacon's approach to flipping is, in a word, methodical. Observing the man working a stretch of cover is like watching warm oil slip down a glass incline — each move is smooth and calculated as he virtually flows from one object to the next. "When flipping, you get into a rhythm," he says. "After a flip, you should pick your next target before pulling your bait from the water. You end up moving from one target to the next with a minimum of wasted action or effort."

As every Bassmaster knows, flipping is a tactic for dense cover, but Bacon carries that strategy to extremes. "I try to put my bait where other anglers won't," he says. "By that, I don't mean flipping into the thickest cover I can find, but rather taking my boat into places most anglers would not work to get to. I get my boat a little dirtier than most folks, but it pays off in boated bass!"

Eliminating water is a key component of any fishing strategy, and Bacon starts his fishing day with a boat ride in search of two things: off-colored water and good cover. Dingy water not only means shallow fish, but also serves to decrease the fish's sight so that the angler can approach

undetected. This, too, is vital to a flipping strategy. Bacon suggests looking for dingy water in feeder creeks, headwater areas, and on windblown mud banks.

Thick cover, be it wood or grass, is essential for the productive flipper, and Bacon points out an inverse relationship between water clarity and the thickness of the cover: "The clearer the water, the thicker your cover needs to be."

After locating suitable cover, Bacon's next step is to check the pH to see whether the water chemistry is suitable for bass to feed actively. If the pH reading is to his liking, he starts flipping.

The angle of approach to a specific target is of the utmost importance, he stresses.

"Some fishermen say that you should never position yourself between the sun and the fish, since that makes it easier for the fish to see you. I disagree with that," he says. "I always try to approach a target from the sunny side, because I know that the fish are holding in the shade." The fish will be in the shade, and the structure will be between fish and fisherman, shielding the angler from the fish's view. Bacon cautions that you should never let your shadow fall over the fish's likely position.

"And when flipping," he continues, "I always want to drop my bait over an object so that it remains where I put it, rather than swimming back to me. Since I know that the fish is in the shade, I want the shade on the opposite side of the object from my boat so that I can keep my lure in the shade and near the fish." Constantly draping the line over objects invites abrasion, so Bacon reties often, cutting off the damaged mono.

In addition to shade, current is influential where bass will hold. In the presence of even a minute flow, fish position themselves with their noses facing into the current.

Bacon is widely considered to be one of the most astute masters of pH and its relationship to fish activity. His Lake Systems Multi-C-Lector device plays a vital role in his summer flipping. In a nutshell, bass are most comfortable in water with a pH (a measure of the acidity or alkalinity of the water) of 7 to 9. Furthermore, feeding fish will relate to the pH breakline, or that depth at which the pH changes most dramatically when measured with a pH probe of some sort.

A Bassmaster Tournament Trail regular, Bacon lip-lands a largemouth he caught by flipping into a milfoil bed on Kentucky Lake in summer. Photo: Chris Altman

"A pH meter is an extremely valuable tool for fishermen, because it allows them to eliminate vast stretches of water without having to spend the time fishing them," Bacon says. "For example, I will rule out any water with a pH less than 7 or greater than 9, if I can find good water with a pH of 7 to 9. Ideally, I would prefer to fish water with a pH of 7.9 to 8.4, since fish here will be most comfortable and therefore most active.

"In the summer, one of the things you will find in many lakes is a very high pH level, especially near the surface and around submerged vegetation, because of the alkaline products released by photosynthetic aquatic plants," Bacon notes. A probe lowered gradually through the depths will, however, most often reveal a more suitable pH. Bacon also recommends checking the pH whenever you notice a change in water color, since the dissolved and suspended materials muddying the water will usually change the pH.

In many thermally stratified lakes throughout the country, the pH breakline, or "pH cline," is usually located just above the thermocline. Because a pH cline associated with the thermocline is relatively deep, an angler might believe that discovery would rule out shallow-water fishing.

"Not at all," Bacon says. "If you check the pH again in shallow areas like coves and banks, you will often find another pH breakline in just a few feet of water. When I can find that situation, I'll most often use a flipping strategy." If he is unable to find another pH breakline in the shallows, or finds it in water too deep to flip, Bacon stashes the flipping rod and resorts to a deeper strategy of some sort.

Aquatic vegetation seemingly poses a dilemma for anglers during the summer because as the sun beats down on the plants, photosynthesis occurs at a rapid rate, thus drastically raising the pH level. "At first glance, you would be tempted to skip the grassbeds completely," Bacon says, "but that would be a mistake.

"In thick vegetation, the sun hits the plants near the surface, but the plants underneath remain in relative darkness. If you check the pH at the surface, it might read 10 or so. But if you lower the pH probe down into the plants, you can often find a good pH a few feet below the surface," he adds. In that situation, you usually can find the bass congregated down in the thickest parts of the grass, and they are a prime target for the flipper."

Bacon goes on to recommend switching to a heavier sinker and working the bait a little longer with each flip. Because the fish cannot move swiftly through the thick grass, it takes them a bit longer to reach the lure.

Historically, flipping is one of the most productive techniques ever devised in the world of bass angling. With these tips from one of America's finest "flippers," you can flip up bucketmouths during the hottest days of summer. For your protection, don't forget to take along plenty of non-alcoholic beverages and apply sunscreen liberally.

— JUNE 1990

PRO-STYLE TECHNIQUES FOR THE NEW BREED OF BASS

By DOUG ODOM

With increased fishing pressure, and the natural aging of cover in the man-made reservoirs, largemouth bass' habits are changing. The more aggressive bass are giving way to a more passive largemouth that is harder to catch . . .

To catch today's "changing" breed of bass, you need to specialize in bass-fishing techniques. If you question the fact that bass are changing their habits, ask yourself the following questions:

Are bass strikes as vicious as they once were?

Do the bass strike repeatedly?

Can you still catch as many fish out of a particular hole before the bass turn off?

Have you been forced to change fishing areas completely?

The answers hold the key to improving your modern-day bass fishing.

First, I believe bass are changing their habits. For sure, the massive man-made lakes created during the late 1940s-1960s are a "changing environment." Significant amounts of fishing habitat are lost each year to increasing infestations of grass and moss like hydrilla and Brazilian elodea. Many reservoirs are losing some of the very best spawning areas to indiscriminate shoreline development. But, as much as anything, the deterioration of normal shoreline cover due to the aging of the lake is the major reason bass habits are constantly changing. To the bass angler, the most noticeable change is the rotting away of shallow-growing willows and stick-ups, and the silting-in of creek and river channels.

These changes Bassmasters can see happening and generally accept as fact. Now, let's take our premise a step further. It is my opinion that bass fishermen are altering the characteristics of largemouth bass, especially in reservoirs or lakes under heavy fishing pressure.

With their improved angling abilities, modern-day bassers are "selectively breeding" a strain of bass that are much less aggressive, or should we say more conditioned, at least as far as fishermen are concerned. By selective breeding, we recognize that certain desirable traits can be bred into animals; for example, speed in a horse, fat on a hog, a good nose on a dog, or growth rate in chickens. The list is endless.

In the changing situation with bass, the increased interest in bass fishing has resulted in catching many more of the more aggressive fish, thereby allowing the passive, harder-to-catch, "intelligent" fish to reproduce. An example is the change in the way I've caught bass over the last five years on South Carolina's Santee-Cooper lakes. At one time, my method was retrieving a weedless lure rapidly across the 'gator grassbeds in upper Lake Marion, and having huge bass viciously, and repeatedly, strike. I didn't catch a largemouth this past season that struck with the viciousness of bass five years ago.

If you can accept that selective breeding results with domestic animals, then there's reason to believe that passive, intelligent bass will breed more of the same characteristics. Over the years with bass-fishing pressure increasing, I've seen bass become harder to catch. Some suggest there are fewer bass, and to a point, I agree. But, by adapting new methods and techniques, I still catch as many bass, even though the strikes are now almost imperceptible and require a greater degree of skill and concentration on the part of the bass angler.

Crashing the willows is a method I stumbled on a few years ago while guiding on the Santee and Congaree rivers near my Orangeburg, S.C., home. Once this technique is understood, you can consistently catch bass behind even the best fishermen. This technique is at its best during a shad spawn or run in late spring and early summer.

The normal method used for fishing riverbank willow trees is to drift downcurrent and cast spinnerbaits, crankbaits, or plastic worms to the bank and retrieve in the traditional manner. The larger willow trees that stretch out over the water from the banks are generally considered obstacles; something to maneuver around with the electric trolling motor so the fisherman can cast back to the bank.

There are several important keys you should consider: (1) Bass are not going to fight the current. They seek a slack or calm pocket. (2) These fish are not going to move far or fast for a lure; they're not the same breed. (3) Shad are free-swimming fish, preferring open water, but requiring something solid to spawn against. If you've observed a shad spawn, you know they create quite a ruckus.

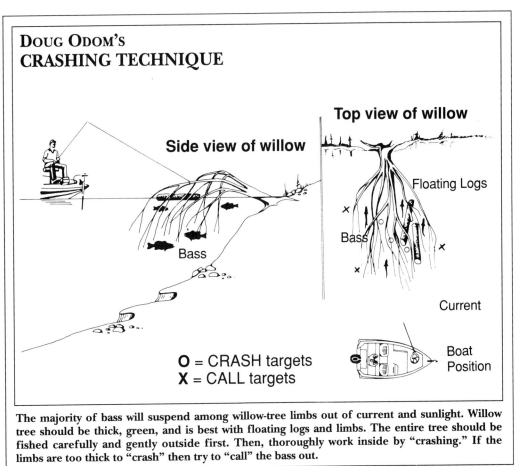

DOUG ODOM'S CRASHING TECHNIQUE

Top view of willow

Side view of willow

Floating Logs

Bass

Bass

Current

Boat Position

O = CRASH targets
X = CALL targets

The majority of bass will suspend among willow-tree limbs out of current and sunlight. Willow tree should be thick, green, and is best with floating logs and limbs. The entire tree should be fished carefully and gently outside first. Then, thoroughly work inside by "crashing." If the limbs are too thick to "crash" then try to "call" the bass out.

OK, we've determined that bass are holding under and inside the outer limbs of these larger willows. The bigger and thicker the tree, and the deeper the limbs extend under the surface, the better. Also, something solid, like floating logs caught in the branches, greatly improves this cover situation.

How To Fish The Crashing Tactic

You've got a mental picture of the tree we're going to fish. Here's how to fish it. Fish upstream against the current so you can hold the boat still, and work this tree for 5 to 20 minutes. This upstream position puts a strain on your electric motor. I've found that a powerful foot-operated trolling motor like the Magnum MotorGuide is a must.

My tackle includes a 5-foot, medium-heavy, Skyline graphite rod (a sensitive graphite rod really helps because the strikes are super soft), and Stren fluorescent 20-pound-test line. The all-important lure choice is a 1/2-ounce single-spin Bushhog that has the top shaft shortened just a little. I've selected this lure because it is extremely durable, well-balanced, and this weight size will "crash" through the mass of willow limbs and leaves, and can be retrieved without fre-

quent hangups. Most top-quality spinnerbaits, such as Ray Scott's balanced BASS Spinner, can be adapted for this technique. The heavier, well-made lures will stand the repeated slamming into the willow tops.

Your first few casts should be presented soft and easy around the entire outside edge of the tree. Successive casts should be aimed deeper and deeper into the willow. The outside casts will catch the "easy" or more aggressive fish.

Now, let's crash the bush. Move the boat in close — to within 5 or 6 feet. Select a thin spot in the willow, and drive or crash the spinnerbait with all the strength you can muster in an overhand cast straight down through the top of the tree. You must be standing so the cast is directed down into the branches and leaves of the tree. If the spinnerbait does not reach the water, then jerk it back out, and crash the same spot again.

Now, your spinnerbait is inside the tree and down in the water. This is where the new breed of bass lives. Bass won't move far, though many times they will come to the crashing sound, apparently reacting to a shad spawn taking place.

Lower your rod tip, and allow the spinnerbait to sink as far as possible into the limbs. If the bait drops to the bottom of the underwater tree limbs, that's perfect. Now start jigging — raise the spinnerbait toward the surface until you hear the

Look for bushes that bunch up against other structure such as standing trees, and work them thoroughly with your crankbait.

Photo: Gerald Crawford

blade "spit" as it breaks the surface. You must listen. It is difficult to see the bait inside the heavier willows. And, too, this is when many strikes occur.

Then, repeat the process. Drop the lure to the bottom of the tree and jig up until it spits. Work the lure a minute or two — that's not too long to tease these bass. When you retrieve the lure from the willow, don't move to the next tree — go to the next limb in the same tree. Many times, I've caught 10 bass from one tree without moving the boat, and any willow that produces a single strike usually will hold many more largemouths that will strike.

A tactic I employ prior to fishing tournaments is to ride the lake searching for these willow trees, and tear small openings (holes) in the tops so I can more easily crash spinnerbaits through later. Don't make the holes too large, and other anglers will seldom notice the casting targets.

How do you get the bass out of the trees? If you hit the fish quick enough and hard enough, you'll jerk the bass out — most of the time. With the bigger fish, you may have to actu-

ally go into the tree after it, and that's when the fun and fireworks really start. My best bass caught with this crashing method weighed 10 pounds, 14 ounces, and was all pure muscle. I'll never forget that fight!

At the 1976 South Carolina Invitational on Santee-Cooper, I boated 22 bass to place second with 62 pounds, 3 ounces, including a first-day catch of 33 pounds, 2 ounces for a 10-bass limit. The fish were caught by crashing a Bushhog spinner through overhanging willows along the Santee River.

How To Call Bass From Cover

There's a twist to this crashing technique that may seem odd, if you don't already wonder about this method. You can actually "call" bass out from under trees that are too thick to crash through. Start with the same tactic by carefully fishing the outside perimeter of the tree. Cast well beyond the tree and work the spinnerbait back along the sides and outer ends of the overhanging tree. When the outside area is fished thoroughly, move in close and pick a target at the edge of the thickest part of the tree. The downstream side is usually the best place to find bass.

Now, start "slamming" the spinnerbait on the surface as hard as possible on the same spot again and again. Then, "splat" the lure on the surface, and release a foot or so of line, and feel the bait down until a bass holding under the overhanging tree could spot it. Now, move the spinnerbait toward you slowly for a couple of feet, then burn it back, and repeat this tactic over and over. If you've got a fishin' partner, take turns hitting the same spot. Believe me, you can call bass out of the thick cover with this method.

On a bright spring day on the upper Santee River, I proved it would work to a friend, Reese Early. Up until then, Early had never called anything but his bird dogs, and looked at me like I'd finally gone bananas when I explained how the tactic worked. We approached a big willow covered with wild grapevines, much too thick to crash. I boated a 1 1/2-pound bass on the downstream side, and a 4-pounder on the outside end by gently working the Bushhog around the edges.

Then, I started slamming the lure as hard as possible on the surface near the lower side of the tree, and seven casts afterward landed a 3 1/2-pounder. By this time, Early's jaw had dropped open. A dozen casts later to the same spot, I hooked and landed a largemouth in the 7-pound class. Early saw it, but didn't believe it. That tree produced seven nice bass, and one new converted bass "caller."

Bass apparently sense that all the ruckus is a shad spawn, and will move some distance to investigate. When bass approach the edge of the tree, and the spinnerbait drifts down in front of their nose, they can't stand it. This tactic works especially well in stained or muddy water. By "muddy," I mean so thick you can almost see coon tracks crossing the river. (All the muddy water does is scare off fishermen who don't know better.)

Parachute Worm Inside Cover

Another successful method for catching passive bass is one I've labeled as "parachuting" a plastic worm. First, let's again set the stage. Locate a fairly steep point, but not too steep, leading from the deeper water in an area with nearby shallow flats. This particular point has dozens of bushes along the banks in about 3 1/2 to 4 feet of water.

You've determined that bass are using this point along a migration route to and from their feeding grounds. The water is clear, and the sky bright. In this case, the clearer and brighter, the better. When conditions are cloudy or overcast, bass won't hold as tight in cover, and it's harder to pinpoint their locations. The normal method for fishing bass holding on bushes, stick-ups, etc., is to cast to the bush with a plastic worm or past the structure with a spinnerbait or crankbait.

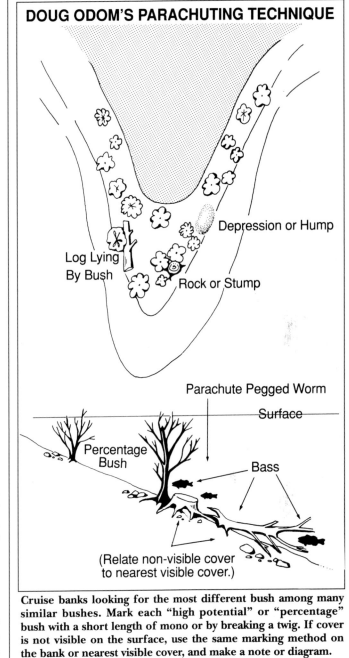

DOUG ODOM'S PARACHUTING TECHNIQUE

Depression or Hump

Log Lying By Bush

Rock or Stump

Parachute Pegged Worm

Surface

Percentage Bush

Bass

(Relate non-visible cover to nearest visible cover.)

Cruise banks looking for the most different bush among many similar bushes. Mark each "high potential" or "percentage" bush with a short length of mono or by breaking a twig. If cover is not visible on the surface, use the same marking method on the bank or nearest visible cover, and make a note or diagram.

Also, most bass fishermen will change to light line in these clearwater conditions.

The tackle I'm going to use to parachute a plastic worm is a short, stiff spinning rod, again preferably graphite, and 17-pound-test Stren line. The lure is a 6-inch Mann's Jelly Worm. I like lime or watermelon in fishing clear water. The worm is Texas-rigged with a 3/16-ounce slip sinker pegged with a toothpick tight on the worm head.

To parachute the worm, cast it high over the bush — stop

When parachuting a plastic worm into thick cover, peg the 3/16-ounce slip sinker with a toothpick tight against the worm head.
Photo: Gerald Crawford

The trick was total concentration on the bush and the line. Often the only hint of a strike was a slight movement of a twig or realizing the worm was not sinking as far as it should into the bush.

Sometimes, to reach a particularly good-looking spot, the line would be draped over limbs 4 feet above the water. That's why at least 17-pound-test line is necessary. With very little line actually in the water, the heavier line doesn't seem to matter to the fish. The trick was the presentation, and the detection of the strike.

This method can be very effective in tournament fishing situations. Once you've established this pattern, spend time locating these type places and bushes, and mark the "highest-potential" or "percentage" bush. I look for a particular bush among many other bushes that has something different about it. For example, a big rock or slump right beside it, a hump or depression under it, just anything to make it the most outstanding bush.

Mark these special bushes by tying a short piece of monofilament to a twig or by just breaking a small limb. I especially use this tactic on structure that is not visible on the surface. Pinpoint the hidden cover by stacking two rocks as a marker on the shore, tying monofilament or breaking a twig on a bush nearby and making a note and diagram on your map.

I always investigate a fallen tree real close because there's one super spot around it that is usually best. If you know exactly where to cast into that big tree, then you're cutting down the odds of a wasted cast.

Once you've familiarized yourself with the high-percentage bushes, you should return and fish them several times during the day. At different times, a bass migration moves in or out. One or more bass will hold on that percentage bush at least part of the day.

During the 1976 Virginia Invitational, I caught five fish from one bush during the course of the three-day tournament, and there were many bushes I took two fish off the same spot. If you locate enough high-percentage bushes on different points, you can establish a milk run, and not ever need to cast to the other hundreds of identical-looking, but not as productive bushes, that everyone else is beating to death in their quest for fish.

There's no doubt that bass habits are changing. But, then, so are fishermen. A new breed of "bass hunter" has emerged from the angling crowd. The new pro-style Bassmaster is strong, innovative, and will try anything to catch fish.

— MARCH/APRIL 1977

the worm, and drop it straight down into the center of the bush with as little disturbance as possible. Allow the worm to settle to the roots or into the bush, then jig it up and down very slowly. At the 1976 Virginia Bassmaster® Invitational on Kerr Reservoir (Buggs Island), I caught 23 tournament bass with this method, and must point out that I did not catch a fish that I felt strike. I finished ninth with 42 pounds, 12 ounces after a frustrating first day in 41st place.

I realized the full use of this parachuting technique during the tournament practice. I'd cast into a bush located on a small hump of rock along the side of a point in about 3 feet of water. The plastic worm dropped into the bush properly, and sank easily to the bottom. I began to lift the worm up through the bush and felt resistance, like the line was binding on a piece of bark. I lowered the rod tip, and the lure sank to the bottom.

"That's not right," I thought, and now I was really paying close attention. When I raised the worm the next time, a 4-pound bass eased to the surface. When I lowered the rod tip, the bass swam back toward the bottom. That crazy fish had my lure in its mouth! I led the fish to the surface three more times before finally setting the hook.

This particular bass was locked in its home, and not actively feeding. When the worm dropped into its front door, the bass just sucked the lure in. Why should the fish swim off with the bait? The bass was already where it wanted to be.

The only times I felt the familiar "tap" or jerk on the worm was when the bass realized it had grabbed something phony, and was spitting it out. I did not catch a bass after this point.

How To Catch Visible Bass

By TIM TUCKER

Shaw Grigsby has become a master at the difficult art of sight-fishing for bass . . .

It can be the most exciting and frustrating fishing of all.

Sight-fishing for bass, the way the guides in the Florida Keys stalk bonefish on the flats, ignites an adrenaline rush like no other type of bass fishing. Visual fishing has the same allure as topwater fishing, but with one major difference — in this game, you get to see the fish even before it strikes the lure.

It is this visual element of clearwater fishing that creates such an intimidating and frustrating experience when the fish don't cooperate. It's unsettling enough not to get bites in stained or muddy water when you can't be sure a bass is near the lure. But it's doubly unnerving when you can see the fish and it refuses to strike.

Shaw Grigsby is one of the masters of the specialized art of catching visible bass. His prowess with catching bass he can see has paved the way to much of his tournament success, which includes qualifying twice for the prestigious BASS Masters Classic®.

Two prime examples: En route to winning the 1988 BASSMASTER® Invitational on Sam Rayburn Reservoir, Grigsby used light line and finesse lures to coax heavily pressured bass into biting and then wrestled them from some bad places. Grigsby first spotted every bass he caught, both spawning and pre-spawn fish. An impressive opening-round five-fish stringer that weighed 26 pounds, 3 ounces, paved the way to his first B.A.S.S. victory.

Although he finished as the runner-up in the 1989 B.A.S.S. MegaBucks® Tournament on Florida's Harris Chain, Grigsby ran away with the four qualifying rounds,

sight-casting to bass in the tannin-tinted clear waters of a canal to catch more than 60 pounds.

The 33-year-old Gainesville, Fla., angler is among the most versatile of the touring pros, but his forte — and favorite method — is "visible" fishing.

"I like clearwater bass fishing because it's a challenge," Grigsby says. "It's real exciting to see the fish ahead of time, work the bait just right to get it interested and then watch it charge the bait. It's a neat feeling to sit there and watch it bite the bait before setting the hook. To me, it's the ultimate.

"I prefer to see my prey before I catch them. But most people — even the top tournament pros — are just the opposite. They automatically look for dirty, stained water because the fish there are probably going to be more aggressive. But I tend to find fish that are a little larger and almost untouched."

Anglers who avoid clear water figure that if they can see the bass, the bass can see them, and that makes it harder to draw strikes.

But Grigsby says the lack of fishing pressure on these visible bass works to his advantage. "I will often have an area to myself, rather than having to share stained-water areas with other fishermen," he says. "A lot of people get psyched out because they may see a lot of fish, but only catch one out of 100 if they're not real adept at this type of fishing. It's intimidating to see fish and not be able to catch them."

Contrary to popular opinion, visible-bass fishing is more than just bed-fishing for spawning bass. That certainly is a productive time for sight-fishing, but it is by no means limited to spawning season. Grigsby and others, including 1988

Shaw Grigsby pitches a G-2 tube jig to an unsuspecting clearwater bass holding behind a bush.

Classic® champion Guido Hibdon, have proved that along the national tournament trail.

Grigsby seeks out clear water and visible bass in his travels throughout the year, with the exception of the coldest times, when most bass migrate to deeper water.

As with other types of fishing, conditions dictate when sight-fishing will be most productive.

Obviously, good water clarity is required. Through years of fishing the crystal-clear waters of Florida's springfed rivers, Grigsby has developed an uncanny ability to spot bass most anglers would miss. In the process, he has learned to read shallow water that is slightly off-color or has a slight tint to it.

The ideal conditions for chasing visible bass are a bright, overcast day — enough clouds to hide the sun, but plenty of sunlight penetration for seeing beneath the water's surface — and little or no wind. The cloud cover makes clearwater bass slightly less wary, Grigsby says. The exception to his preference for cloud cover is spawning season, when bright days are best. Bass that are protecting a nest are more likely to hold in that position and less likely to spook away from the bed under sunny skies.

"Spawning bass are a whole different game from regular visible-fishing," Grigsby explains. "Bedding fish don't want to bite, so you have to really work those fish. Generally, they're harder to catch. They're finicky because they are not feeding, they are protecting. It takes a different style of fishing to catch them."

Grigsby utilizes a variety of lures for visible bass, including minnow plugs, tube jigs like the Fat Gitzit, small worms, a downsized jig-and-pig, in-line spinners and noisy surface lures such as the Zara Spook and Rebel Pop-R.

His most productive lure choices are the G-2, a tube jig made by Lucky Strike, and a 4-inch Gillraker, a small-diameter plastic worm. The G-2 is fished most often on a 1/16-ounce jighead, but Grigsby uses more weight depending on the water depth (1/8 ounce for 5 to 10 feet and 1/4 ounce for below 10 feet). The tiny worm is impaled on a 1/0 hook and coupled with a 1/16- or 1/8-ounce bullet weight. Grigsby sometimes fishes the worm without a weight, which slows its descent, for non-aggressive bass.

"The G-2 is an outstanding lure for catching visible bass — probably the best of all," explains the Florida angler. "I think that's because it resembles a minnow when it's floating and a crawfish once it hits the bottom and you pop it so it darts backward."

Critical in sight-fishing is to use a lure you can see easily. You need to be able to watch the bait as you're working it and when a strike occurs.

Catching visible bass demands using light tackle and thin line. Grigsby uses a 6-foot medium-action Quantum Quartz-Lite rod and a Quantum Brute 4W reel, which features a wide spool. The wide spool is important, he says, because it

A good pair of polarized sunglasses is helpful in spotting bass before they spot you.   Photo: Grady Allen

will handle a variety of line sizes. Most of Grigsby's visible-bass fishing is done with 6- to 10-pound-test Du Pont Magna Thin, a small-diameter monofilament line that he believes is practically invisible to the fish.

One of the most important pieces of equipment for sight-fishing, Grigsby says, is a pair of quality sunglasses with good polarization and with ultraviolet protection. Grigsby utilizes two different models made by Hobie Precision Optics: an amber-colored pair for low-light conditions and a dark-blue pair for brighter skies.

Perhaps most crucial to stalking visible bass is the initial approach. Unlike a camouflaged hunter in the woods, an approaching angler has a good chance of being seen by clearwater bass.

"You have to present a bait to the fish before it can see you, because once it sees you, it gets real tough to catch that bass," Grigsby says. "You can still catch it, but it's difficult. I think that's the toughest part of sight-fishing."

By following those procedures, Grigsby usually is able to entice a bass to strike. What he sees — most of the time — is what he gets.

— MARCH 1990

BASIC FLIPPING AND PITCHING

By DENNY BRAUER

The 1987 B.A.S.S. Angler-of-the-Year describes his favorite close-range fishing strategies for catching inactive, stubborn bass . . .

If you were to ask me the most effective methods of lure presentation to bass, I would answer, without hesitation, "flipping and pitching."

Professional fishermen have been flipping on the BASS-MASTER® Tournament Trail since 1977, and dozens of tournaments, including the BASS Masters Classic®, have been won with the technique. It certainly has become one of my favorite ways of fishing for stubborn bass.

Pitching, which is a refined method of long-distance flipping, has only become a widely accepted technique within the past two or three years, but already it has won several major tournaments.

The advantages of both flipping and pitching are that they allow you to present a lure very quietly and naturally to a bass, and to do it very precisely. As with other techniques, accuracy is extremely important. With sufficient practice, any well-coordinated angler can consistently pitch a jig or plastic worm to a tiny target at 30 or 40 feet.

After accuracy, the most critical aspect of either method is developing an awareness of what your lure is doing at all times.

With fishing techniques using fast-moving lures like crankbaits or spinnerbaits, a fish often hooks itself. But with flipping, you must hook the fish. And that means you have to detect its strike.

More often than not, there is no sensation to a strike during flipping or pitching. Therefore, it's extremely important that the angler learn to identify the "spongy" or "heavy" feeling that could mean a bass has taken your lure.

What's more, you need to know how fast your lure falls,

in case it only drops 2 feet in 3 feet of water. And you need to learn how to properly work cover to ensure that you are putting your lure in places bass are hiding.

In its most basic form, flipping might be described as a type of vertical jigging in shallow, off-colored water. It is done at very close range, often from a distance of less than 10 feet. I seldom flip water deeper than about 5 feet, because I believe I can work deeper depths more efficiently with other lures.

Pitching is working this same cover from farther away; the "pitch" is an underhand flip-cast which, like flipping, keeps the lure close to the water so it does not make a noisy splash. We use pitching when fishing shallow, clear water to avoid spooking the fish. Recent BASSMASTER Invitationals on Lake Okeechobee in Florida have been won by pitching plastic worms into the reeds.

(Editor's Note: Denny Brauer won the 1987 BASSMASTER Super Invitational on Kentucky Lake with a combination of flipping and pitching, and his success there enabled him to win the B.A.S.S. Angler-of-the-Year title.)

Naturally, the closer you can get to a fish, the better the hookset you'll get and the easier it will be to control that fish. There are times, however, when you just can't get close enough to flip, and that's when pitching takes over. Once your lure is in the water, lure control in pitching is exactly the same as in flipping.

When flipping, normally you'll work your lure up and down as if you're jigging. You seldom will need to keep jigging the bait for long, because you've either put the lure in front of a bass or you haven't. If the fish is there, it will usually hit.

Pitching, on the other hand, may require repeated presentations to the same spot. You have to crawl the lure most of the time, since it's difficult to work the bait vertically from such a distance. When you pitch into a bush, however, you may have the chance to let the lure work vertically as you climb it through limbs and branches.

What's important in either presentation is total concentration on what you're doing and what is happening to the lure.

Line watching is critical, but even this doesn't always mean you'll detect a strike. You almost have to develop a sixth sense, something inside you — like a hunch — that tells you there's a fish on the line.

One way to develop this awareness is to set the hook whenever you even remotely think you have a bass on the

Denny Brauer won the 1987 BASSMASTER Super Invitational on Kentucky Lake with a combination of flipping and pitching, and his success there enabled him to win the B.A.S.S. Angler-of-the-Year title. Photo: Gerald Crawford

line. In the beginning, many times, you won't have a fish, but it never hurts anything but your pride when you set the hook into a bunch of air.

Sooner or later, you will set the hook into a fish, and by catching that bass, eventually you'll develop confidence in your senses and begin to recognize the different ways a bass strike can feel.

Boat positioning and control is another key to mastering flipping and pitching. As you become more proficient in flipping or pitching, you'll develop a "comfort range," a distance from which you will prefer to flip. You'll be able to vary your flipping and pitching distances, of course, but you'll have a preferred range, and keeping your boat at this distance will allow you to have the maximum amount of control over your line and lure.

The techniques are easier to do than to describe.

For flipping, begin by holding your rod tip up, and pull an arm's length of

line out with your free hand. There should be about 7 or 8 feet of line extending off the tip of your rod. Your reel should be in free-spool.

Raise your rod tip to start the lure on a pendulum-like swing back toward you, then after it has swung back, lower the rod to make the lure swing forward, giving it momentum toward the target.

DENNY BRAUER'S PITCHING TECHNIQUE

Put the reel in free-spool and let out a rod's length of line. Hold the bait in your free hand, even with the reel. Dip the rod tip toward the water and quickly snap it upward while letting go of the lure. The lure should swing forward, close to the water on an almost straight trajectory. As the lure moves forward and starts pulling line off the reel, begin lowering the rod up to control the lure's height off the water.

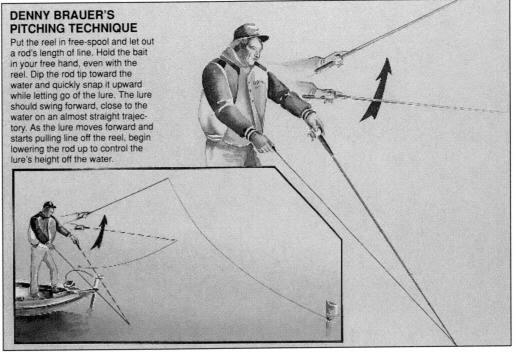

DENNY BRAUER'S FLIPPING TECHNIQUE

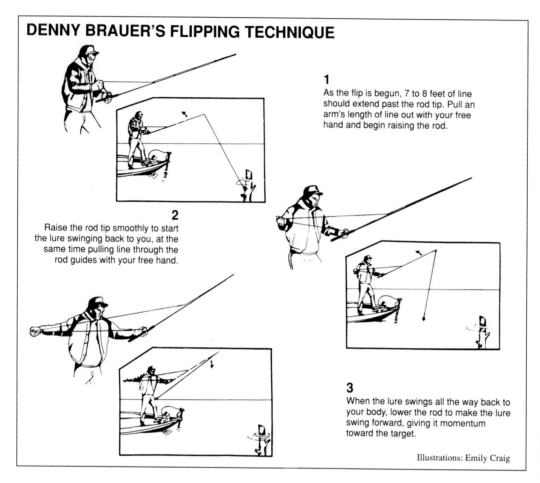

1
As the flip is begun, 7 to 8 feet of line should extend past the rod tip. Pull an arm's length of line out with your free hand and begin raising the rod.

2
Raise the rod tip smoothly to start the lure swinging back to you, at the same time pulling line through the rod guides with your free hand.

3
When the lure swings all the way back to your body, lower the rod to make the lure swing forward, giving it momentum toward the target.

Illustrations: Emily Craig

This technique, one which some have called high-speed flipping, takes a great deal of practice to perform smoothly, but it is extremely effective in so many bass-fishing situations.

Another way to make the pitch cast that I use sometimes is to let about 3 feet of line extend past the rod tip, letting the lure dangle freely. This pitch is made with a quick roll of the wrist. Hold the rod at about waist level, bring it back, then move it forward with a quick, short, underhand roll. The cast can be made with short rods or long ones and with one hand or two.

Some fishermen prefer to pitch with open-face spinning gear, although I personally prefer baitcasting tackle. The spin-fishermen use very stiff, medium-heavy action, 7-foot rods, and they make more of an underhand toss, as if they were pitching a softball. Lure control is achieved by feathering the line as it comes off the spool.

As the lure gains momentum, feed the line you've been holding in your hand back through the guides. Don't let go of this line; simply let your hand move up to the rod so you're ready to grab the rod and set the hook instantly. I'm left-handed and flip with a right-handed casting reel, so as my right hand feeds line, it comes up to the reel and into position to engage the reel. A right-handed person can do the same thing if he uses a special flipping reel with a thumb-bar over the spool.

In the most popular style of pitching, I begin by holding the rod in my left hand (since I'm left-handed) and the lure in my right. The reel is in free-spool. I point the rod toward the target, then dip the tip toward the water and quickly snap the rod upward while letting go of the lure. This sends the lure forward and low to the water on an almost straight trajectory.

As the lure moves forward and starts pulling line off the reel, I begin lowering the rod tip to control the lure's height off the water. Distance can be controlled by thumb pressure on the spool. It is vital in pitching as well as flipping that the lure not get very high off the water, or it will splash down noisily, negating the advantage of a quiet lure entry that makes pitching and flipping so effective.

In hook-setting, the speed with which you move your rod is critical, and the more speed you can develop, the better the hookset you'll get. I believe too many fishermen set the hook from the wrong position, and as a result, they miss a lot of fish. I keep my rod high so I can better feel what's happening to the lure and so I can see the line. And when I feel a fish, I lower the rod, make two quick reel turns to take up slack, and set the hook. This is where having a fast-retrieve reel really helps; in those two cranks of the handle, I'll retrieve about 4 feet of line, and it only takes half a second to do it.

I use the same rods and lures for both flipping and pitching. I prefer a rod that is light enough for comfort but heavy enough to fight a big bass. My own flipping/pitching rods are 7 1/2-footers with an 80/20 action — 80 percent backbone and 20 percent tip. My reel is a Daiwa PMA 33 with a 5-to-1 retrieve ratio, and I usually use 25- to 30-pound-test line.

The two standard flipping/pitching lures are jigs and plastic worms, and I use both.

Jigs seem to work better in colder water, and I prefer either a 3/8- or 1/2-ounce rubber-legged jig with a fiber weedguard. The weedguard is essential. My feeling is that if the cover isn't thick enough to warrant a weedguard, then it's not thick enough to flip.

I always add some sort of trailer to my jigs, usually a jumbo pork frog (Uncle Josh No. 1), a standard frog (No. 11), a pork lizard (No. 800), or a plastic worm. Because flipping and pitching are designed basically to catch bass that are spooky or inactive, I also like to add an attractor scent; I soak my pork trailers in Fish Formula before using them in a tournament.

When I'm flipping with worms, I use either a 5- or 6-inch length, but I

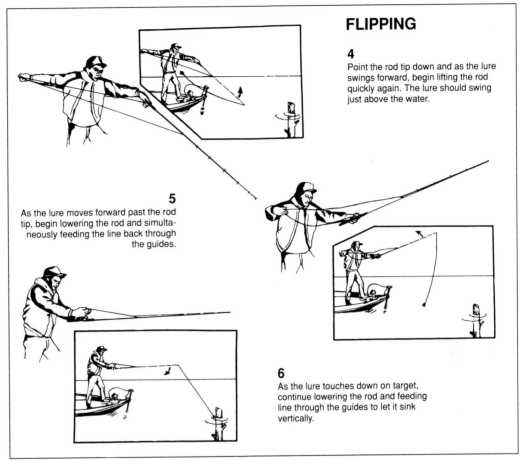

FLIPPING

4
Point the rod tip down and as the lure swings forward, begin lifting the rod quickly again. The lure should swing just above the water.

5
As the lure moves forward past the rod tip, begin lowering the rod and simultaneously feeding the line back through the guides.

6
As the lure touches down on target, continue lowering the rod and feeding line through the guides to let it sink vertically.

have used worms as long as 12 inches. I like a light slip sinker for shallow cover, and a heavier worm weight for thicker cover, and I always peg the sinker on the line with a short piece of toothpick.

I'll use the flipping or pitching technique whenever and wherever I feel it's the best way to catch fish, but I do have two favorite types of cover for those techniques: weedy vegetation and flooded willow trees.

In the vegetation, such as milfoil, it's important to concentrate along the edges, keying on irregular features like points, cuts or pockets along the edge. Bass that hang out in the grass tend to roam more than those that stay in brush, simply because there is so much cover available. That's why concentrating on the irregular features in grassbeds is so important.

I like to fish willow trees because the fish there always seem to be right at the base of them, enjoying the cover from the root systems and the shade from overhanging branches. Sometimes bass key on certain types of willow trees, such as green ones instead of brown ones, and most of the time pitching is more effective than flipping. And you can bet your best jig that the largest bass will be holding in the thickest part of the cover. Other bass may be holding around the edges of that cover, though, so I always fish brushy cover by working the outside edges first, then I drop a lure into the middle.

I can't close this discussion of flipping and pitching without emphasizing the importance of developing a sense of what's happening around you, not only to your lure as it drops into that brushpile, but also how the fish are reacting to it. Let them tell you how they want the lure presented.

A basic rule of thumb in flipping or pitching is that the more adverse and unstable the weather conditions, the slower your lure should fall, and the calmer and more stable the conditions, the faster you can work your lure.

I'm asked quite a lot how I decide when to flip or pitch, and it's a good question. Although I always have a flipping rod in the boat with me, I seldom go out on the water with the intention of doing nothing but flipping or pitching.

If I see obvious bass cover, such as flooded bushes, I may work the area first with a topwater plug. Then if nothing happens, I'll try a spinnerbait for several casts.

If that doesn't work, but I'm convinced that the spot ought to hold bass, I may try pitching a worm or jig from a distance. And finally, if I still haven't contacted a fish, I may move in and try flipping.

Once I establish that the bushes do hold bass and I can catch them by flipping, that's how I'll spend the rest of my time on the water.

— NOVEMBER 1987

SHORELINE FLIPPING

By CHUCK OLSON

The amazingly productive technique of flipping can make you a better bank-bound BASSer . . .

Most fishermen who were on the water that day would say it was a tough one for fishing. But a small, brush-laden cove near the boat ramp looked worth checking before calling it quits.

Up ahead, a bank fisherman was intently flipping a jig and pig into a large brushpile. Quickly, he snatched a nice bass out of the submerged cedar tree. After releasing the fish he clipped off the jig and headed for the parking lot.

"Nice way to end the day," I called after him.

Stopping to light his pipe, he responded, "Had two more today that were bigger than that and four a little bit smaller." Considering that I had fooled only one 13-inch fish, I was anxious to know more about his technique.

"Caught 'em all from that 100-yard stretch" he explained. "And I used just two lures — a 6-inch worm and this jig combo," he said, holding up a 3/8-ounce black jig and pig. "I'd flip 'em into that heavy cover and after about six or eight casts to each brushpile, I'd nail 'em!"

What was that angler's secret? It was no secret, only a successful attempt to adapt to the fishing conditions imposed upon him. Being on foot meant that he could only fish a limited stretch of the lake's shoreline — so he picked a site with a combination of good structure and cover to fish.

And since he wasn't in a hurry to get to the next spot, he fished slower and employed a technique best suited for this pace.

In the Deep South, people have been "bank doodlin'" for ages. Long before high-speed boats and high-tech tackle, bank-walkers were hauling in massive catches of large-

mouth bass. Armed only with a 10- or 12-foot pole, heavy string (forerunners of our flipping gear) and a piece of pork hide or live bream, these fishermen have caught lunkers that many of us present-day BASSers only dream of catching.

So that fellow on a Midwestern lake had rediscovered one of the best bass-catching methods around. For boatless BASSers it may be the best thing since waders. And even for those who do own boats, it allows productive bassing on ponds, streams and other water where boating isn't feasible or is extremely difficult.

The obvious "drawback" of fishing on foot — the lack of mobility — actually is a very valuable, if not so apparent, asset. Because the boatless BASSer is forced to fish a smaller area, he naturally is going to fish it more thoroughly and cover all bases.

And flipping is a technique that is very well-suited to this slow and thorough pace.

Few angling techniques have revolutionized bass fishing like flipping. This long-rod/stout-line method has become a mainstay of many avid bass anglers' arsenals, and for good reason.

It is deadly for nailing big bass and big numbers of bass the fish.

An integral feature of flipping is its slow, methodical approach to bait presentation. This fits perfectly the mobility constraints of the shoreline angler. You're not making long casts, but rather swinging lures to precise targets in the middle of thick cover.

The bait lands softly, so you're not spooking the fish

Boat docks are havens for lunkers, and they can be reached effectively by shoreline flippers.

Photo: Chuck Olson

with noisy casts. What's more, the bank-walking angler can hit the shoreward side of a brushpile — a place that isn't pounded by boating BASSers.

Another selling point is that the technique is relatively easy to master with a little practice, and the investment in tackle isn't great.

Flipping rods are heavy-duty, 7 1/2- or 8-foot casting poles. A number of good models are available, and you should pick one that's labeled for flipping. Any casting reel you already have will do, but new models with the "flipping feature" (which allows you to pull out extra line while the thumb bar is depressed and which engages the reel upon release of the thumb bar — without your having to turn the handle) are good to have.

Line needs to be 20- or 25-pound-test to overcome the abrasion it'll get from being in thick cover and to hoist a bass out of the woodpile before it can wrap around an obstacle.

There's no need to lug around a big tacklebox. All the lures you might ever need can fit into a pocket tacklebox or fishing vest. Mainstays for shoreline flipping include jigs, worms and other plastic baits, pork rind, spinnerbaits and spoons.

Jigs can be either hair- or rubber-bodied and are usually 3/8 ounce or larger. Pork rind favorites, used either in tandem with jigs or alone on weedless hooks, include the pork frog, spring lizard and split-tail eel models. The choice of worms is as limitless as the sizes, colors and styles available. Rubber frogs and crawfish top the list of bogus plastic baits, an overlooked yet deadly group of lures. Finally, any one of the popular big-bladed spinnerbaits or weedless spoons round out the lure selection.

Two necessities for shoreline flipping are a fishing vest in which you can carry pliers, clippers and other items, and polarized glasses, which allow you to see through the surface glare and get a better view of the subsurface cover.

Even outfitted properly, though, you won't catch fish with even the best technique unless you're working the right shoreline.

Start by getting a good lake map and look for classic bass attractors — creek channels, old roadbeds, springs, feeder creeks and the like. Next, outline the shorelines nearest these features and go check them out.

Are the shorelines fishable? Can you walk along them? Do they contain good cover such as timber, weeds, rocks and brushpiles? Probably most important, who owns the land? Always obtain the landowner's permission to use his property and fish his waters.

When you find the right spot, you'll have to remember the two golden rules for flipping from shore. First, assume there's an 8-pounder lying under every bit of structure you can fish. Concentrate on each and every flip-cast, and be prepared for either a jarring strike or a subtle twitch of the line.

Second, approach each target area as though you were stalking a big buck on a quiet autumn morning. Tread lightly, wear subdued colors and move slowly up to the target area.

Remember, you'll be within a few feet of your quarry, so concentrate on making a stealthy approach. Once in place, stay put, keep your movement to a minimum, and only move on when you have saturated the cover.

There has been a passel of articles and even a couple books written on flipping. For those anglers who have never used this technique it would be a good idea to read some of these. Even better than that would be to find a friendly BASSer who's an accomplished flipper and get him to show you first-hand how to do it.

Once you've identified the stretch of shoreline with the best nearby structure, checked out the terrain and (if necessary) received permission to fish there, you're now ready to narrow your sights in on specific target areas. While bass have been taken from nearly every conceivable type of shoreline, four specific areas offer the best bet for shoreline flipping success: boat docks, fallen trees, weedbeds and riprap.

• **BOAT DOCKS** — Most B.A.S.S. members know that boat docks can be havens for lunker largemouths. Here, in the shade and security of the planks, hungry bass wait for an unsuspecting frog or panfish to swim into range and then grab it.

Flip to the likely ambush points — pilings, corners — and work these spots repeatedly and thoroughly. Look for nails or pieces of loose board: loop your casts over these, yo-yo the bait and hold on! This undulating motion is often too much of a temptation even for a bass in a neutral feeding mood.

The best baits to flip under these conditions are worms, the jig and pig, plastic frogs and pork frog chunks on a weedless hook. The real sleeper bait is a No. 11 or No. 1 Uncle Josh pork frog in a green-and-white pattern. When used with an unweighted weedless hook, this bait hits the water, swims, looks and tastes like a genuine frog.

Docks with good crappie structure such as Christmas trees nearby commonly attract bass of all sizes.

• **FALLEN TREES** — Downed trees, of course, offer more ambush points and a much larger area of cover than does standing timber. Flooded brush and hedgerows can also be considered in this class of cover.

There are two key ambush points on a typical fallen tree: The point where the trunk enters the water. Bass often slip back under there, where they're close to prey that falls off the bank. The second type of ambush point is any junction of the main trunk and one or several branches. Work these spots thoroughly and from several different angles and directions.

The best baits for these conditions are the jig and pig,

plastic worm and a spinnerbait or weedless spoon. The spoon and spinnerbait are worked best with a lift-and-flutter action. The jig, worm, and even the spinnerbait can be worked along the length of the tree in a swimming motion. Again, take advantage of overhanging limbs; cast your bait over these and work the bait up and down. Always be prepared for the bass to take the lure on the fall and don't hesitate sticking it to it.

Finally, an especially productive zone for big bass is right in the middle of the thickest cover you can find. Have patience and work your jig or worm down through the tangles until it reaches bottom, then work it back up and down again. This is where your heavy-duty gear will come in handy.

• **WEEDBEDS** — Of all types of shoreline cover, weeds and other vegetation are the toughest for flipping, but don't avoid them — they can be bass magnets. Key ambush points in weedbeds are cuts, points and holes. Keep in mind that active bass usually will cruise the outside edges of weedbeds. Neutral or inactive bass often back into the weeds, facing out.

Excellent lures for flipping weedbeds include plastic worms, pork frogs on weedless hooks, plastic frogs and weedless spoons.

If the weeds are submerged 4 inches to a foot below the surface, try flipping a weightless worm or pork chunk or a plastic frog. Swim the bait back over the tops of the weeds, pausing periodically to flutter the bait down through holes in the weeds. I've seen bass come bustin' through a mat of weeds to nail a worm swimming temptingly overhead.

• **RIPRAP** — This type of cover is present on almost every man-made body of water, often in many different parts of the lake. Look for riprap shorelines along bridges, launch ramps and along the face of the dam.

The target areas on riprap will not be as concentrated or identifiable as will other types of cover. Bass might cruise parallel to the shore or hold off in deeper water, moving up to the shallows only to feed. One place bass do set up in ambush is alongside a rock or boulder that is much bigger or otherwise stands out from the other rocks around it.

While riprap attracts minnows and fry in abundance, the key bass forage here is crawfish. Any attempt to nail bass on riprap should somehow appeal to its yearning for these crustaceans. One of my favorite lures for flipping riprap is a plastic crawfish fished with a light (1/8-ounce) sinker or leadhead jig. The lighter weight will help prevent the bait from getting wedged between rocks.

The deadliest retrieve is to "hop-and-pause" your fake crawfish or 4-inch worm parallel to the shoreline. Overlap your casts in deeper and deeper water until you can't keep the lure in constant contact with the bottom.

Bass can be caught on other types of structure, but

How To Flip From Shore

Flipping from shore is not very different from flipping from a boat. The slight difference comes in the fact that you'll be retrieving the lure from deep to shallow water, instead of the reverse, and that you'll have to avoid shoreline obstacles when making the flip-cast.

Here's how to do it: (Instructions are based on the assumption that you're right-handed.)

1) Hold the rod in your right hand with the extended butt resting on the underside of your forearm. Point the rod straight up, extending your arm above your head. Now let out enough line for the jig to touch the ground.

2) Lower the rod, engage the reel and with your left hand grasp the line just behind the first guide. Pull it back and hold it out to your left side.

3) Raise the rod to cause the jig to swing back toward you (like a pendulum), then lower the rod tip as the bait approaches you. When the jig is back at its farthest point, the rod tip should be pointed at your target.

4) As the jig starts forward, raise the rod tip smoothly and quickly, propelling the lure toward the target and keeping it just above the water. Let the line slip through the fingers of your left hand, but don't let go of the line.

5) The lure should slip into the water with hardly a ripple. Immediately let go of the line with your left hand and grasp the rod just in front of the reel. Be ready to set the hook.

6) Let the lure fall straight down by lowering your rod slowly; the rate you lower the rod tip is the rate the lure will sink. Work the lure close to the bottom, climbing it over any obstructions and letting it flutter back to the bottom. If needed, pause to reel in line — never have more than a few inches of slack line, and don't let your rod tip get any higher than eye-level. Remember, you'll have to move the rod tip about 2 or 3 feet when setting the hook, so give yourself plenty of room.

these four are the classic flipping sites. They exist on almost every lake, they're easily identifiable and, most importantly, they almost always hold fish. Furthermore, the most effective way to fish these areas from the shore is to flip 'em.

Bank fishing, often thought of as a futile exercise, can be a pleasant surprise to BASSers who try shoreline flipping.

— OCTOBER 1985

RUSS BRINGGER'S POKING TECHNIQUE

By TIM TUCKER

When surface vegetation is too thick for lures to penetrate in the usual way, try this trick . . .

It had the makings of a bass fisherman's nightmare.

A cold front had passed through overnight, dropping the temperature by 18 degrees. On this particular morning, all semblance of wind had disappeared and a bright, cloudless bluebird sky greeted anglers.

These were apparent signals that a tough day was ahead.

While other tournament fishermen fretted about the conditions, Russ Bringger calmly began rigging up his flipping stick. But he wasn't preparing for just any flipping technique. He was readying his heavy-cover special, a tactic designed to produce results during the toughest times — cold-front conditions and hot summer days when the fish bury themselves deep into heavy cover for shelter and protection, and stay there.

When the day was over, Bringger had collected another good limit and cashed another top 10 paycheck. Another day at the office.

Once again, a technique he calls "poking" didn't fail him.

"These types of days can be the most frustrating days of all for fishermen," explains Bringger, a talented, 35-year-old Pompano Beach, Fla., pro and champion of the 1986 Florida BASSMASTER® Invitational. "You can be on the fish hot and heavy to the point where they're chasing your bait, and go in there the next day after a cold front has come through and you'd think somebody had seined the place. You'd think there was not a bass in the whole lake.

"But we know from experience, from what biologists tell us and from everything that has been written about bass that the fish have a tendency to get as far up under heavy cover as possible, where there is shade, warmth and protection from the elements (during cold-front conditions)."

Bringger says the same situation occurs in the summertime, when bass hide under thick cover to get shade and comfort from the heat.

"I've found that big bass really have a tendency to do this. But in Florida, where I live, the problem is that the fish will often get under grass so thick that you can't get a lure to them — at least not with conventional methods," he says.

Although most of Bringger's success with the poking technique has come in his native Florida lakes, the fundamentals of this tactic should give BASSers another weapon for grass-fishing everywhere, including the thick milfoil beds of Tennessee's Nickajack Lake, the jungle-like hydrilla found in Texas lakes and the coontail moss of Lake Seminole.

Bringger's poking technique was devised as a way to penetrate thick mats of hydrilla and water hyacinths that blanket the surface and grow so dense that the bottom vegetation (and even the roots of the hydrilla stalks) die. That creates a huge, open cavern beneath this blanket of greenery, the ideal habitat for bass, particularly big bass that recognize it as a protected comfort zone.

But penetrating this sphere of safety isn't easy. Weedless lures like plastic worms and jigs are required, but conventional flipping is often useless. Enter Bringger's poking

Bringger literally pokes his rod repeatedly through thick vegetation and lets a worm sink to the bottom to entice lunker large-mouths like this one.

Photo: Gerald Crawford

technique into the scene.

The technique involves using a long rod (a flipping stick is ideal) with plenty of backbone, heavy line (20- to 30-pound-test), a pegged, 1-ounce bullet weight and a large plastic worm (8 or 9 inches in length).

The technique begins with the worm and weight reeled up tight to the top guide. Then with the reel in free-spool and a thumb holding the spool securely, Bringger begins literally poking the rod into the vegetation, wrestling with the surface cover until he finally penetrates the thick mat. Once the rod tip manages to puncture through the vegetation, he then releases the spool, allowing the worm to sink to the bottom. After jigging the worm a few times, he repeats the process in another spot along the vegetation. He works an area thoroughly, sometimes poking just 6 inches from his previous point of penetration.

"You literally have to shove the rod tip down anywhere from a foot to 3 feet deep to get through the stuff," Bring-

> *"You may poke all day long and get only three strikes, but, usually, you'll have three good fish."*

ger says. "These are times and places when flipping is absolutely no good, yet there are fish in these places. Poking is the only way to get a lure in front of these fish."

When selecting likely cover for poking, Bringger concentrates on the thickest vegetation that has the deepest water beneath it. It stands to reason that the deeper the water, the larger these open-water caverns will be. He works the edge of the vegetation first, but then runs his boat up into the vegetation and begins poking around the boat. If the water is deep enough (more than 5 feet), Bringger believes this activity usually will not spook fish in the vicinity.

"I've found this to be a good big-bass technique," Bringger says. "You may poke all day long and get only three strikes, but, usually, you'll have three good fish. And it's exciting. Think about it: you have an 8- or 9-pound fish with only 8 or 9 feet of line out. You really can have a battle on your hands."

— NOVEMBER 1987

CHAPTER FOUR

FISHING APPROACHES

*W*ays and means of
getting to the fish once
they are located.

Photo: Dave Precht

Photo: Gerald Crawford

Photo: Larry Teague

Photo: Jim Vincent

RIVER SLIPPING FOR BASS

By DAN D. GAPEN

Odd as it sounds, maneuvering a boat and fishing at the same time can be tricky in fast-running water unless you take a backward approach . . .

With the force possessed only by a thousand demons, the Nipigon River pushed and thrust its way past the rusting iron and tarred wooden railroad trestle. The canvas-covered freighter canoe, powered by a 4-horsepower Champion motor, hung dwarfed beneath the immense structure. Boiling eddies pushed from the right, then from the left.

Machelle Daba, an aging 72-year-old Ojibway Indian, grimly held tight to the outboard motor's extended handle. With the motor at what appeared to be full thrust, the craft drifted slowly backward, beneath the structure. The mighty river was winning.

Forward, perched upon a wooden apple crate, sat a young man nearly 15 years of age. Preoccupied with forcing a too-short fly rod to perform, the youngster had little concern for the predicament that appeared to prevail. The craft in which he rode was being forced backward downstream, but apparently it was of little concern to the youthful, angling Nimrod.

Five casts had been directed with little success at a rock and wooden piling that supported the bridge abutment. On presentation No. 6, the fisherman's brightly colored red-and-white fly evoked a huge boil as it passed through the lower edge of an eddy created by the structure. With grim determination, the line was set.

Daba, a river veteran of some 60 years, watched as his companion worked a heavy fish. Ever so slowly the motor throttle was decreased as the fish tired and began to succumb to power created by the weighty river currents. By decreasing power, the old native was able to keep up to

his angler's tiring fish. The bow of the canoe remained pointed upstream.

Two hundred yards downstream from the railroad trestle, Daba placed a landing net beneath 5 pounds of fire-red brook trout. His young angler beamed a smile of delight and accepted his catch for inspection. Without so much as a glance, the old Indian reached behind him, thrust the motor throttle forward to wide open and headed for the opposite bank.

Moments later, after taking advantage of the slower river surface currents there, Daba headed back cross-stream. He positioned the canoe at a point above the Paramachine Bridge on the world-famous Nipigon River. Again, he eased the motor throttle back ever so slightly and repeated the process that had yielded the big trout. Slowly the craft began to drift backward toward the bridge. Without knowing it, Daba was "river slipping."

As a growing boy in the northern reaches of Ontario's bush country, I was to receive many more lessons from the old Indian, but none that would so affect my future ability to fish running water. Slipping running water has over many years enabled this Bassmaster to considerably increase total fishing ability by as much as 50 percent. Let me explain:

River slipping most certainly has been a part of river angling for as long as man has traversed flowing bodies of water. It didn't receive any particular attention until the late 1960s or early 1970s. River guides in states such as Arkansas and Tennessee have been utilizing this method for years, but never really refined the art.

Trout guides on western rivers, such as the Snake and

Madison, worked boats styled to represent the craft used by ancient whalers with oars to slip these white-water western streams. Where normally motor thrust propels the craft against the current, oars perform the task. The disadvantage to this method is seen when really fast water is encountered and oar power is unable to suspend the craft in a holding pattern. Instead, due to a lack of power, the boat with its occupants is forced downstream in a too-fast drift, thus preventing fishermen from fishing the water properly.

Those who have worked salmon streams from Maine to Newfoundland, via boat or canoe, have experienced river slipping in one form or another. Working Atlantic salmon with a fly rod from a moving craft can only be accomplished by a "bow-upstream, stern-downstream" method. The angler who works flies for salmon or trout must have the boat, from which he casts, remain steady and suspended at one point while he fishes. This is essential if the angler is to present the fly effectively.

What does all this have to do with the BASSer who seeks smallmouth and largemouth bass from a local creek or stream? Surprisingly, a great deal.

I began river slipping, as previously described, on the Nipigon River in Canada in the early 1940s when only a boy. During the last 20 years, I've used a similar method to fish the huge network of rivers in the northern half of the United States in pursuit of all game fish. No longer do I utilize the canoe as the vehicle but instead have transferred to the more stable johnboat. This craft, with its flat bottom and broad beam, holds a much more stable course while responding in a manner that better suits the needs of those working running water.

The Equipment — During over 40 years of slipping rivers, there have been very few craft not used by this angler: canoes, V-bottoms, semi-Vs, glass, aluminums, tri-hulls and johnboats all have worked beneath me at one time or another. If I had to pick one rig for "Average River" U.S.A., it would be a 14-foot aluminum johnboat with three separate seats. The center seat should contain a manual livewell. By "manual livewell," I refer to one which contains no mechanical pump but instead works on gravity feed via two inlets, one on either side of the boat.

The boat width can vary, but I prefer the wider models. The extra width creates better stability, thus enabling a more relaxed angler to better fish the passing-water structure.

Some johnboats have sharply pointed bows while others retain the look of a cement-mixing box with bow and stern width being nearly equal. Years of research show that a boat with a bow slightly narrower than the stern works best when river slipping. I do not like the narrow front ends for river work.

The johnboat's depth may vary with the area you fish. Most river anglers prefer 16- to 20-inch sides. Depth is usually controlled by water conditions. Heavier and more rapid-water conditions necessitate deeper-sided craft. Where rivers run slow and sluggish, johnboats with sides of 14 to 16 inches often are used. My overall preference is 20 inches. This enables you to work most of the nation's fishable rivers, and in no way detracts from ability to work slow water.

Motors that make suitable companion pieces to a 14-foot johnboat vary with each region visited, but probably fall within the 2- to 18-hp range. I prefer the 5- to 6-hp sizes. These are big enough to have built-in reverse shifts and slip clutches.

I don't believe there's a river I've worked bass in that a motor bigger than 6 hp was needed. Some western rivers may require bigger boats as well as bigger motors, but they are in the minority and generally are considered "trout streams." For the average bass angler who seeks smallies or largemouths, the 14-footer with a 5-horse will do just fine.

Five Horses Are Plenty — Why not a bigger motor? Several reasons come to mind:

The investment cost of a river-slipping rig is one factor. All one has to do is compare prices of a 5-hp to an 18-hp motor to realize the advantage in a smaller motor.

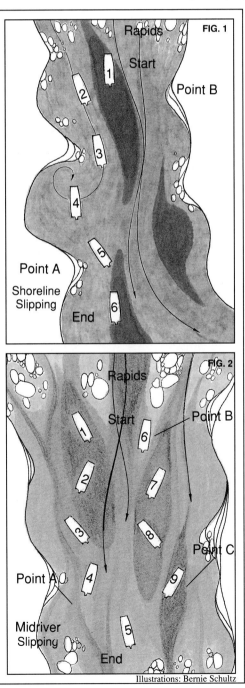

FIG. 1
Rapids
Start
Point B
Point A
Shoreline Slipping
End

FIG. 2
Rapids
Start
Point B
Point A
Point C
Midriver Slipping
End

Illustrations: Bernie Schultz

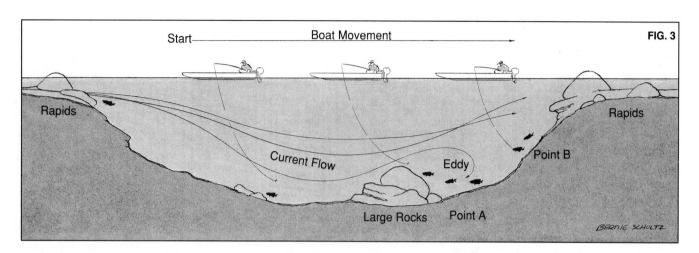

The cost of repairs is another reason. River running can be a damaging experience for equipment, especially for the beginner. Repair charges on larger motors, such as for replacing a lower unit, can be extremely costly. Smaller motors cost less to repair.

The ease with which you handle smaller equipment must be weighed, too. Consider the energy and labor expended to drop in and take out smaller and lighter units. One also must think about water depth. The bigger the motor, the deeper the shaft. Smaller motors enable you to work a greater variety of the river's shallow structure.

The ease with which operators can work a small motor enables them to fish better. I find that by using a 5- or 6-hp motor I'm able to sit upon its top cover, hold the throttle handle upward to my left, steer the motor between casts with my left hand and successfully land a bass without changing position. A bigger motor just won't respond to this type of operation.

The most obvious reason is cost of operation and compactness. With gas prices soaring, and the need to conserve energy, it's obvious that this size motor is more economical to run.

Those of us who run rivers for love and a living find that no matter how fast currents become, there are always eddies and boils by which a river traveler can traverse upstream. Any of you who have watched the Ojibway Indians of northern Canada work 18-foot freighter canoes up the whitewater rapids of rivers, such as the Winisk or the Albany, know all that's needed is a reliable 5- or 6-hp motor at the stern.

The Method — "River slipping" is a term generally used when describing a method of traveling backward downstream while still in complete control of one's craft. That's the easy way to say it. However, describing slipping in detail is not that easy. Not only does it afford complete control of the craft, but, when properly executed, river slipping will allow all passengers to fish at ease. It also will enable you to present lures in a proper manner to

fish holding in the current.

Slipping can be performed via two adaptations: (1) when anglers want to fish the shoreline by casting artificials; (2) when anglers find it necessary to get down to bottom-hugging bass in areas such as slicks and centerstream channels. (These methods are shown in Figs. 1 and 2.)

General adaptation to slipping can be accomplished by any BASSer who runs a river. Let me explain:

Slipping Running Water — To "slip" running water, all you need to do is point the bow of the craft upstream, accelerate the motor in forward thrust and begin a series of maneuvers. With the bow faced into the current and the proper distance obtained from shore, the motor operator throttles down to a point where the craft has begun to fall backward, downstream. The motor's thrust is no longer great enough to keep you going forward, and you find the boat sliding backward. That's easy!

Boat Control — Next, boat control must be maintained. To test yourself, accelerate forward a bit and drop off a couple times. You'll find that though you're moving forward and backward along the stream bank, boat control seems to be maintained. The fact is that a point of pivot is established on your craft that allows complete control. Were you to attempt to steer or maneuver the craft from a center or upstream spot in the boat, pressure exerted on other portions would overpower the point of pivot. When this happens, boats are swung sideways, or at least are set into side-slips that are difficult to master. Thus, the man running the motor would spend most of his time fighting the current.

Having experienced going forward and backward with the bow pointed upstream, you now turn the motor slightly. You will find that the boat slips sideways. It does not turn the bow to the side as one might suspect. Because your point to pivot (fulcrum) has no downstream, it slides to the side with the entire craft following suit.

The handle control is just what one might suspect. Turn the motor so the propeller thrust pushes toward the direction you want to go. Once the craft begins to slip sideways, immediately turn the propeller thrust away from the direction in which the boat is moving. This will correct the boat's side drift. One thing the beginner will note is that this sideways slip is similar in feel to power steering on a car. It doesn't take much turn of the handle to set a new course.

You now have the two most important functions accomplished: (1) backward movement with the motor in forward thrust, and (2) sideways movement without having to realign the bow. Everything else in river slipping is adjustments and practice.

For Bassmasters who are going to make an attempt to "slip" a river for the first time, there are a couple other points that are worth remembering:

Rivers that flow with a current speed less than two miles an hour are really not suitable for this method.

When beginning a river trip in which a great deal of slipping is intended, remember to start far enough upstream to allow use of time allotted. Any time river slipping is programmed, begin upstream from the area you intend to work. That may seem a simple point, but many an angler begins downstream just on the basis of instinct.

Specific use of river slipping is best accomplished two ways: (1) to work shoreline, (2) to work the centerstream. The first, shoreline adaptation, is probably the easiest and most commonly used.

Shoreline Slipping — Let's take a typical river that just may be the one near your home. (See Figure 1.) Its shore contour juts out into the currents, then recedes inward to allow waters the opportunity to form eddies and boils. Keeping the proper fishing distance from the shoreline can best be accomplished by slipping.

Move the boat to the start position indicated in Figure 1. Here, close to rocks and rapids formed by a small descent on land structure, you begin to cast upstream toward the shore. The upstream-casting method allows the angler to present lures in a manner similar to movement of natural bait. Current pressure forces dislodged natural bait downstream in rivers.

Slowly the boat is allowed to work its way backward to Point A. Here anglers have a choice — they can continue on downstream to work the eddy around the next point or go forward to Point B. At Point B, a repeat of the slipping method is executed on the far shore. You'll note that the boat bow is always faced into the current flow. This positioning is held easily as long as boaters do not allow themselves to become entrapped in the current flow of eddies and backwaters.

Slipping The Channel — The second most popular adaptation of river slipping is used when hard-to-get-at areas, such as slicks (areas below pools where water smooths out), are worked or when following channel areas. It also is an excellent method to cover deep areas between rapids or fast-water areas. (See Figure 2.)

Slipping these areas can be started at a similar point as described above. Instead of casting, anglers now use a trolling-type technique to produce results. By casting line out behind the boat, allowing it to work backward as slipping is accomplished, all downstream waters are covered.

To keep lures or live bait from fouling on bottom, I find that lifting the rod tip, allowing water to elevate the line, then lowering to allow the lure to speed on downstream, gives the bait a natural downstream movement. This action represents live bait such as crawfish being swept away with the currents. Hair jigs with spinners attached, or lures such as Gapen's Ugly Bug, work extremely well under these circumstances.

To fish the entire centerstream point, you have but to utilize the sideways movement and control previously described to slip the johnboat. By moving back and forth as you descend with the current, you can cover an entire water system. It is a more effective way to cover water than casting.

As illustrated in Figure 2, once you leave the start point, backward movement continues in a zigzag manner until you reach Point A. Here, if the river is wide enough, motor your craft up to Point B where the downstream slipping procedure begins once again until you reach Point C.

This second style of river slipping is one of the best ways to reach big bass during midsummer days when heat and low-water conditions drive them from shallow areas near the shoreline. It provides a method to catch the bigger bass that inhabit "hole-up areas" in rivers.

Two such hole-up hot spots are shown in Figure 3. Point A is a sunken rock such as is found often near centerstream in deep water. Smallmouth bass dearly love this type of structure. Most anglers working rivers drift right on by, never thinking a thing about the boil on the surface that indicates such a structure exists below. River slipping is most effective at producing bass from this spot.

The second area indicated by Point B is an excellent holding area for all game fish, but is especially ideal for bass. Here, just above the rapid waters, bass find a staging area where the river current is not nearly as strong as that near the surface. Food is swept down to the bass as in Area A, and the fish are somewhat protected from heat and the brilliance of the sunlight.

This type area probably produces more big smallmouth bass for the experienced river angler than any other. If a school of 2- to 4-pound smallies is located at this point, it is not unusual to find as many as two dozen within a space similar in size to the johnboat's bottom.

River slipping may not have all the answers to producing limit catches from running water, but rest assured — it is a key that will open a great many doors to better success for the average bass angler.

— MAY/JUNE 1980

TRY MIDLAKE TROLLING TACTICS FOR MORE BASS

By GLENN E. REEVES

What, you troll for bass? This Alabama Bassmaster bad-mouthed the tactic, too, until a veteran BASSer revealed his success method for taking spotted bass on Lake Martin . . .

What, troll for bass in this heat? You've got to be kidding."

Those remarks were directed at my next-door neighbor during a late-August heat wave. I was elated with the idea of going bassin' until he announced plans to troll. You see, I had just moved to Wetumpka, Ala., and was having quite a time learning local waters and techniques preferred by bass. Many times, I had seen my neighbor, Fred Ruffin, come in with huge stringers of bass, even during the hot dog days, while I repeatedly struck out.

If you asked local bassmen today what sort of BASSer the late Fred G. Ruffin was, they'd tell you Fred Ruffin was quiet and reserved, kept to himself and almost always fished alone. Anyone lucky enough to share a boat with him felt privileged, indeed.

I was indeed surprised when Fred asked me to accompany him to Lake Martin. But I was rather astonished when Ruffin announced we would troll, and he expected to take a good bunch of spotted bass. I'd never been much for trolling. Ruffin sensed that I had my doubts, but his was a take-it-or-leave-it attitude and I knew he'd not ask again if I declined. I took him up on the trip and tried to hide my misgivings.

Lake Martin is a deep, clearwater impoundment covering 40,000 acres with 700 miles of shoreline in Elmore and Tallapoosa counties in central Alabama. Instead of the usual 4 a.m. hot-weather ritual I had been following, we left about 8 a.m. The sun was up and blazing; it didn't take a weatherman to know what the day was going to hold. If the bright sun and hot temperatures bothered Ruffin, he certainly didn't show any indications. It seemed to be old hat.

I decided the best thing was to keep quiet, observe, and learn something. I had assumed we would motor along the shoreline, dragging a couple of lures behind the boat. Boy, did I get fooled!

The launching ramp was in a long, wide inlet about a quarter-mile from the lake's main body. As soon as the engine smoothed out at its slowest trolling speed, Ruffin let out line. He had chosen a deep-running lure about 4 inches long. I wondered about his lure. I had always caught spotted bass with small lures. But I tied on one as near like his as I had.

We had traveled about as far as the length of three football fields when Ruffin killed the engine. The curve of his rod indicated a good fish. We were still in the middle of the inlet over what I figured was very deep water. Evidently, Ruffin had no intention of trolling the shoreline. I reeled in to give him plenty of room. I need not have been in a hurry. My lure was only about 35 yards behind the boat. For what seemed like an unusually long time, Ruffin continued to reel steadily, keeping firm pressure but never rushing the bass. I grabbed the net and got ready to do the honors as the 2-pound spotted bass came up shaking its head several yards behind the boat.

With the bass in the ice chest and underway again, I paid close attention as we released line. My lure was out 35 or 40 yards and I was ready to engage the spool, but Ruffin was still letting out line. I thought he'd never quit.

Ruffin noticed I was imitating his actions. He explained experience had proved the lure would run at its maximum 16- to 18-foot depth when trolled approximately 90 yards behind the boat. He had marked the line at this point. This satisfied me as far as lure distance behind the boat, but why were we trolling so far from shore? This question remained unanswered in my mind as we reached the mouth of the inlet. Instead of turning to follow the shoreline contours, Ruffin headed straight across the lake, which was a half-mile wide at that point. I was expecting to reel in and run on across the big water and troll the coves and inlets on the other side — but we kept on trolling.

Somewhere near midlake, my plug started bumping bottom. "Bet we get hung," I said. "My plug's hitting bottom." If Ruffin heard me, he didn't reply. He just leaned into his rod as another bass tried to make off with that fake minnow. I started cranking my lure to give him room, but it never made it. A spotted bass decided its dinner was about to escape. After an eternity of turning reel handles, we had two good spots flopping in the boat.

Looking back, I think this was the turning point in my attitude toward trolling for black bass. We continued to troll through the heat. Instead of taking time out for lunch, we ate sandwiches one-handed and held onto our rods. We stopped only to land a bass. The halts were a lot more frequent than I ever had anticipated. We trolled the midsection of large inlets and coves; then made the return trip across Lake Martin at a different location. Not once did we troll the shoreline. About 3 p.m., Ruffin decided to knock off.

On the trip home, he summed up the success reasons for his trolling technique. Ruffin had found out years earlier that hot-weather bass were deep and trolling near the shoreline produced only hangups and lost lures. He moved farther out to give the deep-runners room to operate. The midlake technique was harder to learn because of the expanse of open water and because this was before most anglers used depthfinders. On each side of the main river channel, the lake bottom is covered with hills, ridges, and humps. Some extend to within a few feet of the surface. Before the lake was built in the 1920s, the land alongside the river was cultivated in fields of corn and cotton. The only thing now to hang up on is a few rock piles that farmers had piled in the fields.

The author is shown working ridges and drop-offs located around a midlake island on picturesque Lake Martin in central Alabama.   Photo: Glenn Reeves

Here's a selection of trolling lures and tackle used by the author with success. Pictured are a few nice spotted bass.
Photo: Glenn Reeves

The coves and inlets we trolled were branch heads in earlier days. Most were cleared just before the lake filled. In the 1920s, timber was so plentiful it wasn't economical to haul out the trees. They were cut, chained in great piles, and anchored in areas that would be covered with water at least 50 feet deep once the lake filled. This structure helped make Ruffin's midlake trolling successful. The bass used these huge log piles as deep-water sanctuaries. To feed, the bass moved along the humps and ridges after spottail shiners and threadfin shad; both were stocked along with bass.

Ruffin and I fished Martin many times. We always trolled the same way, in the same areas, and seldom were we skunked. Ruffin had learned the configuration of the bottom structures with the aid of an anchor rope marked at 5-foot intervals. It was a slow process that required much effort, but it was worth it. He boated bass when others were cooling their heels in the shade.

Once introduced to the technique, I did a good deal of experimenting and forfeited a lot of bass, but things I learned then are no doubt responsible for a few extra bass in the livewell today. I used as many as a dozen different lures just to see what would happen. Ruffin used only two types — imitation threadfin shad and long, slim, deep-runners that resembled spottail shiners. His idea was to match the baitfish on which bass fed. It proved to be best. I seldom ever matched his catch while changing lures.

During days when bass were hard to come by, we varied the trolling speed from ultraslow to a fast pace that put a definite bend in our rods. Many times bass hit only when we were executing a wide arc or turn. This caused the lures to speed up as they followed the arc of the line, and hits there were the best indication a troller needed to speed up the presentation on the straightaways.

One question we were never able to answer was why we only caught spotted bass. We never caught more than half a dozen largemouths in our many trips. The spot is the predominant species in Martin and our method was more suited to catching them. Spotted bass have a tendency to school and roam like wolf packs in search of food.

The Alabama Power Co. lowers the level of Martin during fall months in readiness for winter and spring rains. Many BASSers turn to other lakes, but the trolling technique described continues to produce when the lake is falling as much as a foot per week. Some shallow areas must be avoided, but midlake structures can still be worked effectively.

The best tool or fishing aid for this type of fishing is a depthfinder. It will reveal in a matter of hours what it took Ruffin years to discover using his anchor and rope. When I purchased a depthfinder, Ruffin wasn't too impressed at first, and justifiably so. It only proved the facts that he already knew. It was a different story, though, when we tried another area. After a couple of days trolling new territory, we knew almost as much about the bottom configuration as we did the familiar areas we had been fishing.

Even though I learned to accept trolling and caught fish, I still thought that once fish were located we could do better by anchoring and casting to them. Ruffin agreed we probably could, but warned if we did, our spot would be ruined. Other fishermen would see us sitting still, and were sure to investigate as soon as we left. If they hit the spot, and some surely would after depthfinders became fairly common, the structure would be ruined. Ruffin believed constant fishing pressure would cause the bass to seek a quieter, more peaceable area. He didn't believe trolling pressure would be heavy enough to alter fishing, because many anglers turn their noses up at the thought of employing this technique.

Successful trolling, though, is much more than just dragging a lure behind the boat. Whether or not it's an art, I won't argue, but it is a systematic technique that required certain refinements to make it an effective and enjoyable way of bassin'.

For fishermen interested in trying, here are some suggestions:

(1) Use lures that resemble the bass' natural forage.

(2) Experiment until you find the distance behind the boat that allows the lure to work at its maximum depth.

(3) Use a line as light as possible under prevailing conditions. Large-diameter line causes too much drag and won't

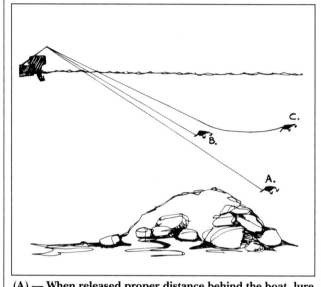

(A) — When released proper distance behind the boat, lure will reach its maximum depth.
(B) — When trolled too close to the boat, lure runs shallow.
(C) — When trolled too far back, lure also runs shallow because of belly that forms in line.

allow lures to reach the maximum depth.

(4) Vary trolling speed from very slow to as fast as the lure will run without twisting and spinning.

(5) Work structures from several different angles. Sometimes bass will only hit lures traveling in one specific direction.

(6) Always carry a good lure retriever or plug-knocker. Regardless of where you troll, you'll get hung.

(7) Troll with only one rod when alone. Your chances may be better with two lures, but believe me, when you troll through a school of hungry bass with two rods, you'll find your hands too full.

As far as the best times to troll, I prefer late summer or early fall. Anytime is productive, from immediately after spawning to the coldest part of winter. In my area of Alabama, I've never had much luck during January, February or March. I think it's because a trolled lure, even at the slowest speeds, is a bit too fast for bass, whose reactions have slowed due to cold water. Of course, during spawning, bass are scattered and spend more time in the shallows.

There are no contour maps available of Lake Martin or many of the other Alabama Power Co. lakes built in the early 1900s before such mapping. For this reason, trolling is the best way to learn these lakes. It allows you to cover a lot of water and, at the same time, use a depthfinder to learn the configuration of the bottom and structures. It also keeps your lure in the water where it belongs. No other method offers as much, in my opinion, and yet allows you to catch bass in the process.

— *SEPTEMBER/OCTOBER 1975*

DRIFTING AND DRAGGING

By RONNIE KOVACH

The reel does little work in these two Western fishing techniques, until it's time to wind in a fish . . .

Many lakes in the West are typically deep and clear with minimal shoreline structure. Bassmasters accustomed to running and gunning along a bank lined with ample cover may at first be overwhelmed by the stark terrain of these Western reservoirs.

However, bass fishermen in this part of the country have learned to devise strategies to work these impoundments effectively. Two such tactics are "drifting," which uses the wind for propulsion, and "dragging," which relies on the trolling motor for moving the boat and the bait.

Both methods have become popular in Western bassin' circles as a means to fish deep while surveying large expanses of open water, often in foul weather, with maximum efficiency.

Drifting With The Wind

The main feature separating the drifting strategy from dragging is the lack of reliance on an electric trolling motor. Winds that whip across these barren Western lakes can generate considerable swells, waves and chop. These are tough conditions in which to try to power a

A rather modified doodlin' approach, drifting often will trigger strikes from lethargic, deepwater bass. Photo: Ronnie Kovach

fully loaded bass boat with an electric trolling motor.

West Coast bassers instead set up different drift patterns in which their boats are pushed across the water by the wind.

For example, to drift across shallow flats in a large cove — a typical pattern — you would motor to the far, lee side of the cove. After positioning the boat parallel to the bank, you then allow the wind to push you across the cove. Once you reach the other shore, start up the big motor, drive back to the leeward side and begin another drift.

A considerable amount of territory can be covered by drifting in this fashion. Similar drift patterns might be established between two points, along a rocky dam, over submerged trees or along an old creek channel. Drifting allows the Bassmaster to concentrate more upon the baits bouncing along the bottom than having to fight the elements while maneuvering the trolling motor.

A multitude of different lures are highly adaptable for drifting. By far, the simplest to use are soft-plastic baits.

The standard Texas-rigged worm bounced on the bottom with a 3/16- to 5/8-ounce bullet weight makes a perfect drift bait. The heavier sinkers are often necessary to maintain solid bottom contact, particularly with a fast drift or in deep water.

It is important to note that worm fishing on the drift is different from using this bait from a more stationary casting platform. First, you must be ready to drop the rod and instantly give the bass slack when you feel the first "tick" in the line. Sometimes, the worm is plowing so fast along the bottom rift the fish can hardly stay up with it. You must give the bass a moment to eat the bait.

Also, because the drift is moving the worm for you, it is best to imbed the hook barely through the outer layer of plastic, rather than into the middle of the body. "Skin-hooking" the worm like this will make it somewhat less weedless. However, a quick, efficient hookset is facilitated with this ploy.

The Carolina rig is another excellent combination to try with the drifting strategy. Use anything from a 1/4- to 1-ounce bullet weight or oval egg sinker butted against a swivel. Attach 18 to 36 inches of leader line, then a worm hook to the end.

The heavier sinkers will provide for adequate bottom contact with even the fastest drift in the deepest water. A plastic worm, curley-tail grub, or featherlike reaper can be drifted with this Carolina setup. These baits will, to some degree, float up off the bottom. This can be a deadly combination when drifted over submerged weedbeds or rockpiles where bass are holding.

You also may want to switch to a specially designed plastic-foam floating jighead for drifting in deeper water. Lace on Garland's Spider or Haddock's squid-like 18-Tail to the floating head and drift these baits well above the bottom for bass.

Another variation on this theme is to use Jack Chancellor's well-known Do-Nothing worms. These bland-looking baits are rarely used out West, a fact which Dave Nollar, one of the pioneers of the deep-water game, uses to his advantage. Nollar routinely drifts a simple smoke-colored Do-Nothing worm on a Carolina rig to nail quality fish while other anglers are fighting the wind.

"The fish haven't seen the Do-Nothing worm very often," observes Nollar. "When I drag this bait, the dying, fluttering action simulates the way shad move in deep water. The turbulence created by the larger sinker plowing along the bottom also helps to attract bass. This is one of those methods that

takes time for people to discover."

In addition to the soft-plastic baits, other lures have some intriguing applications as drift baits. Heavy 5/8- to 1-ounce slab spoons such as the Hopkins No. 075 or Haddock's Jig'N Spoon can be "yo-yoed" over deep ledges as the boat drifts along with the breeze.

On windy days, it is almost impossible to maintain good boat position over these offshore "breaks" while using a spoon in the traditional vertical-jigging fashion. But with the drifting technique, you simply let the spoon sink to the bottom and then give a few pronounced lift-and-drop motions with the rod. As the boat drifts along, let out more monofilament to maintain good bottom contact with the spoon. At some point, you will find that you cannot let out much more line and still have control of the lure. Quickly reel up, vertically drop the spoon below the boat again, and start the spoon-drift all over.

Dragging relies upon the trolling motor to keep the boat headed upwind while the angler drags a lure on or near the bottom.
Photo: Ronnie Kovach

Other more traditional reaction baits such as crankbaits, spinners and surface lures can also be tried with the faster drifts. Anglers working from either the front or back seat of the boat can make a series of rapid-fire casts to open water or shoreline cover while the rig is being pushed in the wind.

With these kinds of lures, one of the new high-speed baitcasting reels can be a real boon. A baitcaster with at least a 6-to-1 gear ratio will help you fire off casts and retrieve your lures quickly, and keep pace with fast-moving drift patterns.

Finally, drift fishing is not limited to artificial offerings. Live-bait enthusiasts have been employing the drifting tactic for years as a means to catch bass in rough water. Nightcrawlers, mud suckers, shiners, waterdogs and other bait can be drifted along the bottom with a 1/8- to 1/2-ounce lead shot crimped 12 to 18 inches above the bait. Here again, as with plastic-worm drifting, be prepared to give the bass a modest amount of slack line and a chance to eat the bait.

Dragging Behind The Boat

In contrast to drifting, dragging relies upon the electric trolling motor to maintain more precise boat position. Essentially, the angler keeps the trolling motor on, heading the boat upwind, while dragging a lure on or near the bottom.

It is important to note that for competitive-style bassin', the dragging method does not constitute trolling, which is illegal on the BASSMASTER® Tournament Trail and other circuits. As long as the contestant makes intermittent casts while dragging over a long stretch of water, technically speaking, he is not trolling.

Both the Texas-style worm and the Carolina rig will work equally well for dragging baits over deep, underwater terrain. However, most BASSers prefer to add a modicum of rod-tip action to the soft-plastic lures while moving along with the trolling motor.

One variation is to rig a 4- to 6-inch worm Texas-style, behind a 3/16-ounce slip sinker. Drop the worm straight below the boat, or make a cast away from your rig. Once the bait hits the bottom, throw the reel into gear, pick up the slack line, and rhythmically shake the rod tip.

As the boat glides along, this modified doodlin' approach, sometimes termed "doodle-slidin'," will often trigger strikes on lethargic, deep-water bass. It has been a consistent winner on many deep Western tournament lakes, including Mead, Mojave, Havasu and Roosevelt.

It is not necessary to give the fish any slack before setting the hook with the doodle-slide. Whereas the worm may be moving quickly on the drift, the boat operator governs the speed of the bait while dragging.

Some anglers opt to drag worms threaded onto an open-hook leadhead. Small 1/8- to 1/4-ounce darter or P-head jigs are often used in lieu of a Texas setup.

Recently, however, Western pros are finding that a specially rigged worm with tandem open hooks may be an even better alternative for deep-water draggin'. These baits are relatively simple to construct.

Select any 4- to 6-inch worm in which you have confidence. Thread it onto a 1/8- to 1/4-ounce leadhead. Next, tie a short, 2- to 3-inch-long piece of 10- or 12-pound-test monofilament to the center of the open jighead. Then tie the other end of this line to a No. 2 to No. 6 long-shank hook. (Some pros simply use a plastic-worm hook while others prefer a Carlisle or Aberdeen style.) This rear hook forms the "stinger" for the lure.

As the tandem-hook worm is dragged along the bottom, use your rod tip to add a "twitching" motion. Many bass will be nailed with the rear stinger. "Shake the tandem-hook worm vigorously," comments B.A.S.S. pro Mike Folkestad. "Do it in a manner similar to doodlin'. Your trolling motor will do much of the work for you all the way down to 50 feet. I like to drag and bounce this bait through broken rocks. Always be prepared for a 'pressure bite' (a soft strike) while dragging these worms."

Plastic, fork-tail jigs such as Haddock's Kreepy Krawler, Garland's Spider and Canyon Lures' Cap'N Gown also are used frequently as drag baits. Folkestad similarly employs these lures on lakes such as Roosevelt and Mead, where there is sloping terrain, and small rocks with the points gen-

tly tapering off from the bank.

"On these lakes you can actually see the bass near the bottom with your graph," says Folkestad. "Free-spool a heavy, 3/4- to 1-ounce jig with swimming plastic tails and just troll-motor this bait above the bottom in 25- to 60-foot depths. Let the jig bump over the bottom and swim above the structure. If a fish is down there, it will usually eat the bait on the drag. I find that I actually catch more bass with dragging if I use hardly any rod-tip action. Just let the trolling motor do all the work."

The twin-spinner is another "sleeper" lure to use with the dragging method. These are basically leadhead jigs with vinyl or live-rubber skirts and two wire arms with spinner blades that extend out from the bait. With the blades spread apart, the twin-spinner appears rather insect-like with prominent "feelers." These lures are perfect for making good bottom contact, particularly in the colder months. As the twin-spinner slowly is dragged across the bottom, the whirling blades may call in otherwise sluggish bass to investigate. Add a pork-rind trailer for an even more sensuous-looking drag bait.

A final tactic worth trying has been used extensively for saltwater species, but rarely in serious bassin' ranks. Dave Nollar frequently guides for highly sensitive Alabama spotted bass at Lake Perris in Southern California. Invariably, the spots will follow migrating schools of threadfin shad down to 90-foot depths. Nollar has found that a floating Rapala minnow worked at these extreme depths can be a phenomenal bait for deep-water spots.

Nollar uses a special dropper setup to get a small No. 7 floating Rapala down to the 50- to 90-foot range. He ties his main line to a three-way swivel. Then he ties on about 12 inches of leader to one of the swivel eyelets. To the other end of the leader, he ties on a 1- to 2-ounce spoon sinker. Next, Nollar adds an 18- to 24-inch length of leader to the remaining eyelet and ties the tiny Rapala onto it.

The heavy sinker takes the floating minnow down quickly. The Rapala then suspends 18 to 24 inches above the sinker, floating well off the bottom. Using his trolling motor, Nollar simply drags this floating minnow rig over areas that show fish and bait activity, and occasionally gives the lure a quick twitch with the rod tip.

Although drifting and dragging have become staple methods for Bassmasters fishing deep Western lakes, these techniques will work anywhere the angler has to confront wind, depth and large expanses of water. You will find that largemouths, smallmouths and spotted bass can be taken by drifting or dragging lures along the bottom.

However, don't become lazy when employing these two tactics. Each still requires proper bait selection, well-balanced tackle, precise hooking techniques and a high level of concentration to make them perform under adverse conditions.

— APRIL 1990

BELLY BOATS: THE SIMPLE APPROACH TO BASS FISHING

By BYRON W. DALRYMPLE

These techniques, used from a tube or float, are probably the best-kept success secrets in bass fishing . . .

Most bass fishermen know what a tube float is, but only a meager percentage of the nation's bass fishermen have ever used one. The late Paul Young Sr. of Laredo, Texas, who spent most of his bass fishing hours in a tube, used to offer to take on any of his boat-fishing friends in a contest. He'd let them pick the water and the hours to be fished, and bet that in his tube he could beat them for poundage and size of fish. Young, a fine flyfisherman, never had any takers.

Oddly, it is a fact that of the hundreds of bass-fishing tournaments held annually across the nation, very few allow tube equipped fishermen to compete.

Is it simply that they would clutter up the water and, perhaps, get run over by the big-boat boys? Is it that the boaters, fishing in the modern and traditional manner, feel that the tube fishermen wouldn't get a fair shake? Or is it just the opposite?

Perhaps the reason is because pairing anglers in boats helps guarantee that tournament rules will be observed by all competitors. Regardless, fishing with a tube float or with one of the other one-man, lightweight devices that allows a fisherman to get close to his work is an astonishingly effective approach. Among the provocative attributes are a low profile, silent maneuvering, and getting into crannies and corners bass boats, or even skiffs, can't manage.

Of the several inventions that fall within the general "float" category are the tube, foam-plastic rings based on tube design, larger rectangular foam-plastic floats on which the angler sits, and the dinky one-man inflatables. Each has its selling points.

The plain inner tube with a canvas seat in its doughnut center, much improved in added conveniences from its early days,

was the forerunner of them all, and is unquestionably still the most popular, simplest, most economical and, just possibly, most effective.

Most boat fishermen have never taken the "belly-boat" tube very seriously. You're either that kind of fisherman or you're not. But this attitude misses the important point. It's true that some BASSers have become so enamored of the tube float and its effectiveness that they hardly ever fish any other way. A very few, however, have discovered that as an extension of the bass boat, the tube is — like the innumerable other gadgets used in bass fishing — simply a very important device for reaching bunches of bass in places where a standard boat is totally shut out.

These anglers keep their tubes in the boat. They fish in conventional manner part of the time, and go over the side the rest of the time — when they have come to the end of the line with the big boat.

So the tube-fishing matter simmers down to something like the old arched-back feeling between bowhunters and rifle hunters. Each looked askance at the other — until they both discovered that they could lengthen their seasons, expand their legal take of game and double their enjoyment by doubling in weapons. Instead of kicking each other, today the factions have, to a great extent, amalgamated.

This rationale, if applied to floats and bass boats, could enhance catches, put more trophy bass on stringers and give bass anglers the best of two worlds.

The trophy matter is a hot selling point for the tube. When bass get large — then larger — they usually, with age, become more and more lethargic. They don't cruise around, but take up a lair where forage in large mouthfuls can be scooped up at close range.

And they select, very commonly, places well protected — back in the drowned timber, under a stump surrounded by cypress knees, in any of innumerable situations where no boatman can possibly get to them handily — and there they stay until they're caught.

The gent who is astute in manipulating a tube can squeeze in among the trees, wangle a precise spot to work from and drop a lure or bait practically into Mr. Monster's mouth.

Notes About Floats

The tube float in its most primitive form originated, so far as is known, in the South. Along the large Southern rivers there are many oxbow lakes bulging with bass, places to which it was — and is — next to impossible to get a boat or even a canoe.

There are thousands of ponds, swampy sloughs and small low-country lakes to which either no roads run or else the waters are too small to bother boating, or too shallow or small to accept any boat larger than a flat-bottomed pram. So, years ago, clever anglers began using inner tubes, with some sort of seats contrived in them. A few even

What many a boat sitter doesn't realize about a belly boat is that one's profile is so low that much closer approaches to bass can be made.
Photo: Byron Dalrymple

simply pulled the inflated tube up under their arms and kicked their way around, barely tippy-toeing muddy bottoms.

These uses sparked better equipment. Many tube floats were homemade, and still are. Two 8-inch strips of canvas are laid with substantial sag across the center hole, wrapped around the partly inflated truck tube and strongly stitched. Thus a seat is formed in the center.

It is mandatory to make the seat fairly low-slung. Some originals had the seat too high, which placed the center of gravity — the angler's main weight — too high. It was possible to turn over and such an occurrence could be dangerous.

The proper design is to get the tube high enough around one's middle so the elbows can rest on it, yet not so high one cannot comfortably cast. So balanced, overturning the tube and occupant is nearly impossible.

The next improvement to these primitive floats was a pair of suspenders affixed to the canvas. This held the tube in place with the suspenders, over the angler's shoulders. When he moved into the shallows, the tube was held in place around his middle and he could walk as needed.

From here on the float tube began to be improved and mar-

keted. Today almost any sporting goods store that outfits anglers either sells or can order a complete tube harness with all the trimmings.

Accoutrements and improvements are numerous. Many tube harnesses are a complete canvas cover into which the tube is stuffed and zipped. There are suspenders, zippered pockets, and pouches for stowing tackle, lunch and whatever else one wishes to take along. There are items such as a rod holder to use while changing lures or removing fish, a place to attach the stringer, a place from which to secure and hang a small paddle, and even, on some, an accessory inflatable backrest for full comfort.

The great advantage of the full canvas cover on the tube is that it wards off any possible chance of puncture. In certain waters — Texas ranch tanks for example — drowned thornbush, such as mesquite, can be a problem.

The way that hurdle used to be handled was simply to hold a finger over the hole as air sizzled out and kick like all get-out for shore. Tube fishermen, however, have little to worry about so far as punctures are concerned, even in the thickest cover, and particularly so with the heavy canvas cover.

Original propulsion simply was produced by kicking one's feet. In warm water, of course, no boots are necessary. Many tubers just fish in old jeans and sneakers. In colder waters, chest-high waders are used.

The problem with "swimming" the tube by kicking the feet is that it's slow, a bit difficult in a breeze, and there is a tendency to keep turning around. If it circles, a big bass on a line can turn the foot-kicker 'round and 'round.

That's no immense disadvantage. Almost any Bassmaster would be pleased to disco to the tune of a singing line and a circling trophy bass!

Some tube enthusiasts have used swim fins. They work well enough, but they move the fisherman backward. The same disadvantage is evident when using one of the foam-plastic floats on which one sits. Fins keep you looking over your shoulder. In the dense drowned timber, where tube floats are most advantageous, moving backward is a handicap.

To cure this problem, several manufacturers have designed and marketed plastic or aluminum flaps or fins that attach to the ankle. These are curved a bit, and hinged so they fold back as the foot is reached ahead, then catch water on the backward push of the foot to give forward thrust.

With a bit of practice, tubers can maneuver in great style with these foot fins. Most, however, simply kick their feet, unencumbered. And they fish in the snug places where they have to move very little. Needless to say, tubers — and the other light floats, and even one-man inflatable boats with miniature aluminum and plastic oars — definitely should not be used in large, open waters where wind may put one out of control in a hurry.

A homemade tube rig can be shaped up for only a few dollars. The average canvas cover and seat with basic "trimmings" runs about $40. And for $100, or a bit more, a Bassmaster can put together a complete outfit, including chest-high waders.

As an extension of the bass boat, or even as an extension of bank and wade fishing, this is an economical means of getting into countless areas of prime bassin' that in many instances are wholly unfished.

Inflatable Boats

The one-man inflatable boat is quite a different approach. It can be stowed in a backpack, with a pump, and carried to pack-in spots. A few of these miniature craft weigh as little as 12 or 15 pounds, with tote bag and small oars.

They have advantages for larger waters — bays of large lakes, smaller primitive lakes without launch facilities. They have not gained, however, the popularity of the tube.

For one thing, they are less comfortable. The angler almost lies down to fish. They are not immune to punctures and many have evidenced valve trouble — inflate and deflate valves that come apart, or lose function with moderate wear. Granted they are a means to an end in some instances, and are in some ways an extension past the habitat of the average tube fisherman.

Foam Floats

Foam-plastic doughnut-design floats have, to date, not caught on emphatically, simply because the inflatable tube in its canvas cover is less bulky to transport, and in general more convenient. The larger, rectangular plastic-foam floats have picked up quite a few adherents. These are a totally different concept from the tube. Several have been marketed. One of the first was the "Water Wagon," built in Texas.

These floats are a kind of fishing platform, light, sturdily built, about 8 inches thick, as much as 4 feet wide by up to 6 feet or more in length. With the Water Wagon type, the angler sits on the float with feet and lower legs through an opening. The float can be paddled, but keeping it steady is tricky. The smallest breeze turns or skids it. So does the motion of casting, or playing a fish. A small paddle can be used for propulsion and steadying. Most users don swim fins for either forward or backward motion.

The newer such floats, as the Mascot Boats of Arlington, Texas, are "boats" with a motor bracket that will take either a small electric or a motor up to 3 1/2 horsepower. Under such power, however — 3 1/2 hp — they should be used with caution. They are lightweight and can be cartopped.

Learning to operate one of these floating platforms requires practice, but they are quite efficient rigs when one becomes accustomed to the routine. And they are, of course, unsinkable. However, users should wear life jackets, and some users run a safety line and snap from their belt to the tie-up ring on the float. In the event of a fall overboard, the user thus is ensured that the float will be easy to grab and can't drift away.

Bass fishermen use these foam "boats" for silent approaches in small bays or in timber spaced widely enough to maneuver them. They carry one piggyback on a bass boat and pull it overboard at destination. These platform floats, well-designed, cost more than the other devices. The total investment is several hundred dollars, especially if a small motor is included. However, with today's increased costs in gasoline, they are viewed as bassin' bargains.

Tips And Tactics For "Belly Boats"

All told, the "belly boat" has gained, and holds, the greatest popularity. Most modern BASSers think of it just as a gadget for small-pond fishing. They would be wise to take a broader view of them.

One area of bass fishing that is much overlooked is largemouths in streams. The float trip by canoe or flat-bottomed boat for smallmouths on swift streams has long been a popular endeavor. Almost no one goes after largemouths in streams, except in a very few large, slow rivers where boats are used.

The tube float is virtually perfect for stream fishing for largemouth bass. It can operate beautifully in streams too small for anything larger than a kayak. It does likewise in streams that are made up of numerous shallow riffles, too "thin" for boats, interspersed by deep holes, or too deep to wade.

Here, indeed, is a whole new world of bass fishing that is barely touched by anglers. Many sloughs and marshes have the same handicaps for boaters; too many shallow spots for boating, yet too many deep pockets for wading without a tube.

Yet these uses — and the millions of small ponds too large to cast across from the bank — are by no means the most important facets of bassin' to which the tube is peculiarly suited. There are literally hundreds of thousands of acres of backwaters, brushy tributary stream mouths, drowned timber stands, stump fields, and similar expanses in the hundreds of large impoundments scattered across the nation that are totally untouched by bass anglers. Even on heavily pressured reservoirs, many such areas remain virgin.

They're untouched because they cannot be fished by boats, even very small boats. Nor can they be fished from the bank. They stretch too far and are too dense to cast into or through.

Nor can they be waded. They're mostly too deep.

Yet the tube fisherman can squeeze between trees, push through brush, and ease among the stumps. He can penetrate far beyond the perimeters where the boats ply their trade. He can fish for (and catch) bass to which no other fisherman — not even the inflatable one-man boat or plastic-foam platform rider — ever casts.

Close Approach

Because of the ease of a close approach to target areas assumed to hold bass, short casts can be made. These require a minimum of physical exertion and thus add to the silent technique. They are, also, pinpoint accurate. With a longer rod or Flippin' Stik®, or a fly rod, short flips or casts to the targets can be accomplished easily .

A great many of the most successful bass fishermen who use tubes, however, make almost no cast at all. All sorts of names have been applied to their technique: from "doodle-socking" to "yo-yoing." The most succinct way to describe it is fishing a lure vertically.

The standard tackle used by many, especially in dense cover, is a fairly stiff, long rod. This allows reach, and a no-nonsense haul-up of fish hooked in dense cover. Line must be heavy enough — 15- to 20-pound-test unless water is exceedingly clear — to hold fish short and to withstand scraping on timber or brush. The lures most commonly used are weedless jigs, plastic worms, or a jig plus a plastic worm.

Bait is deadly, but on the whole so much more bother under the circumstances that most tubers forego it. Artificials do just as well. Exceptions are the expert users of cane poles. They are in a class by themselves, dropping a frog or minnow or other bait practically down the mugs of countless big bass.

The silent approach, and reaching out a long, stiff rod to drop a jig or other lure on the button, is without question the most accurate presentation possible to impart.

The tube floater who uses this method can place a lure precisely:
• Sliding it down the bole of a drowned tree.
• Slipping it between two submerged stumps.
• Daintily dropping it through an inconsequential hole in brush.

No caster can possibly match the performance.

Whatever type of float you use, this whole facet of bass fishing will bear examination with an open mind by those who've never probed it. This is an extremely economical way of outfitting.

It is utter simplicity — toss the float into the car and go. But most important of all, it is an absolutely lethal way to fish for bass — big bass!

— 1980 BASS FISHING GUIDE

CAN TUBERS COVER ENOUGH WATER?

Q — How can a bass fisherman, restricted by a tube float, cover enough water to be effective?

A — He doesn't need to cover a lot of water. That is one of the fallacies too many boatmen accept as truth — the more water covered, the more bass. The floaters cover a small water area more thoroughly.

Q — Isn't it a fact that a fisherman with his legs and feet dangling in the water is going to spook the fish?

A — Quite the opposite. Bass are not especially shy of seeing an angler's lower torso, as long as no quick or violent moves are made.

Q — These light floats can't operate, however, out in big water, can they?

A — Not safely. But they don't need to. They do just the opposite. They get into tight places in brush or timber where bass never see a lure, and that's one reason tube fishermen catch so many.

Q — Why don't bass see, at such close range, the tube fisherman above water, and get scared off?

A — The floater presents an exceedingly low profile. Bass vision above surface is limited to a cone of view in such a way that the lower the object to the water, the less it is seen, and vice versa.

Q — Most boating bassmen wouldn't want to give up their big boats and take to a tube, would they?

A — They don't need to give up anything. The tube works wonders as an extension of the boat, letting an angler fish places he can't cover from his boat.

Q — How does a fellow carry enough gear when he's in a tube?

A — You don't need much. And modern floats have zippered pockets and pouches in which to stow lures and extras, plus rod holders and a place to attach a stringer.

Q — How does the tube floater move about?

A — By kicking his feet. There are even ankle fins to attach over boots or wading pants to assist, if one wishes to try them.

Q — If these floats get into timber and other places where big boats can't, how does the fisherman cast in such places?

A — Many don't cast at all. They reach out a long rod and drop a lure vertically, then jig it.

Q — Do these tubers ever get any big bass?

A — They mop up bass of trophy size, because they can get to the types of lairs where big bass like to lie.

— BYRON DALRYMPLE

ONE ON ONE WITH BASS

By JOHN WONGREY

Now's the time to slip into a pair of chest waders and hit the water. These basic guidelines are applicable where wading and bass are compatible . . .

When it comes to fishing for bass, I'll own up to my prejudice rather quickly — I'm a wade fisherman. And this is especially so in the spring when largemouth bass enter the shallows to feed and enlarge their winter-lean frames.

So let's slip into a pair of chest waders and go wading for some bass.

The strongest argument in favor of the wade fisherman versus the boat angler is that this method allows the BASSer to achieve better lure placement and permits quieter stalking — two key ingredients to more bass action. The boat-bound fisherman also is hindered by the fact that spring bass are likely to be found in water measuring no more than a foot in depth. The boat fisherman's attempts in such water are usually inadequate because the boat, especially a large boat, impedes movement.

I really can't substantiate that wading produces bigger fish, although I know that some really big largemouths forage the spring shallows. Two springs past, I took an 11-pounder from South Carolina's Lake Moultrie.

• **Where To Wade** — Prime wading grounds must consist of one, or several, or all the following ingredients: grassbeds, cypress stands, sandy bottom, submerged tree stumps, logs, stick-ups and some type of cover bush that attracts a variety of food, which in turn draws predacious largemouths.

Florida's Lake Okeechobee and South Carolina's Lake Moultrie perhaps come close to being "perfect" wading grounds. They not only have vast, shallow-water acreage, but also an abundance of natural cover and feed.

• **How To Fish** — My wading is very deliberate. Once I enter the water, I fish every stick, bush, lily pad, stump, tree and grassbed within a 360-degree casting circle. In short, I investigate every potential target that may harbor a bass.

It is not advisable to wade fish with a lightweight spincast outfit in areas infested with visual and non-visual obstructions, as good wading grounds usually are mined with obstructions of every kind. The rods are just too whippy, making it hard to implant the hook. A baitcasting rig with a line of at least 20-pound-test is needed for fishing heavy-cover habitat.

I also have learned that it's best not to make long casts. A wader's cast, especially if he is in chest-deep water, has no striking leverage. The only position he can employ is the straight-back strike. If this strike is at a considerable distance, he simply cannot muster the power to set the hook. The boat angler, however, is naturally elevated and has far more hook-setting power than the wader. In short, keep your casts short.

• **Baits** — Lure selection is simple. Match the bait to the season of the year and to local fishing reports. I generally fish the plastic worm, but I do like to run a spinnerbait in the early spring. Topwatering improves as the water warms, bringing with it all manner of insects upon which bass feed.

When the shallows are alive with insects and baitfish, I enjoy scooting a Weed-Wing over the pads and grassbeds to arouse the largemouth's predatory instinct.

• **Summer Wading** — Wading in the warmer months can be productive if the wade fisherman thoroughly knows the area in which the fish may hide during the heat of the day. If not, wade fishing can be a hit-and-miss proposition and limited primarily to fishing the early morning hours and the late-afternoon hours when bass move out into the shallows to feed. Cypress stands usually are productive.

• **Waders' Equipment** — I will emphasize the use of waders rather than shorts or swimming trunks since there is always the threat of stabbing or cutting yourself on some form of underwater obstacle. However, if you don't mind getting wet, a pair of old pants and tennis shoes will suffice. Waders will keep you drier and offer more protection than a pair of pants. Never wade barefooted. If you do, then you're courting trouble.

The same waders you employ for other sporting pleasures such as surf fishing, stream fishing or waterfowl shooting are suitable while wading for bass. However, you may find the insulated waders a bit uncomfortable.

Most waders have a pocket on the inside front where you can store tackle and a snack. I generally wear a hunting vest where I can carry additional food and water. Simplify your lure toting by carefully selecting choice baits. A knife and a pair of long-nosed pliers also should be included as part of the equipment. A stringer should be included if you care to keep a couple of fish for the table.

• **Safety** — Going into an area for the first time, the wade fisherman is confronted with uncertainties since he has no previous knowledge of drop-offs and water depths. One way to analyze this problem is to look at the water-standing trees. If there are no distinct water marks on the trees, expect unusually high water. During low water, the once-covered portion of the trees will have a definite change of color.

If you are somewhat awkward in the water, a walking staff will help keep you upright and also will provide a means of rest if a tree or stump is not nearby. You can attach a small length of rope to the staff and tie the other end to the wader strap. Allow the stick to float behind you until you have need of it.

If you can't swim, don't take any chances while wading. Even if you can swim well, don't wade recklessly.
— *MAY/JUNE 1981*

In wade fishing for bass, investigate every potential target that may harbor a large-mouth bass.

Photo: Jack Bissell

TROLLING TRICKS FOR BASS

By DON WIRTH

Trolling for bass is a skills-demanding, highly specialized technique that works. Here's how to do it successfully...

To many Bassmasters, a fisherman who trolls for bass is as lowly and unethical as an attorney who chases ambulances to get clients.

But is this attitude toward trolling justified? Is trolling simply "dragging baits" behind the boat? Or are there skills and techniques involved? The answers are no, no and yes.

While trolling isn't permitted in bass-tournament competition, many pros — including several whose names you'd recognize — admit to using the technique to find fish when they're not competing in tournaments. They are aware of two facts: trolling works, and fishermen, by and large, do not understand the practice.

Trolling is widely practiced for other freshwater game fish. Indeed, it's often the only practical way to catch such species as salmon or walleye. I've trolled for chinook and coho salmon in the Great Lakes and have always found the fishing immensely enjoyable. So why not troll for bass?

I posed that question to Doug Hannon of Tampa, Fla., "the bass professor" whose angling exploits we've covered in Bassmaster (see "Doug Hannon on River Fishing" in the Sept. 1984 issue).

"Some bass fishermen consider trolling to be a low form of fishing, unethical and unsportsmanlike," Hannon says. "Or people regard it as a no-skill approach to bass fishing. Maybe they think you only have to throw a lure out behind the boat, keep the motor running and sit back and drink beer."

There's much more to trolling than that , as anyone who's ever dragged deep-running plugs for stripers will attest. To be successful, you've still got to understand bass structure and how fish react to various weather and water conditions.

"Sure, you can troll by simply dragging a bait behind the boat while you're taking a nap — just as you can make sloppy casts," he says. "For casting to be productive, the angler must choose correctly from a wide array of variables, including line size, retrieve speed, lure types, bait presentation and bass hideouts. Productive trolling, too, involves every one of these variables."

One reason Hannon is a good source of information about trolling is that he's familiar with both sides of the issue. His expertise in live-bait fishing is well-known. What isn't always recognized is that Hannon is a well-rounded bass angler, one who much prefers to try various types of fishing than to downgrade any of them.

Instead of scoffing at trolling, Hannon studied it, learned all he could about it, and then incorporated it into his total fishing approach. "Those who fish with me for the first time often are surprised that I'll troll for a while, use live bait sometimes, cast in the conventional manner and flip — all within the space of a day's fishing," he says. "I enjoy all facets of fishing, and I try to keep an open mind about various methods of lure or bait presentation. I know this has contributed to my success on big bass." Hannon has caught — and released — over 400 bass exceeding 10 pounds apiece, and he credits his holistic angling approach for a good portion of his achievement.

Not only is trolling a surprisingly effective way to catch bass, Hannon notes, it has very real advantages over conventional casting in certain situations, notably in learning a body of water with which you're not familiar.

"It's a good idea to study a topo map of a lake you've never fished, but it's also important to motor around the lake and evaluate what it has to offer," Hannon says. "Trolling is the best way I know to fish a strange lake and cover a large amount of water at the same time.

"Perhaps you could hit the water and start spot-casting to places you picked out on a topo map, then run to other places and do the same thing. But until you actually see the lake and explore large areas of it, you're at a great disadvantage. A good overview of the lake is essential for fishing success, and trolling enables this."

Once fish have been located, trolling might be the best means of keeping your lure at the right depth. Let's say you're fishing 20-foot depths with a plastic worm, he suggests. If you cast the lure 100 feet, it probably will begin falling toward you as it sinks to the bottom; then it rises off the bottom as it approaches the boat. That means the worm will be in the productive zone a relatively small amount of the time.

But with trolling — especially with the side of a downrigger — you literally can set the desired depth and pay attention to keeping your lure in the fish zone.

Trolling is especially useful in covering a specific, large piece of structure, Hannon says. In the summertime, when bass are on vast flats in many reservoirs, casting may never pinpoint the bass, even though the fisherman is correct in assuming that the fish should be on this type of structure at this time of year. In some reservoirs, flats may cover several miles, yet the bass may be bunched up on a relatively small spot on the flats, maybe relating to a certain feature of the structure that you can't determine — such as single stumps apart from a mass of stumps. Trolling allows you to cover these large areas quickly and efficiently. When you locate bass at a certain place along this structure, you then may stop and cast to them, if you like.

But trolling needn't be limited to covering unfamiliar waters quickly.

"Buck Perry, the man many regard as the father of structure fishing, utilized trolling," Hannon notes. "This combination of structure fishing and trolling may seem a paradox to

some, but the fact remains that Perry was a master at putting the lure in a target area with a precise presentation. His Spoonplug (still a great bass lure) produced legendary catches as Perry trolled it over humps, around creek channel bends and similar structure." Perry's unorthodox ideas shook the bass-fishing world at the time, and the lessons he taught about structure fishing and trolling are viable today.

Another benefit of trolling isn't so easy to define, yet very real, nonetheless. "Trolling is very relaxing, and it allows you time to reflect that you simply cannot get when casting," Hannon says. "As the hours pass, you can become more a part of your environment. True, many types of trolling require paying close attention to your depthfinder, but even then, trolling is not nearly as demanding as is casting. It can be relaxing, and when you're fishing with a companion, trolling lets you carry on a conversation without the fear that you'll get distracted and miss a fish."

When To Troll

Hannon believes trolling is most effective when bass are staying more than 8 feet deep, in the summer and fall, especially. And the fish don't have to be in open water, over barren flats and drop-offs for it to work, either.

"I've caught big bass by trolling over submerged weedbeds, along stumpy creek channels, even next to shoreline weeds such as hyacinths," he says. "Of course, different situations require different trolling techniques and, in some cases, special aids such as planing boards or downriggers."

He recommends that fishermen start by trolling systematically along general contour lines, such as 8 or 10 feet, then moving progressively deeper until they get a strike.

Hannon says bass relate closely to a certain depth under specific conditions, and they do not like to leave the depth zone they're in, even to chase forage. This is strictly physiological, he explains.

"Bass have a swim bladder — in essence an air bubble in their backs — to control buoyancy," he says. "Once they've acclimated their buoyancy to a certain depth, they find it uncomfortable to move more than about 8 feet above or below that level." As evidence, Hannon cited the time he

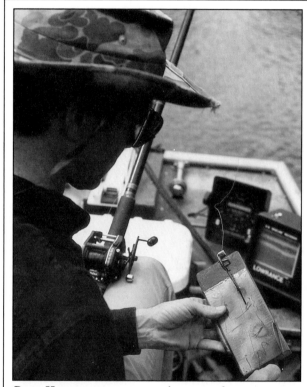

Doug Hannon uses sonar equipment to locate structure that's right for trolling.   Photo: Don Wirth

spotted a congregation of bass on his chart recorder, hanging above a weedy bottom in 12 to 15 feet of water, and trolled a wild, live shiner over them. Every time the shiner passed over the "honey hole" it swam to the surface and, surprisingly, the bass wouldn't follow it. He used a downrigger to get the bait down to 12 feet and immediately began catching bass.

Hannon uses his knowledge of bass habits to decide which types of structures to troll in the various seasons. In summer, he works the large flats and weedlines; in the fall, he concentrates on points. Spring finds him trolling in the coves and creeks. If he trolls at all in winter, it is along deeper shorelines. But extended, cold weather is a poor time for trolling, because sluggish, cold-water fish demand a slow presentation — generally slower than you can troll bait, he says.

The Trolling Motor

Trolling motors, whether gas or electric, must be capable of propelling the boat at a slow rate of speed while a lure or bait is being pulled behind.

If a gasoline motor is used much for trolling, it will work better with air-gap spark plugs, instead of the surface-gap plugs that are standard in most outboards. Air-gap plugs will not load up and tend to stay dry when run at idle for long periods, he says. Check your engine's service manual for the recommended air-gap plug substitution.

Electric motors can be effective in many types of trolling, especially when a few modifications are made.

"First, use a minimum of 6-gauge copper wire — I use 2-gauge in my own boat — which delivers far more thrust than does the 10-gauge wire commonly found in many bass boats," he says. "Going to this larger wire often is the equivalent of adding two or three higher speed settings to your electric motor's output."

Hannon modifies his foot-control motor by bridging the on-off switch with a regular 35-amp toggle switch. When he flips it on, the motor will stay on, whether or not the foot control is depressed. When it's off, the trolling motor's pushbutton on-off switch takes over. He also uses a rheostat for his speed control; this allows him to increase his speed gradually, which is less likely to spook shallow fish, Hannon believes. "I have long felt that bass acclimate themselves far more easily to a constant noise than to an intermittent noise," he explains. "By trolling with my motor on constantly, rather than starting and stopping it, and by increasing the motor's speed with the rheostat, which gradually shifts the power, I avoid sudden disturbances in sound. We often hear that bass are spooked by trolling motors, but I think it's more likely that they are spooked by a sudden change in the sound in their environment." (Hannon uses a Memcor Model R-100 rheostat, rated at 1 1/2 ohms, and he says that this

device also will help increase battery life. Your marine dealer should be able to install these modifications.)

Does a gas engine spook fish? As far as Hannon can tell, it does not, if run in a constant trolling mode. "If I'm working a shallow weedline, however, I much prefer to use my electric motor, as the fish are going to be spookier," he says.

Lures For Trolling

"In trolling, as in casting, I stick to a few proven lures," Hannon says. Among his favorites:

• Shad-type vibrating baits such as the Cordell Spot, Rat-L-Trap, or Burke Crankstar.

• Minnow imitations such as the A. C. Shiner or Rapala.

• Deep-running crankbaits such as the Bomber Model A, Rebel Deep Wee-R, Rapala Shad Rap. (Note: The world-record smallmouth bass was taken on a trolled Bomber.)

• Fluttering spoons, such as the Daredevle.

• Plastic worms, such as Burke's Swimmin' Worm, which Hannon designed.

• Small, soft-plastic grubs and jigs with various types of trailers.

• Topwater plugs like the Jitterbug.

• Spinners like the Mepps or Rooster Tail.

"A Rapala or A. C. Shiner is absolutely one of the best lures you can troll for big bass," Hannon insists. "It should be trolled at a fast clip — up to about 7 miles per hour. It's one of the few lures that's tuned well enough in the factory so that it won't roll over and skitter across the top when trolled at high rate of speed," Hannon says. He recommends a lure of 5 inches or so in length when fast-trolling these minnow imitators.

Conversely, Hannon recommends trolling deep-diving crankbaits slowly. "With these lures, it is vital that you check the action of the lure by dragging it alongside the boat at trolling speed," he says. "If the bait isn't running true, adjust it or use another bait."

Spoons are very good lures for trolling, especially when fished on a downrigger, Hannon says. So are plastic worms. "I love to fish the Swimmin' Worm along shallow structure such as a weedy shoreline with this lure — trolling at a slow rate of speed — and have caught bass over 13 pounds on it," he says.

Jigs and grubs are best fished slowly with an electric motor, as are spinners — just fast enough to turn the blade, Hannon advises. One surprising lure on his list of trolling favorites is the Jitterbug. It should be trolled at a speed that will cause the Jitterbug to emit that familiar "plop-plop-plop" sound, especially along the banks.

With some of the other lures, Hannon often adds a weight in front to control the depth. He prefers weighting the lure to using a long line, which invites tangles and is more time-consuming to retrieve when it hangs up. He slips a worm weight onto the line, adds a swivel, and then about a foot of line to which the lure is tied.

Special Trolling Tools

Virtually any rod-and-reel outfit suited for bass fishing can be used for trolling, but a rod of 6 1/2 or 7 feet is especially helpful. With a longer rod, you can pick up the slack quickly and set the hook more effectively when you get a strike, he says. Those who wish to get into bass trolling more deeply might be advised to get a specialized 8- or 9-foot trolling rod, but as a rule, trolling requires no specialized tackle. Hannon uses rod holders, and he fishes up to three rods out of his boat at once — the legal limit in Florida, where he lives.

As in other facets of fishing, specialized equipment can make trolling more productive, and Bassmasters might consider purchasing one or more of these devices. Downriggers, which utilize a heavy lead weight to place the lure at an exact depth he desires is indicated on a counter — usually built into the device, but sometimes a separate component. When a fish hits, the line — which has been pinched between two rollers — is pulled free, allowing the fishermen to fight the bass without the burden of the lead weight. "Most bass fishermen can't imagine using a downrigger to catch bass," Hannon acknowledges. "That's because they think of these devices in terms of salmon fishing, in which lures must go down 100 feet or more. But I've used them successfully in water less than 10 feet deep.

"They are extremely helpful when bass are holding tight to a certain type of structure — say, hydrilla growing 6 feet off the bottom in 25 feet of water. If a lure is presented 3 feet above the weeds, a bass probably won't rush out and take it. But if it's dragged a foot over the weeds, your odds of catching fish are greatly enhanced. Downriggers offer the fisherman precise depth control, without running out great lengths of line. I also use a downrigger to fish lures that ordinarily would be next to impossible to fish at a certain depth, such as a Floating Rapala in 15 feet of water, or a Swimmin' Worm 12 feet deep."

Hannon recommends fine-tuning the line release to adapt whatever lure you're fishing: with a plastic worm, an extremely light release should be used; with a crankbait, a firmer release is acceptable. For bassin', Hannon likes downriggers comparable to the Little Jon (manufactured by Big Jon Inc., 14393 Peninsula Drive, Traverse City, MI 49684; (616) 223-4342).

Planing boards are great for shallow-water trolling, but they rarely are used by bass fishermen. These boards have a retaining clip, much like that on a downrigger, that holds the line; when in use, they cause a trolled lure to swing out to one side — not straight behind — the boat. The advantages of this are tremendous to the bass fisherman, Hannon

believes. "It's hard to troll in shallow water, because you're constantly in danger of hitting a stump or rock with your trolling motor," Hannon says. "You also run the danger of spooking bass when the boat runs over them. With a side planer, or planing board, the lure runs where you haven't been. Your boat doesn't go near the places that your lure goes. You have tremendous control over your lure, too; by raising or lowering your rod, you can cause the side planer to move in and out of irregular weedlines or other shoreline structure and virtually can guide your lure to where the action is."

Since there's no boat running over the bass, you can troll with a side planer on a very short length of line — 20 feet or so, as opposed to 60 feet or more in conventional trolling. Hannon likes to use a Rapala with a planing board, and he has taken several huge bass in this manner.

"Planing boards have not been exploited to anywhere near their potential in bass fishing," Hannon feels. He uses the Red Rover planing board (manufactured by Troll Sports Co., Route 3, Deronda, WI 54008). Planing boards come in pairs — a left and a right; the ones Doug recommends are $28.95 a pair.

Trolling Tips

As a rule of thumb, Hannon recommends trolling your deepest lures on the shortest lines. "This may seem backward to many folks, but a deep-running lure with very much line out tends to develop a lot of bag in the line and is more apt to get tangled," he believes. He'll run deep crankbaits 30 or 40 feet behind the boat, but never more than 60 feet behind, whereas longer lines may be utilized for shallow-running lures such as the Rapala.

When trolling for bass in rivers, Hannon says it is very important always to troll upstream. "Bass will position themselves to avoid the current, and they generally will be along the shorelines where the current is slack," Hannon explains. To get the right lure action while trolling downstream, you'll have to run the boat faster than the current. And that doesn't give the bass enough time to look over your lure. Troll upstream.

Try Trolling

Keep an open mind about trolling. Instead of scoffing at it, consider it to be one more skill to be mastered in the quest for all-around bass-fishing excellence. Trolling involves a tremendous amount of know-how — certainly as much as other forms of bass fishing — and it remains, perhaps, the last truly unexploited frontier in bass fishing. Give trolling a try. You may discover a whole new world of bass-fishing enjoyment.

— APRIL 1985

THE ABCs OF BANK FISHING

By BYRON W. DALRYMPLE

The problem for a miniwater BASSer isn't finding the fish, but getting your lure to and the fish out of the water . . .

Sometimes it seems every bass angler has forgotten in our world of modern bass fishing, that there are a myriad of miniature bass waters practically in everyone's backyard. These are where bass fishing actually began, and not even from a boat. The bulk of original bass fishing lore slowly accrued years ago from the experiences of fishermen who fished from the banks of small lakes, ponds and streams.

Many a modern-day Bassmaster doesn't even realize that, and, further, has never fished from dry land out into a stump-filled or weedy pond, or perhaps cast a lure to the undercut opposite bank of a rivulet in which a mounting-size bass could barely turn around. Oddly, too, though these small waters would seem to be the easiest ones on earth to fish, many a modern BASSer would have no idea how to anchor himself bankside and fill a stringer.

In our present day this is a situation that needs attention, and remedy. It can be an immense pleasure to get acquainted with this old-fashioned kind of bass fishing.

Focus on unsung creeks, ponds and miniature lakes becomes a renaissance of sorts, a rebirth of where and how bass fishing began. It can also be an eye-opener. For the bass, now and then even of mounting size, are present.

There is one important additional selling point of this fishing that no family bass fisherman should overlook. Fishing from the banks of small waters is tailored perfectly for starting youngsters, and that is an important consideration.

You may at first feel inhibited by being tied down to the shore. But remember how kids lose interest quickly, want to move around, are fidgety after a short time in a boat? Here, they fit the situation. The lake or stream is just their size.

The kids can drop a rod and move around when they please, chasing frogs or daydreaming, then start over. They can drag a fish ashore easier than tussle it into a boat. And bear in mind that a great many old grownups of today started bass fishing just this way. It is ideal for families, both for wives who fish only casually and for kids.

Furthermore, because at least some of these waters are everywhere that bass range, in our changing world acquaintance with bank fishing, your neighborhood waters could become something of a necessity. The energy you use doing so is strictly your own.

Nor is downsizing bass fishing to standing flat-footed on dry land beside a rivulet or pond by any measures less dramatic than winding up a hundred-horse motor on a 20,000-acre impoundment. It is different. It can be a challenge, a provocative learning experience, indeed a new world of bass fishing in its own right, and a pleasingly economical one.

• **Back To Basics** — Early bass anglers commonly fished these miniature natural waters from the bank for very simple reasons. First, there weren't any huge impoundments. Natural lakes and streams were where the fishing was done, and throughout most of the domain of the black bass, these were small. Thousands of lakes of less than 200 or 300 acres, tens of thousands of ponds dotted the basslands, streams easy to cast across coursed everywhere. Many of the same waters are still there, plus the addition of literally millions of man-made farm ponds.

Those early bass fishermen seldom had boats, either. Marinas were unheard of, rental boats few. Nor was fast

■

transportation available. Mostly there was none except for the occasional early chug-along auto, more often by horse or "shank's mare."

The average early bass fisherman simply gathered his tackle, walked to a nearby creek or pond, and began fishing. Interesting is the fact that almost all early, and often still-famed, bass lures of the 1800s and beginning 1900s were first fished from the bank, in small lakes, ponds or streams, cast by an old-fashioned steel rod or dangled from a line at the end of a long cane pole.

James Heddon sat on the bank of Dowagiac Creek in Michigan, whittling and experimenting with his first plugs. Original Creek Chub Darters were cast from the bank into the St. Joseph and Maume rivers in Indiana. The renowned old Snagless Sally and Indiana Spinner both were baptized by lure maker John Hildebrandt from the bank of the Wabash River in Indiana.

The early-day small-water bank fisherman had one immense advantage over his modern big-water brethren: he had a much smaller search area in which to locate fish. He also had what might be seen as a distinct disadvantage: he was bound to bankside and thus, far less maneuverable. Today's counterpart faces the same basic advantage and disadvantage.

There are a myriad of small waters in every Bassmaster's bailiwick. A short drive and a brief hike will get you to the fishing.   Photo: Byron Dalrymple

• **Pluses For Miniwaters** — Consider first the problem of finding the fish. We are talking here about lakes in general, of sizes from around 100 acres down to ponds you can cast across, and among streams, the small, slow, meandering rivers amenable to largemouths, plus small creeks tributary to them, and, in addition, the smaller, swift smallmouth streams.

Ponds a cast will reach across, or at least halfway across, are seldom very deep. The same is true of the miniature lakes. From shore, by moving slowly around the perimeter, one can reach every square foot of the ponds, top to bottom, and such a substantial portion of most miniature lakes that,

by diligence, you certainly can locate fish. The small streams, if one learns to "read" them, are even easier. There are only so many places bass are likely to be when feeding, or when resting.

Just because acreage is small, finding bass does not guarantee that they are going to strike. But the choices of location on small waters are so compressed that at least a fisherman quickly can try them all. This eliminates one of the most aggravating quandaries the big-water bass chaser faces: to whit, have I missed even showing my lures to bass, or are they simply indisposed?

The small-water angler knows without any question — in all instances where he can reach the major portion, or at least a substantial sampling of the water — that he is presenting his lure or bait to bass. They've seen it. All he has to settle, if they won't communicate, is what changes to make to arouse them. Or, he can simply persevere until a feeding period begins.

• **Any Disadvantages?** So now look at the disadvantage mentioned already — a lack of maneuverability — because one must fish from shore. The significance of that factor immediately pales. It isn't the hurdle the BASSer accustomed to a boat may at first believe.

If, on a small water, the angler can reach most of it, or samples of all situations it offers, doing so quickly and without endless travel, where is the disadvantage of being bank-bound? The fact is, small waters are tailored for bank fishing. You fish quietly, not disturbing the quarry with boat or motor sounds and motions. If you watch the sun's angle, being careful not to throw your shadow out onto what may be bass lairs, since you are bank-bound and can maneuver only in one plane along shore, you don't waste endless time with aimless probing.

In an earlier BASSMASTER® Magazine article of the "How Bass Live" series ("Mini-Bassin' Waters," Sept.-Oct. 1980 issue) it was noted that searching for fish in small lakes and ponds is chiefly a search in a horizontal plane. That is, because depth of these waters is not broadly divergent from place to place, the bottom of most being a shallow bowl-shape, searching for fish in a vertical plane is not as important. Water temperature and oxygen content differ only modestly, surface to bottom.

It was further noted that what most bass fishermen call "structure" that holds bass — chiefly bottom contours and objects — is virtually eliminated. We might say that "above-surface structure" is what counts, in the form of emergent vegetation or vegetation slightly submerged, but seen from surface, plus such items as stumps, blowdowns, partially submerged logs, at-surface rock ledges, and so on. Small lakes and ponds are easy to decipher.

In creeks and small rivers, the limited lie-up spots for bass are even more obvious. Boulders with hiding places beneath them in slack or slow water, the slide or glide downstream from a boulder or modest-sized rock in swifter water, an undercut bank, an overhanging bush, a log lying out into the water, a deep, dark hole below a riffle — all such places will hold bass both when they are feeding and when they are resting.

Largemouths seldom feed on riffles, but smallmouths commonly do. Their stream habitats have more riffles because they are swifter. All the places a largemouth may be in a stream, a smallmouth may also be, but in addition the latter often moves periodically from a pool up onto the riffles above it to feed on minnows or aquatic nymphs.

• **Bank Walker's Tackle** — So, this gets us to tackle. You have to make up your mind some lures will be lost, an occasional length of line with them. However, the attrition is seldom any greater than when you are in a more maneuverable situation, in a boat.

For weedy, small lakes and ponds, those with brush along the edges, such as submerged bottom willows, others with logs and stumps, the bankside Bassmaster should stick with stout tackle, just as you would when fishing a debris-covered bottom in deep water from a boat. You need to be able to horse a lure out of weedy hangups, and you need to be able to manhandle a bass out of the same.

This means, for such waters, a line of perhaps 15-pound-test — perhaps in some situations 20-pound-test — and a rod with ample body. Large reel (line) capacity also is most helpful at times. For example, on hundreds of ponds with clean (non-timbered) edges, a lure hung on some obstruction on bottom way out in the middle can be saved — if you have enough line.

Simply walk around the edge, paying out line and keeping the rod tip up and line barely snug, until you're on the opposite side of the pond from where you hung the lure on the retrieve. Most times it will come free with a gentle tug.

Stout tackle is not needed everywhere. Use judgment. On a perfectly clean farm pond, for example, with no bottom debris, no shoreside brush, no weeds, lighter tackle is suitable. Particularly if such is a clear-water pond, fishing light is likely to be more productive.

When there are shoreside weeds that may inhibit a lure, regardless of how strong or fine your line, learn the "kid's art" of reeling to the outer edge of the weeds, then raising the rod tip slowly, gently — giving the lure a flick to get it ashore without hanging. Lose a few feet of retrieve water to save a hangup.

• **Fishing Miniwaters** — During much of the year, even on warm days in winter, many small lakes and ponds are warmer than the large impoundments, and bass commonly feed in them more often on or near the surface. A rule of thumb is always to start out with a topwater lure. These hang up less if carefully maneuvered. Several topwater types also are available with a single upturned, fixed-position hook at the rear, swathed in a skirt. They're virtually weedless. Select your surface lures to get those that are as weedless as possible. If the bass won't hit on top, you have to go down after them.

In any truly weedy small lake, it is poor practice to select just the lures you happen to like, regardless of their weedless qualities. Remember that getting the lure back after the cast, with proper action en route, is the fundamental hurdle.

Stick with such items for underwater as a weedless spoon, perhaps with a pork-rind trailer, or the close-to-weedless safety-pin spinners, or plastic worms hooked in the weedless Texas style, or fish the worm with hook point buried and cast without any sinker, so they simply waft down gently. Jigs are also feasible for this work. But lures such as sinking plugs with multiple trebles are just begging for trouble.

In other words, select lures that will perform best with the least difficulties from the bank. In addition, it is vital to learn to control your casts.

The short, exceedingly accurate cast is much of the time the best bet on all these waters. If you cast across a stream to an undercut bank on the far side, the lure must land, and float along, not a foot from the bank but 2 or 3 inches from it. Be assured, this technique will catch three times the fish the inept "foot-from-bank" casts will.

On the ponds, keep in mind that bass, especially large ones, have selected, from a limited number of choices, very precisely placed lairs. Drop your lure within an inch or two of that stump, log or lily pad.

Learn, also, to maneuver slack line. Slack tangles in weeds are far more difficult for a bank fisherman to unravel than for one able to move a boat at will. So, watch incessantly where the line tracks. Don't let it slip under a lily pad, or around a thin bulrush. Always, whether using surface or underwater lures, as you retrieve out of deeper water into weedy shallows, raise your rod tip high, get the line clear of nearby weeds or brush, and steer the lure deftly as you reel, using the high-held rod tip to manipulate it.

Incidentally, rods should be chosen according to individual waters. On a lake or pond you can't cast across, but one with an open shoreline, use a long rod with good action, so you can reach out to test long-cast spots. On a small-sized pond, a shorter rod will do. If a lakeshore has much timber close to the water, keep the rod length moderate. Most bass-fishing streams have a lot of bank cover. A short rod is the least exasperating here.

For all of these waters, don't stick simply to the traditional overhand cast. Learn agility. Sometimes a sideswipe, a sharp underhand lure pitch or toss will put a lure into a spot you can't reach any other way from the bank.

• **Appraise Your Chances** — For the still waters, one of the most important parts of the bank-fishing technique is learning to make detailed appraisals of the shoreline before you start. There are certain to be a few bankside openings in brush or weeds that will give you a casting advantage. There may also be physical attributes of the shore-line — an abrupt turn, an indentation, a watery gut running up to an inlet — that present beautiful casting opportunities.

Keep in mind always that a cast and retrieve parallel to a section of shore, if feasible, is likely to be more effective than one at right angles. It presents the lure continuously to more places a bass may lie, or to more than one bass.

Even more so than in big-lake fishing, prime lie-up locations along the perimeter of a pond will be endlessly productive. They may not be numerous, but they are easy to mark or remember. The same is true of specific bass lairs in a creek. Once you take a good fish, file the exact place in memory, or mark it. In due time another bass will be there.

These places have the ingredients needed to attract mature bass, and will continue to do so as long as the shore-line is not altered. Spring spawning areas also may be very limited. Once you locate a suitable bedding area in use, you can bet it will be used season after season.

The truly successful small-water bank angler must practice a certain amount of restraint not needed by boat fisher-men. For example, suppose the long, heavy roots of an old stump stretch out from it several yards at right angles to where your cast must be made. The far side looks like just exactly where a big bass should lie. If the roots are slightly submerged, a deft caster might well drop a surface lure bare-ly on the far side, and at the explosive strike "jump" his prey over to the inshore side of the obstruction. But it's chancy. And, once that big one has been hooked and fouled on the far side, perhaps breaking off with the lure in its mouth, it

On small waters, every likely fish location can be checked quickly.
Photo: Steven van de Woert

won't be eager for a long time. Or, perhaps the strike is missed and the lure hung.

There has been for some time now a slow but noticeable increasing interest in the old-fashioned idea of bank fishing the small lakes and the creeks. A good many readers even have written to BASSMASTER® Magazine to ask questions about bank-fishing techniques. Part of the heightened interest may stem from the overwhelming popularity nowadays of old things and old customs. But a great part also comes from the need of many Bassmasters to discover economical, yet enjoyable, ways to pursue their sport, even though the approaches may be changed somewhat from what we have known.

Perhaps there's a message in all this: take a look at the small bass waters, still or moving, near you; take a look at the banks and think about how you might catch a bass from dry land. For a substantial percentage of today's bass fisher-men, this just might be — what with current wild talk of future taxes on gasoline anywhere up to $5 a gallon — an important part of the picture of tomorrow's "Bass Fishing U.S.A." Maybe it wouldn't be all bad. After all, Jim Heddon walked to the bank of Dowagiac Creek — and his heirs are still doing pretty well!

— JANUARY 1981

Photo: Tim Tucker

CHAPTER FIVE

WATER WAYS

Learning the factors that govern the environment of bass is the key to success.

Photo: Gerald Crawford

SUCCESS TACTICS FOR TIDEWATER BASS

By MIKE PANE

Tidewater rivers and creeks harbor largemouths all along the coast, and most of them are underfished. Here's where, how to use the tidewater current to catch more bass . . .

I've got something on here, but it must be weeds. It's not moving," my wife Ginny said.

"Look, Ginny! You've got a crab!" I yelled. She had snagged the blue claw crab while jigging a Little George tailspinner along the edge of a hole in the swift current of Totusky Creek. I really shouldn't have been surprised, but it was a little unusual to catch a crab while fishing for largemouth bass.

The reason I shouldn't have been surprised was that Totusky Creek meets the Rappahannock River near Tappahannock, Va., about 30 miles upriver from the Chesapeake Bay. This slightly brackish section of the river not only contains freshwater fish such as largemouths, crappie, and sunfish, but anadromous fish like striped bass, shad and white perch and, believe it or not, saltwater species such as bluefish and sea trout! But we were just after the largemouths, and so far, it had been challenging but rewarding fishing.

I first heard about Virginia's tidewater largemouth fishing shortly after I moved to the Washington D.C. area. It was some time before I got around to trying it because of the excellent reservoir fishing provided by lakes such as Gaston, Kerr, Smith Mountain and, more recently, Anna, where I guide bass fishermen. I'm sorry I didn't get to it sooner.

I'm not the only BASSer guilty of this negligence, though. Except for a handful of dedicated tidewater fishermen, most of the state's bass fishermen don't realize the potential of the tidewater areas. This situation is rapidly changing. One of the results of this change is that this year's Virginia B.A.S.S. Federation State Tournament will be held on the Chickahominy River, which is one of the better-known tidewater streams in the state.

It took a whole year of intense fishing for Ginny and me to become reasonably proficient at tidewater bassin'. The basic theories of structure fishing are still important but have to be modified somewhat because of the effects of the tides. This is something we had to learn the hard way — by spending many hours studying the water and the bass.

At first, Ginny and I concentrated on fishing only the abundant visible cover such as pilings, fallen trees, and lily pads. We caught bass, but only a few, and most of them were small.

We gave up fishing the visible cover and started fishing underwater structures such as bends in the channel, holes, sunken logs, and drop-offs. This produced a little better, but still we weren't doing as well as we though we should. Many days we couldn't buy a strike. Other days, we caught just enough bass to keep our interest up.

The same day Ginny caught the crab, we were slowly moving up the creek against a moderate outgoing tide. We were casting to the bank cover and watching the depthfinder for bottom structure.

"Hey! Did you see that?" Ginny asked excitedly.

"See what?"

"Over there, in the mouth of that gut I saw a fish boil, and a bunch of minnows came out of the water like something was after them," she said.

"Probably a catfish or gar," I told her. We had seen both channel cats and gar chasing baitfish in the shallow water along the bank.

"Not this time. It looked different. Let's move over to casting range," she said.

We eased over, and Ginny whizzed a cast up the mouth of the little feeder ditch. She reeled the black double-spin just under the surface, but it never got out of the gut.

"Got one!" She grunted as she laid the steel to what looked like a very hefty fish.

It was a 4-pounder, and the first of nine we took in about 15 minutes of furious action. Then the bass quit like somebody turned off a switch exactly at the same time the tide stopped moving.

"That's it, Gin," I said. "They feed in the mouths of the guts on the outgoing tide. The tide probably carries baitfish out of the shallow swamps and guts into water deep enough for the bass to feed on them. When the tide stops, the feeding stops because the bait starts moving back into the shallows."

We fired up the big motor and cruised up the creek, looking for another gut. The next gut produced

When the tide is low, bass often will hold around cypress trees away from the bank.
Photo: Gerald Crawford

no action. Nor did the next, even though the tide had started moving in. In fact, we caught no bass at all on the incoming tide. We figured we had found the pattern.

The next time we tried the tidewater bass, we went to Piscataway Creek, also on the Rappahannock. The tide was low and coming in, which meant about a six-hour wait until the conditions were again right according to our newly discovered pattern.

To pass the time, we decided to try to find where the bass were schooled while waiting to move into the mouths of the guts.

I guessed they would be in the holes formed on the outer edge of bends where the current gouges the bottom as it sweeps along. Some of these holes are 30 to 35 feet deep, but most average 15 to 20. Of course, the depth fluctuates as the tides change, but only a few feet. We had tried these holes before, but without paying much attention to the current.

I anchored the boat above a hole near a gut, and we started working it with plastic worms. We fished hard for an hour, hitting the hole from all angles. We even tried anchoring right in the middle of the hole and casting to the edges. We couldn't buy a pickup.

I was certain this had to be the place they rested in while

waiting for the outgoing tide. Rested in — the thought hit me like Ford's Better Idea. The current was moving through the hole pretty swiftly here on the outside of the bend.

"If I were a bass, I wouldn't like having to fight that current," I said to Ginny. "I'd be over there on the inside of the bend, on the downcurrent side, where the flow is slower."

"But it's only a few feet deep over there," she answered, getting the drift of my thinking. "Everybody knows bass rest in deep water, and this hole is the deep water."

"That's true except when deep water doesn't have the right conditions to keep a bass safe and comfortable," I answered. "That spot behind the bend is close enough to this hole to make the bass feel secure, yet they wouldn't have to fight the current as much."

We eased over closer to the inside of the bend. I canted the worm upcurrent and let the flow sweep it around the bend. By feeding line slowly, I was able to let the worm settle naturally into the slow water where the flow was deflected by the bank.

It never reached the bottom. Something grabbed it and ran for the deep part of the hole. I quickly boated a fat 3-pound bass. We caught five, all more than 3 pounds, from that spot before the school spooked.

We never did get to fish the mouths of the guts, because

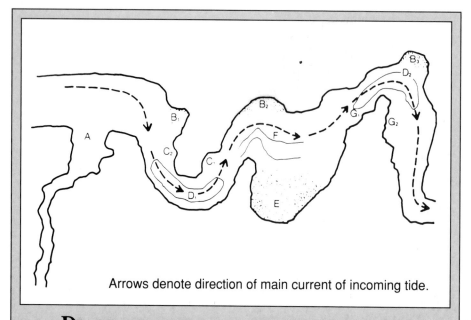

Arrows denote direction of main current of incoming tide.

DIAGRAM OF TYPICAL TIDEWATER CREEK

(A) is the mouth of a gut. Fish on outgoing tide.

(B1, B2, B3) are potential spawning areas. The slight indentations away from main current will have little or no current. Especially good if shallow with hard bottom.

(C1) is a prime spot on incoming tide. Main current will follow outside of bend. Deep hole (D1) nearby and gut (A) nearby. The area inside the bend and downcurrent of the point is where bass will concentrate.

(C2) would be less-productive, but similar spot to try on the outgoing tide. Just as it starts to go out, fish will stop here to rest on their way to the mouth of the gut. A few fish will stay behind here also.

(G1) and (G2) are same as above.

(F) is a gradually sloping point. The author sometimes finds bass where this drops into the main channel if the current isn't too swift. Bass will sometimes stop here on way to and from feeding and resting areas.

(E) is a broad shallow bay with 2 to 3 feet of water along the bank. The main current is so far away that there is actually little or no water movement here. The author caught large numbers of 1- to 2 1/2-pounders here at times; usually on high tide.

(D1) and (D2) are deep holes gouged in the stream bed by the flow of the current around the bends. Not all bends have them.

the fish, we didn't have any trouble catching them.

We caught bass in the mouths of the guts on the outgoing tides because the current carries bait out of the shallow swamps, and the bass ambush the bait in the deeper water at the mouths. We also learned that guts with underwater cover in the mouths produced best.

The best fishing on the incoming tide is wherever the current slows down because of a sharp bend or point, with deep water nearby, and preferably close to a gut.

Another area that is sometimes productive is wherever the bank widens into a large, shallow bay-like area, especially if the bottom is hard. Bass cruise the banks in 2 to 3 feet of water, and take black or yellow double-spins, plastic worms and Rebels.

These bass usually average smaller than those we catch in the guts and on the points, but when they are there, we catch a bunch.

Some of the creeks have large lily pad fields, usually in the upper, shallow end or in the wide shallow bays. Although some BASSers do well in the pads at times, we have never been very successful in them.

The best times to fish tidewater are from April through November, with May, June, October and November the top months. When the water temperature plummets, the bass are too difficult to catch consistently enough to warrant fighting the harsh conditions.

A few sunny days in midwinter can warm the shallows up enough to cause a short feeding spree, but your timing has to be perfect, and you have to be careful to fish only those banks where the tide is very slow. The bass are even more reluctant to fight the current in the winter.

Since we've learned to use the current, our success has skyrocketed. We learned the bass spawn wherever there is a hard bottom in moderately shallow water with little or no current. The current is the most important factor. We've found spawning bass over mud bottoms and in deeper water, but never where the current was moving swiftly. I believe the faster current washes the eggs away, covers the

long before the tide turned, we had caught more than 20 bass between 2 and 5 pounds. All we had to do was locate the right combination of bend, nearby deep water and slower current, and we found bass. There were plenty of spots like this all along the creek.

We finally had caught on to the real key to tidewater bass fishing. It didn't make any difference whether the tide was going out or coming in, as long as it was moving. It was the movement of the current that affected the location of the fish. During slack water, the fish were busy changing locations, scattering to feeding or resting areas. Once we found

beds with silt, and makes it hard for the bass to remain stationary on the bed, so they have adapted. Remember, bass can't make their beds on the downcurrent side of obstructions as they would in a regular stream. In tidewater streams, the downcurrent side changes about every six hours.

Our favorite spring lures are plastic worms and spinnerbaits. We buzz spinnerbaits across the spawning areas, and the strikes are downright vicious. Great care must be taken when fishing plastic worms when the bass are on the beds, though, because they will only be moving the worm out of the bedding area and will then promptly drop it. Use a highly visible line, like Stren Mod II, and hit the fish at the first sign of a pickup.

In early spring, before they are actually spawning, we use shallow-running minnow imitations like Zebco Z-Plugs, Rebels, Rapalas, and Mepps spinners along with plastic worms and spinnerbaits. In

Good fishing can be had on the incoming tide wherever the current slows down because of a sharp bend or point.

Photo: Gerald Crawford

fact, this combination of lures is the best basic arsenal throughout the year, with the addition of the Little George tailspinner and jig-and-eel for the deeper holes in midsummer and late fall.

Occasionally, the bass seem to want a lure like the Mud-Bug, Bomber or Arbogaster. I believe this is because these lures resemble the crabs and crawfish that inhibit tidewater streams. It's hard to fish these lures in the shallow areas, but along the holes they can sometimes be deadly.

The water color is almost always muddy or murky, so I prefer dark-colored lures for most of my tidewater fishing. Black spinnerbaits, with yellow for a second choice, black, purple or blue worms, black tailspinners and jigs, and brown or black crankbaits are the most productive. The only exception is that I like silver Mepps and Rebels and, occasionally, a silver crankbait or a blue Z-Plug.

Some of the better tidewater largemouth spots in Virginia are the Rappahannock River from Fredericksburg to about 10 miles below Tappahannock; the Mattaponi River; the Pamunkey River; the York River; the Chickahominy and the James rivers, and the creeks entering these rivers.

The techniques described here will work on all of them. In fact, I've used these techniques successfully on the Blackwater and Pocomoke rivers on Maryland's eastern shore as well. Similar tidewater rivers and creeks harbor largemouths all along our coast, and most of those areas are underfished.

One word of caution is in order: Fishermen should be extremely careful with their boats. These tidewater areas can be treacherous, especially at low tide or when the wind is strong. Many fishermen, including myself, have run aground on mud flats and spent hours getting off. Also, there are many pilings, fish nets, and sunken logs just under the surface. And when the wind is blowing right, johnboats and even small bass boats are impossible to use and can be risky. Navigate these waters with extreme caution until you get to know them, or fish with someone who already knows the water.

Try tidewater bass fishing for a change of pace. It probably won't make you give up reservoir fishing, but you'll enjoy the challenge.

— JULY/AUGUST 1975

DIRTY TRICKS
TO CATCH BASS

By JAMES A. BRANG

*Knowing where and how to fish mudlines can
mean hitting a bassin' jackpot when
others come up busted . . .*

Beware the ides of March in southern Indiana. Usually accompanied by southern winds, balmy, warm weather, sunny skies and fantastic bass fishing — normally the best of the entire year — there are exceptions. For example, last year spring arrived late. Mid-March offered cold, biting winds, an abundance of sleet, snow and rain, and prolonged cases of fishing fever for most Hoosier BASSers. But not for me.

I was fishing every day, regardless of the elements, and happier than a bear in a beehive. I was catching trophy bass like never before — 7-, 8-, and even 9-pounders. It was almost like shooting fish in a barrel. No, I didn't have any "secret lures." Nor was I fishing hidden, private lakes. Chunking the same lures other BASSers have been tossing for years, I was concentrating on lakes that receive the most fishing pressure. But I did have one ace-in-the-hole: the type structure other BASSers bypass; most don't even know it exists.

This "structure" can change location, depth and even shape, from one day to the next. It can even disappear, at times. It is never detectable on a conventional depthfinder. Still, it is as influential to the bass' movement, and activity, as any type of permanent visible structure. And it is present in all of the nation's lakes, ponds, strip pits and rivers, at one time or another.

This secret structure is a mudline, silt line, or plankton line. Depending on the season, and water conditions, it can be either a horizontal or vertical structure, or a combination of both.

These observations started about 25 years ago during my early scuba-diving research. Even in lakes and pits that appear to be crystal clear on the surface, at various water levels, there are silt lines — places where dirty and clear water are separated as though a plate of glass is slipped between them. The change is abrupt, and under normal conditions one layer does not mix with the other. I always found bass associated with these areas. But my study and research didn't stop there.

Not that the silt line wasn't a dandy place to prospect for bass. It was extremely productive, and still is today. BASSers around the country are catching strings of big bass from "down where the water darkens." But the silt line occurs only during summer months, and usually is quite deep. The silt line is located easily with the use of a light meter or temperature gauge, since it is related closely to the thermocline. This constitutes one of the forms of changeable structure we are discussing, although the silt line is the least effective of all types.

More useful to the bass angler is the form of horizontal structure that exists when muddy or dirty water forms on top with clear water underneath. This frequently occurs when late fall, winter and early-spring rains dump runoff waters into an impoundment. At these times, the incoming water usually is warmer, hence lighter in weight, than the lake itself. Consequently, the runoff remains near the surface and spreads out over a large area. On occasion, I have seen coves and tributaries for several miles where such conditions existed. If you can determine the depth of the prevailing mudline under such conditions, you are almost certain to load the boat with bass. (See FIG. 1.)

Basically the same conditions happen during summer months when prevailing winds from one direction blow masses of plankton to the windward shore. During the peak season of plankton blooms, this literally can turn the surface of a given area into "pea soup."

These types of horizontal, changeable structure are the best, especially the runoff mudline, since it frequently covers a larger area and extends deeper. Depending upon the difference of air and water temperature when a spring storm hits, the amount of runoff, the surrounding watershed and other variables, the incoming water will warm the cove of a lake to a certain depth. Usually the wider the temperature variation, the more distinct the mudline will remain for a period of time.

Strong winds that blow into an area can mix shallow-forming mudlines, and severe cold fronts also can dissolve a distinct mudline after a few days. In major drainage tributaries, the mudline will penetrate deeper, but still can be just as distinct.

As mentioned, water of varied temperatures does not mix easily under normal conditions. Where the temperature variations are abrupt, so can the color differences be. In scuba diving I actually have encountered levels as completely different as if a plate of glass were keeping them apart. I could remain in comfortably warm and clear water under such conditions, yet stick my finger or hand into a dirty layer that seemed as cold as ice water.

As an example of water's resistance to mix, on Lake Monroe here in Indiana where I fish, water is frequently withdrawn from the middepths through the control tower at the dam. This affects the middepths 10 or 15 miles up the lake. It just sucks that one level of water out of the whole lake, instead of removing only water from the dam area.

• **Finding Horizontal Mudlines** — Obviously light meters, as used in finding silt lines, will not work. Since the dirty water is on top, it blocks out the light near the surface. So, even if the water is clear underneath, the light meter indicates very little light.

Unless the mudline forms near the surface, where clear water can be detected by running a boat through an area or by stirring up the water with a sculling paddle or push pole, the best method of pinpointing the exact depth of such a mudline is by use of a water temperature gauge. Start on the surface and keep checking deeper until you find a distinct change in water temperature.

If the water is 8 feet deep and the temperature is the same

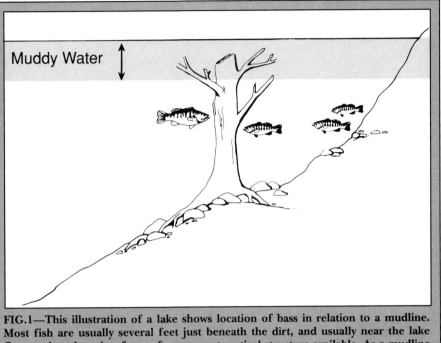

FIG.1—This illustration of a lake shows location of bass in relation to a mudline. Most fish are usually several feet just beneath the dirt, and usually near the lake floor, unless there is a form of permanent vertical structure available. As a mudline moves deeper, the bass continue to retreat or back off to still deeper water to maintain this magic distance of 2 to 5 feet from the muddy water.   Illustration: Emily Craig

from top to bottom, you can assume the water is muddy all the way from the surface to the bottom. If you move out into deeper, say 12 feet of water, and the temperature gauge registers a sharp change at 10 feet, you can assume the bottom 2 feet at that location offers clear water. Once you locate the mudline, attempt to work your lures just under it. Then, you will have quickly eliminated a lot of empty water. You will be putting the lure right on the bass' dinner table. But even then, in large tributaries this "magic depth" could cover a lot of water.

Let's go one step farther to cover the very best spots, in the least amount of time. Use this changeable mudline structure in combination with existing permanent structure. If, for instance, you know where there is a creek channel at a depth of 10 to 15 feet in that cover, or an underwater hump or ridge, or a brushpile or anything else at the same depth, concentrate on these places. Bass do not like to be squeezed between the mudline and the lake floor. If the mudline is at a depth of 10 feet, do not work a flat area that is 11 feet deep. An uneven bottom where the bass could sink below the mudline would be excellent, especially if an opening to deeper water is available. (See FIG. 2.)

Most larger bass prefer a little room to roam. A clear-water area of from 3 to 5 feet beneath the silt has been most productive for me. A deeper band of clear water is not good. Then, the fish move shallower until they come closer to the mudline. If and when the mudline moves deeper, the fish retreat somewhat or move to a different permanent structure

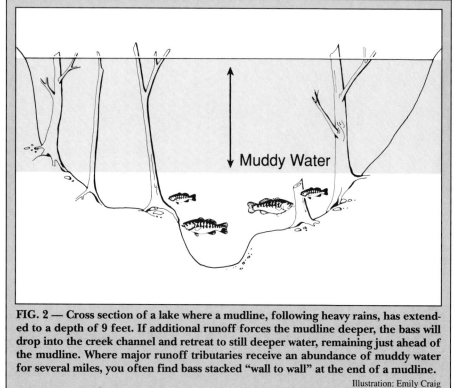

FIG. 2 — Cross section of a lake where a mudline, following heavy rains, has extended to a depth of 9 feet. If additional runoff forces the mudline deeper, the bass will drop into the creek channel and retreat to still deeper water, remaining just ahead of the mudline. Where major runoff tributaries receive an abundance of muddy water for several miles, you often find bass stacked "wall to wall" at the end of a mudline.

Illustration: Emily Craig

to maintain the desired distance.

One bright, crisp April afternoon I was heading up the Mud Creek tributary of 1,200-acre Dogwood Lake in southern Indiana to wet a line. Just as I rounded the junction and began heading north I met a fishin' friend, Norm Fromme, coming out of the area. We stopped to exchange ideas. "You'll need a shovel to dig a hole, so you can get a lure in the water up there," Fromme laughed. "Even then the fish couldn't see a lure if you hit 'em right on the head."

"Maybe if I'm lucky I can hook one in the back," I replied, and proceeded up "mud alley." At that time, I had not perfected and refined my mudline tactics, but had an inkling that possibly the muddy water might not extend from top to bottom. I thought that if such a condition existed, this would be a perfect place to do some experimenting.

I took temperature readings at several locations and depths before concluding the mudline was at a depth of 12 feet. This ruled out much of the area I had intended to fish. Thinking the bass should have been shallower in preparation for the approaching spawn, I almost abandoned the area in favor of some shallower, clearer coves back down the lake.

But something, possibly the hardheaded German instinct in me, persisted — don't give up without at least a try. There was a sharp creek bend covered with scrub brush and sunken logs in 15 to 18 feet of water in the area. I had taken a few summer bass at this spot in previous years. I fired out a long cast with a 1/4-ounce black weedless bucktail jig with a

pinched-off, 6-inch blackberry Jelly Worm trailer and allowed the combination to settle to the bottom.

An 8-pound, 2-ounce largemouth must have watched it drop through the muddy upper layer of water, because when I twitched it the big bass climbed all over it. Successive bass of 5-4, 7-2, 7-1, 6-7 and 3 1/4 pounds followed the big bass into the boat in short order. And I had new 17-pound-test monofilament popped twice in the process by bass too big to handle, down in the brush.

On the way home I stopped at Uebelhor's Bait & Tackle in my hometown of Jasper, Ind., to weigh the fish. To this day, Charlie Uebelhor claims that was the "best limit of Indiana largemouths" he has ever seen. The next day I returned to the same area and again took a braggin' limit that averaged over 5 pounds, plus a number of other good fish that were returned to the lake. But by the time I had another chance to return the following weekend, the mudline was dissolving and the fish had moved to a different area.

• **Vertical Mudlines** — When incoming water is about the same temperature as the lake itself, the muddy water will mix with clear water equally from top to bottom, as far as the runoff can force its way into the lake. Again, depending on the amount of water entering a lake, this vertical mudline can move only a short distance, or up to several miles, down the lake.

At times, vertical mudlines can be just as productive as horizontal ones, but the line separating each is usually not as distinct and usually breaks up and mixes with surrounding water quicker.

As an example, some years ago in preparation for the four-man Indiana bass team championship on Lake Monroe, Dick Williams, Fred Willis, David Land and I found heavy concentrations of bass along a massive vertical mudline in the upper reaches of a major tributary. The fish were on the clearwater edge several feet from the dirty water, and they kept backing off as the mud and silt moved toward them. For three days we moved with the mudline, and the fish. When possible, we concentrated on permanent structure in combination with the mudline. At the end of the tournament, we had moved a couple of miles from where we had initially started fishing, but we still were catching bass and easily claimed the championship.

As mudlines move down a lake, they keep pushing a

majority of the bass back. It doesn't take long to visualize what is happening. The bass from the ends of a cove are pushed back into an area occupied by others. As the mudline continues downstream, these groups continue to retreat into areas occupied by still others. Eventually you could have a wall of bass at the edge of a mudline, especially one that has moved a great distance.

• **Best Lures** — A variety of lures work well for fishing this changeable structure. For shallow water, spinnerbaits and crankbaits are tops. In deep sections, jigs 'n eels, Little George tailspins, plastic worms, grubs and spinnerbaits are all effective. Black, brown and other dark colors seem best; I can't explain why, unless possibly because fresh, incoming water stirs up crawfish and other bottom-dwellers.

Since schools of baitfish move with and feed on massive sections of microscopic plant and animal life as they are pushed by the wind, baitfish-colored lures are head and shoulders above anything else for working plankton lines.

For working deep silt lines in midsummer, any color lure that normally produces in clear water is good.

• **The Methods** — The most effective approach for working vertical mudlines is to toss the lure into the dirty water and retrieve it back into the clear water. Most strikes will be violent, impulsive attacks that usually occur just after the lure enters the clear water. The vertical mudlines are the easiest to fish since the exact location can be seen. Keep the boat back in the clear section far enough to avoid spooking the school.

When working horizontal mudlines where the top section is dirty water, several different methods are effective. For shallow mudlines, retrieving spinnerbaits or crankbaits down through the dirty water is deadly. For deep mudlines, working bottom-bumping lures downhill along the lake floor until they enter the clear section is the easiest and surest method of arousing action.

If the exact depth of a mudline and location of a combination permanent structure is known, the dead-fall tactic is lethal. A fluttering spinnerbait, lightweight jig and eel or slowly falling grub entering a school of bass will be attacked instantly.

Early last spring, I found a mudline at a depth of 9 feet in the upper reaches of Indian Lake in southern Indiana. This section of the impoundment contains an abundance of standing timber where only the trunks are still erect. Concentrating on depths of 10 to 15 feet, I cast a large-bladed, black/orange single-spin close to every big tree I could find and counted it down. As the spinner fluttered into the 11-foot depths beside the remains of an oversize oak tree, I saw the line twitch, which indicated a bass had engulfed the lure. I jerked back hard enough to rip the hide off a full-grown alligator, and the stainless-steel 4/0 hook sank into the tough jaws of a big bass, a 7 1/2-pounder.

I continued to probe every likely tree, and before day's end I had brought 23 bass into the boat. All of them came from the magic 11- to 12-foot depth along the bottom edge of the horizontal mudline. I actually began to anticipate the strikes as I counted the bait down, and knew it was approaching the contact point.

The more types of permanent structure you can use in combination with a mudline, the more likely are the results. Creek channels are probably the best stationary structure available. This is frequently the route bass use to retreat, as the mudline spreads and deepens.

The contact points of mudline fishing almost are identical to any other types of structure fishing. Look for a break or change, the same as you would along a weedline, treeline, creek channel, underwater ledge, cove covered with bonnets, or anything else. Once you learn to locate and fish this productive, changeable structure, the most confusing part is keeping track of it, moving as it moves and changing as it changes. And at times, it can move or change very quickly.

Cold fronts, strong winds, additional rain of a different temperature, or time can change a horizontal structure into a vertical structure or vice versa. During rains — and short periods of up to a couple of days immediately after — are best, before winds and lake currents mix the water and heavy sediment and mud particles begin to settle.

Always check each cove or tributary separately. No two sections are the same. Just because the magic horizontal mudline was at 15 feet in one tributary doesn't mean it will be anywhere close to that in another. In certain instances where incoming water is just slightly murky, bass in a clearwater lake are attracted to it like flies to honey. Instead of holding at a point where these two waters meet, though, they immediately penetrate any existing colorline and spread out into the dingy water. Do not confuse slightly murky water with muddy water.

And even when certain sections of a lake become muddy enough to plow, a few bass, which are usually smaller specimens, will remain in the dirt. Most bass, though, will retreat until the muddy waters become somewhat diluted.

Under the right conditions, horizontal mudlines with the dirty water on top offer the best cover and structure I have ever seen or fished. They can be much better than beds of hyacinths, lily pads or other types of heavy cover. Mudlines provide the surest method of beating cold fronts; frequently severe cold snaps follow the heavy, rain-producing winter and spring storms. The dirty water provides cover and shields out the bright sunlight. The bass feed all day long, as though it was the best overcast, threatening day.

It can be difficult, even frustrating at times trying to find and follow a constantly changing mudline, but once you hit the jackpot of big bass at the other end, you will consider the rewards well worth the effort. In fact, if you are like me, you'll soon start hoping for more and bigger spring storms. It can become your "ace-in-the-hole" when other anglers consider such conditions hopeless and give up easily.

— JANUARY 1981

FISHING INDUSTRIAL WATERS

By STEVE PRICE

A shoreline industry may provide a pipeline to bassin' success for you . . .

At first glance, it looks like the last place you'd never want to cast a lure: a pipe from the shoreline spewing a stream of off-colored water into your favorite lake or river, polluting it with who knows what kinds of contaminants.

This is what B.A.S.S. Tournament Trail pro Hank Parker calls "industrial water," and regardless of what it looks like, it's worth a few casts.

"By 'industrial water' I'm describing both intakes and outlets where water is either pulled out for use by a factory, or put back in a river or reservoir after use," explains Parker, a former BASS Masters Classic® and Super B.A.S.S. winner.

"Normally, these places are easy to recognize," he adds. "Outlets are characterized by one or more pipes that simply have water pouring out of them, while intakes are located below the surface and are sucking water into them. Signs may or may not be present, but you usually can see a factory or industrial plant nearby.

"Sewage treatment facilities, electric power plants, pulp and paper mills and other businesses that use water in large amounts will have these intake or outlet pipes, and at times fishing around them can be outstanding."

Several factors contribute to this. Outlets,

Industrial-discharge outlets may look unsightly, but they can produce outstanding bass-fishing action.

Photo: Steve Price

which usually are better than intakes, frequently are pouring some type of nutrients back into the water. This actually can be what starts a food chain, since the nutrients feed plankton, which in turn are eaten by small minnows. The minnows attract bass and other predators.

"As water pours from an outlet pipe, current is created," says Parker, "so everything around the pipe is constantly in motion, a factor that not only keeps bass in the area, it keeps them active."

To fish an outlet pipe, Parker recommends plastic grubs, crankbaits, spinnerbaits and even topwater plugs. His personal favorite is a 2-inch grub on a 1/4-ounce jighead. Casts should be made directly into the boiling water and worked out.

If the current around the outlet is especially strong, Parker will direct his casts more to the edges of the swift water rather than directly at the pipe. Boat positioning should be such that retrieves will bring lures with the current rather than against it.

Intake pipes are not as common as outlets, and often require slightly different tactics. Parker fishes them with weedless jigs, worms or grubs, which he tight-lines around the edges of the inlet. The lures are worked in short hops, but care must be taken to keep the lure from going into the pipe.

Larger factories may locate intake and outlet pipes in small canals or creeks rather than the main lake or river. If this is the case, the entire canal can be a fish producer, although the best spots may be directly around the pipes, or the mouth of the canal. For this, crankbaits, jigs and worms are top lure choices.

Outlets and intakes are most productive when water is being pumped. You can determine pumping schedules by on-sight visits, or by factory inquiries. Whenever possible, try to be fishing shortly after pumping begins.

Parker remembers one outlet pipe along the Alabama River, site of the 1981 and 1982 Classics®, where he found bass schooled during practice.

Once the tournament began, however, he couldn't get near the spot because local boats had anchored there. He later learned they caught and kept more than a dozen bass in the 2- and 3-pound class on one of the tournament days.

— *FEBRUARY 1986*

Factory outlets sometimes warm surrounding waters, and attract baitfish and bass during cooler weather.

Photo: Grady Allen

FALLING-WATER BASSIN'

By JACK WOLLITZ

*Declines in lake levels can be unsettling to bass —
but it doesn't have to upset
your bass fishing . . .*

The lake is falling." Those four words can strike fear in a bass fisherman's heart and cut as deeply as Chicken Little's immortal declaration about the sky doing likewise. Heads will nod, shoulders will shrug and the weak-kneed even might turn and head back home. With a little luck, they might arrive in time for the kickoff of the early game on TV.

But anglers who have done their homework will not be in quite the exasperated despair as the ill-informed bunch. In fact, the bass will tend to concentrate a little more during the annual autumn drawdown on many reservoirs.

While there won't be too many times when such conditions will yield a bass here and a bass there, the chances are that when fish are found, they will be in a good-sized school. It is possible, then, to pick up several before the school scatters into deeper water.

Bass definitely react severely to those times when lake management agencies decide to pull the plug to draw the water down to winter pool. While the bass' reaction to the cooling water of fall is to feed voraciously on baitfish, the fish also pull away from shorelines and become more difficult to locate.

Such times are tough even for the most seasoned of professional anglers.

"It certainly is one of the most difficult conditions you can encounter," says Randall Romig of Spring City, Pa., a veteran of several BASS Masters Classic® championships. "When the lake is being drawn down, the fish are difficult to locate. They tend to pull off the banks and suspend."

Another Classic® veteran, the affable Woo Daves of Chester, Va., says falling water definitely means one thing: "That's when you need to spend a lot more time with your LCR (or other liquid-crystal depthfinder) looking for ledges and drop-offs, underwater bridges, humps and stump beds."

Charlie Ingram, a three-time winner on the BASSMAS-TER® Tournament Trail and a former Classic® qualifier, found one of those underwater honey holes several years ago in November as the water was falling at Apache Lake in Arizona. "I caught 44 pounds in two days on a 3/4-ounce Hopkins spoon in 52 feet of water."

So while conditions are tough in times of falling water, the pros' experiences show they are not impossible.

Their advice essentially is to scan the lake bottom for deep-water objects and contours that should hold bass spooked into the depths by the drawdown.

"In the fall, when they are dropping the water, that's one of the toughest kinds of fishing there is. You can just about forget bank-running," Daves says. "You will find fish on the structure holes, though, and you can 'get well' in a hurry."

Daves says the deep-water fish will react less quickly and less drastically to falling water than their shallow-water cousins. "If you concentrate only on structure fish, in 10 to 20 feet of water, you should catch some. You might find, so to speak, a little honey hole."

Daves, Romig and Ingram recommend looking for falling-water bass congregated in areas where creek channels touch points, on bends in channels or on ledges, humps and other bulging contours.

"Those kinds of spots are going to produce sometime," Daves notes. "Stick with them and go back to them a couple of times; you're going to find fish there eventually."

Once you settle on an area with underwater structure that looks suitable for bass, turn up the sensitivity on the depth-finder and seek out the baitfish that may be there, too, Romig recommends.

"In the fall, look for the deep brush and stumps, but primarily the thing to look for is the baitfish. Look for the bait on the flasher, and then fish under them. You should contact some bass," says the Pennsylvania angler.

Romig also recommends anglers consider that, while bass drop back from the shores and tend to suspend, they will choose to suspend in vertical cover when it is available. "If you have standing timber or vertical cover on deep creek channels — like at Lanier (Georgia) or Truman

With falling water levels, bass move to deeper hideouts such as submerged humps. Photo: Jack Wollitz

(Missouri) — fish will pull off the banks and suspend in the limbs of the trees," Romig has found. "They will be much more catchable in that condition than when they are suspended over open water."

Still another trick is noted by Ingram.

"I try to find the warmest water in the lake," he says. "For instance, at Wheeler Lake (Alabama), one river runs a little warmer in the fall than the other tributaries, and I like to go into it and flip or pitch the vertical bluffs with a brown jig."

Bass in the autumn that are dealing with falling water levels and temperatures are less cover-oriented than they are at other times of the year, Ingram says. "They're there for one reason — to feed up for the winter — so if you find the bait-fish in 10 or 15 or 20 feet of water, stick with them. The bass will be there sooner or later."

Smallmouth and largemouth bass react the same to the falling water, Romig says, and both species' instincts tell them that whatever they do, they should do it quickly.

"The fish will move fast once they sense the water is falling," Romig says. "Even in the spring, the fish will pull off the banks when they are in shallow to spawn and the lakes start to drop."

He has found that once the water level is stabilized, the bass seem to relax.

"It won't take but two or three days for the fish to feel comfortable and move shallow again."

Daves, too, has found that bass greeted in the spring by falling water don't lollygag around cover in the shallows. "In the spring if the bass are on the flats and the water starts dropping, they might go anywhere. If they are up in the back of a creek, they can go to the channel or to the next deepest bushes or stumps."

He says fishermen should look for deeper cover — even as little as 6 or 8 inches deeper — than what the bass were using before the water started fluctuating. They will scoot from the shallow stuff to the relative security of the next deepest cover.

If the first objective in autumn drawdown fishing is locating likely fish-holding water, the next step is to figure out how to put the bass into the boat.

Most veteran bass fishermen recommend deep-diving crankbaits as the most efficient tools for plucking the first fish from a school.

"I start with a Bagley DB3 in a Tennessee shad pattern or

Bass pro Woo Daves says forget about bank fishing when impoundment water levels are dropped in the fall.
Photo: Gerald Crawford

one with some chartreuse in it," says Daves. "Then, after I catch one or two from a spot on a crankbait, I'll use a worm and maybe catch two or three more. And then I probably would go back to the crankbait. I like to change it around a little bit so the fish don't get lure-shy."

For deep-water worming during the autumn drawdown, Daves often goes with a large lure. "I'll tie on an 8- or 9-inch worm then — whereas during other seasons, I'll use a 6-inch or even a 4-inch worm," he says.

He fishes the worm on a 1/4- to 1/2-ounce sinker, going with the heavier weight when the wind is higher.

"And sometimes I'll pinch the weight on a foot or two up the line so the worm floats up — Carolina-style," explains the Virginia fisherman.

Romig also likes to do his prospecting with a crankbait, and then switch to another lure as a follow-up.

"Sometimes you can catch them on a creek channel with a deep-diving crankbait, or you can count down a jig and swim it through where the bass are holding," Romig says.

Ingram says the jig-and-frog is an excellent lure to fool larger bass holding in a particular area, while vertical jigging will take a greater number of fish due to the fact it can be worked more quickly, allowing the fisherman to cover more water in a hurry.

Some anglers have been experimenting quietly in recent years with slipping a tube lure like a Fat Gitzit over the long slab spoons similar to those made by Hopkins, Jack Chancellor and others. The plastic sheath, Ingram notes, gives the spoon a soft texture so that when a bass clamps down, it will tend to hold the bait a moment longer before trying to eject it.

The extra second, or even a half second, could mean the difference between a hookup and a missed strike.

Fishing friend Jeff Hahn and I gave draw-down bassin' a try last November, when we traveled to a U.S. Army Corps of Engineers flood-control reservoir near our homes in northeastern Ohio — even though we knew the water level was falling rapidly.

We selected our first spot: a hump that rises sharply from 20 feet off the creek channel to top off at 5 feet before dropping off again to a

10-foot-deep trough between the hump and the shore. The top of the crest has several large stumps. The fish apparently had been chased off the top and sides of the hump by boat traffic, so we moved on to our next hole.

It was a vertical shale bluff from which we hooked and landed a few "keeper"-sized bass. They struck 1/2-ounce Hopkins spoons worked off the bottom on a gravel slide 12 feet deep.

Our next stop was at the steep side of a point that runs parallel to the creek channel. Hahn connected with a freight-train bass, but the struggling fish pulled free before we could get a look at it.

Disappointed and shaking from the experience, he moved his boat to our last stop of the afternoon: a riprap bank at a bridge that crosses the lake arm. Such sites are excellent choices because they offer deep water, hard bottom and current — three prime ingredients.

On — literally — the last cast of the day, I connected with a 3 1/2-pound smallmouth bass that belted a 3/4-ounce Silver Lucky. I was hopping it down around the break in the riprap where it bottoms out with the sandy channel bottom.

The smallmouth fought vigorously — as expected — and jumped several times in the 49-degree water as it tried to detach itself from the treble hooks. I carefully released the fish after we snapped a few pictures, and we happily recounted the day's bass. Later we discovered that other bass fishermen weren't doing so well on that dreary, drawdown day. Our game plan apparently had worked.

Our experience also showed that deep-working lures such as jigging spoons and flashing, vibrating, sonar-style baits such as the Heddon Sonar, Silver Lucky, Silver Buddy and other blade-and-lead lures can be the secret when the bass have withdrawn to deep sanctuaries.

These lures give anglers the option of working them quickly in steady crankbait fashion. Or they can be retrieved in a hop-stop-sink motion like a jig-and-pig or plastic worm. They also work very well in a vertical-jigging presentation such as is used with slab spoons.

Bass usually will hit the baits as they are falling, whether in the hop-sink or vertical jigging.

Deep-water bassing — required in drawdown situations — can be intimidating to fishermen, but Daves says there is a positive side to it. When you're out looking for bass holding offshore on structure, he says, at least hordes of other anglers won't be pestering you.

Randall Romig looks for baitfish and vertical structure, and fishes a crankbait or jig to catch bass that may be suspended. Photo: Gerald Crawford

"If you look hard and find a couple of channel bends or humps or ledges that hold fish, not many other people are going to find those," he says. What is more, Daves says, the lessons a fisherman learns by seeking out deep-water haunts also can be applied to summer fishing.

"In the summer, you're going to be fishing deep anyway, and falling water won't affect bass at those levels very much," he says. "In fact, whatever current is created by the drawdown may even help the fishing."

So look on the bright side, as Daves does. While discovering that the lake you're going to be fishing is in the midst of a dramatic decline in water level can be a disheartening experience, you can deal with the dilemma.

It all boils down to the most basic of bass fishing truths: Find baitfish in conjunction with classic bass structure. The rest, as they say, is up to you.

— DECEMBER 1989

FAST-WATER BASS

By TOM STERLING

Currents and moving water hold bass throughout the year. Read on to learn how to catch them . . .

During the 1979 BASSMASTER® Tournament Trail, a 21-year-old rookie pro from California roared into the competition like a tornado, winning one tournament outright, earning money in all six and finishing fourth in the BASS Masters Classic®. He missed claiming B.A.S.S. Angler-of-the-Year honors by less than 2 pounds — one bass.

His name, of course, is Gary Klein. And many believe he will become one of the bright new stars in professional bassin'. He has the desire, associates will tell you, and certainly the self-confidence and enthusiasm. Klein also has something else going for him that is overlooked by many of his competitors. He calls it his "fast-water bass pattern."

In a word, this blond gypsy from Oroville, Calif., likes to fish moving water and currents, and in fact, begins practically every tournament diligently studying maps to locate such conditions and plotting how to fish them.

"It's pretty much a carry-over from my learning days in California," Klein admits. "Our Western bass are deep, finicky fish that are always moving as they chase shad. The only shallow-water bass you can ever depend on are always in moving water where food is washing down to them."

• **Movin'-Water Pattern** — Klein believes moving water offers some distinct advantages in fishing, too.

• First, it positions the bass. With experience, a Bassmaster can spot those positions immediately, and thus work an area much more quickly.

• Secondly, moving-water bass are generally easily accessible, for they are along shorelines in water less than 10 feet deep.

• Third, they are frequently larger fish.

• And fourth, fast-water largemouths are usually more active than their calm-water cousins, because the water is cooler and more oxygenated.

"There are disadvantages to fishing moving water, as well," Klein points out, "and these should certainly be considered by anyone trying to fish this type of area.

"Boat control may be a problem, as the current will continually sweep the angler beyond his target area. Just finding moving water may involve long runs up a lake to a particular river or creek channel, and even then, bass might not be on a definite pattern. When you fish currents, you very well can be fishing for individual bass," he says.

"Perhaps the rising cost of gasoline will slow down some of us who like to run long distances," Klein says, "but everybody thinks the grass is always greener up the river. I get that out of my system on the first practice day. If the fishing is good, then I'm ahead in the game. If it isn't, I've already seen it and can concentrate in another area."

• **Pattern Particulars** — The primary question concerning a moving-water bass pattern is, where do you begin looking for bass along a shoreline? After all, what makes bass prefer one portion of a river-bank over another?

"That is the question I have to answer in every tournament I fish," Klein laughs, "and it's different in every lake. Basically, however, there are some things to look for that can help narrow the search for fish.

"Cover must be present, and the heavier the better. Current will always be stronger to the outside of a river bend than on the inside, and floating debris often will be caught in such spots, but permanent-type cover, such as a fallen tree or big boulder, is always better.

"Depth should always be noted. In many lakes, the main river channel will swing against a bank providing that classic shallow/deep-water combination that bass seem to like. A good map and sonar depthfinder can help you locate spots like this.

"Anything unusual in the shoreline itself is also worth studying. I like to work the mouths of cuts and inlets, but a friend I know can't pass up an island if water is moving quickly around it. A lot of finding fish like this boils down to experience on the water, I think. All of us spot places that just 'look fishy,' and many times, they do hold bass," Klein explained.

• **"X" Marks Spot** — Klein's search for current and moving water begins with map study. Normally, the best current will be in the upper end of an impoundment where the lake actually narrows down to river-like conditions. Another consideration for current is studying the surrounding countryside, for a hilly, rolling topography indicates feeder streams will also have good, strong-water movement that attracts bass.

"Because a tributary creek has moving water doesn't necessarily mean it will be a good spot for bass," Gary Klein cautions. "Bass have other requirements, too, primarily cover, and many feeder creeks are too shallow to hold good concentrations of fish. Smaller creeks, too, are often heavily silted, which is usually detrimental to bass."

California's Gary Klein has made a rocket climb on the BASSMASTER Tournament Trail. He depends on bass in moving water. Photo: Steve Price

Klein prefers, then, to stay in the major river channel or in the largest tributaries. He goes upriver and works down, and he stays on the outside of the river bends. He works any type of cover, such as fallen logs, overhanging tree branches or the mouths of creeks and coves; and his favorite lure is a hand-tied jig with a worm trailer. He uses 7 1/2-foot Fenwick Flipping Stiks exclusively, and lines testing 25 to 40 pounds.

• **Lure Presentation** — "Because the moving water positions the bass very exactly," Klein explains, "lure presentation becomes critical. Thus, the situation becomes tailor-made for flippin' or jigging. That means most of the bass caught are going to be at very close range, and for that I want stout rods and heavy lines that I don't have to worry about breaking."

Klein gave me a demonstration of just how important lure presentation can be when fishing current. At his request, I tied on a plastic worm. While he eased the boat up to a partially submerged log extending out from the bank, I saturated the log and surrounding water with casts. I did not get a single "tap."

Klein moved to the bow, announced that any bass on the log would be "right there," and on his first flip, brought in a 7-pounder!

"First," he laughed, "remember that bass will always be facing upstream, letting water filter through their gills. That also means they can see food washing down to them naturally, and anything that moves upstream against current — like your worm was doing — is not natural, so they shy away from it.

"Second, bass are frequently in two major areas by any protruding cover in current. They are behind it where the force of the water is actually broken, and they don't have to continually fight the current; or they are holding right along the outside edge if the current is not as swift.

"Many times you'll see a complete tree that has fallen into the water, and the branches will spread out in all directions. In a situation like that, work the outside first, then work any small pockets or openings on the down-current side.

"You'll have to consider the speed of the current as well as the level of the water, too," Klein points out. "In faster water, the fish will require more cover or protection so they don't have to fight the current. That's when you want to work behind the logs or rocks, and especially the mouths of coves, inlets and other shoreline irregularities. These places offer that type of protection, but still give the bass the chance to see what's being washed downstream.

"In high water, you may be able to fish a little closer to shore, since new cover is generally made available to bass as water rises, and the shoreline itself slows down the force of the water. Depth is one of the most important factors in bass fishing, even in moving water," believes Klein.

• **The Jig Rig** — With these considerations, it's easy to see why Gary Klein uses a jig. Depending on water conditions, the jig weights vary from 1/8 to a full ounce. The

■

faster the water, the heavier the jig. The colder the water temperature, the less active the bass will be, so the lighter the jig.

In very heavy brush with active bass, Klein likes a 1/2-ounce model. He ties his jigs with a nylon weedguard, and advises any brush fisherman to do the same.

"Fishing moving water is not really a casting game," he concedes, "although I'll toss worms, crankbaits and spinnerbaits parallel to the bank if action is slow, and I want to work a long stretch of water in a hurry."

Klein uses the long Flipping Stiks for his casting, too, and is seldom without at least half a dozen of the long rods in his boat.

"Basically, it's a flippin' or jigging situation," he says, "because the bass are only going to be very close to cover. It's a waste of time to cast, for that puts the lure in front of the fish just a fraction of the entire retrieve. Jigging puts the lure on a bass' nose, and if it doesn't hit it after a few seconds, you move to another part of the cover."

• **Boat Control** — Klein's favorite fishing depth is from the shoreline down to about 5 feet, which often places him within arm's length of solid ground. Boat control is critical, for one bad move will send him crashing into the shore or into the very cover he is fishing. Klein operates with a trolling motor as much as possible, and has equipped his boat with one of the strongest he could obtain. If he's in extremely fast water, Klein works with outboard power, balancing the boat's forward thrust against the downstream push of the current, but it's not something he likes to do.

"If the current is moving that quickly, it also means it's washing your lure downstream at top speed, too, which makes line control difficult and strikes hard to detect. When you're in a situation like that, look for protected water, such as the mouth of a cove, and pull into the eddy behind it. Then, carefully work the edge of the fast water — there will be a distinct eddy line where fast and calm water meet — and that's where bass will be.

"Cast upstream into the fast water so your lure comes down with the current across that eddy line. Crankbaits are an excellent choice for this type of water, as are plastic worms and plastic grubs. If you're fishing something deep, try to let it bounce right above the bottom, and don't expect a big strike, only a sudden hesitation as the lure stops moving."

• **Bass In Fast Water** — Some radio transmitter tracking studies performed by biologists with the Tennessee Valley Authority on Pickwick Lake and the Tennessee River have come up with some additional information regarding smallmouth bass in fast water. Outstanding smallmouth fishing is available in the first several miles of Pickwick's upper end below the Wilson Dam. For the most part it contains steadily moving current, even when a minimum of water is released through the dam.

In periods of extremely high water when most of the flood gates were open, the biologists found their transmitter-equipped smallmouth bass were swimming down along the edges of the main Tennessee River channel or into whatever deep potholes they could find, as if to get under the push of the current, but still be in position to watch for food washing past.

The biologists knew exactly where the bass were, but the water was much too rough and fast for anyone to try to fish for them. Klein's strategy of positioning his boat in an eddy and working the deep edge of the fast water is about the only option available to Bassmasters in such situations.

Klein believes, and has proved to his own satisfaction many times over, that bass living in moving water are frequently larger than those encountered in calm water. One reason, he thinks, is that these fish get first choice of anything being washed downstream. The water itself is normally richer in nutrients, which attracts smaller members of the food chain, such as crawfish and minnows.

With this abundant food supply, the bass do not have to expend as much energy chasing it, either. Klein's best-ever largemouth, a 9-pound, 3-ounce lunker, came from the currents of the St. Johns River.

• **Seasons & Reasons** — Currents and moving water also have another advantage that Klein is quick to point out, which is that they hold fish throughout the year:

• In summer months, when oxygen levels may be extremely low in some parts of a lake, they always will be higher where the water is moving.

• In spring, rains will ensure a continuing supply of fresh food washing downstream.

• In winter, when bass don't like to move far for anything, the fresh food supply still will be washing by in front of them.

• In fall, with weather fronts blowing across the nation, bass instinctively seek heavy cover, and much of that cover is right along a riverbank in the current.

To be sure, fishing current and moving water the way Gary Klein does can become an added weapon in any Bassmaster's arsenal. In most cases, it is an individual fish pattern, although Klein occasionally has taken three and four bass from a single fallen tree. Often, after he has caught bass from such a spot, he can return several hours later and catch another bass that has moved in to occupy the vacancy.

It is also a technique that requires sound boat handling and expert lure presentation. Klein began fishing currents and moving water when he began flipping. In the second tournament he ever fished, Klein finished fourth, behind a fellow named Dee Thomas, who won by Flipping. Klein spent the next three years trying to learn the tactic, but did not have much success until Dave Myers of the Fenwick staff ironed out his flaws.

— JULY/AUGUST 1980

Tailrace Tips

By STEVE PRICE

BASSer Jim Skelton has a knack for
catching big fish below dams . . .

For more years than he can remember, Jim Skelton of Leeds, Ala., has been fishing in the tailrace below Logan Martin Dam on Alabama's Coosa River. He understands the water patterns there, knows the locations of the rocks and deep holes, and has a knack for catching big fish that swim up below the dam.

In March 1982 Skelton caught a 16-pound, 3-ounce hybrid striped bass, which stood as the state record for a year. He'd caught dozens of hybrid over 10 pounds each before landing that whopper, and literally had watched them grow up as Alabama began stocking the white bass-striped bass hybrid in the Coosa River. This past spring he caught and released a 24 1/2-pound striped bass in the same tailrace.

Tailrace fishing, like Skelton enjoys, offers its own unique action and excitement, especially when the prize may be such a heavy fish. It also can be very specialized fishing, where one boat enjoys constant strikes and another catches nothing.

Safety is another prime consideration for this type of fast-water fishing. Hidden rocks, boiling currents and fast-changing water levels add an element of danger that does not exist in flat-water lake fishing.

Here's how one of Alabama's top tailrace pros handles such conditions:

• **Fish Selective Spots** — "I think one of the most important things to realize when fishing tailraces is that not all the water is productive," emphasizes Skelton. "Just like on a lake, fish in tailraces very often seem to use or hold in selected areas. I caught my big striped bass while anchored in the exact same place where I caught that record hybrid, for instance.

"I've seen schools of spotted bass move into one particular place where you couldn't cast without getting a strike, but miss that place and you couldn't buy a fish.

"I believe the formation of rocks and boulders, combined with the force of the water flow, has a lot to do with where fish might be," Skelton continues, "and this can change throughout a day as water levels rise and fall. I have several different places I like to fish below the Logan Martin Dam, and I move from one to the other until something pays off."

• **Work Edge Of Current** — Skelton never anchors his boat in the fastest water, but rather, puts it to one side or the other where he can still reach the strong current with a long cast. He likes to work the edge of that current and fishes along the bottom. Stripers, hybrids, spotted bass, largemouths and other species use holes and rocks for resting areas against the force of the water; fishing deep in such rock-filled current means losing lures, but Skelton feels it is the only way to consistently score on big tailrace fish.

"For tailrace fishing I use either a large white bucktail jig or a 3- to 4-inch grub on a leadhead jig. To get them to the bottom in the current, I like 1/2- or 5/8-ounce sizes, and I fish them with 20-pound-test line on a stiff casting rod.

"The trick is to cast upstream, then let the current wash the jig down. Control the lure with your rod tip, letting the jig bounce and skip along the bottom, and after it washes past, you reel in and cast again," says Skelton. "That's really all there is to it. In a full day of fishing tailraces, you'll make hundreds of casts to the same place, but you never know when fish will move into the area."

• **Clues To Observe** — You may not know exactly when fish move in, but you can look for clues that tell you fish might be present. Watch for baitfish activity, diving gulls and surfacing gar. Each is a positive signal that larger game fish may be nearby.

"Baitfish activity is really important," notes Skelton, "because when minnows are jumping, it's an indication fish are active and moving, and sooner or later larger fish will come in after them. Diving and circling gulls often mean baitfish are moving, even if you can't see them, but stationary birds frequently indicate they're waiting just like you are. Active garfish also means bait is in the area."

Like many tailrace anglers, Skelton prefers to fish when water actually is being released through a dam, and he generally notices an increase in activity anytime water suddenly rises.

In a way, this changing water acts like a tide change in the ocean. Baitfish get washed around and away from their hideouts as the current strengthens, while at the same time increased water depth offers added security for larger predators, and allows them to move upstream out of their own deeper holes.

• **Currents Will Change** — Again, Skelton cautions, not all the water below a tailrace will be productive, even when the current is moving swiftly. Current patterns — and thus, bait movement — will be influenced strongly by where water actually comes through a dam. At electric power-producing facilities that may have half a dozen generators, only one or two may be in use at a time, depending upon demand. Water from them will position bait one way, while current from another generator or combination of generators can position baitfish in a totally different location.

"It's important to watch for changes like this," Skelton notes, "because they can occur anytime. Whistles from the dam aren't always used to signal fishermen, either. I watch the fishermen around me. If my place isn't producing, but someone on the other side is hauling them in, then I think about moving to a new spot."

Reading the water in a tailrace so you can cast to potential hot spots is something that comes only with repeated experience in the same tailrace at different water levels, says Skelton. "You generally can see the edge of the fastest water," he explains, "but something to look for are smooth, slick areas on the surface in that fast water. They indicate rocks down below, and what you want to do is cast so your lure bounces beside them.

"Only trial-and-error casting will show you how big the rocks really are because you'll get snagged if you're not careful, but these are the places big fish use. I think a lot of tailrace fish tend to move in schools, because I have found rocks like this and have caught a dozen fish in a dozen casts from them, and seen other fishermen do the same thing."

• **Use Quick-Release Anchor** — Because many of the fish in tailraces are big, one thing Jim Skelton recommends all anglers use is a quick-release anchor that has a float attached on the line. A heavy hybrid or striper can strip 50 yards of line

In tailrace fishing, water currents generally position the baitfish, so study the currents carefully to help decide where to anchor. Most anglers anchor in calmer water where they can cast to faster-moving water. Photo: Steve Price

off a reel long before an angler has the fish under control, and, with both current and sometimes crowded water conditions, the only practical way to fight a fish is by drifting downstream with it. For this, some type of fast-release anchor assembly is needed, and because there is rarely time to bring up the anchor, a float is used to mark its location so it can be used again.

A favorite release hook is one similar to those used on trailer winches to hook the bow of a boat, and floats can range from empty gallon milk jugs to old propane bottles. Practically anything that won't be pulled under by the current can be used.

Quick-release anchors also serve another purpose, which is to get a boat out of trouble if water rises suddenly. In many tailraces, drift fishing is not feasible due to the large number of rocks or other boats, so anchoring is a common practice. An expected rise in water will produce a wave that easily can sink an anchored boat, but a quick-release anchor at least allows the craft a chance to get out of danger.

Another safety precaution Skelton recommends is wearing a life preserver, even if you're an expert swimmer. If you fish within 800 feet of a dam, it's an Alabama law anyway, and also may be in your own state. A few life preservers are finally being designed by fishermen for fishermen.

Tailrace fishing normally peaks in spring and again in autumn, although big fish can come anytime. Spring is best for hybrids and stripers, because they migrate upstream to try to spawn, and congregate in large numbers below the dams. In fall, the cooling temperatures again bring fish upstream from open water into the tailraces.

Regardless of whether you try tailrace fishing in spring or fall, try some of Jim Skelton's pointers. He's proved they work for him, and they'll work for you, too.

— MARCH 1984

BASS ON THE RISE

By WILLIAM BOOK

*When the lake level is rising, the savvy
BASSer beats the banks . . .*

On the Ozark lakes I fish, the deep, clear nature of the water forces Bassmasters to fish deep, hidden structures most of the year. Much has been written about the supposed joys of crawling plastic worms through 40 feet of water, and if you are planning a visit to a hill-country reservoir like Table Rock, Bull Shoals, Norfolk, or many others along the Arkansas-Missouri border, you'd better bring plenty of lead.

But, occasionally, relief is offered from this s-l-o-w, often tedious angling. In spring, summer and fall, Mother Nature sometimes provides gully-washing thunderstorms that send torrents of dirty, debris-filled rainwater swirling down creeks and hollows to pour into the gin-clear lakes. Bass are drawn almost magically to the backs of coves where the water is stained, and to where it is rising rapidly into the grass and brush above power pool level. For the savvy Bassmaster this concentration of shallow, aggressive bass is the key to beating the deep-water blues.

I call it "fishin' the rise," and there are two lake conditions that come under the heading:

• When localized runoff is not so much bringing the lake up as it is staining the water and washing food and debris into the lake.

• When the lake is rising rapidly, flooding previously dry shoreline.

I learned about the first condition as a youngster. My father and I spent two humid June days trolling Bombers and sliding purple worms through the slime-slickened cedar trees of Table Rock. Bass were scarce, and small. We returned to our cabin the second night of the summer sojourn frustrated and ready to quit.

During the night the humidity became unbearable, making sleep in the hut, which lacked air conditioning, impossible. Finally a breeze blew in, peals of thunder echoed off the bluffs, and a torrential downpour swept across the lake in a blitzkrieg of water. By daylight the storm had vanished, but the water in the narrow cove where our boat lay moored had turned perceptibly murky, and had risen several inches up the bank. A raft of shocks, leaves, and other debris had amassed at the back of the cove, washed into the lake by the freshet that was still splashing down the hollow above us. Dad was the first to notice the swirl in the midst of the floating garbage.

"See that?" he exclaimed, pointing. "There's a big carp swimming in that mess."

Not seriously expecting anything, he tied a white single-spin to his pet casting outfit, stepped onto the dock, and made a short cast to the spot where he'd seen the swirl. The lure fell at the water's edge, Dad lifted with the rod, and the spinner blade began to pulse just beneath the trash on the surface. A second swirl appeared, the spinnerbait twitched sharply to one side, Dad set the hook, and the first decent fish we'd seen on our trip climbed from the water like Roland Martin going after prize money.

We spent the next 12 hours pitching spinnerbaits and topwater plugs into the backs of similar coves. We ended the day with the nicest limit of bass we've ever taken from Table Rock. And we learned a lesson applicable to virtually any bass water anywhere: When the water is rising, beat the banks.

Rising waters inundating previously dry shorelines often spell feeding time for big bass.

Photo: Gerald Crawford

• **When Bass Turn On** — The second condition that draws bass to the shallows is found when a lake is rising rapidly, flooding previously dry shoreline, even though there may not be any runoff in the immediate vicinity. Such a condition may be caused by upstream dams, or by failure to release water from the lake you are fishing. Let me give an example:

Truman Reservoir in Missouri is gaining a nationwide reputation for its exploding population of largemouth bass. Truman is chock-full of cover, an inland sea of flooded trees. Bassmasters from local and Kansas City bass clubs fish it daily, and are becoming intimately familiar with its snaggy confines. Many will tell you that the best bass fishing on Truman comes when heavy rains in the Osage Valley above the lake cause the impoundment to escape its conservation pool boundaries.

The headwaters of the lake become quite muddy, and virtually unfishable. But in the main portion of the reservoir, in the general area where the major arms join near the dam, the swiftly rising water stays relatively clear. Anglers in the know grab the first buzzbait they can lay hands on, and make a beeline for one of Truman's many grassy flats. As the lake rises, inundating the previously dry, overgrown shorelines along these flats, big bass swarm over these spots like carp in a flooded rice field. They swim right into the thick stuff and feed ravenously.

The newly flooded areas are rich in potential food, and cover. Lunker bass that before may have been scattered along miles of shoreline suddenly congregate in the grass like gamblers at the Super Bowl. Bassmasters work the flats 'til their arms ache and make phenomenal catches.

This situation is not exclusive to Truman. Several farm

ponds near my Independence, Mo., home rest snugly in lush meadows. When warm rains cause the ponds to spill over into the meadows, bass are attracted to the edges. I remember an expedition my father and I took to Bull Shoals a few years back. The lake level was 14 feet over power pool and rising. Water that flooded onto flats choked with heavy June vegetation brought with it countless hungry largemouths, and even a few walleye.

We motored slowly along the deep edge of the flats, casting Storm's Thin Fins into just a couple feet of water over green grass and around willow trees. Bass roamed over the grass, and walleye lurked in the willows. The lesson is still the same: When the water is rising, beat the banks.

• **Where The Bass Prowl** — Informed Bassmasters are aware of the importance of deep water to bass movements, a principle which must be remembered when "fishing the rise." Whether you are searching for runoff in the backs of coves, or for a bass-loaded flat on the main lake, keep in mind the most productive spots will be those with either immediate access to deep water, with a clearly defined route to deep water, or with a clearly defined route to deep water nearby. Careful study of a topographic map should allow you to detemine if an area has bassin' potential.

Does the grass flat extend over a considerable distance, with a shallow, undistinguished slope toward a river channel half a mile away? If so, the extreme distance from deep water probably means fishing it is a waste of time.

If the flat is 100 yards across, with a sharp break into 40 feet or greater depths, it may be a bass feedlot. The same idea applies to the search for shallow bass in dirty coves. Concentrate your efforts in portions of the lake where either the coves enter directly into the main lake channel, or where a definite structure exists that extends from deep water into the back of the cove and acts as a migration route. High water doesn't alter the basic requirement of nearby security.

During rising-water conditions of either type, bass move to the banks for one big reason — to scavenge up a meal. They are feeding and aggressive. This makes even the wariest of hawgs incredibly vulnerable.

• **Lures To Consider** — When making your lure selection, keep in mind that the bass are looking up, watching for the telltale surface commotion that indicates a struggling critter frantically out of its own element. This generally calls for surface lures, the noisier the better. Buzzbaits and single-spins are excellent choices, as they both make a racket and both retrieve through grass and debris with a minimum of hangups.

Tandem-bladed spinnerbaits are my first pick. I've found I just can't beat the versatility of the spinnerbait. I can "V" it over heavy grass, crank it thrumming beneath a raft of flotsam, and slide it easily through the maze of branches of newly submerged cedar trees. The spinnerbait is a universal lure that calls bass the way a smorgasbord calls overweight eaters.

Buzzbaits, like the Lunker Buzz, run a close second. They are *the* preferred lure on Truman when fishing flooded grass flats. While not as versatile as a single-spin, the buzzbait makes up for this by producing an irresistible noise when sped across the surface. And when used in discolored water, this noise and sputter allows bass to home in on them with deadly accuracy.

Color choice for spinnerbaits and buzzbaits depends on water clarity and light conditions. If the water is clear, as it generally is at the dam end of a lake, white is my favorite. If the water is murky, I go with a more visible color like chartreuse. Black-and-yellow is effective on overcast days, as is black-and-white.

• **Add A Stinger Hook** — When fishing spinnerbaits and buzzbaits over drowned grass or weeds, I always use a trailer hook. The trailer runs little risk of hanging up in the grass, and pays off with an increased hooking percentage. I've landed some awfully nice fish that were hooked only on the trailer. When I'm dragging spinnerbaits through accumulated debris that has washed into the lake, I remove the trailer hook. It takes too darn much time to keep cleaning sticks and leaves off the extra point.

It must sound like spinnerbaits and buzzbaits are the only lures to use when fishing the rise. That isn't true. Surface plugs are potent, especially ruckus-raisers like the Zara Spook. Walking a Zara over submerged grass and through the back ends of freshly dirtied coves draws explosive, heart-stopping strikes. For years, on lakes like Table Rock and Lake of the Ozarks, Bassmasters have relied on the Spook when rains bring the bass to the banks.

At other times, surface lures may be ignored altogether in favor of crankbaits. Several years ago I fished Pomme de Terre Reservoir in south-central Missouri. Three days of warm April rains had brought the lake up 3 feet, and muddied the water considerably. Clay banks along the water's edge that had been high and dry all winter now were partially submerged, and crawdads by the thousands emerged groggily from their winter sleep. Casting brown crankbaits right up against the clay banks and retrieving them like crazy, I saw more large bass taken from the Pomme that day than I have in all the time since. It was murder! And it once more illustrates my point! When the water is rising, you've gotta beat the banks.

Fishing the rise offers Bassmasters some of the most exciting angling many of our lakes have to offer. The combination of cover and abundant food creates for many impoundments the largest concentrations of shallow bass outside of the spawn. Their aggressive state provides an optimum opportunity to make a fine catch. And the techniques employed are just plain fun. The next time you encounter these conditions, be ready.

— APRIL 1983

Photo: Dave Precht

Photo: Dave Precht

Photo: Gerald Crawford

Photo: Fishsport

Photo: Gerald Crawford

CHAPTER SIX

SEASONAL
SECRETS

*B*ass fishing is a four-season
sport and the rules that govern
it change through the year.

COLD-WATER BASSIN'

By CHUCK OLSON

You can extend your bassin' to a year-round sport,
if you know where to find fish in
cold weather . . .

BASSers who live in warmer climates are spoiled. When the water temperature goes much below 50 degrees, many of them quit fishing until the first good weekend of spring.

For anglers north of the Mason-Dixon Line, where I live, ignoring bass fishing when the water is less than 50 degrees means foregoing as much as six months of potentially prime bassin'.

True, you can't expect quite the amount of action in December as in May, but you certainly can catch bass.

They may get sluggish as lakes approach the freezing mark, but bass don't quit feeding altogether. There are plenty of knowledgeable bass fishermen who would wager their boats that bass can be caught in water even as cold as 35 degrees. I am one of those deranged northern anglers who regularly participates in that odd ritual known as ice fishing — and I have caught hundreds of largemouth and smallmouth bass. If bass can be caught regularly in 35-degree water, it is reasonable, then, to assume that they also can be fooled into striking when the water is 40 degrees.

To be successful at nabbing cold-water bass, you must have a basic understanding of bass behavior and some knowledge of the body of water you plan to fish. You also must possess the determination and patience to concentrate on fishing despite harsh weather.

It's been thoroughly discussed that bass are cold-blooded creatures, which means that their body temperatures match that of the water. Simply stated, their bodily functions slow down as the temperature declines. Naturally, a lethargic bass isn't going to burn up much energy and therefore isn't going to need to eat very much.

But the important thing to remember is that bass in cold water do eat. When and where they eat are the keys to catching them.

Finding their hiding and feeding spots is especially critical in cold water. More so than during any other season, bassin' "blind" during the winter surely will lead to empty livewells. A good topographical map and depthfinding equipment are musts.

When the water drops below 50 degrees, the great majority of bass abandon shallow water and the visible shoreline structure that offer shallow-water anglers casting targets. The fish move down points to deeper water and slip into submerged creek channels.

To find these hot spots, you'll need to rely on maps and sonar.

Choosing which electronic aids to use is governed mostly by your budget. Chart recorders are the most expensive and the most helpful in "reading" the bottom. The new LCD recorders promise to be almost as revealing, and they are much more affordable. Traditional flashers are the least expensive, but they don't provide a "picture" of structure and fish as the recorders do.

Whatever depthfinder you can afford, its value is enhanced tremendously when used in conjunction with accurate, up-to-date topo or navigational maps. You also must know how to use the maps. An underwater hump could look like an old pond unless you understand contours. Have a knowledgeable person show you how to read these maps or pick up one of those handy how-to booklets offered by the U.S. Geologic Survey, Army Corps of Engineers, or other

agencies that produce the maps.

Next, you'll need to figure out where bass likely are to be at various water temperatures.

Using months as guides for identifying bass patterns is about as useful as tying on a buzzbait for ice fishing. February bassin' in North Carolina could involve hunting prespawn or even spawning fish, while in Minnesota, February is a time for resharpening ice augers.

The real key to patterning winter bass is water temperature. Furthermore, the most accurate guide is average subsurface-water temperature.

An example of this point is a phenomenon that occurs in late winter and early spring. In well-protected, south-facing coves, the sun's rays may drive the surface temperature in the back of the cove above 50 degrees. However, the average subsurface temperature of the rest of the cove might still be in the low 40s. If you determined your fishing pattern solely according to the surface-water temperature — and many BASSers do — you'd expect to find aggressive fish in less than 3 feet of water. In reality, few bass will have climbed out of deep water and into the shallows, and they definitely won't be aggressive.

To avoid being fooled by the surface temperature, get an inexpensive temperature probe that can be lowered on a 10- or 15-foot cord. With it you can determine the water temperature at various depths and quickly compute the average subsurface temperature.

With a little practice, you'll soon be able to draw a mental map of the temperature zones of the area you're fishing and, in conjunction with your depthfinder and structure map, you'll be able to guess where to fish and you'll know precisely which lures to use.

Lure selection is easy. Experience has shown that basically four lures/baits consistently will catch cold-water bass: jigging spoons, spinnerbaits, the jig and pig, and live bait such as chub minnows. On rare occasions bass may be caught on other offerings, but for the greatest chances of success, stick to these four.

The question of which bait to use, and when, depends upon several factors, including the average subsurface-water

A weedless jig and pig often will coax wintertime bass into striking, but concentration and persistence are the real keys to finding — and catching — cold-water bass.

Photo: Ron Wright

temperature, the structure being fished, the aggressiveness of the bass, the weather conditions and, finally, your confidence in the bait. In general, though, these "rules of thumb" are valid.

When the water is less than 40 degrees, or whenever you're unsure of which lure to use, go with live bait. In thick cover, use a weedless, 5/8-ounce jig and pig. Around bluffs or points, the jigging spoon works best. And for fishing relatively shallow water, spinnerbaits are perhaps the most versatile baits you can use, especially for covering a lot of territory quickly.

Those are only guidelines, however, and you'll be wise to experiment if bass aren't swarming to what you're using.

The old saying, "The only thing predictable about a bass is that it is unpredictable" always should come to mind when any guide to bass fishing is laid out. It is with that caution that the following key to water temperature and its effects on bass behavior is presented.

• **COOL: 45-50 degrees.** The shorter days, lower angle of the sun and the arrival of the first Canadian cold fronts all combine to push the water temperature below the "magical" 50-degree mark. The few degrees of temperature the water gains during the daytime are usually more than offset by the loss that occurs when the cold night air literally sucks the warmth from the water.

At the other end of winter, the sun's rays begin to strengthen, the cold fronts become weaker and the water begins to warm up. As different as these environmental changes are, the bass' behavioral responses are relatively similar, so similar that in 45- to 50-degree water — regardless of the season — bass will behave in the same, predictable way. In general, the majority of the bass in a single body of water will exhibit one of two behaviors: staging or feeding.

The main difference between staging and feeding fish is, again, water temperature. When the water temperature is at the low end of this range (45-46 degrees) or when it is falling from the upper 40s, bass will most likely be in the staging mode. Conversely, when the water temperature is at the upper end of this range (49-50 degrees) or when it is warming into the upper 50s, bass ought to be in the feeding mode.

The best analogy I've heard is, "staging means they're ordering from the menu; feeding means they've dug in."

The first place to start looking for bass in the staging mode is on "the breaks." First, find what looks like prime

Cold-water bass fishing offers more of a psychological obstacle than a physical one to most BASSers. Because we don't experience action the few times we fish in cold water, we psych ourselves out of pursuing it.

spawning territory — that is, a south-facing cove with a good gravel and mud bottom and protected from the wind. Next, find the nearest deep-water sanctuary and draw a line connecting the two. The break or drop-off that occurs on that line is the best place to try for staging bass. More times than not, you'll find the bass on the deep side of the break, usually in water more than 15 feet deep.

It's even easier to find bass in the feeding mode. Start with the locator system you used for finding staging bass and then just slowly and thoroughly work shallower water. You even may find that the bass just have changed position by about a foot or two in water depth. Always keep in mind that this is not the season of plenty when it comes to forage. There won't be much food in the water and that which is there, primarily minnows, more likely will be limited to deeper water also.

• **COLD: 40-45 degrees.** This range represents the coldest that most lakes will get in most of the Southern states, but it may persist at that level for much of the winter. Therefore, skills for fishing these waters can come into use for a relatively major part of the year. The farther north you go, the shorter the time span that the water temperature is in this range.

In my home state of Ohio, for example, the water temperature drops into the low 40s relatively early in winter, around the first week of November, and it gets even colder by the end of the month.

With water temperature in this range, bass definitely exhibit what most of us call "turned-off" behavior. It doesn't matter much whether the water temperature is 40 or 45 degrees, the bass behave the same way — lethargic.

The fish will be deep, and they will have to be coaxed into biting. Savvy anglers can use this situation to their advantage by realizing that these two conditions make fishing easier by greatly reducing the choice of locations and lures. You can immediately eliminate 75 percent of the lake you're fishing — and you need only bring along a handful of tackle.

To find the 25 percent of the lake worth fishing, go back to your locator system of drawing lines between good spawning areas and the adjacent deep water. This deep water is the place to start hunting. Then use a depthfinder to pinpoint brushpiles or stumps along these creek channels and/or schools of baitfish. Remember that the bass still will feed occasionally, and they won't want to go far to chase prey.

Finding these cold-water bass is the easy part. Coaxing

them into striking is what sets the best BASSers apart from the rest.

Remember that the bass' metabolism is slowed down substantially — but it's still running. Don't expect any bursts of energy from these fish. Just plan on being in the neighborhood when they get into the mood to feed.

I rely on the peak-activity times identified in the solunar tables to tell me when to be fishing the best spots.

When they do feed, I figure that it's most likely to be on a small jig and pig or, if that fails, a live chub.

• **SUPER-COLD: Less than 40 degrees.** In many respects this water temperature range signals a good time not to go bass fishing. The water is too cold to launch the boat in, and too warm to go ice fishing. Unfortunately, in many northern states there is a long period of time when the water stays in the upper 30s and before it freezes.

In reality, bass behave basically the same in 35-degree water as they do in 45-degree water. Whether the temperature is a few notches above or below 40 degrees, the same strategies and lures should work.

There is a direct relationship between the average subsurface temperature and the air temperature. It's usually colder on top of the water. And since humans aren't cold-blooded, they've got to prepare for adverse winter weather.

Dressing warmly and wisely is important, if you're to be an efficient, successful BASSer.

No one should venture out for winter bassin' without the proper clothes and accessories. A snowmobile suit, wool socks, gloves, and a warm hat are essential. A vacuum bottle filled with a hot drink will help, too.

Also, winter anglers should be able to recognize the early signs of hypothermia — the dangerous lowering of body temperatures — and know how to treat it. Boating mishaps during this time are life-threatening.

Nobody has to convince Lonnie Stanley that jigs will catch bass when water temperatures dip.   Photo: Gerald Crawford

Even prepared for the cold, I've found, it's difficult to keep your mind on fishing. I recall suffering through a December snowstorm in the middle of windswept Dale Hollow Lake, where I was hunting for one of those legendary, huge smallmouths. I couldn't decide which was worse: the bone-chilling ride down the lake, the frozen rod tip, the blinding snow, or the fact that neither my partner nor I had had a strike all day.

Just when I had narrowed it down to either the snow or the frozen tip, my 1/8-ounce jig was pounded by a big fish. My hookset was several seconds late.

That was a hard, painful lesson on cold-water bassin' — the importance of mental discipline. Every B.A.S.S. member knows well that along with confidence, concentration is one of the most essential ingredients for successful bassin'. But it's hard to concentrate when your fingers are numb and your feet are cold.

Cold-water bass fishing offers more of a psychological obstacle than a physical one to most BASSers. Because we don't experience hot-and-heavy action the few times that we fish in really cold water, we psych ourselves out of pursuing it seriously.

But by putting in a little more preparation time and stepping up our level of patience, bass anglers everywhere can make their bass fishing season last a full 12 months, the way it should.

— JANUARY 1986

MIDSUMMER BASSIN' TACTICS

BY JAMES A. BRANG

Bass are like people, only wetter.
When the sun bears down, look for fish
in the shade . . .

The scorching days of midsummer are a time known for the "doldrums of bass fishing." Ol' Bigmouth lies dormant, inactive in the depths during the day, only invading the cooler shallows to feed at night. Right? Wrong! That's ridiculous, a hundred times incorrect. The bass are active at night, all right, and often in or near shallow water, but daytime, midsummer bassin' can be just as terrific. Allow me to explain:

After years of chasing bass all over the country, both day and night, oftentimes catching them in shallow, 80-degree-plus water during the hottest part of the day, I'm positive it's not so much the heat that bothers Mr. Bass as the direct rays of the bright sun.

If you have any doubts, let's think about it for a minute. Although the air temperature does change substantially from midday to night during summer, the water temperature remains almost constant. I have checked it dozens of times, and under normal conditions, have never found the water temperature to change more than a degree or two at most. Definitely not enough to influence bass activity. In small ponds, following severe cold fronts, there was a more distinct change — but, oddly enough, these were times when night fishing was the worst.

During the hot, dry periods of late-June, July, and August, water clarity is frequently the clearest of the year; the weather the calmest and the sun almost directly overhead. These conditions allow more sunlight to penetrate into deeper, open water than at any other season. It is my belief that bass will search for areas then that contain some type of shield and protection from the sun.

Where To Look For Bass — Numerous types of structure, cover, weather and water conditions influence where bass will be in midsummer. Areas containing heavy, thick surface cover are excellent and easy to locate. Old ramshackle duck blinds, logjams, brushpiles, beds of hyacinths, lily pads or other types of thick, almost solid cover or vegetation with some space or open water beneath are prime summer bassin' spots. And the closer to deep water these areas are located, the better the odds of finding abundant and larger bass. On the other hand, where certain types of thick moss grow from the surface to the bottom — with no openings — you will encounter few, if any bass.

Summer bass also are attracted to "vertical structure" such as standing trees, underwater ledges, sunken islands, the edges of tall weedbeds, shoreline bluffs and overhanging trees. The key is one word — shade. Fish frequently move completely around an obstacle or section of cover as the sun moves from east to west during the course of the day. Along creeks or ledges, bass may switch from one bank to another, or move a short distance up or down a creek to find a bend or submerged cover that provides shade.

In open bathtub-type lakes with little structure or cover bass will retreat to the deeper sections. Even clear water filters out some sunlight as the depth increases. And even crystal-clear lakes and pits have deep-water silt lines where there is a band of cloudy water. (See "Dirty Tricks To Catch Bass," January 1981 BASSMASTER.)

Wind and rough surface water help block out some sunlight, too. Even when the water is clear, the waves and chop break up the surface, which prevents a portion of the sunlight from penetrating to the depths. In summer, windy weather can be a BASSer's best friend. Many times fish gather along windswept shorelines, especially where silt is stirred up along a clay or mud shoreline or bottom, to mix in with the surrounding water, which provides a "sun shield."

Overcast conditions that accompany weather fronts frequently offer some of the best opportunities for summertime bass angling. The darker and more threatening the weather, the better it is for fishing. Consider staying on the lake when it begins to rain — unless there is lightning, strong winds, or obviously unsafe conditions. In addition to bringing insects and food into the water and a fresh supply of oxygen, heavy rain-

On bright summer days, bass stay close to cover that provides plenty of shade.

Photo: Gerald Crawford

drops break up the surface even more than a strong wind.

In summer, dirty water and plankton blooms are other conditions to seek. Silt particles or microscopic plant and animal life can cloud the water to hinder light penetration.

If a river or current flows through your fishing lake, this is always a prime location to do some daytime, midsummer prospecting for bass. Such currents usually carry stained water, and even if not, the current itself breaks up the water and creates a barrier that helps block out some sunlight. Too, in warm water, a current is as refreshing to fish as a gentle breeze to anglers on a sweltering day.

Shallow-Water Tactics — Since shallow-water cover is easier to locate than many deep, invisible hot spots, and shallow-water fish are frequently active fish, begin by probing shallow sections if suitable cover is available. Rule of thumb: the brighter the day, the thicker the cover needed. If you have an option, always select an area with the wind blowing into or through the vegetation or cover. Seldom consider any cover to be too thick at this season. Even if the cover is so thick you cannot see the water, or get a lure into it, bass will occupy such areas — if they can get under it.

One method to check out such heavy vegetation for the possible presence of bass is to drift or pole your way into an area and observe the stems of underwater weeds. If they are covered with an abundance of scum or algae, do not waste too much time in the spot. If they are clean, it usually indicates an abundance of baitfish; baitfish eat this algae from the weeds. Then, your chances of locating bass are good. Surface scum and algae is a different situation; bass love to hide

beneath it, especially when it is matted together solidly like a carpet or putting green on a golf course.

And always be aware of fish movement on the weeds, sometimes noticeable only by shaking lily pads or reeds. With more than one type of weed growing in an area, look for sections where the different varieties meet, such as where lily pads and reeds merge. Here there is usually a change in the bottom composition. Any other type of cover or structure located in the weeds, whether visible above the surface or not, makes an area even better. Ditches, stumps, duck blinds, submerged brush and bushes are a few examples of potential hot spots for bass.

If the wind is blowing, such as through weeds that extend above the surface, always fish into the wind. With the breeze in your face, the weeds are bent toward you; this enables your line and lure to slide over and through the vegetation. Avoid casting across or against the "grain."

Due to numerous and ever-changing weather patterns, barometric pressure and moods of the bass, always attempt to establish a pattern within the weeds. Just because bass are in the vegetation does not mean they're everywhere in the thick stuff. At different times, the bass may be near tiny openings back in the weeds, under the thickest "cabbage" available, in the thin grass along the inside or outside edges, along the points of the weedbeds, or elsewhere.

In fishing over the thick cover a slow, steady retrieve is easier for bass to "track" or follow. Where it is impossible for fish to actually see the lure riding above the surface over weeds, bass actually can follow the movement the line and

■

lure cause in the weeds. Then, when the bait enters a small opening, bass frequently explode after it. Old-timers call the openings a bass' "picture window." In areas that contain heavy floating scum and algae, large bass will keep such spots open by periodic tail-fanning. Cast 10 or 15 feet beyond the opening and directly over the middle.

Retrieve the lure so it swims or crawls through the opening, and you're almost assured of an arm-jerking, heart-stopping strike.

When crawling lures over a vegetation-cluttered surface, explosive strikes often scatter weeds, water and bass in different directions, without your even hooking the fish. Other times, short-strikers hit behind the lure. Bass miss the lure because of poor visibility in the thick gunk. In many instances, they depend on sound, vibrations and movement more than sight.

Try to keep your cool when a lunker tears the cove apart and still misses the lure. Continued casting, and slightly slower retrieves, where possible, usually produce one or more additional strikes in the same spot. But even if you cannot raise the bass immediately, chances are you will do so later. Allow the area to rest. Then, return and try again. If your efforts still do not persuade the bass to attack, mark the exact same spot and return the next day or later. Once a large bass has taken up residence in an area containing abundant and suitable cover, the fish is not likely to move or surrender it to another smaller bass.

Deep-Water Techniques — If your waters do not contain dense, shallow-water cover, but feature sunken islands, deep, winding creeks or river channels, submerged forests and the like, you're still in luck. There definitely is no need to sit beside the air-conditioner. The trick is to change fishing locations and position your lures in areas shaded from the sun. In the morning, most bass are behind the east creek banks or on the west side of vertical structure. During afternoon hours, they reverse their positions. During midday hours, they may be on the north side of the structure, beneath dense brush, other underwater cover or in water too deep for bright light to penetrate. In standing timber, search around the bases of the largest trees.

One summer hot spot I found was a stump-covered sunken island near the mouth of Mammoth Furnace Creek in Barkley Lake, Ky.. The top of the hump was 10 feet below the surface with the surrounding depths dropping into 35 feet of water. During some of the hottest weather, I've never failed to catch a bunch of bragging-size bass. The pattern is as dependable as my pocketwatch. At daybreak or dusk, the bass are on top of the mound in and around the stumps and roots. When the sun is shining, the bass always bunch up along the shady side. And the higher overhead Ol' Sol is positioned, the deeper the fish descend. During the midday hours, the fish usually are on the deep, north side in submerged brush.

Many creek channels and similar structure provide basi-

cally the same conditions for bass. Once you find such a deep-water hot spot, it usually remains productive all summer. This is one season when there is seldom major fish movement for long distances, as during spring and fall. Fish usually are congregated tightly in these choice, deep areas, and even when not actively feeding, will take a lure just to prevent another bass from getting it.

Silt Lines — In gin-clear lakes or other waters that have no shade-producing cover or structure, fish will descend into deeper water — how deep depends largely on the weather conditions, and the depth of the clear water. A water thermometer or light meter will pinpoint the thermocline and silt line, which usually are located in close proximity.

Even in ultraclear lakes, there will be a silt line but it may form in extremely deep water and frequently as deep as 40 feet or more beneath the surface. To BASSers unfamiliar with this deep-water hot spot, the silt line is merely the place where the clear upper layer of water meets a cloudy or dirty band of deeper water. On bright days, the fish are just beneath the mixing line where it intersects with permanent structure on the lake floor.

By locating areas of hard, clean bottom or whatever structure is available with the intersecting thermocline and silt line, you quickly can pinpoint the best spots in the lake. Bass use this silt line the same as they do a weedline, treeline or shoreline, even if the silt line is deep.

If you do not have a water-temperature gauge or light meter, but the lake contains some type of deep-growing moss or weeds, you can use this vegetation as an indicator as to where to begin. Weeds will grow as deep as the sunlight penetration. Begin fishing at the deepest edge of the weeds and gradually work deeper.

Weather Fronts — The weather patterns affect fish behavior throughout the year, but especially during hot, midsummer months. Always pay close attention to weather reports and approaching frontal systems through television forecasts and newspaper weather maps. Try to determine when the front will be approaching your area, and arrange to be on the lake at that time, if possible. When the barometer takes a sudden nosedive, and wind and black clouds begin rolling in, bass often go into a feeding frenzy.

Some systems zip through rapidly, and in a couple of hours everything is over and back to normal. If BASSers are not on the water at the right time, in a productive location, they likely will miss the action. Avoid long, time-consuming boat runs that can eat up the prime fishing time.

Some of the slower-moving systems have enormous bands of heavy clouds that may hover in an area. These are the weather systems for which I wait. When one approaches, you will find me on the lake from daylight until dark. I have taken days off from work to fish local waters when such conditions existed, and by doing so have enjoyed some of the best fishing of my life — even better than those long vacation trips to famous bass factories in different parts of the country.

On two trips to Lake Monroe, in Indiana, I fished slow-moving summer weather fronts that came through exactly one week apart and caught limits of bass that averaged over 6 pounds per fish. To this day, one boat-dock proprietor asks me how I always could hit a perfect day when "the fish were biting."

When fishing summer weather fronts, be extra cautious of wind and lighting, which can kill you. The most difficult thing for a BASSer to do is to leave a bunch of feeding bass, but for safety's sake, it is necessary, especially when your hot spot is located in open water.

This is one reason I attempt to locate several areas that attract fish close to shore or in protected coves with high banks. Since most summer

In deep water along bluffs, bass may move up and down in the water, depending on light penetration. Here, vertical fishing may be the answer.   Photo: Gerald Crawford

storms in my area approach from the west, the western shore is the logical area to search for such hot spots. Under storm-front conditions, the fish usually will be near the same structure and in the same vicinity as on bright days. The difference is they may be somewhat shallower and scattered over a wider area, rather than bunched up in a small, shaded area. For instance, they may be all over and around a sunken island and

on both sides of a winding creek channel, the same as at daybreak and dusk on a clear, hot day. Just because there are existing overcast storm conditions doesn't mean bass will move several miles up the lake or back into large coves to get to a certain shoreline or stump bed. If bass already are taking up summer residence near such areas, they may provide good fishing at such times. Always attempt to locate the "home" of summer bass, whether shallow or deep.

Once a front passes and the skies become even partly sunny, the action usually dwindles. At times, even partially overcast days — when the sun pops out and disappears, only to shine again in a few minutes — offer even poorer fishing conditions than bright, cloudless weather.

Whether fishing during hot summer days or on cooler nights (or at

any other time, for that matter) always try to be a thinking BASSer. Use logic and common sense in figuring out areas where you might locate some fish. Before long, you'll no longer dread the so-called "summer fishing doldrums." As a professional guide once said, "Fish are just like people, only wetter."

— JULY/AUGUST 1981

Fish into the wind when fishing weeds, because grass stems will be bent toward you and lure presentation will be better.   Photo: Gerald Crawford

TACTICS THAT WORK ON BIG SMALLMOUTHS IN SUMMER

By EARL SHELSBY

The first step in catching river bronzebacks is getting in position to cast where they are. In hot weather, big smallmouths move to the backs of the pools . . .

There are so many smallmouth bass in the Potomac River that the little ones get your lure before the big ones have a chance," I used to claim after catching more than 100 bass of 1 pound or smaller.

I wasted a lot of time (if you call catching bass wasting time) on those small-size fish before I learned a surefire summer technique for finding the big ones. The tactic was developed on the Potomac, but the technique will work on other good smallmouth rivers.

The reason I was not catching larger smallmouths was that I was so busy fishing that I didn't take time to think how to catch big fish. I didn't consider what makes up a good smallmouth river. I never thought about the stream structure. I never thought about the larger fish that were spawning all those little bass.

Smallmouth rivers are a series of pools (relatively deep holes) separated by riffles or falls, depending on how rapidly the water level drops toward sea level. These pools vary in size from a few hundred yards to a half-mile or more. The smaller bass will wander over these pools. Usually the larger fish will be confined to that section of the pool just upriver from the riffles or falls.

The first step in catching big smallmouths from streams is getting in position to cast to where they are. Most smallmouth rivers are clear in the summer. If you get too close, the bass will spook. A good rule is to position your boat where a comfortable cast will land right in front of the riffle.

Not anchoring or securing the boat is the reason anglers miss connecting on big smallmouths. Most anglers just float right through the best fishing water without casting. In most cases they are busy keeping the boat straight or they are moving so fast over the riffle they don't get proper action on lures.

Besides staying a cast upriver, you should be in position to fish in front of the riffle, where most of the water is going. It's a matter of reading the water. The riffle will form a "V," or more than likely a "U." The larger the V or U, the more volume of water going through it. The higher water flow means more bait flow, which increases the chances a lunker smallmouth will be there.

If you secure the boat in position, you can plunk the lure smack in the point of the V or the center of the bow in the U. If a lunker smallie is there and, of course, if it's in a feeding mood, the bass will strike on the first or second crank of the retrieve. Be ready!

What kind of a lure should you use for stream smallmouths? Swimmers, jigs, spinners, and surface lures in small sizes are the general rule.

In swimming plugs, the 4-inch Rapala is good. Gold has been a top color for me, but silver is popular. The fast-back Rebel plug is one of the most consistent lures on the Potomac. Black back with silver sides is the favorite color combination. Crank them very slowly upriver, and the current will add the action needed to entice a strike.

White or yellow jigs in the 1/4-ounce size have netted results for me. I pour my own leadheads, paint, and add the bucktail. Dan Gapen's Ugly Bugs, in the same colors, have produced also. I work jigs so they skip along the bottom in about 1-foot hops. It is just a matter of snapping the rod upward, taking up slack, and repeating.

In spinners, the No. 3 Mepps with silver blades and white

bucktail is my choice, but C. P. Swings and Rooster Tails are popular in other areas. I usually go to a spinner when the water is a little murky. If the water is muddy, I usually don't bother fishing for smallmouths. Spinners are fished just fast enough to keep from snagging on the bottom. Since I fish upstream, the current spins the blades and attracts the fish.

My favorite surface lures are Heddon's Tiny Torpedo and minisize Crazy Crawler. Since I only fish the surface when a mayfly hatch is coming off, I use white or silver lures. Fish the Tiny Torpedo in short jerks to activate the propeller, and work the Crazy Crawler in a steady retrieve so it makes a gurgling sound.

West Virginia's Cacapon River is another small-mouth river that has produced lunkers for the author.

Photo: Earl Shelsby

Old-timers quietly catch stringers of smallmouths like this to make us youngsters appreciate the wisdom they have gathered over years of fishing. Photo: Rick Taylor

The heavy worm rod with 20-pound-test line used for largemouth bass in reservoir fishing is too much tackle. Trying to fish lures that weigh a fraction of an ounce with this kind of tackle ceases to be fun. Besides, heavy line can be more easily seen by bass in clear smallmouth rivers.

Because most smallmouth rivers are a stairstep of pools separated by rocky shelves or riffles, today's modern bass boat is of little use. A shallow-draft johnboat or a canoe is much more practical. You must navigate through shallow riffles to reach the nest pool. A stout, 10-foot pole is a very useful accessory. It can be stuck in the bottom to hold the boat in perfect casting position. Likewise, you can push upriver against fast water where oars or electric motors are useless. Two mushroom anchors are also good gear for the smallmouth-river boat. They don't wedge in rocks like some other type of anchors do.

OK, you have secured the boat in position. You put your spinner lure at the edge of the riffle and catch a nice 5-pound smallmouth. What do you do next? Do you move downriver to the next pool? Not yet! Stay put because there are likely more smallmouths where you caught that one.

Many times a Potomac limit of five smallmouths has been taken from the same pool. My general rule is to fish the pool for 20 minutes after taking a fish, before moving. That gives the other lunkers, which may have been spooked in landing the first fish, a chance to settle down and get back to where you can catch them. Usually, you can expect to take a second fish within five minutes, if it is there.

You might be asking, "Is this a year-round scheme for taking smallmouths?" Unfortunately, the answer is no. This is a hot-weather technique. After the spring runoff is over, the river settles to its summer level and the hot sun begins to send the river temperature up, big smallmouths move to the backs of pools. Why?

There are two reasons. First, smallmouths like cool water.

Tackle is a matter of personal preference, but whether it is baitcasting, spinning, or spincasting, the general rule is don't go too heavy or too light. My choice is a medium-action rod with a Zebco Cardinal 4 reel loaded with 8-pound-test line. I would never recommend line of more than 10-pound-test because, remember, you are fishing clear rivers for smallmouths and stouter line may make them wary.

There was a time, I would not fish anything but ultralight tackle with 4-pound-test for smallmouths. I caught some 5- and 6-pounders on light tackle, but believe me, I just happened onto some fish that had run out of luck altogether. You need enough tackle to handle the fish rather than having the fish handle you. Remember, you are fishing right at the edge of riffles, and most of the big bass are going right down through the riffle if you don't have enough backbone in your tackle to stop them. That 5-pounder with fast water to help it is suddenly like a 10-pounder.

About 60 degrees is their favorite temperature. The slow-moving water, at the top of the pool, heats up the most. The water picks up speed in the back of the pool as it heads toward the riffle or falls. The faster water is closer to the preferred temperature for bass.

The second reason is that the back of the pool is like a funnel that brings food to the wise bass that has learned to rest and wait, while yearling bass run all around the pool looking for food.

After a normal spring (normal in the amount of rain and temperature), you can expect the bigger bass to show up in the backs of pools about the first week in July. They remain until the end of September. During mild falls, I have found bronzebacks in the Potomac as late as early November.

Working the back edges of pools is not a technique that is unique to the Potomac River. It has worked on every good smallmouth river I have fished in recent years. I have taken good-sized bass on my first visits to New Hampshire's Contoocook, West Virginia's Cacapon and Cheat rivers; Maine's upper Penobscot; Pennsylvania's Susquehanna; Virginia's James and Shenandoah; and Missouri's Meramec and Big Piney rivers.

When we talk about "catching 100 smallmouths in a day" on the Potomac, we are talking about those days when the conditions are right. The water is low, clear, and cool enough to have the smaller bass on the move. But 100 bass up to 13 inches long is not my bag. I like action as well as the next bass angler, but what really gives me a charge is to show up at the local watering hole and pull a lunker out of the livewell. There

is something about the curious looks that satisfies my warped ego. That's why I pass up the little bass and head right to the backs of the pools, just in front of the riffle.

While I get an extra kick out of catching bass on artificial lures, there are many veteran bassmen on the Potomac that catch more than their share of braggin'-size smallmouths on live bait. Minnows are very popular. Most old-timers trap the minnows right out of the river, and fish them about 18 inches below a bobber. Others fish the minnows on the bottom with enough lead pinched about a foot up the line to hold the bait down where fish will see it.

Hellgrammites and crawdads are what smallmouth bass like for dessert. They probably would be used more if they were available in bait stores. They can be caught in most streams that run into good smallmouth rivers. These should be fished on a No. 6 hook with just enough pinch-on lead to keep the line on the bottom.

The Potomac River divides Maryland, Virginia, and West Virginia. The entire river can be fished with a Maryland freshwater license. The section that borders Virginia can be fished with that state's freshwater license and the same is true of the West Virginia section. There is no closed season on the Potomac River.

We typewriter-totin' Bassmasters have a tendency to make all fishing sound too easy. There are times when smallmouths have had their fill or just are plain contrary, but you can bet that from July through October, the big ones are hanging in the backs of pools close to the riffles.

— *JULY/AUGUST 1975*

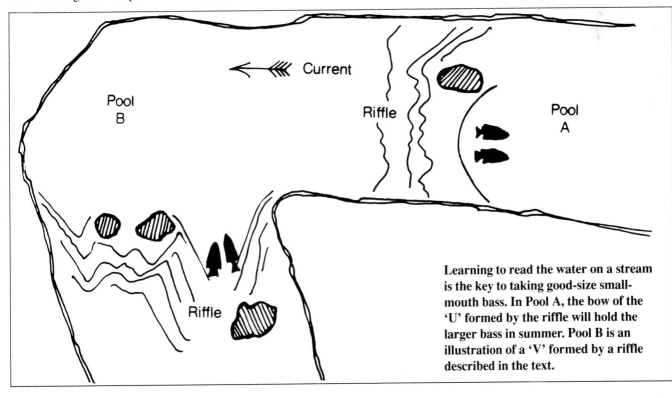

Learning to read the water on a stream is the key to taking good-size smallmouth bass. In Pool A, the bow of the 'U' formed by the riffle will hold the larger bass in summer. Pool B is an illustration of a 'V' formed by a riffle described in the text.

SUREFIRE TIPS FOR WINTER BASS

By MIKE PANE

Don't be cabin-bound by cold weather. A slow-and-easy approach with tailspinner or jigs can produce bass even on the most frigid days...

There are lots of reasons for not going fishing for largemouth bass in the winter. For openers, it's often abominably cold and uncomfortable. Also, it takes a pretty good basic knowledge of bass habits and structure fishing to find them. Then, it demands some highly specialized techniques that take plenty of practice to perfect in order to get the bass on the hook once you find them.

It definitely is not a pastime for the occasional fisherman who just wants to get outside for a while. However, there is one overpowering reason why Bassmasters should go bass fishing in the winter — you can catch a whale of a lot of good bass.

The main thing to keep in mind about winter bassin' is that, although the bass don't completely stop feeding when the water turns cold, they do slow down. The bass' metabolism slows down so far that they feed very little, but they do still feed. Also, bass can be caught even when they are not feeding by adjusting fishing methods to their slower metabolic rate. This is the real key to winter largemouth fishing. By using the right techniques in the right places, you can catch bass in the winter even when they are not feeding actively.

Where are these right places? Well, this is the hard part. I like to concentrate on medium to deep water where there is a well-defined vertical change in the bottom. Look for any spot where 10-15 feet of water drops steeply into 35-40 feet or even deeper. Use a depthfinder to locate places where a rocky bank rapidly drops into deep water. Such places especially are good if they contain some type of cover such as brush, stumps or rocks.

There are other kinds of places that will produce winter bass as well. I have caught bass in deep, sharp bends in creek channels, on underwater bridges and brushpiles in creek channels, on rock ledges near deep water, or over old road beds and even in water as shallow as 3 to 4 feet under very special conditions in cold weather.

I believe bass don't want to move far in the winter. Steep drop-offs let them move to feed or adjust to changing water conditions without having to move far or lose contact with the major structure. So fish deep, sharp drop-offs more than any other kind of structure.

Once you locate a drop-off that looks good, only half of the search is over. Now you have to search along the drop-off for the school. This can be a ticklish job, as you have to fish carefully to make sure you cover the entire area thoroughly at a pace suited to the fish's slow metabolism.

I use a depthfinder from the bow of my bass boat to follow the contour of the drop-off with the electric positioning motor. Move along this contour very slowly and cast into the deep water. Then work your lure up the drop-off until you locate the fish or run out of structure without catching a bass, turn around and repeat the process, except cast to the shallow water and let the lure fall off the drop. If you don't pick up a fish this way, look for another drop-off.

I have two proven lures that I use almost exclusively in the winter. Both produce equally well at times, and at other times, the bass show a definite preference for one or the other. By keeping two rods rigged up and alternately casting each of them, I can find out which works best.

The two lures are a black jig and pork-rind eel and a lead tailspinner, like the Little George. I prefer the 3/8-ounce jig

Adjust your fishing tactics to a S-L-O-W crawl, and fish the right places to catch cold-weather largemouths. Hunt for well-defined vertical changes in the bottom structure. Rapid drops are the key spots to fish .   Photo: Gerald Almy

and the Uncle Josh 4-inch, split-tail eel. The Little George selected is black in muddy water and chrome in clear water in the 1/2- or 3/4-ounce sizes. When the fish seem reluctant to hit, I go down in size to 1/4-ounce jigs and Georges. This often turns the trick.

This winter I plan to test the new Little George II. It has two blades instead of one, which makes it fall slower and the blades turn better at slow speed.

Many winter bass fishermen occasionally do well with safety-pin spinners (single-spins), using them the same as I do the jig and tailspinners. I believe I do better with my lure selection because winter bass seem to take the smaller lures more readily than the larger safety-pin spinners.

The way to work these lures is slow — the slower, the better. Remember, these bass have slowed down and they don't

want to chase a bait. They want it to fall or crawl right into their mouths. Cast out, let the lure settle on a tight line and simply reel it back right on the bottom or right against the side of the drop-off as slowly as you can turn the reel handle. I have to reel the Little Georges a little faster than the jig and eel to keep the blades turning over. Sometimes I'll add a little hop to the lure just to make it interesting.

Often bass are suspended somewhere along the drop-off between the top of the drop and the bottom, usually at about 15-25 feet. The bottom might be 60 feet down, but the fish rarely are that deep. Suspended bass hug the side of the drop-off, so the lure must be kept against the vertical side as it is retrieved slowly.

Detecting a hit is the hard part of this technique. Sometimes the bass inhales the lure as it falls on the cast. That is why you should let it fall on a tight line. The tight line enables you to maintain more sensitive contact with the lure on the fall than a slack line would. What you'll feel when a suspended largemouth takes the lure on the fall is a light "tick" or the lure will go weightless. Sometimes the lure will simply stop falling before it has had time to reach the bottom as the suspended bass takes it. Another indication of a hit is that the line will twitch or move ever so slightly to the side. Be a line watcher, and be alert.

If the lure reaches the bottom unmolested, let it rest for a few seconds, then give it a little hop. Sometimes a bass will follow the lure down and hover over it, waiting for the bait to move again before nailing it. Watch carefully, and if the line twitches as the lure settles back down, hit 'em hard!

If nothing happens, start your retrieve. Now you should expect a light tick or the lure will just stop dead if a fish takes it. This demands a good sense of feel of the lure. I've found that the new graphite rods help immeasurably for feeling this kind of hit.

That's why I never wear gloves when I fish for bass in the winter, no matter how cold it gets. The delicacy of the hits demands that you be able to keep as close contact with the lure as possible to feel those slight changes that mean a bass is doing something on the other end. Of course, I wear gloves when running or otherwise not fishing, but when you get down to the real nitty-gritty, just grit your teeth and fish barehanded.

Other than this special advice on gloves, I would recommend that you dress as if you were going on an Arctic expedition. Down or wool long johns; felt insulated rubber boots; thermal, hooded sweatshirts; face masks; insulated or wool hats; Fiberfill II or down jackets; rubber raingear to cut the wind; snowmobile suits; and insulated or down-filled jumpsuits are all welcome in my boat during winter. I've even been known to bring along a catalytic heater on very cold days. Otherwise, hot soup in a thermos usually will do a good job.

This brings up a point that is often overlooked by winter fishermen. Choose your boat partner with care. Be sure he knows that you intend to make a day of it. He should love fishing enough to put up with a bit of discomfort, and he should know enough about the outdoors to understand how to dress for cold weather. If your partner is miserable, it will ruin your day as well as his.

Now that you have some idea where to fish, what to fish with, how to fish, and how to beat the weather, you don't have any excuse for missing out on the winter bass bonanza. It might not look like good bass fishing weather when the leaves are on the ground and the boat deck is covered with frost, but when you locate that school of lunker largemouths, you'll change your mind in a hurry.

—JANUARY/FEBRUARY 1976

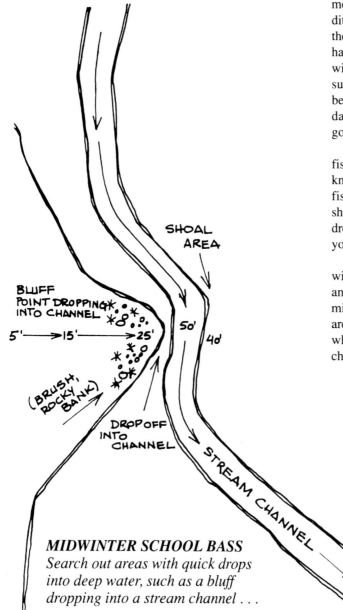

MIDWINTER SCHOOL BASS
Search out areas with quick drops into deep water, such as a bluff dropping into a stream channel . . .

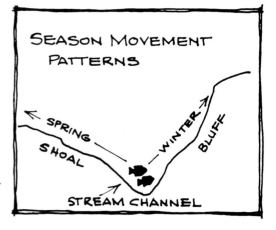

SEASON MOVEMENT PATTERNS

Some anglers never wear gloves, regardless of how low the temperature drops, so they can feel delicate strikes better.

Photo: Gerald Crawford

Photo: H. Lea Lawrence

Photo: Gerald Crawford

CHAPTER SEVEN

WHEN BASS ARE IN BETWEEN

*F*or those times when fish are nowhere to be found, here's where to find them.

Photo: Wade L. Bourne

SOLVING THE IN-BETWEEN BASS PUZZLE

By TOM STERLING

There are basic tactics for catching shallow- or deep-water bass, but even the pros fret about what to do with suspended fish . . .

Bassmasters in every corner of the country always can be certain of one factor regarding the whereabouts of their favorite quarry: the bass are either on top, on the bottom or somewhere in between. Most BASSers can catch ol' hawgjaw on top, and some regularly trick 'em down deep, but nearly everyone has trouble when the rascals are suspended in middepths.

"I'd rather fish for bass anywhere than when they're suspended," says Rick Clunn, two-time winner of the BASS Masters Classic® and a tough competitor anytime. "There are basic techniques for fishing shallow-water bass and also for deep-water bass, but I seldom feel really confident when I'm after suspended fish."

Why Bass Suspend

Bass suspend for a variety of reasons:
• The availability of oxygen is a critical factor.
• Water temperature is also important.
• The passage of weather fronts may make bass suspend.
• And, they often hover at midrange depths during major seasonal migration.
• Light penetration is another factor that may cause bass to suspend at virtually any time.

Bassmasters have been conditioned that fish don't like bright sunlight. So, bass go deeper to avoid it, as long as oxygen and temperature levels remain agreeable. Quite possibly the reason bass seem to suspend so often after a weather front is because fronts (especially in fall months) are often followed by a day or two of bright, sunny weather.

Oxygen content and water temperature can be related directly to the condition of the lake itself, and understanding that can help you understand why bass suspend. Depending on what part of the country you live in, a large impoundment can go through several distinct stages during the year. These include a summer stratification, fall "turnover" and a spring turnover.

In spring, surface waters begin to warm as air temperatures climb. Spring is normally a windy season, too, and these strong winds force the warmer surface water to circulate throughout a lake. And water temperatures become fairly constant in all portions of the lake. At this time the bass are active and fairly easy to catch.

But, as spring turns into summer, the winds normally die down — stopping natural circulation — and the lake surface becomes hotter. This warmer water is lighter than deeper water since it contains more oxygen. And, thus, a lake stratifies into two distinct regions. Bass usually do not remain for extended periods in the hot, oxygen-rich shallows, but they cannot stay in the cooler, oxygen-poor depths.

So, they suspend.

The warm upper-lake level and the cold lower region are separated by a transition zone known as the thermocline. Theoretically, every bass in the lake should be stuffed into this "intermediate" layer of water, where they seek out the proper "comfort zone" and temperature. Seemingly, all a Bassmaster would have to do is locate this layer with a thermometer — drop his lures into it — and catch a boatload of bass.

Such is not the case; although some thermoclines may

span 20 feet or more in depth, as a scuba-diving instructor I've found the span quite thin, where water temperatures dropped 20 to 30 degrees in less than 3 feet of actual depth change. Any bass swimming into that thermocline would probably bounce off it!

This condition may last until the lake turns over in the fall. This phenomenon is a reversal of the summer stratification process. Colder air temperatures chill the surface water, whereupon it sinks and mixes with the deeper waters until the overall lake temperature becomes uniform once more. The bass start moving into shallow water again and become more active. Thus, fall bass fishing is eagerly anticipated after summer's slowdown.

Try Shaded Structures

Fortunately, you don't have to spend your summer months searching for lake thermoclines and waiting for cooler weather. There are much easier ways to locate and catch summer bass. Keep in mind, as you do look for summer fish, that depth assumes major importance. Don't keep plugging shallow coves and shorelines after the sun gets hot. Bass seldom will stay in such places.

Try casting around floating piers, boathouses and bridge pilings. Spots like these offer shade, cover and often deep water very close to shallow water. Because most BASSers are oriented toward shallow water anyway, this "visible structure" offers a casting target that wide-open water does not provide.

Tom Anderton, one of Vicksburg, Mississippi's, top bass hunters who is known for his ability to outwit suspended largemouths, starts virtually every fishing trip working bridge pilings and floating piers when he believes bass are suspended.

"For some reason, bass remain relatively shallow when they're around structure like this," Anderton points out. "I seldom catch bass more than about 10 feet down, even though the water may be 40 feet deep below them."

Anderton is primarily a plastic-worm fisherman. And for suspended fish, he simply counts a weighted worm down a few feet, then with his rod tip high, retrieves it with slight but steady twitches. With light line (6- to 12-pound-test mono), an attentive BASSer can feel even the lightest hit by a bass.

Bass often suspend along flooded roadbeds, following them as migration paths between deep and shallow water. This angler is fishing a fencerow that parallels an old roadbed.

Photo: Steve Price

Rick Clunn, two-time winner of the BASS Masters Classic®, studies a depthfinder when searching for suspended bass. Graph recorders show locations of fish, but suspended bass can be difficult to detect. Be a line-watcher.

Photo: Steve Price

Bridge pilings also should spring into your bassin' mind if you're fishing in rough weather. On windy days, bass often suspend when the waves start rolling, maybe just to keep from getting tossed about themselves. Bridge pilings break up the wave action, as well as provide an angler shelter from the weather and a place to tie the boat.

Often, too, bass suspend for certain periods during major seasonal migration movements, particularly after spawning. Even on bass-loaded Toledo Bend this is true, and bass become tough to catch. Fortunately, this fishing frustration lasts only three to five weeks.

"When they're suspended, they're the spookiest bass I've ever seen," says Toledo guide Larry Nixon, the 1978 B.A.S.S. Champs winner, and a full-time guide on this 181,000-acre Texas/Louisiana-border impoundment. "They move out to water 25 to 40 feet deep and suspend between 10 and 17 feet down in underwater trees."

Bass Up A Tree

For most weekend bass chasers, this is an impossible puzzle to solve. However, Nixon seems to have solved at least part of the suspended-bass problem. The Bee Branch, Ark.,

native has found bass suspended on Toledo Bend in the exact same spots year after year. Here's how this BASSer, who fishes an average of 300 days each year, attacks the problem:

He prefers to cast a plastic worm into the treetops and twitch it through the branches. Bass take a lure on the drop, and normally engulf it lightly. If largemouth bass are suspended deeper, say 20 to 25 feet down, then Nixon switches to a 5/8-ounce jigging spoon and fishes it vertically. The veteran guide uses the same 12- to 17-pound-test mono he always fishes and doesn't modify his plastic worms or topo spoons. Nixon does use a 5/8-ounce slip sinker with the worm to enhance detection of the light strikes.

"I've found I cannot catch a lot of bass from the same tree, but I can catch a lot from the same area. My best results are very early each morning, too. Normally, my clients and I can have limits (15 bass each) by 8 a.m., but by then the action is pretty well over for the day," admits Nixon, who ranked eighth among the top bass fishing pros in 1978.

Another suspended spot to look for in-between bass is over the very same structure you fish when probing for bottom-hugging bass. This includes flooded roadways, bridges, treetops, submerged house foundations, and especially underwater points and creek channels. As Nixon has experienced, largemouth bass may suspend over the same structure year after year. So, if you fish the same reservoirs each season, keep a record of where and how you caught bass. A fishing diary could save a lot of time on your next trip.

Open-Minded Bass

One important key to finding suspended bass in more open water, is being able "to see fish" on a depthfinder. Unless you can afford to use a graph recorder — that readily shows fish on a printout — reading a flasher depthfinder is largely just a matter of practice and experience. This "bass-spotting" is a little simpler if you're over a hard roadbed. The road itself will give a constant flash as the bottom signal, and any red flashes that show between the bottom and surface most likely will be fish. If the boat is moving, the sonar flashes won't be constant like the roadbed, so be alert and have a buoy ready to mark the fishy location.

World champion Rick Clunn catches suspended bass in places like this by drift-trolling. After pinpointing the fish location with marker buoys, he moves off 20 or 30 yards and free-spools a lure to the approximate depth and fishes vertically, right over the edge of his boat.

"A plastic grub of 1/16 to 1/4 ounce is by far the best lure to use here," Clunn explains, "and you can accurately count it down." Much has been said about all lures falling at a rate of "one foot per second in water," but keep in mind that line weight and spool tension can vary this considerably, advises Clunn.

"If you have two rods on board, use them both," Clunn continues. "Count the plastic grubs down a little deeper than the depthfinder shows the fish because as you begin drifting or trolling with the electric motor over the bass, the lure will rise slightly.

"Move very slowly right over the fish. And, don't try to add any lure action at all — simple boat movement will make the grub hop and swim enough to attract a strike," Clunn says.

If bass are suspended fairly shallow, in open water, you might try casting instead of Clunn's drift-trolling tactic. On most suspended fish, you'll find a productive zone of only about 2 feet of depth. It's difficult to keep a diving plug in this strike zone for any length of a retrieve, since a plug travels in more or less a half-moon direction as it is retrieved.

Another problem with casting to shallow bass is that boat noise easily spooks them. This forces you to keep your distance and make long casts. Thus, drifting quietly over the bass usually is more productive, although certainly not as exciting.

The "Strike Zone"

Suspended bass, especially those out in more open water, do not hit a lure hard. Nor do they move far to get it. Very often, the only feeling you'll encounter is a slight "nibble" that simply becomes a heavy weight. At other times, it's more like pulling a lure through a mossbed — there is a growing resistance during the retrieve as if moss (weight) is being collected.

To set the hook on these bass, don't jerk it suddenly, just raise the rod tip quickly and forcefully. Normally, you'll be using lighter lines, preferably in the 6- to 12-pound-test range. And, you won't be able to horse these fish aboard quickly. The lighter line allows natural lure action with the light grubs, and a greater feeling of sensitivity up through the rod when a bass does hit.

If you have trouble picking up suspended bass — repeat drifts go untouched — vary lure depths even more. And, move more slowly through the fish. It could be that you've found the bass in a non-feeding stage and it's going to take a bit of coaxing to get them to strike.

Try forcing the fish down to the bottom — a technique that occasionally gets them to hit if the water is not extremely deep. Run your outboard over the suspended fish several

Bass suspend anytime of year, but do so most often in summer and fall. Be alert to the fact the bass may suspend relatively "shallow" over deep water, in the case of bridge pilings. Check likely areas top to bottom. Photo: Tom Sterling

times, causing a wake and really stirring up the water. Then, come back and drop a plastic worm or a jigging spoon to the bottom and start working it vertically. Bass will swim into areas of poor oxygen and uncomfortable temperatures for short periods before moving back into their suspended stage, and you'll have to act quickly to get a strike. You'll seldom catch more than one or two fish before they do move back up into the in-between zone.

Suspended bass usually do not congregate in tightly knit schools, like crappie (speckled perch) and bream. As you drift over fish, keep a close eye on the depthfinder. The fish may move or you may locate another group nearby. This is what makes depth presentation so important in fishing suspended bass. You're showing the lure to a smaller target. The tighter those bass are suspended, the more critical the correct depth becomes.

When suspended bass are slow to respond, you may be able to pull them up to the surface by using a shad-type lure or possibly a sputtering buzzbait on the surface. Spring and early fall are good times to try this technique, especially if you can see baitfish activity nearby.

"On Toledo Bend, during the suspended-bass period, I always begin throwing a Zara Spook, Rebel Chugger or Dalton Special and work it with a lot of commotion," says Nixon. "If the bass are active, they normally will come out of the treetops to hit on the surface. But if baitfish aren't present to begin with, this technique rarely works."

Many Bassmasters like to race a buzzbait over sunken timber for several casts, then slow it down so the lure just barely stays on the surface. Fish will surface from as deep as 10 to 12 feet down just to see what is causing all the disturbance. Often, these bass will strike and miss. When they do, you may be able to catch them on the very next cast by pitching a plastic worm into the same spot.

The next time you head out after suspended bass, try some of the tactics outlined here. They've all worked for the pros on the Bassmaster® Tournament Trail on different lakes across the country. And, they can work for you, too. Suspended bass are never easy fish to catch, but they can be caught. Swallow your pride and try drift-trolling. Pay more attention to your depthfinder and you'll soon be able to catch suspended bass even on the slowest days.

— 1979 BASS FISHING GUIDE

WHOLE LOTTA SHAKIN'

By LARRY WILLIAMS

A deep-water technique for catching suspended bass is catching on in weedy, cover-filled waters as well . . .

There's been a "whole lotta' shakin' goin' on" in California recently, and it has nothing to do with a Jerry Lee Lewis concert or one of the frequent earthquakes that rattle windows from San Diego to San Francisco.

The "shakin' " phenomenon that has made such an impact on the Golden State is a bass-fishing technique that has gained converts at a rate that would be the envy of many a late-night TV evangelist. From the winding Colorado River impounds to the sprawling water-storage reservoirs that dot California's landscape, "shakin' " has become a popular solution to unlocking the mystery of catching quality bass under even the toughest of conditions on heavily pressured lakes and rivers.

In its simplest form, shaking is a technique of jiggling a soft-plastic bait — usually a grub or small worm — in or near a suspected bass hideout. The action ranges from a relatively vigorous shake to a more subtle tapping of the rod shaft to impart an erratic movement to the bait. As a method of presenting a plastic worm, it has been around since the days "B.C." (Before Creme). As an integral part of a fishing philosophy or system, however, it only recently has become widely used as a principal means of consistently taking finicky bass.

One of the individuals most responsible for spreading the word about the shaking technique has been Jerry Corlew, a 35-year-old tournament angler and lure manufacturer from Lake Isabella, Calif. Corlew heads Anglers Pro Specialties, a company specializing in the manufacture of the grubs, hand-poured plastic worms and specially designed jigheads that

are the basic components of the system.

Not unlike the story of many other successful lure manufacturers who specialize in bass baits, Corlew began his operation on his kitchen table. "I didn't start out with the intention of going into business," he explains. "I was trying to 'build a better mousetrap' for my own use. After a while, though, the demand for the jigs I designed was so great that I quit my job as a photographer and went into the tackle business full-time."

Corlew credits B.A.S.S. legend Dave Gliebe with giving him inspiration and confidence to experiment with new designs and ideas.

"I had the good fortune to meet Dave in the early '80s and became his non-boat practice partner for probably 15 or more professional tournaments. Dave is nothing short of a bass 'vacuum' and I learned early on that if I was going to be successful fishing from the back seat behind him, I would have to look for subtleties in structure, breaklines and bait presentations."

While Gliebe is best-known for flipping and pitching jigs to shallow-water cover, Corlew says, "Dave wouldn't hesitate to go to small baits, light line and deep water if the conditions changed. He is a constant tinkerer, never fishing a bait as it comes from the factory. He would widen the throat of virtually every hook he used to get a better hooking advantage. He'd trim the rubber, paint lures right there in the boat, shave lead off jigheads to give a better balanced presentation — anything to put fish in the boat.

"He gave me the confidence to test and create new ideas and designs, and he critiqued my early lures relentlessly with no concern over our friendship. During one tournament on Lake Mohave, I watched him flip 3- and 4-pound bass out of very heavy cover using 4-pound-test line and tiny 'finesse' baits . . . the original finesse flipper. The time I spent with him changed my concept and outlook on bass fishing forever. Watching him modify lures gave me the idea to make small baits with big hooks and to seek a natural appearance in my creations."

As early as 1983, Corlew used the early version of his system to take fourth place in a tournament on Lake Eufaula, Ala.

"They were laughing at my baits and equipment back then . . . until I collected my trophy," he recalls. Over the next four years, Corlew spent thousands of hours on the water, refining his baits as well as techniques for their presentation. As a result of his on-the-water research, Corlew has developed not only a balanced jighead series but an extensive line of salt-impregnated Shake'N Grubs and hand-poured Shake'N Worms as well as a series of other 'finesse baits' to complete the system.

"I certainly didn't invent shakin' or dabblin', as I call deep-water vertical fishing, but I think I've taken the basic concepts and refined them somewhat. In my research sessions on the water, my intent has been to develop a system that any fisherman — novice and pro alike — can use successfully in deep, clear water conditions as well as shallow- and dirty-water applications."

Shaking is a light-line technique, but not necessarily a light-tackle technique. Corlew is emphatic about this when discussing his system.

"It is not a system for noodle-like, buggy-whip rods," he declares. His rods are 5 feet, 4 inches and 5 feet, 8 inches long. He helped design the rods, and asked for a sensitive tip, a stiff shank section and a medium-heavy to heavy butt. He says a good shaking rod must have the strength to set the hook. He demands a quality reel with a good, smooth drag; Lew's Speed Spin reels are his favorites. He tapes the reel to the rod handle, Tennessee-style, to enhance the balance of the rig and aid sensitivity.

Line size is important, too. Corlew's rule is to use the lightest line practical for the conditions. He normally uses 6- and 8-pound-test, but has adjusted up and down according to situations. In thick cover and stained water, line as heavy as 12- or 14-pound-test will work.

"In heavy cover, the secret to landing a bass is to maintain pressure on the fish, keep its head up, and go dig it out of the hydrilla if you have to."

The point to remember, according to Corlew, is that you are fishing a relatively small bait that you must make appear "natural." Especially in open-water situations, heavier lines tend to interfere with the balance between the jighead and the bait, and they distort the action of the bait.

"Balance" is a word that comes up often in a conversation

Tournament angler and lure manufacturer Jerry Corlew is a prime mover and shaker behind the popularity of the shaking technique. Photo: Larry Williams

with Corlew.

"That is the real key to the whole system," he says. "There was a lot of trial-and-error in our early jighead designs. We were working with 2/0, 3/0 and 4/0 (bass-sized) hooks on small, dart-type heads. It took a lot of shaping and reshaping of our design to reach a point where the bait and jig were balanced. They couldn't be nose- or tail-heavy."

Corlew even used computer-assisted research to achieve the balance he sought. It wasn't easy, because most of his baits are between 3 3/4 and 5 3/4 inches long (similar in size to the common forage), and the jigheads had to be small and lightweight with a large-throat, oversized hook.

The system evolved initially to take hard-to-catch bass from deep, clear, western impoundments that receive an inordinate level of fishing pressure.

Because of the water clarity and fishing pressure, bigger bass often are suspended — or at least, deep — in open water. The key bait for that situation always has been the plastic grub.

"The grub-type bait is the most versatile and adaptable lure on the market for the large majority of fishermen," Corlew notes, "because it is such a 'forgiving' bait. It's hard to fish it 'wrong.' And since it is usually fished on an exposed hook, the bass often hook themselves when they come up and inhale the bait."

The shaking technique is surprisingly simple to master. It consists of casting the bait and retrieving it with a rhythmic "shaking" of the rod tip and a slow, steady turn of the reel handle. Corlew allows the bait to fall to a desired depth on a relatively tight line, then steadily shakes the rod tip from a 9 o'clock position to a 10 o'clock position — moving the rod tip only about 4 inches — then lets it fall back to 9 o'clock and repeats while slowly retrieving line.

Rather than using the arm to move the rod tip, he imparts the action with his wrist.

"Vary the rhythm and pause occasionally," Corlew advises. "Many times the bass will hit the bait when it changes its movement pattern."

Patience is the key to the shaking technique. When they first try it, many fishermen fish the bait too fast.

Most shaking is done while swimming the bait through the water, but larger bass often are to be found near cover or on the bottom, especially around creek-channel ledges, where an exposed hook invites hangups.

Corlew has developed a weedless Shake'N Dart series of jigheads for those situations. These jigs feature a small barb at the head similar to the Keeper Hook design. The head of the grub or worm is pushed onto the barb and the hook is inserted into the plastic body, Texas-style.

"The key to fishing the weedless Shake'N Dart is confidence as well as patience," Corlew explains. "When the bait encounters a limb or some other obstruction, rather than pulling on the bait and hanging it up, give a little slack and shake the rod tip as you slowly lift the bait up and over the obstacle. Many times the fish will hit the bait on the fall after it has been pulled over a snag. It is really important to concentrate on your line movement," he adds.

Each of the western lure manufacturers has its staunch supporters who feel strongly that "their" brand is the best. Anglers Pro Specialties has a loyal following as well.

Western pro Gary Robson, who often dominates tournament action on the Colorado River system, is a believer in the APS system, as are Bobby Sandberg of San Diego, who has caught more than 400 bass over 10 pounds (including an 18-pound, 12-ounce lunker), and 1987 BASS Masters Classic® qualifier Claude "Fish" Fishburne of Atlanta, Ga.

In addition to his tournament credentials, Robson enjoys a reputation as one of the top producers of big bass on the West Coast. His biggest largemouth, a 14-pound, 9-ounce fish, and his 8-pound, 2-ounce spotted bass from fabled Lake Perris (a little more than a pound shy of the world record) were both caught on Shake'N Grubs fished on dart heads.

"The Colorado River system is a tough fishery," Robson notes. "Water releases, weather fronts, wind and heavy recreational use all create conditions that can change almost overnight. To be successful on the Colorado River system, you have to be able to adapt because the fish can be down as deep as 50 feet, and the water color can be anything from crystal clear and smooth to chocolate brown and choppy.

"With the weedless Shake'N Dart, I'll throw right into brush or shallow rock structure, using as light as 1/16- or 1/8-ounce heads. If the water is dingy or stained, I try to keep the bait in contact with objects. The idea is to make the grub or small worm look like injured forage. My rule of thumb is to turn the reel handle about an eighth of a turn for each two shakes of the rod tip."

Robson relies on his electronic depthfinders extensively, especially when bass have moved to offshore structure. He looks for "balls" of baitfish and perhaps schooled bass — especially those that appear "related" to the baitfish.

He drops a 1/8-ounce Shake'N Dart with a translucent or salt-and-pepper grub to the proper depth, and brings the bait through the fish while shaking it very slowly.

A safer bet is to find bass hovering near structure, because they tend to be more active than those in open water. If the bass are suspended 20 feet deep over a 40-foot bottom, he looks for structure such as tapering points or secondary breaks nearby and at the 20-foot depth. Then he uses the same shaking methods there.

To work the bait at the proper depth, Robson counts down the lure after the cast. He knows that a 1/8-ounce head drops about 10 feet in 10 seconds, while a 1/16-ounce jig takes a count of 13 or 14 to drop the same distance.

Fishermen using "finesse baits" like these know how difficult it is to detect bites. "The bite, over open water, is usually just a 'heavy' feeling of weight," Robson says. "And if the grub or worm is being presented as a swimming bait, the bite can be just a feeling of 'nothingness.' "

Bobby Sandberg, a huge bear of a man, looks almost out of place fishing small baits on light line; you might consider him the Billy Westmorland of the West.

"There are times when shaking is the only appropriate response to the conditions," he explains. "I use shaking baits a lot in tournaments when I'm fishing "used water" behind other fishermen, and I like them as follow-up baits when bass swirl at a topwater or spinnerbait.

No doubt, shaking is as simple as it is versatile. Already it is gaining acceptance on the nation's heavily fished bass waters — including Lake Eufaula, where they once laughed at Jerry Corlew's funny little jigs and lures.

— JANUARY 1989

INTO THE DEPTHS

By DON WIRTH

*New tackle and techniques are opening up
the deep-water realm to
bass fishermen . . .*

When I was about 6 years old, I had a favorite record, one I played so often I wore the grooves smooth. It was a musical story about a little boy who puts on one of those 1940s diving suits and goes down, down, down into the sea, where all sorts of mysteries, dangers and adventures awaited him. He talked to the fish and, of course, they answered.

Today, many Bassmasters have a similar sort of fascination with deep water. It's something fishermen have always been drawn to, but something few really understand. And when it comes to talking to those deep fish — well, it takes more than verbal encouragement to make deep bass bite!

"As fishermen, we have done an exceptionally poor job of conquering deep water," believes Nashville, Tenn., bass guide Tony Bean. "Mentally, bass fishermen are buffaloed by water over 20 feet deep." Bean, who specializes in trophy smallmouths, reminds us that 20 feet, while sounding like the Mariana Trench to most bass fishermen, isn't that deep for a giant smallmouth. "I've taken big smallmouths from water over 40 feet deep," Bean says. "If you think fishing 20 feet deep is tough, try 40."

Bass fishermen just are beginning to awaken to the promise that deep water affords. "Deep fishing has typically not been the domain of the bass angler," Bean emphasizes. "But new lures and tackle, plus advances in electronics, are making deep-water bassin' easier, more productive, and more fun than ever before."

How deep do bass occur? The numbers are bound to surprise you. "The largemouth bass, as a species, prefers shallow water," says bass researcher Doug Hannon of Tampa,

Fla. Hannon once analyzed catches of Florida bass over 15 pounds and found that 90 percent of these bruisers were caught in 3 feet of water or less.

However, largemouths can, and will, go deep — very deep. "Largemouths have been caught down to about 60 feet," Hannon says. "Some have been caught even deeper, but I'd put 60 feet as their depth limit in 99 percent of the cases."

Hannon indicates that several factors can force largemouths into the depths. "A thermal inversion, where warm water gets pushed very deep, can often send largemouths far deeper than most fishermen might believe," he says, adding this phenomenon is most often found in large, wind-swept reservoirs.

Other reasons cited by the experts why largemouths can be found in very deep water include the following:

• Bait movements into the deep-water zone.

• A shifting and lowering of the "comfort zone" so that comfortable water temperatures are found only in deep water.

• Fishing pressure.

Smallmouth and spotted bass, more so than largemouths, can properly be thought of as deep-water species. Fred McClintock, a smallmouth-bass guide on Tennessee's Dale Hollow Reservoir, reports catching bronzebacks 76 feet deep in the dead of winter.

"These fish were mixed in with a school of lake trout, which is generally considered to be the deepest species in Dale Hollow," McClintock says. "I caught both smallmouths and lakers off the end of a deep point on live bait."

And if you think that's deep, spotted bass occur even deeper! The International Game Fish Association's annual publication, "World Record Game Fishes," states that "Kentuckies" have been caught as deep as 100 feet.

Now that's deep!

Deep Water And Structure

Bass are structure-related fish, so merely fishing deep isn't enough. "When I'm trying to locate a big smallmouth, I think of deep water as their primary structure," says Tony Bean. "It's the most important thing I can look for, but it isn't everything." Bean says he likes to look for "deep water and . . ." indicating a long list of secondary structures:

"Deep water and a long point, deep water and a river or creek channel, deep water and a hump, deep water and cover, deep water and a shallow flat, etc."

This primary/secondary relationship between deep water and structure applies to all species of bass, not just smallmouths. For when bass are very deep, there's usually some sort of structure close at hand.

For purposes of this story, let's arbitrarily label "deep water" as anything over 20 feet. This may sound extremely deep to many largemouth-bass fishermen, but shallow to some experienced, smallmouth- and spotted-bass anglers. "Deep water is a relative term," Bean reminds us. "Smallmouth- and spotted-bass fishermen are often more successful fishing deep than are largemouth fishermen for

Paralleling a bluff bank is a time-honored method of keeping your lure in the deep-water payoff zone. Photo: Don Wirth

be fished in deep water. The few that are include:

• Jigs (hair and rubber) and leadhead baits such as grubs and Sassy Shads.

• Plastic worms, including the various California modifications (more on these in a moment).

• Jigging spoons.

• Metal tailspinners, including the Little George and Spin-Rite.

• Thin metal vibrating lures, including the Gay Blade and Silver Buddy.

• The new 20- and 30-foot crankbaits available from many manufacturers.

Of the baits listed above, two categories recently have been the object of considerable attention from BASSers nationwide: the California-style plastic worms and leadhead jigs including the Fat Gitzit grub and various tiny, slender plastic worms; and the new wave of super-deep-diving crankbaits. California-style fishing has yet to catch on in many regions, but deep-water crankbaits have hit the scene in a big way. "Many fishermen are getting their first taste of deep-water bassin' with the 20- and 30-foot crankbaits," believes Bean.

Deep-Water Tackle

The need for specialized tackle for deep water will soon become evident to the angler who elects to probe this zone. A perfect example is the evolution of new rods and reels especially designed to handle the popular super-

the simple reason that they've been forced to do it to catch fish. For many who are accustomed to catching largemouths, fishing deep will be a completely new ballgame."

Deep-Water Lures

Starting on the business end of your line, it's easy to see that many, if not most bass lures simply are not designed to

deep crankbaits.

"Not long after the super-deep divers came out in 1986, we began getting feedback that bass fishermen were having trouble fishing them," says Zebco's Rich Feehan. "The first thing we discovered was that fishermen were running these baits too fast with standard baitcasting gear. And they were putting far too much stress on their arms. Even touring pros like Paul Elias couldn't fish these baits more than three or four hours a day without burning out."

Zebco personnel met with several lure manufacturers to come up with a rod-and-reel combination better suited to these specialty baits. "We reaffirmed what we have long believed, that most bass fishermen have a preconditioned, 'generic' cranking speed," Feehan says. "They tend to crank a wide array of lures, including super-deep divers, deep-divers and buzzbaits, at the same basic speed."

Rather than try to change the way fishermen crank their lures, Zebco officials decided to design tackle that would compensate for this 'generic' cranking speed. "The super-deep-diving crankbaits need to be fished slowly," Feehan says. "If they are fished too fast, they actually lose their action, and may even roll over."

Zebco's new equipment for deep cranking, introduced into their Quantum line, will slow down these lures and have the power needed to move a heavy fish out of deep cover, Feehan promises. "Our Quantum Cranking Reel has a 3.8-to-1 gear ratio, which actually reduces by half the force needed to keep these big baits moving," he says. "Most bait-casting reels run in fourth gear, so to speak. This one runs in second." The reel mates with a 7-foot Crankin' Rod, which has a medium-heavy body and a fast tip.

This year Penn is offering the "Speed Shifter" baitcasting reel, which runs normally at a 6-to-1 gear ratio but down-shifts automatically to 2-to-1 when a fish is on the line or when a big crankbait offers extra resistance.

Ryobi, another bass-tackle manufacturer, also has designed rods and reels especially for deep crankbaits. "To many fishermen, these lures have been their first introduction to deep-water fishing," believes Ryobi's Ed Briscoe. "An unpleasant experience when trying to fish them is likely to send these anglers back to shallow water." Briscoe believes that winching power, not speed, is what's needed in a baitcasting reel when fishing deep.

"The fast-retrieve reels give you tremendous speed, but little power," he says. "Many fishermen have found them ill-suited to forcing a deep bass out of heavy cover." Ryobi's T-2 baitcasting reel, on the other hand, primarily is designed for conquering the depths, especially when using the super-deep-diving lures. "This reel has a 90-millimeter handle, which is exceptionally long for a freshwater reel," Briscoe explains. "It also has a large spool capacity, which bass fishermen using heavy line must have when fishing deep. And it has a 4-to-1 gear ratio, perfect for cranking the super-deep baits down deep and keeping them there." Mated with this reel is Ryobi's new heavy-action cranking rod. "This rod is long and stiff — two factors that are need-ed when fishing deep water," Briscoe says. "Its 7-foot length gives you more 'sweep' when you set the hook, so that more line is moved."

Briscoe added that a stiff rod is essential when fishing any kind of lure in deep water, not just the new super-deep crankbaits.

"The fisherman often has to put some sort of action into a deep lure, especially one such as a jig or metal spoon," he believes. "These lures, unlike crankbaits, have little or no built-in action of their own. You have to twitch the rod tip, shake the lure, snap it off the bottom, etc. With a soft rod, the lure is far less responsive. You lose touch with the bait when you have 20 to 40 feet of line separating it from your rod. And of course, it's very hard to detect a strike in deep water with a soft-action rod."

One buddy of mine defines "difference of opinion" as "two or more bass fishermen in the same room." Out on the West Coast, expert Riverside, Calif., bass expert Woody Woodruff fishes deep with equipment that might be described as the opposite of that mentioned by these tackle manufacturers. "I seldom use deep crankbaits when fishing for deep bass," Woodruff explains, "but I prefer using small baits and light line."

"Small" may be the understatement of the decade, for Woodruff has been known to catch big largemouths and spotted bass on 2-inch worms and grubs! "These baits might be more accurately referred to as crappie lures than bass lures," Woodruff says. "Unless you're from California, you'd probably laugh if your partner broke out a bait this small. But out here, it's standard procedure."

Fishing pressure, clear water and other factors make deep fishing a way of life for Woodruff and his pals. And the tackle he chooses may turn a few heads. "I use 6-pound-test, sometimes 4-pound-test, with baitcasting gear," Woodruff explains. "But my baitcasting gear is designed to complement, rather than impede, my fishing with tiny lures."

He uses a Berkley Series One 6-foot, medium-light rod and an Ambassadeur 3500C reel for this unique assign-ment. "The key to deep-water fishing is that everything has to match: your lure size and weight, line, rod and reel. With today's ultrasensitive lines and rods, it's far easier to fish deep than it used to be." Woodruff has a remarkable record of boating big bass from deep California lakes on light tackle. Early in '87, he guided two fishermen to world-record spotted bass at Lake Perris just days apart! (See "World Record Spot Caught and Released," April 1987 BASSMASTER®.)

"No matter what kind of bait you're fishing, you've got to be able to maintain contact with it in deep water, or you're wasting your time," believes Bean. "I like to use the lightest fly (or hair jig) that I can when fishing for deep small-mouths, but I'll go to a heavier bait when the wind starts blowing a bag in my line."

Sometimes going to a light line will compensate for the wind and allow you to maintain your feel with a light lure, but Bean recognizes that most bass fishermen are leery of light line. "I fish mainly with 6-pound-test line, which most

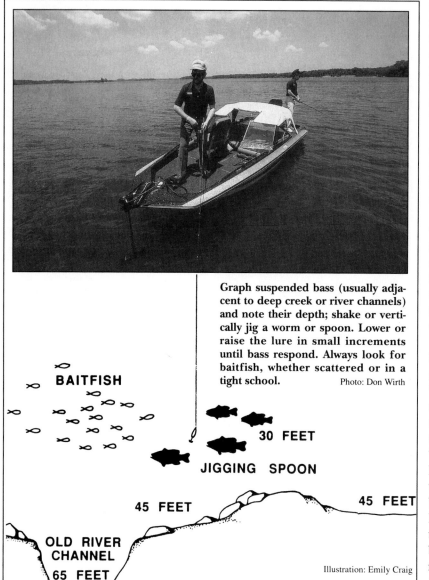

Graph suspended bass (usually adjacent to deep creek or river channels) and note their depth; shake or vertically jig a worm or spoon. Lower or raise the lure in small increments until bass respond. Always look for baitfish, whether scattered or in a tight school. Photo: Don Wirth

Illustration: Emily Craig

temperature drop of 1 degree every 6 to 10 feet, until I hit the thermocline," Woodruff says. "Then, the temperature will drop drastically, a degree for every foot or so that you lower the probe." In many of the California lakes he fishes, Woodruff typically finds the summer thermocline at 30 to 40 feet down. This is where the bass tend to locate, he says.

Another method of locating the thermocline is to turn the sensitivity or gain of your chart recorder or liquid-crystal sonar up high, Woodruff advises, and look for "snow" on the screen.

"I run my graph at its highest paper speed, with the grayline barely turned up," Woodruff says. "Since I find active bass near structure, and not suspending, I try to find areas where the bottom corresponds with the depth of the thermocline. For example, if I found the thermocline at 30 feet, then I look for 30-foot water and fish on the bottom."

Woodruff looks for timber, bushes and brush (for largemouths) and gravel or rocks (for spots) in his deep-water honey holes. "Often I will spot a ball (tight school) of bait and will try to fish deep cover close to this school," he says. To help him keep on the structure, Woodruff relies on marker buoys. "I use two different colors of marker buoys," he says, "to help delineate various parts of the structure. For example, I may use orange buoys at the shallow end of a drop, and yellow buoys at the deep end." Woodruff advises that caution be exercised when chunking out buoys. "Some fishermen try to toss them out right on top of the bait, structure or bass," he says, "but I like to throw them at least one boat length away to avoid spooking the fish."

bass fishermen probably feel is too light. But this line gives better feel in deep water and puts you in control more than does heavy line."

Deep-Water Approaches

"I do most of my deep bassin' during the summer," says Woodruff. "Then, bass are deep, but not as sluggish as they are during the winter." Woodruff uses electronic gear extensively to locate deep bass.

"I often use a Lowrance temperature probe, lowering it slowly to get a temperature profile at various depths," he says. He finds that when surface temperatures are high, say in the mid-80s, the thermocline tends to compress and go deeper. "When I'm lowering the probe, I might pick up a

Next, Woodruff whips out his arsenal of itty-bitty bass lures. "I rely a lot on the doodlin' method for deep bass," he says. Using lightweight baitcasting gear, 6-pound-test line and a 3/0 hook on a leadhead, Woodruff rigs a 4-inch Workin' Girl worm, or a grub, so that the hook is exposed. He drops the bait directly over the side and, once the lure is on the bottom, shakes the rod tip so that the bait shimmies. "This is vertical bottom fishing," Woodruff explains. "You're fishing straight up and down, but your lure remains on the bottom. The strike can be very soft. If you feel anything, set the hook." Naturally, with such light line, your drag must be adjusted to compensate for a vigorous hookset.

If bass are on a ledge or drop-off, Woodruff shakes his worm from shallow to deep, then back from deep to shallow, until bass are located.

"Vertical fishing is the ultimate way to fish deep water," Woodruff concludes. "When you cast, your lure is likely to fall back toward you with a pendulum motion, and may totally miss the mark. By fishing vertically you can target your lure's presentation precisely in deep water."

Bass pro Jack Chancellor of Phenix City, Ala., has made his mark on the BASSMAS-TER® Tournament Trail by concentrating on deep structure. His Do-Nothing Worm and Jack's Jigging Spoon are two fine deep-water baits. The Do-Nothing, an offshoot of the Carolina worm rig, utilizes a 4-inch worm and 1-ounce sinker.

"In a tournament, I can't sit and wait all day for my bait to get to the bottom in deep water," Chancellor says. "The heavy Do-Nothing sinker gets the worm into the business zone quickly."

Likewise, Chancellor relies on his 5/8-ounce jigging spoon when bass are hanging tight to submerged cover and drop-offs in deep water. I vividly can recall fishing with Chancellor on West Point Reservoir one hot September day. We pulled up on a deep ledge, out went Chancellor's spoon, and up came a 9-pound bass. Out went the spoon again, and up came a 6-pounder!

"When bass are deep, they're likely to be stacked together tightly," Chancellor says. "The spoon is the best lure to catch them when they're on deep structure. It's a great tournament lure, because it can be fished quickly and efficiently." Chancellor utilizes a whip-crack-style rod snap to pop the slack out of his line and hop the spoon up off the bottom.

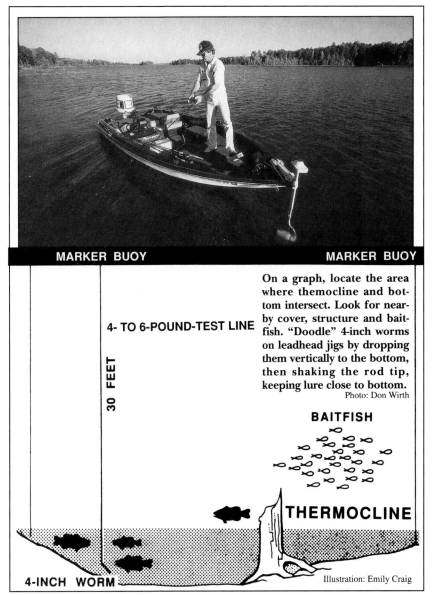

MARKER BUOY   MARKER BUOY

4- TO 6-POUND-TEST LINE

30 FEET

On a graph, locate the area where themocline and bottom intersect. Look for nearby cover, structure and baitfish. "Doodle" 4-inch worms on leadhead jigs by dropping them vertically to the bottom, then shaking the rod tip, keeping lure close to bottom.
Photo: Don Wirth

BAITFISH

THERMOCLINE

4-INCH WORM

Illustration: Emily Craig

Paralleling the bank is a time-honored method of keeping your lure in the deep-water zone much of the time. "During much of the year, I'll seldom catch smallmouths shallower than 20 feet," Bean says. "Rather than casting in toward the bank and drawing my lure back out into the 20-foot zone, I'll parallel the bank, keeping the lure at the right depth for a much longer period." Some baits, such as the Silver Buddy or jigs, are perfect for this approach, Bean feels.

Sometimes bass are not only deep, they're suspended, as well. These can be the toughest fish to catch, but they're still catchable, our experts agree. Woodruff uses 2-inch crappie-style worms and grubs and light line for these fish. "I use a spinning outfit for suspended bass, and a 1/16-ounce sinker or peahead (leadhead). After locating the fish on my graph or flasher, I'll get right over them and count the bait down to

their depth." As an alternative to counting down, Woodruff marks his line at the appropriate depth with a waterproof marker. "Once the bait is where the fish are, I shake it, and keep it right in front of their noses," he says. "If they don't hit, count your lure down deeper the next time and try again."

Take The Plunge

With today's deeper-running lures and specialized bass tackle, it's easier than ever to fish deep for bass. Give it a try soon! But be patient. Use the lures and approaches recommended by our experts. You'll discover that there's a whole new world of bass fishing waiting for you when you get down, down, down . . . into the depths!

— JANUARY 1988

DOWNRIGGER BASSIN'

By BOB McNALLY

*Add a new dimension to your bass fishing —
try downriggers for deep-
water bass . . .*

Mention downriggers to the average B.A.S.S.® member, and it's likely he'll contort his face, squint his eyes, shrug his shoulders and grumble about how much he hates to troll.

That's understandable, since downriggers and trolling go together like bass boats and baitcasting. But for the angler who wants to catch bass in areas seldom worked by average fishermen, the downrigger is a remarkably effective means to that watery end.

A savvy BASSer who knows how, where and when to fish lures and baits deeply and precisely with the aid of downriggers will catch more and larger bass under certain conditions than will those anglers who employ some other fishing methods.

Admittedly, downriggers and trolling are not for everyone. And indeed, downriggers aren't a never-fail aid to livewells full of fat fish. But for the angler who looks at the downrigger as a simple, refined fishing tool that's part of a total arsenal of bass-catching techniques, it's a good bet he'll experience fewer fishless days afloat.

In its simplest form, a downrigger is merely a heavy weight attached to a cable that is lowered to an exact depth. The weight assembly features a clip that holds fishing line and carries the lure to that depth. As the boat moves forward, the lure trails behind and at about the same depth as the downrigger weight. When a fish strikes the lure, the clip releases the line, and the angler can fight the fish without the encumbrance of the heavy weight.

Downriggers were invented for Great Lakes salmon and trout fishermen who needed to get lures very deep and to precise depths. When a sliver of a spoon or a tiny plug had to be taken 50 to 100 feet down to a school of salmon, no method existed that would permit anglers to get small lures to great depths at a variety of speeds. The downrigger was, and still is, the ultimate tool utilized for deep-water salmon and trout fishing.

In recent years, downriggers have been employed extensively by striped-bass anglers and fishermen seeking other deep-water freshwater species such as walleyes, pike and muskies. Marine anglers also are fast discovering the tremendous advantages of downriggers for catching all manner of saltwater fish, including giant tuna and billfish.

Yet for the bulk of the nation's bass fishermen, the downrigger still is a foreign device. Some simply don't like trolling; others believe that their unusual techniques are effective enough in reaching deep bass; and still others disdain having a minicrane cluttering up the sleek lines of their built-for-show-and-speed bass boat. That's too bad, since the use of downriggers makes just as much sense for BASSers as it does for anglers seeking other species.

Let's examine each objection separately:

TROLLING. While almost all downrigger anglers troll, the use of downriggers for bass fishing is far more versatile. Anywhere there is flowing water, for example, anglers can anchor upcurrent of a structure, set out lures or baits with downriggers, and "troll" without moving the boat. This kind of fishing is deadly for working river structures, such as deep points, channel drop-offs, and man-made objects like riprap, bulkheads and bridges. Hot-water discharges and tailraces below dams are other places B.A.S.S. members can

Precision trolling with downriggers allows the angler to present a bait at exactly the correct depth and speed to produce strikes.
Photo: Bob McNally

use downriggers from an anchored position.

Plugs, spoons, spinners and other lures wiggle and wobble seductively when they're taken deep with downriggers in current. Live shiners, shad, even crawfish and earthworms all can be fished easily with downriggers while the boat is at anchor, too.

For the angler who dislikes trolling, downriggers likely are not for him. But to state that it's "boring" or requires less skill than casting is to overlook the refined tactics needed by downrigger trollers who consistently catch fish.

It is widely known that the deeper bass are found, the more concentrated are their schools, and the more difficult they are to catch. So in no other kind of bassing is proper interpretation of structure more important than when deep water is probed.

In addition, the angler employing downriggers constantly must be aware of the slightest change in bottom contour, and the presence and location of thermoclines, which are the borders between layers of water of different temperatures. He must alter lure speeds with deft precision, and he must be acutely attuned to the preferences suspended bass have for the lures and baits he's trolling.

The angler who is bored while trolling is not fishing effectively, because he's not concentrating as he should on the task at hand. An angler who properly fishes lures deep with downriggers tirelessly monitors his depthfinder, hydrographic maps, boat speed and lure action.

Successful deep trolling is a far more taxing fishing method than, say, chunking weedless lures to lily pads. So it follows that because of its difficulty, deep trolling is at least

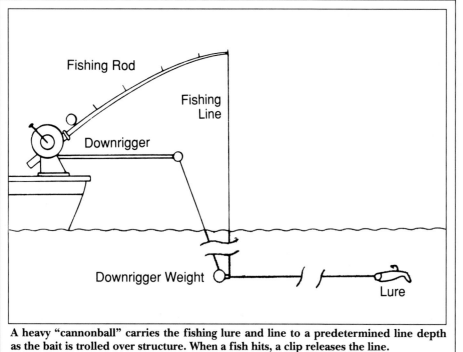

A heavy "cannonball" carries the fishing lure and line to a predetermined line depth as the bait is trolled over structure. When a fish hits, a clip releases the line.

as interesting and sporting a method of bassing as dragging fish out of shallow vegetation.

DEPTH. Anglers who believe bass rarely are so deep that downriggers are needed — at least some of the time — had best bone up on their knowledge of bass and their inherent relationship to structure. Nowhere in America is deep-water bass structure so seldom fished as in my home state of Florida. Bassing still is so good in the Sunshine State that anglers who flail weedbeds through the course of a day on most waters usually will score on a few largemouths.

Further, the bulk of the state's lakes and rivers have comparatively few structures deeper than 15 feet, which is the beginning depth at which downriggers are most effective. Yet one of the first items I installed on my Ranger Rawhide bass boat was a pair of Walker downriggers, and they've proved valuable on a number of occasions on various Florida waters.

Last winter, for example, close friend Bob "Z" Zientara of Chicago and I launched into the St. Johns River late one afternoon for a go at striped bass just south of Jacksonville. Stripers to 10 pounds had been available in good numbers around midriver bridge pilings, with the bulk of the fish caught on crankbaits and jigs. Trouble was, the striper action was very short-lived, with anglers catching just a few fish in a few minutes during the course of a day.

Zientara and I figured the stripers were moving up onto the bridge structures from very deep water to feed for brief periods. So we reasoned that if we fished lures and baits deep with downriggers near river drop-offs close to the

structures, we'd catch stripers for longer periods than by simply casting crankbaits.

I'd like to report that we murdered the stripers, but we didn't. During three days of deep-trolling the St. Johns, we boated about a dozen striped bass to 11 pounds — not great action by anyone's measure. But on the average, we caught more and bigger stripers than any other angler we spoke with that week.

More importantly — and most surprisingly — we had even better fishing for largemouths around the bridge supports than we did for stripers.

The weather was cold and windy — just right for stripers, but poor Florida conditions for bigmouths, at least for shallow-water action. Schools of 2- to 5-pound largemouths had vacated the river's eelgrass flats and were suspended around the downcurrent sides of bridge pilings in 12 to 30 feet of water. The largemouths were schooled extremely tight, and were easily spotted with a chart recorder. But they were difficult to coax into hitting.

In fact, we initially thought the schools were stripers, and we trolled every good striper lure I had through the schools. We never caught a largemouth until we put down small "river" shiners.

The stripers we took that week hit jigs, plugs, spoons, and shiners trolled downriver, but the bigmouths only would take live baits, undoubtedly because of the weather. Even with shiners, the baits had to be set down precisely a foot or two above and upcurrent of bass to tempt them to hit.

On our best day of St. Johns downrigger trolling, Zientara and I caught nine bass between 3 and 6 pounds apiece. Interestingly, none of the striper fishermen we spoke with who worked the same bridge structures with plugs and jigs caught more than two largemouths per day. The use of downriggers and live baits has since saved many a day of largemouth fishing for me on a number of other waters.

Precision downrigger trolling around structure (especially bridges, river-channel edges and deep, tapering points) scored well for me on Florida largemouths last year on lakes Talquin and Seminole, the St. Johns and St. Marys rivers, and the Harris Chain of Lakes near Leesburg, site of the $730,000 B.A.S.S. MegaBucks Tournament.

Friend and B.A.S.S. pro Terry Lacoss of Amelia Island, Fla., my father-in-law Jim Riley of Chicago, and I took a healthy stringer of largemouths with downriggers one day from a deep borrow pit located within a stone's throw of I-95 in north Florida. The bass were schooled deep near a brush-lined bank in 25 feet of water.

By trolling shiners with downriggers just off the bottom and along the brush, we enjoyed constant action all morning. Riley caught the biggest bass of the day, a plump 9 pounds, 13 ounces — his best largemouth ever.

In summer, deep trollers should take careful note of water temperature and thermoclines. Any prime deep structures such as humps, ridges, riprap, channel edges and the like that occur at the same level as the thermocline (easily seen on good depthfinders) likely will yield largemouths.

The beauty of working such deep structures with downriggers is the exacting precision with which anglers can present baits and lures. There is no guesswork regarding lure presentation. The downrigger allows the lure to be positioned at the right depth and speed to entice strikes.

Working suspended bass, even if they're not extremely deep, can be done most precisely with downriggers. Find the depth at which they're holding, then set your downrigger at just above the level, and you can offer them your lures quickly and efficiently.

Precision trolling with downriggers has tremendous applications for other bass species, too. Spotted and small-mouth bass that habitually hold deep along steep, rocky bluffs are suckers for downrigger trolling. Striped and white bass in open reservoir waters can be frustrating for BASSers who use standard casting techniques. But such fish are setups for deep-water structure searching when downriggers are employed.

Night trolling with downriggers is another whole new fishing method yet to be fully explored that should produce hefty catches of all bass species mentioned.

APPEARANCES. Another significant reason some fishermen reject downriggers is the thought of having downrigger paraphernalia on their beautiful bass boats.

Too, drilling holes in a bass boat's transom or stern deck to install downrigger plates is a palm-sweating endeavor, especially for anglers who intend to sell their rig a year or two in the future. But in recent years downrigger companies have devised some remarkably ingenious installation systems that alter a boat's looks very little.

What is more, downriggers can be installed and taken off a boat very quickly.

Companies like Walker, Cannon, Big Jon, Penn and others all market downriggers that can be rigged easily to any small skiff or bass boat without detracting from its beauty.

The Walker downriggers I put on my Ranger, for example, simply required that I drill four, 1/4-inch holes through the boat's rear deck for each of two stainless-steel downriggers' mounting plates. The holes are so small that they cannot be seen, as the boat's deck carpeting covers them. I used stainless-steel bolts and nuts to prevent rusting. To guard against water leaks into the rear storage area, I coated the plate bolts with silicone sealant, which will also act as a bolt lubricant when it's time to remove the plates. At that time, I'll fill the holes with more sealant, which will make the rear compartment as watertight as when I got the boat.

The 6-inch-square stainless-steel deck plates rise only 1/4 inch above the deck surface, so they're unobtrusive when the downriggers are not on the boat. The swivel bases for mounting my two downriggers can be installed in seconds by simply tightening two stainless-steel thumb screws that fit into the deck plates. In less than two minutes I can put the downriggers on or take them off.

Other "quick-fit" downrigger installation systems for small boats feature special mounts that drop into oarlocks, and some have screw-clamp mounts that tighten on the gunnel or transom. One of the best mounting systems is a downrigger base that has a long post that drops down into a built-in rod holder on the gunnel. Most large boats have such rod holders, and they can be installed easily on most fiberglass fishing boats. When the downriggers are not in use, only the gunnel-level rod holder shows, with no plates or swivel bases evident.

For B.A.S.S. members who still dislike drilling holes in boat decks, gunnels and transoms for rigging downriggers, they can do like my father, Tom. When he rigged his Ranger for downriggers, he simply used a 1-inch by 18-inch plywood board that was cut to the width of this boat. He fastened downriggers and rod holders to the board and quick-fitted it to his boat with "C-clamps" (available at hardware stores) whenever he needed it for trolling.

Refinements in downriggers' use for bass anglers are many, and more are being developed constantly.

For example, "scent pads" are available now for downrigger balls. The fabric pads stick to downrigger balls and absorb commercial fish scents, which in turn attract bass to the lures trailing behind. For BASSers trolling downriggers through deep weedbeds or similar cover, Cannon markets special banana-shaped downrigger weights, which are less likely to foul in cover than standard, round downrigger balls.

Another consideration bass anglers must take into account is the length of downrigger arms used on small skiffs. If more than one downrigger is used, it's wise to have arms at least 4 feet long to keep lines well away from each other, as well as away from the motor.

Finally, downrigger bassin' isn't for everyone. It's an extra expense; catalog prices for downrigger systems range from $90 to more than $300.

It's not an easy system to master, nor is it a lazy man's method of putting fish in the boat. There are no guarantees that it always will produce bass. But under the right conditions no system of fishing will better allow anglers to present lures and baits to deep bass, and that ultimately equates to more fish. That's all anyone can ask of a fishing system.

— 1986 BASS FISHING ANNUAL

UP THE DOWN TREETOP

By C. C. RISENHOOVER

Some anglers regard these fish as being dormant and almost impossible to catch. With the right approach, suspended bass are super aggressive . . .

Locating and catching suspended bass is no great mystery to Dick Collier and Jerry Cawthra, two Missouri Bassmasters who seemingly have solved the puzzle that baffles many of their peers. And, if you can buy the theories espoused by these two Show-Me-State anglers, you're never again going to worry about fishing water that is too clear.

Cawthra, 36, and Collier, 33, do most of their bassin' in Missouri's famed fish bowl — Table Rock Lake — a body of water normally so clear you actually witness a bass hit the lure 20 feet below the surface. Even at night, using an artificial Moonglow light, Collier says you can see a bass hit 7 feet below the surface.

That's clear water, but these fishing partners wouldn't have it any other way. They claim Table Rock as their "home lake" and, if you can believe other BASSers in Arkansas, Oklahoma and Missouri, who fish the White River reservoir regularly, Collier and Cawthra are almost unbeatable on the big Missouri-Arkansas-border impoundment.

In less than five years of tournament bass fishing, almost exclusively on Table Rock, the Collier-Cawthra duo has boated more than $50,000 in cash and prizes. And their jobs prohibit them from fishing anything other than one-day weekend tournaments.

Step into Collier's Champion bass boat and you're in for some good fishing, and quite a few surprises.

• **Tackling Suspended Fish** — "Where are your tackleboxes?" I ask my hosts, as I see only a cardboard box filled with several jars of Uncle Josh pork baits, several cards of Bass Trapper jigs, maybe a handful of cupped silver spoons, two Zara Spooks and a couple of topwater Rogues.

"Don't need a tacklebox," Dick Collier explains, "I've got some Bass Buster Scorpion spinnerbaits in a compartment there, but other than those, you're lookin' at the only kind of lures we ever use."

It's a warm day, the sun is shining brightly, so I muse, "Are you telling me that you use a jig and pig on a day like this?"

"We use a jig and No. 11 pork frog 12 months a year," says Cawthra, "and we use it 90 percent of the time."

"I always thought of the jig and pig as just a winter bait," I say.

"A lot of other people think that way too," Collier laughs.

The big outboard is purring now, pushing the boat through relatively heavy wave action caused by the wind. It's not an ideal fishing day.

Because I've heard so much about these two Bassmasters, I pay attention to every detail, and ask questions, lots of questions.

For instance, Collier and Cawthra each have only two rod/reel combos rigged and ready for action. Having observed the fishing techniques of numerous pros — who normally have several outfits rigged and ready — I wonder aloud about the "skimpiness of their battle gear." The explanation is that, since they rarely use more than two different types of lures on a fishing trip, "there's no point in cluttering up the boat."

Another surprise is the line size used by the anglers. It's 15-pound-test (Maxima monofilament), considered by many Bassmasters to be too heavy to use in such clear water conditions.

"I always thought," I remark and begin to sound like a broken record, "that a fellow had to use light line in water this clear."

"A lot of people think that," Collier mouthed through a grin.

Their rods are 5-footers, heavy graphite with medium tips. The reels are Ambassadeurs.

For this outing, Cawthra has shucked one of his heavy-duty rigs, though it is tucked safely inside one of the boat's compartments. He's testing a spinning rig, spooled with 10-pound-test line, and his complaints about it start before the boat exits the marina. He won't be using it with a jig and pig. It's strictly for use with the Rogue, a thin, minnow-like lure.

As the boat slices through the waves, Collier watches the console-mounted Lowrance chart recorder, a piece of equipment he lauds as being vital in finding suspended fish.

"Before I got the graph recorder," he shouts above the noise of the wind and engine, "finding suspended fish was a lot tougher."

• **Seeking Suspended Bass** — Collier soon shuts the outboard down and lets the boat glide into an area with no visible surface structure. Both anglers select casting gear equipped with black 3/8-ounce jigs and black No. 11 pork frogs; black being the color they use almost exclusively for day or night fishing. The live-rubber skirts on the jigs have been trimmed, allowing the pork to show more.

Collier drops the electric trolling motor into the water, and both Bassmasters station themselves on the front casting platform, the foot-control of the electric between them. They begin making long casts into seemingly open water.

"There's one big tree out there," Cawthra volunteers, "It's one of our best spots."

"The water is 60 feet deep at the tree," Collier says, "and the top of the tree is about 5 feet below the surface. We're throwing into the treetop and using a countdown method to get the bait to about 10 feet before retrieving. If they're not at 10 feet, we'll just keep moving down the tree."

The jig and pork frog combo plays a key role in the search-and-catch method for suspended bass in Table Rock's clearwater conditions.   Photo: C. C. Risenhoover

The anglers are using a pumping motion to retrieve their lures.

"Oops," says Cawthra as he tenses. "I got a bump. There, it hit again, and again." Cawthra sets the hook and the fish shoots toward the surface.

"Kentucky," Collier states matter-of-factly. He quickly has retrieved his lure and casts it almost in the same spot where Cawthra's fish is tugging. "Got one," he yells, setting the hook.

The anglers work their fish toward the boat, and I have the dubious distinction of netting both. As the twosome display almost identical spotted bass, Cawthra confides, "It's not uncommon to get a double hookup like that. With these suspended fish, you'll often have a half-dozen or so follow one that's hooked. If you can get another lure right in behind a hookup, chances are pretty good that one will nab it."

The netted spotted bass are each 18 inches long. Both, uninjured, are returned to the water. Except for a record fish, Collier and Cawthra return all their bass to the water.

"Another thing about these suspended bass," says Collier, "is that 99 percent of what we catch are keepers." Missouri has a 15-inch, 6-fish limit on bass.

• **Table Rock's Spots** — Collier says that on numerous occasions, he and his partner have taken limits of Kentucky spotted bass that averaged 4 pounds each, from the trees.

"The word is getting out all over the country about the Kentucky bass fishin' in this lake," Collier says. "There is no place that can compare with it. I think the 15-inch size limit is what has made it so good."

They're casting again now, and Cawthra says, "In five years of fishing like we're doing now, we can darn near count the non-keepers we've caught this way. What that means is that if you can get six strikes, chances are pretty good that you can win a tournament."

Collier's biggest largemouth, to date, was an 8-pound, 4-ouncer. He has also landed a 6-pound Kentucky and a 4-pound,

USING PORK TO PEN THE HAWGS

Just because Dick Collier and Jerry Cawthra like to fish for suspended bass doesn't mean they pass up shoreline action. When Table Rock bass move in shallow during spring, these two Missourians are very adept at making the fish gobble a jig and pig.

"You'd have to say that we're kind of bullish on pork," Collier admits. "The reason is that you can fish the stuff about any way a lure can be fished."

Collier hasn't cast a plastic worm in more than five years, not because he is conducting a vendetta against modern-day plastics, but simply because he thinks "hawg hide" works better.

Come April and May, Collier and Cawthra will tease bass with a topwater Rogue, a minnow-shaped lure, but they're best known for working spawning areas with a jig and No. 11 pork frog. They cast past a spot, let the bait drop, retrieve to the nest, then begin twitching the bait. Results are often better than excellent.

On Table Rock Lake, you can stand on the casting platform of a bass boat and, because the water is so clear, it's relatively easy to see the spawning sites. The clarity of the water requires long casts.

For springtime bass, Cawthra says run the boat parallel to the shoreline and cast toward the deeper water.

"It's better to run the boat along the bank and to cast out," he thinks. "You eliminate a lot of smaller fish that way."

While the two Bassmasters fish the jig and pig fast or slow and top to bottom, they do use other lures.

"In January and February, we often use a white or chartreuse spinnerbait," confides Collier. "Of course," he laughs, "we use it with a No. 340 white or chartreuse Ripple Rind. And we always use a single-spin Bass Buster Scorpion with a No. 4 or 5 silver blade."

Collier says they use the spinnerbait with a Sampo swivel that spins the blade freely.

Though the two anglers don't use many baits, they're very particular about the ones they do use. "I like a blue-skirted Scorpion at night, and a white one in the daytime," says Cawthra.

A favorite technique of the partners in March is swimming a jig and frog near the surface.

"We just toss it past cedar tops, let the lure fall as it gets to the tree, pump once and start swimming it back," explains Collier. "We even make the jig and frog 'wake' like a spinnerbait buzzed along the surface.

"It tickles me to fish with a crankbait fisherman. If he doesn't go 100 miles per hour down a bank, I have no trouble competing with him with a jig and pork frog," Collier says.

Collier and Cawthra sometimes use flutter-type spoons on suspended bass. These are 3/4-ounce chrome jobs that enable long casts.

"You use a little faster cadence with the spoon than with a jig," says Cawthra. "After one of us gets a hookup on a jig and frog, the other often throws a spoon where the fish is fighting. Following fish will often hit the spoon."

However, both admit a preference for the jig and pork frog because they think suspended bass share their enthusiasm for the soft texture of pork, especially when they're feeding on crawfish.

— *C. C. RISENHOOVER*

13-ounce smallmouth. His best stringer, back when Missouri had a 10-fish limit, was 51 pounds, 8 ounces.

In May of 1979, Collier experienced some incredible largemouth fishing at Table Rock. That month he caught three bass on a topwater Zara Spook, and each bass weighed more than 7 pounds. The largest was a 7-pound, 13-ouncer.

Cawthra, on the other hand, has landed an 8-pound, 10-ounce largemouth, a 5-pound Kentucky, and a 4-pound smallmouth. His best stringer, also 10 fish, weighed 35 pounds.

"We don't catch that many largemouths," Dick Collier says, "but when we do they're normally not deeper than 20 feet. I'd say the norm is 8 to 12 feet. We've caught smallmouths as deep as 45 feet, but that's not really normal.

"The deepest I've caught a Kentucky was 60 feet, but the deepest norm would be more like 35 feet."

Cawthra, battling another fish toward the boat, says they catch largemouth, smallmouth and spotted bass all out of the same tree.

"Gar can be flipping all around us, and we'll be catching bass right and left," Cawthra says, while releasing another good Kentucky.

"What astounds me is the size of the fish," Collier says. "We can't really depend on largemouths, but the spotted bass will average 3 pounds. They're our bread-and-butter fish."

• **The Countdown Method** — Cawthra says the countdown method is the key to getting strikes. He states that a 1/2-ounce jig and No. 11 pork frog will fall at about 1 foot per second, and that adjustments to the speed of the fall can be made, depending on the size of the jig.

"Watching your line is very important," Cawthra warns. "Sometimes there will be a slight twitch in the line. It's important to keep the slack out of the line. It doesn't have to be tight, but it should be taut.

"You don't have to set the hook immediately, either. If one misses the lure, another will get it. A hard set is important, because the bass may be hitting a long way from the boat, and it will be hitting deep most of the time."

Cawthra has barely concluded his dissertation when Collier puts a hard set on a fish. The rod tip arches, and he battles the fish to the boat. It's a large rock bass (goggle-eye), and results in some good-natured ribbing about his fishing skill.

Collier admits that he and Cawthra have spent hundreds of hours locating their suspended bass.

"Finding the places is the most difficult thing, and the most important," he says. "It's time-consuming, and most people would rather be fishing than looking.

"But when you do find the places, it's so easy it's kind of scary. At first, I thought it might be some sort of a freak deal, but we've had six schools located for the past few years. We can pretty well depend on them to hit sometime during the day. Usually, the best hours are 10 a.m. until 2 p.m., even during the summer."

• **Finding Suspended Schools** — So, what sort of place do you look for that might have and hold suspended bass?

"You need a gut," says Collier. "Channels are great, but not all suspended bass relate to a channel. It helps to have sort of a 'V' or gut coming off the bank, though it doesn't have to be all that well-defined. It's important to remember that some bass never relate to shoreline."

"The areas that suspended bass seem to frequent are isolated spots," adds Cawthra. "Isolated treetops, brushpiles, ledges and ditches — anything that might offer cover — can hold suspended bass.

"Most of these spots are going to be off the shoreline, and they're going to be passed up by most fishermen," Cawthra points out.

Collier says that bass on Table Rock will suspend from the surface to a depth of 35 feet most of the time, with the 12- to 20-foot layer, over 45 to 60 feet of water, being the most productive.

"Cold fronts, rain, bright sun and other types of weather changes don't seem to affect suspended bass as much as they do shallow or bottom-feeding fish," Collier says.

Cawthra, busy dislodging a jig from the mouth of another Kentucky bass, goes on record that fishing for suspended bass is not slow, methodical and boring. I couldn't agree more, since I've watched him catch and release several fish.

"It's a fast method of fishing," he says. "You're using relatively heavy tackle and you're encouraging the bass to strike on impulse."

Cawthra explains that the jig and frog is allowed to sink to a predetermined depth in a treetop or brushpile, then retrieved quickly with short jerks that allow the bait to rise and fall.

"The bass doesn't get a real good look at the bait and takes it on impulse before it gets away," Cawthra says. "If a fish misses, let the jig drop again, and most of the time the bass will strike again."

"Yeah, that's something that is contrary to what I used to hear," says Collier. "A lot of fishermen talk about suspended bass as being dormant and almost impossible to catch,

but we've found them to be super aggressive. Sometimes they will strike a lure five or six times before engulfing it."

• **Summing Up Suspended Bass** — Collier and Cawthra say they have practiced their methods on numerous other lakes with tremendous success, that it's not just a phenomenon peculiar to Table Rock.

"It will work in any kind of lake," Cawthra says, "and in any kind of water. We always look for the clearest water we can find in a lake, because that area is normally not fished as hard. Most bass anglers prefer dingy water. We like ours crystal-clear."

Collier says the countdown method of fishing is a must, because the bass may be at a different depth every trip. "After determining the places we're going to fish," he says, "we start our countdown method at 5 feet and work down to 25, or until we hit some fish. They're pretty easy to pattern.

"Even though a front is coming or has just passed, don't eliminate the surface-to-5-foot layer. Start there," he says. "There have been many days when we fished after a cold front — bluebird days when you would think fish would be deep — and we've found good schools at about 5 feet over a treetop in 50 feet of water. The treetop might even be 25 feet below the surface, but they were still relating to it."

Cawthra warns that suspended bass easily are spooked at times and require long casts in clear water.

"And you need to get the fish to the boat quickly," he says. "A lost fish almost always spooks the school."

If a school is spooked, however, Cawthra says to just move on to another treetop. You've probably got them patterned. And you always can go back for seconds

Collier says the fish are normally suspended every month except April and May.

"July and August are excellent months, as good a time as any for suspended bass," he says. "A lot of people think you can only night-fish in July and August, but I prefer day-fishing. At night there's nothing to relate to except the water and your sonar locator. It's harder fishing at night, and we catch just as many fish in the daytime."

Collier says that in the hot summertime at Table Rock, a type of freshwater jellyfish about the size of a nickel begins to show up in open water.

"I don't know the connection," he says, "but you can always find suspended bass close by."

Collier, in the amusement business — jukeboxes, pinball machines, etc. — at Springfield, Mo., and Cawthra, a sheet-metal worker from nearby Nixon, drew each other as partners in a B.A.S.S. Federation Tournament in 1972. They've been fishing together ever since.

Quite a few big bass suspending around treetops had just as soon they had never met.

— JANUARY 1981

Photo: Ed Mendus

CHAPTER EIGHT

DEALING WITH STRUCTURE

There are many habitats for bass, and just as many ways to unlock their secrets.

Photo: Doug Stamm

Photo: Charles Beck

HOW TO FISH HYDRILLA

By TIM TUCKER

Learn to fish hydrilla weedbeds in the plant's various stages, and you'll be more successful at bassin' year-round . . .

It is the scourge of skiers. It is cursed by boaters. It is despised by most fishermen.

But creative, experienced anglers know it can be a boon for bass.

It is hydrilla, an exotic, fast-growing, stringy form of aquatic vegetation that has long dominated many lakes in Florida and has begun to make its presence felt throughout the South in places like Texas and Alabama.

With a growth capability of an inch per day, hydrilla, at its worst, restricts boat movement, alters the class distribution of resident fish populations and causes oxygen depletion, which results in fish kills. But those problems occur mainly when the vegetation has completely overtaken a lake or waterway.

At its best, hydrilla can breathe new life into aging reservoirs and lakes where most of the natural brush and vegetation have disappeared

A few years ago, hydrilla was regarded as a complete nuisance. Now BASSers see it as a haven for big bass.
Photo: Tim Tucker

over time.

David Fenton knows that as well as anyone.

Fenton, a qualifier for the prestigious BASS Masters Classic® in 1985 and 1987 and winner of the 1986 Georgia BASS-MASTER Invitational on West Point Reservoir, guides on Texas' Lake Conroe near Houston. Fenton has fished Lake Conroe extensively before, during and after the emergence of hydrilla, and he swears by its fish-producing ability.

"I love hydrilla," he says. "It provides the best fish cover there is. It provides everything a bass needs — food, cover, shade and ambush points. It's fantastic cover.

"It saved Lake Conroe from dying and returned good fishing to us. I believe most lakes have a cycle. They reach their peak after six years or so and then start to go downhill. I believe hydrilla prolonged Lake Conroe's productivity. At the point when they started eradicating

Bernie Schultz believes the key to fishing hydrilla is to adjust tactics as the vegetation goes through its annual growth.

Photo: Tim Tucker

the hydrilla, Lake Conroe was 11 years old, yet it was still one of the top-producing lakes in Texas.

"When they got rid of the hydrilla, it really hurt our fishing. Now it's going through a double downhill fall, because the lake is old and now, all of a sudden, there are no weeds."

While Lake Conroe regulars like Fenton, Rick Clunn, Randy Fite and Zell Rowland (all tournament champions and Classic qualifiers) found hydrilla to be a plus for their home water, the vegetation fell prey to real estate developers who believed a shoreline choked with hydrilla would detract from their ability to sell lots, according to Fenton.

But that's not unusual. There is a war on hydrilla in several states, particularly Florida, where biologists from the Game and Fresh Water Fish Commission, who have no authority over herbicidal spraying of hydrilla, constantly battle with the various Water Management Districts that control the state's water supplies.

Forrest Ware, bureau chief of the commission's Division of Fisheries, is a fan of hydrilla and its ability to transform aging bodies of water into productive fisheries.

"Hydrilla has received a lot of bad press over the past

decade," Ware explains. "In Florida, hydrilla has been very successful in improving the quality of fishing on big lakes like Orange and Lochloosa (near Gainesville).

"But in any water, whether it be Okeechobee or the St. Johns, you've got to have a good vegetation response to get a good crop of game fish. It's like a steak-and-potatoes relationship as far as Florida's natural lakes are concerned. Man, in his never-ending efforts to better manage Mother Nature, sometimes interferes with that process. If we can get these people to change their attitudes about hydrilla, we'll be better off."

Rather than trying to wipe out everything, if lake managers would let the vegetation remain at a manageable level, the state could produce tremendous fishing in these lakes that have declined over the year, Ware says.

Fishermen, who don't understand how to fish hydrilla-infested lakes, regard the weed as an enemy. They know it gets caught up in their outboard props, stops their trolling motors and clings to their lures.

Instead of considering it a nuisance, though, bass anglers should learn to adapt to hydrilla, the bass pros recommend.

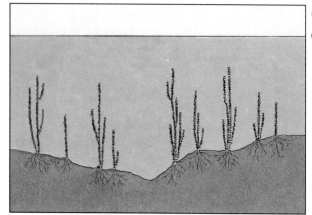

GROWTH STAGES OF HYDRILLA

SPRIG OR ADOLESCENT STAGE: Individual strands stretch from lake bottom to heights of 3 to 6 feet. Best lures: Plastic worms rigged Texas-style; rattling shad-type lures (Rat-L-Trap, Hot Spot); topwaters (Rapala, Devil's Horse, Bass Baffler).

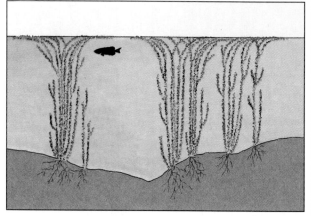

CROWN STAGE: Weeds are beginning to mat the surface. Strands have reached the surface and are branching. Strands remain buoyant. Matting of weeds begins to restrict light penetration and surface sections begin to provide shade. Best lures: Plastic worms rigged Texas-style for flipping crowns; topwaters cast into open pockets.

Illustrations: Bernie Schultz

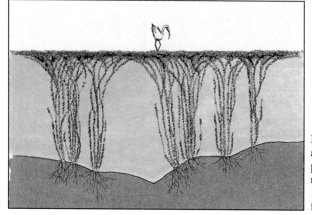

MATTED STAGE: Plant has grown thick at the surface and begins to discolor. Blockage of sunlight to lower portions of the plant causes thinning. Best lures: Texas-rigged plastic worms with weights heavy enough (3/4 to 1 ounce) to penetrate mat; topwaters and crankbaits for fishing contours.

CAVERN/DEATH STAGE: Matting has become extremely thick. Mat may be 2 to 4 feet thick in some areas. By this time waterfowl have begun to eat the plant. Roots tear free. Best lures: Crankbaits and surface lures fished around contours for schooling fish; flipping is still productive around thinner areas or along edges.

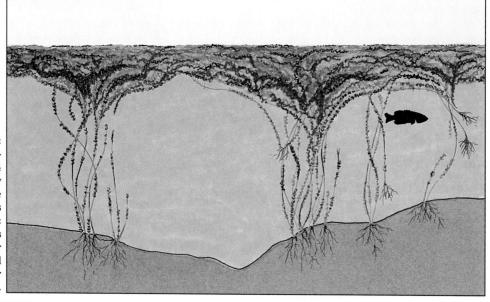

Bernie Schultz, a talented angler who lives in Gainesville, Fla., and regularly fishes Orange and Lochloosa lakes — two hydrilla strongholds — probably understands the plant as well as most biologists, and he regularly uses his familiarity with it to produce great bass catches.

He says there is an art to fishing this type of vegetation. It's very different from working a lily-pad field or flipping into holes in milfoil flats.

The key to successfully fishing hydrilla is to adjust your tactics as the vegetation goes through its annual growth routine, according to Schultz. The cold temperatures of winter kill off a large percentage of hydrilla (except in southern Florida), and the plant starts its growth cycle all over again.

"Several things must be considered when fishing hydrilla," says Schultz. "The most important one is to recognize the stage of the plant's development in its growing season," he explains. "The plant goes through very definite growth stages from the time it first starts to appear until it is fully grown and matted over on top of the water.

"If you pay attention to exactly which stage the hydrilla is in and change your tactics as it reaches each new growth stage, you'll be surprised how many different types of lures will catch fish in these weeds. Most people think you only can fish hydrilla with a plastic worm, but there are times when you can use a variety of different baits and you'll be more successful." Through years of experience, Schultz has identified five distinct growth stages of hydrilla.

After the winter die-off of hydrilla, the first stage is what Schultz refers to as the "adolescent stage," which usually lasts a couple of months. At this stage, the plant is between 5 and 30 inches in height and can best be found by using a flasher depthfinder. Once these submerged grassbeds are located, if the water depth is suitable, he actually graphs the larger beds and looks for pockets, cuts and edges that could serve as ambush points for bass.

The hydrilla at this stage is little more than wispy, free-standing fingers of grass. "There are certain readings you'll find with a depthfinder that will indicate this thin, sparse growth, which is perfect for crankbait fishing," Schultz says. "You actually can run a crankbait through these fingers without much problem. And a bright, vibrating lure like a Rat-L-Trap or Storm's Texas Shad really will catch fish at this stage.

"But crankbaiting the fingers is not for everybody. It's not the most enjoyable way to fish. It's a very effective way to catch fish, but you will get hung up a lot. I get a lot of impulse strikes when fishing hydrilla. When the bait gets hung on a finger of hydrilla, I rip it through from the strand and, as it pulls free, I often get a strike. It's happened too many times to be an accident. I think it triggers a strike similar to the way bouncing a crankbait off of a stump or dock piling does."

Another productive tactic during this stage is swimming a worm across the top of the underwater vegetation.

The second stage, which usually lasts through the spring, is the "crown stage." At this point, the hydrilla fingers have grown to the surface and just are beginning to curl over the top of the water. The plant is developed almost fully, and its stalks are thick — too thick for crankbaits.

The most effective technique now is flipping the edges along open water or small, open holes in the middle of the hydrilla. Also, spoons and minnow-type topwater lures worked quickly along the edges of this vegetation can be effective early and late.

In the summer, hydrilla reaches its full maturity and blankets the surface, still rooted. During this "matted stage," Schultz concentrates on working huge openings in the grass — places that are big enough to get a boat into and still make long casts. These big pools may be hard to reach, but they often hold good concentrations of fish.

Schultz casts worms, topwater lures and crankbaits throughout the day in these open-water areas.

In late summer/early fall, hydrilla begins the downward side of its cycle. In a sense, the plant smothers itself. This stage of the plant's growth is characterized by huge mats of hydrilla, which block off sunlight from its stalks, and kills that portion of the plant. Though hydrilla can remain alive for several months while unattached to the lake bottom, it creates huge open-water domes or caverns that provide shade from the intense summer heat and hold large numbers of bass.

This "cavern stage" is Schultz's favorite.

"Try to visualize huge, floating mats of vegetation with big caverns of open water underneath," he says. "They are void of weed growth below the surface, and they are excellent areas for bass. They are like boat docks almost in that they offer shade and ambush points."

To penetrate the 3- to 6-inch mats of surface vegetation, Schultz uses a 3/4- or 1-ounce bullet sinker pegged with a toothpick on the line above a ribbon-shaped plastic worm such as a Gillraker. Once the worm breaks through the barrier, strikes often are immediate. Texas anglers use specially designed jigs with cone-shaped heads to penetrate the hydrilla during this stage.

The final phase of hydrilla's growth is the "dying stage," in which the hydrilla has begun to disappear, and large, open pockets remain which often are inhabited by schooling bass that forage for food on the outer edges of grassbeds. A Rat-L-Trap crankbait is very productive during this time when the schooling fish are abundant.

When fishing hydrilla, Schultz doesn't place much emphasis on lure color. For crankbaits, spoons and topwater lures, he sticks with silver or chrome to imitate shad, or gold to copy the native golden shiners, a bass delicacy. Dark-colored worms, along with the shad-pattern models, have been the most productive worms in hydrilla.

To some, hydrilla is a nuisance. To others, it's a mystery. But by paying attention to the characteristics of the plant, you will find that hydrilla is also one of the very best havens for bass known to man.

— NOVEMBER 1987

DEEP-WATER STRUCTURE TECHNIQUES

By CHRIS ALTMAN

For year-round action on big bass, look for drop-offs at the ends of points, Charlie Huskey says . . .

I t's the middle of the summer, and it's hot enough to fry eggs on the fiberglass deck of your boat. You've got the day off and you're going fishing, and neither sunburn nor heatstroke will keep you from it.

When you get to the lake, you find the surface temperature in the mid-90s. The fish are deep. You know they are down there, but where down there?

Charlie Huskey, a tournament fisherman from Knoxville, Tenn., knows where. He's so familiar with finding bass in deep water, in fact, that he can attribute over $100,000 in recent tournament winnings to his structure techniques. Huskey, a fireman-turned-boat-builder and now the president of Admiral-Craft Boat Co., spent years developing his skill.

Strangely enough, it all started in Vietnam.

As he relates: "My wife sent boxes of fishing magazines to me there, and I spent my free time reading about the sport I missed so badly. I read a few articles about fellows catching bass from 20, 30, even 40 feet of water. I had always believed that there were more fish in deep water than in shallow, but I had never learned how to catch them.

"So just before I was discharged and left Vietnam, I wrote my wife and asked her to order a depthfinder for me. This was in 1969, and sonar equipment was difficult to come by. She found one, a Ray Jefferson portable unit, in a Sears and Roebuck catalog. And once I got back to Tennessee, I began experimenting."

If Huskey had been an inventor rather than a fisherman, he probably would be wealthy beyond measure, for his experimentation was exceedingly fruitful. It has taken years to master, but Huskey's "bluff-point" techniques are perhaps the most productive deep-water structure methods currently in use by anyone, anywhere. (While fishing with Huskey for the first time, this writer watched in awe as he caught, in a period of three hours, 29 pounds of bass, including a 7 1/2-pound largemouth and two 5-pound smallmouths!)

Huskey's structure? Nothing more exotic than a point extending into the old river channel. He calls it a "bluff point."

"What I'm looking for," says this 46-year-old pro angler, "is a fairly steep, rocky point extending into the original river channel. The point itself is of little importance, but the structure on it is crucial." By identifying and fishing only the best bass-holding structures and eliminating the rest, Huskey has turned point fishing into a veritable art.

"When I'm using this technique," he says, "I'm fishing small bluffs on the points. The technique itself is not hard, but locating these drops on the points is very tedious and time-consuming. You must first master your sonar equipment and develop confidence in what it is telling you. Then you must spend a lot of time easing the boat around and searching for the small bluffs on the points. I use a Lowrance flasher for basic scouting, and then I use a Lowrance X-16 paper graph to mark the drop clearly."

His search for the right structure begins not with his depthfinder, but with his eyes.

"By observing the portion of the point that is out of the water, you can eliminate a lot of territory," Huskey states.

Charlie Huskey's favorite deep-water structure bait is a jig-and-pig.

Photo: Chris Altman

"Rocky points usually have a lot of small drops on them, while smooth mud points rarely have any. And once you locate one of these drops, mark it on a good topographical map. Try to find some objects on the shore to 'triangulate' the spots so that you can come back and locate the drop without having to spend a lot of time searching for it."

Furthermore, be sure to record the depth of the water over the drop when you mark it on a map. "Many times," says Huskey, "you establish deep-water patterns by fishing drops at a specific depth."

Huskey reports that the drops do not have to be large ones. "A drop of just a couple of feet will hold a tremendous number of fish." He goes on to say, "If you see fish suspended up over the drops, they will not be feeding. Fish that actively are feeding will hold tight to the drop."

Why are these deep structures so productive? Huskey answers: "Because they offer the fish everything they need. The drops are close to deep-water sanctuaries and to shallow-water feeding areas, and they give the fish something to orient to, something that gives them a sense of security."

Huskey believes that these small-point bluffs will hold fish virtually year-round.

"During the hottest part of summer

Huskey finds bass throughout the year on "bluff-points" — steep, rocky points extending into the original river channel.

Photo: Chris Altman

Arkie jig tipped with a brown, black, blue, or orange Uncle Josh No. 101 spin pork frog. It's a heavy bait, and it will get down to the fish quickly. Plus, it keeps me in better contact with the bottom and gives me more lure control. When you are trying to drop a jig off a small bluff 30 feet underwater, you need all the bait control you can get.

"I also recommend using heavy line, say, 17- to 20-pound-test, because it will be rubbing against a lot of rock and, again, because I am after big bass. These small drops are the finest deep-water structures in the lake, so the bigger fish will dominate them.

"In the winter, when the fish are less active and I want the lure to fall more slowly, I'll switch to a larger, No. 11 Uncle Josh pork frog, or sometimes change baits entirely to 1/4-ounce fly-and-rind (a hair jig with small pork rind trailer) on spinning gear."

and the coldest months of winter, these drops will hold more fish than most of the other structures combined. Bass still will hold to them in the fall, but they will be on shallower drops than they will be in the summer and winter. You even can find bass here in the spring during the spawn."

Remember that not all bass spawn at the same time, so some fish will be moving up the points toward the shallows, while others will be moving back to deeper water after they have spawned.

"Without question," says Huskey, "the technique is reliable. In fact, when the fishing is poor everywhere else, you can rest assured the bass will be on these drops. A bluebird day (one with very high, bright-blue skies that usually gives anglers fits) is one of the best times to fish them. And a bluebird day in August, when there is some current in the lake, is just about the best fishing that I know of." And yes, bass will be on these drops at night, too.

But the icing on the cake has to be that these deep-water structures will hold both largemouths and smallmouths, though not usually at the same time, Huskey believes.

He uses a "jig-and-pig" combo 90 percent of the time on deep structure. "Catching the bass is the easy part," he says. "Although a worm will catch fish on these structures, I have found that a jig-and-pig will consistently catch more, and larger, bass. I use a brown or black 1/2-ounce

Another bait Huskey uses on these deep-water drops is a 1/2-ounce spinnerbait. "At night, I like to slow-roll a brown or black spinnerbait down the drops. Sometimes this will produce more fish than the jig. And at night, after I have worked the deep-water drops, I'll move my boat in close to shore and cast a white or chartreuse spinnerbait along the top of the point. I retrieve the spinnerbait as fast as possible without allowing the blade to break the surface. This technique is deadly on smallmouths in summer, especially on those clear nights when a full moon is shining."

One final tip: "While scouting the lake, be sure to run your depthfinder alongside sheer cliffs that drop into the water," says Huskey. "You can often locate a point that stems from the cliff but begins under the water's surface. These have proved to be some of my more productive points, and I think the reason is that, because they are not in plain sight, no one else fishes them."

Without question, Charlie Huskey has developed one of the finest deep-water structure techniques in the world of bass fishing. Spring, summer, fall or winter, day or night, in sun, rain or snow, he catches bass. Heed the advice of this professional Bassmaster, and with a little time and effort, you can catch these bluff-point bass as well.

— JULY/AUGUST 1988

DON'T LEAVE THE DOCK

By CHRIS CHRISTIAN

In the middle of summer's "dog days," the best bassin' may be under your feet. Certain docks are bassin' hot spots. Try this shallow-water pattern when the sun is bearing down . . .

The deep summer doldrums. It's a frustrating time for most Southern bass chasers. Gone are the idyllic days of spring when the shallows fairly teemed with active bass and about all a BASSer had to do was keep chunking spinnerbaits at the stick-ups.

Now, high water temperatures make bass sluggish and send them deep. They're tough to find, and even tougher to catch. The old-timers don't call this the "dog days" for nothing, and there will be little change in the picture until the cooling fall waters spark some activity from the bass.

Of course, bassin' folk are a pretty hardy lot, and we've learned to cope with all this. Some BASSers make an annual enlistment in the "dawn patrol," and arrive bleary-eyed at 4 a.m. for a few hours' casting before the rising sun shuts down the shallow-water action and sends them heading for the shade. Others, eyes glued to depthfinders, diligently probe the offshore waters in search of the proverbial bassing "honey hole." A few serious souls even adopt a somewhat vampiric approach and arise in the dead of night to stalk the dark waters in search of monster bass.

Not many Bassmasters would consider working a "shallow-water pattern" on a searing midsummer day, but those who do can frequently find a summer bass bonanza — particularly if that shallow-water pattern happens to be boat docks.

Now, nobody has to tell a veteran bass chaser that boat docks and bass go together like politicians and promises. Fishing this type of cover is certainly nothing new; a few major tournaments have even been won this way. What may surprise some BASSers, though, is that this pattern is at its best during the hot, midday hours when even the bugs won't bite. Under midday conditions, at the peak of the summer, the Bassmasters carefully working the docks can be right on top of one of the best bassin' patterns available to them.

• **The Dock Attractions** — For a highly object-oriented fish, like the bass, an old wooden dock always will be an attractive holding point. The tightly clustered supporting pilings provide a neat underwater hideout. The overhead deck means continual shade. And, docks are generally built in the littoral zone where food is plentiful. On all types of water, bass will use docks to some degree, but on some types of lakes (particularly during the brightest part of the day) these factors can make a boat dock one of the choicest lies available.

During the midday hours, the factor that determines a dock's place on the bass' list of preferred cover is the amount of deep-water cover available. The deeper, man-made impoundments may see only a few fish scattered around the docks. This type of water provides an abundance of deep-water cover as well as clearly defined stratification. The bass, particularly the bigger fish, may find alternatives to boat docks for escaping the midday sun.

A shallower body of water, like many of the natural lowland lakes and impoundments, presents a different picture. These offer little in the way of defined offshore structure, and are generally too shallow to show much stratification. In many cases, the bass are forced to seek their havens in the heavier cover of the littoral zone.

On this type of water, a lot of largemouths will be

homesteading the shorelines for the summer. Dim-light periods will see them actively feeding, and brighter periods will have them holding tight to heavy cover. Given the bass' natural pecking order, the best spots will be taken by the bigger fish. A boat dock is a prime piece of cover under these conditions, and midday periods can see a lot of big bass jamming up underneath the docks.

• **Dry-Docking The Bass** — Getting the bass out from under the docks can be a little tough. Homesteading bass are not active fish. They will be holding tight, and deep, under the dock. The presentation must be one that triggers a strike, since few of these fish will chase a bait. The lure must be put on their heads, and sometimes, it may take repeated casts to trigger the bass to hit.

The bass angler trying to work a boat dock from 40 feet out will be passing right over the better fish that are using it. Small bass may take up positions on the dock's outer edge, but the bigger bass will be back in the tight spots that most fishermen can't (or won't) reach.

The key to hooking dock-hugging bass is to get in close enough to reach out and grab the dock, then flip the lure into every nook and cranny under the dock. Sidearm, backhand, underhand or even skipping a lure into the tight quarters is called for, if the dock is to be thoroughly covered.

It's a close-range, short-cast type of game and most of the fish will be hooked with less than 12 feet of line past the rod tip. Hitting a big bass at that range is explosive, to say the least. One of those dockside encounters with a lunker is usually all it takes to start a bassin' love affair with docks and piers.

Working in such tight quarters can be tough on equipment. Long rods are definitely a handicap. Flippin' might look like the answer, but the long sticks won't serve nearly as well as will a shorter rod. Most serious dock fishermen rely on short, stout spinning rigs (like the Skyline SSK 410) and lines in the 14- to 17-pound-test range.

A short spinning rig is much more maneuverable in tight spots than is a more conventional rig. The shorter rod allows casts from most any position, no matter how awkward. This will put more fish in the boat simply because the BASSer will reach more of the secluded spots — places that other folks pass over as being too tough to reach with their baits.

The most effective bait for this technique are "fall baits," like the Texas-rigged worm and countdown

Small bass may take up positions on the dock's outer edge, but bigger bass will be in tight spots most fishermen can't or won't reach.

crankbaits, like the Rat-L-Trap. Just which one to use depends on how the dock is constructed.

• **Fishing The Docks** — Some docks are cluttered underneath, a veritable maze of pilings and cross members that make lure presentation a matter of bouncing it off something and hoping it falls in the water. A lightly weighted, 1/16-ounce worm weight with the sinker pegged in place is the best bet here. It can be bounced, skipped and ricocheted into places that otherwise would be unreachable to the angler.

The lightweight sinker allows the bait to fall slowly, and that's where most of the hits will occur — on the fall. It's a s-l-o-w way to work a dock, but very thorough. This is the bread-and-butter technique of the serious dock fisherman, and the one that will put most of the big bass in the boat.

Docks that are relatively open on the underside can be covered most quickly with a crankbait. The bass most likely will be holding tight to one of the supporting pilings, and a bait cranked into the piling, then bounced off, should bring some response. By thoroughly covering all the pilings (on all sides), a dock can be checked with a plug more quickly than with a plastic worm.

Here the lure is tossed past the target, allowed to sink, and then retrieved rapidly along the bottom by the piling. If it can be bounced off the piling as it passes, so much the better.

One veteran dock angler summed up the technique by saying, "That fish is going to be right up next to the piling, and if I buzz that lure by real close, the bass has either got to move out of the way, or hit it. Now the fish may not 'bust' the bait the first time it goes by, but after I move the bait a few times he's going to get ticked off and smack that Rat-L-Trap the next time I put it on his head."

In a nutshell, that sums up dock fishing. Keep putting that bait in front of the bass until it gets mad enough to take it. If the bass doesn't hit on the first cast, keep throwing. If it's a "good dock," chances are there's a fish under it.

It can take a fair amount of looking, and a liberal dose of casting to determine the really top docks on any lake. However, once a BASSer stakes out 15 or 20 of these bassin' gold mines, you've got a midday "milk run" that can produce bragging-sized bass during times when most other fishermen don't venture out. Somehow, that makes the dog days just a little easier to take. Just lay around the docks and catch your share of big ol' good 'uns.

— JULY/AUGUST 1981

As anglers such as Gary Klein know, docks provide a neat underwater hideout for bass in the middle of summer's dog days.

Photo: Gerald Crawford

LEDGE-FISHING BASICS

By DAVE PRECHT

Paul Elias gets an edge on other pro anglers by fishing the ledges . . .

If Paul Elias could have his way, the BASSMASTER® Tournament Trail would begin the season on Lake Eufaula on the Alabama/Georgia line and end it on Kentucky Lake in Tennessee/Kentucky. Along the way would be stops on Lake Seminole, West Point Reservoir and several of the Tennessee River impoundments.

Never mind that none of Elias' three BASSMASTER tournament victories — including the 1982 BASS Masters Classic® on the Alabama River — occurred on any of those waterways. What matters is that Elias loves to fish ledges, and those are his favorite ledge-fishing lakes.

"I've done well on open-lake structure in several lakes we've fished tournaments on," says Elias, a veteran pro from Laurel, Miss. "I've done well on Kentucky Lake practically every time we've been there, and I've caught some big fish on Eufaula several times."

Elias loves open-lake structure, particularly the ledges or drop-offs at the junctions of creeks and river channels. He says bass found at those spots are relatively easy to catch and, what's more, they aren't usually loners.

"If ever you catch one on a ledge, stop and anchor," he declares. "Bass will bunch up on a ledge."

The term "ledge" is a broad one, even in bass-fishing jargon. Basically, it applies to the edge of a comparatively shallow flat or gently sloping bottom that is cut by any channel. Every reservoir has river ledges, but not all ledges are productive, and not every spot on a good ledge holds bass, he is quick to point out.

"Some of the really deep reservoirs don't have any shallow water near the river channels — that's definitely criti-

cal," he explains.

The ideal drop-off is distinct, and it occurs at the edge of a flat between 5 and 12 feet deep, he says. The channel itself plunges 25 or 30 feet below the surface. And the best ledges have some form of cover on them, including stumps, brush, rocks, and aquatic grass.

Finding these open-water hot spots is simple, if you've got a good topographical map, a depthfinder and the knowledge to employ both tools.

Elias studies his map to find expansive flats about 5 feet deep (or at least 8 feet in hot weather). Arriving at such a shallow area, he idles along and watches his depthfinder (a Humminbird LCR 4X6) until it shows the bottom dipping sharply into a creek channel. Then he turns the boat and follows the channel until it intersects with a deeper creek channel or the main river. There, at the juncture, he expects to find bass.

"On each side of the creek channel is a point, and that's what I like to fish," he says. Elias positions his boat over the tributary channel, lowers his trolling motor and begins searching for bass.

He uses two baits, primarily: a deep-diving crankbait designed to dig into the bottom, and a Carolina-rigged plastic worm. Those two baits scour an area efficiently and quickly — especially the crankbait.

"I've always believed that a fish will eat another fish before it will eat anything else, and crankbaits resemble fish," Elias says. "If you try to find fish with the Texas-rigged worm, you'll waste a lot of time. I can go along, searching with a big, deep-diving crankbait like the

(Mann's) 20+ or a Carolina rig and cover a lot more water. Then, when I find the fish, I can zero in on them and catch more bass on the Texas rig."

Elias uses two varieties of Carolina worms. One is a two-hook affair called the Mann's Limit Finder. It's similar to the Do-Nothing worm with which Jack Chancellor won the 1985 Classic, except each hook is covered by a soft-plastic nipple designed to make the lure weedless.

The other rig he calls the "Do-Something," and it is merely a large, Texas-rigged worm incorporated into the Carolina setup. In either configuration, the worms are fished at the end of a 5-foot-long leader that is attached

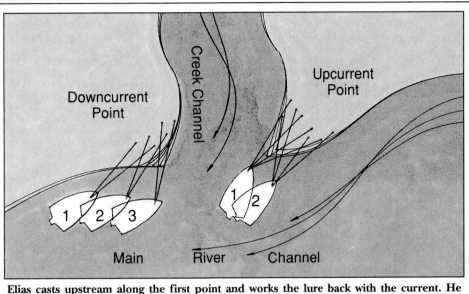

Elias casts upstream along the first point and works the lure back with the current. He then moves to the next point and repeats the procedure. His boat always is positioned on the downstream side.

Illustration: Bernie Schultz

to a swivel. Above the swivel is a plastic bead and a 1-ounce bullet weight. The bead cushions the knot against damage from the weight banging against the swivel. Sometimes he uses an 8-inch worm on his Do-Something rig, but Elias' favorite lure in that arrangement is a 12-inch Mann's Auger Snake. He inserts a 5/0 worm hook through the top of the snake and then imbeds it in the body of the lure to make it weedless.

"The Limit Finder seems to work better in hot weather when I'm searching for fish, but when I find them, I throw the big worm," he says. "Big fish will bite the little, two-hook worm, but I have more confidence in the Do-Something worm."

While most fishermen, including Jack Chancellor, simply reel in the Carolina-rigged worms steadily and quickly, Elias often hops or pumps them as he would a traditional worm.

He positions his boat over the creek channel, usually casts upstream, and works the lure back toward him with the current.

"Even if they (dam operators) aren't generating power and there isn't any current, I still like to bring my bait downstream. I feel that the fish position themselves facing upstream, even when there isn't any current." He says it's easier to work the lures properly by positioning the boat over deep water and casting toward the shallows, but if action slows, he often tries the opposite tack, and drags the bait up the drop-off.

Elias has learned over the years that it isn't easy to pinpoint bass concentrations on open water and stay with them. And it would be impossible to do so without a marker buoy, which he considers one of the most important tools for deep-structure fishing.

"Let's say you have found an island in the middle of the

lake," Elias suggests. "The top of the island is 12 feet deep, and it's surrounded by deep water. The top is bare, slick, except for three stumps on one end.

"You're casting along and not getting anything until you cast across those three stumps and hit a stump and — *bam* — you get a 3-pounder. You let off the trolling motor and fight the fish. Now the wind's blowing the boat. You unhook the fish, jump back up to cast and you think, 'Well, where was it?' You might cast 50 times and never hit those three stumps again."

To remedy that problem, Elias sets a marker buoy on the edge of his bow as he fishes. As soon as he gets a strike, he kicks the buoy overboard and notes the position of the strike in relation to the buoy. The marker gives him a reference for locating the productive spot again.

Anglers unfamiliar with river ledges may want to mark a long section of the ledge with several buoys, which gives them a better idea of the shape and location of the underwater structure.

Ledge fishing is a productive pattern year-round, according to Elias, although it's most successful on his favorite lakes between the spawn and the first really cold weather. September and October are among his favorite periods, he says, because bass are inclined to gather in thick bunches along river channel edges, intercept baitfish, and enjoy the relatively cooler water along the river.

"The bass is a shallow-water fish," Elias explains. "It likes water 15 feet deep or less, and in warm weather it likes cooler water.

"If a bass wants that cooler river water, with shallow water nearby, a ledge is the place to go."

— NOVEMBER 1988

CATCHING BASS IN TREES

By STEVE PRICE

Study the timber and let the trees tell you where the bass are located . . .

The first thing most Bassmasters think of when they see a lake full of standing timber is heaven. They expect to find bass beside every tree.

After an hour or so of fruitless casting, however, their thoughts often change. There isn't a bass beside every tree, and in some instances there may not be any bass beside any of the trees.

"Fishing timber can be a very humbling experience," says Toledo Bend fishing guide and B.A.S.S. Tournament Trail pro Tommy Martin. "The main problem is that at first glance everything looks so good, but when you fish timber you really have to define your pattern carefully because there are more variables than most anglers consider."

Two-time BASS Masters Classic® champ Rick Clunn agrees with Martin. "First, you need to analyze the timber itself," he points out. "Try to determine if it is young or old timber. That is, are you fishing a newly impounded lake, or one five to 10 years old or older? This will have a direct influence on where fish may be.

"Next, look at the trees themselves. Is the timber thick or spread out? Are the trees in shallow water or deep water? Or are the trees submerged? The answers to these questions will tell you where and how to start fishing."

"Basically, this is known as 'reading timber,'" adds 1983 B.A.S.S. Angler-of-the-Year Hank Parker. "One of the ways this technique helps you find fish is that the formation of trees will also show you the configuration of the bottom structure. Points, channels, ridges, depressions and humps can all be pinpointed very easily as you watch the growth pattern of the trees.

"In my opinion, bass don't relate to the timber as much as they relate to the structure. They simply use the timber as cover on that structure, and they move more because they have so much cover available."

Based on these considerations, here are some of the ways pros like Martin, Clunn and Parker successfully attack timber reservoirs:

• **Young Timber** — "Normally, young timber in recently impounded lakes is very thick," explains Clunn. "In the early days of Toledo Bend, the trees were so thick you couldn't get a boat back in them at all.

"In thick timber, bass tend to be more edge-oriented. The shad run the edges of the treelines, and so do the bass. The edge of a treeline frequently marks an old roadbed, fence-line, or perimeter of a field," Clunn says, "so study the shoreline to see what the bottom might look like."

"In a young lake up to about six years old," Parker notes, "fish are generally more shallow. In really thick cover, I just forget about the trees and concentrate more on the structure (bottom contour). Look for humps, marked by taller trees, or points and indentions along the edges."

Martin likes to look for something different in the thick cover, such as a cluster of cedars growing amidst a forest of oaks. At other times, only the trees with green branches may hold fish while those with dead, brown branches don't. Still another consideration is to look for smaller, isolated patches of trees away from the main stands of timber.

Fishing techniques and lure selection for young timber depend largely on what's available for a casting target. Some timber is so thick you can't cast into it without snagging.

When edge fishing, crankbaits, plastic worms and spinnerbaits can be tried. Vary your retrieve speed and style until something clicks. A hopping worm is often very effective in places like this, but if you happen to find bass schooled on an old roadbed, ripping a crankbait down through them may be more efficient. Remember the first bass you catch and how you caught it.

• **Older Timber** — "In older lakes it is often important to actually identify the trees in order to find fish," says Clunn, "because knowing the type of tree can tell you where it was growing before impoundment, and the type of bottom there. Pines, for instance, tend to grow along higher ridges, while hardwoods are found in the lower bottomland. The bottom around the oaks will likely be muddy, decaying vegetation and not necessarily suitable for bass. Birch trees, on the other hand, are more often found along creek channels, and these are excellent places to look for bass in older tree-filled reservoirs."

As lakes grow older, the timber begins to thin. The drowned trees lose their branches and eventually rot at the waterline. This presents a dangerous navigation problem, and also changes the habits of the fish.

"Believe it or not," says Parker, "when timber really begins to thin out, you start looking for bass in the thickest timber still remaining. Very often, especially in shallow water, the key is fishing fallen timber. The reason is that one tree lying down in the water offers a lot more shade and cover than several trees still standing."

"As the years progress," Martin continues, "it seems fish become more strongly oriented to humps and channels. We've certainly seen this on Toledo Bend where we don't pay much attention to the trees anymore. The bass move deeper if there is deeper water available, and frequently they suspend if they stay in the timber at all."

The basic fishing techniques for this type of timber vary with the depth of water. In shallow water, a spinnerbait, buzz-

Hank Parker works the edge of a timberline. Crankbaits are effective in such cover, especially in fall or late spring.

Photo: Steve Price

bait, or even a topwater plug may be used successfully. What's needed is a lure that generates activity and pulls fish toward it. Repeated casts may be required.

If the fish are not aggressive, then flipping may be a possible solution. In warm water, use a plastic worm with the sinker pegged in place and concentrate on the heaviest cover

Big bass will stake out a place in the thickest part of flooded timber.

Photo: Gerald Crawford

you can find. In colder weather, switch to a jig and look for channel edges, extremely heavy cover, or perhaps green aquatic vegetation that is frequently found with standing timber.

Crankbaits can be productive in deeper, older timber, particularly in late spring and early fall when bass suspend or begin to move. Stop-and-go retrieves, in which the lure actually bumps a tree trunk, often generates vicious strikes just as the retrieve is restarted.

• **Submerged Timber** — "Submerged timber is the worst of all to fish," feels Clunn, "because you never see it. The best graphs on the market will show some fish in the treetops, but most graphs don't. What you really use a graph for in this situation is to show the bottom configuration so you can concentrate on structure fishing."

"The basic fishing technique for deep, submerged timber," says Martin, "is to jig vertically with a worm, spoon or jig. You can try dropping the lure to the bottom, then working it back up through the trees a foot at a time with short jigging motions,

Jigging vertically with a plastic worm will pay dividends like this.
Photo: Russell Tinsley

or you can fish from the surface down, jigging progressively deeper.

"Another technique for this type of timber," Martin continues, "is to drift through it with the wind, or move slowly with the trolling motor, pulling a worm or grub down through the trees. With any of these, you need strong, abrasion-resistant line and at least a semi-weedless lure if possible. Check your line often for fraying, too."

"Fishing timber is largely a mental game," concludes Clunn, who is recognized as a master when it comes to figuring out finicky bass. "When you fish the trees, you have to expect lures to get snagged and your boat to get scratched. You have to shorten your casts and make more of them, and you have to realize that bass may not hold in the same areas day after day."

Fishing in the trees can be feast or famine, but the main thing is to study the trees and let them tell you where the bass are, and if you have to, act like the trees aren't even there and concentrate on structure.

— 1984 BASS FISHING GUIDE

RIPRAP BASS

By BOB McNALLY

Riprap — rock-lined levees and jetties — is one of the easiest bass structures to locate, and often the most productive . . .

Bill Syzmanski pointed at the channel marker floating 50 yards out from the west shore of Lake Pepin. He said we should cast between the bank and the marker, let our lures sink deep, then bounce them around the rocks.

Four of us, including Tim Sampson and Greg Moats, sat in two anchored boats and looked heron-like at the ridiculously small patch of opaque, obviously deep, swirling water that stretched upcurrent before us. It seemed absurd for four adult and otherwise sane anglers to all be casting to a spot roughly the size of a school bus on a Mississippi River impoundment as massive as Pepin.

But few people argue with Syzmanski ("Syz" to his friends). Not only is he as knowledgeable and selective about fishing deep structure as a pawnbroker in the process of buying a watch, but he's built like a well-fed black bear from his native state of Wisconsin.

So we did as he instructed.

Four little, 2-inch-long, 1/4-ounce Fuzzy Grub jigs plopped down on Pepin's surface about the same time, and it took only a few seconds for the lures to hit bottom as they pulled the 6-pound-test deep. With the light spinning gear it was easy to feel the rocks on Pepin's floor, which didn't surprise me since I knew Syz wouldn't be wasting his time fishing barren bottom. I wasn't surprised, either, when Syz whipped his spinning rod back hard and fast and said, quite matter-of-factly, that he had a fish.

I was amazed, however, when Sampson and Moats each hooked a fish, too. I promptly fouled my jig fast to the bottom.

Syz drew his 2-pound smallmouth to the boat without fanfare, though such a bronzeback is a good bass anywhere, especially from Pepin — which isn't noted for smallmouths and is as hard-fished a body of water as any I know in Wisconsin.

Sampson landed a 2-pound white bass and Moats boated a little largemouth.

Syz never spoke. He never looked at me to acknowledge the action . . . at least not until he hooked a fish that simply refused to budge from the bottom.

"Get the anchor in, man, and start the motor or I'm gonna lose this 'un for sure," he growled in the tone a black bear uses when it protects its food. "There are some big pike in here, and I think I got one . . . sure can't put much force on 'em with no leader and 6-pound-test."

I obeyed immediately, and closed the gap on Syz's fish, until he fought it from directly above. Minutes later we saw a long white form well up from Pepin's black depths and I slid the net under a pike a few ounces shy of 10 pounds.

An hour later, when Syz's gold mine of a fishing spot finally played out, the tally for the two boats was four smallmouths up to 2 1/2 pounds, 17 white bass to the same weight, six largemouths to 3 pounds, a pair of 3-pound walleyes, and that pike, which was the biggest I'd ever seen taken from Pepin.

After an hour of casting bottom-scraping jigs around the area, I had a pretty good idea what the structure looked like, since the rocks had collected several dollars' worth of leadheads. But when we were done fishing, Syz outboarded slowly around the deep structure and showed me the area in detail with his boat's depthfinder.

He explained why it held so many good-size fish. The rocks were connected to a riprap shoreline that ran for miles along Pepin's west side and protected a railroad-track bed from erosion.

"It's no secret that the west shore riprap holds fish," says Syz. "My dad showed me about fishing the riprap here when I was a kid. But I never learned about the place where we caught our fish today until I hooked another big pike while trolling a plug tight to the riprap bank. It was a 12-pounder and I couldn't horse it. So I followed the fish with my boat when it ran, and it ran far out from the bank toward the bar and hump of rocks that we caught fish from today. From that day until now, I've caught some bass from the structure almost every time I've fished it."

"Syz's Hump," as we now call the place, is a submerged, ridge-like bar of riprap that extends farther away from the bank and closer to Pepin's main deep channel than any other point of rocks along the riprap railroad bank.

Although flipping for bass around riprap requires a high degree of patience, it may be the best method for taking bass out of the rocks.
Photo: Bob McNally

Right near the channel, the rocks form a high spot and provide storybook structure for virtually every game fish that inhabits the lake. Such rockpiles are not uncommon wherever extensive riprap is found. Sometimes during riprap construction, newly placed rocks fall away from the bank that is being reinforced, and at times a veritable landslide of riprap can occur. This forms major points or even humps that reach far out and away from the riprap at sharp angles to the bank, which in turn serve as ideal migration routes for bass and a myriad other sportfish species. When the riprap slides extend to deep-water sanctuaries — as in the case of Syz's Hump on Lake Pepin — the spot can be a honey of a fishing hole.

Such structures along riprap banks invariably are the ones that hold the most and biggest fish, and all species of bass, as well as pike, walleyes, stripers, muskies and catfish are attracted to them. Such structures are the ones all anglers should seek whenever they fish riprap in rivers, reservoirs and natural lakes.

The structures hold fish for two reasons: 1) fish (including forage species) relate to anything that's different along a long line of riprap shore; 2) the more remote the structure off a riprap bank, the less likely other anglers have fished it and,

therefore, the more big fish will be found holding there.

Many of the best bass-holding riprap structures are comparatively nondescript. Some are not visible above the water's surface. But savvy BASSers should always check thoroughly the riprap around lakeside roadways, railroad embankments, marinas, launch ramps and other man-made sites.

Even small residential lakes, borrow pits and golf-course ponds have productive riprap. But once he locates a riprap bank, a fisherman's job is just beginning.

"Sub-cover on a riprap structure is the key to finding the most and biggest fish along a rocky bank," says Gary Jenkins, a fisheries biologist for the Tennessee Valley Authority at the Land Between the Lakes (LBL) area on the Tennessee-Kentucky border. "To catch the most fish consistently from riprap, you've got to locate key changes in the rock-bank features — things like little points or bulges, logs, brushpiles — even the slightest thing different along riprap can hold fish, and it consistently will be the place to find bass.

"It's smart to note where creek channels swing in closest to riprap, too, because these are primary spots for bass to make contact with the rocks."

Jenkins does the bulk of his bass fishing on the waters he helps manage for LBL, including lakes Kentucky and Barkley. He knows the lakes as well as any angler, and has placed high in tournaments held on those waters, with some of his best and most consistent catches coming from riprap banks.

Jenkins makes it a habit to look over riprap banks during periods of low water, usually in winter. He runs his boat along riprap and watches for irregularities in the rocks, and he keeps a sharp eye for logs, brush and anything else that may hold bass. Sometimes he even creates his own bass-attracting structure on riprap by sinking brushpiles or repositioning shoreline logs and stumps so they will be more attractive to bass when the lake level rises. Jenkins marks all such "sub-cover," as he calls it, on a lake map for future reference.

Best conditions for riprap bassing is when water color is stained slightly, which prompts shallow migrations of fish.

Fishing at daybreak, dusk and night along riprap is especially good. And any time strong winds and waves buffet a riprap bank, baitfish and bass seem to be attracted to the rocks.

Jenkins employs some unique lure techniques to catch

most of his riprap bass. His favorite way of fishing riprap is done in early spring for pre-spawn bass. About 70 percent of the fish he catches this way are spotted bass, the rest largemouths. He casts an 11G Rapala tight to the riprap bank, and "pops" it during the retrieve.

Jenkins doesn't fish the Rapala right out of the box; he modifies the lure by replacing the No. 6 rear hook with a larger No. 4 Eagle Claw treble. Then he wraps a bit of fly-tying "lead ribbon" around the hook shank. That gives the lure weight in the rear, causing the Rapala's head to rise at about a 40-degree angle while its tail settles below the surface. Instead of diving underwater when he twitches the bait, the modified minnow plug pops like a chugger or slush bait. And it has resulted in huge catches of spotted bass.

Perhaps Jenkins' most deadly riprap tactic is one most savvy B.A.S.S. members already have in their arsenal of angling tricks, yet seldom employ when fishing the jagged-rock banks.

"About two years ago a friend and I were fishing riprap with standard lures, and the bass kept striking short. They'd roll on the lures but not take them," he explains. "That gave us the idea of flipping jigs for them. Since the lures are compact, they're tantalizing, and when a fish hits, you've got it hooked securely. We tried flipping that day and really mopped up on the bass."

Since that first flipping trip on riprap, the technique has become one of Jenkins' bread-and-butter methods of consistently catching bass. He's used it to win several tournaments. Lots of 4- to 6-pound bass have fallen to his riprap-flipping tactics, with about an equal number of spotted and large-mouth bass caught.

Occasionally, he catches smallmouths from riprap while flipping, and he's sure it would work well on bronzebacks in lakes where they're abundant.

Jenkins employs stout-flipping rods, 20-pound-test line and Stan Sloan's 3/8-ounce Zorro weedless jigs. With nylon weedguards and a flat-bottomed head, the Zorros seem to hang up less in the rocks than typical, round-head jigs. He uses brown or black jigs tipped with No. 1 or No. 11 Uncle Josh pork frogs. He uses the bigger No. 1 pork frogs when fishing dingy-color water, and he always contrasts the color of the frog to the color of the jig — brown jig and black frog or black jig and brown frog.

In clear water, he slices some of the meat from the pork to make the jig-and-pig combo fall faster, which, in his experience, is preferred by bass.

"Flipping jigs and pork frogs is deadly on riprap because these baits perfectly imitate crawfish, which are extremely abundant around the rocks, especially in spring," the biologist explains. "Crawfish instinctively head to riprap in spring because it provides cover and the water is a bit warmer because the rocks absorb heat. Bass are near the riprap for the same reasons, plus there is a ready supply of crawfish for food."

The best riprap for flipping is one on which the deep edge is no deeper than 10 feet, and the most productive riprap edges abut gravel or similar hard bottom. He prefers stained (not muddy) water for flipping, and he wants the riprap to slope at about a 45-degree angle.

By keeping his boat in 8 or 10 feet of water and carefully monitoring his bow-mounted depthfinder, Jenkins is able to keep his flipping jig precisely on the edge of the riprap. He works it around sub-cover wherever he finds it.

He varies the retrieve of the jig and pork frog to water temperature (fast when it's warm, slow when it's cold) and according to how active the bass are. Standard technique for him is to flip the jig to the edge of the riprap and let it fall to the bottom. Then he raises his rod tip slightly and shakes it to make the jig rise slowly and then fall down the slope of the riprap. Hits usually come on the fall.

While flipping likely is the most deadly method of catching riprap bass, it's not well-suited to cover a lot of unfamiliar water quickly.

A better way to search riprap is to troll crankbaits that sport large, sturdy lips that allow the plugs to bump bottom without coming apart. Crawfish- or shad-colored crankbaits are preferred, since they imitate the forage most often found along riprap. Shad-like lures are especially good choices when working riprap on waters that hold stripers as well as largemouths, since such plugs are most likely to score on both species.

Live crawfish, shad and shiners are natural baits for working riprap, too. Minnows are easy to troll when hooked through the lips, and they make for a deadly riprap bass "searching" system.

Another way to locate bass on a long riprap bank is by using a buddy system to scour the area quickly.

Two anglers can work as a team, both fishing from the bow and casting parallel to the riprap as the trolling motor pulls the rig along. The boat should be positioned right over the deep edge of the submerged rocks (usually 8 to 15 feet deep). One fisherman might work a jig or plastic worm (pegging the slip sinker with a toothpick helps prevent hangups) parallel to the bank, and the other angler can fish a crankbait or a heavy, single-spin spinnerbait to the rocky shore and down under the boat. Lures should maintain contact with the bottom throughout the retrieve.

Riprap bassing may not be the most picturesque or aesthetically pleasing type of angling, nor is it always the easiest type of structure to fish effectively. But year-in and year-out, on bass waters from Maine to Montana and California to the Carolinas, few other structures consistently will harbor more or bigger bass than that long, man-made jumble of rocks most anglers roar by on the way to their favorite hot spots.

— FEBRUARY 1987

HOW TO FISH
A DROP-OFF

By C. BOYD PFEIFFER

If you can find a drop-off like this one in your favorite lake, you should be able to catch bass, our pro panelists say . . .

The first and biggest problem in fishing deep-water structure spots — like the one our bass-pro panel will discuss— is finding the places.

Nothing juts up above the surface to let you know how good a honey hole lies below. You need a map or a lot of luck to find it. The pros on our panel (Basil Bacon, Charlie Ingram and Randy Dearman) agree that a topographical map is helpful in searching for underwater structure.

"The first thing you should have is a map," notes Bacon, six-time qualifier for the prestigious BASS Masters Classic®. "It will give you a general idea of what is down there — the lay of the land. With a good map and a flasher, you can tell an awful lot about what's down there. Naturally, if you have a graph recorder, that would be the best way to go."

For this article, each of the pros was given a copy of the chart-recorder etching and asked to tell where and how he would go about catching fish on a drop-off like this. The structure drops off into 25 feet of water on one side, and it has a flat top averaging about 10 feet deep. Brush or debris has collected at the base of the drop-off, and standing timber is along one side. For purposes of this discussion, the panelists were asked to concentrate on the sides and top of the main structure, not the ditch or other contour changes.

Dearman suspects the structure itself is a steep ridge. "I would follow it with a flasher or chart recorder while looking for points dropping off into deep water."

Bacon agrees that a spot like this must have some special feature about it to attract fish. "That's got to be the end of a point or something, the end of an island for fish to hold on it," he insists.

All three of these experienced pros would expect to find a few bass scattered but not holding well on the top of the drop-off; fishing would be far more consistent in the trees and brush along the sides and at the base of the drop-off.

Ingram feels that the fish on top could be easier to catch; those in deep water or in any depressions would be more difficult.

Two of the three pros would pick the same lure for first choice. Bacon and Dearman would start by working crankbaits from far away. Basil would start far away, making a cast that would just reach the bottom of the hump, then work his lure down the side, bouncing it through the stair-step pattern of the breaklines or working a crankbait along the steep sides and down into the brush at the bottom.

"If I knew where this place was I might throw a crankbait at it," Bacon explains. "For that I would move farther out and cast to just barely reach the top of that hump and then work a lure down the side of it into the 18-foot depth (the right side on the picture) and into the trees. I would make a couple of casts on that and work the lure right down in there."

"I'd make a long cast with a fast retrieve to get the bait down and then a slow retrieve to keep it bumping the bottom as long as possible," says Dearman. But, while Bacon would stick to casts across the top, Dearman would work his deep-diving crankbait along the sides and parallel to the breaklines.

"The casts should be long and parallel with the drop-off," explains Randy. "The bait should be kept as close to

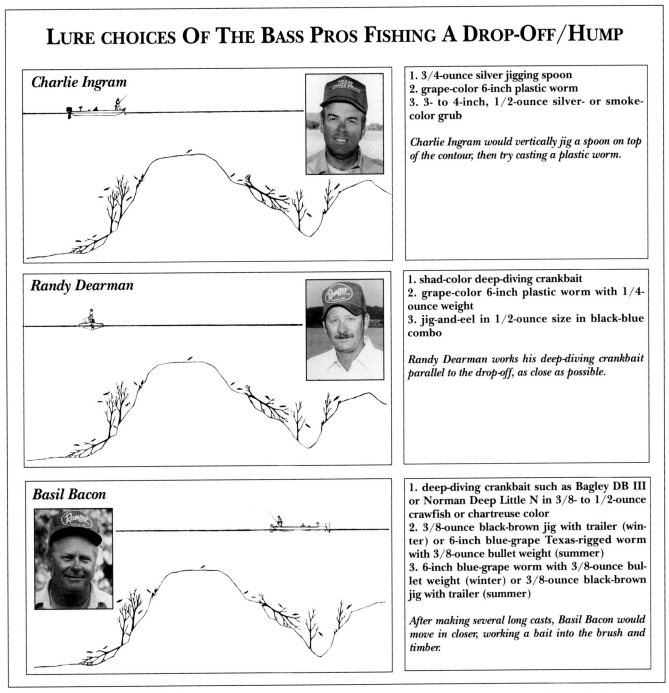

LURE CHOICES OF THE BASS PROS FISHING A DROP-OFF/HUMP

Charlie Ingram

1. 3/4-ounce silver jigging spoon
2. grape-color 6-inch plastic worm
3. 3- to 4-inch, 1/2-ounce silver- or smoke-color grub

Charlie Ingram would vertically jig a spoon on top of the contour, then try casting a plastic worm.

Randy Dearman

1. shad-color deep-diving crankbait
2. grape-color 6-inch plastic worm with 1/4-ounce weight
3. jig-and-eel in 1/2-ounce size in black-blue combo

Randy Dearman works his deep-diving crankbait parallel to the drop-off, as close as possible.

Basil Bacon

1. deep-diving crankbait such as Bagley DB III or Norman Deep Little N in 3/8- to 1/2-ounce crawfish or chartreuse color
2. 3/8-ounce black-brown jig with trailer (winter) or 6-inch blue-grape Texas-rigged worm with 3/8-ounce bullet weight (summer)
3. 6-inch blue-grape worm with 3/8-ounce bullet weight (winter) or 3/8-ounce black-brown jig with trailer (summer)

After making several long casts, Basil Bacon would move in closer, working a bait into the brush and timber.

the breakline as possible," he concludes about fishing with this first choice of a deep-diving crankbait.

"Vertically jig a spoon, preferably on the top of the contour," suggests Charlie Ingram, winner of three B.A.S.S. tournaments in 1984, and two-time qualifier for the BASS Masters Classic.

Ingram would follow up this vertical jigging by casting his second lure choice — a plastic worm — into the deep water, hopping it up to the top of the drop-off. His third choice would be a reverse lure presentation with the grub,

working it down the steep sides and into the brush on the bottom and in any depressions.

After first making several long casts, Bacon would move in closer and work a lure in short casts right down into the brush and timber, teasing the fish with an up-and-down movement of the lure. Following this, he would move in close with his third-choice lure to vertically jig the deep sides of the hump, working the lure into the brush on the bottom.

Just which lure he would use would depend on the time

of year. Bacon would pick a jig as his second-choice lure in the cooler months, followed by his third lure choice of a worm. For the summer, he would reverse this, still keeping the crankbait a first choice in all seasons for the possible quick catch of fish on the top.

In both his second and third choices, however, he would stick with the same colors for winter or summer. For the jig, it would be a 3/8-ounce black-brown jig with a trailer. "With the jig I'd use some kind of trailer," he notes. "I may use pork, or I may use a plastic crawfish."

Randy Dearman would come up with a similar solution for his second lure choice of a worm. "I'd work a worm slowly all around the wood and along the break," he notes, also suggesting the same method for this third lure choice of a jig-and-eel.

As you can see, the pros were in agreement on lure choices, and on colors, too. With regard to worms, two would use grape color; one, blue-grape. And of the jig combos, two would be dark colors, either black-brown or black-blue.

Figuring out a piece of structure like this — even assuming you can find it easily with the help of a topo map and flasher or graph — is no easy feat.

Unlike many of the shallow-water structure types we've looked at and the few deep-water types covered so far, this one offers many different ways of fishing, from long casts to medium, deeply worked casts to vertical jigging.

Boat positioning, too, can be critical if you're going to get the most effectiveness out of the fewest casts. With so many trees, bushes and debris piles, it's a trick to hook fish instead of snags. Our experts prove that fishing drop-offs is not insurmountable, however. In fact, they even tend to think of the challenge as just one more mental hill to climb in learning about bassing — even if that hill is underwater.

—*FEBRUARY 1986*

Charlie Ingram prefers a grape-colored worm for fishing the drop-off.

Photo: Gerald Crawford

FISHING FOR BASS IN GRASS

By STEVE PRICE

Veteran guide Jerry Sims treats each type of greenery differently and employs a variety of tactics . . .

For the past 13 years, Jerry Sims has been one of the most popular — and busiest — guides on Georgia's Lake Seminole. The 37,500-acre impoundment has long been a favorite of America's Bassmasters because of its shallow grassbeds and big fish, and Sims has used his years as a guide at Jack Wingate's Lunker Lodge to become an expert on year-round grassbed fishing.

Many anglers feel all vegetation can be fished the same way, but Sims disagrees. He treats each type of greenery differently and employs a variety of fishing techniques.

The vegetation types found in Seminole — lily pads, hydrilla, moss, milfoil and various blade grasses — grow in lakes throughout the United States, and the methods Sims uses to fish them can apply to all locales. Here are some of his "Pro's Pointers" on fishing different vegetation in early summer:

• **Milfoil, Coontail —** "This is my favorite type of grass for fishing because you can fish it all day long in the heat of the summer, and where you find one bass you often find several more," says Sims, who has caught numerous bass over 10 pounds from the Lake Seminole grassbeds.

"This type of vegetation grows to the top and blankets the surface, but it has definite edges. Whenever you find one of the edges, you know the water depth changes, and this is what makes coontail and milfoil so productive.

"One way to fish it is to look for small, open pockets inside the surface mat and toss a small topwater plug into those openings. Let the plug just sit there quivering — don't do anything special to it — to see if a bass hits it," explains Sims.

"If nothing strikes, cast a weightless worm beyond the hole and swim it into the opening, then let it free-fall down to the bottom. If a bass is present, it'll generally hit as the worm is settling down," says the veteran guide.

Sims also uses a plastic worm to probe the edges of the vegetation, but other lure choices include buzzbaits and spinnerbaits, especially during early-morning hours. A buzzbait can be worked across the top of the vegetation and out over the open water or parallel to the edge.

"In many instances this type of grass actually continues growing along the bottom in deeper water, although it does not come completely to the surface," points out Sims, who spends about 250 days on the water annually. "The grass stairsteps down," he says.

"To fish these steps with either a spinnerbait, buzzbait or worm, I move my boat in close to the surface edge, cast to deeper water, and bring the lure up through the vegetation," continues Sims. "Of course, you also can walk a lure, particularly a weightless worm, down the steps, too.

"The key with this type of vegetation, which often covers huge areas, is to look for points, indentions — anything different along the edge. Bass use these as holding areas, and often I've caught several fish from one area like this."

Later in the day, when the sun may be hotter, Sims advises finding an edge in slightly deeper water, possibly one that falls into 12 to 15 feet of water. These he fishes the same way with a worm.

• **Peppergrass —** "This grass grows on a stalk and covers the surface with small leaves," notes Sims, "in water 2

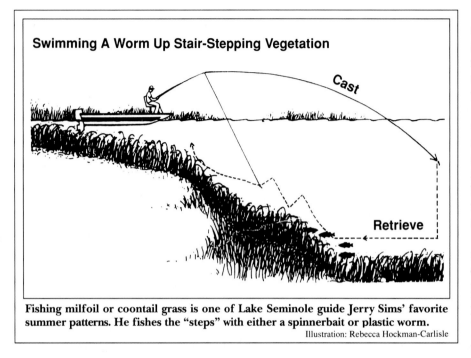

Swimming A Worm Up Stair-Stepping Vegetation

Cast

Retrieve

Fishing milfoil or coontail grass is one of Lake Seminole guide Jerry Sims' favorite summer patterns. He fishes the "steps" with either a spinnerbait or plastic worm.
Illustration: Rebecca Hockman-Carlisle

to about 12 feet deep. Sometimes you find a patch of it the size of a card table and other times it will be as big around as a room.

"I fish this with a buzzbait, cast to the edges first, then work right through the middle of it. If there is a light chop on the water, I use a larger buzzbait, but if the water is calm and clear later in the summer, I use a smaller model."

Sims also will fish peppergrass with a lightly weighted worm, and cast along the edges as well as into the middle of the vegetation. He lets the worm sink, then swims it up through the greenery.

• **Hydrilla** — Hydrilla has found its way into many Southern reservoirs, and is spreading rapidly to other lakes across the country. It is disliked by anglers, boaters and biologists alike because it becomes so thick it can't be fished well. It virtually stops boats, and once started, can't be eradicated.

"Sometimes you can fish hydrilla along its edges," notes Sims, "but that edge may be in 20 feet of water, so you need to pay attention to depth. Fish may be ganged up in it one day but gone the next.

"Spinnerbaits, worms, and even buzzbaits can be used around hydrilla," he points out, "and occasionally you can catch bass over the top of hydrilla if a lake rises quickly and bass move up. Late in the winter, hydrilla may break up into small patches and become more fishable, but in the summer it's very difficult to fish.

• **Blade Grasses** — These grasses, such as cutgrass, cattails, and bulrushes, often offer good early-morning fishing, especially when they grow out from the bank in water 12 to 24 inches deep.

When Sims finds conditions like these, he prefers to fish small openings and points in the grass with a topwater plug or a floater/diver, like one of the Rapala lures.

"Here the strikes normally will come very close to the edge of the grass, so your casts need to be accurate," he says. "If you work a plug several feet away from the vegetation and haven't had a strike, don't work the lure all the way to the boat; just retrieve it and make another cast to the area.

"Another lure that also is productive here is the weightless plastic worm, which can be cast far back into the grass

When fishing stands of blade grasses, cast the lure as close to the edge as possible.
Photo: Gerald Crawford

and slithered out right through it just under the surface."

• **Lily Pads** — Lily pads are most productive in those lakes that have few other types of vegetation cover. They're also better when they're found growing in slightly off-colored water. Like coontail, the edge of a lily-pad field often signals deeper water.

"The time-honored lure for lily pads is a Johnson Silver Minnow spoon with a pork or plastic trailer," says Sims, "and it's certainly a good choice. Worked right across the surface, it has caught a lot of bass over the years.

"Other lures, like a rubber frog or even the weightless plastic worm that is worked up and down through the pads, can be just as good. Sometimes, you can work a buzzbait through pads, and when you do, be sure to continue your retrieve well out from pads in case a fish decides to follow before striking. It happens often."

Learning to fish a plastic worm without a lead slip sinker is one of the most important parts of becoming a successful shallow-grassbed fisherman, Sims believes, because some of a worm's best action is its natural fall.

"When I'm fishing a weightless worm in any type of vegetation," says Sims, "I'm also a line watcher. If my line hasn't twitched as it makes its initial fall, I don't start crawling the worm back to me.

"Instead, I raise the rod tip just to see if a bass might have the worm, and if there is any heavy feeling at all I set the hook. If not, I just twitch the rod tip a little to make the worm shake, then I let it settle again. I do this two or three times without really moving the worm anywhere, and if there is no pickup, I reel in and cast again."

Sims begins with an 8-inch, straight-tail worm in the spring and changes to a 6-inch, swimming-tail version later in the summer as the water warms. As he begins to fish deeper water, Sims will start to add weight, too, with 1/16-, 1/8- or even 1/4-ounce sinkers. He starts with 17-pound-test mono and gradually drops to 12-pound-test as the water clears.

Like many grassbed BASSers, Sims has his own favorite spots he likes to fish year after year. One such grassbed, a combination of milfoil and coontail only 8 feet wide and 300 yards long, has produced hundreds of bass for him over the years at Lake Seminole.

"It's on a hump with open water both in front and behind," Sims explains. "During the past two years when I have fished it at daylight with a buzzbait, I have never caught less than eight bass and even as many as 30. This is by making a run down the grassline, back up it and then down it again. Most of those fish average 4 pounds, and I've caught some as heavy as 9 pounds there."

Sims also caught his largest Seminole bass, an 11-pounder, from a grassbed on a plastic worm. Vegetation definitely holds fish, so follow some of his tips and perhaps you'll add more weight to your next stringer.

— JULY/AUGUST 1984

In the spring, large numbers of bass move onto grass flats to spawn. Weightless plastic worms, or Carolina-rigged worms, are good lure choices.

Photos: Gerald Crawford

Grassbeds are havens for baitfish and the bass that prey on them.

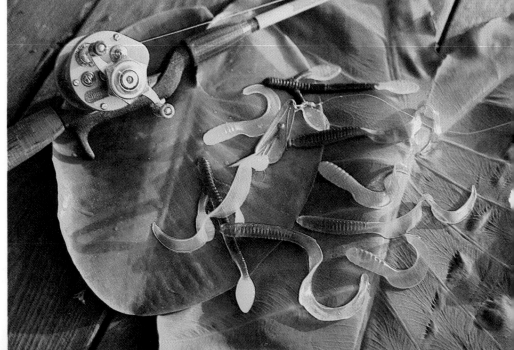

CHAPTER NINE

PLASTIC-WORM POINTERS

The plastic worm has been around awhile, but anglers are inventing new ways to fish them.

DOUG HANNON
ON WORM FISHING

By DON WIRTH

Not all plastic-worm fishing techniques are equal.
Try these innovative ideas to catch,
and release, more bass . . .

Perhaps no single individual in the world of bass fishing today knows more about the largemouth black bass than Doug Hannon, a Tampa, Fla., resident who has devoted his adult life to the scientific study of this fish. But Hannon is no "ivory-tower" researcher; he's a bassin' man, too, with over 300 bass topping 10 pounds apiece to his credit. His radical conservation stands have made him scorned in some fishing circles, while others view him as a shining example, and pass his conservation message along to others like a gospel.

You see, Bassmaster Doug Hannon releases every big bass he catches, and views lunker largemouths swimming free with his yellow tag in the sides of their mouths as "ambassadors" of his cause. Suffice it to say that Hannon is a zealot when it comes to the conservation of the largest of the species. He once guided with the understanding that his clients could keep only one bass brought into the boat, and then only after holding the fish in an aerated and chemically treated tank overnight. More often than not, the next morning would find the clients opting to release their trophy. Hannon's message usually was heard loud and clear.

Today, Hannon guides infrequently, and carefully screens those he chooses to take fishing. His backyard pond, complete with glass inserts in the walls, serves as an observation tank for his bass studies. Ten-pound-plus bigmouths fin slowly among the lily pads under Hannon's watchful eye; yet he knows that a controlled environment never will provide all the answers to the mysteries of the largemouth bass. So Hannon frequently hooks up a camouflaged aluminum johnboat to his truck and heads for some remote Florida lake or river,

in hopes of catching and tagging yet another monster bass . . . and expanding his knowledge.

I've fished with Hannon several times, and the information this Bassmaster has to pass along to fellow BASSers truly is staggering. Yet because he views the largemouth bass as a part of its natural surroundings, not as a solitary "target" to be conquered by an eager fisherman, what he says fits together in a cohesive, easy-to-understand pattern. "Most fishermen never think of a bass as a living thing, acting and interacting in its environment," Hannon says. "Once you realize that a bass isn't just an 'object' but a living creature, you gain more respect for the fish — and become a much better fisherman, too."

In previous trips with Hannon, we fished huge live shiners and caught, tagged and released bass up to 13 pounds. In fact, Hannon is known to far too many people as a "live-bait-only" fisherman; this is a gross misunderstanding of his total capabilities as a bass fisherman. You see, Hannon is a total bass fisherman, "The Compleat Angler," as Izaak Walton would have undoubtedly described him.

"The plastic worm is the artificial lure most likely to fool the next world-record bass," Hannon said as we drove to central Florida for a plastic-worm fishing session in the lakes around Lake Placid. "One of the reasons I believe this is that a worm is a quiet lure . . . it doesn't buzz, rattle or pop."

"I always thought you had to catch a bass' attention in order to catch it," I said, watching the steady beat of the windshield wipers and praying the rains would stop.

Hannon On Bass Behavior — "From observing bass both in the wild and in my tank, I've come to the conclusion that a bass, especially a big bass, can learn very fast. The way they learn not to hit a certain lure, a crankbait, for example, actually is by getting hooked by such a bait and getting away, or by observing other bass in their environment take such a bait and get caught. The bass learns to associate the noise of the lure with danger under such conditions. When they experience these baits firsthand and escape, or see others of their kind get hooked and jerked from their environment, the most successful bass — the ones that will live longest and grow biggest — actually do have the ability to learn from this experience," he believes.

"A plastic worm is a silent bait," Hannon continued. "Therefore, it's much harder for a bass to learn a negative response to the lure. It's strictly a visual lure to the bass; it makes very little noise the way a crankbait does. The bass has no way to associate noise with danger, as with the crankbait. It swims more in harmony with the water, the way a living thing would — not fighting the water like a crankbait.

"Don't misunderstand me, crankbaits can be excellent lures, especially when fish are feeding already. Their frantic action can simulate the distress behavior of an escaping baitfish. But you rarely catch a truly huge bass — one over 15 pounds, for example — on a crankbait. These fish have learned to associate the lure's noise and frantic action with danger; they cannot do this so easily with a plastic worm," opined Hannon.

A worm's natural appearance is more than enough to attract a bass, according to Hannon.

"A big bass will approach a plastic worm readily, in much the same manner as live bait," he noted, "because it closely simulates a living thing to the fish. You don't need a lot of excess noise or action if you're using a worm," he said.

"We've been conditioned to believe that you have to get out there and use every trick up your sleeve to talk Mr. Big into hitting your worm," Hannon said. "In the advertising copy of the lure manufacturers, we read that the big bass is a lazy, sulking creature that constantly has to be coaxed into attacking and eating its prey. Nothing could be farther from the truth. I've observed time after time that a bass will approach its target readily — a plastic worm, for example — and that it wants to be convinced that it's a living thing,

"If more fishermen would go underwater and look at fluorescent fishing line from the point of view of the bass, they'd question using it, too . . ."

Photo: Don Wirth

a safe thing to eat. It's an eating machine; it needs that morsel dangling in front of it. I've dropped live frogs from my hand and watched the reactions of the bass. A frog will freeze motionless when it hits the water and senses a huge bass hovering beneath it. I've seen the bass grab the frog by its hind leg and pull it under the water, then release it; when this happens, the frog swims frantically away and the bass engulfs it immediately.

"In much the same way, I've watched bass in the wild approach my plastic worm and stop, hover a few inches in back of it, and wait for the lure to convince them it's an acceptable food object. The bass typically will approach the worm from behind, stop two to three inches from it, and watch the lure closely. I've seen them grab the worm by the tail and run a short way with it, then drop it suddenly and watch it again. These are often the 'pickups' that fishermen miss when they go to set the hook. It's waiting for you to convince it that the worm is real. It wants to eat it!"

According to Hannon, the bass that are more sure of their prey are the ones that survive and grow the largest. "The small bass that randomly attacks a lure without scrutinizing it somewhat is the bass that gets caught," he said. "The bass that is more careful — the one that literally looks before it leaps — is the most successful bass, the fish that grows biggest and lives longest. And it's easier to convince a big bass that a worm is more edible than most other lures."

Hannon Talks Scents — I questioned Hannon on his observations of a bass' ability to smell, what with so much being made recently about certain "worm sprays" and the like. "A bass has an excellent sense of smell, but from my studies, I've concluded that their sense of smell acts as a secondary reinforcement to their sense of sight," he said. "A bass has a double nostril, which is a clear indicator that it does, indeed, rely somewhat on smell when feeding. A pike has a single nostril; smell is not as important to these fish. Within the nostrils are hairlike organs called cilia that pull water through one nostril and out the other, 'reading' it as it flows. However, I know that you can soak a worm in gasoline and still catch a big bass on it, providing the visual cues are strong enough. The fish often will disregard scent information when its sense of sight is enticed sufficiently."

Although Hannon is skeptical of the effectiveness of various worm scents as fish attractors, he does not decry their use. "They certainly can't hurt," he says, "and may tip the balance in your favor when a bass is being extremely cautious in its food selection. Often I'll catch a bass and wipe my hands on my plastic worms after handling the fish — you couldn't get a more natural scent than that, and it doesn't cost you anything."

Worm scent becomes more important at night and in deep, dark water, according to Hannon. "In clear water during daylight, the visual cues of the lure are by far the most important," he said. "If I were fishing extremely deep water, or at night, I would rely more on scents in my worm fishing, because the visual cues obviously are fewer and weaker to the fish."

Comments On Colors — I asked Hannon about the bass' ability to perceive colors. "A bass can see colors at least as well as humans can," he said. "A major point of difference between the color sensitivity of a bass is that it has a much stronger perception of reds than we do. A purple worm may look fluorescent. Our eyes are very insensitive to red light; we are much more keyed to the blues than reds. As the light becomes dimmer, red is the first color to 'drop out' for humans, but not for the bass. We have heard that a bass is color-blind beyond a few feet; with red, this simply isn't so.

"Red is the deepest penetrating color. It will be visible to a bass in the darkest conditions where other colors wouldn't be seen. This is why red is an excellent choice for deep fish. If you examine a section of bass' retina under a microscope, you would find many red/green color cells; a human retina would have many more blue/yellow color cells."

Hannon said that he is "a lot more basic" in his selection of plastic-worm colors than many other fishermen. "I never take a huge tacklebox with me when I fish; I prefer to travel light and not get overly complicated with my tackle. This frees me up both physically and mentally to be more observant of the bass in its natural surroundings while I'm fishing.

"Many bass fishermen arrive at the lake with an entire arsenal of worm colors. I prefer to keep it simple. In most of the waters I fish, I have found that purple, motoroil and black are productive colors. If I require a little more visibility, I might switch to a metalflake version of the same color worm. On a sunny day in clear water, I've found that most any worm color will be OK, as long as the bass doesn't perceive it as totally unnatural. On a cloudy day on clear water, I'd add blue and green to the spectrum of colors I might use. And if I were fishing extremely deep, dark water, I'd go for choices more in the red category."

The "Big Bait" Debate — Everyone has heard about those snake-sized plastic worms used down Florida way — some of them over 12 inches long. Hannon dismisses these as "too expensive and unnecessary" for most bassin' situations he encounters. "I've used those huge worms a lot in the past, and have caught big bass on them by pulling them over pads and moss — where you want to cast a big shadow and give the bass plenty of opportunity to see the bait through the vegetation. But they're a nuisance to fish; they hang up and tear in two. Overall, I don't think they're extremely productive as a big-bass lure. It's hard to hook a bass on these baits. When I used to guide a lot, people would call me and say they're bringing some huge worms down with them to fish. 'Big worms don't mean big fish in my experience,' I'd tell them. I caught 12 bass over 10 pounds on a 6-inch Creme Scoundrel worm one summer; most of the successful big-bass fishermen I know rely on a 6- to 7-inch worm — nothing larger — to take their lunkers."

Hannon has taken largemouths up to 13 1/2 pounds on these smaller worms, and knows of verified accounts where other fishermen have taken bass over 17 pounds on the 6- or 7-inchers.

Hannon usually begins his plastic-worm fishing when the water temperature reaches 80 degrees. "Before then, live shiners usually will outfish plastic worms for big bass. From the summer through October, however, the worm usually is the more productive bait," he believes. To verify this, Hannon related a story about Florida's legendary Lake Jackson near Tallahassee, which held what he believes to be the most phenomenal big-bass explosion of all time back in the late '60s. "One of the fish camps on the lake kept a log of all the big bass brought in, and recorded the baits they were taken on," he said. "It followed what I've said to the letter — shiners accounted for a vast majority of the big fish until the water got in the 80s; worms worked best usually through October."

Hannon said that it wasn't uncommon to catch "10 bass over

When rigging a worm Texas-style, Doug Hannon places the barb in the very edge of the lure. He uses a green marking pen to camouflage his monofilament fishing line.

Photo: Don Wirth

10 pounds in 30 minutes of worm fishing on a good day back in the late '60s" on this fabled lake. "Jackson had perfect bass habitat," he said. "There were huge expanses of shallow water with plenty of deeper, cooler water adjacent to it. This is necessary for a fish to live a long life — acres and acres of mossbeds full of eels, lily pads and moss over 12 feet of water, so thick you hardly could get a boat in there. These areas held big bass that were easier to catch. We'd go into those mossy areas and count the number of 'three-syllable strikes' we'd get in one day fishing those big worms over the pads. That's a strike that doesn't go 'BOOSH,' it goes 'KA-BLOOO-EEEY!' "

Hannon On Wormin' Tackle — I questioned Hannon on the kind of tackle he uses for worm fishing. I figured he used something unusual, like the 9-foot surf rods he prefers for shiner fishing. On the contrary, his gear seemed pretty "average" to me.

"I like a good, stiff worm rod, 5 1/2 to 6 feet long, with a narrow-spooled baitcasting reel and 12- to 17-pound-test line," he said. He was adamant about his line selection: "I

will not use fluorescent lines. If more fishermen would go underwater and look at these lines from the point of view of the bass, as I have, I believe they'd question using them, too. I've used 30-pound-test clear line and have gotten more strikes than another person in my boat who was using 6-pound-test fluorescent line! If you're careful in your fishing, and develop a good sense of 'feel,' you don't need the crutch of being able to see a fluorescent line better. It glows like a neon tube to a bass," opined Hannon.

Hannon uses Trilene XT line for his fishing. "I've found that by using this line, I've actually been able to drop down several notches in test and go to a thinner line size," he says. "XT typically tests out as stronger." Hannon rarely exceeds 17-pound-test in his worm fishing.

Coupled with a lighter-than-you'd-expect line, Hannon insists on razor-sharp hooks. "None of the hooks you buy are sharp enough to really penetrate the jaw of a big bass consistently, in my opinion," he said. "I sharpen my hooks on a lapidary wheel until I can drag the hook across the back of my fingernail and it won't skip across the surface. When it hangs

"I believe a worm fished Texas-style shouldn't resemble a worm at all to a bass, but rather should simulate a baitfish in action, like the bottom darters . . ."

Photo: Don Wirth

up with the lightest pressure, it's ready for fishing."

The type of hook Hannon uses depends on the kind of plastic-worm fishing he'll be doing. "For typical Texas-rig worm fishing, I've found that the Tru-Turn hooks work well," he said, "but I have had some problems with these hooks penetrating the eye socket of the bass when I set them, which I wish they wouldn't do because I release all my bass. The factor I look for most in a hook, besides sharpness, is angle of penetration. A 40-degree angle is best; a Mustad-type hook is an excellent worm hook because it has this quality."

As to hook size, Hannon allows that he'll use "the smallest hook I can get away with." Too many worm fishermen use hooks that are too big, according to Hannon. "Most people will go to a 4/0 or 5/0 worm hook; they're surprised to see me thread a worm on a 1/0 or 2/0 hook. A smaller hook is easier to set than a big one, and you'll hook more fish that strike."

Hannon often uses a weedless hook, and insists that they are extremely good "hookers." "It's not unusual to hook more bass on a weedless hook than a hook which is buried back into the body of the worm Texas-style," he said. "I prefer a weedless hook when flipping, which is an excellent technique in extremely heavy cover, and one which I would urge all serious Bassmasters to master."

We arrived at our destination, and were met by even heavier thundershowers. Strong winds whipped the lake into heavy swells. Hannon quickly assessed that fishing such conditions would be unwise in his aluminum boat. A phone call to his friend Vernon Fulmer of Okeechobee, Fla., resulted in some better news. "Vern is on his way up with his bass boat, so maybe we can get out on the lake after all," Hannon said. (The 14-foot aluminum craft Hannon uses for most of his bassin' may be perfect for the weedy lakes and rivers he frequently chooses, but he'll be the first to admit it's not well-suited for big open water in high winds.)

Fulmer arrived shortly, his big fiberglass bass rig in tow. The brawny Florida fishing guide is a Hannon "convert"; his T-shirt advertised his guide service and featured a smiling cartoon bass and the slogan, "She's Smiling 'Cause She Was Released!" Fulmer is one of the few guides Hannon will name when people ask his recommendation for someone who can be counted on to produce bass. "Vern Fulmer is a fine big-bass fisherman, and he realizes the importance of releasing big bass," Hannon said.

Fulmer will allow his parties to keep one big bass, but only one. Like Hannon, he's found that most people get into the spirit of tagging and releasing big fish once they understand how fragile the lunker population of any given body of water can be. (Bassmasters interested on fishing the Florida waters from Lake Okeechobee to Lake June can reach Fulmer by writing to: Vernon Fulmer Guide Service, Box 32, 7th St. BHR, Okeechobee, FL 33472. His phone number is (813) 763-5744. Fulmer charges $100 a day for one person, $150 for two; all tackle and gas is included, with the exception of live shiners.)

While waiting for the torrential rains to stop, we chatted with Fulmer about worm fishing in the Lake June area. "I usually use a Texas-style worm and seek out beds of shrimp grass and hydrilla," he said. "This is a real challenge, because these beds are being sprayed for weed control constantly. I've found huge concentrations of big bass in weeds one day, only to return the next and discover that they're spraying the weeds, thereby destroying some wonderful bass habitat."

Unlike many Florida lakes which are bowl-shaped, Fulmer explained that Lake June has a tremendous amount of underwater structure. "Both Lake June and nearby Lake Placid have troughs 40 feet deep running out into them, and deep holes adjacent to the shoreline. A chart recorder is a tremendous help in locating holes, ridges, weeds and bass." Both Fulmer and Hannon use Lowrance recorders; Hannon swears by his Lowrance X-15 computerized chart recorder and calls it "one of the best tools a bass fisherman could have."

We fished on and off for three days in extremely poor weather, and managed to catch bass up to a little over 9 pounds on plastic worms. During this time, Hannon demonstrated several of his "worm secrets" to me.

"You'd be surprised how many people call me and ask me for worm-fishing advice," Hannon said. "These folks are frustrated. They've read about plastic worms being great big-bass producers, yet they can't seem to connect. Many of these fishermen have been conditioned to believe that a Texas rig is the only way to fish a worm because that's the way the pros do it. It's a great technique to use under certain conditions, but it's only one of several techniques you can use to take big bass."

Perhaps more than any other aspect of Doug Hannon's personality, his insatiable curiosity helps make him a great bass fisherman. He's also an inventor. He developed the Hannon weedless prop for the MotorGuide trolling motor folks. He constantly is tinkering with new ways to do things related to bass fishing. This, combined with his keen awareness of how a bass behaves in its natural habitat, has resulted in some truly remarkable worm-fishing techniques; unusual ways of rigging and presenting plastic worms which Hannon freely shares with other Bassmasters in hopes that they, too, will catch and release more big bass.

Hannon's Swimmin' Worm — This worm method has resulted in more fish for the "bass professor" than any other artificial lure. Hannon uses the swimmin' worm in waist-deep water around weedy shorelines or structure. It's a method that's difficult to describe, because it involves threading the worm on the hook in a highly unusual manner.

Hannon describes the hooking technique this way: "Use a No. 186 Eagle Claw hook, No. 1 size. Take a 6-inch Creme Scoundrel worm or similar earthworm-type plastic worm with no frills. I prefer a natural-appearing worm for this technique. Thread the worm onto the hook, starting at the top of the head to about 1/4 inch below the egg sac. Next, take the worm and roll it. You will expose the barb of the hook, but because the point is exposed at a bend in the worm, it remains quite weedless."

To the hook, Hannon ties 14 inches of 30-pound-test line as a leader. "The heavy leader lets you catch a lot of fish without retying," he indicated. At the end of the leader line, Hannon ties a swivel and uses this to attach the completed swimmin'-worm rig to his 12- to 17-pound-test line . . . with-out a sinker.

The swimmin' worm is cast out into the shallows and brought back with a slow, steady retrieve, without imparting any rod action to the lure. Because you usually can see it coming through the water and often can see a bass swim right up and take the worm, "it's one of the most exciting ways to fish that I know of," he said. "Watching a 10-pound-plus bass charge this lure is enough to give you heart failure!"

Hannon doesn't claim this technique to be his sole invention. "I learned it from Jesse Payton, the great bass guide from Altamonte Springs, Fla. This is the only lure he ever used, and he documented three bass over 17 pounds taken on this worm rig. I've caught as many as a dozen over 10 pounds in a single season from the lake I live on outside of Tampa. It's the best artificial lure I know of."

Hannon has altered Payton's original swimmin'-worm rig somewhat, and uses a brass saltwater swivel of the kind used in billfish tournaments. "These are the finest swivels but the traditional design will work just as well."

Hannon's Swingin' Worm — This worm-fishing method works best in extremely clear water where the lure is highly visible to the fish. It is particularly effective in small, tight areas, such as underneath an overhanging tree with surrounding weed growth or stumps, where a great deal of action is required in a restricted space.

"I've found the swingin' worm to be very effective in small farm ponds and creeks, and around the edges of larger rivers and lakes where the water is shallow and the cover often heavy," he said.

Here's how to rig the swingin' worm: "Use a 3/0 to 5/0 hook and drive it straight through sideways 1 to 1 1/2 inches down from the head; sort of like you'd hook a live crawfish," Hannon instructed.

"When you cast the worm out — again, with no weight — you jiggle the rod tip, then reel in the slack. When you pull in the line, the worm 'swings' or writhes, imitating the action of a terrestrial creature like a caterpillar or inchworm that's ended up in the water and is unfamiliar with moving through this aquatic environment. This is why I like to fish this worm rig around shoreline trees and weeds. The bass sees this thing wriggling and writhing and smashes it just as it would a caterpillar that's fallen off a limb into its lair," Hannon commented.

Hannon indicated that the swingin' worm is one plastic-worm technique that's especially well-suited to spinning and spincasting tackle. "If your hook is extremely sharp, you can use light tackle and take big bass on this lure, as I have," he said.

Hannon's Texas-Rig Tips — We fished Lake June's weedbeds using a Texas rig, and I learned a lot of new twists to this technique, one with which I thought I was totally familiar. "Unlike the swimmin' worm and the swingin' worm, I believe a worm fished Texas-style — with slip sinker and the hook buried in the worm — shouldn't represent a worm at all to a bass, but rather should simulate a baitfish," he revealed.

"On the bottom of almost every lake or river, you'll find a group of fish known as darters," he explained. "These are small fish that are typically narrow and somewhat pencil-shaped, usually camouflaged to look like the bottom. They don't swim the way we think of a fish swimming; they just dart and settle. Their manner of movement is much like that of a Texas worm rig, in my opinion," said Hannon.

Rather than seeking an enticing wriggling worm action, Hannon prefers to let the bait move up and down "like a stick" in the water, for, as he indicated, this is the manner in which the bottom darters in the bass' environment move about when frightened. "The bass isn't used to seeing a wriggling-type swimming creature such as a caterpillar or worm in the deeper structure where a Texas rig is best utilized," he said. "That's why an ordinary Scoundrel-type 'stick-shaped' worm often pays off when fished Texas style."

Hannon said he often uses swimming-tail worms when fishing a Texas rig, and does not refute their effectiveness, but, according to him, such designs become much more important when light visibility is lower. "I'll go to a metalflake worm and/or a twister-type tail when light conditions are poor, such as in deep water or on overcast days, because these worms are more light-reflective."

Hannon's favorites for Texas-rig fishing include the Culprit worm, which is, in his opinion, "the finest plastic worm on the market"; he also speaks highly of Mann's Jelly Worms (particularly the new "electric-grape" Augertail variety, which we used successfully on this trip), and Creme brands.

Hannon believes that a great many BASSers using Texas-style rigs with twist-tailed worms, "don't put enough weight on their line to make the tails twist." He says that the fisherman should observe the action of the tail with a particular weight of slip sinker; if it doesn't twist as it falls, a heavier sinker should be used. "I like to use a sinker that's heavy enough to let me know when it's on the bottom with a good 'clunk' transmitted through my line," he said.

Hannon demonstrated his manner of retrieving the Texas rig, and this, too, was different. "Cast out and let the worm fall to the bottom," he instructed. "Then, engage your spool and snap the worm up off the bottom, bringing the rod tip to the one o'clock position."

The next step is what separates the successful worm fisherman from the also-rans, according to Hannon: "Now, keep your rod at the one o'clock position and let the bait fall down toward you, in a pendulum motion. When you feel it hit the bottom and see the line go slack, lower the rod to three o'clock, take up the slack, snap it up to one o'clock and let it fall toward you again, repeating the process until it's back to the boat. A lot of people pick up the worm, then immediately let their rod down. The idea is to 'swim' the worm over the

bottom; when retrieved in this fashion the worm most closely resembles a bottom darter. The majority of strikes will occur when the rod is held at one o'clock; because you're letting the lure fall toward you on a tight line, you'll feel the strike more clearly," Hannon said.

When burying the barb of the hook back into the worm, Hannon sticks the barb into the edge. "Hooking the worm lightly at the very edge allows the hook to exit and enter the fish more quickly and efficiently, which results in more hooksets," he said.

Hannon uses a "slack-line" hook-setting method. He starts at one o'clock, then drops the rod abruptly and brings it back up overhead sharply. "Many people try to tighten down on a big bass and then set the hook; this often merely turns the head of the fish and it will spit out the worm. The slack-line method allows the hook to penetrate much more effectively," he claimed.

Hannon's X-15 chart recorder showed plenty of big bass suspended just above the weedbeds on Lake June. We found that by snapping the worms off the bottom in the manner he described, the worms would pop up on top of the grass into the fish zone. At first, Hannon had all the strikes. Once I went to a heavier weight with the Mann's Augertail worm, I began catching fish, too. It's like the "bass professor" said: "You need a heavy enough slip sinker to make a twisty-tailed worm twist, no matter how shallow you're fishing."

About the resemblance of a plastic worm rigged Texas-style to bottom-darting baitfish, he added: "Many fishermen wonder why small, no-action lures such as Charlie Brewer's Slider or Jack Chancellor's Do-Nothing worm catch so many big bass when they're relatively inconspicuous. It's no mystery at all, really — these lures are imitating darting baitfish, not worms. Maybe we shouldn't refer to these lures as 'worms' at all; it would probably make their purpose more evident to the bassin' man."

Hannon's Neon Worm — One of Hannon's more dramatic methods of presenting a plastic worm involves the use of a phosphorescent material contained in disposable "light sticks" used by campers. "I use the product called Cyalume Light Sticks, which are available at many camping and hardware stores," he said. "These sticks are filled with two chemicals. When you bend the plastic stick, it breaks the vial within, and allows the chemicals to mix. What results is an intense phosphorescent glow, as bright as neon, which lasts for many hours . . . most of the night, if you were camping."

For bass fishing, Hannon instructed the BASSer to "take a hypodermic needle, break open the stick, and suck up the chemicals into the hypo. Then take a plastic worm and inject the hypo into the lure, squirting the chemical into the worm as you withdraw the needle. What results is a hot, glowing line of light that can be extremely visible and attractive to fish."

Hannon said that commercial fishermen know of this technique and utilize it in cut minnows. "This method is used off the Georgian Banks in Massachusetts," he said. "Commercial fishermen actually tie baitfish injected with this material to their nets."

Injecting "neon" into your plastic worms is especially effective in extremely deep water, or when night fishing, Hannon said. "I'd like to try this in a deep, canyon-type reservoir sometime," he said, "perhaps injecting a grub in this manner and throwing it down a bluff bank on a jighead." (Hannon's desire to experiment with "something different" is contagious; he had me itching to get back to Tennessee and try his "neon worm" in the deep, clear reservoirs near my Nashville home.)

Hannon's Butterfly Worm — A relatively new development that Hannon is still experimenting with looked like a surefire fish-getter when I saw it. I call it his "butterfly" worm because of its similarity to the softly iridescent hues of a butterfly's wings. Making these lures involves the use of certain paint pigments which Hannon first became acquainted with through the wildlife sculpture work of his wife, Lynn.

Hannon's Swingin' Worm (above, at left) and Swimmin' Worm are both effective in shallow water. Swimmin' Worm (at right) is viewed on light table.   Photos: Don Wirth

"Lynn specializes in bird sculptures, and some of the paints she uses in her work must simulate the iridescence of the feathers of certain birds. These paint pigments are in a dust-like form. I decided to try them out on artificial lures, because they have the same kind of qualities as butterfly scales — in fact, that's what they looked like. If you've ever picked up a butterfly and noticed the soft, fine 'dust' on your fingers that rubs off its wings, you'll know what I'm talking about," he noted.

Hannon said he put a little of the paint pigment into a bag full of plastic worms and shook it up "just like you're making chicken with Shake 'n Bake." The results were amazing. "The worms become evenly coated with this iridescent dust, and it stays on the worms — water won't wash it off," he said. The "butterfly" worms Hannon demonstrated to me were incredible in their appearance. "Many living creatures have colors exactly like the ones you can impart to your worms through these iridescent pigments," Hannon said. "I'm extremely excited about utilizing these materials on plastic worms and other lures, and look forward to testing them extensively."

Hannon's Line-Disappearing Act — This final tip I learned from Hannon is useful for all kinds of fishing, but

especially helpful to the plastic-worm angler. It's certainly simple enough: "Take a permanent green Magic Marker — one that won't wash off," Hannon instructed. "Make a green stripe across your line spool by rolling it back and forth about one-fourth of the way across your spool, while the line is fully retrieved. Then, when you cast the line, you'll notice that it has a permanent green mark every few inches all the way down it. In other words, it's become a dotted line, and that's exactly how it appears to the fish. As you might imagine, a dotted line is far less conspicuous to a bass than a solid, unbroken line.

"I'd especially recommend this technique to those who insist on fishing fluorescent lines; it helps make them less visible to a fish. With lines such as the Trilene XT that I use, it tends to camouflage the line," said Hannon.

I tried this tip, and he was right, again. It was uncanny the way the line seemed to disappear when the spool was marked as Hannon instructed! "I have used 40-pound-test line treated with this method, and have outfished people who were using 6- or 8-pound-test line in clear water," Hannon said. "One advantage to the plastic-worm fisherman is that it permits you to use a much heavier line test than would otherwise be possible. Green is an excellent color to use because it's a natural color to the fish; a great many things in its world are green. This is especially true in clear water, due to photosynthesis. If the water is cloudy, you don't have to worry so much about the line visibility anyway; so much of the water I fish is clear that I've found marking the line in this manner greatly improves my chances of taking a big bass."

Fishing with Doug Hannon is like browsing through an encyclopedia. This Bassmaster is a veritable storehouse of information, all of it interesting and useful. His worm-fishing secrets are only the tip of the iceberg, too. Hopefully, I'll have the opportunity to relate more of Hannon's knowledge to BASSMASTER Magazine readers in future issues. But even more than his vast knowledge of the largemouth bass, the thing that "rubs off" — like the scales of a butterfly, perhaps — is the man's great respect for the fish he fishes for. Doug Hannon's hope — and mine — is that through a greater living creature called the largemouth bass, Bassmasters will realize the importance of preserving and protecting this, the most sought-after game fish in the world!

—MAY/JUNE 1983

WHAT RIG IS BEST FOR FISHING PLASTIC WORMS?

By BILL DANCE

A lighter weight gives a worm more lifelike action and allows it to fall slower through the strike zone...

I've seen the time you could thread an imitation plastic worm on a hook like a hotdog on a bent coathanger and catch fish. It just points out how effective these phony nightcrawlers really are. Oftentimes the bass seem to prefer the fakes over the real red worms. But there are more effective methods for rigging the plastic worm.

The first plastic worms on the market came pre-rigged. These natural-looking, colored worms were attached to a length of monofilament nylon or "catgut" leader with two or three hooks plus a propeller spinner and a couple of brilliant red beads out front. These rigged worms worked. They caught fish, particularly in shallow, cover-free ponds. But the more innovative bass fishermen began figuring out ways to get the worm into a largemouth's den and not get hung up on every other cast.

Over the years, the "Texas rig" has become the more popular and most effective rigging method. Not every bass fisherman will agree with this opinion. I've discovered it works best for my particular style of worm fishing a majority of the time. Most of the top B.A.S.S. pros on the Tournament Trail use an adaptation of this self-weedless, slip-sinker method of rigging.

I've strayed from this style at times, when rigs used by local anglers seemed to favor the immediate fishing conditions, but basically the slip-sinker rig hasn't changed in my method of fishing for bass.

All that is needed to rig a worm Texas style is a plastic worm, a hook (2/0 to 6/0, depending on the worm length) and a cone-shaped, sliding lead sinker. After slipping the sinker (point forward) up the line and knotting the monofilament line to the hook eye, insert the hook point dead-center into the wig-

gler's head and 1/2 inch into the worm. Bring the hook out 1/2 inch from the worm head. Then pull the hook back through the worm until the eye of the hook remains embedded about 1/4 inch in the worm. Then turn the hook around until the barb faces the worm and can be inserted again into the soft plastic to cause a weedless lure.

Remember this: For the best action, and to reduce line twist, the worm should be completely straight with the line. To accomplish this, be sure to pinch the worm forward just a tad when embedding the barb, thus, when the barb is inserted, the worm comes back straight and even.

There are special "worm hooks" on the market. You may prefer to test several. I've come to the conclusion that the Sproat-style hook is best because the Sproat hook has a small eye which won't tear the soft texture of the worm's head. It also has a shorter distance from the barb to the throat of the hook, which greatly aids in setting the hook.

Special worm hooks are designed with small barbs or off-set bends to hold the worm in position on the hook cast after cast without need of straightening the worm by hand. Eagle Claw has several different styles. Among them is the popular No. 295 Wormmaster with a special 90-degree bend in the shank. Stembridge Products (Fliptail) features a hook with two small "spikes" near the hook eye that stop the worm from sagging. Also, special hooks are marketed by Lindy's out of Brainerd, Minn. O. Mustad features a complete line of quality wormin' hooks.

Before the special hook came along, some anglers used a common toothpick to run through the hook eye, clip off, and hold the worm in place. This method is still used by some veteran wormers.

Some bass fishermen go a step further and soak toothpicks in a special blend of one part anise oil and three parts mineral oil before inserting it into the hook eye and clipping off with fingernail clippers. This mixture adds an additional fish-attracting and human cover-up odor.

Another twist is to peg the slip sinker in place by forcing a round toothpick between the leading hole in the sinker and the line. This keeps the sinker firmly in place against the worm, and in effect creates the same action of a jig-n-worm.

All these methods are quite effective but, in my opinion, defeat the purpose of the slip-sinker rig, which I've experienced to be the most effective worm rig. Allow me to explain my opinion:

First, let's define the purpose of a slip sinker: (1) Gives added weight so the worm can be cast more easily and, of course, takes it to the bottom where you want to fish it almost 95 percent of the time. (2) Gives a "feel" of the bottom cover and structure to the fisherman. (3) Serves as a protective cover or helmet for the worm head and helps keep it straight on the hook, which, as mentioned, is essential to productive worm fishing.

When a bass sucks in a worm or hits it, the fish usually strikes it from the head — moving the slip sinker up the line and away from the worm. Without the weight of the slip sinker at the head of the worm, where it would be if pegged with a toothpick, the soft texture of the worm feels natural to the bass "mouthing" it. With the additional hardware and sinker, it's open for debate that the bass will sense something strange, and reject the worm. This is what may have happened the last time you felt that "tap-tap" on the worm and then nothing else — the bass vacuumed in the worm, realized it was counterfeit, and just as quickly got rid of it. This isn't always the case, and many times you barely hook the bass in the lip.

Normally, with a slip sinker, after you set the hook and the bass crashes through the surface, you'll spot the hunk of sliding lead 2 to 3 feet up the line, and that's where you want it. You don't want it jammed up at the point of hookup where Mr. Largejaw can use that extra weight to its advantage. A bass is a mean alley fighter, and it'll take every advantage. You don't have to give it a wide-open cheap shot.

The more a lure weighs, the easier it is for a bass to jump and throw it. The same principle would apply if you stuck a hook in your hand. You could shake the bare hook all day and probably not get it out, even if you could stand the pain. However, stick only an additional 1/4 ounce of weight on the hook and the odds of throwin' it are much better.

The additional weight at the hook head isn't as critical in catching largemouth bass, which seem to gulp a worm in when they decide to take it. But, in the case of finicky critters like spotted (Kentucky) and smallmouth bass, the less line drag and

Does the weight of a slip sinker make a difference? Professional bass fisherman Bill Dance believes it does. Dance, a seven-time winner in B.A.S.S. tournaments, tells how to get the most out of the slip-sinker rig.

Photo: Don Wirth

weight, the better the odds.

Pegging the sinker also "bruises" the line, in my opinion. The added stress increases the chances of breaking the line on the hookset. This is particularly the case when water clarity conditions, bright sunlight and spooky fish require using lighter (6- to 10-pound-test monofilament) line. This line stress factor isn't as important when the line size goes up to 10- to 15-pound-test.

The slip weight also creates more of a "natural fall" to the worm in cover. True, the pegged slip sinker does act as a weeder at times and is easier to navigate through heavy brush, but after you've felt that worm crawl up through the limb and drop over, the pegged sinker drops like a rock. Often this sharp fall will stimulate a bass to strike, but in most cases the slow, natural fall that results with the weight sliding down the line a few feet nets more strikes.

This brings us to another point: "Does the size and weight of the slip sinker make a difference in the number of strikes?" You bet! Many, many worm fishermen are guilty of this mistake. Trip after trip, they stick to one size and weight of sinker. You should carry a selection of several sizes.

The Bill Dance Rule for Slip Sinkering says: "Use the lightest sinker you can to get the job done." I've gone the route from the standard 1/4 ounce and lighter to full 1-ounce anvils. I'm convinced the average bass fisherman will net more results by using a slip weight that's as light as possible.

A last-minute shortage of 1/4-ounce weights almost caused me some sad memories. Loading my tacklebox for the 1968 All-American B.A.S.S. Tournament, I discovered my sinker supply had run low. At that time, you just couldn't drop by any tackle shop and grab a handful of any size sinkers you wanted. In my desperation, I ended up cutting the wires out of several 3/8-ounce bell-shaped sinkers and packing them. I figured they would work fine, but the heavier weight troubled me. I even strung them up on monofilament line and dipped them in different colors of paint, which I learned later was a big waste of time. I've caught just as many bass on dull, unpainted sinkers.

I still had my doubts about those "heavyweight" worm-drowners when I started practice at Sam Rayburn. But after rigging one up, swishing it back and forth on the rod tip, it felt great and you could chunk it a country mile, even in a head wind. I reasoned further, "If the bass hit this heavier weight, I'll be ahead of the game. The worm will get down to the bottom quicker and I'll be able to work out an area much faster."

What really was noticeable was how well I could feel the bottom. But could the fish also detect me easier on the other end of the line?

My concern ended at the next brush point. A bass "glommed" the worm, and I followed that 3-pounder into the boat with four more fish. A succession of events followed that put me in the heavyweight class. The 3/8-ounce "ruined" me. I caught enough bass, 71 pounds, 13 ounces, to win the tournament, but that was just the beginning.

Later, at Lake Eufaula, Ala., I ran into big Ray Murski, a Dallas, Texas, pro and Jerry McKinnis, then of Little Rock, Ark., and now known for his television show, "Fishin' Hole." They had been tearing up the big bass. They confided that the secret was a bullet-shaped 1/2-ounce sliding sinker.

"Gosh," I thought, "if that 3/8-ounce worked so well (at Sam Rayburn), a bigger 1/2-ounce size should be much better." Yep, the bigger weight did work well in a river impoundment like Eufaula, where there usually is some current and smaller weights are too light. But this didn't register at the time. After that, it didn't make any difference if the water was 4 feet deep or 40 feet, moving or dead. I used the big weight everywhere. I still was catching fish, and didn't dare change even though several times I got some weird looks from tournament partners.

It was another experience at Sam Rayburn in the 1970 Texas National that proved to me finally that slip-sinker weights do make a difference. I'd found a good creek channel in the Black Forest section with a sharp bend where the bank was 27 feet deep and the bed of the creek dropped off to 45 feet. Besides that "good drop," there was good cover and, best of the lot, it held some bass. I caught bass the first practice day on a 7 1/2-inch blue worm and a 3/8-ounce slip sinker. This pattern continued through the practice rounds. They were good bass — from 3 to 6 pounds — but it took almost two hours of steady fishing to get two or three fish.

The final day of the tournament found me, as usual, scrambling. I needed a good string of bass to place high, and really didn't know where to get 'em. The only "hole" I had was the drop-off in the Black Forest. It would take about 45 minutes per fish to coax a good string out of there, but it was my only hole card.

There was a lone 4-pounder that hit in the first 90 minutes. I left to search for some faster action on the same pattern elsewhere. By early afternoon, I still had that single 4-pound largemouth. Back to my only hole. I thought, "Wait 'em out. You can't catch enough to win this thing, but at least you might stay up high in the standings."

After another 45 minutes of patiently inching the worm through that small section of real estate, I had one more bass. The boat was tied to a tree, and I'd been casting about 40 feet into the hole. Time was running out!

I reasoned, "If I move the boat right over the hole and jig the worm straight up and down, it'll be faster, and easier fishin'."

Jigging the worm, I could feel the brush and something like a very faint "tap." Later there was another light touch, but not a strike.

What's wrong? Is it the worm color? Wrong length of worm? Or was it the fact that worm was falling back to the bottom too fast after each jigging motion?

I reeled the worm up like a madman, tied on a smaller 1/4-ounce sinker, and dropped it back in the hole. The worm never got to the bottom. In the next 45 to 60 minutes, I put 22 bass in the boat. The best 15 weighed 48 pounds at the dock. That "simple little thing," changing the slip sinker, meant the difference in winning or losing the tournament.

You might suggest that the school of bass perhaps moved into the hole just about the time I changed size weights. I wondered about that, too. Matter of fact, after filling that 15-bass limit, I put the heavier 3/8-ounce sinker back on my line, returned and fished the hole for about 15 minutes without a hit. When I switched back to the smaller size sinker, a bass jumped on it the very first jig. I left with no doubt in my mind that the worm-lead weight had made a difference in that case.

Several other experiences after that proved to my satisfaction another Bill Dance Rule: "Light weights often make a heavy difference (in your stringer)."

Worm action and bass strikes can be affected by line size, too. If you are fishing a 1/4-ounce sinker on 10-pound-test mono, the worm will fall much slower than it would on 12-pound-test line. In other words, keep in mind the smaller line with the same weight sinker and worm size will fall faster toward the bottom.

I'm not saying don't use the heavy weight! They do have a place in your tacklebox. Remember, one of the reasons for the success of the plastic worm is that it is versatile. At times you'll need to go to the heavier weights to catch fish. Think light! Most times you'll be right! The lighter weight gives the worm more lifelike action; it falls slower. This gives the bass a better chance to nail it on the trip down.

You'll discover the lighter weights are more difficult to cast on a baitcasting reel. You may want to invest in a good open-face reel. With lighter sinkers, it's harder to feel the cover and contour and frustrating to get down in the heavier cover, but try 'em. Let the results speak for themselves.

In this case, I can't come up with a set rule to follow. The size of the sinker will be governed by line size, length of worm the bass are taking, water clarity and the depth the fish are holding. However, here are a few general things to consider:

In the spring, when fishing shallow, clear water, use 3/16- or 1/8-ounce slip sinkers on 6- to 12-pound-test line with 4- to 6-inch worms. Use the lightest line possible, cover and terrain permitting. In shallow water (1 to 10 feet), use the lightest weight possible. Wind conditions may govern your choice.

In deeper, clear water (10 to 20 feet), try the 1/4-ounce sinker and go up to a 3/8-ounce size if necessary. Fish the

worm much slower. From 20 to 50 feet deep, I usually increase the sinker size, and have fished a 3/4-ounce to "feel" the terrain.

There are times when you'll want to discard all the weight except the worm and the hook. These occasions will be apparent when you locate fish shallow, or suspended above the bottom, or in heavy vegetation such as pads, mossbeds or grassbeds. This is slower fishing, and you'll have to adjust.

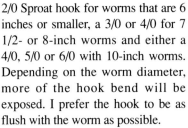

Hook size is most important. Keep this in mind when mating your hook choice to the worm size. I recommend a 1/0 or 2/0 Sproat hook for worms that are 6 inches or smaller, a 3/0 or 4/0 for 7 1/2- or 8-inch worms and either a 4/0, 5/0 or 6/0 with 10-inch worms. Depending on the worm diameter, more of the hook bend will be exposed. I prefer the hook to be as flush with the worm as possible.

Be sure you're fishing with sharp hooks. File or hone hook points, even new hooks right out of the box, until they are needle sharp. You'll need a sharp hook to drive the barb into a bass' tough jaw, as well as to punch through the plastic worm when rigged the self-weedless Texas style. Also, check the point in the worm frequently to see that it hasn't worked out through the plastic and is subject to hangups.

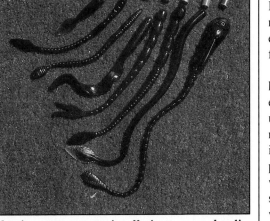

Plastic worms come in all sizes — so do slip sinkers. Match them correctly to catch more bass.

If you do get hung up in deeper water out of reach of the rod tip, move your boat directly over the worm, slowly tighten the line up, then give it slack. Often, this will cause the sliding sinker to climb up the line, then drop, possibly dislodging the worm. Often, just jiggling the rod tip will flip the worm free.

However, if you're anchored on a good hole and are catching bass or suspect you will on the next couple of casts, don't bother. Break the lure off by pulling the line with your hands. Don't take a chance on messing up the fishing hole. With heavier line, wrap something around your hands, or you'll get a dandy case of line cuts.

There are several types of slip weights. You can cut the wire out of pear-shaped sinkers and use these. The bell-shaped sinkers usually are used for bait fishing and are marked at No. 9 (1/4 ounce) and No. 10 (1/8 ounce). If you insist, you can get painted sinkers color-coordinated to match your worm. But it's not necessary. However, I do strongly recommend slip sinkers with a tapered, cone shape. These slide more easily through brush, weeds and snags. Carry a good selection in the 1/8-, 1/4-, 3/8-, 1/2- and 3/4-ounce sizes.

— 1974 BASS FISHING GUIDE

WAYS TO MAKE WORMS WORK

By TOMMY MARTIN

One of bass fishing's most successful pros tells how to select and use the right plastic worm for the job at hand . . .

As a full-time guide and tournament fisherman, I've accumulated enough different bass lures over the years to stock my own tackle shop. If I had to choose just one lure to use for the rest of my life, however, it probably would be a plastic worm. I've met a lot of anglers who don't like to use a worm, but in my opinion it's one of the most effective lures you can cast.

It's really more versatile than many people realize, since you can fish it at any depth — even as a topwater lure — and you can fish it just about anywhere you want.

Worms can be rigged several different ways, too, and fished with casting, spinning or spincasting equipment.

Choosing a selection of plastic worms for your tacklebox is really pretty easy if you keep several basic thoughts in mind.

First, I use relatively few colors of worms, so that choice is fairly simple. In stained water with 2 to 3 feet of visibility, I use dark colors such as grape or black with a blue tail. And in clear water, I go to a lighter color, such as green or red, that offers a little more visibility.

I really pay more attention to the size of the worm than I do the color, but don't be afraid to experiment if you're not getting strikes on the color you're using.

Remember that you can fish worms in practically any lake in the country, but that water clarity and available cover in that lake usually will determine the size of the worm you use.

For example, in lakes with a lot of cover and where the water is normally stained so visibility is about 2 to 3 feet, I choose a larger-diameter worm with a big swimming tail. Here, I'm fishing shallow water usually, so I want a worm that falls slower but which makes more commotion as it sinks. A larger,

6- to 8-inch worm is my choice for this situation.

On the other hand, lakes with clear water and fairly sparse cover generally mean deeper fishing. A thin, 4- or 6-inch worm will fall faster and doesn't create quite as much disturbance in the water.

The one exception to this rule, and it holds true mainly in Florida, is that when I'm fishing a lake known for producing really big bass, I use a big worm. My choices range from 7 to 10 inches, and they usually are worms with wide tails that really swim or ripple when I move them. I believe that larger bass will hit larger lures.

Another thing to remember about choosing plastic worms is that you need to match them with the proper hooks. In heavy cover you need a strong hook, but not necessarily a larger one. I normally use a 2/0 hook with a 6-inch worm, and a 1/0 hook when I fish smaller worms in clear water. You want a hook just large enough to fit in the worm; you certainly won't want a 4/0 or 5/0 hook in a little 5-inch worm. The only time I use hooks that large is when I'm working a worm 10 inches or longer.

Choosing sinkers also poses a problem for many worm fishermen and, indeed, I firmly believe sinker weight can have a bearing on the number of strikes you get. I keep my own choices as simple as possible, and you should, too.

Basically, if I'm fishing water 10 feet deep or less, I use a 3/16-ounce slip sinker. If I'm fishing extremely heavy cover like hydrilla or milfoil, I will use a 1/2- or even 5/8-ounce sinker. In extremely deep, clear water, when I'm using a small worm, I also use a 3/16-ounce slip sinker, even though it takes much longer to reach bottom.

A good rule of thumb often repeated about sinkers is to use

the lightest one you can, and I agree with it. To me, heavy sinkers are best used to pull a worm through cover; the rest of the time they'll deaden your sense of touch as well as alert a bass that something's not right.

The trend in bass fishing today is to use longer rods, but I really think a 5 1/2- to 6-foot rod is the best overall choice for worm fishing. It's easy to use, sensitive and lightweight, and, in medium action, will provide enough power to set a hook. The one time you should consider using a light-action rod for worm fishing is when you're fishing deep, clear water with light line.

In most of my worm fishing, I rig Texas-style. This is an all-around rig that makes the worm weedless for use in heavy cover, but it also works just as effectively for suspended bass as well as for fish holding on structure. If you're just getting started as a worm fisherman, this is how I'd recommend you begin.

Sometimes a Carolina rig may be better, especially if you're fishing in current. My good friend Jack Chancellor won the 1985 BASS Masters Classic fishing one of his 5-inch worms rigged Carolina-style. This rig also employs a slip sinker, but in contrast to the smaller bullet-shaped weights used on a Texas rig, the sinkers normally are much heavier. Chancellor, who's a master at fishing the Carolina rig, uses a 1-ounce sinker.

The difference between the Texas rig and Carolina rig is that the Texas rig is designed to take the worm to the bottom. The sinker slides up and down the line ahead of the worm. The Carolina rig, on the other hand, lets the worm float or swim above the bottom because the sinker is kept higher up the line by a swivel. The worm is tied on a leader 1 to 4 feet behind the swivel.

I use a Carolina rig when I'm fishing a relatively clear bottom, or if I'm working in river current. A lot of fishermen also like to fish a Carolina rig when the bottom is covered with grass — the sinker slides along the bottom but the worm

Tommy Martin considers the plastic worm to be the most versatile lure in a bass fisherman's tacklebox.

Photo: Steve Price

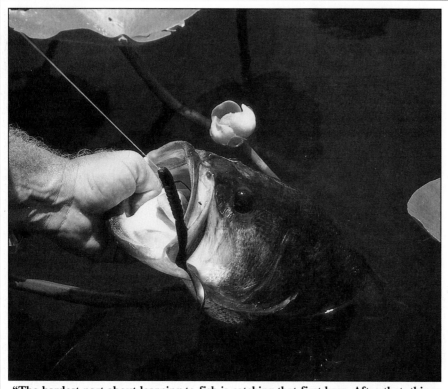

"The hardest part about learning to fish is catching that first bass. After that, things get easier."

Photo: Gerald Crawford

floats up over the vegetation.

You can also fish a worm on the surface, especially in the spring and around vegetation. You can tie your line directly to the hook or to a swivel without a sinker and trail the worm behind so the worm can be eased along the surface like a small snake swimming along the top.

Basically, plastic worms are three-season lures — spring, summer and fall — when the water temperature is 60 degrees or warmer. Water temperature and the amount of cover present determine how I fish worms.

In cooler water when temperatures are between 60 and 65 degrees, I fish worms slower and drag them more along the bottom. On the initial cast, I let it lie for a few moments, then crawl it an inch at a time so fish have plenty of time to study it.

In warmer water, I hop worms more, although I still keep them on the bottom. After the worm falls to the bottom, I move it by rod-tip action, trying to jump the worm in little skips. If I'm fishing specific, visible targets like pilings or brush tops, I'll usually reel straight back after the worm moves past the object and cast again.

On Toledo Bend and other lakes that have thick vegetation, one of my favorite fishing techniques is jigging. Underneath the mats of vegetation on the surface, the water often is open and, if you can get though it, you're likely to get a bass. The trick here is to use a heavy slip sinker that will break through

the greenery. Once I get through, I simply jig the worm up and down four or five times, about 6 inches at a time.

When bass are on the bottom of a sloping point or drop-off, I like to fish a worm down that drop-off. I cast into the shallow water and hop or crawl the worm into deeper water. When fish are suspended up over the drop, however, I generally work from deep to shallow so my worm either falls through the school of fish or pulls through them.

In my guiding, I've taught a lot of clients the basics of worm fishing, and believe me, it's not as difficult as you might think it is. The hardest part is catching your first bass, because after that things get progressively easier. Here's how I tell people to start:

Keep your rod pointed directly in front of you, never more than at a 45-degree angle to the water. Move your arm slowly along the bottom, concentrate very hard on what you're doing, and watch your line. If you feel anything you think might be a fish, reel in slack line — about two reel turns — and set the hook with your hands, wrist and forearms, not your body.

About 50 percent of the time when you're getting started like this, the resistance you feel will be a fish. As you catch more, you'll quickly gain confidence in the lure and will be able to distinguish between fish bites and the obstacles that feel like bites.

I recommend practicing hooksets in your yard, if possible. Just tie your fishing line to a tree, then back off 15 to 20 feet and set the hook. Don't move your body to set the hook, because that takes time, and time is something you don't usually have a lot of once a bass strikes. About 90 percent of the time when you miss a fish when setting the hook, it's because you're too late; the bass already has detected something wrong and has spit out the lure.

When you feel that "tap," the bass has your worm. Don't wait to set the hook. Reel in slack and let the fish have it. If you want to know if it really was a fish, check for teeth marks on your slip sinker.

Because worms usually are worked slowly, they're not the best lures to use when trying to locate bass. Crankbaits and spinnerbaits that can be worked rapidly are better suited for this. But if you catch one on a fast-moving lure and then can't get another to hit, switch to a worm. Chances are you'll soon be right back in the action.

— NOVEMBER 1985

WHACKY WORMING

By DANIEL L. DAVIS

*Here's a light-line, finesse-fishing technique
that is deadly in shallow,
thick cover . . .*

Whacky worming may be today's most productive bass-fishing technique. It certainly is for me.

Since being introduced to the worm-fishing strategy by my friend Dickie Colburn in 1984, I have used this technique to catch well over 1,000 bass and have had the pleasure of sharing the technique with friends and bass-guide clients. And I think you'll agree that whacky worming is a deadly system for bass wherever you fish.

Essentially, the whacky-worm technique involves using a lightly weighted worm hooked through the middle (instead of Texas-style) and fished over weeds and around other structure.

Early practitioners used 6-inch Creme Scoundrel worms, which have a thin profile and relatively hard plastic, and these still are preferred by most anglers using the technique. (In fact, Creme has capitalized on the popularity of the fishing method by introducing pre-

The whacky worm works great in thick cover close to shorelines. Six-pound-test line is recommended.   Photo: Gerald Crawford

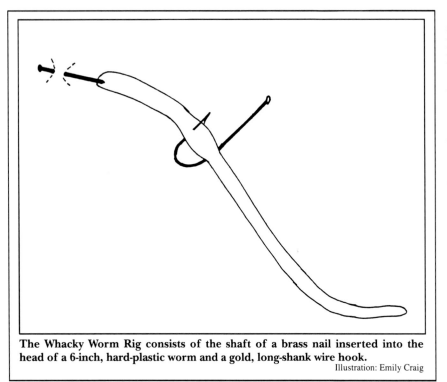

The Whacky Worm Rig consists of the shaft of a brass nail inserted into the head of a 6-inch, hard-plastic worm and a gold, long-shank wire hook.

Illustration: Emily Craig

rigged worms and obtaining a trademark protection for the name, Whacky Worm. Write Creme Lure Co., Dept. B.A.S.S., P.O. Box 87, Tyler, TX 75710.)

The worms are weighted by inserting the shaft of a brass nail (clip the nail head off with side-cutters) into the head of the worm, and the lure is hooked through the egg sac with a 2/0 or 3/0 gold, long-shank wire hook.

The technique works best when the lure is fished on 6-pound-test line with a good-quality graphite or boron spinning rod in a medium-heavy action. A spinning reel with an excellent drag system is a must, since this setup attracts big bass.

Rig the worm by placing the hook through the worm sac as shown in the illustration. Cut about 1/4 inch off a nail and insert it into the head until it is completely buried. As an alternative, insert a worm rattle and a smaller section of nail.

The object is to add just enough weight to the worm to make it spiral down at a rate of about 1 foot per second. You may have to experiment with different weights to determine the preferred sink rate on any given day.

Whacky worming works best over submerged hydrilla beds, where the worm can fall into holes and along edges adjacent to creeks. Other good cover includes stick-ups in 2 to 6 feet of water and around boat docks. It is very difficult to fish this technique more than 10 feet deep because the drag on the line will distort the action and disguise strikes.

Once you've found a good-looking spot, cast downwind 10 to 20 yards and let the bait fall as the boat drifts toward it. Long casts hamper lure action. Too, these shorter casts permit working an area more thoroughly when bass are scattered.

Let the worm settle to the bottom while taking in slack. After the worm lies on the bottom for 15 to 30 seconds, raise the rod tip to make the worm rise about a foot and move toward you about 2 feet. Then let it settle back to the bottom again. Repeat this procedure two or three times each cast, occasionally wiggling or shaking the rod tip as you lift the worm.

Watch your line constantly, because 90 percent of strikes will be no more than a soft pickup with slight line movement to indicate a bite. Set the hook immediately when you detect a strike.

Sometimes you won't know you've got a bite until you pick up on the line and feel slight resistance. Don't wait for the fish to apologize, because it will spit out the worm as soon as it feels pressure.

Remember when setting the hook that only 6-pound-test line connects you to the fish. Since you're using an exposed hook, a quick, firm hookset with your wrist will be adequate. Check the line frequently and retie at the first sign of abrasion or nicks.

A variety of worm colors work, including black, grape, blue, blue-black, purple, red, strawberry and even blaze-orange and chartreuse. The new metalflake finish works well in clear water.

Starting out with the darker colors early in the morning has proved effective. I switch to purple, red or strawberry during the middle of the day and back to dark worms as the sun descends. On overcast days, I tend to stay with the darker colors and, in murky or cloudy water, blue seems to work best. However, as in any bass fishing, the fish don't always follow the rules. When all else fails, try the blaze-orange and chartreuse worms. You may be pleasantly surprised, especially on bright days in exceptionally clear water.

Whacky worming is finesse fishing at its best. It requires patience, dedication and a desire to learn a new, very productive technique.

Remember how frustrating it was before you caught that first bass on the traditional worm setup? This technique, too, can be somewhat trying until you catch a few fish. But once you get the hang of it, you may not go back to regular worm fishing.

— JUNE 1989

NEW KNOT SYSTEM FOR FLOATING-WORM RIG

By WILLIAM J. MCBRIDE

Rigging a worm South Carolina-style is easy once you master this knot system . . .

Many methods have been developed for fishing plastic worms. Like most fishermen in the Southeast, I have advanced from the basic Texas rig to the floating South Carolina rig, which bass seem to favor in this general area.

In its basic form, though, the South Carolina rig has some drawbacks. You must tie three knots. This, of course, greatly increases the chance of line breakage and loss of Mr. Hawg. With the new "system" shown here, only one knot is used.

I cannot take credit for this system. It was related by a fellow Bassmaster. I have used the system since, and found it quite adequate with improvements over rigs that employ swivels and beads as weight-stops on the standard South Carolina rig.

To use the new system, the angler first builds a basic Texas rig. Place the slip sinker on the line and attach the hook with an improved clinch or Palomar knot. Then take a piece of monofilament of the same strength and position it parallel to the running line between the hook and worm weight. Hold both lines between forefinger and thumb, then grasp tag-end of the extra piece of line with forefinger and thumb of your opposite hand. Now, take four turns around the forefinger being used to hold the two pieces. Upon completion of the four turns, the tag-end is pushed under the four loops. Pull the knot tight by grasping the tag-end and primary line with one hand and the trail-end and primary line with the other. Pull knot until you reach desired tightness.

To finish off, clip the trail-end near the knot, clip the tag-end, or side near the worm weight, but leave a short end extending out of the knot. This extension acts as a cushion as the worm weight falls against the knot in actual use.

There are two apparent advantages in this new system. First, the two knots normally used to attach the swivel are eliminated. Secondly, the finished knot can be slid on the line to adjust the distance between the floating worm and weight. This cannot be accomplished in using a swivel, unless you take time to retie.

In normal use, the knot will not slip down the line, unless the weight is lodged between rocks, etc. Regardless, it can be slid back up the line to normal fishing position.

— NOVEMBER/DECEMBER 1975

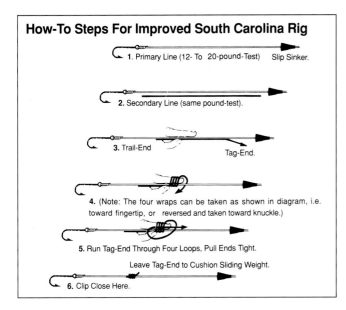

How-To Steps For Improved South Carolina Rig

1. Primary Line (12- To 20-pound-Test)   Slip Sinker.

2. Secondary Line (same pound-test).

3. Trail-End   Tag-End.

4. (Note: The four wraps can be taken as shown in diagram, i.e. toward fingertip, or reversed and taken toward knuckle.)

5. Run Tag-End Through Four Loops, Pull Ends Tight.

Leave Tag-End to Cushion Sliding Weight.

6. Clip Close Here.

HOW TO CRAWL A CHAMELEON

By JOHN WEISS

Nobody knows why for sure, but plastic salamanders make great smallmouth baits. Here's a few pointers on how to choose and use the fake lizards...

It really is not known why, but plastic worms have rarely been effective against smallmouth bass. So the development of plastic salamanders bridges a gap that has needed spanning for a long time. Discussing the matter with numerous scientists involved in lure design and production has confirmed overwhelmingly the suspicion that coming years will see the plastic chameleon shake out on top as the No. 1 smallmouth bait. And it's expected that soon all major producers of plastic worms for largemouth will be marketing an extensive line of plastic chameleons for smallmouths.

Stembridge Products of East Point, Ga., spearheaded the campaign with its Fliptail Lizard, a salamander-shaped plastic bait that measures 6 inches in length and is identical to plastic worms in composition and available in about as many colors. Later, the Burke Lure Co., of Traverse City, Mich., presented its line of plastic Spring Lizards and Salamanders, also available in various colors and in both 3- and 6-inch sizes. Finally, Cordell Tackle Co. presented the ultimate in plastic chameleons, a bait that would actually change color underwater in exactly the same manner as a frightened chameleon trying to escape its enemies.

Consider these features: like the plastic worm, the plastic salamander can be fished slow or fast; it can be worked in deep water where bass are most likely to spend the hot summer and cold winter months; and, it can be worked in the heaviest cover without hanging up — where the largest bass call home. If these factors are important, even more desirable is the fact that plastic salamanders closely resemble a food highly preferred and sought out by smallmouth

bass. Exactly what an odd-colored plastic worm resembles is often the subject of heated debate.

If plastic chameleons are ideally suited for smallmouth bass, they are likewise ideally suited for smallmouth anglers. If you are presently only a fair plastic-worm angler and you feel more at home slinging plugs, spoons and spinnerbaits, you'll probably find yourself quite proficient at fishing plastic chameleons.

Some fishermen use a single weedless hook secured through the head of the bait and others rig three hooks in series along the length of the body. But by and large, the most popular method of rigging is exactly the same as that used when fitting out for plastic-worm fishing. A slip sinker is employed and a long-shanked hook is buried in the plastic body.

I've conducted a number of tests with plastic chameleons in shallow, crystal-clear water to determine the most effective ways to fish this bait. Like most plastic worms now on tackle dealers' shelves, plastic lizards are of the floating variety. As a result, the hook buried in the forward part of the body and the slip sinker riding the line just ahead causes the bait to nose into the bottom. While the head is held down, the tail gyrates and attempts to float upward, rendering continual movement and a very enticing appearance.

This is an ideal circumstance because it perfectly simulates a live chameleon on the bottom, poking its head into crevices and rock piles as though searching for a hiding location. Retrieving the bait in slow, erratic movements gives the illusion that the chameleon has found no hiding place under the shale or rock and is darting quickly to other cover.

There's No Guessing on Strikes

One curious aspect of plastic-salamander fishing is the way in which strikes occur. With a plastic worm you almost have to develop a sixth sense that tells you when the bait has been picked up as largemouths often take the bait very delicately. Just the opposite occurs when fishing a plastic chameleon. A very discernible "bump" is felt and there can be no doubt that you've had a pickup.

Why a smallmouth hits a plastic salamander harder than a largemouth hits a plastic worm is not difficult to understand. A smallmouth has learned from past experience to kill a salamander quickly on the strike because any lizard represents a family of aquatic quadrupeds that can hide quickly. If a chameleon senses danger, it will quickly try to crawl under a flat rock, piece of shale or into a rock crevice. Or it may even attempt to scamper out of the water completely and into vegetation cover on a nearby bank. When this happens, as Mr. Smallmouth is well aware, the fish has missed out on a highly delectable morsel.

Since the strike is always quick and hard, plastic-salamander fishing for smallmouths is perhaps just as easy to learn as conventional plugcasting. When you feel the bump of a smallmouth hitting the bait, you simply lower your rod tip, reel in the slack until you feel pressure or resistance at the end of the line, and drive the hook home, hard.

Compare this with the more difficult art of plastic-worm fishing in which a bigmouth may engulf a worm "on the fall," take it lightly without the angler being aware of a hit, grab the worm by the tail and swim away for a distance before taking the entire bait into its mouth, or torment you with a myriad of other antics. It's easy to see why many newcomers to plastic-worm fishing experience acute frustration and give up in despair.

In fishing plastic salamanders, however, the strike is usually predictable, though nothing about any type of fishing ever can be stated without reservations or exceptions. For one, if the bait is moving along at a fast clip, the strike is likely to jolt your arm from its mooring. If the bait is crawling at a snail's pace and doesn't give the impression that it's trying to escape, the hit may be much lighter, though it is sure to be a quite detectable "thunk."

As in fishing with plastic worms for largemouth bass, using plastic salamanders for smallmouths likewise necessitates setting the hook hard. Remember, you first have to drive the point of the hook through the spongy plastic before it's in position to

Fake salamanders come in all colors and shapes that appeal to small-mouths.
Photo: John Weiss

penetrate the smallmouth's rather tough mouth. Often, I set the hook twice, just for insurance.

If you're using a quality rod and the same heavy line customarily used in plastic-worm fishing, you need have no fear of breaking anything. And since a smallmouth flares its gill covers and literally inhales the entire salamander like a vacuum cleaner, it's never necessary to let a smallmouth run with a chameleon. The reflex action of striking and setting the hook, in my opinion, should approximate that which you would use if fishing with conventional plugs or other artificial lures.

Until now, the lures most favored by smallmouth fans usually have consisted of brightly polished spinner or spoon variations. These baits are limited severely in their use applications, however, since they are incapable of being worked very slowly and frequently hang up, even in the lightest of cover. So plastic salamanders fulfill a valid need as they round out a smallmouth angler's repertoire of angling tactics by enabling him to fish effectively for bass under a majority of varied conditions — the same conditions under which the plastic worm has gained such a noteworthy reputation.

— JULY/AUGUST 1974

DEADSTICKING: LET A SLEEPING WORM LIE

By EWELL PARKER

This isn't the worm-fishing technique for all seasons or all reasons. But on a slow bassin' day, "deadsticking" may be the best tactic to make bass come alive . . .

The bass guides call it "professional overrun." The rest of us know the baitcaster's plague as "backlash." It's the burden that must be borne, the dues that must be paid by those of us who swear by levelwind reels — and it's the reason we sometimes swear at them. It's a bird's nest in the hand, a tangle of monofilament that proves beyond doubt that surgeons really can tie knots without letting go of the thread.

There's only one good thing you can say about a backlash. And as far as I know, I'm the only one who can say it: it introduced me to "deadsticking." Mark that new term down in your glossary of bassin' lingo. You'll hear it again.

It was a midsummer day on my home water of Greenbelt Lake in the Texas Panhandle when I first discovered the promise of the deadstick technique. Those of us on the lake were suffering from a mixed-blessing wind. Blessed on the one hand because it kept crowds of fishermen off the lake and water-skiers on shore; but cursed in another way because the breeze refused to let the small plastic worm cast as far as my reel wanted to turn.

I knew right where the fish were located — on a ledge where the water dropped from 5 to 9 feet, and then on into the main river channel and deeper water. But there was only one way to get to them, and that was casting into the wind. Even when I was lucky enough to cast up into the 5-foot water and slide the worm off onto the lower ledge, I wasn't getting hits.

But one time, the line knotted up and the worm fell short of the 5-foot ledge. It lay there on the lower shelf for at least a minute, while I argued with a championship bird's nest in the reel. When I reeled it up to try for a better cast, there was a bass on the other end. Two more backlashes and two more good bass later, the realization walked up and slapped me smartly: this is exactly what the fish wanted — a motionless, lifeless worm. The bass were picking up the worm as it lay there, doing nothing.

Skipping the backlash step the next time, I cast directly onto the lower ledge, and permitted the worm to sink slowly to the bottom. There was nothing. I watched the line closely and resisted the urge to twitch. Nearly a minute went by. "Well, so much for that trick," I said to myself. As I tightened up the line, though, another bass was waiting for me to begin my part of the battle.

There had been no indication of a strike. There was no strike at all, in fact. It was just . . . there.

The ledge produced eight more bass that day. But not a single one fell for a conventional plastic-worm retrieve. The bass did not want a slow-moving worm. They were telling me that they wanted a dead worm, lying on the bottom. And for once that day, I listened.

Topwater enthusiasts have been using something similar for years. They cast their topwater killers near a bass hideout and let them lie there without a trace of movement until, finally, the bass is tempted out of its hideout. They call their trick, "the deadwater method." I call its worm-fishing application "deadsticking."

It takes no special tackle and no unique talents to fool bass this way. It requires only patience not to move a muscle, and confidence the fish are where you're fishing. It is, simply, putting a plastic worm into that certain spot along structure and letting it stay there until a bass picks it up.

You probably already have the ideal deadsticking tackle in your storeroom. Light line works best, I've found. Ten-pound-test mono is preferred, but you may have to switch to 14-pound-test line in brush. The line ought to be as nearly invisible to the fish as it can be. At the same time it has to be highly visible to the fisherman — who will detect many more "strikes" by sight than by feel. That presents a problem to a Bassmaster who has the prejudices I have against fluorescent line. I'm not convinced that bass can't see that bright orange or yellow stuff, but you should make your own decision.

If you have trouble seeing the clear blue Stren line that I prefer, try tying a 4- or 5-foot leader of clear line onto the fluorescent type.

Whatever the line color, the limpness of the line is most important. The worm must sink naturally and lie on the bottom naturally. A stiff line, or one that coils, will pull the worm out of the hole you're trying to fish.

As with any type of fishing with plastic worms, use the lightest weight you can possibly get by with — certainly no more than 1/16-ounce for 10-pound-test line and 1/8-ounce for 14-pound-test line. I've had no success with heavier weights.

Rig the worm Texas-style (hook

It takes no special tackle or unique talents to fool bass by "deadsticking" a plastic worm. It does take patience not to move a muscle, and confidence that the bass are where you're fishing.   Photo: Jim Vincent

buried in the worm), with a cone-shaped slip sinker that can slide freely up and down the line. There's an exception to that, however. There'll be days when the bass won't seem to bite just right.

You'll feel the fish, set the hook, then, during the battle, your hook, worm and sinker will come flying back to you. Here's what I think happens: the bass picks up the lead and the worm at the same time. It closes its mouth. You set the hook, but the bass has its mouth shut, and the lead pulls up into the corner of its mouth. The hook doesn't penetrate. After the bass realizes it's in trouble, it opens its jaws, and your lure simply pops out. It's a clear indication this is happening when you lose a bass only to find the hook hasn't penetrated through the plastic worm.

To cure that problem, peg the slip sinker about 6 inches up the line from the worm with the tip of a toothpick. Always peg the sinker from the small (cone) end, where it seems to eliminate damage to the line.

Peg the sinker up the line, too, if the bottom where you're

fishing is full of moss or muck. The sinker will sink into the debris, but the worm will lie on top where the fish can get it.

Light line and light sinkers demand small worms and little hooks. (Or is it the other way around?) I've had best success with Smithwick's 4-inch Fluttertail worms, rigged on 1/0 or 2/0 hooks. Also, the Rebel Ringworm is effective — the smaller, the better. The original straight worm seems more effective with this no-action method than the curly-tailed lures.

To get more hookups, bend the hook point out from the shaft a bit, and the point ought to be needle-sharp.

Lure color is important. Often, two-color worms can make a difference in results, especially when the bass are not feeding actively. Customarily, during a fishing trip I'll try a variety of colors and color combinations around the same tree (which I believe hold fish) until I find the most productive worm.

Use the rod and reel best capable of handling the lightweight terminal tackle. Any rod material will do, so long as it's graphite. My personal favorite is the Lake King graphite rod in a No. 2 light action or a No. 3 medium action in heavier cover and 14-pound-test line. I'm a baitcasting fan, so I've picked the Garcia 1500C reel, but the reel choice is secondary. In deadsticking, the reel merely holds the line and cranks in the fish. The growing spinning-reel fan club will do well with skirted-spool affairs in this type of fishing.

If there's one thing that contributes more to my success in catching hard-to-get bass, I think it's the ability to place the worm right in the "target area." An accurate cast is the first step, certainly.

But after you've dropped the worm up against the shady side of that tree trunk, the task of getting the lure to the fish isn't over. Once the worm touches water, play out line by hand, giving plenty of slack. It's essential that the worm drop straight down to the base of the tree. Any tension on the line, from stiff line, the wind or your reel, will cause the bait to swing in an arc away from the target.

Don't be afraid to get fairly close to the target, especially if the water is several feet deep. Even if you're 30 feet from the tree and give the line ample slack, tension from the line trying to cut through the water will cause the worm to miss the trunk by a foot. That 12 inches your worm misses the tree trunk when it hits the bottom will spoil your chances.

A better idea is to move the boat to within 8 or 10 feet of the tree so you can stand up and toss the worm to the best spot. The worm, without the water tension dragging it away, will settle right where you want it. Plus, you'll be able to detect any line movement that could mean a strike.

In shallower or clear water, try casting a couple of feet past the tree in hopes the worm will curve down into the proper position.

Try this simple test to see what difference a few feet can make: have your companion from the front of the boat cast into the water alongside the stern. At the same time, drop your worm straight down beside where his bait lands. You'll readily see his worm arcing away from yours a few inches. And in bass fishing, inches make the difference.

With so much slack (belly) in the line, it means you're left with only your eyesight to detect a strike. Watch the line carefully as it sinks. A twitch or any kind of movement out of the ordinary — the line stopping too soon or sinking too far — means bass! Set the hook instantly. If you discover fish are hitting the worm on the way down, switch back to conventional worm-fishing methods. It means fish are active and you don't need the deadstick technique.

More often, however, the worm will make it to the bottom without interference. Let it lie there without exerting any tension on the line. "Belly" the line by holding your rod at a 45-degree angle, leaving enough slack for the monofilament to rest in a bow. Then keep your eye on that sagging line. If it tightens up you're in business.

Most of the pickups you will get deadsticking won't be active enough for you to feel anything, even through graphite. If you're lucky, the bass will move the worm enough for the line to twitch. But much of the time you'll only discover there's a fish on when you tighten the line to try another cast.

No one who has tried deadsticking has been able to recognize every pickup. I can't explain this. I would have believed that I always could tell when a bass has hold of a worm, but I can't, and it's probable that you can't either. But you can catch these soft-mouthed fish if you're careful.

After the worm has settled and 30 to 60 seconds have passed, begin to take slack out of the "belly" of the line — not enough to pull heavily on the worm, but only enough to make the line tight. With these small weights, a tight line will be enough to move the worm, and the sag will return. If the plastic worm continues to hang in that same spot, be very gentle. A fish will move eventually or give a little to the increased pressure, but slowly, like cold molasses.

Time and experience will let you determine the difference between a fish's resistance or the "pull" of a tree root.

Time and experience also will teach you which types of cover to try.

Pick out what I call the "dominant cover." If there are several cedar trees growing close together, for example, pick the one that's a bit different from all the rest. Maybe it's bigger or has an extra set of branches lower to the water on the shady side or it's in somewhat deeper water. Whatever the difference that one tree has over the others in the group, if that difference affords a bit more shade or cover for the bass, then I believe the biggest bass in the area will be in that spot.

This dominant-cover theory works just as well in stands of brush or mesquite, rockpiles, or any other object that makes a bass feel secure or shades it from the sun.

Try to picture the fish's home. Then try to match the cover to your own mental image of what it should be.

On ledges and drop-offs, deadsticking works best where the drop-off ends and the ledge begins — that point where the vertical drop meets the horizontal ledge. The technique works so well there because the worm, not impeded by line tension, falls directly down into the corner.

Whenever I discover a new area of cover, I usually try each tree or rock with the traditional, faster worm-fishing methods, then try deadsticking around the dominant tree or rock. If it works there, I return to the other bits of cover and offer the fish a motionless worm.

I've yet to figure out why in the world a bass will pick up a plastic worm that's been lying still for 30 seconds or more then hold on to it for so long.

But they do! They'll fall to deadsticking at times when other fishermen already have worked over the cover, and, best of all, when no other lure or method of retrieve seems to pay off.

Deadsticking isn't the worm-fishing technique for all seasons and all reasons. But on a slow bassin' day, deadsticking may be the best way to make bass come alive.

— JULY/AUGUST 1979

SWIM A CROOKED WORM

By E.R. MCCONNELL JR.

Sometimes adding a little wiggle to a plastic worm
will get Mr. Bass' attention when
other rigs fail . . .

There we were, fishing a thick mess of Santee-Copper stick-ups that require a precision cast to prevent the plastic worm from winding up suspended 2 feet above the water, dancing from a well-fouled line. The backwater we were fishing was darkly stained and varied in depth from 2 to 6 feet. Fishing partner Marvin Rish was giving lessons.

I was using the deadliest bait of all time, a 9-inch plastic worm rigged Texas-style. In addition, I had read all the pros' articles in BASSMASTER® Magazine, and I was doing everything right — except catching bass.

As we eased from one opening to another through the dense stick-ups, I saw a small patch of lily pads roll slightly as a suspended bass flexed its muscles. Carefully, I cast a purple worm to the base of the stick-ups and directly in the middle of the lily pads. I waited. Nothing happened. I made a proper retrieve and tried again — still nothing. I changed to a weighted worm and again, nothing.

Ready to admit defeat and afraid that too many casts would spook the fish, I turned to Rish, "Toss that danged ol' crookedy worm of yours over there and see if you can fool that rascal."

Rish turned and laid that funny-looking worm right on top of the lily pads. Then he pulled it off into the water and let it sink a foot or so before he twitched his rod and made the worm swim. Suddenly his line jumped. Rish "crossed its eyes" as he drove

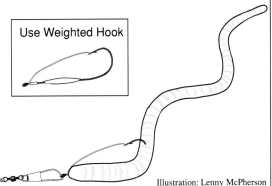

Use Weighted Hook

Illustration: Lenny McPherson

the hook home. A couple of minutes later, I got in some more practice with the landing net. I boated a 3-pound bass for Rish.

That did it! I put away my fancy rigging, bummed one of those crooked-worm rigs from Rish and proceeded to catch bass the rest of the day. I don't mean to imply that worms rigged the regular way aren't fine baits because, day in day out, those soft worms are top-notch bass foolers. However, as Rish showed me, there are situations that dictate using a different type of worm.

The "crookedy worm" he had rigged on that day at Santee-Cooper was nothing more than a 10-inch worm (No. 936 made by the Creme Lure Co.) that was threaded too far down on a weighted 5/0 weedless hook. The result is a worm with a hump-back appearance that can be made to swim or dance through the water by slight jerks or a steady retrieve. If retrieved slowly and steadily, the rig will revolve in the water and sometimes that retrieve method is successful.

The crooked-worm rig has a twofold appeal to bass. First, when allowed to sink, the worm closely resembles a small eel returning to the bottom. Also, tremendous action is imparted to the tail of the worm when the "jerky" retrieve is used. The worm actually appears to be swimming through the water. Give it a try on those days when other worm rigs don't seem to draw attention.

— MARCH/APRIL 1974

The Slack-Line Method

By JOHN R. REED

Among their Texas bassin' peers, Johnny Mayes and Jackie Hewlett are accorded expert status in the art of duping bass with strips of limp, colored plastic . . .

For once it was nice to be ignored. Johnny Mayes was putting the needle to Jackie Hewlett. He held up the yearling bass before ignominiously tossing it back into Lake Conroe.

"That's four to two, my favor," he laughed. He could have made it worse by saying "four to two to nothing," because I was batting a big fat zero.

Ah well, what could I expect? "When in Rome do as the Romans do," is cliché, but it still is apt advice. The two well-known Texas Bassmasters were tossing purple and firetail plastic worms; I'd started with a topwater plug and now was casting a crankbait and picking up a gob of hydrilla on virtually every cast.

I have this thing about plastic worms. I detest 'em.

They simply are not compatible with my high-strung personality. I can fish a worm for hours or so and my nervous system is shot to hell.

Anyway, I like to feel that electric surge of a bass trying to destroy a surface bait or declaring war on a fast-moving underwater lure. A bass often picks up a worm like a picky shopper who gingerly feels supermarket strawberries for ripeness. You can have it!

Mayes, a painting contractor, and Hewlett, an insurance salesman, accept, with thanks. They are worm specialists.

Among their peers, Hewlett and Mayes are recognized as two of the best anglers around. During one four-year span, they had two firsts, a second- and third-place finish in the team division of the prestigious Texas State Bass Tournament, perhaps the largest competitive event of its kind. Their dens are overflowing with huge mounted bass and trophies of various shapes and sizes.

Stubby, effervescent Jackie Hewlett, who appears to be walking around on his knees, estimates he fishes a worm "about 75 percent of the time." But Mayes, slender, of medium build, is more of a diehard. "I would guess that 90, maybe 95 percent of my bass fishing is with worms."

They are, therefore, recognized as experts in the art of duping bass with strips of limp, colored plastic. That is why *Bass Fishing Guide*'s Editor Bob Cobb asked me to fish with them and learn the how-to of their techniques. He did this knowing of my distaste for plastic-worm fishing. (You don't have to be sadistic to be an editor, but it sometimes helps in your dealings with writers.)

The interview took place on 20,000-acre Lake Conroe, just north of Houston, an impoundment that Mayes describes as "a super fishing hole."

It also is a lake caught up in controversy, what with lakeside developers wanting grass carp (white amur) put into Conroe to help eliminate that pest plant, hydrilla, while fisheries biologists and fishermen are united in an attempt to keep them out. "We don't need any more carp," Hewlett says.

We had come to Conroe because Mayes assured me that "we'll get some fish." And I could record firsthand how he and Hewlett did it. It was late summer. The air was almost still, and hot — ditto the water.

I was tying on a torpedo-shaped surface plug when Mayes suggested that maybe it would be wise to use a worm.

"You can have those (bleep) worms," I said.

"Suit yourself," Mayes answered with a shrug. "Just thought you wanted to catch a bass."

Obstinacy, I would soon discover, is no virtue.

Right away I noticed a couple of unusual things:

Straight-Shaped Worms — For one, both were using old-fashioned, pencil-shaped worms, no fan or curly tails. In fact, Mayes said he fishes the Scoundrel, the Nick Creme original. While he is sure they are good fish-getters, he doesn't even have any of the newfangled, curly-tailed worms in his tacklebox.

Slack-Line Wormin' — Another oddity, from my view-point, was the presentation, what both call "slack-line fishing." When either casts, he allows the worm to plummet on a limp line, slack laid across the water. If any tension is applied, Mayes explained, the worm won't fall naturally.

"The more naturally it drops, the more likely it will fool a bass," he stressed.

But the slack line puts a premium on concentration. Both Hewlett and Mayes said they rarely feel a strike; mostly it is a matter of noticing something unnatural, almost anticipating the bite, such as a twitch or a side movement of the line.

Or if the bass picks up and heads toward the boat, Mayes went on, "It is as though nothing is there, as if someone cut your line with scissors."

WHERE — "It is important that you recognize good structure and then get your bait into that cover." We were fishing from Mayes' Ranger and it was equipped with two depthfinders, one over the steering column, another mounted at the bow. No matter his position in the boat, he can take a quick glance and determine what's below.

CONFIDENCE — "You've got to believe that the bait you have on is the one for the job, at that time and at that place. Also you must think that every time you throw out there, you are going to catch a fish. It doesn't always work out that way, of course, but you've got to think positively."

PATIENCE — "The most common mistake is to fish the worm too fast. And the colder the water, the slower the retrieve. In the winter you've got to only barely move it since the bass are sluggish and slow to respond."

CONCENTRATION — "Stay in the ballgame and be aware of what is happening. Watch that line, and strike whenever you

"Watch the line, and strike whenever you detect something unnatural . . . "

Photo: Russell Tinsley

detect something unnatural at the other end."

I watched Mayes at work. After he cast, he would let the worm settle to the bottom and lie there in slack for two or three seconds, and not reel in slack until he was ready to move his bait.

Both Hewlett and Mayes use clear/blue fluorescent Stren, which stands out against the water. Ordinary blue monofilament seems to blend and disappear — "The old eyes are not what they used to be." Neither has tried bright-colored mono but each admits that line choice is a personal hangup more than anything.

"A lot of fishermen use colored line and like it," said Mayes. "Again, it is only matter of what you have confidence in."

That word "confidence" is stiched throughout any discussion you have with the pair about bass fishing generally and worm fishing specifically. Success breeds confidence, and vice versa. So, in essence, it is putting a bait in the water and keeping it there.

Tools Of The Trade — Another factor they emphasize is the importance of quality, supple line, the angler's direct contact with the lure.

"It is the cheapest part of your fishing, yet one of the most important," explained Hewlett. "After two or three trips, I always change lines. That might sound excessive, but after only about a month, monofilament will begin to take a set on the reel, and nicks and abrasions weaken it in places and that might cost you a good fish. And in real hot or cold weather, old monofilament can become brittle," he added.

I interrupted the pair to say that I had been told that the plastic worm wasn't a very effective cold-water lure, that a pork eel was much superior.

"Whoever said that didn't know what he was talking about," Mayes retorted. "One January, for example, we were fishing a tournament on Lake Livingston. Even though it was miserably cold and sleeting, my partner and I caught 79 pounds, 13 ounces in a day and a half to win first place, and every bass was taken on a plastic worm."

Both said they fish worms year-round. With some exceptions, they stay with 4- and 6-inch worms, rigged Texas-style with a 2/0 or 3/0 hook and about a 1/4-ounce slip sinker.

Occasionally, in a lake with little brush along the bottom and when using lighter line, a barrel swivel might be added about 4 inches forward of the worm, to prevent the slip sinker from riding directly against the hook, "where the worm will float off the bottom."

Different Twist — While they use the slim, pencil-type worms — "because we feel comfortable and confident with them" — they believe the twister-tail type might have its advantages and disadvantages.

"It gives more action for the fisherman who isn't real hep on working a worm," Mayes speculated. "As the worm is

lifted and dropped, the tail is moving and twitching and that probably helps attract a bass."

"But in cold water, I still believe in the straight-tail pencil worm," Hewlett added. "You can actually get too much action. A bass isn't going to put out much effort in cold water, and you've got to play the slow game its way."

While at times they might swim worms through submerged treetops on fairly tight lines when bass are suspended, almost all their fishing is on the bottom with the methodical lift-and-drop retrieve. "A mistake is to retrieve with the reel rather than the rod tip," Mayes explained. "I lift the worm, then let it drop, and I don't take up slack until the bait hits bottom."

Feel's The Deal — As for the rod, Hewlett "really likes graphite. It is more sensitive and you get a better feel."

Mayes agreed. "And a stiffer rod will give you a better feel of what the worm is doing than does one of medium-action. Graphite has improved my fishing — that I know," Mayes asserted.

" 'Feel' is so important to success and every component contributes. Mayes uses 17- or 20-pound-test line in timber and brush, 14-pound-test in open water. Hewlett prefers about the same for heavy cover, but in open, clear water goes to even lighter line, 8- to 12-pound-test, and maybe even light spinning tackle — "because it is a lot of fun."

In water 15 feet and shallower, a 1/4-ounce sinker is used most. In moss and weeds they might go as light as 3/16 ounce. And for deep water they employ a heavier sinker; just how heavy depends on the depth and velocity of the wind.

"I remember once on Rayburn, when the wind was howling, I was forced to use a 5/8-ounce sinker," recalled Mayes. "Worm fishing, like any fishing, is adapting to the conditions," he said.

Hewlett noted he believes in the lightest sinker "you can still feel." He emphasized the word 'feel.' "If the sinker is too light, you're only defeating your purpose; you can't feel what the worm is doing."

Feel and concentration, knowing when something is happening that normally wouldn't happen, tells you when to set the hook. While some fishermen advocate striking immediately, others let the bass briefly run with the worm. But Hewlett and Mayes agree there is no hard-and-fast rule. Again, it is a matter of adapting.

"Bass are funny," opined Mayes. "Like the time when Jackie and I were fishing the state tournament at Rayburn. The first day we'd reel down to check if the bass was still on before hitting 'em. But overnight the pattern changed. The next day we had to strike the moment we noticed a bite, no matter what position the rod tip was in. Any hesitation and the fish was gone."

Each said he sets the hook hard only once. "The only time I hit the fish again is if I think I didn't stick it the first time," Mayes explained.

With the slack-line worm method, it's vital that the angler use a high-visibility line. Jackie Hewlett favors clear/blue fluorescent monofilament that stands out against the water.
Photo: Russell Tinsley

Don't Be A Jerk — A bad habit is to hit the fish repeatedly as you bring it in. If you strike more than once, you're subject to losing the fish.

"Every time you set the hook, you're only stretching the skin and making the hole bigger," observed Hewlett. "You might pull the hook right out of its mouth, or the fish will easily throw the worm if it jumps."

"I learned my lesson on a big bass," Mayes interjected with a smile. "I set the hook and had it coming my way, then set back again and broke the line."

Serve 'Em Short — Another temptation to stifle is to throw way out yonder. Unless conditions dictate, such as deep water, Hewlett said his typical cast will be 35 or 40 feet.

Shorter casts serve a threefold purpose: (1) better accuracy is realized; (2) it is easier to feel what the worm is doing; (3) and there is less line stretch when setting the hook on a bass.

Color Of The Worm — Both agree that color does make a difference on some days. If you get in fish, color isn't always that important. Normally the anglers start with darker colors — black, grape or purple — before sunrise, then switch to lighter hues — firetail-purple, red or blue — once the sky brightens. But if they begin with, say, a black worm and it continues to entice strikes even after the sun comes up, they stay with it.

"You always work a color until it quits," Mayes said. "Only then do you experiment with other colors."

Neither has any "pet" color he ties on first; if he has fished a lake before, he lets that dictate the choice.

"Firetail-purple has always been a good color for Lake Conroe, and that's why I started with it," Hewlett explained.

"On another lake it might be some other color. No two lakes are alike. But if one color paid off on a lake last time, give it a good test the next time around before trying something else," Hewlett said.

On this lightly overcast but bright afternoon on Lake Conroe, both my boat companions hauled in bass with some regularity. (I'd caught only one on a spinnerbait.) But they griped because none were large. The fish averaged about 1 to 2 pounds apiece.

After pitching about a 14-inch specimen back into the water, Mayes mentioned that some folks believe he and Hewlett catch big bass every time they go fishing.

"I wish we did, but it just doesn't work that way," he lamented. "You've got to make a lot of casts and cover a bunch of water to get a 5-pounder. They're not hanging around every stump."

"Yeah, you're catching fish and complaining, and all I'm catching is weeds," I mumbled disgustedly.

Mayes made another cast, but took his eyes off his line to glance over his shoulder. "You say something?"

"Hell yes, I surrender," I answered in a loud voice. "Now will you loan me one of those dang worms?"

— 1980 BASS FISHING GUIDE

THE
"EMBREY METHOD"

By REEVES FEILD

*Plastic-worm fishing with a limber wand may go against
the grain of accepted bassin' theory, but
it's hard to argue with success . . .*

Bob Embrey's face, leather-tan after long weeks beneath the sun, was the perfect picture of concentration. As he gently pumped the long, limber rod, I tried to imagine what the 6-inch plastic worm below looked like as it hopped along the brushy bottom of Toledo Bend.

On his second cast of the day, I found out. It looked like "breakfast" to a bass, with a capital "B."

The 7-foot fiberglass rod bowed as the 3-pound largemouth turned tail, and fought to return to the dark depths of the creek channel that once meandered through the vast bottomlands of the Sabine River. Finally, the fish rocketed to the glassy-calm surface, and exploded in a shower of spray against a backdrop of flooded hardwoods and pines.

Embrey's unique worm-fishing equipment dictated that he play the bass carefully. After what seemed like more than a minute, he slid the chunky largemouth into the net and lifted it over the side. It was the first of 30 bass that Embrey would boat that day.

On any impoundment that enjoys a reputation like that of Toledo Bend, 30 bass in a day may not seem all that unusual — not unusual, that is, in the spring and fall, when huge numbers of hungry largemouths are scattered over the shallow, brushy flats close to shore.

My introduction to the "Embrey method," however, took place in early September, a time when many Bassmasters pack up their rods in disgust and turn their attentions to other pursuits.

Sooner or later, however, it was bound to happen — some smart bass angler would up and write a prescription for that seemingly incurable "summer slump."

Bass fishermen — and especially outdoor reporters — are a cynical lot when it comes to accepting new techniques that differ drastically from the so-called "truths." I'm not from the "Show-Me State" of Missouri, mind you, but nevertheless I've learned to chew a little longer than I used to. That way, after tasting something new, I can decide in my own good time whether to spit it out or try to get it down.

After awhile, you begin to pride yourself on being able to spot 'em — to separate those far-out theories that bass fishing seems to inspire from what, as they might say on the lower East Side, is actually "legit." Twelve hours after I first shook hands with Bob Embrey, however, I really had to wonder.

Surely, several million bass fisherman can't be wrong — or can they?

Once in a great while, an outdoor writer does discover something that's totally new and different. Such was the case when the telephone rang at The Shreveport, La., *Times*, my newspaper. After introducing himself, Embrey explained that he had worked out some new plastic-worm fishing techniques that he thought would be of interest to bass anglers.

During the course of the conversation, he mentioned rather casually that he'd been catching limits of good bass regularly at nearby Toledo Bend during the mid-August slump.

I was intrigued, to say the least. For weeks, worm fishing at Toledo had been just short of terrible. In addition, the equipment and techniques Embrey described were totally different from all that had long since been accepted as gospel.

I knew that Embrey was a Bassmaster I had to meet. We arranged a trip for early the following week. "I'll see you about 6 a.m.," Embrey said. Before I could raise any questions, he'd hung up the phone.

Already, I had to wonder, it's a good 90-minute drive from Shreveport to the area of Toledo Bend where Embrey had planned to fish. That being the case, we couldn't possibly get out on the lake before 8 a.m., a time when the hot sun already had most summertime bass fishermen heading for the banks. He'd explained, however, that his best fishing normally came between the hours of 9 a.m. and 4 p.m.

As I loaded my standard bassin' gear into Embrey's station wagon, I noticed all he had brought along was a plastic-worm rod, plus what was undoubtedly the longest levelwind casting rod that I had ever seen. The rod was an Eagle Claw MDRC7, which measures 7 feet

This Toledo Bend basser's technique goes against the grain of all proven worm-fishing methods. Folks chuckle when Bob Embrey hauls out his 8-foot-long wormin' rod, but the laughs don't last . . . Photo: Reeves Feild

from butt to tip. Embrey had to special-order the rod from the factory, since the demand locally for such equipment was anything but great.

Since that trip, Embrey has added a second long rod to his tackle selection that he likes even more. It's a custom-wrapped job that he had made up from a Fenwick No. 844 graphite blank. The blank itself is 6 feet long. Once the handle was added, the rod is a full 8 feet in length.

Embrey noticed me eyeing the long rod. "Folks call that my 'flyrod.' It's what I've been catching most of the bass on," he explained.

The two-piece buggy whip was stiff at the butt, but had all the tip action of a soggy noodle. It was outfitted with a high-speed, levelwind reel and 12-pound-test line.

Admittedly, for several seasons now, the brush-filled impoundments such as Toledo Bend have had most Bassmasters running scared. Line of 20- to 30-pound-test is still preferred, and 5 1/2-foot hawgin' gear with all the sensitivity of a fence post still fills the racks on most bass boats.

The philosophy generally has been to play with the bass after you get it in the boat. Embrey's philosophy, on the other hand, is to worry about getting the bass on before you worry about boating it. The special equipment he uses was selected with just that thought in mind.

Sometime back, while browsing through a sporting goods store, Embrey came across a dusty old Eagle Claw rod, and it immediately shifted his imagination into high gear. The reel clamp was missing — undoubtedly borrowed to put one of the store's more popular models back

into good working order.

"How much do you want for this thing?" he asked.

"Eight bucks," the store owner quickly replied, giving Embrey no time to change his mind.

That $8 was undoubtedly the best investment Embrey would make . . . at least as far as his bass-fishing success was concerned.

Embrey now does at least 80 percent of his plastic-worm fishing with the limber-tipped 7- and 8-foot rods. He's switching more and more to the graphite because of its increased sensitivity.

The primary purpose of the limber rod, of course, is sensitivity. "I'm convinced that most fishermen miss the majority of strikes on a plastic worm. With the light line, however, you get a lot more strikes. And with the light rod, you feel a lot more fish," Embrey says.

The trend toward light line is really nothing new. Top B.A.S.S. tournament professionals, more interested in a limit of keeper bass than in a single lunker, have been preaching the virtues of 6- to 12-pound-test monofilament for some time now.

But the super-sensitive long rod used in combination with the lighter line . . . well, that's something else again.

Embrey fishes the short, 6-inch plastic worms very fast, by most accepted standards. Once the worm settles to the bottom, he plants the handle in his stomach. Then, while holding the rod at the cork just above the reel, Embrey begins his retrieve.

"You find the rhythm that's most in time with how the

WHY A LONG ROD IS BETTER

What are the advantages of a 7-foot-long, limber fiberglass rod that Bob Embrey uses so effectively? He explains it this way:

"You've got to remember . . . it's a package deal that's all tied in with the way I fish it. I jig the worm super-fast with the rod tip out in front. It's done in such a way that the tip flexes with the movement of the plastic worm and sinker.

"Many times, as the worm falls, there's at least some slack in the line. But with the long rod, there's still enough pressure on the tip to feel the pickup the instant it occurs. Throughout the cast, you're in constant contact with the worm."

Embrey said that the longer 8-foot graphite rod has improved his success even more. "The long graphite rod has enough sensitivity to accomplish the same thing. But it's somewhat stiffer than the 7-foot fiberglass, and you can handle a fish a lot better with it."

The graphite is far superior to the fiberglass rod, says Embrey, when the bass are holding in or near extremely heavy brush. With the slightly stiffer rod, he can move the fish away from the cover fairly quickly, and get 'em headed toward the boat sooner.

"Finally, I feel the time lapse between the pickup and the hookset is critical. As a bass moves out of the cover to take a worm, the quicker you set the hook the less time the bass has to get back into cover again.

"With the long rod, I can feel the pickup much quicker, and can begin to set the hook within a fraction of a second," Embrey concludes. "I've noticed that 90 percent of the bass I catch are hooked in the top of the mouth, and right between the eyes, which tells me that I'm getting the hook set pretty darned quick."

— REEVES FEILD

bass are hitting. With the rod almost parallel to the surface of the water, I begin with three short pumps for every turn of the reel handle. If that doesn't work, I may drop down to two, or increase the number of pumps to four, until I find out just how the fish are taking it best," he says.

Embrey keeps the worm moving almost continuously, hopping it 6 to 10 inches off the bottom all the way back to the boat. "The deeper the water, the smaller the number of hops before you take up the slack. If you jig too much without stopping every once in a while to let the worm settle back down, then before you know it, you're fishing 3 or 4 feet off the bottom," he pointed out.

At the first hint of a strike, Embrey turns the reel handle quickly four or five times while snapping the limber rod up as fast as he possibly can. For all practical purpos-

es, he's setting the hook with the high-speed reel and not with the rod.

I was amazed at how many times Embrey was able to distinquish between those subtle pickups and the gentle tap transmitted up the line as the worm and slip sinker bumped the scattered brush.

Finally, my curiosity (along with my vanity) got the best of me. Using 20-pound-test line on a medium-action rod, I was six bass behind when I finally asked Embrey if I could give the long rod outfit a "test."

I tossed the worm out, and had bumped it across the bottom for several feet when I felt something happen that just wasn't right. It was almost as if I had dragged the worm through a small patch of moss. I raised the rod quickly and turned the reel handle as fast as I possibly could, half expecting to hang the biggest brush top in Toledo Bend. I'm not sure who was more surprised — this Bassmaster or the 2-pound bass that came boiling to the top.

Boating the fish, however, was something else again. For a few seconds, at least, the bass did pretty much what it wanted to. Finally, however, I slid the chunky largemouth into the net.

"What do you do when you hang a big bass?" I asked.

"I've caught 'em up to 8 pounds on this long rod," Embrey said. "Me and that fish had a ball. It jumped clear out of the water twice, and made two or three strong runs before I finally got it in."

Embrey has caught a number of bass over 6 pounds each on this special wormin' outfit, including a 6-pound-plus on the day we fished. He was bumping the worm up the sloping band of a flooded slough when the big fish hit. The bass came straight to the top, and cleared the surface by more than a foot. After that, the bass tried every trick in the book to get back down, but the constant pressure from the long limber rod finally turned the lunker toward the boat.

"With a shorter, stiffer rod and heavier line, most bass fishermen have a tendency to try and horse a big fish in quickly before it can hang 'em up. In doing so, they'll actually tear the hook out of a good bass' mouth. With this rig, however, there's little chance of doing that," Embrey asserted.

Embrey is very particular about his equipment and leaves nothing to chance. He uses a straight-shank 2/0 or 3/0 hook, depending on the size of the worm, and sharpens it like a needle.

After inserting the hook point into the plastic worm Texas-style to make it weedless, Embrey pushes it all the way through, and then backs it up — so when he tries to stick a fish, the hook won't first have to penetrate the plastic.

Embrey also files the broad base of his slip sinkers to prevent their sharp edge from cutting the lighter line. He prefers the 1/8-ounce slip sinker in water that's 12 feet deep or less, and the 1/4-ounce in the deeper areas of the lake.

"Everything about this equipment, as well as the way I

use it, is intended to accomplish two things — to feel the fish when it hits, and to reduce the amount of time between the pickup and the hookset," says the Shreveport Bassmaster.

I'll give Embrey credit not only for his ingenuity, but for his fish-finding abilities as well. He's got some productive summer worm holes located on Toledo Bend, and he's constantly finding new ones that apparently haven't been fished.

His techniques work well not only during the summer, however, but virtually 12 months out of the year. Some of his best catches from deep water come in the spring, when most other bass fishermen are beating the banks with spinnerbaits, crankbaits and such, and throughout the fall, when the majority of bass anglers are again back on the banks.

Embrey is president of Remco, Inc. of Shreveport, and Remtex Inc. of Longview, Texas, firms that specialize in precision machining. When he's not working, he's probably fishing . . . and usually alone.

"If I take someone else with me, then I feel kind of obligated to fish those spots where I know we can catch some bass. When I'm by myself, however, I'll spend a good portion of my time looking for new bunches of fish," says Embrey.

This Bassmaster concentrates most of his efforts along flooded creeks and sloughs and in the bends of the old Sabine River channel itself. Most of the fishin' holes are found when the fish give themselves away. Embrey constantly watches for bass "busting" shad on the surface. When a school breaks, he fishes the area thoroughly and checks it out with a depthfinder until he discovers exactly where the bass are holding when they sound.

He also watches for single fish, since one striking bass will often reveal the location of a large school. Shad darting across the surface are also a good indication that something down below has the baitfish on edge.

Finally, Embrey may locate good bunches of bass during the summer months by watching blue herons. Several birds often will be perched like statues on flooded stumps and brush, waiting to feed on baitfish that bass herd to the surface.

Embrey offered one word of advice that would undoubtedly increase the catches of most Bassmasters: "Pick a good area on your favorite lake, and fish it as much as possible. Fish it until you know it like the back of your hand."

Following that advice, Embrey undoubtedly is among the most consistent bass fishermen on Toledo Bend. The ability to locate bass under a variety of conditions has contributed greatly to his success.

However, finding 'em is one thing, while putting 'em in the boat is something else again. When the bass are anything but aggressive, it's technique that separates good fishermen from the hard-luck stories.

— MARCH/APRIL 1977

BUMPER WEIGHTS ON WORM RIGS

By CHUCK BERRY

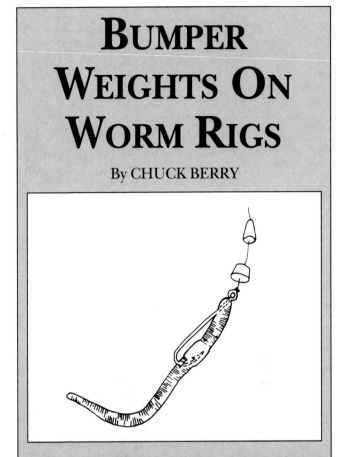

This rig is a variation of the "Texas rig," or, as described in my "Black Bass Manual," the "hidden-point worm rig." But notice the weights; there are two pieces of "sliders" instead of one. I call 'em "bumper weights."

The two pieces of lead bump or knock against each other as the worm rig is moved over irregular bottoms or through grass or brush. On limbs and brush, the two weights slide down a loose line when the worm is snagged temporarily. When freed, as you pick up on the line, the weights slide back toward the hook to create a "bumping" sound, providing the hook eye protrudes from the front of the worm. It's the bumping of the two weights that emit vibrations to attract bass.

In my opinion, this is a superior worm rig for bassin' in turbid water, and especially when retrieved slowly through obstructions. You'll feel the bumping vibrations right down to the rod handle. The bumping may even resemble those first "tap-taps" of a bass. When fished slowly, you'll detect the difference between the weights bumping and the bass tapping.

Cut a few larger sliders in half or use oval sliders (a small one in front of a larger one on the line). Try it. Bumper weights bring in the bass!

— MARCH 1974

Photo: Colin Moore

Photo: Wally Eberhart

Photo: Gerald Crawford

CHAPTER TEN

SPINNERBAIT SYSTEMS

A summary of techniques for fishing spinnerbaits under all conditions.

Photo: Gerald Crawford

How The Pros Fish Spinnerbaits

By NICK SISLEY

Some of the top tournament anglers swear by this bait for most of their fishing. If ever there was an all-around lure, this is it ...

I still remember the first time I saw a spinnerbait and thought, "This has to be a super lure." As I pondered the ways to fish the bait, I couldn't help marveling at how this type lure combined two of the most productive fish-takers that have ever appeared on the American angling scene — the jig and the spinner.

A lot of water has gone over a lot of dams, and I've cast several boxesful of spinnerbaits. However, I'm continually learning how to fish this unique bass lure in different ways at different times to make bass strike. My bet is you have a box full of spinnerbaits. At times, you enjoy good success fishing them, and you're searching for new techniques to make this lure even more productive.

The spinnerbait has become one of the most effective bass takers on the pro B.A.S.S. Tournament Trail. It has figured in five of the six BASS Masters Classic® world finals. Professional bass anglers are using spinners more and more in every tournament. What are the success secrets of the winners?

Why not go to the spinnerbait B.A.S.S. pros, and the spinnerbait lure manufacturers, and pick their brains for the latest trends in spinnerbait techniques? After all, who knows more about how to fish a specific spinnerbait than the lure manufacturer or lure designer? In many instances, the top tackle makers enlist tournament professionals to fish their baits continually — trying to add improvements and to find better methods to entice ol' Mossback to strike under all types of conditions. Here's what BASSMASTER Magazine learned from the pros:

Tom Mann of Eufaula, Ala., is not only one of the most successful B.A.S.S. tournament anglers, his lures, products of Mann's Bait Company, are renowned throughout bass country.

His original spinnerbait, and still a top bass-catcher, was the Wooly Bully. Two other famous lures in his company's stable are the "flavored" Jelly Worm and the tail-spinning Little George.

Marketing Trend To Smaller Lures

In the past few seasons there have been some sophisticated trends developing in the bass fishing market, according to Tom Mann. He could see a growing need for a new type of spinnerbait — one smaller, more compact in size. After a great deal of research, Mann created the TomCat Super Spin, first introduced in the summer of 1975.

Here's what Mann has to say on spinnerbaits: "I created this spinner for a number of reasons. I felt a smaller lure would keep pace with the trend to light-action tackle. More Bassmasters are discovering the art of catching bass on lighter, compact tackle.

"This scaled-down spinnerbait is produced in three sizes: 1/8-, 1/4- and 1/2-ounce. However, the 1/4 ounce is the size fished most. The lure was designed with a smaller pointed head, perfect for fishing through grass and brush, and is fitted with a new concept in spinner blades. The unique perforated blade on the TomCat allows free-spinning action at even slow reeling speed. The tiny cup in the blade also emits bubbles as the lure is retrieved, and the blade spins.

"Although this spinnerbait is available in a wide variety of color combinations, I don't personally feel that color is important in spinnerbait fishing. In most spinnerbait situations, bass strike out of surprise or impulse. Most any color will work under these conditions. The colors I usually fish are white, chartreuse or yellow.

"More important than color is the manner and speed in which a spinnerbait is fished. Water color and water temperature are the most important considerations in lure-retrieve speed. In stained or muddy water, I slow down the retrieve, sometimes to a C-R-A-W-L. In cold water, bass are sluggish and reluctant to move far or fast for any food. Here again, the retrieve should be super slow. Under these conditions, I suggest Bassmasters move the spinnerbait in the same manner they would a plastic worm," says Mann.

Tom Mann's Top Tactic For Spinners

One of Mann's favorite methods for fishing a spinnerbait is "buzzing" stick-ups:

"I like to find an area where the water is 4 to 5 feet deep and heavily laden with stumps, trees, stick-ups or any type of fish-holding structure," he says. "When throwing at a target like a stump or stick-up, make the first cast a foot or two off to one side. If you can entice a bass to come out of its hideout and hit the bait, you'll have better odds of landing the fish. The chances of the bass getting back to its lair and hanging up are less. Secondly, the chance of snagging your lure on the first cast is reduced. On my second cast to the same stick-up or stump, I will throw past the target with a retrieve designed to actually 'bump the stump.' Most strikes come just as the bait bounces off the target," says Mann.

A trailer hook is most important when bass are shallow and/or the buzzing technique is used. When fishing a spinnerbait deep and slow, a trailer hook is not as important, in Mann's opinion.

"After catching a couple of good bass or hanging a couple of stumps, a spinnerbait may stop running true. Continually check the position of the top wire in relation to the lure body and the hook. If the bait tends to turn to the left, the top arm should be moved slightly to the right and vice versa," points out Mann.

Ricky Green is another top-ranking B.A.S.S. pro. He stands fourth on the all-time list of money winners. "I can honestly say 95 percent of my bass have been taken on a spinnerbait," says this Arkadelphia, Ark., basser. "To me, the spinnerbait is without a doubt the No. 1 bass lure." Green now fishes the Strike King spinnerbait, made by a company headed by another top Bassmaster, Charlie Spence of Memphis, Tenn.

Green thinks, "The spinnerbait is the pro's No. 1 lure because of its versatility. This bait can be fished just as effectively in 6 inches of water as it can in 35 feet of water."

Ricky Green's Spinnerbait Tips

Here are Ricky Green's spinnerbait success tips: "Bass seem most responsive when water temperature is between 58 and 78 degrees. In fishing shallow water with these water-temperature conditions, don't let your spinnerbait go more than 6 inches

One blade or two? Which color body and skirt? Nobody has all the answers, and even the pros differ in their opinions about the best spinnerbaits to use.

Photo: Don Wirth

below the surface.

"When water temperature is below 58 degrees or above 78 degrees, the spinnerbait should be fished at a slower rate of speed. Two methods I use are: (1) First, I fish a single-blade a majority of the time. Tandems do not work for me. A No. 5 or No. 6 blade is my preference. I throw the spinnerbait, pull it a foot or so to make sure the blade is turning properly, then let it sink to the bottom. While retrieving, I let the spinnerbait follow the contour of the bottom — reeling it just fast enough to turn the blade. (2) I find this method deadly in the fall. (It's best to have stick-ups or some type of structure in the water, 5 feet or deeper.) I cast past the stick-up, run the spinnerbait right up to it, and stop it as close to the stick-up as possbile. If a strike doesn't occur as it's falling, I yo-yo the spinnerbait all the way back to the boat — raising the lure about 2 feet, then letting it settle back. Strikes usually are light, so keep the slack out of the line, and never raise your rod tip higher than the 10 o'clock position."

Green says the spinnerbait is most productive in murky water. "This lure can also produce in clear water if fishing heavy cover or on cloudy days. In searching for bass when the sun is bright, concentrate your fishing efforts in murky water," he suggests. "I like a white or chartreuse spinnerbait in heavily stained water. If the water is only slightly off-color, I'll choose either a blue and chartreuse or black and yellow. In clear water, my preference is blue or black on cloudy days and white if the sun is bright," notes Green.

Tune Spinnerbaits For Best Action

Tuning a spinnerbait is very important to catch bass consistently. Here's Green's advice: "The blade shaft must be in perfect line with the point of the hook. I also adjust the wire so the blade nicks the point of the hook as it revolves. This adds a little extra noise to the lure as it comes through the water.

"I use a 3/8-ounce spinnerbait 90 percent of the time. I prefer the way it throws and the way this size handles in the water. I use a 1/8- or 1/4-ounce if the water is ultraclear, a 5/8-ounce for deep water. The head design on Strike King allows the bait to fall true. At the '76 BASS Masters Classic, I caught the largest bass that has ever been taken in Classic competition. The largemouth bass weighed 8 pounds, 9 ounces, and it grabbed a 5/8-ounce Strike King. I'd made some adjustments to the lure. I cut 1/2 inch off the shaft spinner arm and added a No. 6 blade. By cutting 1/2 inch off the shaft, the bait falls better when using the larger blades."

Bill Norman, president of Norman Manufacturing in Greenwood, Ark., also emphasizes versatility as the key to why spinnerbaits are such preferred and successful bass lures. Norman Manufacturing recently began marketing Jim Houston's Redman Spinnerbait in three models — single-spin, double-spin, and tandem-spin. Some folks believe Houston is perhaps the top spinnerbait bass fisherman in the nation. He was certainly the "hottest" B.A.S.S. pro on the Bassmaster Tournament Trail last year, winning the South Carolina Invitational en route to B.A.S.S. Angler-of-the-Year honors. Houston uses a spinnerbait at least 60 percent of the time.

Retrieves, Tactics For Spinnerbaits

Houston is on the Bill Norman fishing team, as is Basil Bacon of Rolla, Mo., another top spinnerbait BASSer. The following comments are combined success techniques of Norman, Houston, and Bacon:

BUZZING A SPINNERBAIT — Most Bassmasters know about buzzing a spinnerbait, but there is some misconception about the term. With the proper equipment, you don't have to crank for all you're worth all the time. Using one of the newer, fast-retrieve reels and with the reel spool filled with line, it is easy to hold a quality spinnerbait on top.

STEADY RETRIEVE — This is the most simple form of spinnerbait retrieve — no breaking or bulging the surface. Often it pays to drop the lure down to a medium depth, at least out of sight.

BULGING THE WATER, BUT NOT BREAKING THE SURFACE — Making the water bulge without breaking the surface takes very little practice if you use proper equipment. With this technique, the "V" wake in the water behind a "bulging" spinnerbait attracts the strike. In some instances, bass will come up from depths of 15 feet in clear water to attack a bulging spinnerbait.

BREAKING THE SURFACE INTERMITTENTLY — If bulging the water doesn't work, crank a little faster so the blades break the surface occasionally. The spinnerbait will then sling water drops across the surface, and this commotion on top resembles jumping shad. This technique seems most effective when the water is calm.

"KILLING" THE SPINNERBAIT — Just as the spinnerbait comes up to some type of structure like standing timber, a stump or whatever, stop the bait, and let it fall for 2 or 3 feet beside the structure. Most strikes come right after you stop the lure, and it starts falling. You will see the line twitch. Rear back! If you don't experience a strike, start the normal retrieve. Some strikes occur during the first crank.

DEEP RETRIEVE OVER MOSS BEDS — When you find this type of structure, make the cast, and start a slow retrieve. Feel your way down until the blades are nipping the tops of the moss or grass. This tactic takes concentration. Bass like to hold in this type of habitat, and only will leave the safety of the moss for a short distance. This is why it is important to get the spinnerbait as close to their hiding lair as possible.

TANDEM-SPINS AND DOUBLE-SPINS — Twin-blade rigs have the edge over single-spins when you need a large bulge in the water. This is especially true if there is a little chop on the water. More and bigger blades give you the needed extra bulge.

Houston, who designed the Redman Spinnerbait and developed a rapid-fire rate of presentation for this lure, provides these suggestions: "The more territory you cover, the more bass you are going to catch. I get in close to the structure, bushes or grass, stumps, banks, or whatever, and make very short casts, and lots of them. I developed an underhand toss that permits me to make a cast every four or five seconds. I usually turn the trolling motor on high speed and go right down a bank, knowing that somewhere I'll find a bass that will take the bait I am throwing.

"I never let the bait get out of sight. I see 99 percent of the fish I catch hit the spinnerbait. I always wear a pair of Polarized sunglasses to eliminate glare, and to make it easier to keep in eye contact with the lure. Sometimes you'll see the fish hit the bait, but never feel it. Watch your line, too. If it moves sideways, rear back. This is very important."

"I like oversized blades and prefer the tandem-spin over the single-spin," says Bacon, who believes he introduced fishing large blades to Bull Shoals. He's more or less the "father" of large-blade spinnerbait fishing in clear water. Bacon goes on to say, "Watch your line at all times. In clear water, and especially if you are bulging the water with large blades, you have to be alert continually. If you're not alert, a bass can be on your spinnerbait and you will see nothing but a swirl in the water and maybe a miss. A big blade leaves such a large wake that it takes constant concentration to spot an approaching or striking bass."

SPINNERBAIT COLORS — Bill Norman believes spinnerbait colors are very important, but Jim Houston says they don't make much difference.

LINE WEIGHT — "This is a matter of personal choice, but we advise 20-pound-test when fishing heavy cover and 14-pound-test for clear water and better feel of the bait," says the Norman fishing team.

VIBRATION AND BLADE SIZE — This angling trio doesn't agree with most other B.A.S.S. pros on this matter. They feel the dirtier the water, the smaller the blade. The clearer the water, the larger the blade. Their reasoning is that a larger blade has more power of attraction in clear water. If the lake is murky, they feel bass are attracted to a lure by vibration, not sight. Smaller blades turn faster and thus send out more vibrations into the water.

Fleck's Weed-Wader spinnerbait has been instrumental in

winning three straight BASS Masters Classics — the first in 1974 at Wheeler Lake, Ala., by Tommy Martin, the second at Currituck Sound, N.C., in 1975 by Jack Hains, and the third by Ricky Clunn at Guntersville Lake, Ala. The Weed-Wader is unusual because it incorporates Indiana blades, whereas most other spinnerbaits utilize the Colorado spinner.

Hains changed the back blade from Indiana to willowleaf at Currituck. The willowleaf simply came through the Currituck grass better. Hains also utilized a 1/4-ounce lure, which made it easier to keep the bait on or very close to the surface.

Entice Bass To "Come Up"

At Guntersville, Clunn used a 7/8-ounce Weed-Wader, with an oversize No. 7 and 8 blade combination, but this particular design was about two years old. J.D. Robinson of Fleck Products says the company is not producing the big-blade combo now because the blade sizes were too big for the bait. Fleck now offers the 7/8-ounce Weed-Wader with size 5 and 7 blades. To counteract the larger blade area of the older lure, and for added casting weight in the wind, Clunn used a lead wrap-around sinker as a keel on his Weed-Wader so the bait would cast and retrieve over the milfoil grass at Guntersville better. (See, "Rick Clunn's Classic Catch," Feb. 1977 BASSMASTER® Magazine.)

Robinson feels it is important to try to tempt a bass to "come up" to hit a spinnerbait. He says, "If you can entice bass to come up, you are usually in for a great day of fishing. I usually start fishing by bulging the water. If that doesn't work, I run the spinnerbait 2 to 3 inches under the surface. I next move to 6 to 8 inches below the surface, then to 3 to 4 feet under the surface. If all these experiments don't pay off, I come back and try and break the water."

Hains, who ranked No. 2 on the '76 B.A.S.S. Tournament Trail, had an interesting experience during a tournament. The first day or so he was missing strike after strike. In tournaments, Hains uses a trailer hoook, but on the final day he tried something drastic — adding a trailer hook on a trailer hook! It paid off with six bass, and all were nailed on the last hook. I echoed Robinson's words, "Why didn't I think of that?"

Jimmy Houston, regarded by many as the top spinnerbait fisherman in the country, always retrieves the lure near the surface.

— *MARCH/APRIL 1977*

HOW DENNY BRAUER 'BURNS' A BLUFF

By STEVE PRICE

When bass are hiding tight against a sheer rock wall, try this technique for getting their attention . . .

Steep-walled bluffs are among the most intimidating sights to bass fishermen visiting a new lake, for they nearly always signal deeper water, which in turn means harder-to-catch bass.

Denny Brauer, a top Tournament Trail pro from Camdenton, Mo., has perfected a pattern for fishing these rock walls that is remarkably effective — and easy and fun to use. He calls it "bluff-burning," and it works well whenever bass are suspended and holding tight against the bluffs, especially from late summer through early winter.

Basically, bluff-burning consists of tight, parallel casting with a big-bladed spinnerbait along the very edge of the cliff face. The lure is bulged just under the surface with a fast retrieve, and it attracts bass that may be suspended below.

"The bluffs where this pattern seems to work best," says Brauer, "are those that lead into a bay or main channel, bluffs that circle and form a basin or large bay, and those bluffs located seemingly in the middle of nowhere, where no other structure may be available.

"Bass are attracted to bluffs for many reasons," continues the Missouri pro, "but certainly one of the main reasons is that baitfish often are present. Wind blows bait against these rocks, and bass move in and suspend under them. In some areas, I think bass may stay along bluffs year-round, too."

Brauer believes clear water is an important ingredient in how strong this pattern might be on a particular lake. He enjoys very good results off bluffs in Lake of the Ozarks, a clearwater impoundment on which

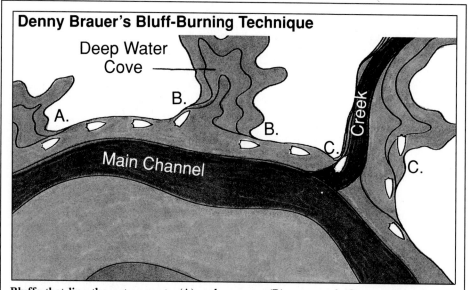

Denny Brauer's Bluff-Burning Technique

Deep Water Cove

A.

B.

B.

C.

C.

Creek

Main Channel

Bluffs that line the entrances to (A) embayments, (B) coves and (C) creek mouths are the best. Brauer positions his boat tight against the bluff face and casts parallel to it. Corners and ends of bluff walls are the most likely places to find bass.

Illustration: Bernie Schultz

Brauer prefers a 7-foot casting rod for bluff-burning because it affords him longer casts and more hook-setting power. Photo: Gerald Crawford

he works as a bass guide. But he has not found it very effective on dingy-water lakes, or those with plenty of surface vegetation.

On these waters, he thinks the bass simply move to shallow cover. In clear water, though, bass tend to move vertically more than horizontally, which is another reason they are attracted to bluffs.

For bluff-burning, Brauer likes to use a 7-foot casting rod, which enables longer casts and greater hook-setting power, and a fast-retrieve reel filled with 14-pound-test line. He fishes a half-ounce spinnerbait with a No. 6 or 7 blade, and he adds a pork trailer to provide buoyancy and a trailer hook to catch short-striking fish.

"The noisy spinnerbait brings suspended bass up," says Brauer, "although it rarely brings up really big fish. This is

an excellent tactic for 'keeper' bass when fishing conditions are tough everywhere else and other patterns haven't produced any fish.

"I move my boat in right against the bluff, often touching it, and keep my casts within a foot or two of the wall "he adds." I retrieve fast, and I keep the boat moving pretty steadily, too."

His favorite bluffs are those lining the entrance into a bay or cove; the most productive spots often are the edges just before the bluff ends or curves in toward the cove. Bluffs at the mouths of large creeks also are among his best spots.

On bright days, this pattern brings best results early and late, especially when there is some shade and the water depth is at least 15 feet. On cloudy days, bluff-burning can produce throughout the day.

"One thing I've noticed about this pattern," Brauer cautions, "is that sheer cliffs that drop straight down into deep water are the best for attracting bass. When bluffs stairstep down in a series of ledges, the bass tend to locate along other parts of the structure."

— MARCH 1988

Typically, Brauer retrieves the spinnerbait so the blade is making a bulge in the water's surface. Photo: Gerald Crawford

RAISE 'EM WITH A RUCKUS

By STAN FAGERSTROM

Racing topwater spinnerbaits across the surface is an old trick for taking bass, especially around heavy aquatic vegetation . . .

The fishing was slow. I had been on the water since the first light had pushed the dark shadows away from the edge of the pad fields. My stringer hung in limp loneliness near the front of my boat.

The sun hadn't managed to poke its bright fingers of warmth through the gray blanket of clouds that shrouded the green countryside. But the temperature was climbing. I slid my hat back, lifted the oars to rest in their holders and relaxed in my boat seat.

I had fished mostly with plastic worms, single-spinners, a couple of floating-diving plugs and an assortment of surface lures. I'd lost a big fish on a plastic worm on my third cast and released a 1-pounder that hit my frog Hula Popper. That had been the extent of my success.

My gaze wandered across the crowded trays of the tacklebox. One of the extra boxes I carried in the bottom of the big box caught my eye. I had marked the top of it with a red felt pen. The top was labelled "Wigglers." Now I knew what my next tactic would be.

I picked an old gold No. 5 Shimmy Wiggler out of the box. I slid a strip of 4-inch white pork rind over the natural bucktail that covered the single hook. Quickly, I tested the point of the hook with my thumb. Satisfied of its sharpness, I slid the lure into my snap and clipped it shut.

My boat was about 20 feet off the edge of the pad fields. I cast 40 feet ahead and let the Shimmy drop 4 feet into the pads. I had it coming back before the water from its splash had even started to settle. Now the lure boiled, gurgled, spluttered and spit as it raced toward me. My right hand blurred over the reel handles.

Suddenly there was movement in the pads 10 feet to the right of the speeding lure, just as it cleared the pad field and broke into open water. The pads bulged, parted, and there was a slashing boil beneath the surface as the bass drove in. Fast as that racing lure was moving, the fish had reached it in the space of a heartbeat. K-A-S-P-L-O-O-S-H! Fish on!

That could have been 30 years ago or yesterday. The high-speed tactic for bass is one I've been using ever since I knocked the hide off my knuckles with the first level-winder I ever cranked way back in the 1930s. It's a technique that has stood time's test and it should be part of every bassman's fishing strategy.

Let me set one thing straight. The fast-retrieve technique I'm going to discuss won't always catch bass, but neither will anything else. Old-timers won't have to be told that and a newcomer to pad-busting is going to learn it for himself soon enough. I've just put the finishing touches on a full-length book on bass fishing. It details my experience with largemouth bass over the past 30 years. One of the central themes of the book is that a largemouth bass doesn't always do anything.

It's hard to convince a beginner a bass will hit something moved as fast as you'll often see knowledgeable anglers work certain of their lures. It's a tough, demanding way to fish. There's nothing about it which bears the slightest resemblance to relaxation. As the years go by, I find it more difficult to employ the procedure for very long at a time because of the complaints I get from a tired right wrist, elbow or shoulder.

Let's consider a few of the lures which are best-suited for

raising a ruckus. Many of them have familiar names. The old Shimmy Wiggler No. 5 is a dandy. The No. 2 Hawaiian Wiggler is just as good. The Sputterfuss of the Hawaiian Wiggler family is excellent, especially for larger fish. The nice-casting little Weed Wing is fine and so is Herb's Dilly. There are others equally effective.

I like the Shimmy best where there is a fair share of open water in addition to pads, grass, brush or whatever the cover happens to be. Much the same is true of the Sputterfuss and the No. 2 Hawaiian Wiggler, though I will use these two Arbogast baits where the going is heavier. Herb's Dilly also works well in heavy cover but the best of the lot where the pads make almost a solid blanket is the Weed Wing.

The retrieve itself isn't very involved. You just crank the devil out of whatever lure you select. Let's suppose we're working along the edge of a pad field like I described in the beginning. Stand up in your boat because it's easier to learn and execute the fast retrieve if you do. Keep your boat in close to the edge so your retrieve can come back parallel to the open fringe of the pad field.

Look ahead 30 to 50 feet. Try to hit one of the little pockets or indentations 3 to 5 feet back in the pads. You want the lure to scurry out of the pads into open water, then run parallel to cover. Never let the lure drop. If you are a right-hander, switch the rod from your right to left hand while the lure is in flight. Move the lure forward as it hits the water and start reeling just as fast as you can at the same time. Now speed up some more!

Bass will "bust" out of cover to smash a fast-moving lure.   Photo: Stan Fagerstrom

What you'll be doing if you are using the technique correctly will be to make the lure raise all the ruckus it can. It should look for all the world like a miniature outboard with 100 horses bucking and snorting as it pushes the cover aside. The little metal prop should leave a bubbling froth as it does its dizzy dance back to the boat.

The BASSer who introduced me to the fast retrieve was a wonderful old guy named John (Tex) Reeder. Before he died, Reeder was making rods in Vancouver, Wash. He had the topwater speed tactic down to a science. Reeder had just one problem. He used the fast comeback to the exclusion of all other methods. When it worked he made a killing. When it didn't, he got skunked. One time the two of us put six fish on the stringer, every last one of them taken on No. 2 Hawai-

ians and No. 5 Shimmy Wigglers. All of those fish topped 4 pounds apiece and the two biggest went better than 6 each. That's not bad bassin' in my part of the country.

The memory of the fishing we had that day is one of the many reasons I spend so much time with my hind end parked on a boat cushion. It's also one of the main justifications for writing about the fast-retrieve procedure. There just isn't another thrill in all of the enchanting realm of bass busting to match the sight of a good-sized largemouth when it comes thundering after a lure you are trying to take away from it.

It doesn't matter what time of day you use the fast-action approach for bass. I've done just as well with it from 10 a.m. to 2 p.m. as I have at any other time. I know fishermen down

Position your boat so you can fish down the side of weedy cover.
Photo: Gerald Crawford

South who make a killing with it at night.

The short casting rod with guts enough to get a lunker's head up and out of the cover is best for this kind of bass fishing. My own favorite is a custom-built, 5-foot stick with a straight handle. My reel is the Ambassadeur 5000.

Line? The best I've found for ruckus-raisin' is Cortland's new Micron. It's small in diameter for its test, spools well and, best of all, has almost no stretch. You can hit old evil-eye just as hard as it hits you and make the hook stick. I prefer Micron in 15- to 20-pound-test for my fast fishing and I use straight Micron with no leader. Your line should never be down in the water anyhow if you are working the lure correctly, so the leader isn't important.

My old friend Tex used to get fish on the super-fast retrieve from beginning to end of the season. I personally find it best from late spring through early fall. Water temperatures are warmest in the lakes I fish then and that's when I find bass most likely to chase down a super-fast topwater spinner.

I think the BASSer who uses only one approach, be it the plastic worm or the fast retrieve, is making a mistake. That's why you'll seldom see me use the super-fast retrieve the first crack out of the box. The speedy retrieve is a noisy, surface-disturbing way to fish. It figures to scare heck out of anything not mad or mean enough to hit. I much prefer to start out with a surface plug, plastic worm, a floating-diving lure, or what-have-you before I turn to the fast retrieve. And that's not because it isn't effective. I just want to give myself every possible advantage and the speed routine may still get fish even though you've tried a half-dozen different approaches in the same area.

There are those days when bass will hit in this fashion more readily than any other. That, of course, is the time to stick with the procedure. If you've never tried it before, you will be surprised how often those days do come along in the course of a season.

As I indicated earlier, the fast retrieve is one which gets largemouth wherever they are found. I've been using it for years in the lakes and sloughs of the Pacific Northwest. I've corresponded with BASSers in other parts of the nation who have been doing the same. One of them is George Thompson, another member of B.A.S.S. from Joplin, Mo. Thompson makes a lure he calls the "Go-Devil." It's designed especially for the kind of hell-raising surface action I've been describing. Thompson doesn't make a lot of lures but the ones he does turn out get fish.

Sometimes I get good action using a floating surface lure, like Heddon's Dying Flutter or one of Gordon Estes' Daz-E-Mae Clippers, by working them just the way I do the sinking lures with the metal prop. The technique is the same. Just cast them out next to cover and yard 'em back like there was no tomorrow.

One more tip — whenever you use this approach to bass fishing, learn to watch the cover on both sides of your lure. If you do, much of the time you'll see the fish move before it starts its charge on the bait. Don't panic and try to jerk the lure away as the fish tears after it. Just keep it coming. If old bucketmouth misses the first time or just boils behind it, keep right on reeling as fast as you can, don't stop. I've actually had bass blast a lure three and four times on one retrieve before they ever made connections. Every one of those hits had the spray flying and my pulse pounding.

You really can get bass by raisin' a ruckus. It's a method that's best around cover in fairly shallow water. Never leave such an area without at least giving it a try. Build the technique into your own approach to bassing. I'll bet 10 Silver Minnows to one Wicked Mama, you'll wind up using it as much as I do!

— *MARCH/APRIL 1972*

How Cliff Craft Fishes Deep-Water Spinnerbaits

By TIM TUCKER

Typically used in shallow water, spinnerbaits can be deadly over deep-water structure, too . . .

Cliff Craft refers to it as "just another fish-catching tool, another weapon in your arsenal."

But if you listen to the legendary Roland Martin, it's an "outstanding fish producer and a consistent method of catching fish in deep water throughout the year."

Both are talking about fishing spinnerbaits in deep water, a vastly underrated technique that Craft introduced to Martin during a tournament on Toledo Bend several years ago.

Martin had caught a large number of quality bass (3 pounds and up) by working crankbaits along ledges and deep-water timber, a pattern with which he figured he could easily win the tournament.

Paired with Craft on the first day of competition, Martin found that the fish didn't cooperate nearly as well as they had in practice. The bass simply were no longer interested in the small crankbaits.

Craft suggested fishing a spinnerbait in that 10- to 15-foot water, but Martin was a little skeptical. Like the majority of bass fishermen everywhere, he had known the spinnerbait as strictly a shallow-water tool. But he quickly changed from skeptic to convert.

Patiently working the fluttering spinnerbait, Craft put 10 bass that weighed a total of 44 pounds into the boat while Martin watched. Craft finished third in the tournament, and Martin added another valuable technique to his treasury of fishing tricks.

"With spinnerbaits, probably 90 percent of the fish are caught in water shallow enough that you can see the object that the fish are hiding near," says Craft, a veteran pro from Sugar Hill, Ga.

Jimmy Houston, for example, invariably works his spinnerbaits just under the surface. "Jimmy's probably known as the greatest spinnerbait fisherman alive, mainly because he fishes the baits 90 percent of the time. And he catches 90 percent of his fish on them," Craft says. "Most people just don't associate the spinnerbait with deep water."

"Deep," of course, is a relative term. On Lake Lanier in Craft's home state, deep water is in excess of 30 feet. Shallow water is 15 feet and less. But in Florida, anything over 10 feet would be extremely deep.

"To me, deep water means the level at which most lures become ineffective, particularly crankbaits," he says. "And spinnerbaits give you another viable lure and presentation to try to catch those deep-water fish."

Craft says the deep-water spinnerbait technique is a more productive tactic for catching the inactive deep-water fish in the extreme temperatures of winter and summer than it is for bass that are feeding actively. "When they are inactive, they can be taken by lures that get reaction strikes — like a jigging spoon or deep-running crankbait, if you can get it down that deep," Craft explains.

"You also can get a reaction bite from a spinnerbait, because of the flash of the blade and the undulation of its skirt."

The depth of the structure automatically limits your choice of weapons. Anything past the 15-foot mark only can be worked effectively with three types of lures (plastic worms, jigging spoons and jigs), he says.

To illustrate that point, Craft refers to an outing on Georgia's West Point Lake a couple of years ago, when he was catching bass in 15 to 20 feet of water on a plastic worm.

Cliff Craft says his deep-water spinnerbait technique is better for catching inactive fish in extreme temperatures than it is for bass that are feeding actively. Photo: Tim Tucker

Suddenly, the bass became inactive. He chose the fluttering spinnerbait over the other standard choice, a jigging spoon, and began to catch those inactive fish.

"I just don't like to fish a jigging spoon in less than 25 feet of water," he says. "There are more productive lures to use in that depth, and the spinnerbait is one of them.

"The spinnerbait has an advantage over the jigging spoon, because it has a slower, more tantalizing fall. With a 3/4-ounce Hopkins spoon or 1/2-ounce Mann-O-Lure, a fish has to be real quick to get it as it falls. But the spinnerbait gives you the same type of fall that you'd get with a jig-and-pig, plus its blades give it more visibility. It falls slowly enough to give the fish time to size it up, so they're more likely to jump on it as it flutters past than they would a jigging spoon."

For fishing a spinnerbait in deep water, Craft uses a 3/8-ounce single-spin model with a No. 4 or 5 blade. A double-bladed lure doesn't produce the tantalizing, helicoptering motion that attracts bass.

He also "doctors" the lure by removing the living-rubber skirt that is popular today and replacing it with an older style of skirt, one with stiffer strands of rubber. That change allows the bait to fall better and the skirt to undulate more enticingly.

While most spinnerbait fishermen add a pork or plastic trailer to the spinnerbait hook, Craft says a trailer's bulk keeps the bait from falling correctly, and its extra length sometimes deadens the blade action.

Using 14- to 20-pound-test line, Craft fishes deep-water spinnerbaits on a sensitive graphite rod and pays close attention to the vibration he feels through the rod.

"If I don't feel it throbbing as it falls, I know I don't have good blade action," says Craft, a four-time BASS Masters Classic® qualifier. In that case, he shortens the blade arm of the spinnerbait.

"Many people aren't aware of it, but you can get a lot of different vibrations just by shortening the length of the arm," he explains. "But you need to remember that the more you shorten that wire, the more you decrease the weedlessness of the lure."

At depths of 30 feet or more, Craft says, lure color isn't an important variable. Visibility is, however, so he uses a hot-yellow or white skirt for fishing all depths. After a great deal of experimentation with blade color, he has settled on copper for most situations but he occasionally switches to nickel or white in clear water and gold in extremely off-colored water.

Deep-water spinnerbait fishing requires some knowledge of electronics to help pinpoint prime structures for this technique — deep-water humps, gullies, drop-offs and roadbeds. Deep treetops and grassbeds are good places for this technique, also.

"Surprisingly, you can fish it in some fairly heavy cover, like boulders and thick brush," he says. "As long as you don't get the spinnerbait arm too short, the spinnerbait is one of the most snagless lures known to man."

While the spinnerbait is an easy lure to fish in deep water, Craft cautions that it takes a persistent angler to succeed with this technique.

"Patience is the key," he explains. "When you're fishing a spinnerbait in 15 to 35 feet of water, it takes a long time for a bait to drop that deep.

"Then as you retrieve it — always using the yo-yo retrieve — it takes a good bit of time, maybe a second or two after each pull, to allow the bait to drop back down."

And concentration is important, because the bass will most often hit the bait while it's falling — a point in the retrieve where many fishermen lose some sensitivity.

Take a tip from Cliff Craft: the spinnerbait isn't just a shallow-water tool. It can save the day when deep-water bass become inactive.

— APRIL 1987

Single-spin spinnerbaits are preferred for deep-water fishing because they have a more tantalizing motion on the fall.

Photo: Doug Stamm

SPINNERBAITS FOR COLD-WATER BASS

By CHRIS ALTMAN

While most anglers offer jigs to deep-freeze bass, these Tennessee anglers are mopping up on spinnerbaits in winter . . .

For most Americans, bass fishing is a warm-weather sport. OK, maybe a cool-weather one, too. But by the time the leaves have fallen and the robin is well on its way south, most anglers have traded their tackle for guns or bows.

"That's just fine with me," remarks Charlie Huskey, president of Admiral Craft Boats. "I enjoy having the lakes to myself during the winter." Among fishermen in East Tennessee, Knoxville-based Huskey is a tournament angler well-known for his catches of big bass from deep-water structure.

Tommy Buckingham, a marine dealer and tournament fisherman from Morristown, Tenn., who now is fishing the BASSMASTER® Tournament Trail, says, "The winter months offer some of the most enjoyable fishing of the year. The fish are there to

Big-bladed spinnerbaits with pork-rind trailers are hard for midwinter bass to refuse.
Photo: Gerald Crawford

be caught, and you will have very little competition for them. Most people just don't like to fish when they have to keep dunking their rod tips to get the ice out of the line guides. And you certainly don't have any trouble with water-skiers!"

These veteran anglers from the Volunteer State have developed several spinnerbait tactics that are extremely effective for ice-water bass. Although the techniques were developed in highland reservoirs, both anglers have proved them (or adaptations thereof) productive in all types of lakes.

Unless Huskey is fishing a tournament and trying to catch a quick limit, you can safely bet that he is fishing exclusively for big bass. One of the first structure-fishing specialists in the state, Huskey spends his angling time developing new big-bass techniques or refining his standard ones to work better.

One of his most productive wintertime techniques calls for the use of a big-bladed spinnerbait. "A jig was always *the* winter bait to use when bass fishing, especially if you wanted to catch a fish of any size," he says. "In the early 1970s, I started playing around with a variety of other lures during the winter months simply because I felt there were other ways to catch these fish."

Over the next few years, Huskey developed a few spinnerbait techniques that not only caught largemouths and smallmouths, but attracted truly big fish of both species.

"My average spinnerbait bass during the winter months averages right at 4 1/2 pounds," he reports. "Remember, these are Tennessee bass, and a 4- to 5-pound average is truly a remarkable accomplishment." Huskey has taken largemouths over 9 pounds and literally hundreds of smallmouths over 5 pounds with his tactics.

"Basically, I fish two different spinnerbaits during the winter months: a short-arm drop bait and a long-arm one. The key is using a bait with a giant blade," Huskey says, "something in the neighborhood of a No. 7 or No. 8 Colorado blade (about the size of a half-dollar). When the water is very cold (high 30s to low 40s), the bass are quite lethargic and don't want to move around a lot. They still have to eat, and I believe that a big fish will try to capture just one big meal rather than a lot of little tidbits. For that reason, I like a big-blade/big-bait combination."

When fishing during the coldest months of the year, or as Huskey says, "When it's so cold you don't think you can stand the next cast," he uses a short-arm spinnerbait and concentrates on structures adjacent to the old river channel. "I started making short-arm baits before they were commercially available, but now I like to use Strike King's 5/8-ounce Spin-Dance bait. Most of the time, though, I'll change to a larger blade."

Huskey reports chartreuse as being his most productive color but says he sometimes uses purple or black if the water is unusually dingy. All of his ice-water spinnerbaits are tipped with a brown No. 1 Uncle Josh pork jumbo frog from which half of the fat is trimmed. It leaves an orange spot on the belly of the pork.

Huskey's favorite target for his drop-bait is a tree that has fallen from a steep bank into the water so that its top hangs over into the channel.

"I believe the fish just suspend in the tree limbs and move only when absolutely necessary. With the boat situated over the channel, I like to cast well up on the channel ledge and crawl the bait slowly along the bottom until I hit the first tree limb," he reports. "Then, you simply pull the bait up and

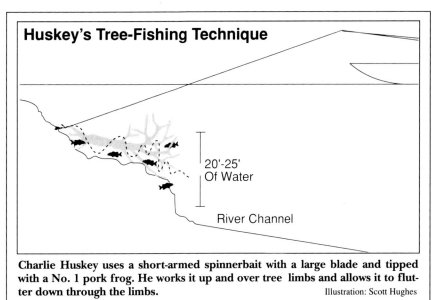

Huskey's Tree-Fishing Technique

20'-25' Of Water

River Channel

Charlie Huskey uses a short-armed spinnerbait with a large blade and tipped with a No. 1 pork frog. He works it up and over tree limbs and allows it to flutter down through the limbs.   Illustration: Scott Hughes

over the branch and let it flutter down through the limbs on a tight line." The up/over/down series is repeated each time the bait or line comes in contact with a limb. "Most of the strikes will occur as the bait is fluttering down through the tree limbs. The fish normally don't hit very hard, so you have to keep a tight line and pay close attention at all times."

Huskey notes that while you can catch fish in very shallow water during the winter months, most of the truly big fish hold in 20 to 25 feet of water.

"I try to find trees that are situated at that depth," he says, "but that's not always possible. Sometimes you have to take things into your own hands and create your own!" Huskey goes on to say that if you cannot locate a suitable fallen tree, the same short-arm drop-bait worked over and down rocky channel ledges is a good back-up plan. "Not all of the fish will be in tree limbs, of course. But I do think they are ideal spots for cold-water bass."

Huskey also looks for trees that have fallen off a bluff in close proximity to the river channel. "If you will watch the tops of bluffs as you head down the lake, you can see where a tree has fallen off the cliff and into the water. Most of the time, the trees are submerged totally, so very few anglers ever know that they are there. These are my hidden honey holes.

"Sometimes the trees fall into the bottom of the channel, so they're in water too deep to hold the fish. But other times, the trees will catch on a ledge or hang up somehow. These are wonderful big-fish spots, and you fish them the same way as a tree lying over a channel ledge."

Huskey generally fishes these fallen trees from December through February, but moves to very shallow water in early March.

"Bass in the spring move shallower far more quickly than

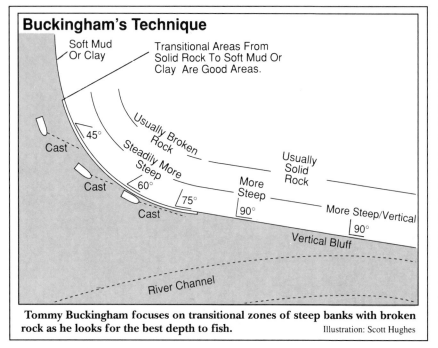

Buckingham's Technique

Soft Mud Or Clay

Transitional Areas From Solid Rock To Soft Mud Or Clay Are Good Areas.

Usually Broken Rock

Steadily More Steep

Cast 45°

Cast 60°

Cast 75°

Usually Solid Rock

More Steep 90°

More Steep/Vertical 90°

Vertical Bluff

River Channel

Tommy Buckingham focuses on transitional zones of steep banks with broken rock as he looks for the best depth to fish.
Illustration: Scott Hughes

cation of a strike is a slight, sideways jump of the line."

In addition to these prime areas, spinnerbaits also are good winter lures to use when you are trying to locate fish on a fairly expansive structure. Short-arm baits are good choices for slow-rolling down riprap banks, and long-arm baits are a top choice when trying to locate fish on a deep-water flat adjacent to the river channel. In the pre-spawn period, Huskey also likes to fish culverts and trestles ("any narrowing through which water is flowing") with his long-arm bait. In muddy water, stick with a large Colorado blade, while a willow-leaf blade is suitable for clearwater use, he advises.

While Huskey prefers big spinnerbaits with big blades, Tommy Buckingham likes tiny spinnerbaits when he is after bass in fridgid water.

"I know that big baits will definitely catch fish during the winter, but I am convinced that I catch many more fish — both big and small — on smaller spinnerbaits, especially in clear lakes," he says.

Buckingham does not use traditional spinnerbaits, but pieces together a unique lure from various components. A 1/4-ounce hair jig is coupled with a No. 2 Hildebrandt spinner, a small safety-pin-shaped wire arm, the bottom of which snaps onto the jig-eye, and a tiny No. 2 Colorado blade fitted to the end of the wire arm. When combined, the duo creates, in essence, a tiny spinnerbait. This astute angler believes that a hair jig is much more productive than a rubber-skirted jig during winter.

To add buoyancy to the bait, he adds an Uncle Josh U-2 or No. 101 spin-pork trailer. "One of the nice things about this rig is that you simply can unsnap the hair fly and replace it quickly. In a matter of seconds, and without having to tie a new knot, you can change the entire complexion of the lure.

"Cold-water bass typically do not hit a bait very hard," Buckingham states, "and often they will just mouth the lure. To compensate for that, you need a very sensitive rod. I use spinning gear most often because I believe it offers greater sensitivity than a baitcasting rig, and I get a quicker hookset with it. Too, this technique is most productive in fairly clear water, so I want to use light line. Normally, I'll use 6-pound-test line, and I never exceed 8-pound-test."

Buckingham's favorite target for the little bait is a bluff-lined channel bank on the main lake. Specifically, he fishes the ends of the bluffs where they taper down to a point or a pocket. "If you will examine a bluff bank, you'll see that in most cases, the ends of the bluff will grow gradually less steep. These are the areas I concentrate on, and not the bluff

most people believe, especially the bigger sows. As a consequence, most anglers tend to fish underneath the bass," Huskey believes.

Huskey's pre-spawn fishing calls for the use of the big-blade, long-arm spinnerbait. "This technique demands a Colorado blade, such as Strike King's Houston Model Magnum. Again, I prefer a chartreuse bait, but I'll switch to black, brown or purple if the fish aren't responding. And I tip this bait with the brown, fat-trimmed, No. 1 pork frog," Huskey says. He most often chooses a 1/2-ounce bait, but if the water is extremely muddy, he'll switch to a 1/4-ounce lure.

"As the water gets muddier, I'll choose a smaller head size and use a slower retrieve. The only problem is that these big blades will cause a lighter bait to roll over, so you really have to just crawl the bait along."

When the fish move shallow, they move extremely shallow, Huskey believes, and he catches the majority of his early pre-spawn bass in 12 to 18 inches of water. "Really, this technique is best when the water is so muddy it looks like you could walk on it. After a hard spring rain that raises the lake level and muddies the water, it's a hard tactic to beat," he says.

For the most part, Huskey fishes these big-blade, long-arm spinnerbaits in typical spawning areas located in close proximity to the river channel.

"If you located some good big-fish holes during the dead of winter, then you should concentrate on shallow flats in those areas. All you do is cast the bait to the shoreline and ease it through the shallows at a slow, steady retrieve. The fish won't usually hit very hard," he says, "and the first indi-

part — I've caught very few fish off a vertical bluff."

Buckingham says these areas not only change in degree of incline, but also rock type. "The bluff part is usually solid rock, but the ends are usually broken rock of some sort. I like the broken-rock areas, especially if they meet a slick, clay bank."

Bass do not hold as deep in the winter months as most people believe, Buckingham argues. "I catch the vast majority of my fish in 4 to 12 feet of water, and rarely will I catch one deeper than 20 feet. That's both largemouths and smallmouths."

On a typical bank with an incline of about 45 degrees, Buckingham fishes bluff ends by positioning the boat about 25 feet away from the shoreline. A 35- to 40-foot cast is then made from the front of the boat at a 30-degree angle toward the shoreline. As the slope of the bank grows steeper, he positions the boat closer to the shoreline. "All of this sounds complicated," he says, "but all it does is keep your bait near the bottom. If you sit way out from the bank and throw directly to it, the lure will swing back to you and you'll never touch bottom."

Actually, he doesn't fish the small spinnerbait directly on the bottom. "These little baits will hang in the broken rocks if you let them touch bottom every time. Once I am able to figure out the depth at which the bass are holding, I'll try to keep my bait at that depth at all times. That's where the pork trailer comes into play. The buoyancy it and the line provide helps me to swim the bait along at the desired depth.

"When fishing an area of this type, you pattern the fish not only by depth, but by the slope of the bank and the type of rock," he continues. "Once you've established the pattern, it will hold throughout the lake until a major weather front forces the fish to move."

Although spinnerbaits are normally considered shallow-water, warm-weather lures, these two Tennessee anglers have found other uses for spinnerbaits — and they have been well-rewarded. Give it a try, and remember, if you ever feel the blade stop turning, set the hook!

— JANUARY 1990

Spinnerbait bass caught during the winter may average over 4 pounds.

Photo: Chris Altman

TRY FLIPPIN' SPINNERS

By JOHN ANDERONI

BASSers are getting turned on to this new technique of fishing spinnerbaits with long rods...

There's no doubt that bass fishing has turned into a highly sophisticated sport. Electronics provide the ability to position us in the bass' ballpark. Ultra-advanced watercraft zip BASSers there in the blink of an eye, then serve as a comfortable fishing platform. Today's tackle designers furnish the tools to yank a bass of any size from any cover, while still being comfortable to use and appealing in looks. But, regardless of the quality, or quantity, of fishing gear, the bottom line calls for the fisherman to convince the fish to "take the bait." And, duping the fish to strike is what bass angling is all about.

Putting a lure in the bass' strike zone is the Bassmaster's chief concern. There have been countless methods envisioned to do the job. However, if you spend your fishing hours on shallow, dingy, flatland, structure-filled lakes, "flippin'" should be high on your bassin' tactic list.

A lot has been written about flipping in recent years, and even though the method has been heavily publicized and refined, the truth is that bass anglers have been flipping lures since Day One. Take a heavy rod, a strong line and your favorite plastic worm or jig rig. Then, find the heaviest, thickest cover around, drop the bait in the middle, work it up and down a couple of times — and hang on.

Fundamentally that's all there is to it. Or is it?

With fishermen realizing that, basically, flipping is really just a reinvention of the wheel, more BASSers are starting to dig into their experiences, or pick the brains of veteran bass anglers, hoping to improve their techniques. And in so doing, another "new" tactic is gaining popularity among Midwestern BASSers even though its users have labeled it top secret.

What is this magic fishing formula that just may guarantee a boatload of bass? For lack of a better name, let's call it "Spinnerbait Flippin'."

• **Seeing Is Believing** — Last fall, during an Ohio bass tournament, my partner and I came across a couple of bass fishermen who normally fight it out each year for the "Mr. Bass" title. They were working long, 7 1/2-foot flipping sticks in heavy cover, but fishing faster and more erratic than you would expect. Our boat passed them by and we moved down the channel, but not before I caught a glimpse of a spinnerbait on the end of a line. When they won the tournament, the mental wheels started turning, and I recalled an incident that had happened over 30 years ago.

Every small community has a "town drunk," but ours was probably the best fisherman I ever met. As a kid of about 10, I sometimes followed him as he caught fish to eat, and nine times out of 10, it was bass. I recall a fall day when ol' Felix started working the waters of Ohio's Miami-Erie Canal, which happened to run right behind my back door. He had a cane pole, black braided line and a Pflueger Tandem Spinner hanging on the end.

He walked down to a couple of logs that rested along the bank, tossed the spinner to the far end and started a sweeping retrieve. He stopped and jigged the spinner a couple of times and continued the retrieve to the end of the log. He repeated the process again, then reversed the pattern. On one retrieve he suddenly changed directions, and made the spinner surge at a right angle away from the log. That's when the bass hit.

It was thrilling to watch him hook and work that big bass on a cane pole, and it was even more thrilling to watch him repeat the show two more times during the same hour. But, with three lunkers that would have put him in the money in any B.A.S.S.-club tournament, he packed his gear and fish and headed back to the piano crate he called home.

The more I remembered the incident, the more I realized that there was just no way he could have worked the bait the way he did with a casting rod. But, using a "flipping stick" . . . well, it's not hard to figure why the anglers who are employing this tactic are having so much success. There is no doubt the technique works. So, let's examine spinnerbait flipping more closely and see why some of the users swear it will increase your catch 20 to 30 percent.

• **Using The Technique** — First, flipping spinners is a year-round tactic but is especially effective in the fall or spring. During these seasons, many of the largest bass are finning in heavy cover, and getting a lure to them is a problem.

True, a skillful fisherman can cast a long-arm, weedless spinnerbait into heavy cover and usually retrieve it without too much difficulty. Unfortunately, during rapid changes of temperature or weather, the angler might be dealing with neutral to inactive fish. If this is the case, most efforts will probably produce little, if any, action. But, flipping the same lures gives some distinct advantages to the spinnerbait users that the caster just doesn't have, and if properly fished can muster a strike from any bass.

Spinnerbait flipping is a tactic designed for close-in fishing. If a flip of more than 15 feet is necessary, the technique really defeats itself. But, let's assume you're working close to a cover-filled bank. What can this approach do for you?

One of the biggest advantages is accuracy. Even though a good caster can generally drop a lure in a bucket at 15 feet, an average skilled flipper should be able to do it at least as well, if not better. Flipping also allows you to feather the spinner into pockets that most casters ignore.

When fish are tight in structure and you're working in close quarters, the quietest presentation is a distinct benefit, especially if you must repeat the cast before a sulking bass decides to strike. Without a doubt, the BASSer wielding a flipping stick is able to cover the area more effectively and faster, and at the same time has better control and feel with the shorter line length between the rod and lure.

• **Working The Lure** — Once the bait is in the water, the real art comes into play. Here's where the BASSer fine-tunes himself to the fish and begins to work the bait, adjusting his retrieve as the structure varies. As the angler feathers his cast into a tight pocket against the bank, he can allow the bait to settle vertically to the bottom, or before the lure crosses a log, he can stop and vertical-jig the spinner, using the structure as a pivot point. This is a dandy tactic for fall and spring when fish are neutral or inactive.

The BASSer might drag the spinnerbait along a log quickly, then, when it reaches the end, suddenly stop it and let it drop — a great time for a strike. Fishing in close with a 7 1/2-foot

rod also gives the angler the option of reversing the direction of the retrieve, which often triggers a fish to strike. Being able to fish behind, as well as in front of cover, also is an angling advantage and speed control of the lure is a distinct plus. When you flip a spinnerbait properly, it is definitely in the fish's territory longer than when casting and this, in itself, will produce more fish.

It takes a certain angling sense to be a good spinnerbait flipper, an ability that comes from experience. Consequently, the method takes concentration. This is mentally exhausting, especially when fishing is tough. And it's physically exhausting due to the weight of the equipment, the amount of exertion and the fact that standing is a mandatory requirement.

To some, the spinnerbait is known as a "heavy-structure idiot bait." Throw it in the brush, get it out and hope that in between a bass decides to belt it. To the angler who flips, the spinnerbait is without a doubt the most versatile, finesse bait in his bassin' arsenal.

As you try the technique, that first strike will be awaited anxiously. When it comes, it can be savage, or so subtle that only line movement gives it away. No matter what the case, you will feel confident in setting the hook and getting the fish out of the cover. The 7 1/2-foot rod gives a definite advantage in pulling big bass from heavy cover in comparison to the average-length casting rig. Fish that are lost are usually the fault of the fisherman. Either a bad knot or the line becomes worn from rubbing against the structure. So, make it a general rule to retie often. This will reduce the amount of fish you lose dramatically.

• **Spinners For Flipping** — As far as spinnerbaits for flipping are concerned, the lighter weights are best. The less the weight, the easier it is to control. The ideal spinnerbait is a long-armed, single-blade in 1/8 to 1/4 ounce. The skirt should be shortened to just cover the end of the hook point. This should take care of short-strikers. Ball-bearing swivels are a must, and allow the lure to be worked slower, yet still retain the proper blade vibration. A No. 3 1/2 or 4 blade works well on either the 1/8- or 1/4-ounce baits. If you're flipping a 3/8-ounce lure, switch to a No. 5 blade.

Spinnerbaits can be flipped in any cover during any season provided the water is off-colored enough to prevent spooking fish. As far as water temperature is concerned, 50 to 80 degrees seem to be the approximate extremes. When possible, fish with the sun to your face. Even though it may be uncomfortable at times, you can see the structure as well as watch your line. Sun coming over your back creates a silhouette and casts a shadow.

Flipping the spinnerbait into a brushpile is the easy part. What you do with the bait once it is in the water is the challenge — the art you should try to develop. And, once this level is reached, spinnerbait flipping becomes a confidence tactic that can produce "bonus bass" when other tactics fail you.

— NOVEMBER/DECEMBER 1982

HOW TO SLOW-ROLL A SPINNERBAIT

By STEVE PRICE

Guy Eaker explains one of the most difficult and deadliest spinnerbaiting techniques . . .

O f all the different ways to fish a spinnerbait, the technique of "slow-rolling" is perhaps the most difficult, and probably the most misunderstood. It can be a deadly method to use, however, when fishing under adverse conditions, when bass are deeper than 10 feet, or when they're holding extremely tight to certain types of cover.

"Slow-rolling is not really a new technique," explains BASSMASTER® Tournament Trail pro Guy Eaker, generally regarded as one of the top spinnerbaiters on the water. "I first heard the technique described by Blake Honeycutt in the late 1960s when I fished with him over knolls and ridges on Lake Norman near Charlotte, N.C.

"Basically, slow-rolling means fishing a spinnerbait deep, say between 5 and 20 feet, over brush, grass or trees. You don't 'drop' a spinnerbait when you're slow-rolling; you 'swim' it down. You cast shallow and slowly turn the reel handle so the lure moves forward as it sinks. The blades turn continuously.

"The spinnerbait never actually rolls or turns over, as the term implies. It simply feathers down over or beside a target."

In his pro career, Eaker has pocketed more than $100,000 in tournament prize money by using a spinnerbait, and much of it has been through slow-rolling. In B.A.S.S. competition, he has two second-place finishes at Lake Okeechobee and a third-place finish at Sam Rayburn that came by slow-rolling.

"You know it's time to start slow-rolling when bass don't come up to hit a spinnerbait, even though you're fishing around good cover," says Eaker. "You have to take the lure to them, but you do it more slowly.

"Many anglers might use a jig or worm under these conditions, but a spinnerbait offers flash and vibration other lures don't have. The key is keeping the spinnerbait as close as possible to the target, even bumping it, and making certain the blades are turning continuously."

Even though his target, such as a fallen tree, submerged grass or row of stumps, may be 10 or 12 feet deep, Eaker begins a slow-roll by casting well beyond that target, and when the lure touches the water, he actually pulls back on the rod as he reaches for the reel so the blades start turning instantly.

His preference is, naturally, his own "Eaker Eater" spinnerbait he designed several years ago (manufactured by Bagley Bait Co., P.O. Drawer 110, Winter Haven, FL 33882), but he candidly admits that other spinnerbaits also can be used in slow-rolling. He recommends a tandem-blade model, preferably a willowleaf/Colorado blade combination in different colors. He likes a 1/2-ounce model with a No. 3 silver Colorado blade and a No. 4 gold willowleaf blade. If he feels more vibration is needed, he changes to a No. 5 willowleaf.

"I'll cast shallow and get the blades turning so the fish hear the lure coming," says Eaker, "and once I start turning the reel handle, I never stop. My rod tip is pointed down at the spinnerbait so I actually can guide it toward specific places. I'll let the lure touch the target, too."

One of Eaker's favorite places to slow-roll a spinnerbait is over emerging grass that is still several feet below the surface. If the bass don't want a fast-moving lipless crankbait like the Rat-L-Trap, then a slow-rolling spinnerbait is an excellent alternative, and it's much easier to fish than a jig or worm.

"Swim the spinnerbait down until you feel it 'tick' the top of the grass," explains the six-time BASS Masters Classic® qualifier from Cherryville, N.C. "Then wind it just fast enough

Guy Eaker's favorite spinnerbait is a 1/2-ounce "Eaker Eater," which he designed, and which features both a gold willowleaf blade and a silver Colorado blade.
Photo: Steve Price

to stay at that depth. Don't try to hop it up and down or make it jump — just reel it slowly and steadily right over the top of the grass. The bass will do the rest."

Because submerged vegetation like this may be quite shallow, Eaker doesn't hesitate to switch to a lighter 3/8- or 1/4-ounce spinnerbait that does not sink as fast as a heavier model. His favorite trailer is a white plastic split-tail eel.

Slow-rolling also can be productive over steep channel banks, especially in fall and winter when a sudden front moves bass from a flat on which they had been feeding to the nearest deep water.

"When I fish this type of structure," says Eaker, "I swim a spinnerbait down to the bottom, then bounce it slowly over that bottom until it reaches the edge of the drop-off. Instead of letting the lure drop over the edge, though, I pump the spinnerbait once or twice as if I were still hopping it along the bottom. If a bass doesn't hit then, I reel in and make another cast.

"The reason for bouncing the spinnerbait slowly along the bottom is simply to have contact with the bottom, so you know exactly when the drop-off occurs. You don't want your lure to fall off that edge because bass are seldom down there. Instead, they're holding out from the edge, often at the same depth."

Still another prime situation in which to slow-roll a spinnerbait, explains Eaker, is any place you've been catching bass with a fast-moving crankbait. Don't leave that hole, he cautions, without reeling a slow, deep spinnerbait through the same places. Very often, you'll catch larger bass on the spinnerbait than on the faster crankbait, simply because those bigger fish aren't as aggressive.

Fallen trees along the shoreline offer still another good opportunity to slow-roll a spinnerbait from shallow water down to deeper depths. When fishing this type of cover, Eaker positions himself well out in deeper water and casts close to the bank, even though he knows bass probably won't be so shallow. Then, holding his rod tip down, he gradually brings the spinnerbait down the tree trunk into progressively deeper water. Along the entire distance the lure remains only inches from the cover.

"The hardest thing to learn about slow-rolling is keeping the lure moving deeper along the retrieve, or in the case of vegetation, at the proper depth just above it," concludes Eaker. "Most anglers use spinnerbaits for shallow, visible cover, but slow-rolling into deeper depths just doubles the effectiveness of the lure."

— MARCH 1988

SPRING SPINNERBAIT TACTICS

By PETE ELKINS

There's a lot more to catching early-season lunkers than just flinging a spinner into shallow water. Here are the bylaws for bassin' success . . .

It was one of those spring days about which Bassmasters dream. Three days of warm spring sunshine had given way to an equally warm, but overcast, rain-dripping day, the kind that soaks down the back of your rain jacket. And, it was the time that sends big largemouth bass into the shallows from the pre-spawn holding areas.

The bass were tight against scattered grass clumps and weedbeds, especially those in small protected pockets near deeper water. The main channel was muddy, but the slough and coves were perfectly "colored" for the best springtime lures of all — spinnerbaits.

I knew the bass was big because its dorsal fin was protruding from the water as the fish finned in a small opening surrounded by grass clumps and verdant reeds. "Buck" or male bass were nearby, their presence marked by occasional greenish swirls in the murky water.

Carefully calculating the necessary path of the spinnerbait into striking range of the sow, I cast 10 feet beyond the cover, and thumbed the spool to ease the gold-bladed spinnerbait into the water. The lure throbbed slowly toward the target. Two feet away, the heavy bass turned toward the noisy intruder. Then, a sudden bulge of brown water and a thudding blow to my graphite rod announced the interception by one of the lurking male bass.

While the frenzied buck bass fought well, I watched the big female bolt toward the safety of deeper water. Even though disappointed, I wasn't unhappy. The female would be back the next day, and so would I. The spinnerbait had already taken more than two dozen good largemouths from the warming shallows, including several in excess of 5

pounds each. The fish had been carefully released for another encounter.

If you live in the South, springtime means spinnerbait time. Other methods are certainly productive. For example, crankbaits can be especially good for pre-spawn largemouths. Venerable jig and pigs always are effective. But a well-tuned and artfully presented spinnerbait is *numero uno* for oversized largemouth.

There is, however, a lot more to taking springtime bass than just flinging a spinnerbait into the nearest shallow water. The when, where, what and how are of critical importance.

• **When Spring Bass Turn On** — "When" depends upon geographical latitude and current climatic conditions. Generally, throughout the South and other areas, peak results occur after the water temperature reaches 55 degrees and above. Rising temperature is important. Once the water temperature reaches approximately 65 degrees, then whether it's rising or falling in temperature isn't quite as critical.

In some southern states, like Georgia, good shallow spinnerbait action may kick off in February, and build in intensity throughout March and April. My experiences also indicate that the action will continue longer into late spring and early summer if the water remains murky. A review of my 1982-83 fishing log reveals that late March and early April marked the best spinnerbait action in the Chattahoochee River and its bass-filled impoundments, lakes Eufaula and West Point, near my Columbus, Ga., home.

Overcast, rainy, but warm weather is also an important

"when" consideration. As an example, my log reveals that on April 15, 1983, I fished a favorite grassy slough with a tandem gold-blade Water Witch spinnerbait from 5:15 p.m. until dark. It was raining and warm. The results included nine good fish, counting one 8-pounder.

By the next day, conditions had changed. A sunny, windy, cold front moved into the area. My partner and I could manage only four decent fish from 3:30 p.m. until dark.

The lesson is obvious: Buy a good rainsuit, still expect to get wet and pray for warm, rainy days. Murky water reduces the adverse impact of sunny skies somewhat. Still, overcast and warming trends are the most important "whens" next to water temperature.

• **Where To Go For Action** — Assuming that the "when" is successfully met, "where" looms next in importance. There are some important differences between lakes and rivers. A natural river, one without dams, tends to flood heavily during the early spring. By April, the water level may be fishable.

There can be some torrid bass action in the overflow portion of natural rivers during flood stages, but it's not something that a bass-boat-equipped angler can really take advantage of. In addition, the fish can be spread out so much in the flooded swamps that only a few anglers know where to find them.

A man-changed river is a different proposition. Good spinnerbait fishing starts early. Bass will be on a shallow weedbed pattern as the water reaches toward the 60-degree mark. Bassmaster Carlos Sellers, an artist with a spinnerbait, from Baxley, Ga., also notes that fish in a man-changed river such as the Chattahoochee seem to move much farther from channels than largemouths in impoundments at the same time.

Impoundment "where" centers on creek channels. A savvy spring spinnerbait practitioner, like Sellers, concentrates on the edges of well-defined creek channels in 6- to 8-foot depths. Definition of the creek channel is vital. Initial contact with spring bass usually will occur where cover is near the original creek channel in 10 feet of water. The more vertical the channel, the closer the bass will hold to its edge.

During the pre-spawn period, big females often are concentrated at the mouths of creeks or coves. If the water is clear, they will hold in 10- to 12-foot depths. If murky, they stay in 5 to 6 feet, again near the channel.

Even though not ready to spawn, the sows occasionally will move into nearby grass or cover to feed. During these feeding forays, as well as during the actual spawning period, the fish will be on the sunny side of grass if the water is still warming and below 65 degrees. Once the water temperature exceeds that mark, then shade becomes a relevant "where" factor.

As the actual spawning season begins, the bigger bass spawn in about 3-foot depths. Smaller fish will move into the grass itself to spawn.

• **Spinners To Sling** — With this general background as to when and where, the next hurdle is "what." Spinnerbaits come in a huge variety, most of which are for general purpose. Some are superior for buzzing or bulging along the surface. Others are ideal for bottom-bumping in cold weather. Only a few are ideal for shallow water and thick vegetation. During the last 20 years of intensive bass fishing, I've tried almost all popular spinnerbaits.

But, I didn't find an almost perfect spinnerbait until last spring. The Water Witch tandem gold-bladed spinnerbait is my answer to shallow bass in the springtime.

The Water Witch features unusually small-diameter wire and gold blades, which apparently combine to create vibration that is irresistible to largemouth bass in the shallows. Because of the lighter wire arms, a large fish invariably bends the wire. Retuning is necessary after most fish, but the added trouble is rewarded.

Most advocates of springtime spinnerbaits prefer nothing less than 20-pound-test mono. Given the murkiness of typical springtime bass waters in the South, line color isn't overly critical. Tackle for throwing the spinnerbait is entirely up to the individual angler's preference. Stiff rods are an advantage. High-speed casting reels with at least a 3-to-1 retrieve ratio are important. Even though retrieve rate normally should be slow, especially in early spring, big female bass react to the strike by immediately bolting for deep water. Unless the BASSer can catch up with the slack line, the first jump often will result in a thrown lure.

Strikes are increased by adding a pork frog to the spinnerbait as a trailer. If there is good color to the water, experts like Sellers prefer a No. 11 Uncle Josh frog. If the water is clear, then a No. 101 frog with a smaller 1/4-ounce single-spin with No. 3 1/2 gold blade is the top producer.

Frog pattern always is good for the Uncle Josh No. 11 in colored water. In clear water, black or solid green are recommended choices. For those BASSers fortunate enough to be near tidal waters in the spring, a chartreuse/brown skirted spinnerbait with a frog-patterned No. 11 "pig" can be deadly.

In typical Southern springtime waters, yellow, white or white/yellow skirts are the ticket with a tandem gold-bladed spinnerbait. Even in extremely murky water, shallow bass can be color-conscious. Veteran spinnerbait anglers have experienced occasions at West Point when largemouth would dart up to white spinnerbaits in murky water, but turn away at the last minute. Switching to an identical spinnerbait with yellow skirt (both with the ubiquitous No. 1 frog) brought a strike.

Trailer hooks usually are not necessary in the spring, except when fishing spinnerbaits very fast in clear water.

HOOKING BASS ON SPINNERBAITS

Largemouth bass do one of two things to a spinnerbait during the spring. They either kiss it or try to kill it, more often the latter.

The "kiss-and-don't-tell" strikes are more common during the very early spring when big bass are still in deeper, pre-spawn areas along creek-channel edges.

Male or "buck" bass always seem to have murder on their minds. Big females on feeding forays into the shallows also are homicide-bent.

Although these two types and strikes are radically different, the solution to both lies in maintaining a tight line.

The more subtle kissing strike is identical to that familiar to winter Bassmasters who bump spinnerbaits down deep ledges or through treetops. Successful hookups require a keen sense of touch and sharp reflexes. Modern rod materials, like graphite and boron, make strike detection much easier. The rod tip should be kept as close to the water as possible. The effective slow, steady retrieve makes this fairly easy to do when fishing the lure in water deeper than 3 to 4 feet. A straight rod lift usually will hook the fish.

At first blush, the problem inherent in hooking a murderously striking bass appears to be minimal. But, the problems are much worse than with the kissing cousins. The problems derive from the fact that a big bucketmouth in shallow water (3 feet or much less) doesn't really like where it is. It's nervous that far from the fishy womb of deep water.

Thus, as soon as that gold-tinted shad it's just mauled suddenly sprouts metal, plastic and a hook, the bass hits the panic button for deep water. The result: a startled fisherman who just felt a sharp tug, then nothingness; a void caused by 15 feet or so of slack line. Unless the fish hooked itself on the initial strike, the potential for a thrown lure on the first jump is very high.

The solution is, as stated, maintaining a tight line to the spinnerbait at all times with minimal rod-to-water-surface angle. Unlike fishing deeper water, it's difficult to fish a spinnerbait properly in only inches of water without dragging bottom while holding the rod tip low. Add a general requirement for a slow retrieve and problems mount.

Carlos Sellers recommends replacing the No. 11 frog with the larger No. 1 size to create added buoyancy in extremely shallow water. This permits a lower rod angle while maintaining a slow retrieve.

A fast-retrieve reel also helps collect the sudden slack line caused by a bass literally knocking the line toward the boat. Sharp hooks are essential and maximize chances for hooking the bass properly on the initial strike.

Total concentration on the part of the angler also permits instant reaction to the strike. The easy way to maintain the requisite level of concentration is to believe that a largemouth is tracking the lure at all times.

Trailer hooks are an obvious solution. Unfortunately, the best springtime bass action is in thick grass or weed cover. A trailer hook's tendency to collect trash or to foul in the cover far outweighs its hooking advantage. My advice would be to try a trailer hook until conditions convince you to remove it.

— *PETE ELKINS*

When using a trailer hook under these conditions, no pork or grub trailer is used, usually.

At times, Uncle Josh's 4-inch "Bass Strip" is an excellent trailer with a tandem spinnerbait.

If the grass is simply too thick to fish a spinnerbait, Bassmaster Sellers recommends a frog-patterned Heddon Moss Boss fished with a fast-twitching motion to make it hop across the grass.

• **Slow-Motion Bassin'** — As good as the spinnerbait is, it needs to be presented properly to obtain maximum results. As a generality, "how" in spring spinnerbait fishing for big largemouth equals to "slow."

When fishing the well-defined creek channels mentioned earlier, the spinnerbait should be cast parallel to the inundated creek channel. The lure should be retrieved as slowly as possible with the blades turning 6 to 8 inches off the bottom. Strikes commonly will occur as the spinnerbait comes up over or nudges bottom cover, then flutters back down. Except for this momentary pause to drop the bait after contact with cover, the retrieve should be slow and steady.

If the early bass are deeper than 10 or 12 feet, canny Bassmasters simply let the lure fall down the bank into the channel until contact is made with the bottom. Then, simply nudging the bait along the bottom will produce strikes. In clear water below 55 degrees, the retrieve should be just fast enough to make the blades wobble to create flash. The blades need not spin. In murkier water, a turning or spinning blade is more critical. But, slow is still the watchword for success.

• **Careful Lure Presentation** — The same basic presentation pattern remains effective as the water warms; however, the BASSer should concentrate on shallower water. Remember that the bigger fish will usually stay in water at least 3 feet deep.

As the water temperature continues to climb, and activity shifts toward the grass and weedbeds in murkier water, short casts of no more than 20 feet are often most productive. A well-placed short cast offers many advantages over a longer one.

One warning, however: be alert to signs that your proximity is spooking fish. Electric motors should be used sparingly and on the lowest speed neccesary.

Any and all viable cover should be fished carefully. Actively feeding bass will maul a spinnerbait as soon as it hits the water. More often the lure's flight path should be carefully calculated to bring it down quietly beyond the target. In clear water shallows, it may be necessary to cast as much as 20 feet beyond fish to avoid spooking them.

When casting large grassbeds, initial casts should target the fringe areas of the thickest grass patches. If nothing happens on the fringes, then the lure should explore the cover itself. In most cases, the bass will detect the lure in the thick cover, track it through the cover, and strike as it drops off the near edge.

One exception to this occurs when fishing cover or creeks that feature grassbeds paralleling the shoreline with several feet of open water between the shore and the grass. I cast onto the shoreline, retrieve through the open water and anticipate a strike as the spinnerbait struggles up onto the grass from the open water. Like those strikes in deeper water early in the spring season, strikes can be subtle, so stay alert.

• **Favorite Spring Pattern** — An isolated patch of grass always is worth serious attention. My favorite pattern is to fish large clumps or hummocks of grass that protrude from the water. Largemouths invariably hold tightly against this cover. Consistent strikes occur only if the spinnerbait actually touches the grass as it passes. Accuracy is essential.

Permitting the lure to hit the water in some situations will spook fish or otherwise fail to attract strikes. I learned this lesson the hard way. Fishing alone, I muscled my aluminum bass rig with paddle, electric motor and sweat over a narrow muddy bar separating the Chattahoochee River from a long, grassy slough.

"Probably too shallow, anyway," I told myself. The slough was shallow, but had 2 to 3 feet of stained water near clumps of grass. I presented my spinnerbait in a conventional manner and dropped it within inches of the grass. The Water Witch and No. 11 frog entered the water relatively quietly. After I fruitlessly covered 100 yards of appealing water, I turned around to give the stretch one more try.

My first cast on the return trip overshot the target and landed in the middle of a grassy clump several inches out of the water. I gently jiggled it free. The spinnerbait slid noiselessly into the water. I turned the reel handle once, felt a solid thud, and saw too much slack line. When I caught up, 4 pounds of irritated *Micropterus* went airborne.

I repeated the same tactic, cast into the grassy clumps, then eased the lure into the water. It yielded six more nice largemouths in the same 100-yard stretch.

Attention to details, proper equipment and spinnerbaits, coupled with springtime-colored water, will provide sufficient action with mean, green bass to sustain a Bassmaster through the trying days of late summer.

— MARCH 1984

KEYS TO SPINNERBAIT SUCCESS

Bassmaster Carlos Sellers of Baxley, Ga., is one of the South's premier spinnerbait fishermen. He fishes the lure year-round, but dotes on its effectiveness during the springtime. His experiences with springtime's shallow bass have culminated in four keys to success:

• **Use Heavy Line** — In the South during the magic and usually murky spring period, Sellers uses nothing less than 20-pound-test mono. The sturdy line is mandated by both potential fish size and abrasion caused by constant line contact with the bottom. Line color isn't as critical in colored water; thus, many people opt for fluorescent lines to ease strike detection. However, the shallow-water strikes usually are easy to detect. Solidly hooking the fish may not be so easy.

• **Use Light-Colored Skirts** — Given the dominant role of shad as forage fish, the best spinnerbait colors in water with "color" are yellow, whites, yellow-whites, or white-chartreuse combinations. Sellers and many other murky-water anglers prefer tandem-bladed baits and reserve single-spins for use in clearer water.

• **Think Slow** — A slow retrieve is the best way to take springtime bass, especially larger fish, while the water is below 65 degrees. A slow, steady retrieve also seems to permit the bass to home in on a spinnerbait in water so muddy that there is virtually zero visibility. After a bit of practice it's possible to feel every rpm of the tandem-blade spinnerbait with a slow retrieve. If anything alters the rpm pattern, think *bass* and react accordingly.

Bassmaster Sellers swears that he can feel a change in the vibrations of his spinnerbait as a bass approaches close to the lure. Although I'm not prepared to palm a Bible on the point, I have experienced many occasions where I could detect a definite change in a lure's "feel" instants before I felt the thud of a strike.

Generally, the slow retrieve should be just fast enough to avoid fouling the lure on the bottom, no matter what the depth. My experiences indicate that as the water warms to 65 degrees and above, the retrieve rate may be increased a bit in water less than 3 feet deep. Indeed, some of my best results in late April and early May come with a retrieve just fast enough to bulge, but not break, the surface.

• **React Fast** — Spinnerbait strikes are sudden affairs, no matter whether hard or soft. A spinnerbait-stung largemouth reacts immediately. Any hesitation on the part of the angler may result in a lost fish. Fortunately, the bass hook themselves frequently enough that gawkers like me still can react quickly enough to set the hook.

— PETE ELKINS

CHAPTER ELEVEN

Photo: Steve Price

GETTING THE MOST FROM CRANKBAITS

*H*ere's why so many bass fishermen are hooked on swimming lures.

Photo: Gerald Crawford

CRANKBAIT TIPS THAT YOU CAN USE

By NICK SISLEY

Crankbaits are designed with built-in wiggles. But no lure designer can build in all the fish-catching retrieves. This fact-loaded article tells you how to fish these plastic-lipped and metal-billed fish catchers . . .

Just what is a crankbait? Not long ago I contended that a "crankbait" was a floating, diving lure with a large metal lip. I placed "alphabet" lures, with plastic lips, in another bass-bait category. Other Bassmasters, tackle manufacturers, and professional bass fishermen have grouped alphabet lures and baits with large metal lips into the same category. Now, both universally are called "crankbaits."

A crankbait is a lure that dives into medium or deeper depths, and usually achieves its most effective side-to-side wobble action with a fairly rapid, steady retrieve.

In the March-April issue of BASSMASTER® Magazine, we presented spinnerbait tips from the experts — BASS pros and lure manufacturers alike. The purpose of this three-part series is to brain-pick the "pros," and hopefully to help you fish different types of bass lures better. In the July-August issue, we'll cover plastic-worm tips. Here's what the pros and lure designers say about fishing crankbaits:

How To Fish Alphabet Lures

Lures that exemplify alphabet-type crankbaits are the Big-O, the Baby-N and Little-N, the Rebel-R series, the Super-R, the Bagley series of balsa crankbaits, Rabble Rouser's new bug-eyed Ashley, and many others.

George Perrin and Lanny West of Rebel provide some excellent scientific-supported crankbait fishing suggestions to consider. Except for Rebel's first running bait, the Humpback, all its crankbaits have been developed in a 36,000-gallon test tank by taking advantage of a vast amount of electronic and technical know-how. Above the round tank are

attached four fishing rods on a motor-driven wheel. A control panel with an observation window at floor level permits adjustment of lure speed. Frequency of lure wobble, lure noise, and other data can be recorded via sophisticated electronic equipment.

In the course of experimentation, the folks at Rebel discovered the old standard bass lures all had something in common. They vibrated at a frequency of between 65 and 75 cycles per second. With this knowledge, Perrin set out to develop a series of crankbaits with action within that range. Perrin also began experimentation with "rattle" sound chambers within this same cycle spectrum.

Rebel lure designers discovered that putting a metal ball inside a lure was not enough. To achieve consistent sound frequency, the metal ball had to be placed in a chamber within the lure. The metal-ball size had to be matched perfectly with the size of the sound chamber.

Using these scientific facts and such things as oscilloscopes, underwater microphones, and other electronic equipment that most BASSers associate with science fiction, Rebel developed the Maxi-R, Mini-R, Tenny-R, and Wee-R lure series (all the same bait with the addition of a deeper-running lip), the Super-R (suspending crankbait), Rebel Racket Shad and, new for '77, the Rebel Shallow-R.

Rebel, and other crankbait manufacturers, emphasize that a "jam knot" should not be used in fishing crankbaits. They strongly suggest you use a small snap or a "loop knot" when tying to the split ring. Some manufacturers package crankbaits with a small lure snap already attached. However, this snap often is removed when a Bassmaster changes lures.

Although some anglers prefer to fish cliffs and steep banks from deeper water, it's often best to cast parallel to such structure. Try it both ways.

Photo: Nick Sisley

When that crankbait is tied on again, a knot probably will be used instead of the snap, and the action is affected.

Remember also that a "jam knot" tied directly to a crankbait's split ring will affect its action. To give your crankbaits the utmost action, use a small snap or a "loop knot." Personally, I prefer a loop knot called the "Uni-Knot Loop ." (See "How To Tie The Uni-Knot.")

The Super-R is an unusual crankbait because it "suspends." It tends to stay at the same depth when stopped. Most crankbaits are buoyant. However, a baitfish, in swimming from place to place, tends to stop often, but doesn't float toward the surface when it stops — the baitfish suspends. A lure that suspends simply looks more natural.

Tips For Fishing Suspended Crankbait

Yes, this is an excellent lure type to cast into standing timber when you find bass suspended among branches. Cast beyond and parallel to the tree, crank to the desired depth, then stop the lure just past the tree trunk or main branches. The bait will suspend, arousing the curiosity of Mr. Largemouth. Sometimes the strike occurs while the lure is stopped.

If it doesn't, jerk the bait with your rod. This often triggers a strike, as the bass thinks its prey is getting away.

Sluggish bass in cool water tend to take a suspended crankbait when it stops. As bass become more active with warmer temperatures, they are prone to strike as the suspended lure is jerked through and around the cover. However, stopping the lure is still advised.

Proper "tuning" of a crankbait is critical. Some are easier to tune to run straight on the retrieve than others. If a crankbait runs off to one side, bend the lure-eyelet (where the line is attached) slightly to the opposite direction. Check to make certain the hook hangers are straight and the hooks are not bent to one side.

Sometimes it pays to "overtune" a crankbait, so it runs off to one side. Let's say you are working a shoreline from right to left, and you're casting at a lot of floating boat docks. Try overtuning a crankbait so it runs off the left. Now, make a cast along the right side of each floating dock. As you retrieve, the crankbait will actually swim underneath the dock — where the bass are. Another trick with an overtuned crankbait is to throw parallel to the shoreline — so the overtuned bait runs in toward the bank.

HOW TO TIE THE UNI-KNOT

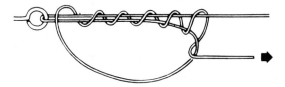

(1) — Run the line through the eye for at least 6 inches. Fold it back to form a double line and make a circle back toward the hook or lure with the tag-end.

(2) — Make six turns with the tag-end around the double line and through the circle. Holding the double line at the point where it passes through the eye, pull the tag-end, as indicated by arrow, until the six turns are snugged into a tight barrel.

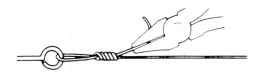

(3) — Now grasp the standing part of the line and pull (see arrow) to slide the knot up against the eye.

(tag-end)
──────────────────────────── (Standing Line)

(4) — Continue to pull standing line until knot is tight. You can trim the tag-end flush with the closest coil of the knot, because the Uni-Knot doesn't allow line slippage.

To Use as "Wiggle Knot"

To tie a small loop into the eye of a crankbait, giving it free movement in the water, tie the same knot, up to the point where the turns are snugged up around the standing line.
Next, slide the knot toward the eye of the lure, by pulling on the standing line, until the size loop desired is reached. Use tacklebox pliers to hold the knot at this point, pulling the tag-end to maximum tightness.
Under normal casting and retrieving the loop will hold. Once a bass is hooked, the knot will slide tight against the eye for better security. In Du Pont tests, for instance, a pressure of about 5 pounds on a 14-pound-test line was required to pull up the loop.

Some anglers shave the plastic lip in an effort to tune the lure properly. This is a serious mistake. Removing material will take the lure out of balance. Tune by adjusting the front eyelet, and by making sure the hook hangers and hooks are straight in line with the body.

Bill Norman's Little-N and Baby-N are very close to the size of baitfish bass eat — shad, sunfish, perch, bream, etc. Bill Norman feels that colors and sizes are very important in crankbait fishing. He suggests matching the color of the lure to the color of the food fish — whether it be crawfish, shad, bream, perch, etc. In muddy, murky, or stained water, Norman prefers yellows and golds. In clear water, he tends to tie on a silver, green, or bright color. The Little-N or Baby-N can be fished fast or slow, or even as a topwater bait. Normally, they require little turning to run straight.

Norman thinks most crankbait fishermen don't concentrate enough. The angler must be aware of how the lure vibration feels in his rod tip. The newer graphite rods help because they're more sensitive. If the vibration stops, set the hook! Norman says many BASSers have better crankbait results with a stop-and-go action.

"Most anglers think bass always strike when the lure stops, but often they haven't realized the plug is already in the bass' mouth. These unperceptive fishermen don't feel the fish until the retrieve is started again," says Norman.

Norman's little Scooper also was designed with "suspending action." Norman feels this lure is particularly effective in colder water when fish are sluggish.

In summer, Norman uses crankbaits, like the Little-N, as a topwater lure, especially if he sees bass breaking the surface or chasing shad. "When bass are in brush or thick cover and you can't get a crankbait to them via the standard underwater retrieve, work a crankbait on top like a crippled shad," says Norman, who also notes that shad change colors, being pinkish in cold water and greenish in the summer and early fall when water temperatures are higher.

Crawfish Color Tops In Spring

Cotton Cordell opines, "The crankbait is the easiest lure for most Bassmasters to use. They are easy to cast, and a steady no-nonsense retrieve usually provides lots of action and strikes." During the early season, this Arkansas luremaker prefers to cast smaller crankbaits, and usually opts for crawfish or bluegill colors — "because these look like early-season bass food."

In off-color waters, Cordell might switch to chartreuse or gold, and he especially likes red hues. "They are simply easier for bass to see in murky water," he says.

In midseason, Cordell selects a Smokey Joe, pearl blue-eye or barfish pattern. The tried-and-true chrome with black back is always his favorite. In summer, Cordell switches to larger crankbaits, utilizing light shades or chrome colors in clear water and chartreuse, bone, and shad colors in dingy water.

Cordell points out that line size does affect the depth crankbaits will run. "Always use the lightest line possible when you are trying to make a deep retrieve," says Cordell, who prefers 8-pound-test for most situations. Naturally, when fishing around thick brush, where bass can wrap your line in nothing flat, heavier lines are in order.

When fishing a normal, steady retrieve, you miss a strike or fail to get any strikes. What should you try? Use a slower retrieve, and/or the stop-'n-start retrieve.

Cover the Waterfront With Crankbaits

Lee Sisson of the Bagley Bait Co. says the advantage to fishin' a crankbait is that BASSers can cover more water. "It's a productive lure because it can be fished on the surface, down to 15 feet, and anywhere in between," he says.

"In the early spring, big bass hold on the first breakpoint from the nesting areas. I tie on a Divin'-B, and work these areas thoroughly, whether they are near a creek, treeline or whatever. Depth is usually 10 to 12 feet. Even in Florida this method works. Last year, off one breakpoint, I took two bass over 10 pounds and another that weighed 11 pounds, 9 ounces," says Sisson.

Once the bass move up on the nests, Sisson chooses a crankbait that will run over the nest. The 2-inch Kill'r-B works perfectly in water about 5 feet deep. The Honey-B is used in shallower water. "Whether bass are on the nest or not, match the lure to the depth of water at which the fish are holding. This is a key point in crankbait fishing," says the Bagley expert.

Sisson thinks crankbaits catch bass because of the vibration patterns they produce. Sometimes it takes different vibration patterns to excite bass. For instance, Bagley's 3-inch Kill'r-B and 3-inch Balsa-B run at approximately the same depth. However, the Balsa-B has a fast, quick vibration. The Kill'r-B has a slower, more pronounced wobble. The different vibration patterns they produce imitate different foods.

A steady retrieve works most of the time, but if Sisson is encountering short strikes, he slows the crankbait down. This maneuver often saves the day. "If fish are hitting short, and slowing the lure is not the answer, try the stop-and-go

When fishing around downed structure such as trees, try to make the crankbait hit the underwater obstructions.

Photo: Charles Beck

method," advises Sisson. If you feel an underwater obstruction, make a new cast, crank the balsa bait down until you feel the obstruction, then stop it.

Sisson feels he's not fishing a crankbait properly if it's not hitting some type of structure. The broad bill on Bagley's bait allows the light balsa-wood plugs to crawl over and through heavy cover without getting hung. One such tactic is to cast beyond, crank down to the base of a tree, then pull the lure toward the top limbs. This prevents the bait from getting lodged in the "V" on a limb.

"Down here in Florida, where most lakes have sandy bottoms with few obstructions, I've found running a crankbait right on the bottom is effective. If I can find a spot where the bottom changes only a few feet, I will usually find fish," adds Sisson. "There is one such ridge in Lake Summit, one of the lakes Cypress Gardens is on, where almost any afternoon during the spring or summer you can catch fish 7 pounds apiece or better. All I do is crawl a 3-inch Divin-B along that ridge," the Winter Haven Bassmaster says.

In addition to bending the lure eyelet to one side to tune or overtune a crankbait, here's another tip to alter its action: "If you want a faster wobble, bend the wire toward the lip. If you want a slower action, bend the wire upward," says Sisson.

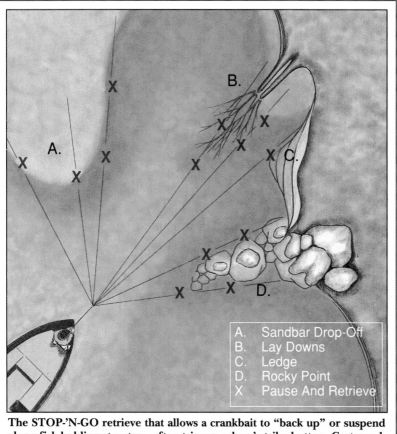

A. Sandbar Drop-Off
B. Lay Downs
C. Ledge
D. Rocky Point
X Pause And Retrieve

The STOP-'N-GO retrieve that allows a crankbait to "back up" or suspend along fish-holding structure often triggers a bass' strike button. Cast parallel to the rocky shoreline, trees, stick-ups, etc. and crank to the desired depth. Then, stop the lure just past a pocket or bush. The lure will float up (back up) or suspend. Sometimes the strike occurs when the bait stops. If not, pull the lure with your rod, and repeat the stop-'n-go retrieve along the structure. Illustration: Bernie Schultz

"Know what each type of crankbait will do under different circumstances. Know what the action is, and know what depth the crankbait will run. This way you know which bait to use when you encounter a specific fishing situation. The best way to find out how a crankbait acts is to try it in a swimming pool," concludes Sisson.

Tactics for Fishing Metal-Lipped Crankbaits

The Bomber is one of the oldest crankbaits in this metal-lipped category. Similar lures are Bomber's Water Dog, Hellbender from Whopper Stopper, the MudBug from Arbogast, etc. The Bomber folks also suggest "topwater twitching," as described under alphabet lures. These types of baits do, however, provide a different action.

Tuning is just as important for metal-lipped plugs. Make sure hooks and hook hangers are straight. As a last resort, try bending the metal link attached to the lip — in the opposite direction that the lure is running. Different Bomber lure sizes

are designed to run at various depths. The smaller sizes run down to 6 feet, while the larger models dig down to 15 feet. Select the size Bomber (lure) appropriate to the depth you want to fish.

Though metal-lipped crankbaits have two good treble hooks, these plugs are remarkably snagless. The wide diving plate usually prevents the hooks from becoming entangled in underwater obstructions. Also, these buoyant lures float free of submerged snags when tension on the line is relaxed. If not, try jiggling the lure with your rod. It often will float free.

Trolling is truly an effective bass fishing method — especially for locating fish holding deep. These heavier, metal-lipped baits run exceptionally deep with a long trolling line. Some will plunge to near 30 feet. The Bomber's Water Dog, available in three sizes, is a lizard-like plug. A spinner on the tail is attached to a snap, and can be removed easily to attach a trailer hook, a fly, skirt, bucktail, pork rind, etc.

Floyd Mabry, one of the experts at Bomber Bait Co. and a renowned Bassmaster, believes a steady retrieve is all that's required for a crankbait to reach its maximum depth — not a super-fast retrieve.

Mabry likes to run a crankbait right up to the bass structure, whatever it might be (tree trunk, limbs, rocks, boat dock, pilings, etc.), and actually make the lure bang into the object. When the crankbait zooms off sideways, in a different direction, that's one move that makes most bass strike.

"It excites them!" says Mabry. "A lure with little action, slithered through a bass' lair without any fanfare, might not entice a nibble."

However, with a fast-moving bait that's bouncing from one limb or snag to another, a bass doesn't have a chance to decide whether it wants the lure or not. The moment of decision is "now."

Another Mabry comment is extremely interesting. He feels that bass over 4 pounds seldom strike a lure. "They simply engulf it," he says. "Smaller bass will whack a bait with gusto, but you don't feel anything when the big 'uns suck in your bait — but the lure stops vibrating."

When the lure action quits, it might be a leaf or a piece of grass, but when Mabry encounters this situation, he rears back on the rod. Mabry keeps his rod tip close to the water surface and this, too, is important, "You can't set a hook nearly as well if the rod is above horizontal," he says. "However, with the rod tip at water level, a long sweeping motion will set the hooks, and the bass is horsed away from its hiding structure."

Mabry uses a stiff rod for crankbait fishing, even though casting is more difficult. When working around brush (which is almost always with a crankbait), the Bomber pro fishes 20-pound-test line.

Change Fishing Depths, Not Lures

Most crankbaits run 4 to 6 feet deep, but bass are often 10 and 12 feet deep. Many BASSers, when they are not having success, change baits, but they often continue fishing lures that travel at the same depth. Why not go to something deeper? A crankbait with a large metal lip is often the answer under these circumstances.

Another Mabry tactic is to fish crankbaits along submerged timber. Position the boat so your casts will be parallel to a line of timber or along a boat lane cut through the timber. With this presentation, the crankbait will be coming past a series of fish-holding submerged trees, rather than just one.

Metal-lipped crankbaits can be most effective under clear skies and/or clear water conditions. That's when bass normally go deeper. Because larger metal-lipped crankbaits dig deep, they pull harder. In many instances, however, the extra effort is worth it.

Use a steady retrieve so the metal-lipped diving bait will achieve maximum depth, but once the lure starts bumping structure, lure speed should be increased to its maximum.

Another of Floyd Mabry's favorite places to fish a deep crankbait is through a "pond" that's been covered by a new reservoir. Such a bottom feature is often the home or sanctuary of numerous fish.

Be sure to keep your reel spooled to maximum capacity, especially when fishing around brush. Under these circumstances, it's often a matter of inches whether or not a bass wraps your lines in limbs. With a full reel spool, you'll retrieve considerably more line per crank than with a half-full spool.

Make mental notes of where you take bass on crankbaits, particularly submerged tree structure. Mabry has found that in Toledo Bend, bois d'arc trees hold more bass than any other type of tree. They have numerous limbs — more places for forage fish and bass to hide. Mabry concentrates casting efforts in such places.

Whopper Stopper's Jodie Grigg says the Hellbender's running depth is controlled by speed of the retrieve. The faster the retrieve, the deeper it dives. Because this metal-lipped lure travels in a head-down position, it will bounce off or flip over most underwater obstructions, making it relatively snag-free.

Here are worthwhile tips to recall from Grigg, who sug-

In early spring before bass spawn, work break points near creek channels or treelines to catch "staging" fish.

Photo: Gerald Almy

gests finding moss beds 5 to 10 feet deep. Control the Hellbender's depth by speed of retrieve, making the lure run just above or "tick" the tops of this bass-holding structure. Also, by casting this type lure toward shore and retrieving to deep water, it's simple to imitate a crawfish scooting along, kicking up puffs of sand, mud, and gravel. And here's another tactic: Cast beyond brush-type structure. Use a fast retrieve to get the Hellbender to the desired depth, then slow the retrieve as the lure reaches the cover. Strikes can be triggered by abruptly stopping the lure next to the spot where the bass is holding. Let the deep-diver float up a foot or so, then resume a fast retrieve, imitating a baitfish about to escape.

Though some BASSers prefer to fish cliffs, steep banks, and points by casting from deeper water, it's often best to cast parallel to this type of structure, digging this metal-lipped crankbait to the desired depth and slowing the retrieve through the productive water. This same type of procedure can be followed when working the deep ends of points, casting creekbeds, submerged islands, or ridges, says Grigg.

Exceptional depths can be reached by trolling the magnum-size, metal-lipped crankbaits. Often a king-size Hellbender is used as the vehicle to hitchhike a lighter, smaller lure — such as a streamer fly, small jig, a light spoon, an unweighted grub, etc. — down to the fish-holding depths. These light lures are tied on a 24- to 30-inch leader, which is attached to the swivel position of the Hellbender's tailspinner.

Some Bassmasters make alterations, removing the spinner unit, attaching a bucktail, rubber skirt, or a different-size spinner blade. By bending the connecting link on the lip to the right or left, these metal-lipped crankbaits can be made to run off to one side — under overhangs, boat docks, or other bass-holding structure.

— MAY/JUNE 1977

MAKING
CONTACT

By DON WIRTH

Give your lures lifelike action with the venerable
bump-the-stump retrieve . . .

"Y ou gotta knock on wood!" go the lyrics of the classic soul tune. And in bass fishing, nothing could be more on target. There are few Great Truths in bass fishing, but one of them is that when you bounce your bait off an object or the bottom, a strike may be close behind.

What is it about knocking on, bumping into, bouncing off and banging against structure that turns a bass on to your lure? What tricks do experts use to maximize contact in critical places with their artificials? And what can the weekend angler do to increase his success with contact baits? We posed these and other questions to some of the best lure fishermen in the country. Their answers may surprise you.

Mechanical Vs. Erratic Action

"A bass lure may look realistic when you pick it up in the tackle shop, but what really counts is how it looks in the water," cautions "bass professor" Doug Hannon. The Tampa, Fla., fisherman has devoted his life to studying big bass, and he's convinced that the best big-bass lures imitate life in subtle ways.

"A lot of fishermen wonder why they catch more big bass on a nondescript bait like a jig than on a wobbling crankbait that might have a very realistic scale pattern painted on it," he says. "Often the answer lies in the general movement profile that the lure presents to the bass, rather than on a realistic paint job."

Fishermen need only spend a few minutes watching live minnows and crawfish swim and move about in a clear brook to grasp a critical element in bass-lure design.

"Living prey exhibits many visual qualities, but among the most basic is that it moves, and that this movement tends to be random or erratic rather than steady or mechanical. Living things move, then stop, then change directions, then move quickly, often all in the space of a few feet," Hannon says. A steadily swimming bass lure has movement, of course, but it fails to offer the random movement that signals "real food!" to a hungry bass.

With most lures, the fisherman can exercise varying degrees of control over his retrieve and can enhance the bait's natural, erratic action tremendously.

"With a crankbait, for example, you can use a stop-and-go retrieve, or you can bounce the lure off stumps and rocks or you can root it along the bottom," Hannon suggests. "Any of these — or all three used in combination — give the bait a far more realistic appearance to the bass. Now the lure isn't just swimming merrily on its way in an unvarying wobble, it's moving more like a living thing."

Hannon says that the flight behavior of living prey often excites a bass into striking. "One of the visual cues that prey 'telegraph' to a chasing bass is flight," Hannon says. "In other words, when the minnow or crawfish is chased, it tries to get away."

Hannon points out that the live-bait fisherman is familiar with how the bait's struggles tend to elicit savage strikes.

"When you fish a big golden shiner for trophy-sized bass, it's not uncommon to see the shiner jump right out of the water in its efforts to escape a bass. This usually triggers even more aggressive pursuit from the bass, which by this time may be blowing and boiling all around the bait as it tries to catch it."

By contrast, an artificial lure doesn't know it's being pursued by a bass, and it may exhibit no flight behavior. "When you're just cranking your bait along steadily, there might be a bass following it, waiting to be triggered to strike. Often when the bait maintains its steady, unvarying course, the bass decides it's not real and turns away," Hannon believes.

But bass fishermen can give their baits the illusion of flight behavior, Hannon points out. Typically, this involves causing them to change speed or direction suddenly via contact. "When you bang your crankbait off a stump or rock or make it veer off by glancing it against a submerged roadbed, in effect you're injecting flight behavior into the lure. What is more, bass tend to hang around such 'contact structure' anyway. So fishermen should begin to look at structures like stumps, rocks, brush, the bottom and dock pilings not only in terms of their power to draw and hold bass, but also as something to help induce flight behavior in their lures."

Hannon says that there's a trade-off when using lures capable of extremely erratic action over those with a steadier, more mechanical movement pattern.

"I'm convinced that baits with a mechanical action are easier for the bass to spot in many cases than are baits with a highly random action," he says. "But merely seeing the lure doesn't make a fish strike. The bass may, and often does, follow a steadily moving lure, but it won't strike unless it is triggered by a sudden change of speed or direction."

Contact Kings

Expert bass anglers feel that certain lures work better in a contact situation, and rank the following among the best bang-bump-and-bounce baits:
- leadhead jigs and grubs
- weighted plastic worms
- spinnerbaits
- crankbaits, especially those with a large diving lips.

"Jigs and worms are heavy-contact baits that have no built-in action," Hannon says. "They depend on the retrieve used by the fisherman and on contact with objects for whatever action they telegraph to the bass. And because they are designed to be worked slowly over the bottom and around cover, they have a maximum amount of erratic action and tend to catch bigger bass as a result."

For giant bass — fish over 15 pounds — few artificials can match plastic worms and jigs, Hannon feels. "The biggest bass are the ones most attuned to the movements and profiles of their preferred forage species. It should come as no surprise

Deep-diving crankbaits can catch fish in shallow or deep water, depending on how they're retrieved. Photo: Doug Stamm

that most giant bass taken on artificials fall for a high-contact lure, rather than one that swims steadily through open water."

Spinnerbait Savvy

"When I'm fishing shallow water, which is any time I can, I'll often reach for a spinnerbait," says Columbia, Tenn., bass pro Charlie Ingram. The BASSMASTER® Tournament Trail veteran is awesomely proficient with this lure. Watching him fish it is a lesson in contact bassin'.

"Many fishermen seem to be afraid of getting hung up, and

so they fail to make sufficient contact with structure," Ingram feels. "If there's a big submerged tree, they might throw to one side of it or reel the bait quickly over the top, avoiding the branches. Either retrieve might catch a bass, but you can bank on a contact retrieve — if a fish is in the tree, a bump will trigger a strike."

Ingram casts his bait so that it hits the structure not once, but several times during the course of a single retrieve. "Instead of slicing a cast across the tree, cast so that the spinnerbait is drawn down the tree," Ingram suggests. "Let the bait tick against the trunk and branches. If it gets hung in a branch, tighten down so it shoots over the limb. I get most of my bites when the bait is banging against the cover I'm fishing."

The Tennessee angler likes to retrieve his spinnerbait at a depth that lets him see the blades flashing. In murky water this might be very shallow. "I'll run it over shallow logs and try to come in contact with the edges of brush or other cover. It's the change in speed and direction caused by contact with an object that gets 'em."

Crankin' For Contact

Crankbaits can epitomize the mechanically swimming open-water bait, or they can be turned into contact lures by fishing them more aggressively, our experts feel.

"I tend to use a deep-diving crankbait, one with a long lip, for both deep and shallow contact situations," Ingram says. "Don't forget that the long lip does more than make the bait dive. It acts as a deflector, allowing the lure to root along the bottom and run into objects without constantly getting hung up."

Ingram likes a deep-runner such as Rabble Rouser's Deep Ashley Probe for his serious contact crankin'.

"Rather than change baits constantly, I'll put the same lure on a different casting outfit, depending on where I'm fishing it," Ingram says. "If I'm fishing shallow, I'll use a rod and reel with 20-pound-test line on it — that cuts the depth potential in half (because the extra drag from heavy line prevents the lure from diving as deep as it would on light mono). For deeper fishing, I might go to 10-pound-test line."

Ingram combines a hesitation retrieve with his contact strategy, making the lure extremely erratic as it moves through the water. "I'll let it root along bottom for a few feet, then stop it just for a split-second. Even the slightest pause seems to trigger a strike."

Contact-crankin' places extra stress on your equipment and may require special tackle. "Bumping and bouncing your baits is especially hard on your casting reels," he says. "Use good-quality equipment, stuff that will take a beating and stay together when cranking." Graphite rods, the gold standard for most bass-fishing situations, aren't as effective for contact cranking as fiberglass rods, or graphite rods with a fiberglass tip.

"Fiberglass absorbs the shock of contact much better than graphite does," he says. "Plus, with a graphite stick you may overreact and jerk the crankbait out of the mouth of the bass. Fiberglass absorbs this 'strike shock' better and lets the bass take the lure deeper."

Offshore Contact

Tournament Trail veteran and past BASS Masters Classic® champion Jack Chancellor specializes in offshore bassin'. He reasons that in reservoirs, many bass move off the banks and relate most strongly to channel drop-offs, ledges, bars and humps. He stays in contact with these choice structures with two baits of his own design: the Do-Nothing Lure and Jack's Jigging Spoon.

"The Do-Nothing looks like a small plastic worm, but it's retrieved more like a slow-moving crankbait," says the Phenix City, Ala., pro. The ungainly looking bait is actually a part of a system that includes a 1-ounce slip sinker, red plastic bead, swivel and leader line to which the 4-inch worm is attached. "The Do-Nothing is a tremendous contact lure, in that it gets to the bottom quickly and stays there," Chancellor says.

He likes to fish this bait in water at least 8 feet deep. "A good contact bait should exhibit highly erratic movements as it strikes objects or the bottom," Chancellor points out. "The heavy sinker of the Do-Nothing rig keeps the bait near the bottom. But the tiny worm suspends off the bottom. The sinker absorbs the contact, and the worm darts and settles behind it. When the sinker gets hung up, I just tighten down on the reel handle until it becomes dislodged. The worm shoots off suddenly, then slowly settles again. This is often when it gets eaten!"

In extremely deep water, and when Chancellor feels there is a good concentration of bass, he'll use a spoon. "I like to look for humps, channel drop-offs and the like that have some cover associated with them," he explains. "I'll drop the spoon right down into these areas and snap it off the bottom." Chancellor finds that modifying his spoons lets them knock on wood without getting hung up so often. "I'll often trim one or two hooks off the treble, or replace the treble hook with a single weedless hook. This lets me probe hard-to-fish areas such as a channel drop lined with brushpiles."

In shallower water, Chancellor prefers to use a crankbait, especially a deep-runner. "When you've got a bait rooting on the bottom or bouncing off a stump, it'll turn on a bass — even a fish that's sulking on the bottom. They'll often bite it even when they're not actively feeding."

Chancellor likes shallow-running crankbaits, too, and he strives to maintain contact with these baits as well. "I like a Rat-L-Trap (lipless crankbait) and a Little N with a small lip. I try to root these baits along points and bars, maintaining an erratic, glancing retrieve."

Diving crankbaits work extremely well for contact fishing in both deep and shallow water. The long lip helps the lures deflect off the bottom and other objects without hanging up. Doug Hannon recommends using a stop-and-go retrieve, as well.
Photo: Don Wirth

Weed-Fishing Wisdom

Making contact with aquatic vegetation tends to produce a dampened effect in your lures. The sharp change of direction that comes when you bump a crankbait off a stump isn't evident here. Instead, the bait usually pauses, perhaps even hangs up momentarily, before continuing on its course. Either motion can trigger a strike, our experts feel.

"I like to use a large Rapala for big bass, but it tends to get hung on grass and wood cover, unless you modify it somewhat," says Hannon. He removes the standard treble hooks and replaces them with weedless trebles.

"Now, contact with cover is more possible," Hannon says. "The trick is to twitch it slowly through emergent grass, stumpfields and other heavy-cover places, making contact with the objects. If you try to fish it too fast, you'll trip the weedguards and hang the lure. I've caught some of my biggest largemouths on this modified bait."

Ingram finds that mossy grasses, including hydrilla and milfoil, tend to entrap a lure and may make the bait hard for the bass to locate. "I like to fish a plastic worm on a jig in heavy moss, and I often add a rattler to the worm to make it a little easier to find," he says. "The trick is to pull the lure out of the dense moss and into the open. When the bass sees it, it'll try to strike it before the bait gets buried in the moss again."

Stay In Contact

Take the advice of our experts and keep your bass lures in contact with the bottom, stumps, rocks, weeds and other objects. Learn how to use high-contact baits more effectively. Master erratic, high-contact retrieves with spinnerbaits, crankbaits, worms and leadheads. Consider modifying other lures to enhance their ability to probe cover without hanging up. And above all, learn to develop a less-timid approach when casting your baits around cover. Remember that the bass are there. Sometimes all it takes to make them come out is a knock on their doors.

— MARCH 1989

HOW TO FISH
CRANKBAITS IN THE CURRENT

By CHRIS ALTMAN

Moving water triggers bass' appetites, and few lures have greater appeal to their tastes in these times than crankbaits . . .

A catalyst, in the field of chemistry, is defined as a substance that increases the rate of a reaction without being consumed in the process. In the realm of crankbaiting, moving water is the catalyst that sparks the feeding and ignites a reaction between bass, baitfish and Bassmaster.

For untold years, small crankbaits have been a boon to small-stream anglers. While puny, in-line spinners have historically been productive fish-catchers, serious brook-waders have relied on crankbaits as the crux of their strategies to attract bigger fish. Lures like Rebel's Wee-Crawfish series and the diminutive Cordell Big-Os have been the mainstays of stream Bassmasters virtually since their inception.

Unfortunately, when many anglers make the move from wading a tiny stream to casting a river's currents from a bass boat, they often leave their crankbaits at home. After all, the lures seem to hang on everything. Anyway, spinnerbaits and plastic worms are our traditional river baits, right?

"Spinnerbaits and worms are the preferred river lures of most anglers," says Rob Kilby, a 34-year-old B.A.S.S. tournament pro who finished third in the 1989 BASS Masters Classic®, "but I honestly believe that crankbaits are the most versatile river lures found in a tacklebox.

"Most anglers believe that crankbaits are too prone to snagging for a structure-rich river. But that's not true," declares Kilby of Royal, Ark. "If you use a relatively deep-diving crankbait with a fairly long lip — something like a 7A Bomber — then you actually can work it through the thickest cover in the river without hanging it very often. If

you pull the bait slowly through the brush, the long lip will work up and over the limbs."

The key is to work the bait over each limb, utilizing the lure's buoyancy when needed, rather than cranking it steadily through the brush. Anglers across the country are learning to work crankbaits in this fashion, and pitching them into heavy cover is becoming a hot tournament strategy.

What is more, Kilby maintains that it is far easier to keep a crankbait amidst a brushpile or other structure — or in the strike zone — in relatively swift water than it is a spinnerbait or a plastic worm.

"A crankbait's bill offers resistance to the water that keeps it running on track against the current. Whereas a spinnerbait or a plastic worm will be washed away from the structure, a crankbait will continue along its course provided you maintain a steady pull on the bait."

That trait alone makes the crankbait a deadly weapon for moving water, he says. Too, a crankbait can quickly cover a lot more water than can a spinnerbait or worm.

Interestingly enough, he often tosses tiny crankbaits on 20-pound-test line when fishing a river system. "I'm not often concerned with achieving the bait's maximum depth in a river, since most fish remain shallow. Instead, I'm more concerned with getting a fish out of heavy cover, so I use heavy line."

Most often when cranking the current, Kilby switches among three lure sizes in three different colors to see which combination bass like best.

"I usually start with a medium-sized bait like a model 7A

Long-billed crankbaits are surprisingly snagless, and they are capable of dragging big bass from deep cover.

Photo: Chris Altman

Bomber, then let the fish dictate the size they prefer. If they're finicky, I'll drop down to a small bait about the size of a Rebal Wee-R. When the bass are feeding on larger baitfish, I'll switch to a larger bait about the size of a Rebel Maxi-R."

In clear water, Kilby likes a chrome bait. A shad pattern works best for him when the water is slightly stained. And in stained to muddy water, or in overcast weather, he most often tosses a fluorescent chartreuse or a fire-tiger pattern.

"The nice thing about fishing in a river is that the current makes the fish predictable," Kilby says. "The current dictates everything, and the fish react predictably to it. They will always face into the current, and when relating to a structure, they'll always be on the downcurrent side so they don't have to fight the flow of water all of the time. It doesn't take a large object to break the force of the current, and that is something most anglers don't realize." It is obvious, then, that casts should be made upstream and retrieved with the current.

When looking for moving-water bass, Kilby recommends searching for objects that break the current.

"Things like stumps, blowdowns and pilings are obvious, but not so obvious are eddy and slack-water areas, and these are the things most river anglers overlook. Creek mouths often hold fish, and wing dams and rock jetties are super fish hideouts. You'd think that the bass would be behind the jetty, but most of the feeding fish actually will be in front of it."

Kilby explains that the current flowing directly into the jetty is dissipated, creating an eddy effect directly in front of the structure.

"When you are fishing river structures, you are most often fishing for individual fish," Kilby relates. "Occasionally, you might locate a deeper channel ledge that will hold several fish, but most often it's one structure/one fish. For that reason, river fishing is a run-and-gun, cast-for-one-fish kind of fishing."

Kilby has learned that river bass usually are patterned according to structure. "Sometimes, however, you can pattern them according to area. For example, at the 1989 Classic® on Virginia's James River, I found fish holding in the first 100 yards of the creeks. Wherever a creek or tributary entered the river, I could catch fish off any kind of junk in the first 100 yards. Once I discovered that, I just ran from creek mouth to creek mouth."

Like most crankbait experts, Kilby believes that the retrieve imparted by the angler is most often crucial, although it is not emphasized enough by most anglers.

"Most often, it varies according to the activity of the bass, so I like to experiment for the first few hours until I can put together a retrieve that makes the fish respond. It pays to be creative with variations of your retrieve," Kilby says, "because it's often the retrieve that separates those who catch fish from those who don't."

In addition to complaints that crankbaits are prone to snag, many anglers lose a disproportionate number of fish hooked on a crankbait. Kilby loses very few crankbait fish, and gives credit to the use of a fiberglass crankin' rod with a soft tip, wickedly sharp hooks, a well-set drag and good judgement when landing a fish.

One of the most desired flat-water situations sought by knowledgeable tournament anglers is the combination of good deep-water structure, the presence of baitfish and current.

"In the greater South, this combination often is found in many of our reservoirs, especially in river-run lakes and those used for hydroelectric generation," says B.A.S.S. pro Paul Elias of Laurel, Miss., "and it is one of the most productive angling patterns from the latter part of April through November. I honestly believe that when this situation exists, crankbaiting main-lake, deep-water structures is the most effective, most productive way to fish."

Elias, winner of the 1982 Classic and a nationally recognized crankbait wizard, says, "In most lakes with a good shad population and some type of current, you usually have a hefty population of bass that tend to remain relatively deep throughout the year, holding to deep structures and feeding primarily when the current is flowing."

West Point and Eufaula, two reservoirs shared by Alabama and Georgia, are perfect examples.

"In lakes like these," Elias notes, "you can crank until you're blue in the face when the water is not moving and never get a bump. But when the generators kick on, the moving water pushes the shad around and turns on the bass."

Elias' favorite deep-water crankbait targets include river ledges in the main lake, isolated humps and underwater islands adjacent to the river channel, and points dropping into the old river channel.

"You sometimes can catch current-oriented fish from secondary points in major creek arms, but for the most part, I prefer to stick to main-lake structures. When possible, I like to find structure with 4 to 12 feet of water over them, and the deeper the water is around the structures the better I like them."

Elias believes that most anglers fail to focus on these structures as often as they should, primarily because locating them is often tedious.

"Start with a good topo map before you hit the water and try to identify potential structures. Then use your depthfinder to locate those structures, any cover on them and baitfish around them. I rarely use my depthfinder to locate bass, but I rely on it to locate depth changes, structures, cover and baitfish, which will hold fish in that area. You've got to have confidence that if the key ingredients needed to hold bass are there, then the bass *will* be there too.

"Locating just one good spot will put you in numbers of good bass," Elias states. "A good example of this was the 1989 Alabama Invitational on Guntersville. I entered that tournament a long way out of qualifying for the Classic, so I knew I had to work hard and find some good deep-water structure that would produce some big crankbait bass for me. I was fortunate enough to do so, and I caught 50 pounds of bass from just one structure."

Counting the bass his partners weighed in, the one area produced 80 pounds of fish. That spectacular showing, which resulted in a 5th-place finish for this seasoned veteran, earned him a berth in the 1989 Classic.

A key to crankbaiting these deep structures is timing, Elias believes. "The fish feed with the current, so you need to be there when the generators are turned on. The distance between the structure and the dam is of the utmost importance, since it takes some time for the water to begin moving throughout the lake. Those structures near the dam usually turn on soon after a current is generated, but it might take an hour or more for the water to start moving in the upper end of the lake."

Deep-divers must be fished slowly in the current.   Photo: Chris Altman

He readily admits that fish can be taken from these deep-water, current-laden structures with a variety of lures. But crankbaits are so deadly, he says, because they provide a baitfish-like silhouette, which is a positive feeding stimulus for the bass.

Too, deep-diving crankbaits allow you to cover the deep-water ledges and drop-offs rapidly, whereas it might take all day to fish one of those spots with a slow-moving plastic worm. And best of all, he emphasizes, big crankbaits simply catch bigger fish.

"You hear a lot about matching the size of your plug to the bait on which the bass are feeding," he notes. "That is generally good advice, but there comes a time when you match your bait to the bass you want to catch. In most of our lakes, there are literally tons of big shad, and big bass like to feed on these larger baitfish. Big crankbaits prompt big bass to strike. So I use big crankbaits, and I fully expect to catch big bass."

Elias' favorite deep-running crankbait is the Mann's 20+, the first of the ultradeep-divers. He says the lure dives more quickly than any other crankbait he has used, which means he's covering more of the structure with each cast. He adds that Bagley's DB3 and some Poe's plugs are effective for deep-structure cranking.

Proper equipment is crucial when working deep-diving crankbaits, Elias believes.

"A long rod is mandatory, since you have to make long casts so that your bait will hit the structure. I use a Quantum Crankin' rod (a 7-foot, medium-light action graphite rod). And with deep-diving baits, you must use a reel with a low gear ratio to provide power for cranking at the proper speed. If you retrieve a big-billed crankbait too fast, it will roll through the water rather than dive." Elias uses 15-pound-test Trilene Big Game line for his deep-water crankbaiting.

"In addition to proper equipment, the retrieve of the bait is important," he says. "I like to pause the bait whenever it hits a piece of cover and then speed up the retrieve. I think it imitates a baitfish that runs into something, is stunned and then decides it had better get the heck out of there before something big and ugly eats it!"

For the most part," Elias notes, "an erratic retrieve is far more productive than a straight one. You should be making hundreds of casts to your structure, so you will have time to experiment with varying retrieves."

You don't have to be a chemist to understand the reaction between current, crankbaits and bass. To enjoy the explosive combination, all you have to be is there!

— *APRIL 1990*

POWER-FISHING MINNOW BAITS

By TIM TUCKER

A long-hidden secret for fishing deep-diving minnow plugs finally is revealed . . .

After 12 years as a touring professional and after three world championships, numerous other tournament victories and the B.A.S.S. Angler-of-the-Year award, it takes something spectacular to get Rick Clunn truly excited about his fishing exploits.

During a remarkable week of tournament fishing on New York's St. Lawrence Seaway one recent June, Clunn enjoyed such a moment. Listen as he describes it:

"It was the most unbelievable fishing. I was out in 15 feet of water, jerking a minnow bait, and all of a sudden there would be about 10 smallmouths weighing 2 1/2 to 5 pounds swimming up under it. I would then stop it and let it sit. And the minute they would start to turn away from the bait, I would just pop it. Every time one of those big smallmouths would come back and explode on the bait.

"I had one big boulder in clear water that I just couldn't bring the bait by without seeing those big brown objects that looked like they were coming from the heart of that rock. It was exciting — the most exciting fishing I had ever done. I hadn't been so eager to go out the next day in a long time. I just couldn't wait to get back out there. It was incredible."

If that kind of fishing action doesn't make your pulse race, you had better check the level of your embalming fluid.

It was at that New York tournament that the jerkbait, a shallow-diving, angled-lip minnow-style lure — also referred to as ripbait — began to garner some serious attention. While the St. Lawrence River harbors the kind of fishing that makes almost every type of artificial lure productive, it was the jerkbait in the hands of several knowledgeable pros that produced the quality bass.

It raised some eyebrows, much to the chagrin of certain pros who wanted to keep it a secret.

"The jerkbait is a very 'confidential' bait among the professional fishermen that are in the know, you might say," Clunn says today. "It's a lot like the Pop-R was. Certain fishermen have really kept the jerkbait to themselves."

Of course, since competitors on the BASSMASTER® Tournament Trail are paired randomly with other contestants each day, it is impossible to conceal the effectiveness of hot lures like ripbaits or the Pop-R.

"You can't keep the bait itself a secret, but you can usually maintain secrecy about the way that you fish it," the popular pro says.

And for a small, select fraternity of pros, the secret of the ripbait lies in the way they fish it.

Jerkbaits like the Bomber Long A, Rebel Spoonbill, Rattlin' Rogue, Rapala, deep-diving Bang-O-Lure, Mann's Stretch-Pluses and Rebel Minnow have suddenly assumed a more important slot in the tackleboxes that travel the national tournament circuit. The pros have discovered that with the right technique, these minnow baits will produce impressive results under a variety of weather conditions and cover and structure situations.

But these lures are most effective in the hands of the fisherman who isn't afraid of working up a sweat and creating a blister or two. The design of these baits creates a substantial drag in the water, which makes them harder to pull. And the only way to drive the bait down and make it perform correctly is to muscle it.

Pros like Clunn, Zell Rowland, Gary Klein and Jimmy

A deep-diving minnow bait, fished with a powerful ripping motion, is deadly on big bass.

Photo: Tim Tucker

Crisp drive the lure down and through the water with powerful sweeps (or "jerks," giving rise to the term, "jerkbait") of the rod, which can create bulging biceps. Coordinating single turns of the reel handle with each sweep, they always leave enough slack in the line to allow the bait to walk from side to side, which many believe is the key to the bait.

The idea is to make the lure dart frantically through the water and then pause to allow it to suspend momentarily. That combination of power-and-pause is important because a bass can either ambush the bait while it is motionless or strike out of reflex action as the lure steams by it.

"Done right, it will wear you out. If you don't have blisters at the end of the day, you're not fishing it right," Clunn advises. "That is the secret with the jerkbaits — how hard you work them. Very few people will commit to working that hard.

"And if you upgrade to the big No. 18 Magnum Rapala that Jimmy Crisp throws, you'll discover what hard work is.

That bait is definitely a secret. It's a deadly, deadly bait when you step up to that size. But there is not one in 100 guys who can work that bait right all day. I know I can't."

It doesn't require the physique of Hulk Hogan to catch bass on these lures, however. Simply retrieved steadily below the surface, jerkbaits will catch fish. But the true power of the bait lies in the power of the angler. That is just one example of what separates the top pros from the rest of us.

The design of the bait, with its long, slender body shape, gives it a natural appeal to bass. Its shape resembles that of a shad, minnow or shiner — all prime food sources for largemouth and smallmouth bass. And biologists tell us that bass are more likely to consume prey with that silhouette than ones with the shape of a bluegill, for example. The elongated shape of a minnow will slide more easily through the throat of a bass.

The jerkbait, Clunn believes, is one of the most versatile

hard baits available to fishermen. The fish-attracting quali- ties of these lures are numerous.

"The thing that makes it special is that it catches numbers of bass, and it also catches quality fish," he explains. "I think that is because of the size and shape of the bait and its unique action. It's an elongated bait that can get down pretty deep — deeper than most people realize. It has the Zara Spook 'walking the dog' type of action, except it's done underwater, which for some reason is very enticing to bass. And you can also hover the bait, stop it and almost suspend it, which, again, is attractive to larger fish."

It is one of the few lures that will allow the angler to quickly cover water in search of bass, yet finesse individual fish holding on an isolated piece of cover into striking.

For most anglers, the seasons for fishing jerkbaits are spring and summer. Clunn will also use it in special situa- tions at other times of the year, like along a wind-blown bank or bluff.

Fellow Texan Zell Rowland also fishes it through the fall and into the beginning of winter. "I've caught fish on a jerk- bait when it was snowing outside," adds Rowland, who credits the Bomber Long A with helping him win the 1986 B.A.S.S. Super-Invitational on Tennessee's Lake Chicka- mauga. "I just worked it real slow and stopped it a lot."

Another reason tournament pros love the lures is that they can be fished in a wide range of cover and structure types. Almost no fish-holding habitat is immune to them.

Clunn believes these baits are at their best when fished over submerged vegetation, but he has been known to drive the big ripbaits through brush as well. With the exposed tre- ble hooks, it takes experience and considerable skill to maneuver it through brush, but it can be done.

Rowland and Cliff Shelby, a talented bass angler and Ranger Boats executive from Arkansas, say the baits are most alluring when used to parallel rocky shorelines like those found in reservoirs like Bull Shoals, Shelby's home lake.

And Bull Shoals has the one ingredient most crucial with this type of fishing: clear water. The clearer the water, the more effective a ripbait is in attracting fish from consider- able distances.

Once a bass is located, these jerkbaits can be trans- formed into enticing finesse lures, thanks to their near- neutral buoyancy. Experienced anglers rip the bait down to the desired depth and then pause it next to the cover, where it can maintain its position for several seconds if enough pressure is applied to the line. Twitching the bait while it suspends is often enough to trigger a reflex strike from an inactive bass.

To enhance its suspending ability, Rowland adds weight to a Rebel Minnow by drilling a hole just above the front hook, inserting a 1/2-ounce piece of lead and resealing the hole.

"But you don't need to do that with the Spoonbill," adds Shelby, who is a firm believer in the persuasive powers of that Rebel ripbait. "In the clear water here at Bull Shoals, you can really get a good idea of how a lure performs. I've found that the Spoonbill is an amazing bait for finessing a bass into striking.

"Not only does it suspend well, but you can actually make it back up 2 or 3 inches. I'm not talking about the tail rising up. With a little practice, you can make the entire bait back straight up. And that initiates a vicious strike from a fish watching it."

At other times, the strike on the Spoonbill will be any- thing but vicious, though. So Shelby advises paying close attention to your line.

Because of the Spoonbill's suspending quality, it is sur- prisingly effective in the late-winter/early-spring period, when the water is still cold (40 degrees or so) and the bass are inactive.

Knowing the bait's ability to draw bass from a distance, Shelby emphasizes the importance of working the lure all the way back to the boat.

The depth these baits run ranges from 3 to 10 feet or more, depending on the diameter of the monofilament used and the brand of lure, Clunn says.

When selecting a ripbait, Rowland has a single criterion: weight. The heavier the lure, the farther it can be cast and the deeper it will dive.

Although line size will help dictate the depth to which you can drive these lures, Rowland won't use less than 12- pound-test. Smaller line cannot withstand the pressure he puts on it with his technique of power-fishing, he says. Like many Bull Shoals fishermen, Shelby uses 4- to 8-pound-test for finessing the clearwater fish.

The choice of rod with this type of fishing is crucial. Both Shelby and Rowland prefer long (6 1/2- and 7-foot) medi- um-action rods with slightly limber tips. The rod should have enough backbone to drive these big baits through the water, yet a tip limber enough to enhance the lifelike action of the bait.

The type of reel isn't nearly as critical. Almost any type of reel will suffice, but a high-speed model makes this type of fishing a little easier.

Rowland relies on two color patterns in ripbaits — shad imitations and chrome with a blue, black, green or gold back. "The way we power these jerkbaits, a chrome finish really flashes under water," Rowland says. "And in this clear water, that flash will attract bass from as much as 25 or 30 feet away."

The attractions of these diving minnow baits are many. And in the hands of a fisherman willing to put forth the effort to fish them correctly, these big jerkbaits simply over- power bass.

— APRIL 1989

TRY CRAWFISHIN' FOR DEEP LUNKERS

By JOHN D. ADAMS

When bass have an appetite for mudbugs, this technique is hard to beat ...

Although the plastic worm rightly has been acclaimed the No. 1 bass lure in the world, there is at least one other deadly method for taking bass off the bottom. This method calls for a much faster and erratic action than the plastic worm. It will score just as many, and maybe even more, bass than its slower counterpart if practiced with consistency.

One sure way to get into a real mudslinging brawl is to tell a bass fisherman he's fishing the bottom too slow. Why should a bass strike something sailing along the bottom, stirring up a fuss, when it won't take a succulent-looking plastic worm crawling tantalizingly along in front of its nose? Well, maybe that creature, causing all the commotion, sets its taste buds in motion. This method reminds the bass of something delicious it dined on in the past.

Bass are fond of crawfish. When plentiful, crawfish make up a large part of their diet. Using this to your advantage can be rewarding, but it will take some special tactics to make it work.

In early December, while fishing a small lake in northern Mississippi, I was greeted with a strike on the first cast with a black spinnerbait. The bass was small, but the secret it told me was not so small. Upon checking, I found that it had been dining rather well on crawfish. Although I had a narrow assortment of baits in my small auxiliary tacklebox, I did have a couple of diving lips. I tied on the one most closely resembling the natural markings of the crawfish — a dark gray with black specks on it.

What followed was some of the best 30-35 minutes of bass fishing I have experienced. I was fishing from a small con-crete platform in the center of the dam where the water level of the lake is adjusted. I was making about 40-foot casts and retrieving in a very fast, stop-and-go action. Nearly all of the strikes came about 10 feet from the dam, where the line was in its most downward angle, giving the bait a very fast and exciting wobble. I was holding the rod at a downward angle and cranking the reel as fast as possible to keep the lure on the bottom.

Every few seconds I would interrupt this fast retrieve with a dead spot by pressing the free-spool button on the side of the reel for a split second. Most of the strikes came either during or immediately following this stop in the action. I landed seven bass that ranged from 2 to 4 1/2 pounds and lost nearly that many more.

Then the inevitable happened. A sour ol' bucketmouth became the proud possessor of my magic lure. In the excitement, I had neglected the task of retying the line after it came in contact with the rough edge of the concrete. I tried the other diving lures, but the color was just not right. I rummaged through other lures in the small box, but the thought of that bass with the "hot" lure hanging in its jaw simply took the heart out of my efforts.

I have used this method on many occasions and, in most cases, take bass with it. A fairly short, stiff rod is essential to fish this method successfully. You can give the lure a stop-and-go action with the rod, but with the strike coming while the lure is stopped, or shortly after, this puts you in an awkward position to set the hook. By using the free-spool button on the reel to stop the lure momentarily, the rod is always in position to set the hook. This is extremely important because of the extra amount of force you must use to compensate for the extra line below the surface.

The depth of the water you are fishing is a decisive factor in deciding what speed your retrieve should be. When fishing water less than 5 feet deep, a slower retrieve is used. The first few cranks on the reel should be fast to allow the lure to dive as soon as possible. As soon as the lure reaches the bottom, the retrieve should be slowed down to allow the lure to bump along without digging into the bottom. In water over 5 feet deep, it is best to keep up the fast retrieve throughout the cast. Slowing down the retrieve in deep water sends the lure on an upward incline and causes the action of the lure to be lost. Moving the rod tip slightly, from side to side during the retrieve, adds a little more motion to the lure and deserves experimentation.

Don't worry about snagging when fishing heavy cover. The diving lip on the front of the lure jumps it over most snags before it will hang up. However, when fishing an extremely trashy bottom, I sometimes replace the rear treble hook with a large single hook to reduce the chances of a hangup.

It would take a mail-order catalog to list all the different lures that do a good job in imitating the crawfish. Almost any lure with a diving lip lends itself well for this method of fishing. Remember, the larger and straighter the diving lip, the faster it will get to the bottom. The depth of the water will determine what size and angle diving lip the lure should have. For water less than 5 feet deep, the small, downward-slanting lips work well, but for water deeper than 5 feet, the larger and straighter lip should be used.

In determining the size and color of lure to use, your best bet is to try to match the lure to the crawfish inhabiting the lake. The best method for this is to check the first couple of bass you catch. See if they are feeding on crawfish and, if so, what the average size and color is. If you cannot determine the size or color, it is usually best to stick with medium-size lures, no more than 3 1/2 to 4 inches long.

Usually the darker the color, the better your success will be. Not only does the darker color closely resemble the hues of a crawfish, it also is more visible to a fish in deeper water. It is usually best to stick to black, dark-brown, or gray colors with specks of white, orange or red scattered on the side. There are times when the direct opposite in color and size pro-

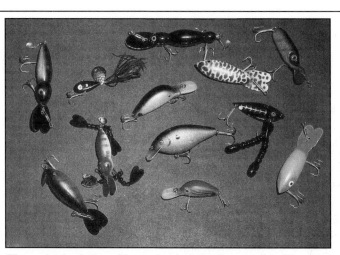

The author's choice of lures that imitate the crawfish. Note the use of short tail ends of plastic worms attached to the treble hooks of two deep-diving lures and the addition of a skirt to the lead-bodied tailspinner lure.   Photo: John Adams

duce. When bass are not in a feeding mood, the larger and brighter-colored baits will sometimes aggravate a strike when nothing else will.

There are some tricks you can do to a lure to give it more appeal. One of my favorite tricks is to take the last couple inches of plastic worms and attach them to the treble hooks on the lure. These will have to be replaced often, because they have a tendency to be torn loose by snags or when a bass strikes, but it is well worth the trouble. I also use, with success, the small rattling devices normally inserted in plastic worms. I glue a couple to the underside of the diving lip. I use the "rattlers" fishing extremely deep water, or stained or very muddy water.

Another type of lure suited for this method is the lead-bodied tailspinner bait. I use this type in very deep water over a clean and/or, preferably, a rock bottom. Floater-diving baits just simply take too long to get to the bottom or won't reach the fish when they are below 15-18 feet deep.

The cast with a tailspinner lure begins like that for a plastic worm. Allow the bait to flutter to the bottom. When the line goes limp, start the retrieve in the same manner as with diving baits. The retrieve does not have to be quite as fast since the weight of the tailspinner lure will keep it on the bottom.

Most of these lead-bodied baits are rather small. I always dress them up with pieces of plastic worms or attach rubber skirts to create a larger target. Since these baits are fished in very deep water, I recommend using only black with a minimum of lighter markings.

One of the biggest advantages this bottom-hustling method has is its versatility. This method lets you experiment with different retrieves and extra goodies that can be attached to the lure. Ask yourself this question, "Excluding the spawning season, how many of my big bass come off the bottom of the lake?" I am sure the answer is, more than half of them. Think of all those times you have gone home with an empty stringer after crawling a worm slowly across the bottom. Maybe the bass were there after all, but you were just moving the bait too slow to find them.

The next time you start to pick up your plastic-worm outfit to fish the bottom, tie on a fast-retrieve diving bait and try a faster approach for deceiving Mr. Bigmouth. The results will add a new and exciting dimension to your bass fishing.

— NOVEMBER/DECEMBER 1974

HOW TO FISH CRANKBAITS IN WEEDY LAKES

By STEVE PRICE

*Alabama fishing ace Don Snider says the secret
to crankbait success is just throwing
and winding . . .*

If you studied the fishing techniques of Albertville, Ala., bass angler Don Snider, you wouldn't think of him as a crankbait expert.

For example, he doesn't use — or even own — any of the newer 7-food graphite rods with the lighter, more flexible glass tips. His rods are 5 1/2-footers with pistol grips, and their actions range from stiff to stiffer.

He has thousands of dollars worth of crankbaits, but he uses only seven or eight individual plugs — over and over again, even after the paint is long gone.

He doesn't study maps to locate prime lake structure. He doesn't use a chart recorder, or even one of the liquid-crystal units. His standby is an old flasher.

As other anglers constantly refine their tackle, technique and approaches to fishing, Snider stays with the tried-and-true. Yet he is considered by many to be one of Dixie's best deep-water structure-crankers. He's only fished two B.A.S.S. tournaments, but he finished 15th in one and first in the other — the 1988 Alabama BASSMASTER® Invitational on Lake Guntersville. Locally, moreover, he's considered a threat to win any of the 25 to 30 smaller tournaments he enters each year.

"It's just a matter of throwing and winding," says Snider, 45, a slim, gray-haired technician who's spent the past 19 years working the third shift at Goodyear so he can fish during the day.

"Deep-cranking is largely a matter of patience and confidence — patience to give the technique time to work, and confidence that it will work eventually. It's hard not to get discouraged after you've fished three or four hours without

a strike, but you simply have to keep doing it.

"I've had plenty of days like that in tournaments, then won those tournaments in 15 minutes when I finally found the fish. I've caught 20 and 30 bass from an area less than 10 yards long — all of them averaging 3 pounds or more."

Snider's been crankbaiting deep bass since 1976, when Goodyear workers went on strike for six months. He and a friend spent their time fishing as often as six days per week; he remembers cranking Rebel Maxi-Rs down the ledges of Alabama's Weiss Lake and being absolutely astounded at the number of bass he was catching.

All they were doing was working old crappie hangouts where the water depth changed along drop-offs, channels and humps. If it worked on Weiss Lake, he reasoned, why not Guntersville, which was just a long cast from his home in Albertville?

"It did work," says Snider. "In three straight days we boated over 200 pounds of bass by crankbaiting. I thought the fishing was easy, and I've been doing it ever since."

Snider's main ingredient for cranking success is finding a dramatic depth change. He looks for a severe drop where the bottom plunges from between 15 and 17 feet to wherever. He doesn't worry about the ultimate bottom depth because he's not fishing there. He works the top of that 15- to 17-foot range.

"My preferred depth used to be 12 feet," Snider says, but that was before the 'big' crankbaits were introduced. Twelve feet was as deep as I could wind a crankbait down.

"Then, the Mann's 20+ and some other deep-divers came out, so now I look for that 15- to 17-foot range; 15

"In three days we boated over 200 pounds of bass by crankbaiting. The fishing was easy, and I've been doing it ever since."
Photo: Gerald Crawford

feet is about as deep as I can get a big crankbait down on 12-pound-test line."

Even though Snider calls these fish "easy bass," there's more to it than simply finding that preferred depth.

"I look for cover, and I look for anything else that might be a little different," he says. "Even one or two stumps, or a little patch of weeds, could be all that's needed to attract the bass.

"For anyone wanting to learn deep-cranking like this, I suggest riding the main river channel of your favorite lake, and just looking for this depth, as well as for something different.

"Stay up on the shallow side of the drop, that is, keep your boat in that 15- to 17-foot water but close to the drop to deeper water."

When Snider first began teaching himself deep cranking, he would drop a buoy to mark his starting spot, and continue fishing along that drop all day. When he stopped fishing, he would mark that spot, then begin at that point

the following day. In the course of days, weeks and months spent on the water, he fished untold miles of channel breaks.

Naturally, certain patterns of the technique began to repeat themselves.

"When you're casting ahead as you follow the channel," says Snider, "try to keep your lure within about 5 feet of the edge. In other words, you're casting nearly parallel to the break, not over it.

"What you're looking for are fish that have come up into that shallower water to feed. They're big bass, and they'll hit a lure. When they're finished feeding, they go back off the edge somewhere into deeper water.

"Forget those bass out in the deeper water, and don't even be concerned with how deep it is. You're not fishing out there. You're working a very specific depth and type of structure that may not pay off for hours and hours, but when it does, you can get unbelievable action."

In addition to channels, Snider also fishes humps and

deep ridges in the same depth range. His years of searching on Guntersville have shown him the locations of many such places — he fished about 25 of them during his BASSMASTER win there — but good lake maps also will show them.

"Work the deepest side of the hump," advises Snider. "Again, you want the most severe drop you can find. The size of the hump doesn't have to be large either, but if it has deep water on at least one side, and maybe some type of cover on the top like stumps or vegetation, you'll probably find bass on it."

One of Snider's favorite places on Alabama's Lake Logan Martin demonstrates how small such a hot spot can be. It's a ridge 2 feet high, 5 feet wide and perhaps 30 feet long. It comes up on a flat and runs into the Coosa River channel. He found it by accident one day when he was running the edge of the channel itself.

"I'm always on the lookout for things like this," he explains. "This little ridge is something different from its surroundings, and it has the severe depth change. I don't fish many lakes outside Alabama, but I'm certain every bass lake in the country has little humps, ridges and underwater islands like this that hold bass."

The season of the year generally determines which end of the lake Snider fishes. In spring and fall, the upper end of an impoundment usually warms first and cools quicker than the lower end. In the spring, those bass will become more active sooner, but in the fall they may become inactive quicker. The rest of his fishing year is usually spent on the lower end of an impoundment.

Surprisingly, perhaps, Snider has not enjoyed a lot of success fishing the channels of tributary creeks. He doesn't doubt bass are present in such places, but he simply has more confidence along channels in the main lake.

Snider's favorite crankbaits include the Rebel Maxi-R, the Model A Bomber, Mann's 20+ and the new cedar crankbaits from Poe's. When using any of these, he doesn't like the lure to stay on the bottom and dig ditches. Instead, he prefers it to bump stumps and other cover along the bottom.

When the lure does hit something, Snider stops his retrieve momentarily, then starts winding again. If a bass is present, he says, a strike often comes when the lure stops, or just after it starts again.

"You don't always feel jarring strikes with deep crankbaits, either," he explains. "More often, there is an instant when the wobbling stops, as if someone has taken scissors and cut the line. That's when the bass has it, and you have to set the hook."

> *"Confidence is the name of the game in this type of fishing, and I have confidence in what I'm using."*

Snider's rods are 5 1/2-foot medium/heavy- and heavy-action sticks. He's been using them for years, feels confident with them, and knows they work. He keeps his rod tip down and pointed straight at the lure as he retrieves.

"I won't tell anyone what type of rod to use or how to use it," Snider points out. "What works for me may not work for someone else, and I certainly won't tell another angler that the long rods with glass tips won't work for them just because I don't use them.

"Confidence is the name of the game in this type of fishing, and I have confidence in what I'm using."

As for reels, Snider plans to try some of the new crankbait reels with low gear ratios that make winding big, deep-diving baits much easier. Currently, he uses regular-speed reels but gets very tired by the end of a day of fishing.

Snider alters his crankbaits to make them more effective. He first replaces the standard hooks with larger VMC hooks that better handle larger bass. He also sharpens all the hook points until they're razor-sharp; you'll find no loose crankbaits in his boat — the danger of getting hooked with one is too great.

Snider does not spend much time tuning crankbaits, either. If it doesn't run nearly perfect right out of the box, the lure is discarded. He gets plenty of wobbling action from the lures by using Berkley Cross Lok snaps.

"If you want to try deep-cranking along a channel on your home lake," he advises, "I suggest you start by simply running the main river channel anywhere you feel like it. The important thing is that you make up your mind to stay with it and not give up after a short time.

"Put your depthfinder's transducer on the trolling motor so you can see exactly what's under you, then try to find that 15- to 17-foot depth. If you fish in the South between late February and early November, this will be a good starting depth.

"Then, ease along the channel break and look for something different. Channel bends are good. Stumps are good. Grass or milfoil is good. Watch for baitfish, too."

He says it's important to keep your lure in the water, but when you do find some place a little different from its surroundings, or when you catch a bass, ease around the area and study it with a depthfinder so you can understand what you're fishing.

"You may catch one bass and think you've found them," says Snider, "but that isn't always the case. Just 5 feet away there may be a whole school of fish hovering around some feature you could easily miss."

— JULY/AUGUST 1989

TROLLING LIPLESS CRANKBAITS

By BOB MCNALLY

A deadly new technique has evolved for catching huge bass on lipless crankbaits . . .

What started as a frivolous Florida fishing fling last spring for a paltry few anglers turned into a deadly fishing technique with a fanatical following by late summer.

The technique is a ridiculously simple one, so simple, in fact, that many sophisticated Bassmasters refused to try it — until they saw bass catches being made with it.

"Basically, all the fishermen do is troll along the edges of weeds and flooded cypress knees with lipless crankbaits, and they catch bass. Lots of 'em. And they're big!" says Ernest Wigglesworth, owner of McGilvray's Fish Camp on 4,000-acre Newnans Lake in north-central Florida near Gainesville. "For years, a lot of our best fishermen have been catching big bass with small, lipless crankbaits that imitate shad, like Rat-L-Traps and Sugar Shads and Spots. But often they'd cast all day and boat just three or four fish. That got some of our regular anglers thinking about a better way of fishing the same lures in the same places where they caught bigmouths."

What a handful of Newnans Lake fishermen determined to do was to troll the lipless lures along the lake's shoreline edges. And what they discovered was one of the most deadly fish-catching methods to come along in years.

While many of these anglers tried to keep the technique quiet, big catches of big bass eventually got plenty of attention. Heavyweight catches became so commonplace on Newnans during the hot, broiling days of late spring and summer — a time when many Florida anglers have trouble catching any decent fish — that newspaper reports of such catches ran almost constantly.

Following is a typical one I wrote for the Jacksonville (Fla.) *Times-Union* last July:

"Minny and Benny Bass are bagging boatloads of bass.

"The husband-and-wife Gainesville fishing team have been scoring well almost daily by trolling fast with Rat-L-Trap plugs on Newnans Lake. Early and late fishing is most productive, and they are catching largemouths and sunshine bass (white bass-striper hybrids) to 6 pounds. They generally troll along the outside edges of lily pads and main-lake points.

"Father-and-son anglers Tom and Allen Cochran, also of Gainesville, are using the same trolling technique on Newnans, and they recently landed 13 largemouths weighing to 7 1/2 pounds."

Lots of 6- to 11-pound largemouths were caught from Newnans via trolling the lures last spring and summer. Most fishermen using the technique worked from small johnboats, many of them rental boats. But as the success of the technique was exposed, bass fishermen in large bass boats tried it with their hefty, sophisticated rigs and big outboards — and they caught fish, too.

Naturally, as the technique caught on with anglers, it spread to other Florida waters. Soon, big catches of heavyweight largemouths were being made by anglers trolling lipless crankbaits on Rodman Reservoir, Lake George, the St. Johns River, the Harris and Tsala-Apopka chains of lakes, many small lakes in the Ocala National Forest, on famed Lake Kissimmee, and West Lake Tohopekaliga.

By late summer, trollers working lipless lures were scoring well on largemouths as far south as Lake Okee-

chobee and as far west as Lake
Talquin, and some anglers began
employing the technique successfully in the bass-rich rivers of
Georgia and on some of that
state's impoundments, such as
Clark Hill Reservoir, Lake Lanier
and Lake Blackshear.

Clearly, trolling lipless crankbaits has made its mark on bass
fishing. The technique also caught
plenty of striped and hybrid bass,
even crappie, pickerel, rainbow
and brown trout, and catfish!

Like most effective fishing
techniques, this one can be simple
or complicated, depending on how
much an angler intends to work at
the method.

To the occasional fisherman,
it's a godsend, since it is a "no-
brainer" method of catching plenty
of good-size fish. They simply tie
on the lures, flip them behind the
boat, and roar off down the lake —
catching bass and most anything
else that swims in their wakes.

For the sophisticated angler,
trolling the little lipless lures takes
consummate skill and great atten-
tion to detail. It requires manipulating many trolling
nuances, any of which can bring additional bassin' success
to any day on the water.

Seasoned bass anglers quickly recognized that trolling
lipless lures along shoreline cover and over submerged
weedbeds like hydrilla and coontail moss was the fastest
means of checking such waters for largemouths.

It is deadly around other shallow structures, too, such as
riprap, bulkheads, pier pilings and bridge abutments. What is
more, it's a fast method of fishing. Speed in working such
areas is especially important during hot or bright weather,
since under those conditions the bulk of the best fishing is
had at daybreak and dusk. So the quicker an angler can cover
a lily-pad-lined or cypress-studded shoreline, the sooner he
finds feeding fish during the optimum hours of the day. Too,
on days when bass are finicky and scattered, trolling
crankbaits results in more fish per hour spent on the water.

Lipless crankbaits are ideal for shallow-water bass fishing for several reasons. The baits — available from several
manufacturers, including Bill Lewis Lures, Cordell, Mann's
Bait Co., Storm Lures, Whopper Stopper and Rebel — are
shaped like favorite forage of largemouth bass — shad and
shiners. Too, slow-sinking lipless lures tend to "plane" dur-

Florida anglers have discovered that huge largemouths will hit a lipless crankbait trolled rapidly along the edge of weedbeds.
Photo: Bob McNally

ing trolling, rather than dive deep like crankbaits sporting
diving bills or lips. With lipless lures, Florida fishermen are
able to quickly check very shallow, weedy, cover-filled
shallows where diving crankbaits with lips would hang up
in the structure.

For example, during a typical trolling pass with a lipless lure, an angler would speed up to get his plug over a
high spot in hydrilla, but would slow down to allow his
lure to fall a bit when he checked deeper water or the
drop-off of a weedbed.

Some anglers modify their lures, adding slip-sinker
weights ahead of the lures for deeper trolling. They use bullet weights up to 1 ounce, which they slip onto the fishing
line, then tie on a barrel swivel, a 2- to 3-foot leader and the
lure. Others drill holes in the baits and fill them with weights
or merely allow them to fill with water during fishing.

For very shallow trolling, some fishermen use stream-
lined, cigar-shaped cork floats ahead of lipless crankbaits to
make them run just a few inches under the surface. This
proves deadly when fishing slightly submerged hydrilla
weeds, which are prime forage areas for giant largemouths.
Many anglers who work dense weedbeds also remove the
forward treble hook of a lipless crankbait and replace the

rear treble with a single, short-shank hook or a wire-weed-guard hook. This greatly reduces lure-fouling in cover and often results in boating more bass because the fish are less likely to tangle exposed hooks in grass, logs or brush.

Trolling lipless crankbaits is basically a shallow-water technique, since the lures do not dive down at higher speeds like other crankbaits. Bottom-bumping crankbaits have been the mainstay of many trollers for decades, so the use of free-swimming plugs for trolling is looked at dubiously by some veteran fishermen, especially those skilled at "spoonplugging" and structure fishing. But even spoonplugging guru Buck Perry of Hickory, N.C., the man generally credited for starting deep-water structure fishing, endorses trolling free-swimming lures.

"Bumping bottom is of paramount importance to consistent bass-fishing success whenever lures are used in deep water, about 8 feet or more," states Perry. "But in the shallows, it's a whole new ball game, because the fish generally are more active, more aggressive. A free-swimming lure, therefore, can be deadly, especially when trolled along the edges of cover."

Many of Perry's spoonplugging trolling techniques have proved very effective when working lipless crankbaits. Perry always has stated that lure speed is vital to success, and Johnny Jacobs of Tallahassee learned that firsthand during a summer of trolling lipless crankbaits.

"I make a habit of trolling fast, then slowing down, then trolling fast, when working lipless lures," he says. "Some days bass want the lure fast, ripping along faster than I ever could crank them with a fast-retrieve reel. Other days they want it slow, or some speed in between.

"A lot of the biggest bass I've caught by trolling along deep (6 to 8 feet) weed edges hit after I stopped the boat to let the lures sink all the way to the bottom, then goosed the motor and ripped them off the lake floor. Fishing that way, I took an 11-pounder last August from the edge of a Lake Jackson lily-pad bed."

Some very successful anglers pump their rods when they troll lipless lures. By pulling, yanking or pumping the rod irregularly during trolling, the angler is imparting an extra bit of darting-and-falling action to the trolled plug. Pulling on the rod gives the lure a spurt of speed and causes it to move up and forward. By dropping the rod tip back down, the lure's forward progress slows, so it falls. When the line comes tight again due to the forward speed of trolling, the lure zips back up. This zigzag, saw-toothed lure pattern triggers bass into striking out of instinct.

A quick change in rod angle or boat path also can incite bass to hit, especially during the dog days of summer. The theory behind this trolling tactic is that bass frequently will follow the lure, apparently undecided about whether to strike. But a sudden dart in a different direction elicits an immediate strike response from the bass.

The same explanation applies when anglers "speed-troll" lipless lures. A crankbait ripping along at breakneck speed causes bass — particularly bass lying in the edge of heavy cover such as weedbeds, stump flats, submerged brush and undercut river banks — to hit the lure instantly, without allowing it time to look over the lure like it could a slow-moving plastic worm or topwater plug. The fish doesn't have time to be selective. It simply reacts.

Other refinements in trolling lipless crankbaits are being discovered all the time by savvy, innovative anglers. Some fishermen, for example, troll two plugs when working cover edges. The bait swimming closer to the cover is a small, lightweight one used with heavy line, a combination that keeps it working near the surface. The heavy line (often 20-pound-test) also is needed to horse bass from the thick cover. The lure trolled on the "outside" of the boat is larger and heavier, and is used with light-test (10-pound-test) line. The lighter, less-water-resistant line lets the heavier lure run deeper, and heavy line isn't as important on the deep-water side of the boat, because it's usually far enough away from the trolled cover edge that any bass that strikes need not be overpowered.

While many trollers prefer using standard, short, stiff-action "worm rods," some have learned that long popping rods or flipping sticks are better. The greater length of such rods lets anglers work trolled plugs better around cover edges and keep lines well away from propellers. Also, the long, two-fisted handles of popping and flipping rods make for less strenuous trolling because the rod butts easily can be held with two hands, or the handle can be rested against the angler's knee or propped against the boat console for extra support.

Although trolling lipless crankbaits has its origins in Florida, there is no question that trolling the little lures is effective in bass waters everywhere.

Anywhere bass scatter in weedy or brushy shallows to feed or station to ambush prey should be prime for trolling lipless lures. Too, "straining" deep water with lipless lures ought to be effective for ledge-living smallmouths, Kentucky spotted bass, and for open-water stripers.

Recently, some bass anglers have begun trolling small, lipless crankbaits deep and slow for bass in fall and winter. The little lures have proved very effective when allowed to vibrate slowly along old, deep, sunken roadbeds, creek-channel edges, underwater humps and similar structures. They enable anglers to check such deep structures for feeding bass quickly, which was the original purpose of the technique in the beginning.

No one is yet saying that trolling lipless crankbaits is a sure cure for all an angler's fishing ills. But as another effective tactic in a Bassmaster's overall arsenal of fish-catching skills, the method can't be discounted.

— MARCH 1988

CRANK LESS, CATCH MORE

By RUSSELL TINSLEY

*The 'crankbait' is a misnomer. The implication
is that you simply toss it out
and crank it back . . .*

The spot looked bassy all right, a half-submerged small dead tree, its underwater branches covered with moss, snuggled near the sloping rocky shoreline. I lobbed a shad-finished crankbait into the pocket and brought it back, feeling the resistance and wiggle of the lure through my rod tip.

Nothing doing. I gave it a second chance. There had to be a bass there.

Again no takers. I glanced on down the cactus-covered bank for another spot to hit.

Meanwhile, A. W. (Mac) McLaughlin, seated at the boat stern, targeted his lure into the same pocket. "You had your chance," he said, and that proclamation was followed by a grunt.

I turned as a good fish boiled near the tree and McLaughlin horsed it into open water. After he got it into the boat, I hung it on the tacklebox scales — 4 pounds, 9 ounces.

That husky bass provided McLaughlin with a measure of self-satisfaction. "You've got to tease 'em into hitting," he said, grinning.

In recent months my buddy McLaughlin has gotten hooked on crankbaits because many bass have, too. He lives on a rocky bluff overlooking Lake Marble Falls in central Texas. At least two or three times a week, sometimes more frequently, he rolls out of bed to plug for bass for an hour or two.

This narrow, deep impoundment, only about six miles long, is no great shakes of a bass lake; so when you catch a good one here it gives you a certain sense of triumph.

The so-called "crankbait" certainly is nothing new; only updated. Deep-diving plugs, like the Bomber and Hellbender, have been around longer than most BASSers can remember. But what was known as a "deep-runner" became the crankbait when the hand-carved, balsa wood Big-O started getting raves from pro tournament fishermen. This resulted in a proliferation of plastic look-alikes.

Ronny Hibler, a part-time guide on the Highland Lakes chain of impoundments in central Texas, put McLaughlin and this bass-chaser on to the crankbait a few years ago. He was fishing nearby Lake Lyndon B. Johnson several times each week, and told us that a wobbling, shad-colored plug was outperforming all others. Hibler gave us each one of the pot-bellied lures to try. And while we both threw it occasionally, this was mostly an act of desperation when other baits weren't producing, which was no fair test.

McLaughlin, like most BASSers, tends to stay with things that have been successful in the past. It wasn't long ago that virtually all his fishing was done with a safety-pin-type spinnerbait with bucktail, a custom model he makes.

His bass-fishing experience spans more than a half-century. Now semiretired, except for writing some newspaper columns about his favorite sport, he did accept an offer to help periodically at a local Marble Falls tackle store, and it was here that he became intrigued with crankbaits.

McLaughlin reasoned that when someone came in and asked about a specific bait and how to fish it, the best approach would be something positive rather than trying to give the potential customer a snow job. So he carried a few of the crankbaits home to test them during his early-morning sessions. They took fish, and the rest is history — well, almost.

The worst thing that has happened to this plug, McLaughlin believes, is it got saddled with the nickname "crankbait." The implication is that you simply toss it out, and crank it back. This is what most fishermen do, and with the fast-geared reels, one really can be streaked through the water.

"Ah yeah, you'll take a bass now and then fishing it that way, even trolling," he explained. "But to catch fish with any consistency, you've got to adapt, to vary the retrieve, changing speeds. The crankbait is a very versatile lure once you get the hang of fishing it."

The model crankbait McLaughlin selects is often dictated by water depth; a short-lipped plug for shallower water, one with a longer bill to go deeper. "And a smaller model usually will take more bass than a jumbo, but with its light weight it requires some familiarization to cast it with any accuracy."

Yet it is what you do with bait once it gets "down there" that is the most critical factor.

"Let's face it, most Bassmasters are in too much of a hurry; we reel too fast," McLaughlin goes on. "You'll catch a bunch more bass on a slower retrieve," he believes.

McLaughlin and I have spent many hours together in a boat, and the veteran BASSer has taught me a lot. He is patient, always concentrating. He also is a firm believer in confidence. Once you get a bait you feel comfortable with, stick with it. You'll take more bass that way.

There is no set pattern to his retrieve. But one of the favorites is to locate likely cover, perhaps a drowned brushpile, and then toss way past it near the shore, or maybe the edge of a weedbed if this is where the structure is positioned. Instead of immediately starting to reel, McLaughlin allows the floating plug to lie there a few seconds; then he switches it to simulate a crippled baitfish that has floated to the surface and is gasping its last breaths. Often this makes a bass lose its cool.

If no takers, McLaughlin says reel rapidly a few times to bring the lure deep before it reaches the cover you intend to probe. Once it gets to the desired level, he decelerates, and moves it with a slow stop-and-go tango.

The crankbait, head down, has a knack of going through heavy stuff without hanging. When you feel it bouncing against submerged brush or limbs, you have it in the right place.

"Most fishermen throw to open water because they are afraid of hanging and losing an expensive lure," McLaughlin says. "They're wasting their time; that isn't where you are going to find bass. No matter what kind of lure you are fishing, you must learn to recognize likely structure, and then fish it properly."

There is no predicting when a bass might hit, but one of the experience-proven times is after the bait has been brought to a halt, then started in motion again.

"Maybe the bass thinks the baitfish has seen it and is about to escape. That makes the predator pounce, whether the bass is hungry or not," he speculates.

But a crankbait isn't only a deep-water lure, even the long-lipped models. A flaw many fishermen have is they switch to something else when they relocate their efforts to the shoreline shallows.

One of the bass' favorite foods in the rocky-sided Texas Highlands lakes, as well as other reservoirs, is the crawfish. A crankbait in shallow water can be rooted along bottom to imitate a crawdad.

"But again, an error is to be fooled by the name and simply crank the bait in," says McLaughlin.

"I used to live in Louisiana, and had the opportunity numerous times to watch a crawfish in action. It retreats in short bursts. It will scuttle along a ways, then stop a spell, and take off again. That's the way you ought to work your crankbait," he asserts.

This lure also is productive when retrieved shallow through treetops in deep water when bass are suspended, or equally as effective along a rocky point, where the water slopes from shallow to deep. McLaughlin casts into the shallows, then stairsteps the plug down the drop-off to make it look like a crawfish trying to escape a predator.

"On any lake, don't overlook those points," he stresses. "That is where bass frequently hang out."

As for bait colors, it of course depends on what the bass prefer on any given day. But McLaughlin stays primarily with light and dark shades; something white, silvery or shad-finish when fishing deeper water. He will plow a darker plug along bottom to look like a crawfish.

"When I find a color that looks good and pays off with bass, I will fish it probably 90 percent of the time," McLaughlin explains. "You've got to feel that you are going to catch a bass every time you cast. This isn't possible if there is some uncertainty about the bait you've tied on the line."

And as for the newest lure-color technology, McLaughlin has had best success with the reflective-type finishes "only because I began catching bass on them and now fish them most of the time."

Those "true-life" printed lures, made to be an exact replica of a bluegill or some other baitfishes, he admits, are eye-catching and no doubt will fool bass. But he isn't convinced they are any better than the older and more conventional paint jobs.

"I suspect they are made to appeal more to the fishermen than the fish," he says wryly. "But that's the point; if you don't convince the fisherman to buy a crankbait and put in on his line, then all this stuff is moot anyway."

— 1980 BASS FISHING GUIDE

How Rick Clunn Fishes Lipless Crankbaits

By TIM TUCKER

Wherever he finds bass in the grass, you'll find this Classic champ casting vibrating, rattling crankbaits . . .

Rick Clunn calls it his primary tool for locating bass, which is lofty status considering the credentials of the man.

The tool is the lipless crankbait, a vibrating, shad-shaped, flat-sided rattling lure that allows anglers to cover water in search of active bass quickly. For the three-time BASS Masters Classic® champion, the Rat-L-Trap is his best bird-dog bait, the lure he ties on when there is lots of ground to cover and time is running short.

Although he fishes it around a variety of structure and cover conditions, the Rat-L-Trap is Clunn's weapon of choice most often for a wide variety of aquatic vegetation, ranging from submerged milfoil to vertical bulrush strands. Vegetation is where a lipless crankbait can best strut its stuff, he says.

For Clunn, lipless crankbaits know no seasonal boundaries. As long as a lake or reservoir has some type of vegetation, he will automatically fish that lure.

"The Rat-L-Trap and lures like it do several things for you," Clunn says. "You can control it over the top of the weeds with the position of your rod tip. With any submerged weedbed, the top of it will vary, and this bait allows you to make quick, easy adjustments and still keep working just above the weeds.

"Weed fishing is notorious for having what I call non-positional fish — which means you cannot predict where the bass are going to come from. With vegetation, particularly submerged vegetation, you have to search for the fish. In a stump row or by a stick-up, you know where those fish should be holding. The Rat-L-Trap is the best bait I know of for locating these non-positional fish. There is no doubt that the bait draws fish to it. The noise from the Rat-L-Trap will draw fish that are buried in the weeds out to see what's going on.

"It's the one bait that you don't have to present properly to the fish."

Clunn's victory in the Alabama BASSMASTER® Invitational in the spring of 1987 on Lake Guntersville is a classic example of the allure of lipless crankbaits to grass bass.

His pattern centered around isolated patches of submerged milfoil that were 1 to 4 feet below the surface in 5 to 13 feet of water. Although a few of the bass still were spawning, most of the fish were in a post-spawn mode and seemed to be holding around the edges of any bare spots on the underwater islands. Clunn conquered these spots with a 1/2-ounce gold Rat-L-Trap fished on 8-, 10- and 15-pound-test line.

The Rat-L-Trap was the right tool for the situation, a bait that Clunn could use to skirt the top of the submerged vegetation and still attract the attention of bass hiding inside it. The lipless crankbait has a bigger role in grass fishing than most anglers realize, Clunn says, but he warns that this type of fishing can be frustrating.

"If you're going to crank weeds, you have to put up with a certain amount of frustration," he explains. "You can hardly make a cast without having to either slap the bait on the water or reach up and clean grass off of it. The average guy won't tolerate it. He'll either move out away from the weeds or find a place where there are no weeds. To be successful, you have to control yourself when fishing weeds and be willing to put up with fighting them all day long. Many times it would be easier to fish a worm or a spinnerbait, but they don't usually produce the strikes the Rat-L-Trap does."

When working a submerged weedbed or the outskirts of a

vertical wall of vegetation, Clunn emphasizes keeping the lure as close to the cover as possible. That will also increase your chance of getting hung up, but popping a bait free from the grasp of vegetation also triggers strikes from time to time.

Serious consideration should be given to the equipment involved in fishing lipless crankbaits.

Clunn uses an inexpensive 7-foot fiberglass rod. He has long been a proponent of using glass rods with fast-moving lures like crankbaits, believing that the graphite rods allow us to respond too quickly to a strike and often take the bait away from the fish.

"The best thing ever made for fishing lipless crankbaits is the 7-to-1 (gear ratio) high-speed reel," Clunn says, in reference to Daiwa's Procaster model PT33SH, the fastest baitcasting reel on the market. "Its value is not in the fact that it is so fast. The real key with this reel is that it is almost a variable-speed control reel. I can really feel the bait with this reel. I can slow the bait down and speed it up without losing that feeling. With most reels, if you slow down, you lose the feel of the Rat-L-Trap momentarily, but not this reel. That kind of control is important when you are trying to run a crankbait just over the top of brushpiles or grass."

Clunn's choice of line size varies from situation to situation. Although he primarily uses 14- to 17-pound-test, he adjusts the size of the line depending on the clarity of the water and the amount of fishing pressure in the area. In his Guntersville win, Clunn began the tournament with 15-pound-test line, but dropped to 10- and 8-pound-test line on successive days. Downsizing his line was a major reason he was able to continue to catch fish off of the same spots, he believes.

Although Clunn swears by the Rat-L-Trap for fishing vegetation, he insists it is a more versatile lure than most people realize for other types of cover.

"I've had good success with it in the fall by repeatedly casting to boat docks," he says. "It may take 25 casts to the same dock before you get a strike, but the good thing about it is that you can follow people throwing other baits like a spinnerbait or worm and catch fish off the docks they just fished."

During a fall tournament on Lake Tawakoni (near Dallas) two years ago, low-water conditions congregated the fishermen around the lake's boat docks, and created a situation where the anglers literally formed a line to fish each structure. Clunn watched as boat after boat struck out on dock after dock with the more conventional lures. But when he followed the parade by making short pitch-casts under the dock, the Rat-L-Trap produced two or three strikes from beneath every pier.

"It's a reflex bait," Clunn says. "I think creatures in nature have to be tuned in to subtleties to survive. Sometimes you can change some little thing to give them a different look, and that is enough to trigger a strike."

The noisy lipless crankbaits are also good tools for jump-fishing schooling bass, as well as fishing muddy water.

Rattling, lipless crankbaits draw fish out of hiding, says Rick Clunn, who uses the lures extensively in tournament competition. Photo: Tim Tucker

For all of its benefits, a problem remains with the Rat-L-Trap and similar lures that fishermen must recognize — its poor hooking ability. The basic design of the bait works in favor of a frantic bass. When a bass is struggling, the weight of the flat-sided bait provides enough leverage to work the treble hooks free of its mouth on many occasions.

To remedy that situation, some of the tournament pros began modifying these lures by removing the rear hook (to avoid excessive fouling with the modified belly hook) and drilling a hole down through the body of the bait. They then would run the monofilament through the lure body and tie it directly to an oversized hook. That adaptation was the forerunner of Bill Lewis Lures' Pro Trap and the Cordell Slidin' Spot.

Clunn does not use the free-swinging version of the Rat-L-Trap, saying the problem of losing fish still exists despite the adaptation, and he does not want to sacrifice the rear treble hook. Instead, he simply replaces the factory hooks with larger models and flares the barbs outward. "My hooks look like I've been pulling them out of stumps all day," Clunn says.

The biggest danger of a bass dislodging the lure is when it takes flight. In an effort to convince the fish not to jump, Clunn immediately buries 2 to 3 feet of his rod tip in the water after setting the hook. Although that is often not enough to stop the initial jump, Clunn has enjoyed good success in keeping the bass from making subsequent leaps — the most dangerous part of the battle.

Despite its flaws, the lipless crankbait remains a viable tool for both locating and catching bass. "If a lake has vegetation in it, you had better be throwing one of these baits," Rick Clunn declares.

— MAY 1990

TIME FOR SHALLOW-RUNNERS

By LARRY GREEN

A s-l-o-w subsurface action with a crankbait will tempt early-spring bass to strike . . .

There is a period early in the spring when good numbers of bass are in shallow water in preparation for spawning and generally are not all that responsive to the likes of artificial baits.

This unresponsive period usually occurs because water temperatures are still in the high 50s to low 60s, still within 8 to 10 degrees below the ideal spawning temperatures.

Ripe with milt and eggs, the sexually mature adult bass are drawn into the shallow waters by the natural urge to spawn, yet because of the cold water, the bass still are sluggish and, for the most part, unresponsive to a good majority of artificials — but not all artificials.

The weedy, structurally inundated shallows call for special lures and a special fishing technique. Deep-running crankbaits almost are useless because they hang up on anything and everything in the shallows. Spinnerbaits are effective, but can often put out a little too much commotion and, in fact, turn off these sluggish bass in shallow water. Plastic worms also are good, at times, but unless you strike a bass on the head with one, or put it within immediate visual range, the bass just won't pick it up. Jigs, generally, sink too rapidly and always are dropping into the thick of the debris. The banging of a leadhead jig on old submerged limbs and stick-ups can, and often does, spook these touchy shallow-water bass.

Surface lures are ideal to work in shallow water, as you can place them anywhere and skip, jump or flutter them from one open pothole to another, but the problem here is, again, one of water temperature. The bass are not responsive to the commotion produced by surface lures, nor are they yet willing to jump on a surface bait.

That leaves BASSers with one artificial bait which really is the most ideally suited for fishing in the shallows in early spring. I'm speaking in particular about shallow-running crankbaits, the kind that normally will either float or suspend themselves just beneath the surface, then turn just barely under the surface when retrieved. Some of the more deadly shallow-runners have very small diving or action lips in front, but have the flotation factor built into the lure in such a manner that when retrieved very slowly, the head or front of the lure is submerged to promote the action, but the tail end or rear of the lure rides high enough to just barely break the surface.

• **Skimming The Shallows** — Properly retrieved, this type of shallow-running crankbait comes skimming along partially submerged, wiggling and shaking and causing just a slight erratic "S" trail across the surface.

I find that this is the very best action attainable for working the shallows and demanding a good response from pre-spawned bass.

You get a s-l-o-w action that lets the bass know something has invaded its spawning territory, yet the slow subsurface action is mild enough to evoke a response from a bass that in the biological sense of the word isn't fully awake yet.

The bass responds because this type of bait and action is within its biological feeding limitations.

You can prove this to yourself. Find a spot in the shallows where you know pre-spawned bass are close to shore looking for nesting sites. The more sub-surface structure, the better.

You'll discover within just a few casts why you cannot work a deeper-running crankbait effectively, and if you're totally observant, you can plainly see that lures or plugs that produce too much action, too much noise, and too much vibration really can spook these shallow-water bass.

I'd also be very surprised if you could evoke any decent response out of a surface lure in water temperatures around the high 50s or low 60s. If you get a bass to bump your surface lure the way green sunfish, or bluegill often do, it is telling you that it does not like this invasion of privacy on its preselected spawning site, but the fish does not really attack the lure.

The answer, then, as I'm confident you will discover ultimately, lies in a shallow-running crankbait when it is retrieved slowly and cautiously through the shallows in such a manner as to catch the bass' attention without alarming the fish.

• **Invading Thin Water** — Remember that despite the bass' sluggish metabolic condition, these early-spring bass keenly are aware that in shallow water they are extremely vulnerable to a wide variety of predators like ospreys, great blue herons, and others.

If suddenly spooked, a bass will expend all its energy in but one quick burst toward deeper water.

Bassmasters fishing in boats should keep this uppermost in mind when approaching the shallows, long before any lure is even cast. The slightest wave or ripple sent across the water toward the shallow shoreline can, and usually does, spook shallow-water bass. What the bass senses is not so much the visible wave or ripple, but the change in water pressure as the wave or ripple passes through the shallows. The bass may suspect a wading bird or whatever other predator it feels may be stalking it. Always use a very quiet approach toward these shallow shorelines.

That first cast can be critically important if you're sure you're over bass-infested shallows. If you must place the lure directly onto the surface of the water, do so with the utmost care and gentleness. I'm always looking for a gentle, sloping, snag-free bank where I can purposely over-cast to lay my artificial bait onto the edge of the shore, then just ease if off the bank and into the water.

• **Fishing The Shallows** — This technique is extremely effective because pre-spawned bass will lie within just a

few inches of the shore, often with just enough water over them to cover their dorsal fins.

Remember that in this cold water, no bass is going to be aggressively chasing any offering, which means that your artificial crankbait has to be placed between the shore and the bass.

The bass will position itself to intercept a seductively running crankbait directly in its path, but on the same hand it probably will not turn and chase a bait that was cast short and retrieved off toward deeper water.

I've watched pre-spawned bass in the shallows on hundreds of occasions and it's almost disgusting how fussy and sluggish these bass can be; that is why it's so important to play up to the bass' slightest whims, and in this respect I feel that a good plug-caster or spin-caster can accomplish this best with the aid of the shallow-running crankbait.

Often in the early spring when you do hook, play and ultimately land one of these moody bass, you may discover that other bass will follow the hooked fish right up to the boat.

I suspect this happens more out of confusion than anything else, or the fact that at this time of year many of the spawning bass are paired up, and where one goes the other follows.

You'll find that if you sit quietly and stop casting for just a few minutes, these following bass will return to the same exact spot where you caught the last one out of the shallows.

• **Selecting Lures** — At this point you're probably wondering which choice of color or style of shallow-water crankbait is best suited for this early-spring fishing. It's a logical question to which there really is no definite answer, except to say that much will depend on the color of the water.

Often in the early spring, many lakes and waterways are in somewhat of a milky, murky or just plain muddy condition. You should remember that the bass will be in the shallows, tight against the shore, regardless of the water coloration.

But coloration will to some degree determine the color of your plug. Your personal experience in each situation really serves as your best teacher, as each habitat differs to the degree it could dictate its own prescription for success.

Minnow- and shad-imitation crankbaits with a diving bill designed for shallow running are the author's favorite lure for duping early-spring bass. Bagley's Small Fry and Rebel's Minnow series are pictured.   Photo: Larry Green

However, here are some standard guidelines that are not necessarily my own, but ones which I have done well to observe over many years of fishing these early-spring bass with shallow crankbaits in a wide variety of water conditions.

It has been determined that fish can see dark colors in muddy waters better than light hues. The extreme of this would be an all-black lure in highly muddied water. There's no reason to suspect that, in this respect, the black bass is any different than any other fish. As the water tones turn clearer, then the lighter-toned lures can be used effectively to catch fish.

I mentioned coloration only because in the early spring months bass anglers do encounter murky, if not muddy, water conditions in any number of waterways. When you so encounter muddied waters, try darker-patterned crankbaits.

I've always had exceptionally good responses out of shallow-water bass in muddy water, using color patterns that include black, brown, orange, olive, tan and red, or any combination of the above colors.

In slightly clearer water I usually stick with the crankbaits that are patterned in natural color schemes such as frog, baby bass, bluegill, crappie, pike, trout or other natural color-pattern imitations.

In extremely clear water you really can't beat the standard all-chrome or silver body topped by a darker-colored back that's either green, blue or black. I particularly like this color combination in the minnow-type plugs.

The style or type of artificial lure is not all that important as long as the plug is designed specifically as a shallow-runner. These plugs usually are identified by a very short diving bill or plane on the front.

• **Tips On Lure Types** — There is a grave misconception about these crankbaits with regard to their plastic lips or diving planes. Some misguided fishermen seemingly refuse to purchase a crankbait that does not have a large diving plane (lip) on the front of it because they feel they are being cheated out of action on the premise that the larger the (lip) diving plane, the greater the action.

That, in most instances, is totally false, and in some cases works in the opposite. It's not the size of the diving lip that determines the action, but more the angle or pitch of the lip.

In actuality, many of the very deep-diving plugs with large, slightly sloped diving bills have a very slow action, but can attain a running depth in excess of 18 feet. On the other hand, those shallow-water crankbaits with very short, steeply pitched dive planes have a great deal of action.

The only way you'll really know how a plug is going to act is to put it on your line, cast and retrieve it. But in so doing you'll discover that it's the angle or pitch of the bill and not necessarily the size of the diving lip that determines the action of the lure during the retrieve.

If you're puzzled, just remember that for good shallow running, the plastic bill should be steeply pitched; in some cases it's almost vertical.

When all else fails to convince you what the action of the lure is going to be like, read the instructions. Lure manufacturers spend a great deal of time, money and research in carefully printing the instructions that are placed within the packaging of every lure. These instructions tell you precisely what you can expect out of a lure, before you purchase it.

Yet, for all their good intentions, the average bass angler seldom if ever reads the instructions. If you feel you're beyond the instructions, you're making a big mistake, as chances are you'll learn qualities about the lure that you wouldn't otherwise have expected. Nobody is above reading the instructions enclosed with any lure. Remember that and you'll be the wiser for it.

If you fail to get a response out of the long, minnow-type plugs, then switch to naturals or fat baits, as long as all are shallow-runners.

Remember that the bass will be very sluggish at this time of year, and the Bassmaster's job will be to tease and tantalize the fish into a strike, which will feel more like just a slight bump than a strong strike.

• **S-L-O-W Down** — The slower you can retrieve that plug the better off you are. With the suspending, shallow-running crankbaits, the best method of retrieve is a pause — retrieve — pause approach. This not only seduces temperamental bass into a strike but, more importantly, it will give any half-interested bass that might be following your artificial a chance to catch up to it and eat it.

Just keep thinking to yourself that every bass in the shallows is acting lethargic. Think in s-l-o-w motion and fish accordingly. Once you locate an ideally suited piece of shallow shoreline, one that looks as if it is holding spawn-ripe bass, take the time to work that piece of shoreline thoroughly until you're positive you've placed your lure on the nose of a bass. In essence, that may be exactly what you'll have to do to provoke a strike.

Keep the hooks of your lures needle-sharp, and be ready to respond to the slightest nudge. Remember that, as underwater films have proved, bass can move up to a running crankbait, totally engulf it and then spit it back out again without the angler ever detecting the pickup.

Bassmasters everywhere are fast approaching that period of the year when the bass will be moving into shallow water and looking for nesting sites.

You should plan to be on hand to intercept and catch these bass, and if you'll follow my advice, I'm certain you'll discover, as I did, the tremendous advantages of using shallow-running crankbaits to score some big successes on early-spring largemouths.

Remember, fish quiet, s-l-o-w and shallow. Good luck!

— APRIL 1983

CHAPTER TWELVE

JIGGING EXPERTISE

A jig is a lump of lead, hook and skirt that doesn't do anything, except catch fish.

Photo: Matt Vincent

Photo: Timothy O'Keefe

JIGGING TIPS AND TRICKS

By STEVE PRICE

Gary Klein says concentration is the most important factor in becoming a successful jig fisherman . . .

In the past four years no lure has generated as much interest or publicity as has the rubber-leg jig. Several major tournaments have been won with the lure, including the 1980 BASS Masters Classic® by Bo Dowden. Today, Bassmasters not only have a variety of jigs from which to choose, but also special jig tackleboxes, jig rods, and a bewildering array of pork and plastic jig trailers.

Through it all, California tournament pro Gary Klein of Oroville has kept one of those "I-told-you-so" smiles, for this blond, energetic 26-year-old has used jigs ever since he began fishing over 20 years ago. He started with jigs because he had to walk shorelines in those days and didn't want to carry a lot of rods and tackle; the jig caught more bass more consistently than anything else he owned. Today he manufactures three highly popular models.

"It's a fascinating lure to fish," says Klein, who used a jig to propel him to runner-up honors for B.A.S.S. Angler-of-the-Year in 1979, "even though it's a non-action lure.

"I feel that with a jig, if I get 10 strikes from bass, I can boat all 10 of those fish. I can't say that about any other type of lure, even those with multiple hooks.

"A multi-hook lure has disadvantages in that the bass rarely totally engulfs the lure, so the hooks are dangling outside to snag on roots, limbs and other cover. And they do, allowing the the fish to get free," Klein said.

In his years of fishing jigs, Klein not only has amassed a wealth of knowledge about how to fish jigs, but also how bass react to them. Here's some of his advice on how to get more out of this "do-nothing" lure:

• **Concentrate** — "I believe concentration is the single most important factor in becoming a successful jig fisherman, even more important than confidence. Because a jig does not have any built-in action, you must learn to watch your line when you fish it, especially on your very first cast to an object.

"Bass tend to hit a jig on its initial fall. I've seen many fishermen miss bass they never realized were present, simply because they weren't watching their lines. In these particular instances, the lure fell several feet, stopped momentarily, then fell again. A bass can hit and exhale a jig that fast and smoothly. You might not feel anything, but you can see it," says Klein.

• **Use Properly Matched Tackle** — "Because a jig is such a small and compact lure, bass usually inhale it completely when they strike. They suck it in, then close their mouths again.

"If you use a limber rod, or light line with a lot of stretch, you simply get the fish's attention when you try to set the hook, and the barb never penetrates anything. The bass comes to the surface, opens its mouth, and spits the lure back at you," explains Klein.

"I strongly recommend using a heavy-action rod, either a long-handled rod like a flipping rod, or a stiff casting rod. When I'm fishing east of the Rockies, or in shallow water, I use lines that test 14, 17, 20 and even 25 pounds.

"In California and the Southwest, shallow water actually is pretty limited and bass tend to be more structure-oriented. The water usually is clearer and our average fishing depth is about 25 feet. With those conditions, we use lighter lines testing about 12 pounds and regular baitcasting rods because the fishing is more nearly vertical.

"What you are striving for is a solid hookset that forces the barb into that upper lip. A stouter rod and line also lets you control the fish once it is hooked. Remember, too, that a jig is a target-oriented lure, so most fish you catch with it are going to be near heavy cover anyway," Klein says.

• **Swim A Jig** — "One of the techniques we use often in California and other deep, clear reservoirs, is to swim the jig, rather than hop it or crawl it along the bottom. This also works in Southern lakes when fish are located along creek channels, as they are in summer and fall.

"It's easy, and it adds a new dimension to your jig fishing. Cast beyond your target, count the jig down to any desired depth, or let it fall to the bottom. Then, with your rod held parallel to the water, crank your reel handle five or six times, very fast.

"Next, stop reeling so the jig begins to fall again. Crank it fast five or six more times, then stop once more. Strikes occur when the jig changes direction, such as jumping up when you begin reeling, or as it starts falling when you stop reeling.

"When you're fishing a creek channel, reel your lure to the edge of the drop-off, but instead of letting the jig fall off the edge, swim it straight back to you. You can put entire patterns together with this simple technique," says Klein.

• **Use Big-Hook Jigs** — "For some reason, manufacturers use smaller hooks, occasionally down to size 2/0, when they make lighter-weight jigs. I think this is a mistake. When I switch to a lighter jig, such as from 1/2 ounce to 3/8 ounce, it's not because I'm looking for smaller fish. It's because existing conditions dictate the use of a lighter lure.

"I don't use anything smaller than a 5/0 hook on any of my jigs. If I want a smaller jig, I use scissors and trim the legs.

"Something else to look for is a good weedguard. Most are either too stiff or too thick. You want the lure to be weedless but not fishless. On my jigs we use heavy-duty monofilament or black nylon you can shape by hand.

"The head design is also important. I like a jig that doesn't have a bulky, blocky head, but instead, offers a smooth taper. I want the top edge of the head to flow evenly and smoothly right into the line-tie eye, which helps prevent snagging," Klein explains.

• **Fish Without A Trailer** — "You can fish a jig successfully without a pork or plastic trailer. The best time for this is just before bass spawn or when they are actually on the nest. The reason you don't want a long trailer at this time, is to force the bass to pick the lure up by the head, because of its small and compact size. If you use a long trailer, the bass will pick it up by the trailer and never be near the hook," he notes.

• **Fish Vegetation** — "You can cast a jig over most moss and milfoil successfully and with devastating results, too. Use

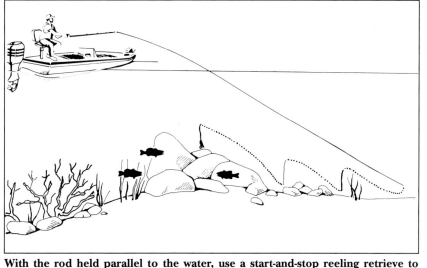

With the rod held parallel to the water, use a start-and-stop reeling retrieve to "swim" a jig over bottom structure. The jig will rise and fall. Strikes occur when the lure changes direction.

Illustration: Emily Craig

a full-skirted jig with a 6-inch plastic-worm trailer, and pull it right across the top. The long trailer will swim from side to side, and create an action like a small snake.

"Drop the jig-and-worm into potholes and openings and let it settle lazily to the bottom, or pull it over the edge of the vegetation and then swim it slowly back to the boat," Klein suggests.

• **Use A Jig In Hot Weather** — "How you fish a jig during the summer usually depends on the type of lake and the water conditions you encounter. If you're fishing deep water, swim the jig off the channel ledges and across points with a fast stop-and-go retrieve that causes the jig to change speed and direction often.

"If you're fishing in a tributary where there is either heavy cover or current, flip the jig into that cover. With stronger current you can make short pitch casts or underhand flips upstream above your actual target and let the water wash your jig down into the cover.

"For suspended bass, you may consider switching to a small marabou jig. In my tournament tacklebox I always have a supply of 1/8-ounce marabou crappie jigs. Anything will hit this jig, including nice bass. I often tie on one of these when I'm getting a lot of hits and want to find out exactly what's doing the hitting," he said.

• **Practice Makes Perfect** — "You need to have confidence in any lure you fish, and jigs are certainly no different in this respect. The best way to get confidence in a jig is to use one and catch fish with it.

"One technique I used when I was learning to fish a jig was to go to a small lake and fish a jig all day, but never let it touch the bottom. This makes you concentrate, you learn about swimming the jig, and you'll catch fish, which leads to greater confidence," according to Klein.

— NOVEMBER/DECEMBER 1984

A BASSer's Guide To Giguer Fishing

By DON MILLER

Dropped into the water it's a big zero — but you can make it dance a bassin' tune...

Now that we've caught your attention, and before we lay some bassin' truth on you, let's explain that "giguer" bit. That's the French word, meaning "to leap," which probably is the great grandpappy of a word with which every bass fisherman is a lot more familiar — jig.

Paint it, trim it, bounce it or swim it, and the lowly jig deserves all the attention it gets plus a lot more. Just dropped into the water, it's a big fat zero. But by using the fishing rod as a conductor uses a baton in directing an orchestra, a BASSer can play sweet music with the jig. He can make it dance and dart; he can make it come alive. He can make it move like a minnow, slither like a crawdad or bump along like a town drunk who bounces off the curbstones.

It's the lively manipulation of a jig that obviously resulted in the name. For more than five centuries, a jig has been a lively dance . . . and "giguer" means to leap. Add it up and you emerge with a fishing lure older by far than the dance itself, but a lure that leaps and dances in lively fashion. By the way, it catches a whale of a lot of bass.

In today's angling circles, the plastic worms hog the headlines. They're usually used with a weight (primarily a slip sinker) and a hook. So what do you have when you use a weight, a hook and some dressing? Ah, you catch on fast, friend — you have a glorified jig!

Excepting the topwaters and the middepth wobblers which are minnow-like in appearance, it's amazing how many of today's most successful plugs hang on the family tree of the simple old jig. That piece of lead and a hook may be spruced up with some feathers or tipped with soft plastic.

It might have a safety-pin spinner ahead of it or a spinner blade revolving around the shaft. But any way you look at it, it's a jig with a little fancy trimming.

It can dance or dart. It can be retrieved slowly or rapidly. It can bump the bottom or swim the middepths. Drape a pork eel on the hook and it becomes a slithering, tantalizing lunker lure, deadly in the submerged timber and rock areas. Dressed with maribou on the hook, it's a deadly lure along rock cliffs, or bounced off rounded boulders deep beneath the surface.

Jigs come in all sizes, colors and shapes. Often, when bass get lockjaw and the kids howl for something to eat, I fish a pair of 1/24-ounce jigs in a tandem and put tasty fillets on the table.

One jig dances along at the end of the line; a second dangles from a 6- or 8-inch piece of monofilament. The long end of a blood knot is used to splice the line. Sometimes even a third jig is used the same way, offering Mr. Bass a regular smorgasbord.

At the opposite end of the jig size, I've dunked 3/4- and 1-ounce jigs, with or without pork or plastic additions, to put many a bucketmouth on the stringer. In fact, I fished the 1/2- and 3/4-ounce jigs with eels for two solid years on the Missouri-Arkansas impoundments of the White River, with generally good success. What the heck — Virgil Ward used 'em, and what's good enough for Virgil is good enough for Miller.

There was just one difference. Ward felt every movement of the jig, and knew precisely what it was doing every moment. I was just dragging it along, with no real concept of how it looked or what it was doing. Then one overcast afternoon, I worked a flooded-timber arm on Table Rock Lake, up the Long Creek arm. Suddenly, I knew what the lure was doing. It was a part of me, an extension of my arm via the baitcasting rod.

I slithered it over logs and bounced it off rocks. I let it slide off a drop-off and eased it through tangled branches.

"I can't explain it," Ken Carney had told me months before, "but you feel it." Carney was right. As a lazy angler, I'd been inclined to rest my elbows against my body, or let the rod lie against the boat gunwale. There was no way to "feel" the jig as it made underwater contact with bass cover.

The big difference came when elbows were held away from the body and the reel was tipped so the handles were upward. Then the left hand became a human switchboard, telegraphing every little bump, jar and movement. Even the monofilament played a part, and moved to one side or another when a bass gulped the jig and began to swim away with it.

The experience was filed away for future use on Table Rock and Bull Shoals. And back home in Ohio, the old spinners and wobblers once again were hauled out of the tacklebox. They had the built-in action and there was no need to get fancy with the rod tip. Then I met "the bug man," sometimes known as Al Luttrell.

Luttrell looked at my tacklebox, shifted a cud of tobacco in his jaw and spat derisively. "Get rid of that hardware and start pitchin' some bugs," he advised.

Luttrell's "bugs" are tiny jigs, from 1/32-ounce on up to huge 1 1/2-ouncers, the latter used on northern pike in Quebec. "Ya gotta make 'em dance," Luttrell insisted.

While he maintained a very slow retrieve with one hand on the reel handle, he made the slender rod sing like a buggy whip. In the depths, the jigs were responding to the tip action incorporated above.

From then on, experience became the teacher. A gentle rod-tip wave produced strikes from rainbow trout. An even softer wave enticed crappie. For white bass, the tip vibrated like a hula girl with a bad case of the chills.

Ah, but largemouth bass — it didn't take long to discover that on my favorite waters they preferred a "lift-and-drop-back" retrieve. The jig would dart up, then drop down and the strike usually came as it dropped. Bass didn't hit these small jigs; they just plain inhaled 'em.

Black jigs and yellow jigs emerged as my favorites for largemouth, with yellow the springtime favorite and black good all year.

On the Beaver Creek arm of Kentucky's Lake Cumber-

land, I got another good jig lesson. It was early spring with water high and muddy. In a boat ahead of us, an old-timer slammed a yellow spinner against the bank and caught bass. So what's so surprising about a yellow spinner producing in dingy water? And why is this safety-pin spinner such a fish catcher today?

Study it with an open mind. The spinner had a hook and some dressing and a — well, sonuvagun! It has a moulded leadhead and body. And we add the famed single-spin to the jig family — weight, hook and trimming.

Further jig experience led me to green and brown as choice colors for smallmouth water. Bounced off rocks in the normally clear and deep impoundments, those brown-green jigs apparently looked enough like crawfish to satisfy any hungry bronzeback.

Spreading the gospel on jig fishing isn't easy, however. Virtually every bass fisherman has confidence in some battered old bait he's used for years, so he's reluctant to change. When he does consent to try jigs, they're usually given a half-hearted and brief effort before Old Faithful is tied on again. The angler forgets that he's been fishing Old Faithful for three or four hours without a strike, so he gives up on the jig after a half-dozen casts.

The cure for that is to take no lures along except a handful of jigs. Then you have no choice. It's a crackerjack way to learn how to use jigs productively. Basic in learning is to remember that unless the rod tip is used to maneuver it, the piece of lead and a hook does nothing. It is lifeless. But by varying the speed of retrieve, and by manipulating the rod tip, the angler makes the inanimate piece of lead and feathers come to life.

An added bonus in jig use is in economy. They can be molded and tied easily and making them is a great way to occupy some of those non-fishing evenings when the snow piles high outside. The last batch I tied cost 1 1/2 cents apiece — and that same jig sells for 35 cents in our local tackle stores. Labor involved, plus middleman and sales-outlet markups, make the difference.

While the same basic leadhead and hook are used, in varying weights and sizes, the dressing is restricted only by the imagination. Plastic worms or plastic grubs are excellent additions. Feathers can be used in creating a bulky lure or a sparsely dressed lure. A tiny spinner can be added to the hook itself, or used ahead of the basic jig to make a spinnerbait.

The combinations and the methods of using them are endless. But best of all, the lowly jig is one of the greatest fish-catching lures ever used by a fisherman to catch bass.

— 1974 BASS FISHING GUIDE

> *Combinations and methods of using jigs are endless, which helps put them among the greatest fish-catching lures of all.*

STEVE DANIEL'S JIG SYSTEM

By TIM TUCKER

A jig with a pork or plastic trailer is a super big-bass bait, even in Florida . . .

When Steve Daniel moved to Florida's Lake Okeechobee a couple of years ago, he brought with him the weapons he used to catch bass in his home state of Tennessee and elsewhere in the country.

Included in an arsenal good enough to garner a coveted spot in the 1985 BASS Masters Classic® were a variety of jigs. Daniel promptly began to experiment with those jigs on Okeechobee, where he intended to begin a guide service. "Experiment" is the proper term, because Florida bass fishermen rarely fish a jig in their shallow, weed-laden lakes. In fact, most didn't believe a jig-and-pig would even be retrievable below the Georgia line.

On one of the first days that Daniel began trying a jig and pork-chunk combination, Lake Okeechobee yielded a pair of bass that topped the 9-pound mark.

"I knew I had something. I knew then that a jig-and-pig would be productive in Florida," Daniel says. "But I really wasn't surprised, because I knew you could fish a jig anywhere in the country and catch fish around any kind of structure or cover. It's a really good big-bass bait."

Daniel, who earned one of the highest finishes ever by a Classic® rookie when he placed fourth on the Arkansas River in 1985, is a versatile angler with many talents. He can fish every lure effectively, from a deep-diving crankbait to a Do-Nothing Worm. He has proved his abilities on waters as different in nature as Lake Mead in the west and Tennessee's Chickamauga and Nickajack.

But he credits a major portion of his success to his ability to fish a variety of types of jigs and to the systematic approach he has developed to cover almost every conceivable condition.

"I am really crazy about jig fishing," says Daniel, who now makes his home in Clewiston, Fla., where he guides out of Roland Martin's Clewiston Marina. "When you have the confidence in jig fishing I have, there is extra anticipation every time you fish it, because you know it's such a great big-fish bait. That anticipation keeps you on your toes.

"And the jig itself is such a versatile bait, regardless of what you use as a trailer. You can fish it so many different ways. I might throw it on a drop-off, into a brushpile or over a log and work it real slow across the bottom. Or I might jig it vertically over a piece of deep structure. It's a good lure for finding fish, because I can cover a lot of water with a jig when I swim it slowly. I fish a worm and a jig pretty much the same way, but I'll fish a jig more often.

"I fish a jig around any type of shoreline cover, especially where there might be crawfish, which is what a jig really imitates. It's also good in rivers for fishing drop-offs and tailwaters with plenty of current. A lot of people don't like to fish current with a jig because it's not easy to do. But if you find areas below dams where crawfish are plentiful, you'll catch a variety of fish — largemouths, smallmouths and spotted bass. I think it's the most effective lure you can use below a dam."

Included in Daniel's jig-fishing system are five combinations: plain jigs (with no trailer), the jig-and-pig, a jig with a spring lizard, a jig and (plastic) crawfish and a small hair jig with a tiny pork chunk. Each has its own applications, although Daniel doesn't limit his jig choices exclusively to certain conditions.

The jig-and-pig combo is probably his favorite.

"It's a good bait for hot weather in that it's a big-fish bait and big bass are lazy, especially the middle of summer. Crawfish are easy prey for bass because they don't move very fast. Even when it's real hot and the fish aren't very active, bass will hit a crawfish when they would pass up other food," he believes.

Daniel's most productive jig-and-pig combination is a brown jig with a black No. 11 Uncle Josh pork chunk. "But I try to match my jig-and-pig colors with the prevalent colors of crawfish," he adds. "For example, in the springtime, they'll have a greenish tint to them, so I use some green in my jigs — black-and-green and black-and-chartreuse."

A significant portion of Daniel's success throughout the year comes on a brown jig tipped with a black plastic spring lizard, a homemade, twin-tailed trailer that resembles Burke's Split Tail Eel.

For Daniel, a prime clearwater combination is a brown jig teamed with a brown-and-black Ditto Fire Claw trailer. "It's a real good bait in clear water where the fish can get a good look at your bait before deciding whether to hit it," he explains. "This combination resembles a crawfish more than any other."

A productive but often overlooked smallmouth lure is a brown-hair jig coupled with a tiny, black Uncle Josh No. 101 pork chunk, which is about 1 1/2 inches long. "This is a super smallmouth bait in rivers," Daniel says. "It's one of my favorites for fishing below a dam."

A jig without a trailer has a place in his system, but Daniel has limited applications for it.

"I seldom use a plain jig, but it's a good bait for fishing real deep and vertically jigging it like a spoon," he says. "Out west they call it 'shaking.' You just drift through an area of deep water and just barely shake it vertically. I don't use a piece of pork on the end of it because that makes it slower to fall and slower to fish."

Generally, Daniel fishes a heavy jig, usually a 5/8-ounce version. He says he needs the heavy jig to work the bottom, which is his approach about 75 percent of the time. The heavy jig enables him to keep in good contact with the lure (which makes it easier to detect a strike) and, he says, "the fish don't seem to care how heavy it is."

Daniel admits he fishes jigs on line heavier than most other anglers use.

"I use a line as heavy as I can get away with," he says. "Even if I'm fishing reeds in real clear water, I'll use 25-pound-test line. The only time line size seems to matter is in open water, where it definitely does make a difference. But as long as you're around a lot of brush or reeds or any kind of cover, you can use heavy line."

Presentation of the jig is critical in clear water especially, Daniel says.

"Lure presentation is the part of jig fishing in which a lot

Although Daniel's favorite jig colors are black and brown, he often matches them with the prevalent colors of crawfish, a major food item for big bass. Photo: Tim Tucker

of fishermen fail, particularly in real clear water," he adds. "In dingy water, you can fish right on top of the fish and flip to them.

"But in clear water, you need to back off and learn to pitch your jig into the water without making a big splash. That's especially important if there's a lot of fishing pressure on the area and the fish are spooky. Presentation means everything in that case. You need to be as subtle with it as you can be."

Finally, Daniel reminds us that jigs are enjoyable — and easy — lures to fish.

"If you went out and bought a 1/2-ounce jig and a bottle of No. 11 pork chunks, you'd be set up to fish anytime of the year, under a variety of water conditions and in many types of structures and have good success," he says. "Any fisherman of any skill level can catch fish on it. I don't think any other bait can beat it."

— DECEMBER 1987

JIG FISHING
WITH A MASTER'S TOUCH

By BOB GWIZDZ

*Lonnie Stanley is a master at making
and using leadhead
jigs for bass . . .*

Lonnie Stanley has fished well enough over the years to qualify for three BASS Masters Classic® championships. But when the world-finals get underway, he usually has a tough time.

Stanley himself recognizes the problem. To borrow a phrase from football, Stanley hasn't "danced with the one that brung him."

Put another way, Stanley has forsaken the bait that made him successful — the leadhead jig. The Huntington, Texas, lure manufacturer has used a jig of his own creation to boat plenty of fish during the fall and spring months of the regular-season BASSMASTER® Tournament Trail.

But by August, when the BASS Masters Classic® is held, Stanley, like most anglers, has put up the jig and gone with more conventional hot-weather bass baits.

"One of my problems has been not having enough confidence in our own product," says Stanley, whose lead-headed, rubber-skirted bass baits predominate in tournament pros' tackleboxes. For too long, he's relied mainly on spinnerbaits and crankbaits in warm water.

Stanley has changed that. Now he's beginning to go to the jig regularly in the summer, too. He employs several techniques for warm-water jig fishing that are a bit different from those used by most anglers.

"During the summer, you can use jigs two or three different ways," says Stanley. When bass are hiding in open spaces beneath hydrilla beds, most fishermen in his part of the country tie on 9/16-ounce jigs, trim some of the rubber out of the skirt to help it penetrate the weeds, then pitch the bait into little openings in the hydrilla. Most use plastic trailers in the summer.

Stanley's own method of penetrating the hydrilla — one he learned from well-known Toledo Bend anglers Larry Nixon and Tommy Martin — involves fishing vertically, primarily. It resembles deep-water doodle-socking, but in weedbeds. The secret, he says, is being able to figure out the best places to fish in a hydrilla bed.

"You have to learn to 'read' hydrilla, just like any other cover," he says. "Bass relate to the weeds the same way they do the contour of the bottom. Usually the thickest hydrilla will be growing up on a hump, and that's usually where most of the fish are."

While Stanley's doodling technique employs a rather heavy jig in rather heavy vegetation, he turns to a different pattern for scattered weedbeds. He swims the jig in sparse grass.

"I use a small jig, and I let it fall until it hits the top of the grass — either hydrilla or coontail moss — and then I swim it through and over the cover," he explains. "As the jig swims over the top of the grass, bass come up and hit it."

Apparently the bass are suspended in the vegetation, feeding on baitfish that seek sanctuary within the weeds.

While those weed-fishing techniques seem to have bolstered his success in summertime, Stanley didn't need much help in the other seasons. His mastery of cool-water jig fishing is well-established.

That's because Stanley has long believed that jigs are the top bass catchers for the cooler seasons. "Nothing can beat a jig from October through April. At least south of the Mason-Dixon Line, the jig is the best bait there is those eight months," he says. "Up north, jig fishing is good from the time the water thaws out until it freezes up again."

For year-round jig fishing, remember these tips from one who is among the best at making and using leadhead jigs:

• Fish a jig slowly. "I like to fish it super-slow. Some of the times I've done best in tournaments is when I can 'finesse' the fish into hitting the bait. I'll throw it out there and shake it in one place, not moving it more than a foot for 20 seconds."

A variation of that finesse technique is what Stanley calls "rattling brushpiles." Cast the jig into a brushpile, let the line drape over a branch and then move the bait up and down in the same place for as long as a minute. "The fish sees it but won't take the jig until aggravated enough to strike," Stanley says. "That's my favorite type of jig fishing."

• Learn the pitch-cast. Too many anglers continue to ignore the increasingly popular pitch-casting technique, an adaptation of flipping that doesn't require getting quite so close to the fish.

"The fishing public will find out in the next two years that pitch-casting is tremendously important," he says. "Even now, if you can't pitch-cast, it's your own fault; all it requires is practice."

Fishing pressure is the main factor dictating the pitch-cast. "Years ago on a Saturday there might have been 300 boats on a lake. Now there's 3,000. You can bet that just about every good-looking spot on a lake has been fished by somebody before you get there," he believes. Bass become spooky, and getting close enough to flip a jig to them — 15 feet or less — will ensure that they won't bite. But a jig can be pitched, using the same low trajectory and quiet entry as flipping, from 30 feet away.

Big jigs attract big bass, especially when the lures are adorned with trailers such as pork-rind frogs.   Photo: Bob Gwidz

In pitch-casting, Stanley holds the jig in one hand and the rod in the other. He dips the rod tip, then raises it as he lets the jig go. As the bait moves past the rod tip, he lets it pull line off the reel. He adjusts the height of the rod tip to keep the bait 6 inches or so above the water. When that jig gets close to its target, he raises the rod tip slightly to cause the bait to drop silently into the water.

• Pay attention to jig colors. Although Stanley manufactures other baits, he insists that jigs will outfish other lures simply because they mimic preferred food items — crawfish and bream. He's experimented with shad-colored jigs, but has not found them to work as well on bass as the standby patterns.

"I've never been to a lake yet where a crawfish color — orange, brown or pink — or your bream colors — blue, red, purple, black — won't catch fish," he declares.

He says his multicolored jigs make a tremendous difference in fishing success.

"It's funny that there have been a million colors of crankbaits and spinnerbaits, but only two or three colors of jigs. When we started developing these jigs back in 1979," he recalls, "we'd go out and test various colors, and we were surprised at how important color could be. We'd fish a rockpile, for instance, where a black/brown/pink jig would catch 40 fish an hour. Then we'd switch to a black/green/chartreuse jig and catch only nine an hour. Then we'd go back to the black/brown/pink and start catching 40 an hour again."

The key to selecting proper jig colors is contrast, Stanley says. He prefers brighter colors in muddy water, softer contrasts in clear water.

"When fishing on Sam Rayburn one time in the back of a cove where the water was stained quite a bit, a black/green/chartreuse jig was killing the fish. When we moved out to the points, a distance of maybe 300 yards, the water cleared up, and the same jig wouldn't work any longer. But when we tried a jig that was toned down — just black and green — we again caught lots of fish.

"I know it seems that we're getting real technical — saying that six strands of colored rubber make the difference between catching fish and not, but it does," Stanley says. "It's the same with any bait — break up the pattern of the bait, and you're going to catch more fish."

Nowadays, Stanley rarely fishes the old standard jigs of yesteryear, solid black or brown. He may use a single color on the skirt, he says, but he always uses different-colored heads, weedguards and trailers — a solid-black jig with a green head, a green weedguard and a green pork trailer, for example.

"I've had real good success with a black jig with a chartreuse head, weedguard and pork . . . in fact, I don't know if you ought to write that. That's one of my tricks," Stanley says.

As to which color combinations anglers should use, Stanley says three factors must be considered: "One is flash, another is to imitate a certain bait, and the third is the confidence factor. If you have something you're confident in — if you think it'll catch more fish — chances are it will."

And nobody has more confidence in a jig than Lonnie Stanley.

— JANUARY 1987

GUIDO HIBDON'S MICROJIG SYSTEMS

By TIM TUCKER

A B.A.S.S.® pro from Missouri is stringing heavyweight bass on ultralight jigs . . .

Guido Hibdon will never forget Alice.

Before his wife gets upset, it should be noted that Alice was a 10-pound female bass with which Hibdon became well acquainted during Super B.A.S.S. IV on Florida's St. Johns River.

"I could see all of the fish I was catching that day," the veteran bass pro from Versailles, Mo., remembers. "There were three bass in one place that would have weighed 10 pounds apiece.

"In fact, I broke one of them off twice in one day. The first time she hit and ran around the trolling motor and broke off. So I waited for about 30 minutes and went back and tried again. Somebody had put a little stick in there to mark the bed and she ran around it and broke off again. And she was still on the bed the next day. I would go by and wave at her.

"That was Alice."

Hibdon left Palatka, Fla., without catching Alice. That's not the significance of the encounter. The importance of their regular meeting for several days was in how he had attracted her attention.

Not to mention the attention of other big bass throughout the country.

Guido Hibdon thinks small.

Hibdon, a two-time winner on the BASSMASTER® Tournament Trail and former qualifier for the BASS Masters Classic®, is one of the few anglers to have mastered the art of fishing tiny microjigs for big bass. And he has proved that the miniature lures produce in bass waters from Lake Mead in Nevada to Georgia's Lake Lanier and the St. Johns River in Florida.

In Super B.A.S.S. IV, his microjig system produced 48 pounds, 11 ounces of bass, good enough for fourth place. Even more impressive was his victory in a national tournament on Lake Lanier in which he weighed in 50 pounds, 4 ounces of bass — in just two days of fishing.

"This is not something a lot of guys have learned to do well," Hibdon says. "It's not the easiest way to fish or the easiest technique to master. But it's worth the effort to learn.

"It's an excellent bait for deep water and shallow water. But it takes patience because it is finesse fishing. It's something I like to do because I know that in a tournament there aren't 90 other people doing the same thing. That's why I enjoy it."

Hibdon's idea of a small, but deadly weapon is a 1/32-ounce Gitzit Jig, although he occasionally uses a 1/4-ounce model. The Gitzit, made by Bobby Garland's Bass'n Man Lures in Arizona, is an ultralight, plastic, hollow-bodied jig that seems to breathe as it falls or is pulled through the water.

He usually fishes the little lure on 4- or 6-pound-test line, but occasionally ties on 8-pound-test line when fishing for big bass, like on the St. Johns River. For the most part, fishing microjigs on ultralight line requires the touch of a surgeon.

"You certainly get more strikes with light line," Hibdon explains. "That's because the fish can't see it as well. I've always figured that you have to get the strikes before you have to worry about catching the fish. If I use 8-, 10- and 12-pound-test line, I believe I cut my strikes just about in half. If I can get the strikes with these little jigs, I'll worry about catching the fish later. Maybe that's all in my head, but that's the way I've fished for years."

Hibdon uses spinning tackle for his finesse fishing. His rod is a Phenix boron, the Don Lovino's Doodling Rod model. "You can set the hook hard with 4- and 6-pound-test line and if you've got your drag set halfway right, you can jerk as hard as you want without breaking the light line," Hibdon says. "This rod has that much give to it. I don't know of very many rods on the market that you can do this with."

On the surface, it would seem that hooking a decent-sized bass with the tiny hook of these microjigs would be a challenge. But Hibdon insists it's not.

"It's not hard to hook fish with this little jig, even though the hook is small," he explains. "The fish usually eat it.

"It's a No. 4 hook, which is like a perch or crappie hook. But if you can get any part of that little bitty hook in the bass, it's yours. These hooks are needle-sharp. They will penetrate bone, so you can land big fish."

Fishing microjigs on light line not only requires patience, but concentration, as well.

"With a jig this small, it's very important to watch your line constantly," Hibdon says. "You'll never feel one of them hit. You have to be aware of the very instant the line stops. A lot of times, it will stop and quickly begin moving again.

"That means a fish is on. And then is when you should set the hook — never set it on the stop. That's when the fish is grabbing it the first time. When the lure moves again, it has already turned and sucked it in. You have to have the patience to wait until the bait moves to set the hook."

Once the hookset is made, Hibdon cautions that even more patience and finesse are required for battling big bass on this light line.

"You've got to be patient when fighting the fish," he says. "You can't horse it to the top. You *hold* a bass more than you *fight* it. The key is to let the fish play itself out. It doesn't take that long. As long as you hold tension on the line, the fish will work its way up."

Although he has experimented with microjigs in all types of water clarity, Hibdon says clear water is where the tiny lures are most effective.

Clear water calls for light-line/finesse fishing," he explains. "The clearer the water, the better this works.

"Most people use 8- and 10-pound-test line and that's extremely light line to them. But that isn't light line to me. In clear water, light line is 2- or 4-pound-test line. You can land

some awfully big fish on 4-pound-test — super-big fish.

"It's vital to fish microjigs very slowly," he says. "If you're fishing a 1/32-ounce bait and you lift it a foot with the rod, it might fall 10 feet in deep water. So you do very, very little lifting. It's strictly a matter of moving the boat around as you fish it. The boat's movement gives subtle movement to the jig; you really don't have to put much action on the jig at all, other than the basic retrieve."

Fishing these tiny jigs requires an attitude adjustment of sorts.

"You have to realize that you'll be making shorter casts than normal," Hibdon says. "You're fishing right around the boat. A 20-foot cast would be a long cast. Any longer and you can't control what the jig is doing. You can't let that much line out and fish effectively. You have to keep in constant contact with the bait."

Fishing for bass with microjigs has put Guido Hibdon in the money in a lot of tournaments.
Photo: Gerald Crawford

In clear water, the choice of color for jig bodies makes plenty of difference, according to Hibdon. "I use smoke colors 90 percent of the time. In Florida, a smoke with copper-and-red flake has been real effective. On Lake Mead, I use smoke with blue-and-silver flakes. These color combinations reflect a lot of light."

Although Hibdon has won a considerable amount of money on the magical little lures, he admits that microjig fishing is so much fun that he'd use them even if they didn't sweeten his bank account.

"I could fish different baits and I could fish heavier line, but I prefer to be doing something different from what everybody and his brother is doing," he says. "That's the reason I fish these little jigs on light line. There's a lot of sport in it.

"I won a tournament on Lake Lanier with over 50 pounds of fish, and every one I caught was on light line. I wasn't doing anything special, except that it was something nobody else was trying.

"That's what separated me from the rest of the fishermen. I had 50 pounds and the second-place guy had 18 pounds. But the others just couldn't, or wouldn't, do what I was doing. A lot of guys knew exactly what I was doing, but they didn't have the experience in this kind of finesse fishing to duplicate it."

But you can bet that America's top bass fishermen have begun to study the basics of microjig fishing since Guido Hibdon took them to school in recent months.

—SEPTEMBER/OCTOBER 1986

Photo: Gerald Crawford

CHAPTER THIRTEEN

SPOONING STRATEGIES

There's something about the metallic flash of a shiny spoon that puts a gleam in a bass's eye.

SPOON-SHAKING FOR BASS

By TIM TUCKER

Here's how Florida's Larry Lazoen catches huge bass from heavy cover . . .

The black spoon skips across a seemingly impenetrable mat of peppergrass and slaps the surface with every turn of Larry Lazoen's reel. Without pausing, he makes another long cast across the top of vegetation so thick that small birds and animals could walk on it.

The rhythmic slapping sound begins again, but it is suddenly interrupted by the sweet music that only a bass enthusiast can appreciate. In between beats, the 1/2-ounce Johnson spoon simply disappears, enveloped by an explosion of grass and water.

Despite the unnerving nature of the vicious strike, Lazoen calmly plays the bass and strong-arms it toward the surface. After several seconds, the bass tires and Lazoen trolls over to it. A little gardening is in order. Having picked his way through the weed tangle to the fish, Lazoen locks his thumb firmly under the bass' lower jaw and pulls it into the boat.

Inside the mouth of this 5-pound-plus largemouth he finds a well-buried Johnson spoon. This fish was so determined to ambush the bait that it had inhaled it, peppergrass and all.

Unfazed, Lazoen unhooks the fish and drops it gently overboard. He's seen it all before.

"That's what happens with this technique," he says as he fires another cast across the jungle-like vegetation. "It seems to agitate them like nothing else."

The technique is called "spoon-shaking" and it was devised by Lazoen, one of the premier guides on Lake Okeechobee as well as one of the country's top tournament bass pros. Lazoen, who lives in Port Charlotte, Fla., and also guides in salt water, is one of a very few anglers to qualify

for the BASS Masters Classic® through both the pro tournament circuit and the B.A.S.S. Chapter Federation system.

His spoon-shaking is a variation of weedless-spoon fishing that has paid handsome dividends in Lazoen's career. In addition to several Florida tournament victories, the technique has played a big role in helping to secure both of his Classic® appearances.

In his first Classic, the 1984 event on the Arkansas River, Lazoen finished fifth — then the best performance ever by a Federation representative. But he never would have gotten the opportunity to compete in fishing's most important event without the help of his spoon-shaking technique.

The trick produced fish throughout the long and grueling road that Federation anglers must endure to qualify for the Classic. Its greatest moment was in the Southern Division tournament, when it produced 51 pounds of bass and lifted Lazoen into the Classic as the top angler on the division's winning state team.

Spoon fishing in vegetation is basically a simple affair. Many thousands of largemouths have been caught by fishermen simply tossing out and winding in a weedless surface spoon, but through years of experience on Lake Okeechobee, Lazoen devised a spoon technique that has paid off in weedy lakes and rivers from Florida to New York.

In the standard retrieve, the spoon runs just below the surface, bouncing off submerged or thin surface vegetation. But that technique often isn't very productive (or a very enjoyable way to fish) in extreme heavy-cover situations such as matted hydrilla and peppergrass or large fields of thick lily pads.

In those situations, even a weedless spoon has difficulty coming through the vegetation. But with Lazoen's spoon-shaking technique, it doesn't have to penetrate the grass, yet it is consistently productive. The spoon simply skirts across the top of the vegetation and creates a commotion as it does.

It is a faster and noisier way to work an aquatic spoon.

"When I'm fishing grass that isn't very thick, I'll run a spoon under the surface like everybody else," Lazoen says.

"But this technique works in heavy cover where there's very little else you can throw."

Lazoen uses a long (6-foot, 10-inch) rod, heavy line (20- to 25-pound-test) and a 1/2-ounce spoon adorned with a plastic-grub trailer.

The long rod is important. After he makes a lengthy cast, Lazoen begins to retrieve the spoon and keeps his rod tip high to ensure that the nose of the lure stays up as he pulls it across the grass. He uses a quick retrieve, similar to that of a buzzbait, but with one major difference.

As he reels the spoon, Lazoen constantly shakes his wrist, which makes the lure slap the top of the weeds and water at regular intervals. The sound it produces under water must be either enticing or aggravating, because the bass respond to spoon-shaking with amazing aggression.

"I think the speed of the spoon causes a reaction-type strike rather than a hunger strike," Lazoen explains. "They hear it coming for so long because it's beating the water as it moves toward them. Once it arrives, they nail it, even if they have to "blow" through the grass to get it."

Lazoen theorizes that the rhythmic noise of the spoon also makes it easier for the bass to draw a bead on it.

The most productive size for this technique is a 1/2-ounce spoon, Lazoen says, because it casts farther and has more hooking power than the 1/4-ounce size, yet it comes through the vegetation easier than the 3/4-ounce version.

Lazoen's favorite spoon color is black. It produces on both clear and overcast days, he says. His trailer choice is a yellow, flat-tailed grub like the Mann's Swimming Grub, although he says a rubber skirt of the same color also will produce.

It's a slight variation of an old, traditional way to catch bass in weeds. But Lazoen's spoon-shaking has a place and a purpose in weedy lakes throughout the country.

— MAY 1990

Larry Lazoen uses heavy line and a 1/2-ounce Johnson spoon tipped with a Mann's Swimming Grub. The rhythmic noise during the retrieve makes it easy for bass to home in on the spoon.

Photo: Tim Tucker

THIS YO-YO AIN'T CRAZY

By MAX HUNN

***Slab-type jigging spoons aren't common in the Sunshine State.
But, yo-yo spoon fishing looks like the coming thing —
when it turns cold down South . . .***

Most BASSers wouldn't pack a 3/4-ounce jigging spoon for Florida. Slab spoons and shallow water don't mix.

Only a yo-yo would do it! Les Wachter looked at this "yo-yo fisherman" and wondered. He wondered if it would work.

Wachter is a transplanted Yankee fisherman who migrated from "up nawth" to Florida to become a fish-camp operator on Lake Talquin. He's quite familiar with vertical fishing techniques for deep-water reservoirs, yet the proposal of yo-yo fishing in late December in Florida's waters startled him.

It was understandable. What I'd suggested was jigging a 3/4-ounce hunk of lead — a slab-type silver spoon with a single treble hook — up and down in Lake Talquin.

He didn't question the technique. The efficiency of spoon jigging in cold, winter water is regarded as a sure-fire system. But, he wondered, would it work in Florida? The system was spawned to catch tightly bunched largemouths in man-made reservoirs — huge lakes, where water depths of 60 and 70 feet are common.

Only well-diggers think that deep in Florida.

The Sunshine State doesn't offer deep-impoundment fishing. Talquin, for example, has a few places that are 40 to 50 feet deep near the dam on the Ochlockonee River. Otherwise, the "holes" are mainly 15 to 30 feet deep where the old river channel twists and turns across the 9,412-acre lake, which is located in the Florida Panhandle near Tallahassee.

However, there were very solid reasons for proposing such off-beat Florida tactics. I'd been fishing on Lake

Seminole near Bainbridge, Ga., before dropping in to see Wachter at the Lake Talquin Lodge. At Seminole, I'd been introduced to spoon-jig fishing. Ol'Sem is another impoundment, termed by some a "big shallow farm pond," not considered suitable for this type of fishing.

But, Jack Wingate and Jerry Sims insisted we say "howdy" to yo-yo fishing. We didn't break any records. We did catch fish, and Bassmaster Bob Gibson of Cleveland, Tenn., provided the clincher in the chilly 30- to 40-degree weather when he landed a 5-pound largemouth with this system.

After hearing of the Seminole success, Wachter was all for experimenting. Talquin, while somewhat smaller, is a similar reservoir.

Only a few hours of daylight were left, but there was no point in postponing things. The water was cold. The forecast was "no change for tomorrow," and I had to go home the next day.

We headed up the lake. The destination was the river channel that twists and turns like a demented snake. We found it, but even in the channel, we couldn't find any holes deeper than 18 feet. As I studied the depthfinder, I wasn't so certain this jigging would work; at Ol'Sem, we'd jigged 25 feet of water.

On the other hand, if bass didn't have deeper water, where else could they go — but to "the deepest" they could find?

We spent an hour and a half fruitlessly yo-yoing the silver spoons, and trying to stay on the twisting channel edge. Spring Creek in Lake Seminole was child's play compared to trying to follow the twisting path of the Ochlockonee River over Lake Talquin's bottom.

It was getting late. Halfheartedly yo-yoing the spoon, I started to say, "Let's call it quits. " But suddenly, the rod almost was jerked out of my hand!

Startled, I hollered, "Watch out! This one's no butter bean."

The ensuing moments were a Harry 'N' Charlie comedy of errors.

First, Wachter tried to reach the net, forgetting his spoon was in the water. The net was tangled under his tacklebox. Then, he realized, his line was a hazard to me as the bass lunged toward the stern.

He cranked in rapidly and not only retrieved his lure but also my line. I managed to hold my cool and the fish. In a couple of minutes, the bucketmouth surfaced, and Wachter — having untangled the net — slipped it under the fish. That bass weighed only 4 pounds, but had made every ounce count, cold weather or not.

Dusk was close. We eased our way to camp through the submerged stumps for which Talquin is famous. There was more than suspicion now that yo-yo fishing would work in this Florida lake, and that perhaps it would work elsewhere if anyone bothered to try.

Still, I had reservations. I checked with such knowledgeable Florida Bassmasters as Tony Cox, Fed Wilson, Buck Bray and Bill DeLisle. They'd heard of the system, but never tried it in Florida. They weren't even certain what the Hopkins-type of slab-jigging spoon looked like.

It was Cox who provided the clinching evidence. He guides on Lake Talquin and fishes for fun when not working. (See "Will the Real Lake Talquin Please Stand Up?" Sept.-Oct.1978 BASSMASTER® Magazine.)

He promised to test the idea, if he could find a spoon. They're not widely stocked in Florida tackleshops. Obviously, he did. A week later, I got an enthusiastic letter and photo.

Cox wrote: "On 14 February (1978), the day after I talked to you on the phone, I caught this 8-pound bass and six more between 3 and 4 pounds each by jigging the slab spoon as you suggested.

"I was over a tight school of fish suspended 2 feet off the bottom in 23 feet of water. The water temperature was a cold 49 degrees. I had no strikes on the worm in that school. Maybe you have something here."

What intrigues me, in addition to Cox's success, is the belief that yo-yo fishing will work in other lakes in Florida, during extremely cold weather. Such conditions existed the last two winters (1975-76 and 1976-77). Florida's shallow lakes cool fast, and reach water temperatures in the 40-degree range.

There's every indication that yo-yo fishing in Florida probably will follow the same pattern it has on Georgia's Lake Seminole. Until the winter of 1975-76, spoon jigging was almost unknown on Ol'Sem. It still isn't too widely

used. Several factors contribute to this situation. One, there are fewer anglers during the cold weather. Second, the word hasn't been too widely spread. And, old methods are sometimes hard to change.

Slowly, Seminole's BASSers have been converting to the yo-yo technique. Basically, it's the same as used in deeper impoundments, but there are slight variations. A depthfinder may or may not be useful because of the heavy debris on Seminole's bottom, particularly in the productive Spring Creek area.

"Sometimes a depthfinder produces," explains Sims, "but there's an awful lot of junk on the bottom, and you get false readings. However, over a clean bottom or searching deep water over the creek channel, particularly around bends, the fish show up."

This same debris that confused the depthfinder readings also caused Ol' Sem anglers to learn to jig through the treetops. In some impoundments, it's only necessary to jig down to the treetops. In Seminole, you have to jig through the sunken trees. And, there're plenty of them in or out of the channels. It also makes fishing challenging. The odds are often in the fish's favor.

While yo-yo fishing will work with tailspinner Little George-type sinking lures, this type isn't as successful in Seminole as the Hopkins-type slab spoon.

As Sims explains, "I prefer to use the Little George-type when hunting fish. It casts easily. But when fishing directly over the side of the boat, I prefer the Hopkins-type. It sinks rapidly, and has a different flash in dropping."

A George-type design tends to foul and hang up when spoon jigging. The elongated slab-lure fouls, to be sure, but because of its design, can be jiggled, and the weight of the lure acts as a "log knocker." In most cases, you can free the elongated spoon by jiggling it. Both types are used, choice depending mainly upon type of bottom.

To further reduce hangups, most BASSers clip off the forward hook on the treble, converting the spoon into a two-hook affair. Seminole's experts have found most fouls with a slab-type lure are caused by the forward hook. Some argue that the chances of hooking a bass are reduced one-third. Theoretically, that is true, but it's also a fact that you reduce fouling possibilities by one-third. You can't have everything.

Wingate says, "The flutter spoons don't work because they hang easily due to their erratic descent. In other words, they flutter and don't drop straight down. From what we've experienced, the spoon has to drop straight down, and fast."

So, if you're heading to Florida this winter, don't leave your jigging spoons behind. There are some lakes where yo-yo spoon fishing works. And, particularly if recent winter weather trends continue.

—NOVEMBER/DECEMBER 1978

How Jack Chancellor Fishes Jigging Spoons

By TIM TUCKER

Heavy, lead jigging spoons can be deadly on all sizes of bass, any time of year . . .

The jigging spoon has gotten Jack Chancellor out of more jams in crucial times than any other lure. You could call it his "rescue lure." He does.

Consider the biggest moment of the Phenix City, Ala., angler's career when he won bass fishing's most coveted title, the BASS Masters Classic® in 1985. America's bass-fishing public knows he won the tournament on his unique Do-Nothing Worm. But very few realize it was a jigging spoon that bailed him out during a frenzied final day.

Although he held an 11-pound lead entering the final round, Chancellor began to sweat seriously when his best spot, a sandbar drop-off, produced just two small fish by the time midday approached. Current in this part of the Arkansas River had ceased, and rendered his Do-Nothing technique worthless and aptly named.

Remembering past river-fishing experiences when the current disappeared, Chancellor tied on a jigging spoon, moved deeper along the sandbar and caught a keeper bass within a few casts. He went on to catch two more sizeable fish and secure his place in B.A.S.S. record books.

One of the experiences he reflected on when that Arkansas River sandbar had him stumped was another Classic three years earlier. On the second day of competition on the Alabama River, Chancellor didn't have a fish at 11:53 a.m. He put aside his Do-Nothing worm, pulled out a jigging spoon and, within seven minutes, caught a 7-fish limit.

"I was on a breakline that dropped from 18 to 20 feet, and I could feel a bass bumping my Do-Nothing, but I wasn't able to catch it," Chancellor recalls. "I picked up a rod that had a spoon tied on it and dropped it straight down under the

boat. It never even touched the bottom.

"I caught that fish, unhooked it, and dropped that spoon into the water again. I caught 11 bass in seven minutes on that jigging spoon — which has to be some kind of record. That's the kind of fast and furious action a jigging spoon is capable of. But it didn't surprise me. I've done almost that well many times on West Point Lake near where I live. A jigging spoon is the fastest way I know of to catch fish."

Although a heavy jigging spoon like a Hopkins spoon or Chancellor's own Jack's Jigging Spoon can outproduce many other lures at times, even some of the country's top bass pros don't know how to fish it properly. It certainly isn't the glamour lure of the BASSMASTER Tournament Trail.

It's an easy bait to fish, says Chancellor, which makes it surprising that some dedicated anglers haven't bothered to master its use. There are few similarities with the weedless surface spoons popular for fishing shallow grass.

Many misconceptions exist about the simple bait.

Most anglers consider its use to be limited to fall and winter, for example. True, bass are most likely to be "bunched up" during those seasons, but Chancellor has found the jigging spoon to be productive almost year-round.

The exception is just before, during and after the spawning period, Chancellor says.

It's especially productive when bass are schooling on the surface. Chancellor likes to cast it past the point where fish are hitting shad on the surface. Then, as soon as it hits the water, he retrieves it fast enough to make it skip across the top of the water. When it reaches the spot where fish are breaking, he stops reeling and lets it sink. Most strikes occur

Jack Chancellor once caught 11 bass in seven minutes on a jigging spoon.   Photo: Don Wirth

at that point.

Another misconception about the jigging spoon is that it is not a big-bass bait. While Chancellor says the lure most often attracts bass in the 1- to 2-pound range, his largest spoon-fed bass weighed 9 3/4 pounds.

Chancellor refers to the jigging spoon as a specialty bait, one that is better suited for fishing bottom-contour structure like drop-offs, humps, roadbeds and sharp breaklines. The lure is much less effective when fished around such structure as stumps, standing timber, treetops and the like, he says.

Because his favorite way to fish the lure is by vertically jigging it over such structure, boat positioning is crucial.

"If I get on a breakline that drops sharply from 15 to 30 feet, I'll put the boat near the breakline in 30 feet of water and pitch the lure 7 or 8 feet from the boat toward the shallower side. Then I'll sit there and hop the lure all the way back to the boat. If I don't find any fish, I'll ease the boat farther along the breakline until I get on top of some fish."

Chancellor's retrieve rarely varies from the hop he refers to above. Using a 6 1/2-foot stiff casting rod (no special reel is needed for fishing jigging spoons, he says), Chancellor raises the rod tip sharply to make the 3/4-ounce spoon hop up off the bottom. He then allows it to flutter to the bottom. He watches his line and concentrates intently as it does. This is the time when most strikes occur — on the fall. Once the spoon hits bottom again, he repeats the hopping motion and

eventually works the lure back to the boat.

"It's amazing how much ground you can cover doing that," Chancellor adds. "Put your trolling motor on low and hop that spoon and you can cover an awful lot of water. That will surprise a lot of people who think the jigging spoon is a slow lure to fish."

Chancellor avoids fishing jigging spoons in rivers with a considerable amount of current, believing there are better tools for catching bass in moving water. But there are times when it is difficult to get a lure down to deep-water fish in that situation.

One little trick has paid big dividends while fishing deep in current situations.

"On a river like the Arkansas River, where there's a lot of current, I've had to add a little more weight to my spoon," he explains. "Instead of switching to a bigger spoon, which does not work well on smaller fish, I take a Slinker (a unique type of bullet-shaped worm weight), which Doug Hannon designed for Burke Lures, and I put my treble hook on it and connect it to the spoon. That makes it heavier, but it doesn't hamper the action of the spoon or the hooking ability of the lure."

If you fish a jigging spoon enough to clear away some misconceptions about the misunderstood lure, you may find that it can be your "rescue lure" as well. It works for Jack Chancellor.

— FEBRUARY 1987

HOW TO BE
THE BOSS IN MOSS

By MORRIS GRESHAM

*Certainly, there are many excellent weedless lures used by BASSers,
but this "floating spoon" is something special
in the thick, green stuff . . .*

Y ou can throw this special surface spoon onto the bank, and drag it back through anything without getting hung up," Raymond Smith declared. "And it will catch bass!" The aggressive angler's remarks were music to the ears of this fisherman, who often has gazed longingly upon a maze of surface vegetation without results. And Smith's belief is not idle observation. He backs it up with results. The 31-year-old DeSoto, Texas, Bassmaster has earned a reputation as a tough competitor. He has won many club championships and placed high in open tournaments.

Smith understandably kept the "special spoon" a closely guarded secret. His strong finish in the fourth annual Muscular Dystrophy Tournament on Sam Rayburn Reservoir, however, ended the secrecy. During the April, 1978 competition, which was dominated by worms and spinnerbaits, Smith clung steadfastly to the special spoon throughout the two-day event. His tenacity produced two limits of bass that averaged 2.9 pounds each. The catch earned the second-place prize, a bass boat and custom trailer. Smith finished just 1.10 pounds behind winner Jerry McMullen.

Smith's "secret weapon" appears innocuous enough. At first glance, the Moss Boss resembles an overgrown teardrop spoon with a billowing skirt. Its spoonlike appearance, however, is the only similarity between a Moss Boss and any other weedless lure.

That's for certain. The Moss Boss is "weedless"—but the hook is totally exposed! There are no wire guards or soft-plastic protectors to impede the strike of an anxious largemouth. The lure's weedless nature relies on its shape, balance and built-in soft landing. The high-riding Moss Boss isn't con-structed of the traditional metals used in other spoons, but of low-density acrylic.

Why Lure Differs

"It's so buoyant that it almost floats," Smith says. "The hook assembly gives it just enough weight to sink slowly. This bait rides with a high front during the slowest of retrieves, and contacts the weeds with only the rounded, slicker portion of the lure body. The overall effect allows a Bassmaster to pull a Moss Boss through cover impossible to work with any type of metal spoon."

Smith emphasized his point with long casts into almost impenetrable mixtures of willowleaf grass, coontail moss, scum and soup. By conservative estimates, fewer than 2 percent of his casts resulted in any fouling of the lure. But more importantly, many of those casts produced spectacular strikes as eager largemouths engulfed the surface crawler.

Certainly, there are many fine weedless lures used successfully by Bassmasters; such as the Johnson Silver Minnow, Weed-Wing, Herb's Dilly or the Timber King Spoon, to name a few. These type baits work well in scattered to medium cover on actively feeding bass. Their heavier metal construction, however, incorporates certain limitations.

Relatively fast retrieve speeds are required to keep a heavier lure above the vegetation. The "speed factor" increases proportionately according to the density of weed growth. The unfortunate side effect of a speedy retrieve is short strikes from sluggish fish or from bass that misjudged their attack in the low visibility of the heavy cover.

The Moss Boss, on the other hand, may be teased along slowly — a nearsighted bass can zero in on it. This plastic floater extends the casting scope of the persistent angler to reach for bass in areas that rarely see a lure. Thus, it adds another dimension to the average Bassmaster's summer bassin'.

"The Moss Boss gives the shallow-water fisherman a chance at big bass even during hot weather," Smith flatly believes. "Big bass primarily seek cool shade and cover during summer months. Heavy growths of moss and grass offer these basic ingredients. Good oxygen content in heavy vegetation will hold dog days' bass in water as shallow as 2 to 3 feet."

Spectacular Strikes

Topwater strikes in such areas are frequently spectacular. Bass "blow" through the grass. Their action seems designed to kill the lure and blast a hole in the grass at the same time. Then, they turn to suck in the exposed bait in almost the same instant, often completing the maneuver before the startled fisherman can set the hook.

"When a bass hits, you've got to hit it back instantly," Smith emphasizes. "You've got to move the fish quickly to keep it out of the moss."

That's the normal routine. But as the case with most bassin' tenets, there are exceptions, such as Smith's close friend, Troy Edwards of Denton, Texas, who has fared well in tournaments with the Moss Boss.

"Fast hook-setting is normal with the Moss Boss," Edwards admits. "But I have seen days when I had to fish it kinda' like a plastic frog. That is, hesitate a second and hit 'em like it was a worm. Maybe they were just hitting it cautiously or sideways or something, but the quick hookset wouldn't work."

Regardless of how soon he strikes, the BASSer should move swiftly once the hook has been driven home. Get the fish's head up, then maintain a high rod tip. Use the bass' body as a planing surface to slide it across the grass or "scoot it through the mess before it buries up," as Edwards puts it.

Such techinques, understandably, require stout tackle; pool-cue-stiff rods and unyielding line. Despite every effort, occasionally you'll hang large bass that tangle in the grass tight enough to frustrate "Superman." Then, there are two options: (1) rely on the rod's backbone and the 20- to 25-pound-test line to pump the bass out slowly, or (2) move the boat to the fish.

Smith says, "I'd suggest forcing the bass on out. Most will finally emerge with a huge wad of grass attached, and you won't spook other bass in the area.

"If it's a big bass and fouled up too solidly to move, however, the only alternatives are to break the fish off or go to it," Smith concedes. "In that case, the solution is to lift the trolling motor out of the water and use a push pole. Normally, the fish remains tangled in the grass until you can dip it out, if you don't exert pressure and break the line."

According to this Texas BASSer, the most productive

retrieve for a Moss Boss is a slow, steady one — especially when working heavy, matted cover. Bass occasionally exhibit a preference for a popping lure action in scattered cover or lily pads. Generally, however, the steady wobble is best.

Lily pads, in fact, actually enable a Bassmaster to work a Moss Boss even slower, and allow the lure to be fished with the nose end dropped. You actually may choose to crawl the lure beneath some pads. Or bump a pad, then work the lure around it. The Moss Boss should crawl directly over any pad lying flat on the water.

Tips For Teasers

For those not-so-aggressive pad bass, both Smith and Edwards employ "a teaser." The teasing trailer may vary from short sections of twister-tail plastic worms, to double-twisters, to corkscrew-type pork rind. Lengths range from 2 to 3 1/3 inches, just enough to add gusto to the bait.

"The shorter length puts the bass' mouth nearer the hook at the strike," Smith says. "It improves your chance of hooking smaller bass."

He either removes the skirt or cuts it off at a point just behind the hook. The short skirt retains some undulating action, but acts primarily as a collar for the worm trailer.

Although some BASSers fish a Moss Boss with a trailer hook hidden in the twister tail, Smith doesn't recommend this rig. In his opinion, the extra hook interferes with the natural action.

"Since I use a worm trailer principally in lily pads," Smith explains, "I don't value the extra hook. Bass have a clearer shot at the lure in pads than in matted grass. A bass usually nails the lure in an opening and gets the worm, hook, lure — everything!"

The worm or pork-rind trailer adds buoyancy to an already high-riding lure that has a twofold effect on retrieves. First, the lure free-falls at a slower rate into pockets and holes in the cover, and produces a seductive flutter that improves the strike ratio at times. Secondly, the trailer tends to lift the rear portion of the lure in the water, and the nose naturally lowers. Therefore, your rod tip must be elevated to keep the nose up at slower speeds and maintain the weedless effect.

For times when a trailer hook is desirable, the Moss Boss is indeed an oddity among bassin' lures. Its weedless nature hardly is affected by the addition of an extra hook! An Eagle Claw 3/0 SS hook (No. 254SS), for example, may be slipped over the existing hook of the 3/8-ounce Moss Boss without any noticeable loss of efficiency. The extra hook swings freely inside the oversized skirt that fully covers the added stinger and helps float it in an upright, straight position.

The barb of the Moss Boss hook must be deflected slightly to pass through the eye of the trailer hook. The barb is not bent enough to affect fish-holding power, however. And the close fit holds the trailer hook in place without a need for an added retainer.

— MARCH/APRIL 1979

CHAPTER FOURTEEN

Photo: Doug Stamm

Photo: Wally Eberhart

TOPWATER TACTICS

A compendium of useful lore on plugging away at fish that are shallow.

GEORGE COCHRAN ON TOPWATER FISHING

By TIM TUCKER

This former Classic champion quietly has become one of the nation's premier topwater experts . . .

Geoege Cochran is a walking, talking contradiction to the myths about topwater fishing that we have held dear for years.

You know the myths:

• Topwater fishing is just something you do in early morning or late afternoon.

• Surface lures only work in the spring and fall, when the bass are most active.

• It takes a calm, overcast day for a topwater plug to be effective.

• With the ever-increasing fishing pressure, bass simply aren't fooled by surface lures like they once were.

Don't try to sell Cochran on these theories. The 1987 BASS Masters Classic® champion and one of the sport's most consistent anglers knows better.

"Although topwater baits have been around forever," Cochran says, "I think topwater fishing is maybe the most misunderstood type of fishing of all."

Surface fishing is easily the favorite universal technique for luring bass. Unlike other types of fishing, topwater baits provide a visual confrontation that startles and overwhelms our senses in the amount of time it takes to blink an eye. It injects the adrenaline rush that most of us commonly associate with memorable fishing trips.

Ironically, we, as fishermen, often deprive ourselves of the very excitement we crave, Cochran claims, by believing the myths that have been spread by the Joe Isuzus of the fishing world. Experiencing the thrills of topwater fishing doesn't have to occur as rarely as lunar eclipses, if you believe Cochran.

Cochran has quietly become one of the country's true surface-fishing experts. His prowess with — and willingness to use — a topwater bait largely is responsible for his eight consecutive appearances in the prestigious Classic. He has developed an almost religious belief in their appeal, which has led him to refine his system of topwater fishing into something approaching an art form.

Allow the North Little Rock, Ark., angler to dispel the myths most commonly associated with surface fishing:

Myth No. 1: Topwater fishing is only effective early and late in the day.

"Anybody who believes that is really limiting the number of fish he can catch," Cochran counters. "To me, the ideal topwater time has nothing to do with what time of day it is. I've caught some of my biggest fish in the middle of the day when the sun was straight overhead. The ideal topwater times have more to do with the conditions than the time of day."

Cochran's largest stringer in a B.A.S.S. tournament (26 pounds) was caught throughout the day on two surface lures on Florida's St. Johns River.

Myth No. 2: Surface lures are most effective in the spring and fall, when bass are most active and aggressive.

Following the BASSMASTER® Tournament Trail, Cochran fishes lakes and reservoirs throughout the country during practically every month of the year. And he can recall few tournaments in which a topwater bait did not play a role in his success. "The Classic was a prime example," Cochran explains. "I am one of the few people who have won the Classic on a topwater bait. It was one of my primary baits and it certainly helped me win the Classic."

The Classic is held in August of each year, a fact that should dispel the belief that surface lures are unproductive in the hottest portions of the summer. The only times when Cochran eliminates topwater fishing is when the water temperature drops below 50 degrees.

Myth No. 3: The conditions have to be perfect for topwater fishing to be productive. It is particularly important that the sky be overcast and the water be calm.

There is no doubt, Cochran says, that those are the ideal conditions for surface fishing, because bass have a tendency to be shallower as well as a little more aggressive in that setting. But some of the biggest fish he has caught were attracted to a noisy propellor cutting through a slight chop on the water. And he has caught countless bragging-sized bass in fairly bright conditions.

Myth No. 4: Bass don't hit surface lures as much as they used to.

"In this day and time, most people don't fish topwaters much," Cochran says. "But I catch as many fish right now as I did 25 years ago topwater fishing. People have gotten away from topwater fishing, but that is a mistake.

"If the weather is favorable and you get on a good pattern, you will catch a bigger stringer on topwater lures than you will with any other lure. For as long as I can remember, the topwater bait has been one of the No. 1 big-bass lures for me."

Although his surface system has been tested and proved on lakes and reservoirs throughout America, much of Cochran's topwater success has come on the Arkansas River near his home. River fishing, it seems, is the great equalizer when it comes to surface-fishing success.

The effectiveness of topwater lures seems to increase with river fishing, Cochran believes. The conditions don't have be as favorable. And the moving, heavily oxygenated water seems to keep river bass in an active mode.

"Rivers are excellent for topwater fishing because most of the time on any kind of river, bass live in less than 5 feet of water," Cochran explains. "So most of the time, topwater baits will work in almost any situation on rivers.

"Some of my best topwater days have come on hot, clear, still days when the fish were suspended. The fish will suspend around vegetation or other cover on the Arkansas and Ohio and other rivers. If you pitch a

An eight-time Classic qualifier and former Classic winner, George Cochran thinks topwater fishing is one of the most exciting, and one of the most misunderstood, techniques for catching bass.

Photo: Tim Tucker

George Cochran says anglers who believe topwater "myths" hurt their chances.
Photo: Tim Tucker

worm or jig around the cover, the only way the bass will hit it is while it's falling. They will be lying close to the surface, and they won't go down to get a lure. They're more likely to come up to hit a lure, so topwaters are the best choice."

Cochran utilizes three types of surface lures, which he categorizes as "darting baits" (original Zara Spook, Zara Spook Puppy, Zara Spook Pooch and Cordell Boy Howdy), "chugger baits" (Rebel Pop-R, Tiny Torpedo, Heddon Chugger) and "propellor baits" (Heddon Dying Flutter and Cordell Crazy Shad). Each have a specific application, depending on the situation.

Water clarity largely dictates lure selection for Cochran. In clear water, he prefers lures that make little noise (the darting baits). In dingy water, he uses either chugger-type lures or prop baits, using the noise to attract bass that are not able to hunt by vision alone. To select the proper size of lure, Cochran attempts to match the size of the prevalent forage fish as closely as possible.

Cochran doesn't experiment much with various color schemes on his surface lures. He primarily relies on light hues and shad colors.

"For river fishing, my primary bait is a prop bait like the

Dying Flutter," Cochran says in reference to the twin-blade stickbait. "The water is never clear, so you need to make noise to attract the fish. A lot of mornings, I will adjust the spinners on a Dying Flutter real loose and fish it like a buzzbait. I throw it around weeds or brush and use a straight, steady retrieve. The bass will hit it like they do a buzzbait, too. But with two sets of treble hooks, you don't lose many fish like you do with a buzzbait."

Successful surface fishing begins with the equipment involved. Cochran stresses that the choice of rod is critical. Many of the so-called topwater rods on the market are much too stiff to handle a variety of surface plugs, he says, particularly the small lures. A good topwater rod should combine plenty of backbone with a limber tip.

Cochran designed a series of five topwater rods for Daiwa that are suited for fishing surface baits ranging from heavy plugs and buzzbaits to the lightest balsa baits. The rods vary in length from 5 1/2 feet (for short-range target-casting) to 6 1/2 feet (for fishing large grass flats).

Line size depends on the size of the bait — with no regard to water clarity. Cochran uses 10-pound-test for the smallest baits and moves up to 14- or 17-pound-test line for the larger lures like the Zara Spook or Dying Flutter.

Pinpoint casting and the proper retrieve are the basic elements of topwater fishing that are obvious, yet overlooked by many anglers.

"With topwater fishing, you should cast the bait about a foot past the target," Cochran tutors. "It is important to bring it as close by the cover as possible. You have to really concentrate during that first couple of feet of the retrieve. If you are around a fish, it will usually hit in that first foot of the retrieve. If I don't have a strike after the first couple of feet, I reel it in and make another cast elsewhere."

Cochran is asked to describe the most common mistake that fishermen make while topwater fishing.

"That's easy — not having enough patience," he says. "When the average fisherman thinks there is a fish around a piece of cover, he gets in too big of a hurry. But that's the wrong approach.

"When I throw a topwater bait, I usually let all of the ripples disappear and let the lure settle there for about 15 seconds in one spot before I ever move it. That gives the fish time to swim out of the cover and get under the bait about the time you get the slack out and begin to move it. I can't stress enough how important patience is with topwater fishing. Don't get in too big a hurry, because you only have to work the bait a foot or two before reeling it in and making the next cast."

Breaking the traditional rules of surface fishing helped pave the road to success for George Cochran. Follow his lead by not falling for the myths involved in topwater fishing.

— JUNE 1990

BORN-AGAIN
TOPWATER TACTICS

By REX GRADY

There's reason to believe that a bass jumps on a topwater bait because it looks too good to resist. Try these proven techniques...

Topwater fishermen are the true Bassmasters. They're artists with artificials, the craftsmen of casting. For a topwater fisherman, the challenge is to create, to wiggle life into dead wood.

To a skilled topwater angler, a "stick bait" isn't a stiff stick. True, simply reeled through the water, it performs nothing. It pulls like a stick. Yet, in the hands of a master, like Don Latta, the torpedo-shaped plug has more moves than John Travolta on Saturday night.

"The bait won't do nothing until you do," explains Latta in his backwoods drawl. "You gotta manipulate the rod tip to make it come to life," says the Forsyth, Mo., angler.

Latta is a BASSer known to veteran, wrinkled anglers in the Ozark hills. His fame is local. In his heyday, the bright lights of the professional tournament trail had yet to be switched on, and bass anglers didn't show-and-tell, as now. Yet, Don Latta was a "pro" even in the late 1950s for eager students like myself, and a fellow named Charlie Campbell, who's now made the pro grade.

"How come you catch so many big ones, when we can't get nothin' over 2 pounds?" That's the opener of a two-part question directed often at Don Latta. "What's your secret?" is the second part of the interrogation.

The personable Latta would pull the curious fisherman aside, as if to share his most closely guarded secrets. Then, with a straight face say, "There's a simple answer. Big 'uns is all I fish for!"

Topwater fishing is something most modern-day Bassmasters only dabble around with in the summer months, at daylight and dark. However, there's a revival taking place that is sparking renewed interest among the bassin' clan.

There's an obvious reason. As Don Latta would say, "For all the fun of pullin' in a big bass off the bottom, there just ain't nothin' like bein' an eyewitness to a lunker largemouth slammin' into a topwater lure.

"Especially," he'd quicky add, "if you're on one end of the line, and that lunker is on the other!"

Fishing patterns change, too. Game and fish departments are experimenting with increased size limits on man-made reservoirs as a bass management tool. Also, the jump from a 12- to 14-inch minimum size limit on the national Bass Anglers Sportsman Society circuit is altering some fishing styles. More BASSers are adopting the attitude of, "the bigger the bait, the bigger the bass."

Do big topwater baits catch many lunkers? "If you're dead set on catching a 10-pounder, you might as well be fishing a broomstick," said Latta. "When one that big decides to hit a surface lure, you'll be too old and feeble to reel it in anyway."

But, if you'll settle for 2- to 6-pound "lunkers," the Ozark BASSer winked, "they're a patsy for topwater lures."

As to why hawg-size bass don't hit on top, Latta judged, "it's probably a combination of bein' wised up, too fat and lazy. Once a bass starts drawin' Social Security, it's rarely in the mood for fresh air."

Latta had an uncanny sense of humor. And, his Ozark hillbilly act was mostly just that. Although he did write a book, *Secrets Of A Big Fisherman*, Latta credited most of those secrets to the fact, "anybody that fishes as much as I do is bound to learn something, accidentally."

But, credit is due Don Latta. Many of the "born-again

topwater tactics" are methods perfected with stick baits by Latta and other Ozark angling legends — over a quarter of a century ago. In the countless times that Latta has fished, I can't recall seeing him fail to catch one or more lunkers during any trip. The fact he always "caught big 'uns" made him a master among BASSers over the 30 years of fishing in the White River Lake Country.

"Maybe I've been out in the sun too long," he'd say, "but I figure most of the time I've got more goin' for me with a topwater lure than the underwater route."

The Latta logic was explained as: "The books say bass hit artificials for only three reasons, (1) hunger, (2) curiosity, (3) anger. That bein' the case, a topwater bait can rouse 'em into hittin' for all three.

"Whereas, I got a notion that big bass don't get overly riled up at the sight of an underwater lure — they're more apt to hit it outa' curiosity or 'cause it's supper time. So, I'll take the topwater bait as the ticket for bringin' a bass' temper to the boilin' point."

And, Latta claimed, "Believe it or not, one of the best times to get a line-buster bass mad is smack dab in the middle of summer when it's sleepy and grumpy."

Latta would swear on a stack of anglers' Bibles that he caught more lunkers in August "in the daytime on topwater baits dropped on top of bass that had tempers as sizzlin' as the weather."

That's not to say that the "dog days" are the best times to go topwatering for largemouths. Normally, the best time is reserved for early spring or late fall, when big bass are most actively feeding.

However, Latta had a hot-weather formula that still applies for finding lunker hangouts. "First, it's gonna want comfort, and this means cooler water. So, its hideout is probably in water deep enough for comfort durin' the daylight hours. A logical spot would be a sharp drop-off along the main channel.

"Second is cover. This might be an undercut bank, a bush, tree, weeds or a drift. And, just because you can't always see the cover don't mean it ain't down there somewhere.

"Last, a big bass wants a spot where it can grab a meal without too much huffin' and puffin'. Here again, the main lake channel would fit the bill, for this is the route the shad schools take. Shad roam up and down the lake, and a big bass knows if it sits tight they'll pass its way sooner or later," concluded Latta.

There's reason to believe that a bass jumps on a topwater bait because "it looks too good to resist." Retrieve patterns and techniques can be perfected that will — more than any other lure — provoke a bass into hitting a "stick bait" out of curiosity, hunger or anger. The following tactics will produce from early spring to first signs of winter.

THE STICK BAIT — Figuring that big bass like a big mouthful, select a big bait, ranging from 5/8 to 1 ounce. This type lure — an old Heddon Zara Spook — resembled a cigar shape that has no built-in action. With practice, the stick can be made to walk, waltz and wiggle over the surface. (See, FIG. 1, "How To Walk The Dog.")

There are three characteristic topwater movements. Baits, like the Dalton Special or Creek Chub Darter, slide or dart sideways. Poppers, such as the Cordell Carrot Top or Gilmore Jumper, are made to duck under, then pop right back to the surface. More advanced topwater pluggers have perfected the "walk-the-dog" pattern with a Zara Spook or Zig Zagger. With the correct rhythm, the lure slips from side to side.

Up to this point, you probably can recite from memory most of the instructions you've heard on topwater techniques. And, most of the "heavy stuff" has been about how-to "walk and talk" a surface lure. This is the basic move for other advanced methods to be discussed. Each new step adds a different move with the lure. To be a skilled topwater fisherman requires hours of practice. If you use the proper equipment, and are willing to practice, these techniques will add lunker notches to your hawgin' stick.

TACKLE AND TECHNIQUES — A 5 1/2-foot baitcasting rod is preferred with a 5-to-1-ratio reel, spooled with 12- to 17-pound-test mono. Spincast reels will work, open-face spinning outfits are more difficult.

The grip is most important. Experiment with three choices. The standard method is the "long grip" with the left index finger around the trigger on the rod handle. This grip puts all the pressure on your wrist. With the "clutch grip," wrap your left hand around the reel to hold it. This style grip is soon tiring and irritates your hand. The "front grip" is the least fatiguing.

Hold the rod in front of the reel with the left hand and four fingers under and around, and the thumb grasped over the top. Cushion the side of the reel with the hand. Rest the rod handle against your inside left forearm. With this hold, the forearm anchors the wrist and kicks the handle back into position each time you pump the rod tip.

Start the retrieve with the rod tip positioned to either the left or the right side and pointed toward the water. Experiment, and you'll find either left or right, or vice versa, is easier to work the lure for you.

To start a stick bait walkin' and talkin' for bass, crank out most of the slack, but not all of it. Jerk the rod tip in sequence straight away from the bait and on an even, lateral line. This movement has to be a pretty good lick. Remember, you're jerking out slack, getting a heavy lure up prone on the surface, and starting a sharp action with the plug.

If the lure doesn't "start" working, the problem can be too much line slack, too slight a jerk or heavy line that drags in the water. Establish a rhythm by jerking the rod tip with the same stroke, and keep the tip level.

REEL CORRELATION — There is no precise jerk-to-reel ratio of retrieve. You don't have to crank the reel handle every time the rod tip is jerked. Hit a happy medium. You must allow some slack in the line, or otherwise the lure can't turn off course and "walk" to the side.

After practice, the more slack you can work, the wider the bait will swing from side-to-side. In the beginning, start with a medium stroke; don't jerk too fast or reel too rapidly. Do concentrate on a consistent stroke with the rod tip and controlled line distribution.

There are any number of sizes of stick baits. The smaller model enables a beginner to establish a simple rhythm, sooner.

FUNDAMENTAL ERRORS — If the lure ducks under, you're jerking the rod tip down — keep it level. This pulls the bait over the water. The bait doesn't walk? It just pivots as it's retrieved. Give it more slack, your line is too taut. When the bait jumps upward, instead of leveling off in a glide position, the rod tip is being jerked upward. Here again, steady the retrieve.

A longer cast with more line to work is helpful in learning to walk a topwater bait. This retrieve is a little like patting your head and rubbing your stomach. You'll overconcentrate on working the rod tip, and forget to crank. Also, remember that the lure will not jump and switch direction unless the jerk is sharp enough.

The walking step can be varied. For the widest swagger, work more slack. To create surface action — turbulence and noise — make sharp, quick jerks with little line slack. At times, you'll want to start and stop the lure.

STOP-AND-START TACTIC — This is a comeback move after you've raised a big fish but it missed the lure. Cast past the spot, and to one side where the fish hit. Take up the slack, and walk the bait to the spot. Then, stop the lure, allow it to run and drop its tail. To stop and start the retrieve, crank up the slack and position the rod tip forward in the start position.

BUMP-AND-RECOVERY MODE— Learn to mimic nature's creatures. Imitate a small animal trying to get out of the water, such as a frog's habit of swimming to a log, rock or pad — bumping the structure with its nose — then climbing out or holding motionless in the water.

With the bump and recovery, you'll hold your breath in anticipation of a smashing strike. A big bass can't turn it down. Try this tactic along a dock, rock ledge, log or fallen tree or any object in the water.

Cast parallel to the object if possible. Start the bait walkin' and struttin' down the side. Opposite the spot you suspect to harbor a lunker, give the bait a hard jerk as it turns toward the

FIG. 1. THE PRO'S TOP TACTIC: WALKING THE DOG

The Zara Spook is a big topwater bait that has been around a long time. In the hands of a skilled angler it can produce some amazing bass action. This bait has no built-in action. All the action is produced by the angler, depending on the variation in the type of retrieve.

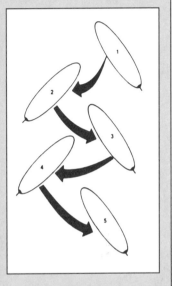

This is the lure Charlie Campbell fished to lead Missouri to the 1974 National Bassmaster Team Championship at Table Rock lake. The lure is manufactured by Heddon. It is a heavy bait, and should be worked with heavy tackle; i.e. a fast-retrieve baitcasting reel, 5 1/2- to 6-foot "worm rod" with a fast tip, and 12- to 17-pound-test monofilament line.

The basic retrieve for the Zara must be mastered before variations can be introduced effectively. This is commonly called "walking-the-dog" type of retrieve. It is produced as follows:

With the lure dead in the water, rod tip at 15 to 25 degrees from the water, and slack out, jerk the rod briskly but smoothly about a foot. This will cause the lure to slide forward and to one side. While this is happening, take up line with the reel so that the original rod position is attained. Then repeat the steps. This will cause the lure to slide forward and to the opposite side, etc.

Here are some tips that will help produce the desired action: The knot recommended is a clinch or improved clinch pulled down very tight so it holds the position on the underside of the screw eye at the nose of the plug. The knot position is important. With this placement, when the lure is pulled, the nose of the plug tends to ride up over the water instead of diving. A notch (groove) also can be filed in the screw eye to secure the knot in position.

Variations of this retrieve are the straight-walking retrieve, which can be used without pauses at various speeds from a slow, very gentle regular retrieve to a very brisk, splashing retrieve that sounds like a small bass striking baitfish on the surface. Any combination of soft and harsh movements can be used and broken up in any manner by pauses, covering a retrieve for most conditions and fish preferences.

— REX GRADY

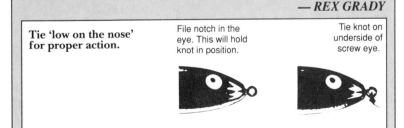

Tie 'low on the nose' for proper action.

File notch in the eye. This will hold knot in position.

Tie knot on underside of screw eye.

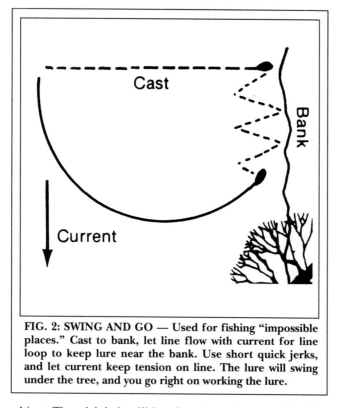

FIG. 2: SWING AND GO — Used for fishing "impossible places." Cast to bank, let line flow with current for line loop to keep lure near the bank. Use short quick jerks, and let current keep tension on line. The lure will swing under the tree, and you go right on working the lure.

object. The stick bait will butt into the structure as if trying to climb out and failed. Stop the retrieve action, let the lure rebound. It will bounce off, turn half around, then drop its tail. Don't bat your eyes. This is when a bigmouth will suck that bait under!

CHANGE OF PACE — A faster, sharper walkin' step creates more water turbulence, noise and improves the range for a bass to hear or see the lure. This change of pace is used to bring a bass up for the second time, which is difficult on a surface strike. Also, a change in tempo might tempt a bass

from a spot fished first with the standard retrieve.

Start with the regular, long-walking step through the target area. When the bait is worked slightly beyond the object, move the rod tip forward and speed up the tip action. Use short, quick jerks which reduce the radius of the walking pattern. The lure will belch water on the pivot, leave a mass of bubbles in its wake and simulate a creature leaving the area in haste.

THE SWING AND GO — This tactic is employed to fish hard-to-reach spots along creeks, rivers or under overhanging brush. Natural forces such as wind, current or tides can be used to an advantage here.

In this situation, cast to the bank away from the "impossible target," and pull off several feet of slack line. (See FIG. 2.) The downstream current (wind or tide) will mushroom the slack line into a half-moon bow as the lure drifts to the target. As the current tightens the line, start the pumping action with the rod tip. Use a slow-pace tip action, do not retrieve the lure and allow the current to absorb the slack line. The surface bait will walk right under the overhanging branches. The current will present the lure perfectly.

Naturally, you might wonder what happens with all that slack line, when a bass socks the lure? This brings up a point on hooking bass with a big surface bait. First, be certain the bass has the lure in its jaws — before you jerk. The rule is "don't jerk the instant the fish hits, jerk one second later." However, if bass repeatedly miss the side-stepping bait, slow the retrieve and shorten the rod stroke. Make the target easier for the fish.

These topwater tactics aren't new. They've been practiced for years by skilled topwater craftsmen. With today's increased interest in "lunkers," they're born again and just as effective.

— JULY/AUGUST 1978

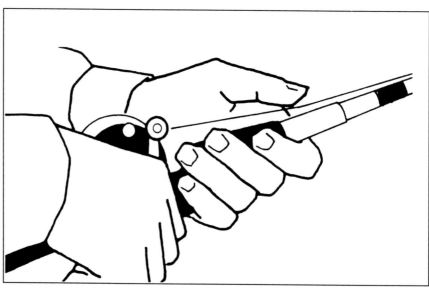

FIG. 3: The front grip helps a topwater angler "walk the lure" without tiring the wrist and hand. The rod handle should rest against the forearm of the holding hand.

SURPRISE A HAWG WITH A FAKE FROG

By MORRIS GRESHAM

Fishin' a rubber frog is made to order for thick moss or grass. Here's how to turn your old crawly creature into a surefire bass catcher with a new stinger-hook hawgin' system . . .

During a lull in the bassin' action, Bassmaster Jim Wells of Garland, Texas, leaned over my open tacklebox. His eyes quickly inventoried its contents with the natural curiosity of most serious BASSers.

"That's a doggone good lure there," he said, indicating my collection of Snag Proof Frogs.

"Yeah," I agreed. "They definitely draw a fantastic number of strikes in moss and weeds, but I miss quite a few fish at times. That delayed hookset can be a little tricky."

"Delayed hookset!" he exclaimed and examined one of the off-the-shelf frogs. "No wonder you have problems. You haven't added 'stinger' hooks to them."

A close look at one of Wells' frogs quickly explained his terminology. His modified frog sported an extra 5/0 hook protruding from the rear with the point up just below the top line of the body.

Perhaps a brief explanation of the old frog-fishing method is in order. The twin hooks on the standard frog hug each side of the hollow plastic body to impart a weedless effect to the lure. An unfortunate side effect is that the body also partially protects the hooks from the bass at the instant of the strike, making a quick hookset almost impossible. With the standard frog, a slight delay is required to allow the bass to mouth the soft frog before setting the hook.

This delay presents a problem for some anglers, not all of them novices. It normally takes a great deal of practice and instruction before the exact timing of the hookset can be mastered. Too long a delay, or one too short, and the result is the same: the frog whizzes past your head, leaving only a massive swirl as evidence of the missed strike.

The stinger hook extending behind the body of the modified frog cures the timing problem. The exposed hook allows the immediate hookset used with any similar topwater lure. Although the hook extends well beyond the plastic body, its orientation retains the near-weedless effect of the basic lure.

The extra hook not only adds a menacing look to the frog; it transforms it from a so-so productive lure into a deadly and effective bait.

A minimum of materials is required to add a "stinger" hook to a Snag Proof Frog: a 5/0 worm hook, nylon thread, and any good epoxy cement.

Begin by putting a slight bend in the shank of the 5/0 hook. Determine the position and degree of bend by placing the hook on the underside of the double hook on the fully assembled frog. When the 5/0 hook extends approximately 1 1/4 inches past the double hook, bend its shank at the fork of the double hook until the point of the stinger hook is approximately 1 1/4 inches below the top of the plastic body. Remove the hollow frog body and legs from the double-hook assembly. Place the 5/0 hook shank along the underside of the double-hook shank and bind the hooks together by wrapping with nylon thread. After tying off the thread, mix the epoxy cement and apply it to the wrapping with a toothpick. Apply the cement liberally but smoothly to provide complete protection for the thread. When the cement has dried, reposition the legs carefully over the enlarged hook shanks. Reassemble the hook-and-legs assembly into the hollow body. Be sure that the lead weight is still in place inside the frog's body cavity. The weight is essential to keep the frog floating in an upright position.

— 1976 FISHING GUIDE

TOPWATER BASSIN' PRO

By CHARLES SALTER

For the topwater fishin' fan, here's some "must" reading. A veteran Georgia surface plugger shares his hard-learned tactics and techniques . . .

Calvin Jaynes walked into the bait shop-cafe at Jack Wingate's Lunker Lodge on Georgia's 37,500-acre Lake Seminole and found the owner dozing in his favorite chair near the cash register behind the counter. One of the South's most highly skilled anglers with a topwater plug, Jaynes tried his darndest to keep a straight face and remarked in a serious tone, "Jack, you told me a lie!"

Puzzled and caught off guard, Wingate quickly sat on the edge of the big chair and asked, "What was that, Cal?"

Jaynes said,"You told me there were 10-pound bass in that area."

"There weren't any 10-pounders?" Wingate asked, slowly breaking into a grin.

"Nope, just 9 1/4 pounds," replied Jaynes, and both men burst into laughter as Wingate reached for his camera.

Superintendent of engineering and auditing for an insurance company in Atlanta, Ga., Jaynes, 51, who resides at nearby Conyers, had driven to the southwest Georgia reservoir late in March 1975 in hopes of hooking a trophy-sized black bass on a surface lure. He had been ribbing Wingate for two days about not sending him to an area of Seminole where some big fish were in a mood to inhale a man-made imitation of a crippled minnow.

By Saturday, March 22, the very heavy rainfall earlier in the northern and central sections of the state had caused the Flint River, which flows into Seminole, to reach its highest level in a number of years. The other major river flowing into the impoundment, the Chattahoochee, also was far beyond its banks, and even the usually clear Spring Creek area had become muddy.

That morning, the wind cut a little chop on the water, and there was cloud cover, ideal conditions for surface lures, so Wingate suggested that Jaynes might find a 10-pounder in a shallow, timber-lined area just off the main part of the lake.

A local fellow drinking a cup of coffee in Wingate's cafe remarked, "They ain't gonna hit when the river is runnin' that high." Jaynes was optimistic anyway, and tied a 5-inch silver Rebel onto his 20-pound-test monofilament line.

"We were fishing in a sinkhole that had big, dead trees in it," Jaynes said later. "An alligator would come up once in a while. We guessed it was 8 feet long. My partner and I had picked up some fish, but they were hitting it with their mouths closed, driving the lure off their beds. One of those fish must have come 2 feet out of the water when it hit that thing and just bounced the lure into the air."

A big fish suddenly swirled in about 4 feet of water close to the timber, and the Georgian spotted the action out of the corner of his eye, then switched on the bow-mounted trolling motor on the Ranger to maneuver into position to cast.

"I threw it right in where the bass was, and I just moved it twice," said Jaynes. "The bass just blew a hole in the lake and looked like it was 3 feet across. The bass really nailed it!"

The fish put on a memorable show, running under the boat, then breaking water and wallowing twice before stripping off more line on the free-spool baitcasting reel. Within spitting distance were trees and logs against which the line could have been cut as easily as sewing thread.

A few moments later, Jaynes grabbed the lower jaw of his 9-pound, 4-ounce largemouth.

Few modern-day anglers are fishing for bass with topwater

plugs, a trend that Calvin Jaynes describes as an enigma.

"I cannot conceive that anybody couldn't get totally carried away with topwater fishing," he said. "My experience over the years has been that when I have had an opportunity to take somebody out and really introduce him to some honest-to-goodness topwater fishing, where the bass just blow a hole in the surface, you make a confirmed Christian out of 'em. I don't have any problem, and they wonder why they didn't do it many years ago."

The long, slender surface baits are fine fish-catchers, he believes.

"They may not get any more strikes than short, stubby ones, but I think that strike for strike you land more fish, get more hooks in them," he said. "Hands down, I prefer the old lures made 20, 30, 40 years ago. I find that no matter how much ballyhoo a manufacturer gives a new lure, if it doesn't catch fish, it doesn't stay on the market."

The most common fault that beginning topwater anglers make is getting out on the lake too late for the early-morning feeding period.   Photo: Charles Salter

Cal Jaynes' Topwater Favorites

In recent years, the Georgian has narrowed down his preferred surface baits to six: the Creek Chub Darter, Heddon Chugger Spook, Rebel, Rapala, Heddon Lucky 13, and black Jitterbug. His choice of Darter generally is either the silver flash or the yellow pattern, and, with the Rebel or Rapala, the silver with black back or the gold with black back. In night fishing on the surface, he doesn't necessarily feel that black is superior to other colors, explaining, "Mostly I use what's on the rod when darkness comes."

He explained, "I don't think color makes that much difference. Sort of like it is in football; on any given day, any team can beat any other team. I think that generally the same thing is true with lures. I have seen in my whole lifetime only two occasions I can recall when one lure, and only one among all those I had to use, consistently produced when no others would draw a strike.

"One was Heddon's Wounded Spook. We had 23 topwater lures with us. I used the lure until I got embarrassed because my partner couldn't catch anything. He was getting his dander up, so we swapped, and I gave him the lure. I thought it was him, not the lure. I switched over to the other 22 lures. Then, he got all the fish, and I didn't get a strike.

"The other time was in the TVA (Tennessee Valley Authority) system. A fellow fishing around us had a no-name lure that was a cigar-shaped affair, chocolate-brown in color. He bought it at a sporting goods store in Michigan while passing through. It was raining and cloudy, real dark. That lure consistently caught fish after fish. The rest of us couldn't catch a fish," Jaynes concluded.

The flat-bellied Creek Chub Darter has been his most productive surface lure over the years.

"It floats high and gives bass a silhouette in two directions, and it has erratic action left and right," Jaynes said. "The effectiveness of a lure is dependent upon your skill in putting the action into it.

"I don't think hard plastic floats as high. This is critical. If a wood lure is heavy, if you have to hesitate before it floats to the top, it won't produce like one that stays on top."

The Georgian's biggest largemouth bass caught on a surface plug weighed 9 1/2 pounds, and his heaviest smallmouth on a topwater lure was a 4 1/2-pounder.

Topwater Targets For Spring

In the spring, Jaynes looks for weedbeds, treetops, boat docks, boathouses, and other places that afford shade and hiding places for bass waiting to ambush their lunch.

"I found, for instance, on Lake Rabun (in northeast Georgia's mountains), a very deep, very clear lake with little cover, that the boathouses were consistently the best place to catch bass," he recalled. "That, and trees, some of which were down so deep you couldn't see them. When a fish came up in midday in July and August when it was so hot you'd just broil in the sun, they'd come from so far down they'd completely clear the water on the strike and do cartwheels."

In the springtime, he starts fishing at sunup and quits at 9 o'clock in the morning or begins casting at 4:30 or 5 p.m. and works his baits until dark.

"I think the afternoon topwater fishing lasts longer than the morning fishing does," he said. "Any given morning could be better than evening, though, in length of feeding period. There are irregular periods that occur during the day, and they can occur anytime, when the bass hit furiously from 1 until 2 in the afternoon or from 11 a.m. until noon.

"Generally speaking, daylight and dark are best," he continued, "early and late in the spring months, starting in April, and by July it comes to a standstill. Then it starts up again in September on through October and mid-November. Some seasons, several years back, on Lake Hartwell (on Georgia's northeast border with South Carolina) I caught bass all through the winter on topwater plugs when they were schooling and chasing shad right on through January and February."

After the surface temperature drops below 60 degrees, topwater strikes are infrequent, he says.

How To Work Surface Plugs

I asked Jaynes to explain how he works his topwater lures.

"That's the crux of the whole thing," he said, "the action that you give to the lure. The maximum amount of agitation with the minimum amount of forward motion of the lure is best. The line is in a plane with the eye, so the average angler has no concept of how far he moves the lure. I've seen people out there who literally moved it 2 feet every time. It moved like a torpedo through the water.

"What I'm trying to do is simulate as best I can an injured or dying fish, which doesn't move like a jet. I want to make an easy target for an old, fat bass that doesn't want to chase it all over the lake.

"At Lake Lanier (about 40 miles north of Atlanta), in that clear water, you frequently can see them. They come up behind a plug and follow it. I had one the other day, 8 or 9 pounds, follow it and you could see it open its mouth and come up to the lure and just kiss those back hooks."

Jaynes knows some anglers who twitch the rod tip twice and pause before resuming the action, but he finds it much more productive to keep the lure in continual agitation and motion across the surface. He doesn't have any quarrel with the guy who gets his kicks out of waiting 20 seconds for the rings on the surface to grow big. For Jaynes, though, the name of the game is maximum exposure with steady action.

"In essence, what I am doing is this: the rod is moved and the slack is taken out of the line, and the rod is held at a right angle to the line, and the rod is moved toward the lure. And, as you move toward the lure, you pick up half a turn on the reel.

"If it's held vertically, you have a bow in the line which takes away some of the action you're trying to put in the lure. I hold the rod at 45 degrees, move it toward the lure, pick up half a turn, which is 9 inches on the standard Ambassadeur 5000, and in the same motion, without hesitation, it is brought back. What we're doing is picking up 9 inches, and then popping the lure 9 inches forward. And, instantly, again without hesitation, the rod tip goes back toward the lure and I pick up the next 9 inches."

Work Topwater Baits Properly

If a Bassmaster gets a sizable percentage of strikes more than 10 feet from where he thought the fish should be, such as in a treetop, he's worked his lure properly — meaning the bass followed it out and decided it was what the fish wanted, the Georgian pointed out.

"If the only strikes are right where you thought the fish was, they are more likely to be impulse strikes," he said. "You know you really are in business when the fish made a calculated decision to hit the lure.

"If you give it an opportunity to follow the lure into open water where there is no obstacle to obstruct its view. . . this is consistently what has made the Creek Chub Darter a favorite with me. They hit it at the boat as much as back there at the stump. And, you pull the rod back, and they hit the lure underwater. This is the mood the fish are in. Some days they want to hit it underwater as much as on top."

During the spring when largemouths are bedding, Jaynes figures there are probably three or more "rolls" at the lure for every fish that hits; the bass, acting in a defensive fashion, are driving the lure away from the nest, and frequently when the fish are hooked, the barb has been imbedded in some place other than its mouth

The Georgian was asked how he sets the hook in the swift, topwater explosion.

"The whole episode is over probably in not more than a quarter of a second. One morning, when I was fishing in a lake near Ellijay, Ga., a hooked bass broke the line that was wrapped around a cable in the swimming area. The next morning I threw in, no strike . . . the wind had a riffle on the water and was blowing the boat over some submerged posts. I threw it over there.

"When the lure was less than 10 feet from the boat, the big bass rolled under it. I knew if I brought the lure back to cast again, the boat would be on top of the posts. I laid the rod down, picked up the paddle and gently backed it away, and the bass just came up and smacked the lure. I thought it was too late, and the bass had spit it out, but I backed up two more boat lengths, and the lure hadn't come to the surface. So, I picked up the rod, and the fish was still swimming around with that Darter in its mouth! It never turned it loose. I boated it, a 6 1/2-pounder."

Short casts work fine for a topwater fisherman, says Jaynes, who used to throw lures a long distance to his targets but finally decided he was wasting time cranking them over stretches of unproductive water back to the boat.

On Top, Clear Water Helps

Jaynes deliberately looks for clear water in 39,000-acre Lake Sidney Lanier, a deep, mostly clear impoundment that has yielded big largemouths for 20 years; spotted bass now appear to be becoming the dominant bass there.

"Clear water does not affect topwater fishing at all," he declared. "They are hitting at a silhouette, and this is the reason that color isn't significant. I think they'll hit on top in clear water when they wouldn't dream of hitting many underwater lures where they get a three-dimensional view of the lure and it actually has some color. At certain times of the day, perhaps the sunlight tends to drive them down."

One spring day, he had success catching bass on a surface lure in slightly dingy water under willow trees, but he believes they also would have struck had the water been clear. In a lake such as Seminole, he fishes in clear water and over grassbeds.

While chunking surface plugs at night on Lake Lanier, he has found the shallow, barren islands quite productive, but rarely would these areas prove fruitful in the daylight.

"I prefer not to make noise," Jaynes said. "I run the boat in so the waves go to the left and the right to a point, and I stop some distance out and turn on the electric motor. But I have had some remarkably good success with noise.

"I was fishing in Lake Rabun once when skiers and boats were going by almost constantly. I threw the lure in water around submerged trees, and the bass would blow it up. The fish get accustomed to the heavy traffic and noise."

Cal Jaynes' Lure Presentation

Sometimes on a warm day in the spring, however, a whole school of bass may rise until their backs are nearly at the surface, to soak up sunshine, and a lure that passes through the air throws out a shadow that spooks them.

How does Jaynes cast to his carefully chosen targets?

"If it is a solitary stump or tree limb or target with water beyond it, I prefer to throw out 5 feet to the other side," he said. "I start the lure back rather than let it smack on top of them. On the other hand, if it's inside a tree partially in the water and partially out, and there is a wedge to throw into, I have no choice.

"But, I prefer to let the lure fall on the water instead of driving it in there with a low trajectory and letting it smash and tumble. I don't think that gets the fish.

"If the bass is there and it's gonna hit, the odds are better than 9 out of 10 times, maybe 24 out of 25, it will hit the lure on the very first cast and first couple of feet. When I'm fishing a tree or a stump, unless I have got time to waste, I don't make

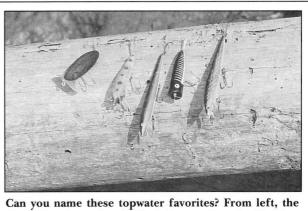

Can you name these topwater favorites? From left, the black Jitterbug, Creek Chub Darter, Rapala, Heddon Chugger, and Rebel Minnow. These are Cal Jaynes' picks, along with Heddon's Lucky 13. Photo: Rick Taylor

a second unproductive cast. If I get one bass, I'll throw back. If I get two, I'll throw back a third time. I usually don't throw a fourth time."

When fishing a river, he casts to the outside of structure away from the bank, figuring the bass are looking for means of ready escape. On the edge of a drop-off, for example, bigmouths can move quickly into deeper water for safety.

In the late spring in reservoirs, he usually doesn't find big fish in the backs of coves, but, instead, locates them out on points and around islands, from which they can move safely in any direction. After the bass have spawned, they will avoid areas in which they could be trapped.

While working a topwater lure around a boat dock, Jaynes likes to cast to the shaded side. If he can make a cast and play it along the edge, he feels the chances are excellent the fish will come out and pounce on the bait.

Best Times for Surface Fishin'?

When is the best time for a bass angler to fish with a topwater plug?

"Hands down, I want the cloudy, rainy days with either no wind or just enough to put a gentle fuzz on the water. The bass on a cloudy day stay closer to the top, and the topwater fishing lasts longer. On a rainy day, the strikes could come all day."

He says a good fisherman should be able to hook at least eight out of 10 surface-striking bass, but he warned that fast reflexes are imperative.

One day last spring while Cal Jaynes and I were casting to a fallen tree on Lake Lanier, the veteran Bassmaster enjoyed a few moments of battle with a 5- or 6-pound bass that finally cleared the water close to the boat, shook its big head violently, and tossed Jaynes' Darter into the air.

Smiling as he reeled in his lure, Jaynes remarked, "Go on your way, old fellow. I've had my fun."

— MARCH/APRIL 1976

CHAPTER FIFTEEN

FISHING WITH NATURAL BAITS

*N*othing catches bass —
especially big bass — like
the real thing.

Photo: Dave Precht

Photo: Doug Stamm

CRAWFISH: THE BAIT BASS CRAVE

By DON SHINER

There are times when smallmouth bass refuse to strike, but rarely do they cull crustaceans . . .

For most of the week we trolled, drift-fished, jigged and dredged the depths on the Big Rideau in the Rideau Chain of Lakes in Ontario. We tried almost every lure in the tacklebox in an effort to catch anything that would strike. Finally, my partner suggested crawfish for smallmouths in deep weedbeds, and, in desperation, we turned to "live bait." At this stage, I would have agreed to almost any method.

A hasty trip to shore, and the bait shop, found us in possession of a dozen lively, sassy crawfish.

It was a sheltered bay, off the main lake, where we pulled in to fish the bait. I peered down through polarized glasses for visible signs of curly leafed cabbage plants, and eventually anchored on the outer fringe of a weedbed.

My fishing companion rigged his crawfish rather quickly. I still was replacing a minnow-shaped plug with a live-bait rig when my partner socked steel into a lunker that was off and running with the bait the instant it splashed into its lair.

I glanced up in time to see the bass explode to the surface. Shortly thereafter, my buddy netted a formidable 20-inch smallmouth, as handsome a

To hold a crawfish without being pinched, grasp it along the back.
Photo: Don Wirth

bass as anyone would want.

Within an hour we had used the last of the crawfish in the bucket, but six fat bass tugged on our live chain. We had released as many more.

• **Uncovering Crawfish** — Most bait shops, on or near bass water, sell crawfish. Had none been available in the shop near Big Rideau Lake where we stayed, we were prepared to catch our own. Most all unpolluted lakes and streams are inhabited with one or more species of crustaceans. These smaller versions of the saltwater lobster thrive in the shallows and hide a good deal of the time beneath rocks or buried in gravel.

Moving or lifting the stone uncovers crawfish which are caught easily by hand. But one must be quick to do so. Crawfish are swift swimmers, escaping backward in a rapid, darting motion. Less than a half-hour search usually yields a sufficient number of baits for several precious hours of fishing.

One can catch crawfish in greater quantity in streams by placing a minnow seine downstream, and then moving rocks and rubble with a hand rake or shovel. Uncovered crawfish are washed with the current into the waiting net.

Crawfish are nocturnal. They come out of hiding at

night to move across the bottom in search of food. One can often find them after dark in shallow water with the aid of a flashlight or lantern.

Since they are scavengers that feed on dead plant and animal matter, crawfish can be baited to a spot with fish heads or entrails. After dark, it's just a matter of going to the baited spot and gathering the bait.

Larger crawfish, with their six walking legs and oversize pincer-claws, look menacing. And, indeed, they are. Even smaller ones can latch onto a misplaced finger and cause considerable pain to the owner.

To counter this, pick one up by spanning your fingers across the thorax or back so the claws cannot reach you. While holding the crawfish in this manner, insert the hook in the tail. Some fishermen break off the claws before placing the bait on the hook.

Bass, too, are somewhat leery of grabbing a large crawfish head-on, with pincers poised in a defensive position. Bass usually attack such prey from the rear, and swallow the crawfish from that position. In so doing, the claws are pushed forward and folded together to offer no resistance.

Crawfish are a mainstay in the diet of bass. Sometimes in clear water, bass can be seen with their heads pointed downward toward the bottom, grubbing among rocks to uncover hidden crustaceans.

Large crawfish are a mouthful for all but the biggest bass. The best size to use includes those of small to medium lengths, which measure from 2 to 4 inches long.

• **Care Of Crawfish** — Live bait can be stored in buckets, but, like minnows, crawfish die quickly in stagnant water. Container water should be aerated if that's what you're using to keep your bait. It is better to stow crawfish in a bucket or box with moistened leaves or moss. If kept moistened, their gills can obtain necessary oxygen from the air.

An examination of the stomach contents of bass often reveals whole or partially digested remains of crawfish, sometimes to the exclusion of other food. But there are times when bass refuse even preferred crawfish baits. During feeding sprees, however, no bass can resist a tempting crawfish, even at midday, when crawfish are usually hidden under rocks.

Crawfish are available in lakes and streams from early spring through fall. As the water temperature recedes to freezing levels in northern latitudes, crawfish burrow into the silt and become inactive. Some fishermen collect crawfish in the fall and, by feeding them occasionally, keep them alive in a container stored in the basement as bait for ice angling.

If you catch your own, unless you are selective of size, the crawfish will range from small to extra large. Most fishermen keep them all as bait. When the bait is not of uniform size, match the hook size to size of bait. Since a 3-inch crawfish is quite bulky, hooks in sizes 2/0 down through 1 and 2 are best. If the crawfish range in size, you should have two or three packages of snelled hooks of different sizes available.

Change the hook size as necessary to match the size of the bait. By fastening the snelled hook to a snap swivel tied to the line, it is easy to change from one size hook to another to suit the bait at hand.

• **Weight The Bait?** — On the day we fished Big Rideau, we were anchored adjacent to the weedbed where we suspected bass to be. It simply meant tossing the crawfish a short distance from the boat. The bait had sufficient weight for casting without adding extra lead. In fact, rather than adding split-shot or a rubber-core sinker, some fishermen prefer to attach a bobber to the line and adjust the float to keep the bait off the bottom. Given the chance, the hooked crawfish will crawl into rock crevices or hide among the weeds and snag the line.

There are times when bass will attack a crawfish, instinctively kill it, and then reject it. When that happens, retrieve the bait in short spurts to simulate an attempted escape on the part of the crawfish. Often, the bass will change its mind and gulp down the bait.

A live crawfish always is better than a dead one. If the crawfish has been mauled by a bass, and appears dead, retrieve it slowly to impart some lifelike action.

The versatile crawfish can be used with any tackle. Even the time-honored cane pole can be employed. Line of suitable weight to match the rod action is adequate. Use a leader of 6 or 7 feet when working a fly line.

Dealers usually buy live crawfish from individuals who are licensed to catch and sell bait. Some states regulate the number of crawfish in possession. Pennsylvania, for example, allows each fisherman to have 35 crawfish baits at one time.

The most satisfactory method of hooking this bait is through the tail, with hook inserted up or down to coincide with the natural curvature of the tail. If the hook is placed anywhere else in the body, it usually penetrates vital organs and kills the bait outright.

During our memorable fishing day in Ontario, the crawfish didn't last long enough to die on the hook. Not only did we run out of bait, but I had used up my supply of snelled hooks, as well. They were cut off and left in smaller bass that were released safely.

It is difficult to judge the best time to set the hook in bass that have seized crawfish or other baits. Smallmouths have the habit of taking off with them, like barnyard fowl eluding the flock. They may run only a few feet, or several lengths of the boat. Any attempt to set the hook before the run is completed results in a blank. Not infrequently, those hooked afterward have swallowed the crawfish and are hooked deep.

We had more action concentrated in one hour of fishing on Big Rideau with crawfish than we experienced at any other time during the week-long trip. Perhaps we could have enticed those bass with artificial crankbaits painted and shaped like a living crustacean. But lacking any, we resorted to the real thing. It was the bait of last resort, and the bass loved it.

— SEPTEMBER/OCTOBER 1980

TRY FROGS
FOR SUMMERTIME BASS

By JAMES RUDNICK

Breathe life into summertime bass fishing by offering the fish one of their favorite foods — a frog . . .

Summer's dog days are back. Hot, humid, no-breeze days. Each lake is like a red-hot mirror. Bass fishermen everywhere sport deep tans, empty livewells and acute cases of the summertime blues.

Dog-days bass fishing can last just a few days, or even weeks at a time. And each bass fisherman who hasn't already given up on fishing in such weather will admit the pickings are decidedly slim.

Slim, yes — but they need not be. Those who want to hook up with bass should consider the following facts: Bass still have to eat, even during late summer. Bass won't be willing to travel very far for a meal, so you'll have to put your bait up really close to any good-looking hiding spot or cover. And maybe most important, you'll have to offer the bass their favorite treats.

Frogs, for instance — real, live frogs. Almost any kind will do. Leopard frogs, green frogs, pickerel frogs. Even bullfrogs work wonders on a lazy bass. It isn't really necessary to be able to tell the difference between each type of frog . . . only that in your local live-bait shop, you pick out good lively ones — ones that tend to jump around a lot to keep from being netted are best.

Keeping frogs alive through a summer afternoon can sometimes be a problem. Putting them over the side of the boat in a minnow pail can cut off oxygen they need to survive and may even make them too warm when the surface waters of the lake are hottest.

To keep them cool and active, place a container of ice in the bottom of a minnow pail, cover it with moss and then add the frogs. The slowly thawing ice will keep them cool and ensure they'll be raring to go when they hit the water for the first time. That's what bass will be looking for — a lively frog that suddenly appears too close to pass up for lunch. It'll work almost every time.

It's also important that you know the proper way to rig a frog for fishing, a way that will keep it most active. In my home waters of Canada, a simple bobber rig seems to work the best.

You'll need a lightweight, good-quality bobber that won't take on a lot of water.

The hook should be of good quality, also, and made of thin wire — to keep the hook from making too big a hole in the frog — but firm enough to hook and hold a largemouth.

Hook the frog through both lips, pushing the hook through and past the barb. Attach a split-shot or two about 2 to 4 inches above the hook. Frogs usually hold a little air inside their lungs and the weight is necessary to pull them down below the bobber.

You'll have to experiment to find out just how far up to set your bobber. The kind of cover and the depth you think bass will be also will dictate bobber placement.

Absolutely the best spot I've found to fish a frog is among weeds, especially lily pads. Tossing a fresh and lively frog near pads is, first of all, a surprise to a summertime bass. Here's a meal — and a good-sized one — seemingly dropped in out of the sky.

If a frog is really active, the commotion almost always will entice a strike from any bass that is nearby. And a hard, fast-moving strike it is.

A bass will hit so hard and so quickly that your bobber will move 10 feet in less than a second. And that's all the time you'll have to set the hook.

— JULY/AUGUST 1988

THE CRANDALL TROLLING SYSTEM

By ROLLA WILLIAMS

Deep-trolling with big shiner minnows on a falling barometer are Doug Crandall's keys to braggin' bass . . .

When Doug Crandall, a 31-year-old house remodeler from nearby El Cajon, Calif., caught the 18-pound, 10-ounce lake-record bass from San Vicente Reservoir, he fooled the fish with a trolled shiner minnow.

A trolled minnow? That's right.

"It's all in the presentation," Crandall explains.

• "Most people want to drift with the wind, but sometimes you have to go into the wind.

• "You have to troll from shallow to deep.

• "You must troll in a straight line.

• "You've got to vary your speeds till you hit the right one, the one the fish want," says the lake-record-holder.

"And one of the biggest things I've learned in the last three years is that the barometer is the best indicator of a good fish bite," he adds.

The best fishing is when the barometer sags about three degrees. And he checks it every time he goes bass fishing.

"It's better than when it's holding. And when the front arrives, it's not good. Before the front is best."

To get his bait deep, where the big bass live, Crandall employs a mix of monofilament and lead-core line. "I don't go all lead-core line like some do," he notes.

His method is to spool 15-pound-test Maxima mono and tie 20 to 25 feet of lead-core line to the end of it. "That gets me down deep," he claims.

To the business end of the lead core, Crandall adds a 15-pound-test Maxima leader about 10 to 15 feet long. "Total lead core doesn't work," he believes. "There's no stretch to lead core. I've tried it with Dacron, too, and that doesn't work, either.

"No stretch and the fish is dead weight," he continues. "You hit a 15-pound bass plus water displacement. It breaks off and goes. If you use a loose drag to compensate, the bass takes the line into the rocks and it's gone. I let the bass run maybe 8 to 10 feet against a tight drag, turn its head and keep it coming my way." Crandall uses a 3/0 bait hook and he pins the shiner — a big one, preferably 12 inches or larger — upward through jaw, mouth and top of its head.

"That makes the bait run straight," he explains. "And it keeps the shiner from hooking up on the bottom."

Crandall has caught 20 bass over 10 pounds from San Vicente over the past two years. An 11-11 and two 10s accompanied the 18-10, and Crandall bagged a 15-10 from the lake two weeks before that eventful trip.

Crandall is not a one-method fisherman, though he prefers trolling and he'd rather use live bait.

"After a spawn," he notes, "the females are ready to gorge themselves. That's when bait fishing really scores."

To get those fish before the spawn, when they're heaviest, trolling deep with 3/4-pound shiners is Crandall's method.

You go downhill, in a straight line, vary your speed and hope for a falling barometer.

It works so well for Crandall that he has invested in a guide license, and works out of Aquatic Taxidermy, Dept. B.A.S.S., 4141 Home Ave., San Diego, CA 92105. He furnishes everything and charges $100 a day.

You can bet — after that 18-10 bass — he'll stay busy trolling, and likely on San Vicente.

— JANUARY 1980

ROLAND MARTIN'S SHINER SYSTEM

By TIM TUCKER

Getting good, fresh, lively bait is half the battle in trophy bass fishing . . .

He prepares like a general going to war.

The battle is still days away, but he has begun to lay the groundwork that will spell victory or defeat. Intent on being properly armed, he spends the week before the battle working hard to ensure success, carefully following each step of a well-drawn-out battle plan to achieve his objective.

Just call him *General Martin*.

Gen. Roland Martin, that is, and he takes prisoners — plenty of them when he goes big-game hunting for trophy bass armed with wild golden shiners.

He's known as the guy who is the most successful tournament fisherman of all time, a man who has won 14 B.A.S.S. events and almost $200,000 for his prowess with an artificial lure. But he's also a shiner-fishing enthusiast because he realizes that the live bait is the key to impressive 10-fish, 70-pound stringers he manages to collect several times a year on his home waters, south Florida's Lake Okeechobee.

Seventy-pound, 10-fish stringers. Imagine.

But by using Martin's time-tested methods of shiner fishing, the average angler can do more than just dream about such accomplishments. Borrowing the tournament king's secrets can put you within reach of what may be bassin's biggest goal.

• **Key to Success** — His techniques are simple. There's no mystery to his success. Preparation, he'll tell you, is the key that unlocks the door to success.

But Martin isn't your average shiner fisherman.

"My whole setup on shiner fishing is just so different from everybody else's," Martin explains. "There're a lot of good shiner fishermen, but very few of them go to the trouble that I go to.

"To get a 70-pound stringer, you've got to mean business. Shiner fishing is unquestionably the best way to get a 70-pound stringer. I caught several 70-pound stringers years ago at Santee-Cooper, S.C., on lures. But that's almost impossible today."

For the last 15 years, Martin has been refining his shiner techniques, adding new, often subtle twists that could make a good day a great day. The techniques he has come up with practically are infallible with the right preparation.

• **Catch And Care Of Bait** — "Half the battle is the bait," Martin says, referring to the care and hard work it takes to catch and keep bait plentiful and alive. Despite trying a variety of methods over the years, Martin admits it still isn't an easy chore.

"One thing I do differently is I believe in getting my own bait," Martin says. "Putting everything in perspective, half of shiner fishing is bait preparation and bait handling. You really have to put a lot of effort into the bait end of shiner fishing. But it pays off in the long run."

Martin prefers collecting wild shiners to using hatchery-raised shiners, which aren't as lively as their cousins and often are unavailable during peak shiner-fishing seasons. To do that, he regularly chums certain shallow-water spots on the southern shore of Lake Okeechobee and the canals around his Clewiston Marina with protein and carbohydrate foods like soybean and cottonseed cake.

Then he collects the shiners using a cast net, a tool he has grown adept at handling. Ideally, he'll have about 100 shiners for his big-bass excursion before he's through. The shiners are well-cared for in a special 50-gallon tank that protrudes from the back of his Ranger. The tank has a good aeration system to keep the minnows frisky.

Martin uses big shiners, theorizing that big shiners mean big bass, a formula he consistently validates with success. The normal golden shiner he uses is from 7 to 11 inches long, but, ideally, he likes an 8- or 9-inch shiner.

• **Tackling Trophy Bass** — For trophy-bass shiner fishing, Martin uses big flipping sticks or light surf rods, 7 1/2 to 9 feet in length. The big, stout rods allow him to cast large shiners with ease, horse a big bass out of a thick weedbed and quickly eat up an abundance of slack in the line when he sees a strike, all functions crucial to successful shiner fishing.

Roland Martin prefers an 8- to 9-inch shiner, hooked through the lips. He keeps as many rods baited as are possible and allowed.   Photo: Tim Tucker

The reels he uses are high-speed models with a 5-to-1 ratio. "And serious shiner fishermen have to have a clicker on the reel," he says. "The most important element to a serious shiner fisherman is to have a lot of good bait in the water. Naturally you're going to spread the bait around the boat and a lot of times you'll be busy on one side of the boat and you've got to be able to hear a strike on the other side. And if you can't get to that rod right away, the clicker puts enough drag on the spool to keep it from backlashing from a hard run and being pulled out of the boat."

The personable Martin believes in being heavily armed in terms of line strength as well.

"For normal south Florida fishing or anyplace where you're fishing heavy cover, I like to use 25-pound-test some of the time, 30-pound-test some of the time and up to 40-pound-test when I'm in heavy bulrushes or reeds," Martin says. "In open water when I'm fishing the edges of canals and deep holes, I'll often use 17-pound-test line. I'd use 12- or 14-pound-test if I were fishing completely open water, but we just don't fish completely open water that often."

Martin prefers big, bronze-colored forged hooks in the 6/0 to 8/0 range. He even makes his own weedguards from coffee-colored, No. 9 stainless-steel wire.

• **The Anchoring System** — An often-overlooked part of successful shiner fishing is the anchoring system, he insists. "Most people don't even own anchors like we use to shiner fish," Martin says. "But you need to be able to stop your boat. That may not sound like much, but it's important. If you're going to fish a bunch of hyacinths, you want to sneak up on the cover and stop your boat in the right position. You don't want to drift into it."

Once the proper preparation is completed, Martin says the easy part is the fishing. He has a simple method for finding fish and positioning the bait.

"My basic approach is structure-fishing shallow water," he explains. "I'm looking at how the wind is blowing, how it's pushing current into and around the points of weeds and stuff like that. Also, the pH is a big factor. By using a pH meter, which tells you the acidity and alkalinity in the water, you can eliminate a lot of water. Generally, if the pH is below 7, you're wasting your time. You want to fish areas with a pH of 7.5 to 8.5. And your best areas are the edge of the pH change.

• **Don't Waste Time** — "Once you determine you're in the right water, there's still thousands of places to fish. So, you've got to move around a lot. If you don't get a strike in 15 minutes and you've got three good shiners in the water, you're probably wasting your time. Don't rely on the fish turning on later. If you know it's a good spot, you might give it half an hour.

"Early in the morning, which is the best feeding period, you'll want to change more quickly. If you pull up to a school of fish in the morning, one is going to hit it right away. You don't have to wait very long. You have a greater problem in the middle of the day. You'll make your move less often then if you know you're on fish. I'll change positions and move about 20 times a day on the average," says the Clewiston angler.

With the proper preparation, Roland Martin, the consummate angler, can show you that a 70-pound stringer is more than just a fantasy. It's within reach.

— *MARCH 1984*

HOW GUIDES SHINE AT BIG-BASS FISHING

By CHRIS CHRISTIAN

This "shiner system" works for Florida's guides, and it can pay off for any BASSer seeking heavyweight bass . . .

When an angler becomes so captivated with his chosen hobby that he forsakes a steady job for a career as a professional fishing guide, he learns life's bitter lessons early in the game. Foremost is that regardless of his past track record, he's now expected to produce bass consistently — not just any bass, but mounting-size trophy largemouth bass.

Couple this with the fact that the guide isn't supposed to catch the fish, but rather the client, whose level of skill may range from expert to non-existent. Thus, it quickly becomes apparent that any guide intending to stay in business had best develop a system for producing good fish on a consistent basis.

A "system" of this type must be challenging enough for the experienced angler to enjoy, but simple enough for the novice to learn quickly. It must be effective under a broad range of conditions throughout the year, and most importantly, geared toward large bass. When viewed in this light, it's not surprising that the majority of Florida's successful bass guides rely on shiner fishing as their bread-and-butter technique.

While some "artificial-only" purists may look upon live-bait fishing as requiring little skill, nothing could be further from the truth. In some cases good fish are taken by less than skilled anglers who simply "soak a shiner and hope," but the overall results of this minnow-dunking approach are so inconsistent, few guides could earn a living, based on that uncertain level of productivity.

The working guides are well aware that consistent results require an aggressive approach. As the master of necessity, they've refined the equipment and techniques into a systematic approach that is every bit as demanding, and precise, as any

other form of efficient bass angling.

• **Shiner: The Guiding Light** — Guides Jim Smith and M.J. Lee, of Welaka, Fla., who work the area referred to as "the Bass Capital of the World," have earned enviable reputations for their innovative techniques on the tough-to-fish St. Johns River. Probably they account for more bass over 6 pounds in a single year than many anglers see in a lifetime. The majority of the fish are caught by clients, fishermen with varied levels of angling experience. The techniques are learned easily, and once applied can boost any BASSer's score on big bass from Florida waters.

Their techniques are geared toward larger, trophy bass. "Small bass — those under 4 pounds — are more aggressive feeders than the larger fish. They roam around a lot, and are quicker to strike than big fish. A good man with a lure will beat out a shiner fisherman, if bass under the lunker mark is the goal" says Smith. "But, most of our clients come for bigger fish. And that's what we are here to provide if we plan to stay in business.

"Bigger bass are different. They really can't compete (for food) with the smaller, more agile fish, so they develop slightly different habits. With the really thick weed cover in Florida, that's where bigger bass spend a lot of time. They'll take over a spot and run the smaller bass out," continues Smith. "Some of these holding areas are virtually impossible to work with a lure; they're just too thick. But if you get a shiner in there, frequently a good fish will hit. After that, it's a matter of muscle to get it out. The reason a shiner is so effective on big bass is that you can work a shiner where you can't work a lure."

Wrestling big bass from Florida's underwater jungles

requires specialized equipment which most guides are happy to provide. Proper tackle is of such importance that few guides are willing to trust the client's selection, and in most cases insist that the heavy-duty gear provided be used.

• **Tackling The Lunkers** — "Each and every aspect of shiner fishing is important, but the proper tackle is the most critical," adds Lee. "If everything else is working right, but the tackle is wrong, the guy is doomed to failure. Improper gear is the biggest single mistake fishermen make. It's a fine line between power and flexibility. The rod, reel and line have to balance out into a smoothly workable piece of equipment. You need the power to muscle a big fish out of the weeds, but the flexibility to cast a small shiner accurately. A rod

The shiner-fishing system perfected by Jim Smith and M.J. Lee pays off with results like this.

needs a little bit of tip action, but not so much that it collapses under stress. The power has to start at the tip and work uniformly down through the butt. A fast-taper rod with a strong butt and a whippy tip won't let you set the hook right, but a rod that's too stiff will kill you when it comes to casting."

Both guides use custom-wrapped rods on heavy, glass, worm-action blanks, Ambassadeur 5500C reels with power handles, and 25-pound-test Maxima line as their standard shiner rigs. (Factory-made rods that possess proper action are the No. 6 Speed Stick, the Bass Pro Shop HB-60 or similar heavy rods.) Surprisingly, both Smith and Lee prefer glass to graphite, having experienced a higher incidence of breakage with graphite than with the glass sticks.

Terminal tackle is simple, merely a float and a hook, but here again the guides get picky. With literally hundreds of different corks on the market, the only one they will use is the Southland No. 3 string float. This little cork looks more at home fishing for crappie, but the guides find it ideal for all but the largest shiners. Why use a small cork?

"The smaller the float, the livelier the shiner will be," says Lee." Look at it this way: how long would you last if you had to drag around a big cork like some of these fishermen use? A lot of people kill their bait just by using a cork that's too big. Also, once a bass takes the bait and starts dragging that big

cork through the cover, it's going to hang up. The bass will feel the pressure and drop the bait. Use a smaller cork and you'll catch more fish."

• **Hooking The Fish** — Hooks merit the same critical evaluation and none on the market have passed. Here hooks must be weedless and very strong. The ready-made weedless hooks are not strong enough to power down on a big bass. Those hooks strong enough are not made in weedless models.

The guides solved this dilemma, with a rather innovative weedless hook, by rigging a strong Mustad hook with a short section of a plastic worm. Since using this hook, their ratio of hookups per hit has improved by 50 percent.

The hook, a Mustad Hollow Point Beak hook No. 92671, is rendered weedless by sliding a short piece of plastic worm up the shank until it covers the eye. A toothpick is inserted through the worm and hook eye to hold it in place. The other end of the worm is slipped over the point of the hook to cover both the point and the barb.

With the short shank, offset point and wide bend, this style hook takes a solid bite and holds. The worm/weedguard outperforms the standard wire-guard models, since the plastic will give and not spring open every time the shiner rig bumps something. The wire-guard weedless hook springs open when jarred, rendering the hook useless.

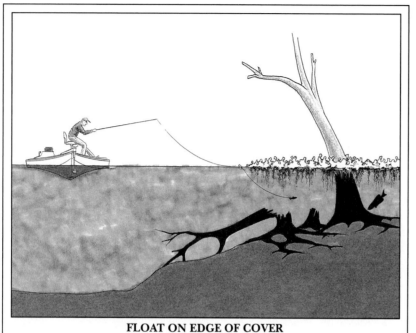

FLOAT ON EDGE OF COVER

FIG. 1 — A cork float is most effective for shiner fishing when water depth is relatively shallow, or filled with debris. The float is used not necessarily to detect a hit, but to prevent the shiner from wandering too far within its given area. When the float contacts the cover, it usually hangs and confines the shiner. Struggling against the pressure of the cork, the shiner becomes appealing to a bass. Use the smallest float possible for the size shiner.

Illustration: Bernie Schultz

Although the worm completely shrouds the hook point, getting the hook set is no more difficult than using a Texas-rigged worm. The big hook rips through the plastic and digs solidly into the fish. And once hooked, few bass are lost due to pullouts, throwing the hook or breaking it. The 5/0-size hook most commonly is used with this worm/shiner rig, but with smaller shiners, a 3/0 is preferred.

• **Handpick Your Bait** — When it comes to selecting the day's supply of bait, both guides are highly critical and actually handpick their shiners. "You've got to have a good, strong shiner that's really going to work for you," says Smith, "one strong enough to work its way into the cover, and then stay lively and kicking when it gets there."

Some shiners, depending on how they're treated after being caught, are in such bad shape they'll go belly-up on the first cast. If you get stuck with bait like that, you may as well go home. You're not going to catch any bass with dead bait."

The highest-quality commercial shiners are those placed in a spring water-fed holding tank and "cured" for 12 hours after capture. This toughens the bait, and helps kill parasites the shiners may be carrying. Shiners treated in this manner will be strong, firm and light golden-brown in color. They'll do what Smith refers to as "work for you." That is, they'll remain lively and kicking on the hook.

Some bait is not worth buying. Obvious signs of such poor

bait would be fungus growth, sores or inability of the minnow to maintain an upright, swimming posture. While it may be difficult for the inexperienced live-bait angler to gauge a shiner's worth just by looking at it, other signs that should be checked include scales missing or coming off when the bait is handled, or a very dark-brown color. These signs mean the bait is in poor condition, and not worth the cost. As a rule there's at least one source of good-quality bait and it's well worth the BASSer's time to seek it.

While shiners are sold in all sizes, most preferred are what the guides call "mediums." These 6- to 8-inch shiners are big enough to work back into the thick stuff, and tempt a wallhanger, but not too large for the 4- and 5-pound bass to handle easily.

On some occasions bass may show a decided preference for either larger or smaller shiners. This is normally a day-to-day trend, so the guides usually try to include a few shiners in the 4- to 5-inch range as well as the 8- to 10-inch size to deal with those sometimes finicky bass.

• **Shiner Shenanigans** — Once the proper bait is obtained, the next step is to get it in front of the bass. In an area the size of the St. Johns River, it's not always an easy task. To simplify this problem, Smith and Lee usually start the search in areas of heavy cover, near deep water. While some exceptions are made due to seasonal patterns, floating mats of hyacinths are the first choice through most of the year.

The hyacinth, a floating water plant with a root structure that extends about 10 inches below the surface, is the home of many small aquatic creatures that nurture both forage fish and bass. Drifting together, the hyacinths form an impenetrable roof-like cover that actually is hollow underneath. If the plants drift over structure, like a creek mouth or an outside bend on a river channel, the searching angler finds an almost certain winning parlay: food, cover and structure. Bass won't be absent for long.

The trick is to usher the shiner underneath the floating cover and hold it there until the bass decides to grab it. This is easier said than done. If bass are in the cover, you can bet the shiner will not join them willingly. The bait must be made to swim in on its own. The two methods used to accomplish this are cork-fishing and live-lining. The only important difference between the techniques is the distance the shiner is allowed to travel into the cover.

• **Corkin' The Bait** — The cork technique is most effective when the water under the hyacinths is relatively shallow, or filled with debris, such as tree limbs. (See FIG. 1.) In this type fishing, the cork isn't necessarily used to signal a strike, but rather to present the shiner from swimming under the cover more than a couple of feet. With the small Southland float positioned about 3 feet above the bait, and pegged in place with a toothpick, the shiner is flipped out to the edge of the cover where it will hopefuly dart underneath.

Should the shiner swim toward open water, it is recast until the bait gets the right idea. Once under the hyacinths, the cork will lodge in the roots and lock the shiner's movements into a small area.

• **Loose On The Line** — If water under the floating hyacinth cover is deep, or free of obstructions, it usually is more effective to allow the bait to roam around freely. When "live-lined," the shiner can cover a much larger area. At times, such as post-frontal conditions, bass are buried so far back in the cover that live-lining becomes the only way to get a bait to them. Everything is removed from the line except for the hook.

While a shiner fished under a cork may be either lip-hooked or dorsal-hooked, the live-lined shiner must be hooked behind the dorsal fin if it is to swim properly. The shiner is cast to the edge of the cover and encouraged to swim as far underneath as the angler thinks prudent. The line fouling on the roots generally keeps the bait in position. (See FIG. 2.)

Detecting a hit with either technique is not difficult. There are no "nibbles" in shiner fishing. The bass "busts" the bait and takes off! For this reason, the reel always is left in the free-spool position. The bass is allowed to run a distance while it swallows the shiner; how long depends upon how the bass are hitting on that given day. It's something that must be determined by trial and error, and hopefully, early in the day.

• **Setting The Steel** — "When the bass grabs the bait and runs, it may move into open water or back deeper in the cover," says Smith. In either case, the line probably will hang on something and put a belly of slack between you and the fish. If you try to take up the slack slowly until you feel the fish before setting the hook, you may feel just the line caught on a root and set the hook without ever getting to the fish. "The most efficient way to turn hits into hooked fish is to stand up, point the rod at the place where the line enters the cover, then reel down fast until you actually feel the fish throbbing on the line. At this point, and no sooner, hit the fish as hard as you can!"

While this may sound unorthodox, Smith points out, "What we're doing with the fast reel down is actually setting the point of the hook into the fish with the reel and the bass' own momentum. The stout strike serves to drive the hook home, and get the fish coming your way.

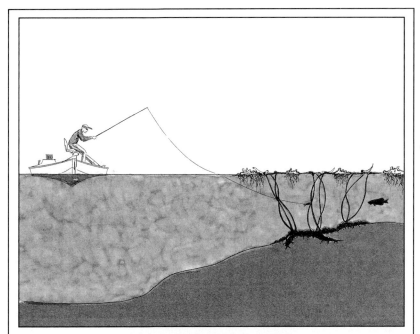

SHINER DORSAL-FIN HOOKED

FIG. 2 — When the water under the cover is relatively free of obstructions, it's frequently more effective to allow the shiner to roam freely on its own. For live-lining, all weights and floats are removed from the line, leaving only the hook. The shiner is hooked behind the dorsal fin to allow it to swim into the cover. (If hooked through the lips, the shiner will frequently turn outward, toward the pull of the line, and not swim into the cover.) Once in the cover, the shiner will not swim with quick tugs on the line. When those tugs turn into a steady, strong pull, the shiner has done its job. Now it's up to the angler to get the bass out of the tangles.   Illustration: Bernie Schultz

"When handled properly, we hook about 85 percent of our hits. No other method we've tried has been more than about 60 percent effective," continues Smith. "Since we're getting all the slack out of the line, we also get a better hook-bite when we hit the fish. As a result, we have very few bass throw the hook. Once we stick 'em, they're generally ours," Smith says.

The shiner system is actually simple, and it's attention to detail that makes it work; the willingness to do all the "picky" little things, and do them right. The guides know that big fish don't come that often; you have to capitalize on every shot you get.

Hooks are honed to a razor's edge; knots are retied after each fish, and lines are replaced after a couple of trips. Monofilament lines get a careful waxing with floating fly-line dressing to keep them on the surface, instead of fouled on underwater vegetation.

Also, these guides — Smith and Lee — spend as much as an hour selecting their bait for the day. Or, as long as 20 minutes working a shiner into "just the right" position. The harder they work, the "luckier" they get. The "shiner system" works for the guides, and it can work for any BASSer who wants to boost his score on big bass from Florida waters.

— JANUARY 1981

Photo: Jim Vincent

Photo: Gerald Crawford

CHAPTER SIXTEEN

TRICKS OF THE TRADE

*F*ishing isn't just a matter
of wetting a hook, but a game
of problems and solutions.

Photo: Jack Bissell

AR 061 AEE

How To Hook And Play Bass

By STEVE PRICE

If you're losing many of the fish you hook, try super-pro Larry Nixon's fish-fighting tactics . . .

Early in the morning of May 28, during the second round of the 1987 BASSMASTER® Super Invitational on Kentucky Lake — the final day during which points for the B.A.S.S. Angler-of-the-Year title could be earned, Larry Nixon snap-set the hook on a largemouth of about 7 pounds.

The big fish came to the boat, swam by, and then simply opened its mouth. The jig came out, and Nixon lost not only the fish, but the Angler-of-the-Year title as well.

"I knew when I lost that bass that I'd also lost the title," remembers Nixon, one of the BASSMASTER® Tournament Trail's most successful stars, "because I was on some really big fish. Five minutes later I caught an 8-pounder, then a 6-pounder, a 3-pounder and two smaller bass.

"The funny thing about it is that I never use a snap-set when I fish a jig, because I lose fish when I do that. I was just so nervous and excited I made a mental mistake, and it cost me dearly."

According to Nixon, improperly setting a hook and then playing a fish poorly are two of the biggest mistakes he sees anglers make. He estimates these two errors cause at least half of his tournament partners to lose one or two fish that would put them into money-winning positions.

"In the past few years many fishermen have gradually switched to lighter rods and lines because the equipment is much more versatile and catches more fish. The trouble is, many anglers haven't adjusted to the different fishing techniques the lighter tackle requires," Nixon points out.

"In the past, we all used stiff rods and 20- and 25-pound-test line for all our fishing. We didn't worry about losing bass because we simply overpowered them.

"Today, however, with the 10- and 12-pound-test lines and limber-tipped rods we're using, you have to be willing to finesse a bass much more.

"Besides, you never know how well you have a bass hooked, regardless of how hard it strikes. Sometimes, too, it seems the harder you pull a bass, the harder it pulls back."

Playing bass really begins with the initial strike, explains the 1988 MegaBucks® champion, because the fisherman must match the hook-setting style to the type of lure being used. The worst lures — those from which bass are most likely to get free — are treble-hook plugs; the best are single-barb lures such as spinnerbaits.

One reason for this is that most treble hooks used today are much smaller than single hooks.

"With a fast-moving treble-hook lure like a crankbait, a bass usually hooks itself," says Nixon, "so when you feel the fish hit, you don't need to do much more than pivot your body about 90 degrees, bring the rod back with you at waist level with the tip pointed down, and keep reeling."

With a single-barb spinnerbait, much the same technique is used, because the lure is generally moving rapidly. Because it is a single-hook lure, however, the hookset made by the angler can be harder and snappier.

The one single-hook lure that requires the most care, believes Nixon, is the jig, which usually is fished slowly. Instead of using a quick wrist-snap hookset like the majority of fishermen do, Nixon uses a sweep-set.

"I just start reeling whenever I feel any type of pressure or weight," he explains, "and I sweep my rod back to the side.

You reel first, then keep reeling as you bring the rod back. You don't jerk the rod at all.

"There seems to be something about the way a bass takes a jig that requires this type of hook-set," Nixon continues. "Maybe the big lump of lead that jumps in the fish's mouth when you snap-set the hook is what makes it open its mouth. I think the same thing happens when you peg a slip sinker in front of a worm.

"You can imagine what happens when you make a snap-set. Suddenly you exert several pounds of pressure at the hook for an instant. The jig is jerked while it's in the fish's mouth and it bangs against the top of the mouth or the lips. The lure rotates, too, because of the head and line-tie eye design. When the fish instinctively opens its mouth, the jig pops out.

"With a more gentle, sweeping motion, the hook-setting pressure is not as great, but it is more natural and it is constant. Because it isn't as sudden, it seems that the fish doesn't open its mouth as much, and the barb has a chance to penetrate.

"Just ask any jig fisherman you know who uses a quick snap-set, and I'll bet he'll tell you that he loses a lot of fish, no matter how good an angler he is."

Lure size has an effect on hook-setting success, as well. Nixon prefers to use the lightest jig he can, usually a 3/8-ounce model, because of the smaller head size. Lighter weight in a jig does not necessarily mean a smaller hook, since most manufacturers use the same size hook on all their models.

Some anglers use this same type of sweep-set with plastic worms, although Nixon admits the chances of missing fish this way actually may increase because the hook must first penetrate the worm. There simply isn't enough barb exposed to do the job. Those who do use a sweep-set always push the barb completely through the worm to clear a path, and some put the hook through the side of the worm rather than through the center.

"It goes without saying that a sweeping hookset requires sharp hooks," says Nixon. "What you want is for the hook to begin biting the instant the point makes contact with anything. That way, constant pressure keeps the barb biting and digging in."

Once a bass has been hooked, says Nixon, the key to getting it safely into the boat is playing the fish properly. The days of horsing a fish across the surface like a wad of grass are over, at least if you're serious about getting that fish into the livewell.

"The only time you really want to play a bass on the surface is when you've made a long cast and need to keep a fish from diving into logs or other heavy cover that could break your line. Otherwise, you want to hold your rod low and try to keep the fish from jumping or even wallowing on top."

First, says Nixon, who is the leading all-time money-winner on the BASSMASTER Tournament Trail, try to bring the bass close to the boat, where you have more control over it. There,

When Larry Nixon sweep-sets a hook, he reels quickly, pivoting at the waist about 90 degrees and bringing the rod back at waist level with the tip pointed down.

Illustration: Emily Craig

use your rod to pressure the fish and guide it from side to side until it wears itself out. Keep your rod tip low and, once the fish does tire, you can reach down and lip-land it, or perhaps swing it on board.

His technique is simple: He lets the fish swim away with about a rod's length of line out. Then he turns the fish to get it swimming back toward the boat and smoothly lifts it up and out of the water, using the fish's own momentum as an ally. If the bass appears ready to jump at boatside, Nixon applies pressure with his rod as it leaves the water, then simply guides it into the boat.

Smaller bass are fairly easy to swing into the boat. But on any bass, Nixon cautions, it's important to make the motion as smooth as possible.

"I cannot tell you how many bass I've seen fall off a lure when an angler really jerked the fish out of the water. All it takes to do it right is a quick but smooth lift and swing to get the fish over the boat," he explains. "That way, if it does fall off, at least it drops into the boat."

Nixon does not use the longer two-handle rods so popular now among the tournament pros. He tried them, but still prefers the pistol-grip models in 6-foot lengths. They're medium to medium-heavy in action, and they have some flex in the tip that helps when playing fish. Flexible tips take some of the pressure off lines, enabling lighter lines to be used.

Nixon, a former bass guide on Toledo Bend, says he's learned a lot about playing bass by watching his clients on the lake. "I watched them making mistakes and then tried to analyze what happened."

Analyze your own fishing techniques and see if you're making some of the mistakes Nixon has seen.

— MAY 1988

HOOK-SETTING: CONTROLLING THE VARIABLES

By GEORGE KRAMER

In fishing — a game of close tolerances — the angler must control as many variables as he can . . .

Surely Murphy, the fabled lawmaker who said: "If something can go wrong, it will, and at the worst possible time," must have been a tournament bass fisherman.

And if anything can go wrong in bass fishing, it's likely to go wrong when a fisherman is trying to set the hook through a plastic worm.

Often failures are his own fault, and they usually occur through simple oversight. Take, for example, the professional angler who hooks and lands 20 fish a day without missing a bona fide "tap." Then on his very next outing with the same Texas rig, he will mystify himself and those around him by missing two or three strikes in a row.

Such dips in his "performance curve" seem astounding at the time, especially since everyone has been schooled from the beginning that any bass of consequence can inhale virtually any plastic worm.

Surely the pros, and most bassin' regulars, could never miss — and yet they sometimes come up short.

A number of variables are associated with the hook-setting process. Some are controllable to one degree or another. Many of them are not.

The wise fisherman will determine the variables he cannot control, accept them as part of the challenge of bass fishing, and focus all his energies on overcoming the variables he can influence with his technique.

Let's examine first the variables within our control.

LINE STRETCH. By nature, all monofilaments stretch. Some, such as Du Pont's Prime or Berkley's TriMax, don't stretch much compared to the wide range of other premium lines. However, this still remains a factor. What's more, thoroughly wetted lines stretch more than dry lines — as much as 30 percent more.

Even if this stretch only equates to a few inches at the end of a 40-foot cast, it can sap the power of the hookset. With standard premium lines, the angler will fare better in setting the hook when the line is comparatively dry, as it is on the first few casts. Otherwise, it is smart to use low-stretch lines when worm fishing.

If the fisherman will be aware of this characteristic of nylon lines, he can make adjustments in the area of rod length and technique to accommodate the additional stretch of the wet line. And in a dry climate, he may be able to limit stretch by alternating rods every half hour or so.

THE ROD. Although the fishing rod is a lever, its advantage is not one of power, but rather one of speed, as has been described in Dr. Paul Johnson's *The Scientific Angler* (Scribners, New York 1984).

What this means is that fishing rods, depending on their length, expedite the energy of the hook-setting motion. The longer rod, of course, pulls the line farther with the same effort than a shorter rod, which should move the hook farther and faster. Stated more simply, most fishermen will stick more bass with a long worm rod than with the standard 5 1/2-footer.

That rod needs to be fairly stiff, too. The more the rod bends under stress, the less energy is available to move the hook. Since one manufacturer's medium-light action may be another's medium-heavy, it's impossible to recommend the perfect hook-setting rod — except to say that it should be on the heavy side.

Curiously, tests showed that rod material made little difference in the area of power or the amount of energy delivered (though it is a factor in other areas). Neither graphite nor boron/graphite outperformed fiberglass or glass composites.

THE HOOK. Much time and energy has been devoted to the area of hook selection, particularly to the sharpness of hooks. Such has been the focus of the new Eagle Claw Lazer points and the Gamakatsus from Japan.

It also has provided the impetus for a variety of hook-sharpening tools from diamond files to the Point Maker grinder (also the Hook-Hone-R). But for all that, there are several other considerations, according to the top B.A.S.S. pros.

Denny Brauer, the 1987 B.A.S.S. Angler-of-the-Year, declares, "Hook diameter is very important. I use the lightest wire I can, because hooks with heavy wire are hard to drive."

What about hook designs incorporating a number of bends in the wire to help position the point properly? Many pros swear by them; others, like Harold Allen, prefer straight styles. With straight hooks, he explains, "the worm balls up quicker on the shank to start the hook penetrating."

California-based pro Gary Klein has introduced his own plastic-worm hook, the Black Weapon. It has a relatively small diameter for its size, a double-tapered round point, and the slightest slice or barb. It is designed for easy penetration while punching the smallest hole possible.

Klein uses a "perfect-bend" design, a symmetrical curvature of the wire that permits all forces on the point to be absorbed more equally. The rigid Sheffield steel construction of the hook contributes to another advantage — controlled flex.

Explains Klein, "Most hooks flex quite a bit when you set. This means the force driving them is partially wasted in pulling the point along until it catches. Look at the hole made by your hook in the upper jaw of a fish sometime. There's a tear sometimes a half-inch or more. When I stick them with my hook, the point doesn't slide."

TECHNIQUE. The impact of a good hook-setting technique cannot be overstated. Consistency in form — including stance, rod position and cranking/striking coordination — characterize the pros.

If an angler is off-balance, for instance, his ability to detect strikes may be compromised. Likewise, he may not be able to handle his rod in the proper manner to drive the hook into the mouth of the fish.

Regardless of whether the reel is "palmed," or the rod is held by the pistol grip or "Western-style" at the foregrip, the

Practicing the correct hook-setting technique will result in catches like this most of the time you rear back on a plastic worm.

Photo: Wade Bourne

body should be square to the target or the fish, and the elbows should be "in" when the angler strikes. To do otherwise limits quickness — and speed, not power, as we shall observe, is the key to hook-setting.

Although a relative term, "loose-line" hook-setting has gained favor among the pros since it was first popularized by two-time Classic® winner Bobby Murray.

Allen likes it much better than reeling until the line is taut, then hauling back. "I set on slack line with a crisp set, because I want the momentum of the line already going forward when I hit the fish. He says his style is like a fighter throwing a jab instead of one caught in a clinch and trying to hit at close range.

Looking at the next set of variables, those which are out of the angler's control, might seem like a futile gesture. However, the better we understand the problems facing successful hook-setting, the better we'll be able to gauge our own performances when fishing.

FISH ACTIVITY. The insiders on the BASSMASTER® Tournament Trail often talk about the "personality" of the bass in a given set of conditions. This, in addition to the daily feeding periods associated with the positions of the moon and sun, offer fishermen a severe challenge.

When bass aren't feeding actively, they aren't going to swallow every rubber snake that enters their niche. In those times, not every tap, peck, twitch, bump or tick will result in a bass.

The fisherman's best move when "the fish aren't taking the worm real good" is to be aware of how the existing conditions might be influencing the fish. Try to determine which method — such as waiting on the fish before setting, or perhaps pulling the trigger instantly — might hook a fish that isn't very active.

ATTACK ANGLES. Closely related to fish activity is the "attack angle" or direction the fish moves as it takes a bait. It is easier to set the hook on a bass that turns away after picking up the worm than on one that rushes from shallow cover directly toward the boat. As the pros fine-tune a pattern, they may try to determine at which angle a fish likely is to strike.

However, no one can anticipate specifically *how* the fish will operate at a particular time, so we learn through missed strikes how long to wait and in which direction to pull to facilitate a secure hookset.

Especially vulnerable to difficult attack angles are fishermen who must operate from the "back seat," as well as those casting from shore or from an anchored boat. They can do little when a bass takes the worm and moves obliquely to an obstruction — dulling the sensation of the bite and compromising the angler's ability to pull directly against the fish.

One other situation that turns many plastic-wormers into crankbaiters occurs when the bass takes the worm in shallow water and then turns and swims directly to deep water, often right at the boat. In such cases the angler usually is caught with a lot of slack and, out of anxiety, swings before he has established a "direct line." Instead, he should keep the rod tip low and wait until the fish is pulling line again before setting.

The following group of factors are "sliding variables," which may or may not be controlled by the fisherman.

HOOK POINT POSITION. Of all the frustrating times when bass spit worms — most can be traced to the spot in which the hook point lodged.

If the barb finds the softer tissue of the sides of the mouth or just above the upper lip, hook penetration is quick and secure. However, if the point hits the bony portions of the upper or lower jaw and deflects, then successful hook-setting is tenuous.

Paul Johnson tested the force necessary to hook a bass with a special hook point sharpened to imitate a surgical needle.

Even with the super-sharp hook, Johnson found it still took as much as 5 pounds of hook-setting energy to imbed this hook into the hardest part of the bass' mouth. It required at least 8 pounds of pressure with a new, although unsharpened hook.

When Johnson measured the hook-setting power of two-time B.A.S.S. Angler-of-the-Year Jimmy Houston, he found that Houston could deliver only between 4 and 4 1/2 pounds of force at a distance of 25 to 50 feet using a 5 1/2-foot worm rod and 14-pound-test Trilene XT.

It is reasonable that even the most skilled anglers may not be able to generate enough power to set the hook into the upper palate of the bass' mouth.

What this suggests is that it is important to react quickly to get the hook point started in a softer location in the fish's mouth. Can anything be done to reduce the chances of contacting the hardest parts of the mouth? In some cases, yes. The Tru-Turn hook has demonstrated an ability to turn its point while compressed in the bass' mouth, and if it avoids the harder plates, this is an obvious advantage.

Too, an angler who is close to the fish and high in relation to the bass is likely to set the hook point straight up and directly into the hardest parts of the jaw. To compensate for that situation, it may be advisable to pause for an instant, then set the hook with a hard sideways sweep to catch the side of the mouth.

Johnson also measured Houston's ability to set the hook while using the sideways set with a 6-foot "mini-flipping" rod and 17-pound-test line. Houston mustered 8 pounds of force, compared to 4 1/2 pounds with the shorter rod. This combination would offer a clear advantage with any hook at close range.

DISTANCE FROM FISH. Hook-setting energy and hook penetration diminish steadily the farther away the angler gets from the fish. Logically, then, the closer one gets to his target, the better his chances of hooking a bass.

Unfortunately, water and weather conditions usually dictate how close we can get. In very clear water, getting close to the fish is not plausible, and neither is the use of thick, low-stretch monofilament line.

STRIKE DETECTION. Although the better anglers would likely conclude that strike detection is well within their realm of control, such is not the case universally.

What's more, based on the observations of divers over a period of years, there is a strong contention that most anglers — including professional-level fishermen — only discern a small portion of actual strikes.

Even with the best equipment and technique, cold, wind and other conditions can dampen the angler's ability to feel a strike. Develop the habit of watching the line where it enters the water, use the most sensitive graphite rods and concentrate hard on underwater sensations. If you haven't tried the Western technique of holding the line over the index finger or between that finger and the thumb, give it a try.

—AUGUST 1987

LAND THAT LUNKER

By DON WIRTH

Getting strikes is fine, but until you've landed the fish you've not finished the battle . . .

The fish flopped right at the boat and got off before I could net it!"

"It jumped out of the water and the hook came out!"

"I had it coming to the boat, but it dove down and my line broke!"

Sad, but true. "The one that got away" is as much a part of bass fishing as are crankbaits, trolling motors and Vienna sausages. Yet more often than not, you could have prevented it. If you've lost one big bass too many, or if losing a good fish has ever kept you out of the running in a tournament, or if you'd like to increase your percentage of catches, not just strikes, read on!

First Things First

"Many Bassmasters devote serious study to improving their strike percentage, yet they rarely think about ways they might improve their catches," believes big-bass expert Doug Hannon. The Tampa, Fla., angler has made a career out of catching big bass — fish up to 17 pounds.

"Hooking the fish is the first and most important step in landing it," Hannon says, "yet most fishermen fail to do a good job in getting the steel into the bass." Even a vigorous hookset may not be enough to drive the hook point into the bony jaw of a big bass. "Even when you jerk back hard on heavy tackle, you usually generate only 2 or 3 pounds of pull where it matters — at the end of your line," Hannon points out. "It may feel to you as though you could move a mountain with your hookset, but much of the energy you expend

gets lost before it ever reaches your hook."

Hannon lists limber rods, stretchy monofilament lines and the drag caused by your line in the water as three villains that rob your hookset of its punch.

Doug believes that most bass are "hooked the way a lure might stick into your hand when you reach into your tacklebox, with the point barely sticking into the flesh and the barb failing to penetrate. This is why so many bass that you hook shake off, and why the hook falls out of many of the bass that you land."

He blames dull hooks and barbs that are too big. A fanatic about hook sharpness, Hannon recently assisted with the development of the new Hook-Hone-R diamond orbital hook sharpener (see "Producing Perfect Hook Points," Short Casts, August 1987 BASSMASTER®). "The hooks on many lures that come right out of the box aren't sharp enough to penetrate the jaws of a medium-size bass, let alone a trophy," Hannon feels. "You've got to pay attention to your hooks if you expect to get fish into the boat consistently."

Hannon also believes that the barbs of many hooks are too large, and inhibit penetration. "You don't need much of a barb to hold a fish tightly," says Hannon, citing the tiny barbs on a porcupine's quill as an example. "I either file down the barbs on my hooks to reduce their size, or flatten them down about halfway with pliers."

Hannon reminds Bassmasters that the barb of their hook may fail to penetrate when they fight a bass. "Because you can't often count on your hook-setting power alone to bury the barb, you need to keep a very tight line during the initial stages of the fight. When you do, the bass will often bury the barb itself as it struggles to get away."

Leapin' Lunkers!

Bass like to leave the water when hooked. It's a tremendous sight, but one that can be mighty humbling to the angler on the other end of the line. What causes a bass to jump when hooked? "It's a reflex action," Hannon believes. "The bass feels something spiny lodged in its throat or mouth, so it jumps up and shakes its gills to dislodge it."

To those who say that big bass don't jump, Hannon answers, "Every giant bass I've ever landed has jumped. It's awfully hard to control a bass over 14 pounds when it wants to come out of the water."

He uses a simple method to maintain control of a bass that's headed for the surface: "If possible, I try to keep the bass from jumping," he says. "I keep a close watch on my line. When I see it cutting toward the surface, I reel as fast as I can and put some pressure on the fish. This often convinces the bass that it's moving in the wrong direction, and it will try to go the other way, which will keep it in the water where I can control it more easily." If the fish does manage to break water, Hannon gives it some slack, usually by extending his arms toward the fish.

"A fish accelerates dramatically when it leaves the water," Hannon says. "It may approach the surface at 3 mph, but once it's in the air and until gravity slows it, its speed increases quickly, since air offers far less resistance to its body than water. Giving a little slack will reduce the force of its jump."

1. It's been said that a 14-pounder won't jump, but you know that it's not true — you've got a big Florida bass on the end of your line, and it's headed for the surface. What do you do? Remain calm. Try to keep the fish from breaking the surface by reeling as fast as you can and putting some pressure on it.   Photos: Don Wirth

2. Work the bass into your rod's "circle of control" — an area within which you can fight the fish and overcome line drag and other negative forces.

3. Once you have the fish ready to come to the boat, pull it boatside, then reverse the pull — in other words, pull the bass to the left or the right and land it "sideways."

4. Reach around from the back of the fish and grab it by the lower jaw. Keep tension on your line. Test your grip before taking the fish out of the water.

Use Your Rod

Hannon prefers long baitcasting rods for most of his bass fishing. "You have far more control with a 7- to 7 1/2-foot rod than you do with a short one," he believes. Hannon likes long rods that have a fairly soft tip for casting artificials. "Most bass rods will indicate a range of lines they're designed to handle. It may say '8 to 15 pounds' or '10 to 20 pounds' on the rod. This is important information. A rod rated for lines testing from 8 to 15 pounds will have enough spring or flex to protect lines testing down to 8 pounds, while enabling you to use lines testing up to 15 pounds without being in danger of breaking the rod under pressure."

A long, springy rod absorbs much of the jumping and pulling power of even a giant bass, Hannon has found. "I've caught big tarpon on a fly rod, which is exceedingly springy. The rod's flex absorbs the power of a big fish's surges and headshakes like a sponge absorbs water. It's a mistake to equate rod stiffness with the stick's ability to put a big fish into the boat."

When Hannon hooks a good bass, he tries to work the fish quickly into what he calls his rod's "circle of control." "Each rod/reel/line combination has a circle of control, an area within which you can fight the fish and overcome line drag and other negative factors," Hannon believes. "A 7-foot rod with 14-pound-test line will let you control a fish up to 30 or 40 feet from the boat, for example. The lighter your tackle, the less control you have at a distance and the more ability the bass has to overcome the spring of your rod with drag." However, Hannon says that you can overcome this effect partially by using lighter lines when you go to lighter rods. "A light line has less drag in the water than does a heavy line. I like a long, light-action rod when I use light lines."

To Net Or Not

Many anglers feel that a landing net is as much a part of their fishing equipment as their tacklebox. But for others, a net is an unnecessary hindrance that only damages fish.

"Most major tournament circuits, including the BASS-MASTER® Tournament Trail, now outlaw landing nets," says Super B.A.S.S.-III tournament winner Doug Gilley. The Winter Springs, Fla., pro cites several reasons for this ruling:

"One, using a landing net unfairly handicaps one of the competitors in the boat. If we're on schooling bass or a good bunch of fish and I holler for the net, you'll drop your rod to net my fish, thereby possibly missing a shot at your own bass. Two, if you get a fish on and I knock it off with the landing net, hard feelings might result. The 'knockee' might go around blaming the 'knocker' for his misfortune. Finally, nets do a lot of damage to bass. If I release a bass that I've netted, it might not survive."

Gilley believes that not using a net in tournament situations "is the only fair way to go. That way, if I lose a fish, I have no one to blame but myself." A staunch catch-and-release advocate in and out of tournaments, Gilley believes that the net is extremely harmful to bass, especially big bass. "When you net a bass, you remove much of its protective slime coating. Then if you release the fish, it's liable to get an infection and weaken or possibly die."

Hannon also frowns on nets. "They knock off scales and split fins," he says. "Just as a skydiver can't float to earth safely with holes in his parachute, a bass can't compete in its world with split fins. When you net a big bass, the weight of the fish pressing against the net really tears up its body." If you must use a net, Hannon suggests, use a rubber one, which is far less damaging to the bass than a nylon net.

Beyond the damage they do to fish, nets are a real nuisance, Gilley and Hannon agree. "When you reach for the net, it's usually fouled in a crankbait or boat cleat," Hannon says. "You just don't need a net to land a bass, even a huge bass. They have no teeth. You can just reach in there and lip 'em."

Doug Gilley says, "Many friendships have been destroyed over a bad netting job. When you're fighting a big bass and it's wallowing around out there, it's easy to lose your cool. Sometimes your partner grabs the net and panics. That's when you're bound to lose your bass." Gilley recalls fishing a buddy tournament where the big bass he'd hung swam around the trolling motor. "My partner grabbed the net, reached out and tried to make every twist and turn that the bass made. He went head over heels into the lake, and I lost my fish."

Lip Service

To many Bassmasters, the thought of entering big-bass country without a landing net may seem like walking into Viet Cong territory without a loaded rifle, but it's possible to land your lunker without netting it, our experts believe. "Lipping a bass is the easiest route for most fishermen," says Hannon. "Bass don't have teeth like northern pike or muskie, so you aren't going to get hurt if you follow a few simple procedures."

Hannon suggests this routine: "Once you have the fish ready to come to the boat, pull it to boatside, then reverse the pull — lay the bass back over to where the spring of the rod would fling the lure off to the side, rather than upward into your face, should the bait come unhooked. In other words, pull the bass to the left or the right and land it 'sideways.' Then if the lure pops out, it won't hit you in the eye." Hannon suggests reaching around from the back of the fish and grabbing it by the lower jaw. "Don't run your hand down the line into the fish's mouth, or hold your hand in the way of the hook. Approach the fish from the side, or from behind. This is easily accomplished when you pull the fish to the left or right."

Once you have the bass by the lower lip, don't try to lift it clear of the water until you're sure you have a firm grip, he says. "This is a critical moment. Your heart is pounding and your adrenaline is racing. You want the fish in the boat. But rushing it may cost you a trophy, tournament points or a nice photograph for your album." Keep the tension on your line, Hannon insists. This will keep the hooks from flopping around and possibly burying into your hand should the bass jump. Test your grip. Take a moment to make sure you've got a strong grasp of the fish before taking it out of the water. Then once you've got it coming out of the water, use both hands to hold the fish if necessary.

Lipping Vs. Swinging

Since the no-net ruling went into effect in most big-money tournaments, bass pros have been facing the dilemma of whether to lip their bass or swing them aboard, pendulum-style. "I'll base this decision largely on whether I'm using a single- or treble-hook lure," says California bass pro Rich Tauber. The Woodland Hills-based angler says that he tends to lip-land bass hooked on crankbaits and other treble-hook lures "because I'm not always certain how well they're hooked on these baits. I'll watch the way the fish is fighting, and pay close attention to it as it's coming to the boat." When Tauber is using a worm, jig or other single-hook bait, he usually swings the bass aboard. "On jigs and similar lures, I'll be using up to 20-pound-test line," Tauber says. "If the bass is under 4 pounds, I swing it aboard. If it's heavier than that I'll lip-land it."

Tauber also swings keeper-size bass that he's convinced are well-hooked on crankbaits and other treble-hook plugs. "Under 2 pounds, I'll swing it," he says. "This applies to light line, too. When you do it correctly, there's little strain on your line or equipment."

Gilley says that the correct method for swinging a bass aboard is somewhat difficult to describe, but has a lot to do with timing and momentum. "You want to get the fish swimming alongside the boat," Gilley says. "When it's moving, it's got momentum. You simply lift the fish out of the water and use its momentum to swing it aboard. Often a bass will swim toward the surface and act as if it's about to jump. When this happens, lift your rod and coast the fish in." Gilley uses this technique for fish up to around 7 pounds that are hooked on jigs and other single-hook baits. When fish are hooked on crankbaits, Gilley plays them until he's able to lip them.

Both Gilley and Tauber caution that there are no hard and fast rules on whether you should lip or swing a bass. "Every situation is different," Gilley believes. "Sometimes you're fishing in grass or heavy cover; sometimes you're in open water. When I'm in cover, I tend to swing the bass aboard, since I'm trying to keep it from getting tangled."

Hannon cautions Bassmasters to exercise special precautions once they've boated their bass. "Sometimes in the heat of a tournament you may be tempted to use your foot to control a flopping fish, so that you can unhook it and make another cast. This will greatly damage the fish. It only takes a second to grasp the fish by the lip and unhook it."

Light-Line Secrets

It's one thing to winch aboard a big bass that you've hooked on that 45-pound-test "well rope." It's completely different when you're using light line. Tauber, a light-line expert, offers these suggestions:

"The key to landing big bass on light line is making several decisions before you hook the fish. If I'm using 4- or 6-pound-test, which isn't unusual in a deep, clear reservoir, I'll probably be using a single-hook bait such as a jig or worm. When a bass strikes, I'll probably 'long-line' the fish." That is, Tauber tries to keep about 20 or 30 feet of line between his bass and his boat. "Use your line's stretch as a shock absorber," he says. "If it's a big bass, you just can't let it swim around. You've got to take command. Put a little force on it, but maintain that long line. Use your rod to correct and direct the bass, never to horse it in."

Smallmouth bass are notorious for "coming alive" at the boat, diving and breaking your line. "Smallmouths are different from largemouths," Hannon cautions. "I've photographed smallmouths underwater, and they just don't want to get near you. A largemouth will let you swim up close, but a smallmouth is extremely evasive."

Hannon recommends using the long-line technique when battling a hooked smallmouth. "Maintain pressure on the fish, but don't try to force it to come to the boat in the early stages of the fight," he advises. "Smallmouths tend to inhabit deep water, and cover may not be a factor. Keep plenty of line (30 to 40 feet for a big one) between you and the fish. Don't let it have an inch of slack — but don't try to pull the fish anywhere near the boat until you're certain it's ready. Most beginning smallmouth fishermen hook a good fish and bear down on it to get it to the boat. But when the bass sees the boat, it panics, shoots for deep water and breaks your line. The long-line technique will tire them out enough so that you can land them."

Coming Aboard!

You've hooked that bass. What happens next is up to you — not just to the fish. Take the advice of our experts. Remain calm. Make decisions ahead of time. Keep some pressure on the fish. And once you've got your bass, treat it with respect. Strikes are nice, but they're even better when you land that lunker!

— FEBRUARY 1988

ANCHORING BASICS

By JOHN WEISS

Here's a short course in how to get
hold of a good fishing spot . . .

Anchor manufacturers are not likely to admit it, but an old hank of rope tied to a concrete block will do just as good a job of holding your boat in place as the most expensive and sophisticated anchoring equipment. That's if holding power is all you want from an anchor and if you don't mind rope burns on your hands, an occasional case of skinned knuckles, and/or the awesome difficulty of raising and lowering the cement block. There's also the fact that it's sure to clunk around in the bottom of your boat and spook fish, and that the abomination looks, well, downright pitiful.

The truth of the matter is that knowledgeable anchoring techniques, along with the use of the proper equipment, can be classified as a very important fishing tactic.

A good anchor should satisfy several angling needs. First, it should be noiseless. This enables you to fish a hole, weedbed or brushpile effectively without sending bass scurrying because of some metallic clanking above them. An anchor that forever is banging around is also sooner or later likely to damage gear aboard any boat — perhaps even the boat itself.

You should be able to raise and lower the anchor effortlessly so that, if need be, you can continually reposition your craft to your fishing advantage. And for further convenience, anchor control devices should be strategically positioned so there is no need to stumble over gear in an attempt to make your way from one end of the craft to the other.

A suitable anchor should, of course, be capable of holding your craft securely in position, even during conditions of the most swift currents and gusty breezes you are likely to encounter.

And lastly, if you're like most anglers I know, you'll want your anchor to look as nice as the rest of your fishing outfit. Tackle and boat gear that is clean and well-cared-for is always a pleasure to use and is not likely to fail or let you down.

That's quite a list of prerequisites for an anchor to satisfy before it deserves a place in your boat. And with the wide variations in fishing-boat design, hull weight and types of water where fish are likely to be found, it should be apparent that there is no single anchor assembly that is better than all others. In fact, you may even find that you need two regular-use anchors (one for the bow and another for the stern) and possibly even a third anchor stowed away somewhere for special-purpose use.

Keep in mind, also, that the anchor that is just right for my boat and my kind of fishing (or another angler's) may be a real bummer for you.

Types Of Anchors

Though there are at least a dozen different types of anchors that immediately come to mind, there are really only two or three "fisherman anchors" that are most efficient and popular with those who pursue finned quarry from craft of less than 18 feet in length. Those are the mushroom, danforth and the mushroom-grapple (which combines characteristics of the mushroom and danforth).

The mushroom anchor especially is popular with bass anglers. It may be found in weights up to 20 pounds. It is short and compact in size, and therefore easy to raise, lower or stow away. The mushroom anchor, as its name describes, is rounded on the bottom and therefore holds your boat in position by

■

Many anglers mount their anchor reels face up, although the author suggests mounting them on the sidewalls where they'll be out of the way.   Photo: Max Hunn

its sheer weight, not by "digging into" the bottom. For this reason, the mushroom anchor is ideal for parking your craft over weeds, brush, trees and other bottom cover that might easily grab onto and prevent freeing of another anchor design. The mushroom anchor also is well-suited to deep-water work especially.

For shallow-water fishing, or for holding in position over "clean" bottoms of hard-packed shell, sand, clay and similar materials, the best type of anchor is one which digs in or "bites" into the soft bottom. And in this category, none is better than the collapsible danforth anchor.

Since the danforth anchor is nearly impossible to rig for use with mounting brackets aboard bass boats, the mushroom-grapple anchor was contrived. This anchor style takes on an appearance similar to that of the typical mushroom anchor so that it may be used with popular hand-winch or electric anchor assemblies. But the base of the mushroom-grapple anchor has grapple-type flanges at the base instead of a rounded bottom. With this anchor you can rely upon its weight to hold the boat in position, or you can let out extra anchor line to drag the anchor on its side and get a bite on the bottom.

For canoes, johnboats, cartoppers, inflatables and V-bottom fishing boats measuring 14 feet or less in length, a 5- or 7-pound anchor usually is more than suitable. For the largest johnboats and V-bottom craft and smaller bass boats (15 feet or less in length), a 10- or 12-pound anchor is just the ticket. And

if you chase after bass in craft of between 16 and 18 feet in length, an anchor weighing at least 15 pounds is advised.

Anchor Mounts And Lifts

Few things are more aggravating in life than having to hand-over-hand haul in an anchor countless times each fishing day, especially if the water is cold.

One of the greatest boons to modern angling and the use of anchors has been the hand-crank lift and socket-mooring. You zip into some secluded bay. Anchor. Fish. Haul anchor. Zip away. All without leaving your seat, banging your knuckles, scorching your hands, straining your casting arm or exercising your storehouse of barroom vocabulary.

When shopping for an anchor lift and mount, examine the product closely before you buy. Look for quality non-rust materials such as cast aluminum, stainless steel, chrome, brass or any combination of these metals, especially where moving parts are concerned. Most reputable marine products manufacturers nowadays use these durable, heavy-duty materials, but there are a few cheapie outfits who care more about your money than your fishing pleasure.

Another reason for close inspection of an anchor-lift and anchor-mounting assembly is because many manufacturers employ different types of mounting brackets for their equipment — brackets which may be ill-suited for installation on the type of craft you possess, or at the location where you desire to have the equipment installed. Generally, the only maintenance that should ever be required by a quality anchor-lift assembly is an occasional shot of oil on moving parts; in some cases, not even this.

Though many anglers locate their anchor reels face-up on the bow or stern decking, I am not in favor of this practice. For one, the anchor rope is not as easily wound on the spool uniformly. And such a mounting also makes for one more gadget that is exposed to knocks and bumps. They may even get in the way when boarding, disembarking, or when playing fish.

I like my anchor reels, one fore and one aft, to be mounted on the sidewalls of the craft next to the seats. In this manner, they are still readily accessible at all times, but never in the way. It might also be mentioned here that the closer the reel to the mount, the easier the rig is to install and use. Otherwise, you may require wheels, pulleys and other paraphernalia strung out the length of the craft.

Anchor ropes deserve consideration too. Nylon seems to be a universal favorite, in either 1/8-or 3/16-inch diameter for most fishing boats. Nylon, compared to rope, is impervious to rot, it stretches slightly to absorb shock and it boasts unusually strong tensile strength per diameter.

Though the amount of anchor line you wind onto your spool will be determined primarily by the average depth of those waters you fish most frequently, a good guideline is to have available seven times the length of rope that the water is deep. If you most often fish waters which average between 15 and 25 feet deep, 150 feet of anchor line on each spool will see you through most fishing conditions with ease. Why you need this reserve line will be discussed later.

Power Anchor Winches

It had to happen sooner or later — raising and lowering an anchor at the touch of a button. Running off the craft's 12-volt electrical system, an electric anchor windlass offers numerous advantages over the hand-crank models.

Traditionally, if you hooked a big fish in heavy cover, a fishing partner maneuvered the craft to open water for you to play your fish more safely. Now, you can do the job yourself, simply by nudging a toggle switch with your finger or even your foot to raise the anchor, then touching the foot-control pedal of the electric motor.

Another advantage has to do with the pure ease with which you can raise heavy anchors from deep water. An electric winch will crank your anchor in at about 1 foot per second. While you are waiting, you can even get in a few more casts.

Lastly, if you anchor frequently over obstructions and experience the annoying problem of your anchor hanging up on rocks and brush, the power winch will normally exert enough pull to dislodge whatever is holding you fast.

Anchoring Techniques

Fishing anchors serve three distinct purposes: to hold the boat for safety reasons, to position the craft so anglers aboard have the best shot at their "holes," and to slow down (but not stop) the craft when drift fishing in the face of strong currents or winds.

Safety-anchoring is required oftentimes, such as when you meet rapids, dams, strong offshore winds or in the event of motor failure. And one of the best ways to get additional "bite" on the bottom, in these circumstances, is to simply let out more anchor line so that a "flat" pull is achieved rather than a vertical one — thus the reason for having seven times the length of rope as the depth of water you're fishing.

When fishing underwater structure during calm-weather conditions, letting down one anchor should be plenty. Sometimes you may not even require the use of any anchor, but need only touch the electric-motor control pedal occasionally.

If there is any kind of current or wind, however, two anchors (one bow and one aft) are the best bet. With two anchors down, the craft not only is held securely in position, but is prevented from swinging about and putting you first too close to your casting target, then too far away.

Since the bow of any craft usually sits higher in the water and therefore is more susceptible to drifting, I like to let the front anchor down first, then the stern anchor. If there are two fishermen aboard, however, both anchors can be let down at the same time.

There is only one disadvantage to using two anchors to secure your boat in position, and it is a problem that has cost many anglers prize fish. Oversize fish that run a good deal while being played, seem to have a knack for finding anchor lines and fouling lures and fishing lines around them. With one anchor out, the problem is not as pronounced and you usually can work around the single anchor line, or prevent the fish from heading in that direction in the first place. With two ropes going to the bottom, however, the situation can get quite hairy. Color the scene even more precarious if two anglers aboard are playing big fish *simultaneously*!

There are two solutions to this problem. The first is the most practical. When a big fish is hooked and two anchor lines are out, pull them both in immediately, either via an electric winch or a pal who is quick of hand. Then, keep the craft in position with the electric trolling motor and foot-control pedal. Or use only one anchor to begin with, sacrificing precise boat control for the secure knowledge that you can handle any whopper that blasts your bait and starts to run.

There is no doubt that fish of all species like rock cover on the bottom—crevices, ledges, drop-offs and so on. And an anchor wedged in these types of obstructions can cause even the most passive of anglers to shout words that can't be printed here. If hanging up on bottom cover is a problem you often experience, you might try rigging a special "trip-line." Such will require extra care and effort in raising and lowering your anchor, but it may save you several gray hairs and several costly anchors.

A trip-line is nothing more than a second line, much lighter in weight, that is affixed to the anchor on a side opposite of where the main anchor line is tied. If a sharp tug on the anchor line does not free the anchor, you simplly pull on the trip-line and *reverse* the line of pull. Practically always, the anchor will move just enough to be freed by the heavier line.

Often, anglers desire to use an anchor not to hold their craft securely in position, but to slow down the boat's drift in the face of strong winds or current — something even powerful electric motors are incapable of accomplishing.

Controlled drifts can be accomplished in several manners. If you have only a heavy anchor aboard, lower it just to the bottom, but allow no slack line out. As a result, the anchor will nudge the bottom but not be able to get a good bite, and the boat will continue to move along slowly. When attempting this slow-drift method, let the anchor out the stern, then use the bow-mounted electric motor to keep the nose of the craft headed in the intended direction.

If your craft is not equipped with a heavy anchor, but two light ones instead, you can accomplish the same thing by letting out only one of these. But before you do so, foul the line around the anchor so that it does not drag properly and thus will be incapable of digging into the bottom.

— NOVEMBER/DECEMBER 1974

GLOSSARY OF TERMS

Bluff-burning: A structure-fishing technique that involves casting a big-bladed spinnerbait parallel with the edge of a cliff face and retrieving it rapidly just under the surface.

Bulging: Retrieving a lure, usually a spinnerbait, just under the surface so the lure bulges the water without breaking the surface film.

Buzzbait: A lure, usually a spinnerbait, designed to be retrieved rapidly across the surface of the water to emulate a frightened baitfish.

Buzzing: Fishing a plug, plastic worm or spinnerbait with an extremely fast retrieve so the lure stays on or near the surface of the water.

Channel: The main bed in a river or lake originally shaped by natural or man-made forces to facilitate water flow.

Countdown lure: A lure that sinks in the water at a predictable speed.

Crashing: Casting into thick cover with a forceful, short cast. Typically, a heavy spinnerbait is used to break through the cover to the water.

Crankbait: A lure, most often made of wood or plastic, designed to imitate a swimming baitfish. Characterized by a plastic or metal bill, a crankbait usually is retrieved under the water with a steady or stop-and-go retrieve.

Dabbling: A vertical-fishing presentation that involves short, underhand casts made with a long, stiff rod. Also see "Flipping."

Deadsticking: A technique that involves casting a plastic worm to a target and then letting it lie still for several moments without imparting any action to it.

Dijacking: Using a cane pole and short line to present a plug in a figure-eight pattern on the surface of the water. Also termed "figure-eighting" or "jigger-poling."

Do-Nothing: A term applied to a fishing technique typified by retrieving a plastic worm on or near the bottom with a slow, steady retrieve.

Double Haul: A fly-casting technique that accelerates line speed to provide longer casts.

Downrigger: A mechanical device used to hold trolled fishing lines under the surface so attached baits can be fished at a consistent depth. A downrigger consists of a base, arm or boom, cable, and weight, to which the fishing line is secured.

Drag: A mechanical device built into a reel that, when engaged, exerts an adjustable range of pressure on the spool to impede the flow of fishing line from the reel.

Drop-off: An abrupt change in the bottom contour, typically at the juncture of a flat and channel.

Finesse fishing: The technique of fishing with small lures and appropriately matched tackle.

Flat: An expanse of bottom with relatively little change in bottom contour or water depth.

Flipping: A technique by which a lure is cast underhand in pendulum fashion to a point a short distance away. The caster imparts an up-and-down motion to the rod to propel the bait forward. Flipping typically is utilized to fish baits vertically in thick cover.

Fly-and-rind: A hair jig with small pork rind trailer.

Gardening: Using a rake or other device to clear a hole in thick aquatic vegetation to allow bait presentation.

Grub: A molded plastic lure normally wormed onto a jighead. The grub body may be molded with a plain paddle tail or a swimming tail that ripples through the water during the retrieve.

Jam knot: Any knot that is cinched tightly against a lure or hook eyelet.

Jig: A popular lure whose lead or lead alloy body is molded around a single, upturned hook. A rubber or hair skirt is fixed to the body so it extends over the bend and point of the hook.

Jig and pig: The combination of a jig and pork rind trailer that's attached over the point of the hook.

Jerkbait: A swimming lure that normally is retrieved with a sweeping motion of the rod rather than with a steady retrieve. The angler sweeps back the rod, reels up the slack line, and repeats the process.

Judas Plug: A hookless lure cast into heavy cover in order to locate bass.

Kneel and reel: A term applied to a style of retrieve by which the angler kneels down in the boat and keeps the rod tip in the water while retrieving the lure. The purpose of such a retrieve is to gain maximum depth with the lure, usually a crankbait.

Loop knot: Any of several different knots tied with a fixed loop. Loop knots are popular with jig fishermen and those who use crankbaits without "O" rings.

Ledge: An edge of a shallow flat or gently sloping bottom that is cut by any channel.

Lipless crankbait: A sinking crankbait manufactured without a diving bill that is retrieved at a consistent depth, depending on the speed of the retrieve.

Lipping: Landing a bass by its mouth by grasping its lower jaw between the thumb and fingers or between the thumb and knuckle of the index finger.

Live-lining: A technique for fishing live bait unencumbered by floats or weights.

Microjig: Any small jig that must be cast with ultralight tackle.

Parachuting: Casting a plastic worm into heavy cover by snubbing the cast and letting the bait fall straight down into submerged bushes or treetops. A short, stiff spinning rod and spinning reel loaded with 17- to 20-pound-test line is the preferred tackle.

Pegging: Fixing a lead weight to the fishing line at the point where the hook is attached. A short wedge, usually a toothpick that is broken off, is inserted into the hole at the head of the slip sinker to keep it from sliding up the line away from the bait. Some anglers also use small split-shot sinkers pinched onto the line just ahead of the slip sinker.

pH: The range of water alkalanity and acidity.

Pitching: A casting method which resembles a modified flipping cast. The bait is swung forward by raising the rod tip, and then allowed to travel forward by free-spooling the line.

Plastic worm: A molded plastic lure originally designed to imitate a worm, eel, or snake. Plastic worms now are manufactured in several sizes, shapes and colors.

Poking: A fishing technique that involves clearing a hole in floating vegetation and then releasing the lure into the water through the hole.

Pound-Test: The point at which line breaks when pulled with a specific amount of pressure.

Power-fishing: A term applied to the jerk-and-reel retrieve used with long, diving minnow lures.

Rattling: Fishing a jig up and down in the same place in heavy cover for several seconds.

Riprap: Rocks piled along banks of rivers and lakes to prevent erosion.

River slipping: Maneuvering a boat stern-first downstream while maintaining control of speed and casting distance from the bank or other targets.

Shallow-runner: A minnow-type lure designed to be fished with a steady retrieve in shallow water.

Shiner: Any of several subspecies of baitfish characterized by silver or golden scales along their sides. Size may range from 2 to 12 inches.

Sight-fishing: Casting lures for bass that are visible to the angler.

Skipping: A sidearm casting technique that propels a bait under cover such as docks or overhanging trees or bushes. Usually, a pegged plastic worm is used and cast with spinning tackle. The force of the sidearm cast causes the bait to skip over the surface and under the cover.

Slack-line fishing: A plastic worm-fishing technique characterized by allowing the lure to fall to the bottom without applying any tension to the fishing line. The objective is to imitate the natural fall of terrestrials into the water.

Slip sinker: A lead weight, usually conical in shape, that aids in casting plastic worms or other baits that are virtually weightless. The weight of a slip sinker selected for a particular fishing situation usually depends on water depth and cover.

Slow-rolling: Retrieving a spinnerbait slowly through the water so the blade is barely turning.

Snap-set: A hook-setting technique by which the hook is set with a quick, relatively short flip of the wrist.

Carolina rig: A plastic worm rigged so the sinker doesn't slip all the way down the line to the hook in the head of the worm. The stopping point on the line, usually several inches away from the worm, may be made by tying a piece of barrier line there, by pinching a small split-shot sinker onto the line below the slip sinker, or by tying a swivel and leader to the fishing line after it has been passed through the slip sinker. Such a rig usually is used in weedy cover or to fish the worm slightly above the bottom.

Spoon: A metal, plastic, or wooden lure often manufactured with a metallic finish to imitate a minnow.

Spoon-shaking: Retrieving a metal spoon on or near the surface of the water by reeling and intermittently snapping back the wrist that holds the rod. The purpose of such a retrieve is to duplicate a frightened baitfish.

Spinnerbait: A jig-like lure characterized by one or more spinner blades fixed to a wire shaft ahead of or above a fairly heavy body, single hook or single set of treble hooks, and rubber or hair skirt. A spinnerbait generally is fished with a steady retrieve.

Sproat: A popular style of hook among anglers who fish with plastic worms, characterized by its relatively long shank and ample gap between shank and point.

Stinger: An extra hook attached to the back hook of a spinnerbait to aid in hooking bass that are striking the rear end of the lure. Typically, stingers are used on spinnerbaits that are retrieved quickly across or near the surface.

Strike zone: The area in the water column where bass will strike a lure.

Suspended bass: Inactive bass that are holding at some point in the water between the surface and the bottom.

Sweep-set: Setting a hook by reeling line quickly and sweeping the rod back at the moment the strike is detected.

Swinging: Boating a bass by raising it into the boat with the rod.

Tailrace: The area below a dam, typified by irregular currents and upwellings.

Tidewater: Coastal rivers, streams and lakes whose depth and water flow is affected by tidal movements.

Texas rig: A plastic worm rigged so the point of the hook is buried in the body of the worm to make it weedless.

Topwater lure: Any artificial bait fished across the surface of the water; typically, a floating lure.

Trailer: A hook, spinner blade, pork rind/frog, or plastic swimming tail attached to the back hook of a lure.

Trolling: Fishing a bait behind a moving boat propelled by mechanical power.

Tuning: Adjusting the eye screw of a crankbait to which the fishing line is tied so it causes the lure to run straight ahead or to one side.

Walking the dog: A term applied to the zigzag retrieve of a topwater lure, caused by jigging the rod tip and reeling at the same time.

Weedguard: A device, usually plastic or wire, affixed to a lure so as to cover the hook point and render it weedless.

Wire-lining: A trolling technique that employs wire line to help sink lures to fish that are holding in deep water.

Yo-yoing: Presenting a flat-sided spoon or tailspinner lure to bass in deeper water with a vertical jigging motion.

INDEX